THE PUBLIC PAPERS OF
THE GOVERNORS OF KENTUCKY

Robert F. Sexton
General Editor

SPONSORED BY THE

Kentucky Advisory Commission
on Public Documents

AND THE

Kentucky Historical Society

THE PUBLIC PAPERS OF

GOVERNOR
WENDELL H. FORD

1971-1974

W. Landis Jones, *Editor*

The University Press of Kentucky

Ford, Wendell H   1924–
    The public papers of Governor Wendell H. Ford, 1971–
1974.

    (The Public papers of the Governors of Kentucky)
    Includes index.
    1. Kentucky—Politics and government—1951–   —
Collected works. 2. Ford, Wendell H., 1924–
I. Jones, William Landis, 1937–   II. Title.
III. Series.
F456.2.F67   976.9'04'0924   77–73702
ISBN 0–8131–0602–8

ISBN: 0–8131–0602–8

Library of Congress Catalog Card Number: 77–73702

A statewide cooperative scholarly publishing agency
serving Berea College, Centre College of Kentucky,
Eastern Kentucky University, The Filson Club,
Georgetown College, Kentucky Historical Society,
Kentucky State University, Morehead State University,
Murray State University, Northern Kentucky University,
Transylvania University, University of Kentucky,
University of Louisville, and Western Kentucky University.

Editorial and Sales Offices: Lexington, Kentucky 40506

CONTENTS

REORGANIZATION [89]

HEALTH AND WELFARE   [165]

EDUCATION   [211]

PUBLIC SAFETY   [257]

CONTENTS

CONTENTS

CONTENTS

HIGHWAYS   [537]

CONTENTS

CONTENTS

GENERAL EDITOR'S PREFACE

THE Public Papers of the Governors of Kentucky is a series of volumes which preserves and disseminates the public record of Kentucky's chief executives. The need to make these records available was articulated by a number of persons interested in Kentucky history, government, and politics. In 1971 the Kentucky Advisory Commission on Public Documents, created by executive order, recommended the publication of the Public Papers of the Governors of Kentucky. The commission oversees and manages all aspects of the project in cooperation with the Kentucky Historical Society.

Approximately every four years the public papers of the last governor and one earlier governor will appear in separate volumes, each designed to provide a convenient record of that executive's administration. While the organization of the material may vary from volume to volume with differences in the styles of the governors, available materials, and historical circumstances, the volumes share an overall guiding philosophy and general format.

It is our hope that the series will prove useful to all those interested in Kentucky government, including citizens, scholars, journalists, and public servants. Not in themselves interpretations of Kentucky government and history, the volumes in this series will be the basis for serious analysis by future historians.

R. F. S.

EDITOR'S PREFACE

THIS volume is designed to make available in readily accessible form the public pronouncements of the three years of Governor Wendell Ford's administration as set out by him in speeches and press releases. This is a carefully selected cross section of the public papers of Governor Ford and therefore contains no correspondence or other private papers.

The emphasis upon speeches and press releases is not solely the result of their availability. Two factors make these kinds of public, but not easily accessible, papers uniquely valuable. First, nowhere else has the full text of these speeches and press releases been printed, and speech texts have not always been preserved intact after the close of a gubernatorial administration. Second and more important, together these speeches and press releases are the publicly pronounced policies of the Governor. They are the articulated public policy of the executive branch of Kentucky state government for a period of three years.

Partly in response to our request to facilitate gathering together these papers, the Ford administration had preserved carefully the speeches and press releases of the Governor. Thomas C. Preston, the Governor's press aide, and Preston's assistant, the late Manette Cupp, had logged and filed all these materials, including background information for most of the speeches. This left for me the primary task of perusing this mass of material labeled by Preston as "speeches, remarks, and press releases" and separated roughly into two categories, "nonpolitical" and "political." I studied the material carefully and analyzed the content of each item to avoid later duplication and to assure that all significant subjects would be covered in the published form.

The material lent itself to organization by topic rather than by chronology. This topical organization may be peculiar to the Ford volume of this series because of Governor Ford's style of administration; it need not set a pattern for any other volume. A complete listing of the speeches and releases in chronological order (both of items included and of items omitted) appears in Appendix 3, and the index will assist also in locating materials which transcend the topical divisions.

The divisions which are used in this volume follow the major themes of the Ford administration's activities, most of which could be discerned in the Inaugural Address which appears at the beginning of the volume. Each of the Governor's speeches other than the far-reaching State of the Commonwealth addresses and the budget addresses was relatively focused on a single topic. Where there were important digressions to another topic, notes have been inserted to direct the reader to other speeches on that topic. With few exceptions all the persons mentioned in a speech are identified the first time their names are cited, and subsequent appearances are noted with a reference to the earlier citation.

Most of the speeches in the original form were not paragraphed and were typed on a speech-size typewriter ignoring capitalization. I supplied paragraphs and in some instances changed awkward lists into paragraph form. Otherwise the speeches have not been changed and appear as they were released or delivered. Governor Ford made most of his introductions and summations extemporaneously, and these are included only where his handwritten notes were extensive and decipherable. Where materials have been omitted to avoid unnecessary repetition this is noted and a reference to duplicate material is given. In a few instances the orally delivered speech and the simultaneous press release have been meshed in this volume. This occurs primarily in the reorganization division where the material is most complex and the audience had copies of detailed organization charts before them. Appendix 2 presents an organization chart which sets out the final organization of state government as the Ford administration ended in December 1974.

This volume, like its predecessor, has not included executive orders or proclamations. These are available in the Secretary of State's office and the relevant orders and proclamations are noted as are pieces of legislation which are referred to in speeches.

The preparation of this volume benefited immeasurably from the pioneering efforts of Robert F. Sexton, who edited the *Public Papers of Governor Louie B. Nunn* and who serves as the General Editor of the series. The Nunn volume then in preparation served as an incentive to the Ford staff to preserve Governor Ford's papers, and it was of assistance to me in substance, style, and citations. Assisting me in this undertaking were Armand Judah, Betty Erwin, and Sandy Hack. Major contributions were made by two thorough and perceptive assistants, Naniene Hammond and Edward Budy. My colleagues in the Department of Political Science at the University of Louisville were most understanding of the peculiar time and space needs of their peer over a two-year period. Wendell Ford while Governor and as United States Senator has been supportive and met all requests for materials. Thomas L. Preston contributed in many ways, particularly in writing a synopsis of the administration.

GOVERNOR WENDELL H. FORD

GOVERNOR WENDELL H. FORD
December 7, 1971, to December 28, 1974

WENDELL HAMPTON FORD was born September 8, 1924, in Daviess County, Kentucky. The son of the late State Senator and Mrs. Ernest M. Ford, he grew up on a farm in the rural Western Kentucky community of Thruston. He attended local public schools and was graduated from Daviess County High School.

After graduation, Ford attended the University of Kentucky, but left school to serve in the United States Army during World War II. He was discharged with the rank of sergeant in 1946 and then attended the Maryland School of Insurance. Upon graduation in 1947, he returned to Owensboro to enter the insurance business with his father.

On September 18, 1943, Ford married Ruby Jean Neel of West Point, also in Daviess County, and they are the parents of two children, Shirley Jean (Mrs. William Dexter) and Steven Milton.

Long active in civic and religious affairs, Ford served as a deacon in the First Baptist Church in Owensboro. He is a past state president of the Kentucky Jaycees and later became the first Kentuckian ever to be elected national president and international vice president. Over the years, Ford has served as chairman of the Kentucky March of Dimes, director of the United States Chamber of Commerce, member of the Kentucky Council on Education, local director of Civitan International, member of the Second Army Advisory Committee of the American Legion, and finance chairman of the Audubon Council, Boy Scouts of America.

Ford left the family insurance business in 1959 to begin his career in public service as chief administrative assistant to Governor Bert Combs. In 1965 he was elected to the Kentucky State Senate and two years later was elected Lieutenant Governor. He was elected Governor in 1971 and served three years before resigning to begin serving his first term in the United States Senate. Ford is the only Kentuckian ever to be elected to consecutive terms as Lieutenant Governor, Governor, and United States Senator.

During his term in the statehouse, Ford was an outspoken advocate of Governors' taking a stronger role in national affairs. In 1973 and 1974 he served as chairman of the National Democratic Governors' Caucus. Ford also was chairman of the Southern Governors' Conference Committee on Crime and Justice and vice chairman of the

National Governors' Conference on Natural Resources and Environmental Protection.

Throughout his career, Ford also has been extremely active in the national Democratic party. He has been a member of the National Democratic Party Advisory Council, a member of the Democratic National Committee, the 1976 National Democratic Party Campaign, and was on the Carter-Mondale Campaign Steering Committee. He presently is the chairman of the Democratic Senatorial Campaign Committee, as well as a member of the Democratic Steering Committee.

In 1954 Ford was named the Outstanding Young Man of Daviess County, and in 1955 he was named one of three outstanding young men in Kentucky. In 1958 he received the American Cancer Association's Layman Award for outstanding contributions in the fight against cancer. In 1973 he was selected Conservation Man of the Year by the Kentucky Association of Conservation Districts and that same year was named Agriculture's Man of the Year by the Kentucky Farm Press Association. Ford also is the recipient of the highest recognition given by the Boy Scouts of America, the Silver Antelope Award.

Ford holds honorary degrees from the University of Kentucky, Morehead State University, Eastern Kentucky University, Kentucky Wesleyan College, and Brescia College. He has also received the highest awards given by the University of Louisville, Western Kentucky University, and Lambda Chi Alpha social fraternity.

INAUGURAL ADDRESS

INAUGURAL ADDRESS
Frankfort / December 7, 1971

IN speaking to you this afternoon, I want my inaugural address to be characteristic of the new administration. I shall not mince words. The attitude of my administration will be one where there is no patience for waste—waste of time, talent, energy, and resources. Let us therefore proceed directly to the heart of the matter, just as the new administration will be geared to a straight course of action, a course to be followed positively, practically, and beneficially to you. We have little time to cut the Gordian knot, because the Governor's term in Kentucky is brief.

There is a portion of the Oath of Office in which I promise before God to be faithful and true to the Commonwealth of Kentucky. This pledge puts an enormous weight on any Governor. But I asked the citizens of Kentucky—I asked you—for such a burden. Today I accept it without reservation or hesitation!

To fulfill the Oath of Office, decisions must be made which are not always immediately popular and with certain groups are never popular. Decisions must be made in view of sudden, as well as long-range requirements. To fulfill the Oath of Office, a Governor must be prepared to say yes or no, whichever the occasion dictates. I am ready to fulfill the Oath of Office! For the test of a man in public life is not how well he campaigns, rather it is how effectively he meets the challenges and responsibilities of office—yes, how faithful and true he is to his Commonwealth, to the people.

Like thousands of other businessmen, I have always tried to conduct my activities in an honest and efficient manner. I will accept no less of those participating in the Ford administration. Therefore, I today reaffirm my intent to reorganize state government wherever necessary. Every agency must justify its right to exist in terms of its ability and willingness to render a full measure of service to you.

Many Kentuckians have come to regard the political process as futile. They have come to regard the institutions of government as irrelevant and unresponsive. The gauging of government is not how popular it is with the powerful and the privileged few, but how honestly and fairly it deals with the many who depend upon it, whose lives are controlled by it.

I am not interested in making an effort to place greater governmental controls on the people. We have already put thirty-five million laws on the books in this great land trying to enforce the Ten Commandments. I am interested, though, in using the structure and controls which presently exist to motivate the agencies and institutions to perform solely in the people's best interest. A statement I uttered countless times during the campaign will be a constant reminder to all of us who will conduct your affairs these next four years; that is, the only reason for the existence of government, at any level, is to serve people. This we can do; this we intend to do.

We cannot individually buy clean air and water. We cannot individually provide safe streets or have the provisions for education. Nor can we guarantee, individually, a system of commerce where all benefit. We can, however, meet these needs through cooperation. We can meet them collectively whenever we apply ourselves to the problems.

Man has gone from oxcarts to moon buggies because of his determination. Man has responded to challenge numerous times, and today, Wendell Ford responds to your challenge! What then is the challenge? It is your mandate. Our responsibility is to the mandate of the people, to the business you have directed us.

You have told us to stretch the tax dollar. We will make it go further. You have expressed your demand for a government of refinement rather than a government of impulsiveness. This you shall have! You have given us the occasion to restore confidence in government and in those who lead government. Every member of the new administration will respect the priority of this opportunity. You have demanded fairness in taxation, a reapportionment of the taxing levels. We shall provide it. You have asked that the farmer be once more remembered. He will be! You have directed us to reevaluate our educational programs, to perfect our educational processes. This shall be done. You have called for economic stimulation. We shall provide it because no one is more aware than we of the direct application of commerce to those other areas touched by your mandate. The army of Kentucky's economy is the clinched fist of the working man, whether he be in the factory or on the farm.

Yet as we respond to your mandate, let me remind you of the well-established fact whereby services expected by the people cannot exceed the people's willingness to endorse. Our alliance these next four years must carry with it an understanding, that as Wendell Ford is faithful and true to you, so will you be to your state. We will strive to eliminate misunderstanding. We ask that you involve yourself in the day-by-day activities of your government by staying intelligently informed. The openness of this administration begins now!

Let us recognize changes taking place in our society, this very hour.

Let us be prepared to meet the requirements that these challenges foster. We must abandon hit-or-miss, piecemeal approaches to the changes of society. This dictates patience on our part and on your part, especially in evaluating our innovations, programs, and results.

The challenge to you, and the challenge to me, is that before we are Democrats, or Republicans, or Independents, before we are any of the things that separate us, let us upon the altar of our state place a personal sacrifice and stop treating that altar as a trough out of which to feed! If you demand wise and honest government in Kentucky, you must recognize that wise and honest government is the product of wise and honest citizens, nothing less. If you demand unfair advantages, special privileges for selected groups, remember that the price of this is the destruction of a commonwealth's character. This I will not allow. If you demand balanced budgets, you must not advocate degrees of expenditures which are without reality. If you demand that Kentucky give you economic security, you must not forget that Kentucky's strength comes from each person standing on his feet. It is not a matter of what we are, but of what we are able to be.

Perhaps on this first day, as on other inaugurations, there are those who consider spoken intentions as impossible. Some look at obstacles and say they can't be hurdled. I say join me now, as we together go over, around, or directly through any obstacle placed before us!

I would be remiss on this thirtieth anniversary of Pearl Harbor, if I didn't compare the trials and tribulations of yesterday and tomorrow and if I didn't reflect on the proven quality of Kentuckians. For on this very day, in 1941, our nation was literally upended from the alien force of physical assault. We were thrust into a period of history which demanded every possible self-denial for the sake of survival. Half of Kentucky's citizens do not remember December 7, thirty years ago. The other half will recall how we were propelled to the brink of human and economic disaster. No citizens gave more of themselves in personal sacrifice than did Kentuckians. I remember that as the fires of Pearl Harbor continued to roar, Kentuckians distinguished themselves in the lines of early volunteers. Huge segments of individual communities suffered torment together, in death marches, prison camps, and muddy foxholes. National restrictions were even more burdensome on Kentucky than other states because we were proportionately weaker in our economic structure.

How many times have we been put to the test? There is no single answer. On this December 7, we are spared the tragedy of global conflict, yet we are surrounded by the tragedy of human failures, of human suffering brought on by self-imposed human limitations. We are confronted by the heart-rendering sobs of orphaned children, hungry children, cold children, and unwanted children. We are confronted by the realization that the pace of criminal and juvenile rehabilitation is too slow. We are confronted by the pollution of skies, by the film-coated waters of once-clear streams, and by the scars of hills and valleys. We are confronted by the dilemma in educational standards, by the non-availability of sufficient treatment of mental illness, and by the grim statistic that today well over 900 persons have lost their lives on Kentucky highways during 1971.

Our acts of omission are often more revealing than those of commission. We see this when we refuse to consider the value of the elderly to society, when we don't listen to the young who do indeed have sound ideas.

The demands of today outdistance the progress being made. I often wonder if the magnitude of need can ever be reduced by man's continued efforts at solutions. I know the greatest tragedy of all would be not to try.

Many of you have offered congratulations and good wishes. I deeply appreciate your feelings. But as I conclude this address, I cannot help but express my greatest desire. That is for you, four years from now, to know in your hearts that I gave every ounce of myself in being the type Governor you wanted and expected.

The job as Governor is a delicate, human task. A Governor intent on accomplishing what he desires, discovers periods of loneliness. These come after all the advice and all the counsel. He finds himself very much alone, when only he, the Governor, can make the final decision which affects so many. The fate of countless Kentuckians rests with such decisions—decisions which must be made from a belief that the future of Kentucky is based on a government and a society in which your children, and your children's children, each in their own time, shall stand equal.

My family and I thank you for coming. I ask that you join me these next four years in seeking God's blessing on our actions.

LEGISLATIVE MESSAGES
AND STATEMENTS

PRELEGISLATIVE CONFERENCE
Gilbertsville / December 13, 1971

DURING several occasions, I have been on your side of the speaker's table during prelegislative conferences, listening to remarks by other Governors. Though I stand here now as the chief executive of the Commonwealth of Kentucky, in many respects I am still on your side of the table, for I have a clear understanding of your role and a firm belief in its vitality. Because of my tenure in the General Assembly, both as a Senator and as Lieutenant Governor, there is a close kinship within me to your responsibilities. I therefore appear tonight with deep conviction for the job you must do, and the job I must do.

As we approach the 1972 General Assembly, we are becoming increasingly familiar with the knotty problems confronting us. We are still seeking realistic and practical solutions to these problems. In a very brief period, it will become your duty, and my duty, to implement effective and equitable solutions. It won't be easy. It never was. Nothing good ever is. As society grows more complex and interdependent the need for cooperation prompts me to solicit your support for the programs I will present in my state of the Commonwealth message when you convene January 4.

The need for cooperation prompts this reminder—that even though there may be segments of individual brilliance within the House and Senate, no heroes emerge from a divided body when division overshadows purpose of action. I expect individual brilliance, because I know you. During the past four years, the General Assembly has made great strides toward becoming a stronger, better informed, and more responsive legislative body. I am grateful for the opportunity of participating in such an effort.

We must have a strong General Assembly. We must have an Assembly that will answer the electorate. We must have an Assembly free to work with the Governor and the courts, as contemplated by our Constitution. We must have an Assembly which controls its internal affairs. You need additional facilities for your operations during and between Sessions, as pointed out this morning by the chairman of your Citizens' Committee on the General Assembly. I pledge to help in developing new facilities for you.

As you know, one of my major objectives is to redesign the administrative structure of Kentucky's government so that it will truly serve the people, rather than itself. Throughout my campaign for the governorship, I stressed the importance of making our state government more responsive to the needs of all the people. You, as the "People's Branch" of state government, can play a key role in achieving this important objective. The overriding theme of this reorganization will be to seek improved delivery of essential services to our citizens. As I said in my inaugural address last week, each state agency will be required to justify the basis for its continued existence.

I have already moved in this regard. Tomorrow, I am returning all higher education budget requests to the Council on Public Higher Education. I am doing so because the council failed to exercise its responsibility, both to the people of Kentucky, and to the General Assembly through its inadequate study of these budget requests.

In addition to this one example, we are finding numerous areas of government in dire need of the restructuring process where fresh understanding, new approaches, and innovation can replace what has become a barrier between government and the people.

Our reorganization plans will be presented to you on a regular basis, for examination, for counsel, for approval. You will not be kept in the dark. In turn, I ask your cooperation in passage of a 1972 executive budget that will be flexible enough to permit executive reorganization—that will be the best bargain ever obtained for Kentucky. We cannot mutually achieve this necessary reorientation of the peoples' government, in the peoples' interest, if either of our hands are tied.

In all matters, let us together respond first to the immediate—yet more importantly to the requirements of the future. Let us accept a covenant whereby individual glory is secondary to purpose for others. Rest assured, my actions will not turn back to the past. Together, you and I can forge for Kentucky a responsible and responsive executive-legislative relationship. This we owe to each other. This we owe to the people who have given us this duty.

STATE OF THE
COMMONWEALTH ADDRESS
Frankfort / January 4, 1972

I APPRECIATE having the opportunity, which you have afforded me tonight, of delivering this address. On a few other occasions I will ask to appear before you in joint Session, including the transmission of my Budget Message in about four weeks. Unlike most new Governors, my appearance tonight is a reunion with many legislative friends. We have worked together before. I am confident we can continue to work together in the best interest of the people of Kentucky. I want your understanding. I want your help.

Although I respect tradition, the four years of my administration will not be inhibited by the past, nor will my remarks tonight. I do not intend to deal with numerous specifics. I want to set forth the philosophy and administrative tone of my administration.

During the brief period since Inauguration Day, I have sought a more businesslike state government. Each individual placed in authority by me has been directed to follow an approach of refinement, whereby the gears of governmental machinery work more smoothly at less expense to the taxpayer.

I am aware of some who scoff about any discussion of government being operated as a business. They say this is an old tune. Certainly, it has been played before. They contend it will be found an impossible dream. Indeed, the magnitude of such an undertaking is awesome. They look upon an order of belt-tightening as one of the early glamor statements, yet one soon forgotten. In times past this has occurred. This will not be said at the end of the Ford administration. Yes, they speak of government as a system incompatible with intelligent business practices. My reply to those who doubt is this: Wendell Ford has not had such an opportunity before. He does now, and knows such a purpose can be accomplished.

My experience in the executive and legislative branches, along with a background in business, convinces me of the vast opportunities awaiting ignition. Together, we must project our regard for the taxpayer's dollar, while accomplishing programs having both an immediate and long-range impact on the betterment of our Commonwealth.

In a very true sense, you 138 members of this Assembly are the people of Kentucky, because you have been entrusted with the power of decision affecting our entire citizenry.

It is not wrong to consider government as a huge corporation. It is not at all unreasonable to approach government in the same tenor an owner approaches his business. I am the Chief Executive Officer of this corporation. You, the Senators and Representatives, are the Board of Directors. The people are our stockholders. They should expect and receive maximum dividends in return for their tax investments. Their life-style rests with our determination of how the corporation should be operated. Their confidence and respect is our only just reward. Their lack of confidence and respect is our just indictment, if we fail to institute sound business procedures.

The people of Kentucky have granted us an awesome responsibility to accomplish their will. That responsibility begins with an evaluation. This is why we are carefully investigating every facet of state government. This is why we have initiated moves to accomplish internal changes which will have a direct bearing on our master plan for reorganization following the General Assembly. This is why our analysis carries a mandate to justify every position held and to instill better management functions at all levels. There cannot logically be any other first step.

Nevertheless, nothing of lasting good can be done overnight. Later in the Session, I am going to ask this Assembly to give me the broadest possible legal latitude so we can put state government in order.

There are many things a Governor can do on his own. Since December 7, we have worked diligently to change the direction of our state government. We have begun to concentrate our efforts toward service to the people, rather than continued growth of government agencies. As I review reports from various departments and agencies, I am convinced of the ample opportunity to carry out my wishes for refinement. Your own studies, from interim legislative committees, have pointed to numerous ills we are presently curing.

One example is the Highway Department. On December 10, there were 9,618 employees there. The number has been reduced by more than 1,000. A review and evaluation of all Highway Department personal service contracts, which number approximately 755, is under way to determine whether they are in the best interest of the taxpayer, and the department. To date, contracts totaling $5.6 million have been canceled, or are in the process of cancelation. In addition, a professional staff to provide a continuing internal audit of finances and procedures will be used to investigate, evaluate, and to make recommendations for more effective ways of administering Kentucky's highway program.

Similar moves are in effect to halt the spiraling costs in the Parks Department. Upon assuming office, we found what I term a "blindfolded attitude of employment practices," there and elsewhere. In Parks, hundreds of seasonal employees, whose real duties had expired after the summer months, remained on the payroll. Lifeguards in December is not my idea of sound personnel practices! Every state park is receiving a magnifying-glass inspection. Every state department and agency will receive this type of inspection in the weeks and months ahead.

We have moved rapidly toward achieving a greater degree of professionalism in the Commerce Department. The environmental impact of industrial and commercial prospects is being evaluated more closely than ever. Environmental quality, side by side with desirable economic growth, can be a reality. To this, I am firmly committed. There is now being developed new emphasis on commercial development, with particular attention to bringing in regional offices for industry, commerce, finance, and private recreational concerns. In modernizing our traditional industrial development program, we are aware that Kentucky must add 90,000 to 100,000 industrial jobs over the next decade to meet demand.

To achieve more exposure by transferring production costs to space purchases, the Department of Public Information has instituted in-house advertising production from its own people, rather than outside sources. The savings will afford this state more advertising space, thereby increasing the interest of those living outside our borders. This is but one of several moves in that department to enhance the image of Kentucky to those who are potential visitors either on a temporary or permanent basis.

During the last two years, I appeared before the people of Kentucky expressing what I thought ought to be done during the next four years. Their expression of favor at the polls is a mandate for action.

I voiced concern for inequities in our tax structure. In the last Session we made some progress. During this Session, I will submit specific proposals to the General Assembly to further make our tax structure more equitable for all Kentuckians.

Regarding environment, I will ask the General Assembly for the broadest possible powers, so together we can build the best environmental program of any state in the nation. Kentucky's natural heritage of wild rivers, beautiful mountains, inland waters, and magnificent flatlands must be protected. I will make specific recommendations to you in order to preserve what is rapidly becoming disgraced through misuse.

A most important privilege granted to Kentuckians and Americans is the process of free and open elections. Our system suffers from its inability to keep pace with the times. We need effective, sensible election reform. Streamlining our election laws will be a major priority in my legislative proposals to assure every Kentuckian the best possible opportunity of expression.

Our system of government also depends upon protecting the rights and property of every citizen. Changes and pressures within our society demand that we have reform in upgrading our law enforcement and criminal justice system. Such a package will be submitted to the General Assembly for action. My budget will contain substantial requests for financing needed changes in the areas of law enforcement, criminal justice and corrections, with special emphasis on upgrading our parole system.

The consumer, the taxpayer, needs protection. Rather than having a sham at the taxpayer's expense, I will recommend a program with teeth in it, which will truly protect the consumer, instead of special interests. You are already aware that I have no patience with the performance of the past. I intend for our efforts to be purposeful and fruitful.

Kentucky, as with most states, has reached the crisis level in financing local government. I will propose specific legislation aimed at relieving, within constitutional limits, as much of this burden as possible. My proposals will call upon the General Assembly to be flexible in the area of municipal and county financing, as well as in statutory grants of authorities that you give counties and cities. We have heard for too long that state government cannot help local government. I am not looking for excuses. I am looking for a way, and I want your advice and help.

No discussion about our obligation to the state would be complete without reference to the plight of urban communities. I will recommend that this Assembly grant home rule where needed and wanted. I will recommend that this Assembly pass a low-income housing bill. I will offer other vitally needed legislation for urban communities, recognizing that the future of our cities and the Commonwealth are inseparably tied.

Kentucky has spent millions of dollars in recent years trying to furnish health and welfare services based on a system that is not suited to our times nor our needs. We must direct our attention to the provision of health and social services at the community level where the problems must and can best be solved. We cannot settle today's dilemma with outmoded approaches which are costly and generally ineffective.

Kentuckians in the past have expressed their willingness to finance education to the best of their ability. We have seen tremendous increases in education expenditures. Still we have far to go. During the campaign,

I placed before the people a twelve-point program, attainable during the next four years, to provide a higher quality primary and secondary education for young Kentuckians. My education legislation package and budget request will finance this program. Over the past twelve years we have seen an unprecedented building program in higher education. New universities, expanded colleges, and community colleges have appeared in all sections of the state. It is now time to put renewed emphasis on the quality of higher education and coordination of these institutions. You can expect legislation from me designed to insure strict coordination and evaluation.

Measures of priority do not end with tonight's message. There are major priorities in agriculture, economic assistance, child welfare, and other areas of government. There are lofty goals to be reached, goals within the grasp of a sound system of government.

Tonight there are serious problems which must be turned into working solutions by the time we leave office. I am approaching the next four years supported by the understanding that adversity can instill a stronger spirit. We have adversity. By the steps taken as partially indicated earlier to you this evening, we are waging a war on adversity. Through the full appreciation of those needs, so apparent today, we shall continue to conquer adversity.

It would be easy to illustrate the prospects of various departments facing a deficit during the remainder of this biennium—a deficit threatened by excessive spending from those who preceded us. However, I will set these out in detail before the introduction of my budget, because it will be necessary for you to have this information for consideration of the budget.

It would be easy to chart the overwhelming problems of unmet needs, now our burden, though not brought about by those of us who must seek solutions. But I do not intend for this address to be a crying towel, as has been the case on some previous occasions. I intend to get on with the work at hand.

There is a mood in Kentucky which cries out for refinement. This is a condition which confronts us. It is not a theory. I believe the mood is justified. Good government is good business. Good business is good politics. The capitol of Kentucky must be more than a mere political center. Let there be no mistake about my firm feelings regarding this creed. I trust that my insistence for moving the center of patronage out of the Governor's Office, out of the buildings of government is proof.

We are confronted at the threshold of this Assembly with a condition of the state's finances which will penetrate every department, agency, and institution supported by government. The first question to be answered is whether or not more can be done through the expenditure of fewer dollars. In other words, do we have the ability to grow in service without growing disproportionately in cost? I say yes.

I am prepared to exercise the leadership you deserve in a delicate cause. I am prepared, willing, and anxious to reshape our political and governmental system to make them responsive to the people they were conceived to serve. Events during the past four weeks have begun to reflect my creed that each agency of state government must justify its reason for existence through service to the people, or it will be abolished.

I entrust with you the provision of equal leadership, and the fulfillment of your duty through a bond of cooperation between the executive and legislative branches. Every Kentuckian has the right to expect no less from each of us.

Thank you, and good evening.

BUDGET MESSAGE
Frankfort / February 3, 1972

BY Kentucky law the Governor is directed to lay a budget plan for the new biennium before the General Assembly. I am here today for this purpose. It is your responsibility to consider this blueprint and authorize revenues and expenditures necessary to operate state government during the next two years.

This budget-making procedure is traditional in our democratic system of government. It is a classic example of the separation and sharing of powers where the chief executive proposes appropriations and tax levies, but only the elected legislators authorize and thereby dispose of his proposals.

The budget touches every man, woman, and child in this state and indeed many beyond our borders. A matter of such significance cannot be treated lightly. I assure you it has not been so with me. It has consumed far more of my time since Inauguration Day than any other task or series of tasks.

Actually, the budget process for me began months ago when I made the decision to seek the office of Governor—when I considered the many unmet needs of our Commonwealth and pledged to improve the quality of life for all our people. It began when I said the harsh tax on food would be removed and when I promised to improve public education by raising the dollars we spend per child through teacher salaries, current operating expenses, and new classrooms. The budget process started with my call for additional vocational education opportunities for our young, with my call for more classrooms benefiting handicapped children who are in the special education category, and with my pledge to give added support to retired teachers on fixed incomes.

I said that two new institutions of higher learning now coming into the state system would be funded and that we would provide for fixed costs and cost-of-living pay raises for professors at our existing colleges and universities.

Budget consideration actually began when I said we would lift the Kentucky criminal justice system out of the past and into contemporary times with revenue-sharing for improved police forces; establish a new professional probation and parole system to replace the patronage-riddled hulk I have inherited; and change the prisons from laboratories for crime to true correctional centers. It began when I promised funds to halt the ravages of strip mining through strict enforcement and long-overdue reclamation and when I pledged reorganization and added support for state agencies which will launch a more vigorous attack on the forces polluting our water and air. Strict attention to this budget was initiated when I said there would be dollars available for new state programs to serve the elderly; when I said we would meet our commitment to completely fund the new state institutions for the retarded at Somerset and Hazelwood; and when I announced that we would make an aggressive start in our treatment programs for alcoholism and drug addiction.

These and other commitments were made to the people of Kentucky with the intention of keeping them. They are clearly recorded in press accounts of the campaign. Each costs dollars. I knew the task would be awesome. But I also knew we could finance them without adding to the tax burden of the people. In fact, I was sure the commitments could be met and the individual tax load lightened.

There were the ever-present skeptics—those who said it couldn't be done and that every promise was an exercise in irresponsibility. Many argued that I could not finance my administration without a monstrous tax increase. They were wrong. I am here today saying it can be done. I am here to show you how it can be done. I want to preface my budget details with this single point of information: the operational cost of government will show the beginning of a downward trend in the percentage of general fund dollars.

EDUCATION

One of the major goals of my administration is improvement in the quality of education throughout the state. I want better public schools, better colleges and universities, and better teachers. But most of all I want to be assured that the new dollars I am recommending for education will go for quality improvements. The 1972–1974 budget attains this objective, providing sixty-seven cents of every dollar from the general fund for education.

Make no mistake, the budget priority is elementary and secondary education just as I pledged in the campaign. New general fund dollars available to the public schools in the biennium over the current fiscal year will total $78.6 million. This compares to $45.9 million for higher education of which $19 million is for the University of Louisville and Northern State College—new additions to the state system.

THE MINIMUM FOUNDATION PROGRAM

The bulk of the money for elementary and secondary schools is channeled through the minimum foundation school program. The new dollars I am recommending in this program will meet the major objectives of educational leaders in our state. Specifically the budget provides an average increase of $400 per teacher during each year of the biennium. This is equivalent to an annual increase of 6 percent, as I promised. These increases are in addition to the increments a teacher receives based on experience and educational attainment. The budget includes an allotment for current expenses that will increase from $1,400 to $1,570 per classroom unit by the end of the biennium. This too is an increase of 6 percent each year and should be considerably more than required to offset the effects of inflation.

The capital outlay allotment is increased by $100 each year, raising the amount of state support from $1,200 per unit to $1,400 in the second year of the biennium. During the four years of my administration this increase will generate additional bonding capacity for local school districts of $81 million and will make possible the construction of 2,600 new classrooms, exactly what I pledged to the people in my campaign. The budget includes 150 new classroom units each year for exceptional children, a program limited only by the number of teachers graduating from our colleges and universities who are qualified in special education.

Additional vocational units are included in the budget to permit full utilization of all vocational facilities anticipated to be available during the biennium. The budget provides for forty new units in the period 1972 to 1973, and 150 additional units the following year.

With regard to vocational education, I have a special announcement. I am recommending $5 million in state funds to be matched with federal dollars for the construction of a new $14.5 million technical institute adjoining the Jefferson Community College in downtown Louisville. The Louisville Technical Institute, located near the city's large medical complex, will provide vocational and career opportunity for 2,000 students. The $14.5 million facility will be dedicated primarily to health occupations and will constitute the first of a three-stage project. Stage two for construction at a later date will expand vocational training in "industrial occupations." The third stage will expand training in "technical occupations." The total project scope is now set at $30 million. The Institute will be administered jointly by the University of Kentucky community college system and the state Department of Education.

The budget provides for a public kindergarten program in the second year of the biennium. In the first fiscal year the Department of Education will develop a plan for the implementation of public kindergartens. It is impossible, even impractical, to have a statewide kindergarten in the space of only two years. Therefore, 100 kindergarten classroom units have been included in the budget for fiscal year 1974. The rate of expansion of this program will be controlled to some degree by the number of certified kindergarten teachers available.

Apart from the foundation program this budget provides $440,000 in the biennium for the production of an educational television series that will put high school diplomas in the hands of thousands of Kentuckians who "dropped out" for various reasons. This major thrust at lifting the state's educational attainment level via television will be developed jointly by the Department of Education and the state ETV Authority.

TEACHERS' RETIREMENT

For thirty years the teachers' retirement program has been a stepchild burdensome to the teachers' retirement system. Therefore, I am putting in my budget $1.5 million to reduce the prior service obligation of the system. Approximately $2 million is recommended for providing retired teachers a 5 percent cost-of-living increase in their monthly retirement checks. For too long the retired teacher, a forgotten segment of our society, has been caught in the inflation squeeze. This money is essential if they are to retain their standard of living on fixed incomes.

LIFE INSURANCE

In keeping with my campaign commitment all certified personnel employed by local school boards will be given a $3,000 life insurance policy. This policy, coupled with the $2,000 benefit provided through teachers' retirement, will guarantee every professional employee life insurance coverage of $5,000.

HIGHER EDUCATION

There is need for new dollars to maintain the quality of the educational programs we now have at the Kentucky institutions of higher learning. In fact there is ample room for improvement, and very simply, it takes dollars to get quality. There has been need in the past for introducing greater rationality into the higher education budgeting process. This we have tried to do and the result attests to our efforts. The higher education budget is based on the relative needs of the respective institutions in continuing their programs as best we were able to assess them. I am more concerned, as this budget reflects, with the necessity of meeting the needs of students than any other single factor.

There can be no doubt the 1972–1974 biennial budget for higher education does things differently. In previous years tuition charges, which represent about one-third of the income available to our colleges and universities, have not been considered in budget-making except at continuation levels. The expenditure level recommended in this budget anticipates tuition increases for in-state students of approximately 20 percent each year, more for out-of-state students. Even with these increases our students will pay less to go to school than their peers in comparable institutions surrounding us.

For instance, in comparison with the University of Kentucky, such institutions as Virginia, Missouri, Virginia Tech, Florida, Alabama, Georgia, and Mississippi will have higher tuition rates. These are only a few of many examples. In comparison with regional schools Miami University, Ohio University, Illinois State, East Carolina, and Indiana State are among those having higher tuition fees.

Projected tuitions, combined with the general fund dollars recommended, fully fund the continuation request of each institution, including a minimum 6 percent salary increase plus all fixed-cost obligations.

To offset the tuition increase for needy students, I am directing the Commissioner of Finance to urge all banks that serve as depositories of state funds to become participants in the federally guaranteed student loan program. This arrangement has proven highly successful in other states and there is no reason it can't succeed in Kentucky. Cooperation on the part of the banks will make hundreds of thousands of dollars available to students who are truly in need of loans. The tuition increase for the community colleges will be $30 less in the biennium than at other institutions. This is in keeping with my aim of making college training as inexpensive as possible for those who wish or must remain at home while pursuing their college studies.

Another unique aspect of this budget for higher education is that funds have been reserved in a pool totaling almost $6 million for enrollment growth in the biennium. The pool will be allotted to those institutions which experience actual growth. This reflects my campaign commitment to put higher education dollars where the students are.

The budget figures I have recommended for the University of Louisville will enable that school to reduce tuitions by $100 in the biennium, bringing them closer in line with tuitions charged at the other state institutions. In the new budget the level of state support for the University of Louisville will increase from 20 percent in the current fiscal year to 37 percent in the 1973–1974 fiscal year.

At Northern State College the general fund appropriation is recommended to go up by 160 percent in the first year of the biennium, which is necessitated by the implementation of a senior class. Funds are included which will double the amount of state support for each full-time equivalent student. These dollars will enable Northern to make more equitable its student-faculty ratio and improve its library holdings, as well as occupy its new campus in the biennium. Moreover, these dollars, I am assured, will provide for the accreditation of the institution in the spring of 1973.

Also in the budget are funds for expanding the Jefferson Community College into Southwest Jefferson County, for meeting the indigent patient costs at the University of Kentucky Medical Center, for beginning the family practice curriculum at both of the state's medical colleges, and for establishing a graduate program for public affairs at Kentucky State College with the cooperation of other state institutions. One advantage will be the upgrading of state employee skills.

Finally, I want to note the funds listed in Senate Bill 54 for the improvement of the Council on Public Higher Education have my endorsement. Along with the bill the attached appropriation can provide the Governor of this state with badly needed advice on planning, coordination, and good management in higher education, something which today, I must sadly report, is lacking.

THE CRIMINAL JUSTICE SYSTEM

The American public is very much concerned about the growing crime rate throughout the land. Let me assure you that your Governor also is concerned. This budget demonstrates my concern. It puts money where heretofore there has been little more than scare talk. Criminal justice experts say we won't make much headway in reducing the crime rate until we deal with every element in the system; from the policeman on the beat, to the courtroom, to the prison, to the probation and parole worker. The criminal justice chain can only be as strong as its weakest link. In this budget, for the first time, we deal with every link.

We begin with the Kentucky Crime Commission. I am recommending an increase in the general fund dollars in the biennium from $2.1 million to $6.7 million. This 300 percent hike can bring 19 million additional federal dollars into Kentucky during the next two years and make sweeping changes in the state's criminal justice system at both the state and local levels.

First, the combination of federal and state dollars will enable the state government to supplement the pay of every policeman in the Commonwealth by 15 percent. However, to qualify for this pay raise the officer must be certified by the state upon completion of a training course to upgrade the level of competence for all policemen in Kentucky. This gives you a better-qualified police officer. Approximately 2,500 officers will be affected by this program. The police salary supplement is estimated to cost $4.8 million total in the biennium.

Second, the Crime Commission's matching funds will enable us to uproot the existing patronage-riddled probation and parole system and expand it with professionals who can give full time to their job and to work actively in helping ex-convicts make a satisfactory adjustment in society. Also we will reconstitute the state probation and parole board and require higher educational qualifications for the members with emphasis on training in the behavioral sciences. The matching funds further enable us to establish a prerelease center for prison inmates at Kentucky Village, which will relieve overcrowding in the institutions and let us do a better job of classifying prisoners.

I am recommending an expenditure in capital funds of $4.9 million for construction of a forensic psychiatry building to serve mentally disturbed inmates now in our prisons. Both the Corrections Commissioner and the Mental Health Commissioner call this the greatest unmet need in terms of facilities in the state correctional program today. The new 150-bed institution will be located on the grounds at Central State Hospital and will be jointly administered by Corrections and Mental Health.

State appropriation for the Department of Corrections is recommended to be increased by 31 percent over the biennium. We must make sure that our institutions are centers of corrections rather than merely places of punishment, and that our efforts are dedicated to rehabilitation, rather than revenge. Also our goal is not to build more walls and fences, but to retrain and release all who can be returned to productive lives in society. Extra dollars permit a new direction for the prisons, to make them something more than hellholes where forgotten men wither and grow hateful during their absence from society. The recommended increase is the largest ever suggested for the state prisons in one biennium.

As for the courts, funds are included in the budget to establish seven new circuit judgeships. With this increase and a redistribution of workload, we can reduce the crowded court dockets, particularly in the urban areas, and make inroads on the problem of "justice delayed." In order to attract and retain worthy individuals, funds are included in the budget for increasing the salaries of circuit judges from $19,900 to $23,500, and appellate judges from $26,000 to $29,000 annually. This increase brings the salaries of the trial court judges to the 1970 national average. For the first time since its original appropriation, we are recommending full funding of the judicial retirement system. Extra dollars totaling almost one million in the biennium are included in the budget which the actuary says is necessary to make the system financially sound.

In the Attorney General's Office we are recommending funds for increasing the salaries of attorneys in order to gain and hold lawyers with experience for their important role in practicing before the appellate courts. The turnover rate there is costly—75 percent during the last two years alone.

The need for preserving the constitutional rights of persons accused of crimes has not been overlooked. While not showing up as an appropriation in the budget, some $2.6 million is reserved for inclusion in a bill I will submit within the next ten days to establish a state office of public defender and compensate attorneys who defend indigent clients accused of major crimes. The public defender will authorize a reasonable fee schedule for attorneys appearing in behalf of indigents. He will otherwise oversee the program for the court defense of poor people accused of crimes as required by the U.S. Supreme Court.

At the state level the general fund appropriation to the Department of Public Safety is recommended to increase from $20.8 million to $30.4 million in the biennium. We will free thirty state policemen for the more pressing duty of patrolling the state highways. These men will come from the boating section.

Through federal funds a new division of boating is being organized that will employ some thirty persons. This is not a re-creation of the old boating organization of years past! The men in this division will be fully trained. They will work full time. They will be employed solely on the basis of merit. Federal officials and I will require no less. During the winter months when not required on the state's waterways, they will assist officers in the Department of Motor Transportation with enforcement of the truck laws and will work with park rangers in providing security for our state park facilities.

In the Division of State Police, we are recommending that detectives be freed from the burdensome duty of arson investigation. This task will be assigned to ten trained employees in the Division of Fire Prevention. Again, federal funds under the Economic Employment Act will be utilized to staff this full-time function. Finally, we are recommending a 5 percent salary increase for state policemen in the new biennium to enable the department to remain competitive in the job market with surrounding states and local governments. This is in addition to their annual increments.

ENVIRONMENT

Few topics generate more enthusiasm or controversy than the protection and preservation of our environment. Words rather than deeds too often have characterized the environmental movement to date. The environmental program I am proposing speaks for itself. Reorganization will be the keystone, reorganization in an attempt to eliminate the proliferation of agencies and commissions and the splintered efforts in this area. The result will be more effective services to people in the battle to save our environment.

Regulation of strip mining will be an important function of the new environmental agency. We must save the mountains, the streams, and the flatlands of the Commonwealth from the onslaught of unlawful mining practices. The law is adequate. Enforcement is poor. To strengthen enforcement I am recommending the employment of thirty-three additional inspectors in the biennium. Our surveillance of strip-mining operations in all areas of the state will be constant, and by whatever means is necessary to see that mined slopes in eastern Kentucky do not exceed twenty-seven degrees as stipulated by law. Violations will bring quick reprisals and the state will at last have the manpower to make its enforcement efforts effective.

Heretofore operating monies for the strip-mine enforcement program have come from fees paid by the mining companies. In effect, the amount that could be spent for enforcement was dependent on the amount of fees collected. The new budget brings a halt to this dubious practice. All fees will be paid into the general fund. Financial support for the strip-mining enforcement program will come from the general fund—in whatever amount is required to get the job done!

I am recommending half a million dollars which will be matched with a like federal grant, which will reclaim 5,000 acres of orphan strip-mine banks per year. We plan to establish a revolving fund for the purchase, reclamation, and resale of the orphan banks, thus the half-million-dollar appropriation will turn over several times.

The new budget recommends an increase in expenditures of $2.2 million in the biennium to abate air pollution. With this kind of expenditure we can lead the nation in providing clean air for our citizens. In the water pollution budget, I am recommending an expenditure of $1 million more in the new biennium. This will be more money for clean water in each fiscal year than for both years of the old biennium. The new dollars will go for additional inspectors to provide greater surveillance of the state's streams and to bring legal action against violators of the law.

To assist local communities in the clean-up of our streams I have recommended legislation creating the Kentucky Pollution Abatement Authority. This Authority lends state participation in construction of sewage treatment plants. Its establishment allows us to obtain maximum federal dollars which will be made available to Kentucky on a matching basis.

I am recommending that the state appropriation for solid waste disposal be doubled. This will permit us to provide increased technical assistance to county and district health departments, train employees of disposal plants, and evaluate and distribute information on new approaches to solid waste disposal methods. I want the mark of my administration in the environmental area to be characterized by personal commitment and financial support. This budget launches us upon such a course.

ECONOMIC DEVELOPMENT

My administration's energies in the vital area of economic development will be divided equally between urban and rural improvements. For people, we will work to attract only those industries responsible to the environment, and we will stand against those having no concern for the ecological consequence of their enterprise.

On the urban side, reorganization will again accentuate my effort. I will follow through with my commitment to organize a Department of Local Affairs with an active community-development arm. In furtherance of community development, the budget includes a $600,000 appropriation to the Kentucky Industrial Development Finance Authority, funds to be used for loans to stimulate the location of industrial subdivisions and plants.

Through the Department of Commerce we will give emphasis to the development of international trade and commercial services. Working through the U.S. Department of Commerce and international organizations, we will seek additional foreign investment in Kentucky plus international markets for our goods. Let me add that this emphasis will leave a positive mark on agriculture too!

I have recommended $2 million in capital funds for the Kentucky Port and River Development Commission. This group has been established by law for several years, but never funded. State funds will be used for grants and loans to local port authorities whose objective will be the construction and operation of river port facilities. With the Ohio River to the north and the Mississippi to the west, plus miles of additional navigable waterways, we have the potential for becoming an important inland shipping state. The advantage of our geographic location in the center of the nation has been ignored for too many years.

I have included in the budget approximately $400,000 for coal research which will be undertaken by the Institute for Mining and Minerals Research at the University of Kentucky. Western Kentucky coal, because of its high sulfur content, faces elimination from the national market in the next few years because of strict air-pollution standards. Unless we find some economic way of removing the sulfur pollutant from the coal, the industry is doomed. Within the next two years full attention will be given to this problem by scientists and engineers at UK. Our long-range hope is to attract privately funded dollars from the nation's major energy corporations for research and pilot plants, located in the state, that will confront and solve the problems identified with this vital energy source.

I have recommended $2.9 million in the biennium for airport development as a means of advancing our economic progress rate. These funds will be matched with both local and federal dollars giving us a $7.9 million airport improvement program.

With regard to economic research, I will submit legislation next week that will establish by statute the Governor's Council of Economic Advisors. The new budget provides additional funding for this research group which is looking toward our long-range economic development.

With regard to rural development, I have recommended funds totaling $100,000 for staffing the Office of Farmers' Advocate, exactly as I promised in the campaign. The bill creating the Governor's Council on Agriculture has been introduced in the House. The Council's objectives will be the development and promotion of a statewide agri-business program, including wider distribution and promotion of the state's agricultural products.

Also, I have recommended $200,000 to fund the Kentucky Farm Development Authority created by the 1970 General Assembly. This Authority will guarantee loans to the small farmer giving him the chance to own and improve his farm while at the same time stimulating the agricultural sector of the state's economy.

An appropriation of $40,000 to be matched with $75,000 in federal funds is included for making a major study of the economic potential along the new Appalachian highway corridors in eastern Kentucky. A detailed inventory of residential, commercial, and industrial sites which have potential for development in eastern Kentucky will be made and carried to industrial prospects.

With your approval of this budget for economic development, I am confident we can show a marked improvement in state productivity, individual earnings, employment, and citizen satisfaction within the next two years.

HEALTH AND HUMAN RESOURCES

No part of the budget is of greater importance than the wise use of funds we allocate for health and human resources. The 1972–1974 budget demonstrates our concern for the mentally ill, the retarded, the elderly, the blind, and the disabled by providing increased general fund appropriations in every area. Our compassion to those less fortunate is shown through the following: $8.1 million for fully funding the operation of the new Somerset Training Center for the Retarded; $1.3 million for operating the Hazelwood Hospital for the Retarded; and $2 million for community mental health and retardation centers to further reduce the number of people who need to be hospitalized. Funds also are included for the development of drug and alcohol programs at these centers. I have a strong concern in both areas and intend to see that drug- and alcohol-abuse treatment, education, and enforcement have top priority in my administration. With matching federal funds we can wage a winning war against these destroyers of mankind, especially among our youth.

Other appropriations include $200,000, or a 75 percent increase, in funding for the control and prevention of venereal disease—a growing problem among teenagers; $100,000 for new hearing clinics in Lexington and Covington to be administered by the Commission for Handicapped Children; $14.2 million to continue the state Medicaid program, including appropriations for new mandatory federal programs; and $1.8 million to implement the federal Food Stamp Law provisions. The number of food stamp counties will be increased from 73 to 100 in the biennium.

We shall include $1 million for the cost of providing increased payments to persons residing in personal-care homes. The increases will be contingent upon improved conditions within these homes. The rules and regulations governing homes will be strengthened to prevent any "warehousing" of our elderly. Homes that don't meet state standards will not qualify for increased payments.

We shall provide $16.2 million for grant programs to the aged, blind, disabled, and dependent children including funds to implement the new intermediate care program and emergency assistance program, $1.3 million for the operation of the new Northern Kentucky Child Welfare Diagnostic Center and the Green River Boys Camp, a residential center for juveniles in Butler County, and $1.2 million for expansion of community services in the Department of Child Welfare. This appropriation will refocus the department's efforts away from institutions and toward community programs that assist the delinquent child in making an adjustment in his home community.

One hundred fifty-six thousand dollars will go to the industries for the blind for a computerized program that will enable some 300 blind persons across the state, with the aid of a talking computer, to compete and hold down jobs that they otherwise could not possibly manage.

Finally in this area $700,000 in state money to be matched by double that amount in federal funds will be appropriated for a $2 million facility for treating children who suffer mental illness. This new fifty-bed hospital unit will be located on the grounds at Central State Hospital in Anchorage and is of highest priority in the capital improvements program in the state Mental Health Department.

CAPITAL CONSTRUCTION

I have already mentioned several construction projects that are funded in the budget. Here are others worthy of your attention: First, there is

$2 million for the renovation of the Old Capitol and Old Capitol Annex. The annex will be vacated next fiscal year when its tenants move into the Capital Plaza. Last session the General Assembly by law dedicated both facilities to the Historical Society. Very costly renovations are required to maintain these historic buildings. Also requested are $1.6 million for the long-overdue refurbishment of the state fairgrounds' athletic field and stadium and $530,000 for renovation and maintenance work on the State Fair and Exposition Center. We shall provide $318,000 for maintenance work on National Guard armories and $2.5 million each year for emergency repairs, maintenance, planning, and minor renovation and construction on miscellaneous projects.

In order that we may begin at once to plan for the new facilities and repair the old, I am asking that a portion of the capital improvements budget be appropriated in the current year.

MANAGEMENT

When I leave Frankfort four years from now, I would like to have a reputation as the Governor who soundly managed the state government. Until reorganization the task is impossible. We will proceed as quickly as possible in the months that lie ahead.

A portion of the funds for this effort are in the appropriation for state planning which I ask be doubled in the biennium. If you grant this request, I can assure you the dollars will be wisely expended. They will be used, in part, to lay the groundwork for the streamlined structure large organizations such as state government demand for efficiency in this day and time.

Also, I am asking that the Governor's Contingency Fund be raised from $1 million to $2 million each year. The contingency fund has been at $1 million now for over ten years. Yet, during that time the size of the general fund has doubled. The $2 million I am seeking represents less than 0.3 percent of the total general fund.

State government efficiency will always be determined, in large measure, by the employees who work for it. These employees have not been overlooked in the budget. Funds are included to pay all salary increments. An appropriation of $900,000 has been put into the budget for the Department of Personnel each year to purchase a single health insurance program effective July 1 for state employees. The cost of this will be shared by the workers. This approach is much preferable to the ill-considered and hastily drawn plan put together in the last week of the previous administration, a plan not in the employees' best interest.

Funds are included in the budget for the salary increases provided in House Bill 111. While considerable criticism has attended this bill, I would point out to you that one of the reasons for its submission is contained in a December study, completed by the U.S. Bureau of Labor Statistics, showing the comparison between salaries in state government and similar jobs in private enterprise in Kentucky. There is a pay gap at all grade levels in the state classification system, but the widest gap is at the upper grades where the top executives and managers in the state's service lag behind their counterparts in private industry by an average of 36.9 percent. This study is available in the state Personnel Department for your confirmation.

Accompanying the executive budget document which you will receive this afternoon is another booklet presenting the budget in a program format for the Handicapped Children's Commission. This pilot effort, a new approach to budget introduction, is submitted for your consideration. The aim of the presentation is to identify the agency's workload and program objectives with greater decision, and at the same time give a much better measure of the agency's performance in the new biennium. This innovation is an example of some of the management improvements we have in mind for state government which will stretch the taxpayer's dollar.

I regret it is necessary for me to ask this Assembly for two deficit appropriations for the current fiscal year. The Department of Finance will require $345,240 and the Department of Corrections will need $249,000 to finish the 1972 fiscal year in the black. Mismanagement in the prior administration necessitates this request.

Also, I am asking for a $600,000 appropriation in the current year to match federal dollars for the state's school lunch program. The federal matching requirements were changed since this Assembly last met. The law change by the Congress makes this appropriation necessary.

HIGHWAYS

I am committed, as I always have been, to the construction and maintenance of an adequate, quality road system within our state. However, four problems have emerged. They must be met head-on.

The first problem relates to the expense of construction. In the most recent year for which figures are available, highway construction costs rose by 18 percent. Moreover, inflation has also hit us hard in maintaining the existing road system. Remember, every mile of highway in our state must be maintained totally with state funds—even though many were financed principally by federal matching dollars. It simply costs more to repair and maintain our road system which is increasing in mileage each year.

The second problem relates to the debt-service cost on the toll roads. Debt service on these highways will increase from $26 million in the current year to $42 million next year, and finally level off at $54.5 million in the second year of the biennium. I am not critical of this increase. Neither am I critical of the toll roads—I voted for them. I am saying the time has come to pay for them, and the responsibility falls on my shoulders.

The third problem I face is the depletion of the highway general-obligation bond funds. The two largest federal aid programs we benefit from are those supporting interstate and Appalachian highways. The federal government provides 90 percent of the cost of the interstate system and 70 percent of the Appalachian system cost. In prior years the state's matching share of dollars for these two programs was provided from the sale of voted general-obligation bonds. This money will be exhausted in the current year. If Kentucky continues to match all available federal funds for interstate and Appalachian highways in the next two years, we must put up $50 million which formerly was provided by bonds proceeds.

The fourth problem is a shameful one. Inspection of Highway Department records during the previous administration tell a disturbing truth. Accelerated expenditures of funds during the past year, a political year, have left the cupboard bare. If the normal trend in previous years had been followed, we would have funds for needed projects. Regretfully, this is not the case. The crisis long predicted in the road fund is here. It falls my lot to deal with it. In considering alternatives, I have ruled out additional general-obligation bond issues. It would be inappropriate to ask the people to vote further debt to finance construction of roads. After much study, I am submitting to you, in a separate bill, a plan to alleviate this great difficulty. You are aware that without financial support the road program would have to be shut down. This matter deserves your most concentrated analysis and judgment.

Other states are experiencing similar problems. In recent weeks Governors of South Carolina and Virginia have included in their budget messages requests to increase the gas-tax levy from seven to nine cents. West Virginia has recently had to raise its tax to eight and one-half cents. Indiana has an eight-cent tax with a sales tax applied on top of it. North Carolina has a nine-cent gasoline tax. Many states have a higher gasoline tax than we. Many others will be forced during the next two years to raise their rates.

My plan for your deliberation in this separate package is that the state motor-fuel tax be increased only two cents. This is minimal, well below speculation, but it will suffice. The additional revenues generated by this minimum increase will let us match all available federal primary, secondary, and urban-aid roads. We can fully match funds available for the interstate and Appalachian systems. We can continue to maintain the existing roads. In short, we can overcome the financial crisis we are in.

Of equal importance, we can begin to channel needed road fund taxes into an area that heretofore has been overlooked. I am proposing that we embark on a bold new program of sharing a portion of the increased gas-tax levy with the cities and urban areas of our state. Therefore, I am submitting legislation that will permit the sharing of one-half cent of the gasoline tax with urban areas, beginning in the second year of the new biennium. These funds will go for the construction and maintenance of city streets and roadways. The total funds available in fiscal 1974 should exceed $9 million.

The next two years are the most critical period the Commonwealth will face with highway financing. In order to get by in the new biennium, it also will be necessary that road fund dollars, which for many years have gone to other state agencies supporting the highway program, be temporarily discontinued. This means that the general fund will have to provide—in the forthcoming biennium—almost $8 million to state agencies that support the Highway Department. Even with these drastic measures, we still will have very limited funds for the construction of highways that must be built with 100 percent state dollars. While the highway budget goes up significantly in the next two years, the new dollars go for fixed costs. What I am proposing to you is a bare-bones budget for operating the Highway Department during the biennium.

FINANCING THE GOVERNMENT

During the election campaign I promised tax reform. Today I stand before you and offer reform. I propose to lighten the tax obligation of the individual, fulfill my campaign commitments, and balance the state budget. To accomplish these formidable objectives I recommend the following tax package for your consideration:

1. The five-cent sales tax on "take home" food be removed on October 1, 1972.

2. A severance tax of 5 percent on gross sales with a thirty-cents-per-ton minimum paid by the coal producer. The tax will be effective April 1, 1972.

3. The deductibility of federal taxes when computing state tax liability for corporations be eliminated, and the maximum tax rate lowered from 7 percent to 5.8 percent, effective January 1, 1972.

Removal of the sales tax on October 1 on take-home groceries will reduce general fund revenues $101 million in the biennium. For the average family of four, the annual tax savings will be at least $80. At the same time, the average family will pay only $15 more on an annual basis for gasoline. The net result is a savings to the average family of $65.

The severance tax will bring $84 million into the general fund during the biennium. The latest available figures indicate that approximately 85 percent of the coal mined in Kentucky is shipped out of state. The weight of this tax will not fall heavily on Kentucky taxpayers. We have for too many years sat idly by while millions of tons of this valuable mineral resource were extracted from Kentucky lands and shipped beyond our borders with no benefit to the Commonwealth except for the direct wages paid to the workers. The time for changing this situation is now.

The corporate tax alteration is a reform that is also overdue. Elimination of the federal deductibility will yield $29 million in revenues during the coming biennium which will be paid into the state's general fund. While this change will increase the state tax obligation of corporations, they can write off almost 50 percent of the increase when they file their federal tax returns. With a cautiously optimistic revenue forecast and a more equitable tax program as outlined, we can meet the service needs of the people, make genuine program improvements, and balance the state budget.

CONCLUSION

In closing let me remind you of an undisputed fact. Never in the history of our Commonwealth have so many programs been available to each of our citizens. Yet we are increasing services while at the same time reducing the citizen tax load, just as I pledged. The programs advanced by me as a candidate are included in this budget, just as I pledged. I respectfully hand over to you what I consider a plan for the betterment of all people and ask that you help me complete the task I began months ago.

I hope you will begin immediate consideration of the budget with hearings getting under way at once. I urge you to complete your deliberations in the shortest time possible so that this Assembly can take up other important matters. The budget is balanced. It has been carefully drawn. To tamper with the revenue side without adjusting the expenditure side would be irresponsible. The fact that I am able to present for your scrutiny and approval a program that meets my commitments without an increase in personal tax liability is a tribute to the Finance Commissioner, Revenue Commissioner, Budget Director, and the staffs of the Departments of Revenue and Finance who have rendered a magnificent professional service. These and other officials you may wish to call are at your disposal until such time as the budget is enacted into law. Thank you.[1]

---

1. The Governor's copy of this address included the following note: "There are numerous other people services in this budget. Quickly, I want to cite only a few: computerization of voter registration in Kentucky to implement the 1970 Voter Rights Amendment; strengthening the public informational functions of the Kentucky Registry of Election Finance; providing a special instructor for blind, retarded children at the School for the Blind; twelve new bookmobiles during the biennium; debt-service grants-in-aid to local communities for renovation and construction of ten libraries; the initiation of a history-mobile program in Kentucky; funds totaling $400,000 to help defray the costs of chronic kidney disease for those who suffer this very expensive illness; and added emphasis on projects for the aging."

STATEMENT RE:
BUDGET PASSAGE
Frankfort / March 15, 1972

IN my message to the General Assembly last February 3, I said: "The Budget touches every man, woman, and child in this state." Little attention was given to that introductory statement, though it signaled an attitude that is spurred on with my signature this morning. While campaigning for Governor, the most frequently utilized word by Wendell Ford was "People." As State Senator and Lieutenant Governor, I gave first consideration to people, just as the tradition of my political party is one of compassion for the man on the street.

This budget, and the supporting revenue measures, clearly demonstrate a new direction for state government in Kentucky. As months pass in the coming biennium, and afterwards, every man, woman, and child in Kentucky will experience a new atmosphere of accountability from their state government. I say this without hesitation when considering the subject of education. I say this without hesitation when considering the subject of safety and security. I say this without hesitation when considering the subject of health and human resources. I say this without hesitation when considering the subject of governmental reform. The bills on my desk reflect this new direction in the environment, in economic development, agriculture, transportation, and in other priorities which dignify the citizen of Kentucky.

We stand ready to accomplish much, and will do so through tax reform, easing the burden on the individual, a burden not only made heavier four years ago, but one which could have been lightened through reform during the last four years. The undisputed fact is that the individual will now pay less state taxes while receiving more services! I predict that the positive significance of these bills will grow as time passes, that the feeling I have today will be shared by all Kentuckians as they see for themselves that indeed, there is an administration responsive to human needs and, at the same time, considerate of the individual's right to tax equity.

Finally, and most important to me, is the fact that I have included in this budget the promises of my campaign. Make no mistake about it, this is a strong beginning, but we will endeavor to do even more in behalf of the individual as each future opportunity is unveiled. I want to especially compliment my staff, members of the Departments of Finance and Revenue, and the Democratic leadership of the House and Senate. History will record their contributions to people, because their attitudes were guided by concern for others.

STATEMENT RE:
SPECIAL SESSION
Frankfort / March 30, 1972

NINE days ago the Supreme Court of the United States decided an appeal from the United States District Court for the Middle District of Tennessee. This was the case of *Winfield Dunn, Governor of the State of Tennessee, et al., Appellants* v. *James F. Blumstein.*

The Supreme Court struck down the one-year residency requirement as a prerequisite for registration to vote. This action therefore has a direct bearing on Kentucky, since our Constitution includes the one-year residency factor. It becomes necessary, therefore, for the General Assembly of the Commonwealth of Kentucky to meet in special session in order that our election laws conform with the Court's ruling.

There is insufficient time to carry out these changes before the May primary election date because of existing constitutional and other legal requirements involving a Special Session, and because of the mechanics of altering our registration process. However, Kentucky must conform before the November general election. I will issue a call for a Special Session in sufficient time to meet the Court's mandate. This will occur early in the summer.

SPECIAL SESSION
Frankfort / June 8, 1972

Your absence from the Senate and House Chambers has been brief. It is my expectation, and I feel sure your desire, that your presence in this Special Session is brief. The 1972 Kentucky General Assembly assumed the responsibility for many pieces of important legislation, which already have, and will have, a positive effect on every person in this state. Numerous items had been long neglected. We have corrected a great number of these injustices. Some of the accomplishments have been cited nationally, with other states already looking to Kentucky for advice and counsel. Still others have been hailed as major breakthroughs in meeting the present and future needs of our people. More substantive legislation was passed by the 1972 Assembly than in any other session of modern history. Perfection is difficult to obtain. This is especially true in the democratic process involving a variety of philosophies, interests, individual hopes, and the uniqueness of your representative areas. Regardless of what some critics might say, as years pass the applause of Kentuckians will increase.

Now we enter a short extraordinary session based on three factors: 1) a recent ruling of the United States Supreme Court; 2) new federal standards; and 3) the need to constantly strive for perfection.

After you adjourned this year, the Supreme Court handed down a decision relating to state voter-residency requirements. This nullifies Kentucky's constitutional provisions governing the subject. Only through a Special Session can we adhere to an order of the nation's highest court. My call has included, therefore, the amendment of the election laws, to set the residence requirements for eligibility to vote in all elections so as to comply with the decision of the Supreme Court. Election reform was a major achievement for us this year. Adoption of the proposed amendment altering voter-residence rules will enable thousands of our citizens to register and vote. These are citizens who heretofore have been disfranchised because they did not meet lengthy resident requirements.

The Ninety-second Congress, in its Second Session, gave states an opportunity to ratify a joint resolution relative to equal rights for men and women. I feel it important that you consider this matter now.

On March 24, as Governor, I signed into law House Bill 430[1] passed by the 1972 Regular Session of the General Assembly. This law prohibits discrimination in the hiring of women or persons between the ages of forty and sixty-five. I have recognized the vital significance of women in government. They are making decisive contributions by accepting the challenge given them in my administration. Already, we have three women commissioners, and a woman holds a key administrative post in the Governor's Office.

As the Regular Session of the 1972 General Assembly began, the Legislature was faced with both congressional and legislative redistricting. As Governor, I recommended to the Legislature that Congressional Districts be reapportioned in a fair and equal manner, making a good faith effort to achieve as nearly as possible mathematical equality between the districts. House Bill 112 was passed,[2] with the variance in population between the largest and smallest Congressional District being less than 1.39. As you know the bill was challenged in federal court on grounds that this legislation had not achieved a precise population equality between Kentucky's Congressional Districts.

After you had adjourned, final official figures from the Bureau of the Census were received in Kentucky. I then indicated by letter to the presiding judge of the U.S. District Court hearing the challenge, that I would include in the call for a Special Session the subject of reapportionment of Kentucky's Congressional Districts. This would enable you to refine House Bill 112 in an effort to achieve a more precise mathematical equality between the various Congressional Districts. Let me remind you however that the Court said our law did not damage the conscience of the Court, therefore indicating that House Bill 112 was indeed a good bill and one that would have been accepted.

Nevertheless, we have an opportunity to seek more perfection and I urge you to do so. The federal Court has retained jurisdiction of House Bill 112 awaiting the action of this Session. I recommend that such changes be made in that legislation as will meet the test of the Court. This can be done by shifting only eight precincts in our present Congressional Districts from which congressmen were nominated in May. The result will be that no district will vary from the "ideal" by as much as a precinct. The percentage variation of 0.1931 will be a national model.

Recent recalculations of the population in urban counties also makes necessary readjustments in some of our state Senatorial and Representative districts. Most districts, beyond a doubt, meet constitutional standards. These districts might well be left undisturbed. Your committees have drafted the necessary legislation to bring all districts into conformance with the Court order and constitutional requirements. It is my firm belief, and I am recommending to you, that no district deviate more than 3 percent on population variance. I know that redistricting never is an easy task. I also know that the General Assembly never has failed to face up to its responsibilities.

Another subject that I have asked you to consider is the enactment of environmental protection legislation. As you well know, both Houses at the Regular Session passed House Bill 294.[3] But this bill, on the last day, was not enrolled in Open Session, as required by our Constitution. The General Assembly overwhelmingly expressed its will on this subject. You have expressed approval of a strong environmental quality program and a strong reorganized structuring of its administration. The State Government Committee, last week, recommended that the bill be reintroduced as passed by both Houses. I concur in that recommendation with four necessary modifications, all of which are incorporated in the bill to be introduced.

The federal Environmental Protection Agency has asked us by letter (which has been furnished to your committees) that two minor changes be made in House Bill 294. These changes will enable us to meet federal standards and permit Kentucky to administer its own program. The draft that I am recommending is technically modified to complement the provisions of House Bill 47[4] which goes into effect June 16. These modifications relate to strip-mining fees and their disposition.

I am recommending for your consideration one other change that I believe was actually intended by the Legislature—that one-half of the increased acreage fees, as well as one-half of the permit fees, be returned to the county in which the mining operation is located. This revenue-sharing is desirable and should be acceptable.

The General Assembly in enacting the 1972 Occupational Safety and Health Law (H.B. 391)[5] took a major legislative step in behalf of Kentucky's industrial workers and their families. This law was patterned on the 1970 federal act and had the full support of my administration. The United States Department of Labor has advised me that two minor changes will make our legislation completely acceptable. This advice has been transmitted to your Labor and Industry Committee. Our state plan must provide for sanctions against first-instance violations of state standards and must meet the federal criteria on citations for violations of the state law. I recommend that you adopt the proposed legislation to that effect and make only those changes necessary to conform to the end that the program can be administered by our Kentucky department rather than by federal administrators.

The final subject in my call is included because of the present concern over state-chartered savings and loan associations. The insurance of deposits with the associations clearly is desirable as is the necessity to make certain the continued operation of the scores of state associations in which thousands of Kentuckians have invested millions of dollars. Your Banking and Insurance Committee has found that the unforeseen effect of 1972 Senate Bill 159[6] is to effectively prohibit loans after June 16, in light of the fact that it takes from eighteen months to two years for state associations to meet federal standards for insurance. The committee and the Commissioner of Banking have drafted a bill to require federal insurance of existing associations by July 1, 1974, and to require insurance before the granting of new charters. I recommend its enactment.

I realize, as you realize, that there are many other items we could consider in a Special Session. However, most of these address themselves to your interim committees for recommendations. I have included in my call those subjects which I consider most pressing and demanding of immediate action. Many of you have advised me of your desire to meet and consider the people's business with dispatch and a minimum of expense. I agree with you. I, and everyone in the Executive Department, stand ready to assist you and cooperate in every way in the performance of your constitutional duties.

---

1. See an act "relating to civil rights," which was approved March 24, 1972. *Acts of the General Assembly of the Commonwealth of Kentucky, 1972*, Chapter 255 (H.B. 430), pp. 1065–76.

2. See an act "relating to Congressional Districts, and declaring an emergency," which was approved on February 23, 1972. This act repealed sections

120.070 and 120.075 of the *Kentucky Revised Statutes. Acts of the General Assembly of the Commonwealth of Kentucky*, 1972, Chapter 17 (H.B. 112), pp. 41–44.

3. House Bill 294, concerning environmental protection, is the famous "Lost Bill," so named because it was misplaced for a critical period of time and thus not passed officially.

4. See an act "relating to strip mining," which was approved March 27, 1972. *Acts of the General Assembly of the Commonwealth of Kentucky, 1972*, Chapter 270 (H.B. 47), pp. 1172–78.

5. See an act "relating to the safety and health of workers employed within the Commonwealth of Kentucky," which was approved on March 27, 1972. *Acts of the General Assembly of the Commonwealth of Kentucky, 1972*, Chapter 251 (H.B. 391), pp. 1048–62.

6. See an act "relating to financial institutions," which became law without the Governor's signature on March 30, 1972. *Acts of the General Assembly of the Commonwealth of Kentucky, 1972*, Chapter 267 (S.B. 159), pp. 1154–63.

PRELEGISLATIVE CONFERENCE
Gilbertsville / December 3, 1973

To introduce the theme of my remarks, I want to go back 116 years to 1857, when *Harper's Weekly* published an editorial entitled "A Gloomy Moment in History." Less than 100 words were written. But in those few words the seriousness of that period came forth loud and clear. *Harper's* said: "Not in the lifetime of most men has there been so much grave and deep apprehension." Apprehension existed because of the domestic economic situation, which was said to be "in chaos." Apprehension existed because of a weak U.S. dollar abroad. Apprehension of prices caused the author to term them "so high as to be utterly impossible." And apprehension grew due to an uncertain political climate, as well as the menace of Russia's decisions in world influence.

This editorial could be printed today with current historical accuracy. I suppose whoever first said, "Times don't change," could smile at the comparison of 1973 and 1857. However, times do change. Yet there are identical problems during various periods of history. Right now, this nation is in the middle of more problems than any of us would prefer. To responsible leadership, they are considered challenges. In what must be a relentless search for proper solutions, the strength of leadership emerges through results. Kentucky and the nation have accepted countless challenges since our founding days. From such an attitude has come success and progress—yet more problems through a changing society and thus more challenges.

Two years ago I stood before the Prelegislative Conference to ask for a cooperative venture in forging a responsible and responsive executive-legislative relationship. This we did. In my opinion, the 1972 General Assembly emerged with distinction. Its membership worked hard. Great legislation having a positive impact on Kentucky was produced. I am proud of the way the executive and legislative branches met various challenges which had been passed over in previous years. I am also proud of the attention you gave other necessary legislation which provides many beneficial measures on behalf of people. You who served should be equally as proud.

Now we face another Session. We do so realizing that much of the groundwork has been attended to in an orderly fashion. Since the 1972 Session, interim legislative activity has been brisk and productive. The pre-filing of bills has given added time for study and review. Approximately 75 percent of this administration's legislation has been sent upstairs for pre-filing—something which has not occurred in the past. You will also find fewer "administration bills" than in the past. As one who came from the legislative branch, I recognize your role and your problems. If our action helps ease the burden, then we will have prevented an imposition on your limited time. The executive branch has also, during the reorganization of state government, kept legislative members advised of those activities, and we have made our staff available whenever other information was requested.

As the 1974 Session approaches, you and I have a clear role in the process of government, at a time when government falls under the critical eye of the citizens. We hear and read much about stalemates in Washington, where Congress and the White House debate publicly the faults of each other and blame each other for snail-paced legislative activity. Kentucky, therefore, can continue to reassure a concerned public that legislative-executive cooperation is indeed real.

There is another federal influence for both of our roles. What happens nationally is felt in each state. Federal-state programs are ever-changing and we must be prepared to respond in one of several directions. Since Kentucky prepares a biennial budget, revenue estimates are subject to greater variations due to a twenty-four-month national economic climate. And now, the energy crisis has brought a frightening chill to what was very recently a warm atmosphere of economic excitement in Kentucky. So the admonition now is caution. We cannot allow our most favorable economic position to be adversely affected beyond expected impacts of the energy crisis. Thus we must weigh prospects of growing unemployment, curtailment of highway funds, changing life-styles, restricted business activities, and other difficulties which will arise due to energy shortages.

Future planning will be more difficult. By facing reality, making tough decisions, and working together we can get through what appears to be a lengthy and difficult period. Anything less will only spark new problems down the road. I have many personal concerns—for libraries, educational advancement, transportation, health and welfare, energy research and development, and a continuing improvement of the environment . . . yes, the list is long. You have expressed to me similar concerns. And I am confident we can find the right approaches despite growing clouds which are not of our making.

STATE OF THE
COMMONWEALTH ADDRESS
Frankfort / January 8, 1974

You have extended an invitation for a report on the status of our state, which I accept with deep appreciation, and great enthusiasm.

In addition to this address, and the biennial budget recommendation, both of which are traditional, I may ask your permission for two other appearances in joint Session. One would be a special energy message due to America's latest crisis. Kentucky's potential for a unique role in helping solve this crisis can have a tremendously favorable impact on our future. The other message would be to speak on reorganization of state government since such an undertaking has not been achieved in nearly forty years.

Tonight's purpose, however, is to place the condition of our state in proper perspective. By doing so, you and others will gauge our present quality of life, how we have advanced in two years, and this Commonwealth's position among other states of the Union.

Certainly, all is not perfect. No Governor, no legislative body, ever accomplishes the sum total that responsible individuals desire. Those who have formerly served would, I'm sure, echo this reality. We have had outstanding Governors and outstanding General Assemblies. But to use an example, though every living Governor, as well as past legislatures, left legacies for others to grasp, each wanted to do more. Years from now, as society changes, other Governors and other legislators will experience the frustrations of trying to perform countless good deeds they will, unfortunately, be unable to complete. This is the history of both our nation and Commonwealth, a history dictating an approach to the rational continuity of administrations—a base I have endeavored to strengthen since December 7, 1971.

In applauding the 1972 General Assembly, as others did following adjournment, I want to say here and now that it was the most productive Session in history, and I challenge this body to surpass the tremendous contributions of service and leadership the 1972 General Assembly provided. Such words as "meaningful, businesslike, peaceful, and historic," were used by the analysts. Naturally they found faults. All of us can, especially when we rely on twenty-twenty hindsight or personal preference. But the justified accolades were there. In my opinion, the justification is now even more warranted in view of Kentucky's posture as 1974 begins.

The health of any state is first evaluated by examining its economic position. In no uncertain terms, the key to progress is when men and women are working. Kentuckians are working, 106,000 more in nonagricultural jobs alone since 1971. Unemployment is declining rapidly and is lower than the national average. Per capita income for Kentuckians has increased faster than the national average. For the first time Kentucky has recorded true billion-dollar farm economies—last year it was one and a quarter billion. Corporations and businesses realized their highest profit levels ever.

Why did all this happen? Because the 1972 General Assembly and I kept our word to the people of Kentucky. Because we tossed away old methods and were willing to try new ones, in the face of howling critics. Because of a determination to make positive things happen, beneficial to all who live in this state. And because the people worked hard to improve their own lot.

At no time since the beginning of World War II, and in many cases at no time ever, has our state's economic growth of the last two years been matched. But the major point is that Kentucky did better than the nation, despite alarming national problems—inflation, impoundments, curtailments of programs, and a paralysis of federal decision-making. It adds up to a Kentucky initiative for which we can all take pride!

At this point, however, caution is indicated. It is imperative that we distinguish between the past two years and the next two years. The past has been conquered! Looking back since the end of 1971, we have hurdled many obstacles which haven't been in Kentucky's way during previous times. Looking ahead to the end of 1975, the energy crisis looms as a definite threat to our state as well as the entire country. Our ability to overcome this and other expected difficulties will be the supreme test. But let me make one point without reservation—there may be an energy shortage, but there will never be a shortage of another resource, and that resource is the spirit and determination of Kentuckians. Adversity builds strength. Warning of adversity on January 4, 1972, in this chamber, I said: "There are serious problems which must be turned into working solutions by the time we leave office. I am approaching the next four years supported by the understanding that adversity can instill a stronger spirit."

This has been the approach. Where there were no federal domestic priorities, there have been state priorities. Where rising costs have burdened especially the poor and those on fixed and middle incomes, Kentuckians are now paying less state taxes and receiving more services.

Our unprecedented economic growth is seen by the $598 per capita income increase. In 1971, unemployment for this state amounted to 5.2 percent. At the end of last year, it was 4.2 percent. We weren't in this condition, for instance, in 1969 when the national rate was lower than Kentucky's, nor in 1970 when unemployment rose, both in Kentucky and America. That climb peaked two years ago. It has been going downward ever since. To expand further, last month only 1.7 percent of our citizens were receiving unemployment compensation. This compares to 2.3 percent in the U.S., again showing Kentucky's outstanding position among other states.

The dramatic rise in workers follows our stable economy, and it comes partially with new and expanded industry—151 new industries with 121 expansions of existing firms. The two-year investment amounted to over $415 million, but that's not all. An additional $231 million was invested in industrial warehousing and electric-generating plants. Confidence is growing in Kentucky!

Agriculture's record-smashing two years were real; federal subsidies were not fed into state figures. Farmers gained their highest net incomes ever. And we didn't do it by selling grain to Russia which caused food prices to skyrocket out of sight. When you put this all together—business profits, unemployment, new jobs, farm income, increased per capita income—with another major part of our economy, coal, it means that Kentucky, often looked down upon by others in the past, stands tall in America!

Look at the coal industry. Its employment has now gone over the 29,000 figure, the highest on record. Coal production neared 128 million tons last year, 20 million tons over our nearest rival, West Virginia! Our first year was also a marked improvement for the coal industry. These things happened—more production, more employment, more money—with fewer strip mines and small deep mines which were generally marginal at best.

What, therefore, is obvious? Despite the perils of a threatening national economy, Kentucky stands out, and someone, just someone, might conclude that in this state we're doing it right!

It is also apparent that by working together, the executive and 1972 legislative branches were correct in instituting tax reform which dramatically improved our economy. When I stood before many of you two years ago with a tax reform plan and a philosophy of operating government as a business, the doubting Thomases were vocal. They have been proven wrong! And who can say this better than the housewife, trying to figure out a food budget in the crunch of alarming price increases? Her family has received even more of a break than first anticipated, a break which resulted when we eliminated the sales tax on food, a campaign commitment you helped me keep.

How I remember those who charged me with irresponsibility in our revenue estimates, who said corporate tax adjustments would harm profits, who said the severance tax—another campaign pledge—would depress the coal industry, and who said the removal of the sales tax on food was ill-timed. Perhaps this will illustrate the foolishness of those who speak simply for political gain, who use scare tactics against Kentuckians, and who are experts at finding reasons why new ideas won't work, rather than being willing to make them work.

Tax reform has stimulated the economy and lessened the heavy load on people, and I publicly thank those men and women who have helped bring us to a new plateau. It has prevented us from merely equaling the national averages, or falling below, as has been the case in the past. It has given Kentuckians a better quality of life, for if we were not where we are today, individuals and families would be paying more taxes, just to keep up, rather than less taxes to move ahead. Furthermore, their struggle against national economic plights would be greater.

The health of Kentucky can be examined through its efforts toward personal safety. Again, Kentucky beats the nation. This time in decline of major crimes, another event which hasn't occurred since before World War II.

The health of Kentucky can be examined through its environment where facts overshadow assumption. Those facts are that in January

1972, 38,000 acres of surface-mined land were in default of reclamation. A positive response has been achieved on 37,000 acres. In doing so, the philosophy was getting the right kind of reclamation rather than pulling the trigger on those who failed to reclaim in the past but would, and have, restored the land through firm, clear direction and firm supervision and enforcement. The greening of Kentucky shows in other ways, with over 14 million new trees planted last year alone; through improved forestry surveillance resulting in the lowest loss by fire recorded in recent years; and through the reclamation of orphan banks, a cooperative venture between the state and Job Corps that is working well and that was funded by the last General Assembly.

The Department for Natural Resources and Environmental Protection's air-pollution-permit system has resulted in an emission reduction of 1.6 million tons per year of pollutants. Twenty-five additional air-monitoring stations have been added to the state network. Open dumps are going, and sanitary landfills are replacing them. Eighty open dumps were closed last year. Water and sewer facility plans and water-quality management plans for all of our Area Development Districts have been completed. The same holds true in planning for hazardous solid waste, water-quality control in mining, and water impoundment regulations. These new standards were reached because the 1972 General Assembly had the courage to support my budget and programs, despite the self-anointed experts who said it couldn't be done.

Kentucky's health is also viewed through her opportunities for citizen activities, whether it be recreation, travel, hunting and fishing facilities, historical events, or the many other advantages a state can provide. Tied with our commercial growth is the tourist industry, which, during the last two years, has reached unprecedented heights in the number of visitors, both from in state and out of state, in the number of miles traveled in Kentucky, and in the dollars spent.

Although major construction at Boonesboro and Tom Sawyer parks has begun, and land has been acquired along with a master plan for the new Kentucky Horse Park already in limited use, the past two years have been a period of necessary refurbishing, of long-needed maintenance and upgrading of our entire parks system. New management techniques have justified themselves by taking some of the red out of the parks budget, a red which has always existed but has seldom been improved upon. These techniques have increased service quality to the 50 million persons visiting our parks in the past two years. I base this on receipt of 40,000 comments, of which 90 percent were favorable.

As you know, the Department of Transportation is responsible for more than 25,000 miles of public roads and assists county governments in meeting their responsibilities for over 19,000 miles. The current fiscal year is also the first for our new Municipal Aid program (state-local revenue-sharing), and I am happy to report that 423 cities have benefited from improvements to 720 miles of local streets. This is the revenue-sharing program the last General Assembly enacted against opposition from those who feared change. But the record already shows it was a responsible and responsive answer to serious needs.

During the first two years, construction projects statewide totaled $297 million. This substantial program notes two unusual achievements. It includes more bridges across major rivers than the total of all such bridge projects for the past fifty years, and had the greatest single project ever awarded, the $17.5 million Pikeville Model Cities cut-through.

Kentucky's health is directly associated with the ability of state and local governments to function as a team. In this area the spirit I mentioned earlier is clear. Never before has there been a more direct line of communications from the community—the citizen and official—to state government. Home rule has proven beneficial. Reorganization has for the first time given local government a direct link to decision-making in the executive branch. The Office for Local Government, our new liaison with cities and counties, provides services to an average of 900 assistance requests per month. Numerous programs in Kentucky have resulted through the full cooperation and input among the state, local governments, and community leaders. Certainly, this is evidenced in our metropolitan areas. It says to you and all Kentucky: Government can be personal, and I think that's the way you want it!

I shall not expand at this time on the results of reorganization or the effects of innovative business techniques applied to the operation of state government. You will have that information in the budget message and other reports. However, I can look you square in the eye and say that, as the last budget called for a percentage decrease in tax dollars for government operations, we did even better by spending less than was appropriated. I can look you square in the eye and say without hesitation that reorganization is working and will work even more professionally as time passes, with, of course, your concurrence. I can tell you that, for example, the entire Department of Transportation now has fewer employees than the old single Highway Department did when I assumed office. I can show you positive signs that the spiraling growth of government can be prevented. Isn't this what we both want? I can assure you that a greater delivery of services, a faster delivery of services, is under way, and this is what government must be all about.

The health of Kentucky is also weighed through its educational opportunities. Education has been under a microscope since the beginning of public schools. It receives the greatest amount of state tax dollars, yet there are those who irresponsibly criticize state government and the legislatures for failure. Exactly where does the amount of money the General Assembly appropriates for elementary and secondary education stand among all fifty states? The answer is ninth best in the nation, and it is no less than disgusting whenever individuals and a few special interest groups backbite many of you and others who have fought against economic odds to improve education. Local funding support does not get such high marks. Community support for elementary and secondary education ranks forty-second, even though there are legal and constitutional steps available to any community willing to expend its own effort for education. So let us distinguish who is doing what and strive to improve the quality of education by ensuring that the massive state funds are indeed student-oriented.

Federal action has brought a cloud over education. Probably the one example among many poor federal decisions which I can give is the drastic curtailment of funds for Head Start, certainly needed in Kentucky. First graders, through no fault of their own, are thrown into classes with those far more prepared for formal schooling. It is an adversity we are trying to overcome, and will overcome, as initiated when the last legislature funded and approved my plan for a public kindergarten, another campaign pledge. Here is one of several areas in which we must move onward.

There are many ways we can improve the quality of education, and once more I must remind you of federal abandonment, this time of libraries. Thousands upon thousands of school children utilize public libraries throughout the state, just as do adults. But the help from Washington suddenly stopped, and we're having to go it alone. And together we will do it.

Educational television now is a tool for 95 percent of our school districts, with 40,000 additional pupils having this special opportunity for learning in the last two years. We must make sure quality is the keynote to KET, just as we must make sure quality teaching is being provided in every county, and just as we must make sure that opportunities for learning are not isolated from any area.

Vocational education, where there has been an 11 percent increase in enrollment during the last year alone, and strong expansion, is another plus for Kentucky, one deserving our continued attention.

Hungry children are handicapped children. The state's effort to eliminate this disgraceful fact of life amounted to 32 million free meals and

600,000 reduced-cost meals during the last two school sessions. May we never again find a hungry child in our schools.

The 1972 General Assembly, acting on my recommendation, moved aggressively in behalf of special education. Again, more must be done, but let's give credit for what has been accomplished.

The last two years have definitely found refinement in higher education, a standard I felt absolutely necessary and one being implemented by the restructured and strengthened Council on Public Higher Education. At the same time Kentucky, by legislative action, assumed a larger financial role by bringing the University of Louisville into the state system, and by providing generous support to Northern Kentucky State College, necessary for its very early years in the system.

Health and welfare for all citizens of Kentucky are one more indicator of our overall status. Recently, I said in a public statement that the Human Resources Cabinet would probably be the most pleasant surprise in total government reorganization. Hopefully you will agree.

Still—before, during, and after reorganization, some startling events happened. They show how we did reorganize without not only disrupting services, but at the same time how we could improve them. I think you will be especially interested in the following: A new procedure instituted in 1972 providing special intensive treatment to juveniles who would have, because of serious crimes, gone to adult corrections institutions, has passed its crucial test. Seventy-five percent fewer juveniles are now in adult correctional facilities as a result of rehabilitation efforts rather than merely putting them away to learn to become hardened adult offenders in later years. Since 1972, the number of children being committed to juvenile treatment facilities has decreased 45 percent as a result of community-based treatment services, certainly a tax savings but even more a human savings.

In early 1972, there was a predicted nationwide explosion of venereal disease. Acting upon my recommendation, the legislature gave increased appropriations to fight this problem. Kentucky's expected increase of 14 percent in new cases of syphilis turned around to a 6 percent annual decrease.

And this one is very significant. The work-incentive program designed to train and place welfare recipients into gainful employment has shown great success. We put the emphasis on productive employment rather than handouts. Job placement has tripled with over 2,500 persons leaving the welfare rolls to assume taxpaying jobs in 1973 alone, and this figure is going up all the time!

In reviewing the status of our Commonwealth, I want to briefly touch on other notable points. Our corrections system will not be classified any more as hellhole institutions. Our parole and probation system will not be under the unsavory light of patronage any more. Our merit system has finally made believers out of skeptics with the addition of 4,200 state employees to its protection (which I will ask you to ratify), with the tightest control ever over dismissal procedures whereby Kentuckians aren't paying for political hanky-panky. To date, only 361 merit system employees have been dismissed for all causes, contrasting with some 1,474 dismissals during the first year of the previous administration. The fight against drug traffic is unparalleled. The success of a much larger enforcement unit can be measured by its effectiveness. In 1971, 369 narcotic and drug arrests were made, in 1972 the figure rose to 532, and in the first eleven months last year, the count neared 800. That unit, plus the attention given by the entire State Police force, is just one more indication of the new assault on crime in Kentucky.

Our state's enrichments came from many progressive pieces of legislation during the first biennium. Consumer protection, a statewide public defender system, refinement of the penal code, court reform, a generic drug law, low-income housing, and state-local revenue-sharing to upgrade community police forces are all people-oriented to enhance the lives of Kentuckians. Wild Rivers protection, the Pollution Abatement Authority, the Technical Institute, and Forensic Psychiatric Center are other noteworthy achievements.

Together, we kept faith with the citizens of the greatest state in America. We did what we pledged to do, proving that there can be credibility in politics and government. The moral, cultural, and physical fiber of Kentucky is strong. Hopefully that strength has been extended through wise, courageous, and responsible leadership.

As I conclude, may these thoughts be left. We have every reason to be proud as Kentuckians. We should be proud of our accomplishments. We saw adversity and were not afraid to challenge it. We conceived new ideas and were willing to try them. We asked for involvement and it came; it came from the communities, the farms, the young, and the elderly. Yes, there is all the room in the world for pride in what has taken place. But there isn't one inch of space for smugness. There is every reason to approach the future with even more determination, expecting the worst in view of our national traumas, yet striving for the best in view of our own status this hour.

I pray that we can look back on this 1974 Session two years from now and say every man and woman in a position of leadership looked the future square in the eye, then took a giant step for human betterment. We can expand Kentucky's role as a national leader by exceeding other states in more categories. In doing so, we will have again kept faith with those who come to us for the answers to their problems, and they will continue to realize that Kenutucky doesn't have to take a back seat to any other state! Thank you, and good evening.

1974 GENERAL ASSEMBLY BICENTENNIAL SALUTE
Frankfort / January 9, 1974

THE purpose of this evening is to introduce the first official event in Kentucky's celebration of its bicentennial era. It is fitting that we gather tonight in these chambers, where in 1970 the General Assembly conceived and created the Kentucky Historic Events Celebration Commission, charging its members with the responsibility of planning and implementing a celebration to recognize and pay tribute to events in Kentucky history.[1]

During our bicentennial celebration, over 3 million Kentuckians will have an opportunity to learn more about their history and heritage. Equally important will be an opportunity for Kentuckians to play a role in projects that will enhance the future of the state and bring lasting benefits to all within its borders. With this in mind, the Kentucky Historical Events Celebration Commission has diligently worked to develop a celebration to span the three-year period from 1974 through 1976 when Kentucky joins sister states in commemorating the two-hundredth anniversary of the founding of our nation. The commission has devoted its efforts toward encouraging citizen participation in bicentennial programs and activities to focus public attention on the proud heritage and future potential of Kentucky.

The promise of greatness has always been inherent in the state's fertile soil, rich natural resources, and its central location. However, it was and is the genius of its people, given freedom and opportunity under a democratic constitution, which has brought our state to its position of cultural and economic prosperity. For this reason, all Kentucky bicentennial activities will be people-oriented, carried out by Kentuckians dedicated to focusing attention on the meaningful contribution of each and every area to the many and varied achievements of the Commonwealth. The eyes of the nation will be upon us as we demonstrate our pride in Kentucky in this bicentennial era. We embark on this, mindful that now is a crucial time in our nation's history, a time when it is more important than ever to show the world we have the strength and spirit needed to meet any and all challenges.

At this moment, I would like you to join me in thanking our state Historical Events Celebration Commission chairman, Clyde Webb,[2] and all the members who have served without payment for shaping the direction of this program as the 1970 General Assembly mandated. Mr. Webb and members of the commission are guests in this chamber tonight.

In preparation for the national bicentennial, sixteen outstanding men of letters have been commissioned by the American Enterprise Institute to present a distinguished lecture series designed to review past national accomplishments and chart courses for future achievements. This lecture series is dedicated to the belief that the competition of ideas is fundamental to a free society. Lectures are scheduled for such historic sites as Liberty Hall in Philadelphia, the House of Burgesses in Williamsburg, and the old Senate Chambers in the United States Capitol.

Kentucky is honored to be selected for one of the lecture programs, and it is with humble pride that we accept our place in this stellar roster of historic sites and welcome today's lecturer, Dr. Gordon Stewart Wood. Dr. Wood is the author of *The Creation of the American Republic, 1776–1787,* and *The Rising Glory of America, 1760–1820.* An educator and historian, Dr. Wood is a member of the American Historical Association. Presently an associate professor of history at Brown University, Providence, Rhode Island, Dr. Wood has also served on the faculty of Harvard and the University of Michigan. Tonight Dr. Wood will question whether or not the American experience provides a model for the evolution of political rights today and in the future. On behalf of the Commonwealth of Kentucky, I want to offer a cordial welcome to all our distinguished guests and present to you Dr. Gordon Stewart Wood.

----

1. See an act "establishing the Kentucky Historical Events Celebration Commission," approved March 30, 1970. *Acts of the General Assembly of the Commonwealth of Kentucky, 1970,* Chapter 128 (S.B. 283), pp. 553–56.

2. Clyde M. Webb (1919–   ), Ashland; vice president for external affairs, Ashland Oil, Inc.; chairman, Kentucky Bicentennial Celebration and the Kentucky Historical Events Celebration Commission (1970–1973); director, Ashland Area Chamber of Commerce and past director, Kentucky Chamber of Commerce. Webb's office, October 27, 1976.

ENERGY MESSAGE
Frankfort / January 16, 1974

THERE are four reasons for this message. One is to outline the serious implications of America's energy crisis. The second is to assess its impact on Kentucky, now and in the future. Next, I want to briefly review how state government has responded to emerging problems of energy shortages. And fourth, I come before you with recommendations to increase energy production in Kentucky, which will create an unprecedented economic boom, and at the same time propel our state into national leadership for research, development, and energy self-sufficiency. If the latter point sounds ambitious, it is! An opportunity which has never before presented itself, and may not again, awaits your decision.[1]

THE ENERGY CRISIS

Like others interested and concerned, you have no doubt asked, "How genuine, how legitimate, is the energy crisis?" So did I, for this is a very complex issue. Many have placed blame on the huge oil companies, believing some joined in an effort to make excessive profits out of a crisis situation. Nevertheless, whether the charges are true or not, those most knowledgeable, and who have been most critical, take pains to admit that a crisis does exist, no matter where the fault is. For our purposes, how Kentucky responds is far more important than the reasons for a crisis.

No single reason exists for the unfortunate predicament just beginning to bring sacrifice and shock to America. However, if we are surprised, our rude awakening should be only because of the timetable. A crisis has been predicted for over a decade. Repeated warnings fell on deaf ears despite conclusive evidence that sometime during the 1970s the United States would begin suffering as fuel reserves declined to a dangerous level. Our dilemma began long before October 1973, when Arab nations invoked their embargo on oil shipments to the United States. The embargo has made matters worse, with the hardest knocks still to come.

In cold, hard facts, the United States with 6 percent of the world's population, uses nearly 35 percent of the world's energy. Our demands are exceeding available energy supplies. Even with conservation, needs will continue to grow unless we are willing to succumb before terrible economic and personal hardships.

Although weather, insufficient inventory figures, and the Mid-East situation hamper government's ability to pinpoint the national energy status on a week-to-week or month-by-month basis, we do know there is from 10 to 20 percent less petroleum this winter than necessary to keep pace with current demands. We know America's annual consumption of natural gas is about eight times the volume used thirty years ago, and gas reserves have rapidly dwindled. We know domestic sources of supply provide 88 percent of the energy used in America. At first glance our reliance on foreign sources (12 percent) does not seem unduly large. However, that reliance was mainly on oil. More than one-quarter of the oil consumed here during 1970 came from foreign sources. We know that by 1985, America will be using twice as much energy as was consumed in 1970. If not, our country will be in a serious depression.

In questioning the true extent of an energy shortage, listen to those already hurt, from the man who has been laid off his assembly job, from the airline pilot, mechanic, or stewardess who must find other work, if he or she can, from the school superintendent who has no idea where to find bus gasoline in the future, from the parent wondering whether or not classes will be conducted on a regular basis because of cold weather, from individuals who must travel to make a living, from the farmer who can't secure fuel for machinery, from the businessman or industrialist who must increase production but can't find fuel.

It is somewhat easier to project future energy needs rather than future sources. Future supply depends upon the pace of discovery and development of reserves, technological improvements, and a broad range of governmental policies, including environmental controls, price regulations, and tax incentives. Studies indicate that in 1985 as much as 40 percent of our energy consumption would have to be furnished by foreign sources, two-thirds of the oil and one-third of the natural gas consumed in America.

Such heavy foreign reliance wouldn't be economically wise, not to mention the international political pressures placed against our country. Projected increases in energy imports imply an increasingly unfavorable balance of trade. The international value of the dollar would steadily decline as foreign energy costs soar.

We are now experiencing similar problems. Thus, the economic implications of our reliance on foreign sources do not lie a decade or so in the future; they are with us now! In other words, it's going to get worse before there is any improvement!

Obviously, America must turn to self-sufficiency. You, probably more than any other legislative body among the fifty states, have the greatest responsibility, and greatest opportunity, in giving direction which will be felt throughout the U.S. as well as in all parts of Kentucky.

I base my contention on several factors—Kentucky's vast energy reserves, primarily coal; Kentucky's potential for economic growth beyond any measure ever achieved; known technology which can produce clean fuel from coal; and Kentucky's obligation to respond with aggressiveness and vision, whenever our future is threatened by adversity.

Without farsighted leadership, without a determination of purpose, the energy crisis will have an even worse impact in later years on our children and our children's children.

IMPLICATIONS FOR KENTUCKY

Kentucky has already begun to feel the impact of shortages of natural gas and oil. This has posed problems for prospective industry as in other states. The shortages of oil have been felt in cutbacks of heating and motor fuel. Because of our climate, we are better off than many states, and we have not experienced an electrical shortage, since Kentucky's electric utility industry is coal-based. But we do have environmental standards to maintain.

Let me emphasize one point which should be remembered throughout this message. The direction I propose for Kentucky will not deter us from improved environmental qualities, whether it be in air emissions or land reclamation. The program I shall propose is designed to produce clean fuel, to stimulate deep mining, and enhance environmental quality and safety standards through research.

While Kentucky will feel the energy crunch from certain shortages, the state's economy is not expected to be as seriously affected as the nation's. Still, we must remain cautious and conservative. We can expect a slowdown of new industrial acquisitions, a decline in the highway fund, and perhaps a curtailment of recreational activity. The energy crisis suggests some unemployment increase, a slower pace of personal income growth, and continuing inflation. Elsewhere, the situation will be much worse, as it already is, especially in many northern and eastern states. Here is where Kentucky steps to the forefront.

Projections of energy consumption in the U.S. clearly indicate a rising need for coal. Coal accounted for about 20 percent of America's energy production in 1970. Output nationally was 600 million tons, with Kentucky supplying about 20 percent of that amount. Every indication points to twice the national output by 1985 or sooner. Last year Kentucky produced approximately 128 million tons. The severance tax brought us over $39 million. Doubling production means twice as much income. Think what this can mean for education, for roads, for human resources, and the other areas of governmental support we agonize over every two years. Think what the added employment will mean. And I haven't even touched on my proposal for research and development which would also generate tremendous economic growth.

There are approximately 65 billion tons of charted coal reserves in Kentucky. Another 50 billion tons are estimated. Kentucky, therefore, is in a most enviable position. A silver lining does appear around the dark cloud of the energy crisis, but unless we act promptly, the silver lining will disappear. Our vast resources require scientific attention. Of the 65 billion tons of known reserves, about 43 billion have a sulfur content greater than 1 percent. Air-quality standards for new plants without sulfur dioxide removal equipment require bituminous coal having not more than 0.7 percent sulfur. Kentucky must find ways of converting its high-sulfur coals into clean fuels if we are to fully share in the future expansion of coal output.

RESPONSE OF STATE GOVERNMENT

We turn now to a brief review of the actions your state government has taken as the oil shortage has brought the energy crisis to its presently acute stage. Last July, by executive order, I established the Kentucky Energy Council.[2] This interdepartmental committee was charged with the responsibility of determining directions and priorities so that this Commonwealth would be prepared for, and able to cope with, the burden of the energy crisis. Since its formation, the Energy Council has also served as our interface with the federal government in the allocation of middle distillates.

I have personally participated in a number of energy meetings with federal representatives. It has been an experience of both frustrations and enlightenment. We have found it difficult to proceed in the positive, assured way we would like, in order to reduce public uncertainties affecting future fuel supplies. However, we have taken, and continue to take, a constructive, supportive approach to the evolving situation at the federal level.

An interdepartmental staff group has performed exceptional service in handling thousands of inquiries about fuel problems, in responding to requests for priority allocations of middle distillates, and, in general, of managing the state's part of the fuel allocation process. We therefore have a functioning staff which can respond quickly to any change in federal policy.

The 1972 General Assembly appropriated $400,000 to support coal research. It was clear that we should begin work on the conversion of Kentucky coals into clean by-product fuels. The $400,000 have been supplemented by a national foundation grant in cooperation with the state and Ashland Oil, bringing our research to over a $1 million effort. The early results have commanded positive federal attention.

PROGRAM TO INCREASE ENERGY PRODUCTION

We must accelerate our research to help assure that certain types of Kentucky coal will remain competitive over the coming decade. Why is Kentucky's position the most promising, the most logical, the most realistic? Understanding the critical decline in domestic oil and gas reserves, as well as the grave dangers of depending upon foreign sources, America must immediately turn to new energy supplies where self-sufficiency can be achieved.

Nuclear power has been long-promised without significant results. Today it is under a cloud of environmental and safety fears, prompting experts to admit we probably won't have sufficient amounts of nuclear energy before the year 2000, or even beyond. Solar energy in massive quantities is extremely costly and also far into the future. Scientists believe a worthwhile solar production system might require a joint effort by the industrial nations of the world. Oil shale tends to be an extravagant, misleading item of hope, though some research is under way. Financial and environmental costs are excessive.

Coal is the most practical solution. We know clean fuels can be derived from coal. We know synthetic oil and gas can be produced in huge quantities. We know the emphasis will be on deep-mined coal. Technology is far enough along for pilot and demonstration projects which will provide the additional research and development necessary for coal to become a major factor in energy production. Last November 16, a navy destroyer completed a thirty-hour cruise, testing the use of coal-derived, synthetic, crude oil in its engines. The results were successful, yet the process used for conversion is far from the sophisticated programs which now must be carried out before commercial production becomes a reality.

The main point is that someone, somewhere, is going to become involved right away! It would be inexcusable if Kentucky did not become the national leader! Failure to act would only reinforce the image of government being unable or unwilling to take necessary steps in behalf of people.

I am, therefore, recommending in the 1974–1976 budget that $3.7

million be appropriated for an expansion of our Kentucky energy resource utilization program. The expansion of activities will not be limited to coal gasification and liquefaction research. They will include further mapping of Kentucky coals, research, demonstration of improvements in mining technology and techniques, support of education and training programs to increase the supply of trained manpower for mining, research on reclamation problems and techniques, and research on environmental effects of Kentucky coals. The major emphasis in the expanded program will be on coal utilization by conversion into clean fuels. The already favorable characteristics, performance, and potential of Kentucky coals in the various processes for gasification and liquefaction will be accelerated.

In addition, I recommend the expenditure of $4 million to construct an energy research facility in Fayette County near Lexington. Laboratory research already conducted proves we need expanded facilities, and clearly we should have one of the nation's major centers for energy research. These measures will place us in a position to command significant financial support from the federal government and private industry.

A third action I submit for your decision is authorization by the General Assembly of a state commitment of up to $50 million over the next three bienniums, enabling the Commonwealth to participate in the design, construction, and experimental operation of pilot and demonstration projects for coal gasification and liquefaction. Under such authority the Commonwealth would be a joint participant with the federal government and private enterprise to accelerate the work of bringing coal gasification and liquefaction processes to commercial feasibility.

A major portion of the state's investment in such projects would be recovered from the projects themselves after commercial feasibility is established. In other words, a buy-back clause would return Kentucky's investment, with the exception of research and demonstration development. The state would not invest in projects after they reach the commercial stage.

There are very good reasons for the Commonwealth to take these steps. I have emphasized the need to accelerate the development of processes for conversion of Kentucky coal to clean fuels and the desirability of establishing Kentucky as a major energy research center. Investment in pilot and demonstration projects will help assure adequate energy supplies for Kentucky and the nation. Moreover, such investments resulting in adequate energy supplies will make our state more competitive for new and expanded industry. State support will be repaid many times in the future, through increased employment, production of coal, new sources of income for our citizens, and tax revenue growth for state and local governments.

We stand at the threshold of acquiring a gasification demonstration plant as well as a liquefaction pilot plant. Both are of such magnitude that private industry cannot finance them alone. It is no secret that the federal government will soon appropriate at least $20 billion for energy research and development. Much of it will be earmarked for coal and probably will be spent by 1980. By participating in a joint venture, Kentucky's share of this money would be considerable. State legislation, however, is necessary if we are to share in the massive federal program.

Part of the $50 million I am requesting would account for total projects of $280 million—the difference coming from the federal government and private sources. This, remember, is for demonstration and pilot projects. Hundreds of millions of dollars more would be spent by industry as commercial operations are conducted, without additional state support. The remainder of the $50 million authorized would, if other pilot or demonstration projects are found beneficial, generate countless additional dollars from either private sources, the federal government, or both.

You have, in your power right now, the ability to achieve the most exciting advancements in the history of Kentucky. You have the power to provide a solution to a national problem. You have the opportunity to advance the economic growth of Kentucky as it has never been advanced and at the same time provide answers to such pressing problems as environmental standards, mining safety, mining technology, and an improved quality of life for all.

When America embarked on its lunar mission, few anticipated the spinoffs. That program gave us new trends in medicine we wouldn't have had for decades. It gave us fantastic advancements in critical weather forecasting. It gave us communication advantages no other country will match for ages. It gave us mapping techniques in countless areas such as natural resources, agriculture, and geology to name but a very few. The same can happen here because you have an opportunity to provide the world with by-products from coal, to spawn new industries through by-product research and development.

Coal is the answer, and the federal government agrees. By giving top priority to a state program, Kentucky will be prepared to respond to federal legislation which will pour tremendous funds into the state for research and development and at the same time enable us to generate our own economic progress. There is no question about liquefaction and gasification. It's going to be produced somewhere. It is feasible, economical, and acceptable. The question is, which state will gain more from this new venture? The answer is the state where those in authority grasp the opportunity first. The people will eventually decide whether, in 1974, this body was willing to make something of a one-in-a-century occasion. If you are, their lives will be enhanced. If you are not, Kentucky will merely rock along in the waves of other states where vision and initiative dominated. Thank you for allowing me to appear, and good afternoon.

------

1. See the section of these papers on "Energy and Environment" for additional material on this topic.
2. See Executive Order 73–577. This order was issued on June 22, 1973.

BUDGET ADDRESS
Frankfort / January 22, 1974

INCLUDED with your budget document is a letter of transmittal relating to a new format and other efforts providing the best accountability ever achieved of state government meeting its responsibilities. The executive branch has tried to work as closely as possible with the Legislature, hopefully easing your burdens during a short but most demanding period. We have endeavored to keep you informed. Whatever additional assistance you desire throughout this Session will be immediately available. For if priorities are met, your line of sight must not be restricted while examining statewide needs.

The citizens of Kentucky have every right to expect wisdom, compassion, and beneficial direction from those who allocate their tax dollars. Funds supporting state services do not belong to either you or me. They are the necessary contributions of working Kentuckians who await our complete and proper management!

The budget plan I offer goes far beyond normal continuation of current state services. Continuation stabilizes the present, but wherever possible we must drive head-on to meet urgent public needs, both now and for the future, with new and expanded programs. Our challenge is to act, rather than merely drift along in complacency! This budget is almost a billion dollars larger than the previous one. It does not require one penny more in new or increased taxes. Even at a $4.4 billion level, the budget is in line with conservative revenue estimates taking into account the energy crisis and other expected national economic trends.

We were especially conservative two years ago in estimating revenue and projecting a surplus. An expected surplus of $80 million in state funds for the first biennium clearly refutes those who said it couldn't be done. I have the utmost confidence in our estimates for the 1974 biennium. When speaking of state government cost savings, you will be pleased to know that up to $27 million less will be spent than was appropriated two years ago.

Let me add an important point. There may be those who believe that all of the new programs we can achieve these next two years come only because of federal revenue-sharing. The truth is that revenue-sharing accounts for less than 4 percent of the budget. The truth is that we must compensate for curtailments of various federal programs and prior fund impoundments. That revenue-sharing for nonrecurring expenses helps our capacity to do far more without any tax increase is due to several factors: the state's economic growth, savings in the cost of state government, the willingness of Kentuckians to work hard, and the remarkable record of the 1972 General Assembly. Federal revenue-sharing money for the coming biennium will grow by $10 million because we didn't rush out and recklessly spend it—we made it work for the citizens of Kentucky through investment, thus giving you a better opportunity of judgment in light of changing national and state conditions.

We have continued all existing programs presently in force with state funds. Due to inflation, the cost is much higher today than twenty-four months ago, and even for agencies where there is no expansion the increase is substantial. Otherwise, state government would have to curtail services. I don't believe anyone in this chamber, and especially the general public, wants state government in such a position! Beyond meeting this particular goal, we have established a long list of new and expanded programs above continuation. These are top priorities in fulfilling the expectations of Kentuckians.

To strengthen our foundation, I have included a 4.5 percent extension to make personnel classification more competitive and a 5.5 percent per year merit increase. These funds provide an average 15.5 percent salary adjustment during the biennium for qualified employees. If state government is to attract, and retain, worthy employees, and if the public is to receive the best value for tax dollars paid, we can't remain as a training ground for someone else. When other governmental units as well as business and industry promote the rapid exit of qualified state employees because pay is better elsewhere, government's ability to function is seriously threatened. This has been the case for too many years, and it's time we wake up to the fact.

On another matter, I made public commitments on three major items at earlier dates and have included them in the budget. They are the University of Louisville Medical Complex, support for the Lexington Civic Center, and matching funds for an Institute to Research Biological Aspects of Aging. There have been a few other public announcements though not made by me. They were pretty accurate, and you'll find most of them in the budget too. Frankly, I started to entitle this address the "Worst-Kept Secret in the History of Kentucky." But I am sure when we conclude you will find a great number of new programs which will make tomorrow's horizon very bright indeed. Now, let us turn to the future, as we examine a new and expanded service delivery system for state government, a system responsive to every man, woman, and child in our great state.

HUMAN RESOURCES

In my 1972 budget message, I pledged that the operational cost of government would show the beginning of a downward trend in the percentage of general fund dollars. I am prepared to demonstrate the fulfillment of that commitment, not just in some small area of government, but in the second most costly function and the largest in terms of personnel. I am extremely pleased to report that the recommended general fund increase the next two fiscal years is the lowest percentage appropriated since 1956. Yet for the first time in memory, it provides 100 percent funding of the entire budget request because of reorganization and innovation.

Many expansions are included in the recommended Human Resources Budget to improve the quality of health, well-being, and living conditions for our people—this is what government is all about. We will improve the quality of life of the aged and handicapped. We are adding $7.6 million each year to support the 20 percent of Kentucky's aged, blind, and disabled who will no longer be eligible for federal aid, since Washington's definition of aged, blind, and disabled is more harsh than Kentucky's. They have quit. We haven't. In a time of unequaled corporate profits, I believe it is tragic to abandon the aged, the blind, and the disabled.

While we have made tremendous strides in medical facilities and professional care, these advancements are useless to the seriously ill or critically injured if they can't get to a hospital in time. I have, therefore, provided $1.8 million new dollars in the Emergency Medical Services Program for purchase of vehicles, communications equipment, and basic emergency medical training. Families with dependent children, where cries of hunger are loud, illness is commonplace, and life is bleak, can expect $3.1 million more in state funds the first year and $7.1 million the second to improve living conditions.

The new Children's Treatment Service Building will soon be completed at Central State Hospital. This budget provides $438,000 for staffing. In addition $312,000 new dollars will be expended for day care. This budget provides service to 8,000 more senior citizens. It responds to requests from small communities and rural schools for prevention of dental disorders. We are also willing to spend a quarter of a million dollars more to assist our elderly citizens at home rather than put them in institutions.

Expanded services in Human Resources call for the establishment of twelve additional Home Health Agencies, new development and improvement for the state's fifteen Regional Health Planning Councils, and replacement of funds taken away by the federal government—$2.5 million—to maintain family and children services, no longer available through title 4–A of the Social Security Act because of federal irresponsibility.

Beyond all of these, and other new programs, I propose over 47 million new dollars to allow for construction and renovation projects. Included are $1.5 million for the construction of a Western Kentucky Reception Center to serve youngsters committed as public offenders from West Kentucky and Louisville.

A visit to our mental health and mental retardation facilities, as many of you and as I have made, shows in no uncertain terms how time and use have taken their toll. Immediate renovations and improvements must be started. I, therefore, recommend nearly $8 million to zero in on deficiencies which have plagued these facilities for so many years. I also recommend additions and modifications to Oakwood. As we concentrate on mental health and mental retardation facilities, I have a special request. Perhaps the most significant new thrust in reorganization of Human Resources is our ability, for the first time, to convert several state psychiatric hospitals and mental retardation facilities into certified intermediate care facilities. By doing so, we will prevent an expenditure of $13 million, which otherwise would be necessary from the general fund to maintain current service levels. This new approach will make them eligible for previously untapped reimbursements for services through federal medical assistance programs and private insurance. This is proof positive that through innovation, imagination, and hard work we can take better care of our citizens with fewer tax dollars. Your concurrence is urged.

One other item I want to note: My request for $31 million dollars to build a medical complex at the University of Louisville is not only for education, but to satisfy health and medical needs of all Kentuckians. I have also included $3 million in the Council on Public Higher Education budget to initiate five regional health centers, which will better distribute health manpower, assuring treatment in all areas of the state. Both appear in the education budget, but we should recognize the human resource/medical companionship these offer. Our purpose is to bring medical services and people closer together—in other words, making them accessible to the citizens you represent.

JUSTICE

Like all Americans, Kentuckians have a special concern for life, liberty, and property. I, therefore, recommend these new programs: increasing the State Police force by 100 troopers in the biennium; providing state policemen an additional 10 percent salary increase each year, in order to retain highly trained and competent officers—this is above the annual 5 percent increment; updating the State Police radio network; state training for approximately 120 additional local police officers each year, above and beyond normal growth patterns; state training for all law-enforcement communications personnel and all local jailers; and additional training for state correctional and judicial officers.

What we have done in the last two years and what is proposed for the coming biennium can be summed up with a statement to the criminal elements from both you and me: "Get out of Kentucky and stay out!" The tougher we make it on the scum of dope peddlers, the stink of organized crime, and the many other elements who prey on innocent and honest citizens, the better life will be in this state.

Other new programs would implement pre-sentence investigations and expand services in shock probation. It is time to implement work-release and study-release in the state corrections system. I also recommend three additional circuit judges to counteract increasing workloads, and I recommend the funding of $1.5 million of the judicial retirement system's prior-service liability. Three additional Court of Appeals Commissioners are necessary if a backlog of 1,000 cases now in our highest court is to be reduced.

As you recall, Kentucky began a unique training program for local police officers last year after months of debate with the federal Pay Board and the Cost of Living Council. No other program of its kind is in America. Available to nearly 3,000 local policemen who qualify through required education, the plan supplements their salaries if they meet strict standards. Limited federal support mandates our expansion of funding to 75 percent of the total. Without the recommended $9.3 million for the biennium, Kentucky will turn its back on one of the most worthwhile assaults against crime we have ever achieved. The training-incentive program's success is found throughout the Commonwealth, with trained police officers, rather than individuals handed a badge, pistol, and life-or-death assignment. We have a long way to go in the battle against crime, and this program is essential.

In addition to the proposed new and expanded programs, the Justice field requires over $30 million in capital construction. Unless we decide to give our correctional system the proper tools for rehabilitation, for separation of prisoners, and for specialized treatment, we will continue in the dark ages with overcrowded mass custody centers. The old ways aren't working. They are expensive and constantly endanger the lives of correctional employees. It's time that we enter the twentieth century by constructing a new maximum-security prison for which I request $15 million.

Prisoner cost is expensive. The expense has mounted for decades because of a revolving-door approach, which is no more than putting them in, letting them out, and putting them in again. A rehabilitated prisoner becomes a taxpayer rather than a tax drainer. Remodeling existing institutions would cost far more than building the specialized prison. I realize there are some who cannot be rehabilitated. These would be separated from those who can. Even with the advancements made, today's structures are inadequate; but with your approval we will be able to make "corrections" what the word stands for. I also recommend construction of a farm dormitory separated from the main institution at LaGrange where work incentive becomes paramount. This plus other maintenance projects at our correctional institutions would total $4.5 million—a lot of money. It should have been spent during the last fifteen years, but it wasn't. If we don't meet a long-neglected responsibility, who will?

Other recommendations are for a new Justice Building to bring all elements of the department under one roof. This frees, for instance, vitally needed State Police space now unavailable for expanded training. There is a serious need for two new State Police post headquarters as well as renovations at several other posts. Funds are provided to accomplish each.

NATURAL RESOURCES AND
ENVIRONMENTAL PROTECTION

Three years ago, when the environmental protection movement was reaching full bloom, Congress began putting final touches on landmark legislation to clean up our nation's air, water, and land. It didn't last long as federal impoundments signaled retreat. Today, in the face of the energy crisis, the federal government is retreating even more from that commitment. Well, they might retreat in Washington, but we're going to continue the attack in Kentucky! I don't believe you want anything less.

In my State of the Commonwealth Address, I outlined measures taken to improve our environment. I am proud to offer a budget which can do even more. To continue work already under way and implement new programs, the next biennium will need $24,900,000. I have earmarked capital construction monies to correct pollution deficiencies at all state facilities. We have a responsibility to clean our own house first! I also recommend the following:

1. An additional $1 million for fiscal 1974–1975 which will stimulate the Orphan Land Reclamation Program, enabling us to reclaim more acreage as the program grows. This is your program and it's positive!

2. Nearly $800,000 the next two years to increase the number of air-monitoring stations and $125,000 to research new or modified indirect sources of air pollution.

3. Three hundred fifty thousand dollars to implement the sediment-control legislation under the federal Water Quality Control Act.

4. One million dollars to repair and maintain dams on state-owned lakes, protecting thousands of Kentuckians and ensuring water sources for hundreds of local communities.

5. Four hundred thousand dollars for the biennium to launch beautification projects in every county, while pushing ahead our efforts to rid the countryside of junk automobiles and orphan dumps. First-time funding of the Wild Rivers Act: $120,000 to regulate the sale or use of pesticides.

One aspect of environmental protection which has never been attempted here is the study of surface disturbances from underground mining. For this purpose, and subsequent action, the budget contains $400,000. Finally, during the next biennium, nearly fifty communities will benefit from funds provided through the Kentucky Pollution Abatement Authority for construction of sewage-treatment plants.

No one can reasonably deny the advancements you and I have made in environmental protection—more in the last two years than in a decade.

I am here now to strongly urge more progress by calling for legislation to strengthen strip-mine reclamation, especially as it pertains to eliminating overburdens and going to head-of-hollow fills.

TRANSPORTATION

The impact of the energy crisis on transportation already has been felt. More headaches are anticipated, and it is in this practical vein that we must approach the area of transportation. In the past two years, Kentucky has made great strides in transportation despite no federal transportation bill a year ago and federal impoundments of funds. Uncertainties over road receipts prompt caution. Despite serious handicaps, we have decided to continue the same levels of service of the past two years by providing $554 million in state funds for the biennium. This requires a supplement of $26.5 million in general fund nonrecurring monies.

Careful monitoring will be maintained to evaluate expected reductions in road funds during this crisis period, one expected to last beyond the 1974–1976 biennium. Certainly, the 1972 General Assembly's decision to establish a recommended municipal street program has become even more important to our cities and towns. This program, along with the rural secondary and county road programs will continue to have my strong endorsement. Even with an emphasis on existing programs, there are five new ones I suggest.

The first is the establishment of a new mass transit program at the state level to provide needed planning and technical assistance to local, regional, and state transportation agencies. Our three largest metropolitan areas—Louisville, Lexington, and northern Kentucky—already have felt the necessity of such assistance, and other sections of our state eventually will be seeking expertise from this office as population grows. A mass transit staff will be assembled within the Department of Transportation to assist both urban and rural areas in planning and completing studies which are a prerequisite for obtaining federal capital-grant dollars. I am recommending an expenditure of a million-plus dollars so we can quit talking and get on with the job of transporting people in urban areas.

Secondly, with the appropriation of $1.1 million in new monies over the biennium, we can for the first time fully implement an overall planning series with the department giving us a long-range, comprehensive approach to all modes of transportation.

The overall impact of transportation on Kentucky's environment will be acted upon by the implementation of the environmental action plan.

New money will be provided for specialized staffing presently not available.

I am asking for nearly one million dollars to comply with federal traffic sign and signal standards by the end of the biennium.

And, last, I am requesting funds for semiannual airport safety inspections, another standard which has never been achieved in Kentucky.

PROTECTION AND REGULATION

A first observation in consumer protection and regulation is the name change. We adopted a good editorial suggestion with the title now being Public Protection and Regulation. Some have characterized Public Protection and Regulation as a "catchall" function. Though not quite true, the cabinet does reach into all 120 counties, serving as an umbrella to shield the public from those who would take advantage by fraud, deception, misrepresentation, and even innocent error. The cabinet stimulates better working conditions, provides educational resources for industry, business, and the consumer, and regulates various activities affecting the general public.

Upon assuming office, one of the most tragic omissions of responsibility discovered had been in banking and securities. Conditions were so bad I authorized $167,000 from my contingency fund to rectify some of them. But more is necessary, such as $150,000 (extra dollars) through 1976 to continue our efforts to upgrade the Department of Banking and Securities' supervision of state banks and state securities. We must add six new examiners.

New programs or expansions call for nearly $500,000 to expand the inspections made under the minimum safety standards program in the Department of Insurance. Only a small fraction of inspections needed for minimum safety standards are being made. I am recommending funds to comply fully with those standards—another first.

Expansions include a $50,000 increase each year in grants to local volunteer fire departments; $150,000 to establish a new program to aid volunteer rescue squads in the Commonwealth by providing grants to purchase equipment and to help train members of the volunteer rescue squads (this will be another first for Kentucky); and $125,000 each year to establish a new program in the Department of Labor, Labor Education, and Research, to better equip the members and leaders of labor organizations, and to encourage them to participate in solving community problems.

Also in the Department of Labor, nearly $131,000 will be granted for enforcing the compliance of apprentice agreements. Funds are provided to add three mine inspectors and necessary equipment.

Finally, I have recommended general fund support for research and security in our racing industry. This recommendation is designed to promote the horse industry and horse racing and to safeguard them against scandals that have hit racetracks in other states.

This budget reflects concern for the protection of the safety, health, and economic well-being of all Kentuckians, as well as protecting the economic integrity of the industries regulated by the agencies in the cabinet. There is another point for your consideration. I favor a no-fault insurance plan that reduces premiums. I urge you to pass such a bill that will also comply with Kentucky's strict Constitution.

DEVELOPMENT

Our economic thrust has been and will continue to be exerted through a combination of activities requiring the support and cooperation of countless individuals and organizations. Maintaining Kentucky's outstanding economic growth, especially through a period of uncertainty, requires even more effort. But there can be no give-and-take, especially as it affects our quality of life.

We have been selective in seeking new industries, rather than throwing open the door for anybody. And we're going to continue to say, "If you pollute, we don't want you!" "If you pay insufficient wages, go elsewhere!" "If you are coming here thinking first of yourself rather than your new home state, don't come!" There are far too many service-oriented businesses and industries, where management is progressive and thoughtful, for Kentucky to be satisfied with anything less than blue-chip firms!

Service-oriented development can be illustrated when the state joins, as I recommend we do, with Lexington by providing $4 million toward its new Civic Center, with Louisville by providing $22 million for the Kentucky Exhibit Hall, and by improving the State Fair and Exposition Center in order to attract hundreds of thousands of new visitors. Service-oriented development comes through research, such as my call for the most challenging program in our state's history, delivered last week in my Energy Message. Service-oriented development comes through tourism—last year a $699 million industry. When out-of-staters visit Kentucky, they support our economy. I have suggested substantial new funds for capital construction and renovations at nearly every major resort and recreation park in Kentucky, including

$4 million for utilities at the State Horse Park and $2 million for development of Dale Hollow. Service-oriented development comes with agriculture, and for the first time we will sponsor the North American Livestock Exposition, another step in the promotion of our growing cattle industry.

But development goes beyond that already emphasized. You are being asked to fund increased laboratory services through renovation of the Hopkinsville Animal Diagnostic Facility. You are being asked to spend new dollars to replace and modernize precision-balance equipment the Department of Agriculture must have for consumer protection in packaging, inspecting retail stores, gasoline pumps, stockyards, and other facilities.

Two years ago, in my budget address, I promised that with legislative approval we would show marked improvements in state productivity, individual earnings, employment, and citizen satisfaction. We did. I call upon you now to break that record and enhance the future of every Kentucky resident.

GENERAL GOVERNMENT

Minimizing the spiraling cost of administering state government was a principal campaign position of mine and has been of foremost concern. Action thus far will not only have an immediate impact on the overhead costs of delivering services to the people, but will create a lasting effect on the ability of future administrations to hold down the amount of dollars required to "support" rather than deliver services.

Two steps taken before the actual preparation of this budget have been and will continue to be significant in reducing the cost of state government: First, I directed last summer that all vacant positions in every organization of state government be analyzed and abolished if possible. As a result, 3,120 positions were eliminated. Secondly, of equal significance is the project now eighteen months old, that of centralizing state government computer operations. I inherited a situation when data-processing equipment of all descriptions was found in nearly every agency. The application of this useful management tool was fragmented, overlapping, and most of all too expensive. As of this date, our actions will save $2.4 million in the next biennium. Reduced equipment, labor, and material cost is netting a savings of $100,000 per month to the taxpayer, not to mention improved quality and accessibility of computer-produced information.

I ask your consideration and approval of a budget for the General Government Cabinet of Agencies that represents the smallest percentage increase in biennial funding for any cabinet of state government. The program expansions set forth are as follows:

1. Three hundred twenty thousand dollars in the biennium to implement a comprehensive, sophisticated emergency operation center in the Boone National Guard Center now under construction in Frankfort. In time of emergency or disaster, this system will give us the ability to communicate freely with all areas of the Commonwealth.

2. Capital construction funds to build two new armories, as well as funds to renovate an existing facility for a third armory. I am also recommending more than $650,000 in the biennium for major maintenance projects at existing Kentucky armories.

3. Because of the fuel shortage, it appears likely that Americans will shorten travel distances for trips and vacations. With this in mind, I have increased the biennial funding of the cooperative advertising program by $230,000. The program emphasizes local and regional travel promotion and matches local funds with a like amount of state dollars. For the state's and nation's bicentennial celebrations, this also provides matching funds for regional program advertising.

4. Fiscal 1975 will be the first full year of operation for the Kentucky Housing Corporation. Already the Corporation is issuing and marketing housing revenue bonds and bond anticipation notes to create funds which will reduce the cost of housing for the poor. The Corporation will operate totally with self-generated funds during the biennium.

5. I have added more than $100,000 to the biennial appropriation for the Commission on Human Rights.

Other programs I have recommended expansion for are: $90,000 to provide marketing assistance to Kentucky's farmers, as well as various assistance and information services through the Kentucky Farmers' Advocate Office (we are also attempting to bring the World Dairy Expo to Kentucky in 1975); additional staff for the Auditor of Public Accounts; additional staff for the litigation program and the consumer protection program of the Department of Law, and general fund dollars for assistance to local prosecutors and officials—a program which had been funded by federal money; funds for the computerization of corporate records which will provide a greater service to Kentucky businesses and corporations (requested by the Secretary of State); and an expanded program in the Department of Revenue for predicting revenue collections.

My total recommendation is $158,187,400. This is only a 6.4 percent increase in the face of a 15 percent inflationary increase in actual costs —meaning we are providing services at less costs through reorganization and businesslike approaches.

HIGHER EDUCATION

The basis for the 1974–1976 biennial recommendation in higher education was provided by the Council on Public Higher Education. I compliment the Council for an outstanding job of evaluating budget requests of our public institutions of higher learning. With their evaluation, we limited our review to the Council recommendation. You should also know that institution requests were the most austere in memory.

The budget recommendation contains over $164.9 million in the fiscal 1974–1975 year and over $177.8 million in fiscal 1975–1976 in general funds for operating our public higher education programs. It does so without any increase whatsoever in tuition! It does so with a reduction in tuition at the University of Louisville which can amount to $100 each year if anticipated funds are realized. And it does so with a $3 million Student Loan Fund, never established before, which will open the doors of higher education to young Kentuckians who today are shut out because they can't afford the cost. The general fund recommendation for the 1974–1976 biennium provides for an adequate level of continuation and addresses some of the exceptional needs of higher education. The Council will develop and implement five regional health education centers in the Commonwealth during the next biennium. A Mining Technology course at Madisonville Community College will provide training for general reclamation procedures.

The budget recommendation for the University of Louisville includes a community thrust program, extending academic, cultural, and service programs to more local residents (particularly those in the West End). General fund recommendations for the University of Louisville and Northern Kentucky State College reflect our strong emphasis on bringing each institution fully into the state system. Louisville's increase over the previous budget is nearly 40 percent while a 57 percent increase has been marked for Northern.

Over $60 million is recommended for capital improvements above the funding already mentioned. The largest amount is $31 million for the medical/health complex in Louisville. Northern Kentucky State College, besides its 57 percent increase over the past two years and the massive funding we appropriated in 1972, is slated in this budget for $13 million more dollars for new and expanded facilities, and this is first-class status in anybody's book.

The University of Kentucky is our principal institution of higher learning. I deem it important to say publicly that in recent months three honors have come to UK which deserve attention. Among the nation's leading Colleges of Pharmacy, Kentucky ranks fifth; among the nation's leading Colleges of Dentistry, Kentucky ranks third; and just in the past few days the University of Kentucky was honored as one of America's major universities for research, along with such institutions as Columbia, Harvard, Johns Hopkins, and MIT. To accommodate the progress recognized at the University of Kentucky, I recommend over 16 million new dollars for a Health/Science Building, a Center on Aging, a Fine Arts Building, and a Technical Institute Building.

Our other institutions of higher learning, at Morehead, Eastern, Kentucky State, Murray, and Western, are provided additional funds in the budget for capital improvements, especially to correct pollution deficiencies. You will be pleased to learn also that no funds are recommended to increase debt service during the next biennium.

EDUCATION AND THE ARTS

Many questions have been asked about new directions for Kentucky's elementary and secondary education. The 1972–1974 budget clearly indicated this administration's determination to emphasize quality—a quality education for our children. When Kentucky had no public kindergarten, we started one. When special education was minimal at best, we prescribed a shot in the arm. When the teachers' retirement system prior-service deficit had been overlooked for years, we cut a small slice from the total amount. And when the state needed 2,600 new classroom units, we made construction a reality.

Recommendations for elementary and secondary education not only guarantee continued massive support, but go far beyond what I believe even the most optimistic would have expected, by providing tools which stress quality. Just to continue the progress we are making will require $697 million during the next biennium. In order to move our Commonwealth forward, I am requesting $120.4 million in new state funds for expansion in the Education and Arts Cabinet, which includes the minimum-foundation program and teachers' retirement. Specifically, these new expenditures include $85.7 million increase for the minimum-foundation program which will increase teacher salary allotments by 7 percent in fiscal 1974–1975 and by an additional 9 percent in fiscal 1975–1976; increase current expense allotments by 7 percent in fiscal 1974–1975 and by 9 percent in fiscal 1975–1976; increase capital outlay allotments by $150 per unit during the biennium; provide 100 additional kindergarten units; provide 450 additional vocational education units (a 25 percent increase to serve 13,500 more students); and provide 1,100 additional special education classroom units.

Education costs will include $7.4 million for construction of new facilities at the School for the Blind and the School for the Deaf, including a new $2 million facility urgently needed for children suffering from multiple handicaps, as is $770,000 for additional staffing at both schools. The multiple-handicap facility will be only one of six in the nation.

Here are more new programs: $13.4 million for construction of vocational-education facilities to serve 19,500 students; $1.8 million for operating new and expanded vocational facilities which will open during the biennium, and for meeting safety and health standards in existing schools; $1.3 million to expand our regional education offices to fifteen during the biennium; $550,000 for the production of both mathematics and science television series for junior high students; $964,000 additional state matching funds to take full advantage of federal school lunch funds; $12.1 million to reduce the teachers' retirement system prior-service deficit to the July 1, 1972, level and begin an amortization program to fund the deficit by 1990; $5.7 million state matching contributions to fund a thirty-year teacher retirement program at age fifty-five, which is long needed and long awaited; $6.6 million to continue the 5 percent cost-of-living increase granted retired teachers during the current biennium and to grant an additional 5 percent during the 1974–1976 biennium; $500,000 to extend our $3,000 school-district-employee life insurance program to cover noncertificated employees; $1 million to establish an emergency loan program for schools hit by disasters; and $196,000 for the Historical Society to operate the Old Capitol, State Museum, and Arsenal Museum. I also recommend, and provisions have been made, to change our cost approach to the weighted-pupil concept the second year.

All of these new and expanded programs in one way or another pertain to public education. But there is one glaring omission—the subject of libraries. No single topic has been of greater concern to me than libraries. Whoever first said "a library is the people's university" offered a down-to-earth awareness that, for some unknown reason, has been tossed aside in Washington. I regret having to again bring up the subject of federal callousness, but facts are facts, and whoever was responsible—the President for eliminating funds to states for library programs or the Democratic-controlled Congress for letting him get away with it—should feel the same degree of shame we in the states feel of disappointment. I'm not going to let this tragedy strike at the heart of Kentucky's outstanding library system! This budget leaves no doubt where I stand. Not only am I requesting money to replace the federal funds which have disappeared, I am recommending expenditures that will add to Kentucky's stature in library services. Two years ago the library program in Kentucky needed $4.9 million in state funds and got it. Now the system must have $11.7 million from somewhere, and if we have to carry the load, we will do it. In the President's new budget I sincerely hope he will restore funds not only here but in the many needed areas for people.

CONCLUSION

Time does not permit discussion of every program or issue. I have covered a wide range of topics, but there are several policy areas with long-range fiscal implications deserving your special attention. They are the retirement systems, road funds, and federal funds.

Three of our four state retirement systems have major deficits. They have been growing since the systems were established long ago. The temptation of providing benefits without accepting the responsibility to appropriate funds for those costs has been wrong. The teachers' retirement system now has a prior-year service deficit of nearly $60 million. The judicial retirement system has a prior-year deficit of about $5 million. Your own retirement program is nearly a million dollars in the red. It is imperative that we take steps to prevent such actions in the future and seek remedies to the problems which now exist. I will recommend legislation to prevent recurrence of this problem and a method to correct the deficits. I have included in my budget recommendations funds to assure that the deficits do not increase in this administration and to begin paying off the deficit in the judicial and teachers' retirement systems. If the three succeeding Governors will make a comparable appropriation, the total prior-year deficit will be funded. My budget recommendation contains over $12 million for the teachers' retirement prior-year service and over $1.4 million for the judicial retirement system. Since the General Assembly prepares its own budget, funds have not been included for that million dollars, but hopefully will be included in the appropriation. It is a staggering amount for us to take from our budget, but it is fiscally necessary and I accept the obligation.

ROAD FUND TAXES

We must seek new approaches to financing transportation costs. It has been traditional in Kentucky and across the nation to rely primarily on consumption of motor fuel taxes and vehicle usage taxes for road fund monies. Where has this led us? Consumption, even without an energy crisis, was beginning to stabilize. Thus, our road fund taxes were not increasing at the rate of inflated costs. An efficient transportation system is too important for us to cut service, and an increase in motor fuels tax is only a temporary solution. I am, therefore, asking the 1974 General Assembly to direct the Legislative Research Commission, during the next two years, to complete a thorough review of approaches to financing transportation needs in Kentucky. That report should be ready for consideration by the 1976 General Assembly.

FEDERAL FUNDS

The trauma of federally funded state administered programs causes uncertainty. Libraries have been cut drastically, and education, human resources, and natural resources and environmental protection also have lost funds. The effect of losing federal funds which were built into recurring costs, plus an unstable economy, necessitate that we devote more of our federal funds to nonrecurring-type expenses. I have said for a long time that every federal grant should be carefully evaluated for the long-range, state financial implications. In this budget we have sought to take that look and will seek even better evaluation the next two years. It is absolutely necessary that before we accept outside funds to start a program, we are assured that state funds will be available to continue that program without reducing service in other programs of state government if those outside funds are lost, cut, or impounded.

We treated federal revenue-sharing the same as nonrecurring state general funds. We built only $7.9 million of these funds into recurring costs in 1975–1976, and that amount is less than 1 percent of the total budget. We can reasonably anticipate the lapsed funds from 1973–1974 and 1974–1975 to be more than $7,900,000. The budget is based upon recurring expenses. Thus, no tax increase to carry on budgeted service levels in the 1976–1978 biennium will be necessary.

The Department of Revenue has carefully evaluated the outlook for our economy during the next biennium. But problems of estimating are compounded with uncertainties not previously experienced. The staff used its best judgment with the information available today, but changes can drastically alter those assumptions. For that reason, I am asking for additional flexibility in the Appropriations Act to make adjustments after consultation with the Joint Committee on Appropriations and Revenue, if the estimates change.

I have asked for flexibility in this budget to permit adjustments based on up-to-date information and controlled by your establishment of priorities. The Appropriations Act includes such a recommendation. It would be irresponsible for us to have underestimated receipts and not be in position to allocate additional dollars where needed. An example would be a priority established by you in granting a tuition reduction up to $100 a year for the University of Louisville.

A balanced budget is submitted. To cover appropriations for the General Assembly, Legislative Research Commission, and other bills with appropriations, $14.5 million is set aside for the biennium. If you appropriate funds beyond these figures, then you must assume the responsibility for increasing taxes to pay the cost or cut services which have been recommended. This budget extends a helping hand into every home, school, business, agency, industry, and all other aspects of life in Kentucky. It does so without the added imposition of new or increased taxes. It does so to stimulate our economy, improve the well-being of Kentuckians, and it responds to the mandate of our citizens who look to us for leadership.

The capital construction portion is an exciting area of development, desperately needed. Reaching north, south, east, and west, capital construction will be found in Louisville, Lexington, Murray, Greenville, Paintsville, Central City, and Ashland. It reaches into Prestonsburg, Elizabethtown, Richmond, Mayfield, Paducah, Somerset, and numerous other communities. Construction will be seen in the counties of Harlan, Bell, Christian, Trigg, Owsley, Marshall, Daviess, Lyon, and many, many more. Every county will feel the benefits of this budget, for we have considered statewide needs. Our concern has no limitations, unlike our resources. Even so, at no time in history has the dollar stretched further.

At no time in history have the Appropriations and Revenue Committees been given so much advance information. For the first time you have had early review of agency requests, review projections, prior briefings, early briefing from agency heads, and detailed explanations of the budget before it was submitted to the General Assembly. I entered the budget process in a spirit of cooperation. These firsts reflect my respect for you and the best interests of the people of Kentucky.

Enthusiasm is a telescope that advances the misty distant future into the radiant, tangible present. I am enthusiastic about our budget, enthusiastic about our present and our future. It is here in our heritage and our resources and, most of all, in our people. I believe you feel as I do that Kentucky can, will, and must emerge to take its rightful place. I believe with all my heart we are on the right track. The budget is now in your hands. Thank you, and good afternoon.

STATEMENT RE:
SENATE BILL 45
Frankfort / March 14, 1974

I WISH to emphasize my full support of the objective of the amendment to Senate Bill 45.[1] I have long recognized an urgent need for industrial development in the coal-producing counties. I have personally been reviewing that amendment to determine its effect on the state revenue as well as the benefits we could reasonably anticipate.

In this review, there are several problems which I see as basic. They must be solved if we are to achieve the objective that both you and I seek.

First, that amendment does not leave adequate funds to cover the appropriations made in House Bill 251[2] and it does not leave any extra funds to cover contingent projects and necessary governmental expense, which occur every year, authorized in House Bill 288.[3] The amendment uses the $916,371,095 figure included in the appropriations bill for 1974–1975 and $933,485,645 in 1975–1976. But that amount does not provide the necessary funds to pay increased costs of pilot or demonstration plants which have been authorized in House Bill 251, nor extra costs such as increased election expenses, back-tax elections, claims awarded by the Board of Claims, court judgments, prior-year claims, unredeemed checks, special legislative claims, and other expenses which the General Assembly had determined to be necessary governmental expenses. These figures include only those appropriations in which a specific amount is appropriated. In House Bill 251 there is an appropriation of $7 million, but an authorization to spend additional funds. If we are successful in obtaining the pilot and demonstration plants for both liquefaction and gasification, additional funds may be, and likely will be, required in this biennium. That legislation permits either payment from the General Expenditure Funds or the sale of revenue bonds. This amendment would in effect prevent the sale of revenue bonds because one-half of the increase in the severance tax would be used for the economic development in the coal-producing counties. No exception is made for severance tax collected on coal used in the pilot or demonstration plants that could be used for paying debt service on revenue bonds under House Bill 251.

Second, this legislation begins to earmark taxes now accruing to the general fund. This practice is generally considered poor financial management. It removes discretion on how tax monies can best be spent and makes the allocation upon the receipts rather than justification of need.

Third, the amendment would, for all practical effects, prevent the allocation of any funds for use in fiscal year 1974–1975. We would not know the total amount collected until near the end of the fiscal year; consequently, no expenditures could be authorized. Let's take the $44 million which is used as the base. Until the actual income from the severance tax exceeded $44 million and the total general fund revenue exceeded $916,371,095, there would be no funds transferred. We need to tie the amount to an actual figure as soon as possible in order that allocations can be made. The $48.5 million will not be known until the end of fiscal year 1975–1976. If we are to proceed with a development fund, then we need to give some assurance that the funds are available and can be expended as soon as possible. This can be done by using previous-year actual taxes collected versus estimates as the basis for allocation. Everyone then knows how much is available.

Fourth, the purpose for which the fund can be used is "construction, reconstruction, or maintenance" of development projects. This purpose is surely too vague for us to undertake administration. Construction, reconstruction, or maintenance of what?

It is obvious that we are seeking to improve and enhance industrial development in these counties. If that is the objective then we need to state more specifically what type of expenditures can be made from this fund and how disbursements are to be made. Regulations and audit guidelines must be established to assure that expenditures are proper.

Fifth, the title was amended to read "revenue and taxation" and the best legal advice to me is the amendment must contain reference to the appropriation or it would very likely be declared unconstitutional. We would be holding out the promise of support knowing very well that it would likely be declared illegal and delayed another two years. It would be most improper for anyone to proceed with that bill with the expectation of such adverse legal action.

In an effort to remedy these problems, I have asked that an amendment be prepared to Senate Bill 281 [4] which I believe achieves the objective of Senate Bill 45 as amended. I believe that it corrects the deficiencies which I have noted and will provide the financial support beginning in fiscal year 1974–1975, rather than having it delayed until fiscal year 1975–1976. The proposed amendment protects the appropriations made in House Bill 251, House Bill 288, and other legislation enacted by the 1974 session of the General Assembly which contains appropriation provisions. The appropriation in the amendment to be considered is based upon the difference between estimated taxes and the actual collection for the previous fiscal year. Thus, we know at the beginning of the year how much money will be available and we will not build up any false hopes. By August 15 each year the fiscal court will be informed of the amount available for that fiscal year.

The appropriation is based upon the severance tax collected rather than the coal mined. We reviewed this provision rather carefully and believe it will simplify administration and give recognition to use dollar value of the coal severance tax rather than the tonnage. What this means is that eastern Kentucky would not be deprived its fair share. The Department of Revenue can require the submission of reports on taxes collected by counties which will simplify administration and place the submission directly to the State Treasurer to make the allocations of monies in the fund. The proposed amendment also establishes procedures by which these funds will be disbursed.

An advisory committee is established consisting of members of the General Assembly from the coal-producing counties to advise and assist the commissioner in the promulgation of regulations governing the expenditures of these funds and the establishment of necessary audit guidelines. The legislation recognizes the role of fiscal courts in the selection of projects and provides the necessary review process by the Commissioner of the Executive Department for Finance and Administration to ensure that funds are wisely expended. The amendment also solves the title legality problem to which I referred in Senate Bill 45.

I emphasize again my support for the concept. Financial aid and industrial development in these counties is most important, and I assure you that I have been exploring ways to provide the necessary support without jeopardizing the commitments that have been made by this General Assembly. I think that you will agree with me that the budget and the energy programs are extremely important to the people of the State and they must remain intact as enacted. I do not believe that it was the intent of the amendment to Senate Bill 45 to jeopardize this legislation.

Just like the amendment to Senate Bill 45, this amendment is no guarantee that funds will be available. It does assure that if funds in excess of the official estimate as reflected in the executive budget of 1974 to 1976 are collected, they will be allocated to the development funds for counties producing coal, and administered in a uniform manner. It does not infringe upon contingent funds for education as provided in House Bill 288. It permits us to proceed with our efforts to obtain the pilot and demonstration plants, and it makes provisions for necessary governmental expenses that we accrue every year.

SENATE BILL 45

The amendment to Senate Bill 45 allocates a portion of the severance tax for Economic Development in coal-producing counties. It was passed by the House yesterday.

---

1. See an act "relating to appropriations and the disbursement of appropriations," which was passed on April 2, 1974. *Acts of the General Assembly of the Commonwealth of Kentucky, 1974*, Chapter 262 (S.B. 281), pp. 502–3.

2. See an act "relating to energy development and demonstration, and making an appropriation," which was approved on March 15, 1974. *Acts of the General Assembly of the Commonwealth of Kentucky, 1974*, Chapter 18 (H.B. 251), pp. 133–35.

3. See an act "relating to appropriations for the operation, maintenance, support, and functions of the Commonwealth of Kentucky and its various officers, departments, boards, commissions, institutions, subdivisions, agencies, and other state supported activities," which was approved on March 19, 1974. *Acts of the General Assembly of the Commonwealth of Kentucky, 1974*, Chapter 80 (H.B. 288), pp. 136–64.

4. On March 12, 1974, Representative Glenn R. Freeman (D. Cumberland) moved that the vote by which S.B. 45 as amended was passed be reconsidered and said motion be postponed indefinitely. This motion was agreed to by the House. Then on March 13, 1974, S.B. 45 became a "dead bill" and was not again considered by the 1974 General Assembly under that number. However, on April 2, 1974, S.B. 281 was passed and was signed by Governor Ford; S.B. 281 was essentially the same bill as S.B. 45. *House Journal 1974*, 2: 1597–98, and *Senate Journal 1974*, p. 978.

STATEMENT RE:
EXCESS FUNDS
Frankfort / September 6, 1974

I WAS served with a summons this morning in which Representative Larry J. Hopkins [1] and Mr. Albert Christen [2] have requested the Franklin Circuit Court to restrain and enjoin the State Treasurer, the Commissioner of the Executive Department for Finance and Administration, and myself from expending excess funds appropriated by the 1974 General Assembly. This appropriation bill passed the Senate by a vote of 37–0 and the House by a vote of 97–0. Every Republican who voted voted for the bill. Representative Hopkins and Representative Overstreet[3] voted for the bill.

Apparently we have entered into another season of politics by litigation, which is just another example of a negative approach by some to Kentucky's problems, its people, its promises. If, for example, we had squandered the taxpayers' money on SSTs, as Marlow Cook[4] has done, that would be a different matter.

But this action today has to be the most callous political move in Kentucky history. Senator Cook and those supporters who have joined in this episode are trying to prevent the state from providing funds for our greatest human resource—our children. I have been in political life most of my adult years and the political action taken today has to be the most underhanded, callous, all-time low point in Kentucky political history.

I made these allocations strictly as prescribed by legislation. An Attorney General's Opinion has declared this to be a valid exercise of legislative authority on the part of the General Assembly, and a valid exercise of executive authority on my part. If this suit were based on merit, it would have been filed at the time of the first allocation of the money in June. That was the season for a move based on merit. This move today is not based on merit; it is based on the fact that we are in a political season. This suit now seeks to create a nightmare for all communities in Kentucky and all service programs in Kentucky.

We must recognize that over half of these funds were allocated in June and commitments have been made which, if changed, will create administrative and fiscal chaos in every region of Kentucky. How will a school board respond to notice at this time that the additional funds for current expense and capital outlay are terminated? How do we handle the great hopes and aspirations that developed as the result of the return of excess severance tax funds to coal-producing counties? And how do we explain to the students who have received assistance under the new state Student Incentive Grant Program that their grants have been canceled? These are just a few examples of the problems created by this suit. Not only does it reflect a negativism which I have already mentioned but also a complete lack of compassion and concern.

Let me point out some things that this suit seeks to stop:

1. Additional classrooms for special education.

2. An increase for the public schools both in current expenses and capital outlay.

3. More money for textbooks in our elementary and secondary schools.

4. Funds to construct the multihandicapped facility at the School for the Deaf, which will be one of only six of its kind in the nation.

5. More money for the public libraries.

6. More money for the blind.

7. Funds for 100 new state troopers.

8. Funds to support the state Student Incentive Grant Program.

9. Funds for the coal-producing counties' development fund.

10. Funds to match a federal grant for improving our court system.

11. Funds to make up the loss of federal monies in our Area Development Districts.

12. Funds for construction of nursing facilities at Eastern Kentucky University, the new Student Center at Northern Kentucky State, in addition to other projects at Morehead, Murray, Western, and Kentucky State.

13. And the makeup of the University of Louisville's loss of city-county money.

I made these choices based on specific authority from the Legislature. I am glad that I did and I only wish that I could have done more. This very question has consistently been upheld by the Kentucky Court of Appeals as cited in the Attorney General's Opinion. This action by the Republicans doesn't do a thing to the Governor. But unfortunately it is a slap in the face to Kentuckians who deserve maximum service from state government. Such an action is only harmful to the blind because of new facilities these dollars would provide. It is only harmful to the deaf because of new facilities. It is harmful to school children who need free textbooks and these texts were being provided through surplus because the Republican economic mess has raised prices 30 percent this year alone. It is harmful to public protection at a time in our nation when the crime rate is soaring, and we in Kentucky are trying to do something about it by hiring more police, giving them the tools they need. It is harmful to the taxpayer who, by delay in programs, will only have to pay more in the future because of inflation.

No, this doesn't harm Wendell Ford. And I'm going to keep fighting for the people of Kentucky who deserve the facilities, the services, and the benefits a surplus can offer.

Everyone knows this is a pure political stunt in behalf of my opponent's Senate campaign, and I am convinced the people of Kentucky will overwhelmingly condemn such base tactics that deprive them of the necessities this surplus would provide.

1. Larry J. Hopkins (1933–　　), Republican from Lexington; stockbroker; elected to Kentucky House of Representatives in 1972; Republican caucus chairman. *Kentucky General Assembly 1974* (Frankfort, n.d.), p. 31.

2. Albert Christen (1894–　　), Louisville; member of State Board of Accountancy (1950–1953); accountant, Jefferson County Republican Finance Committee (1962–1967); Department of Finance (1967–1971); numerous other positions. Christen, C.P.A., is a partner in the Louisville certified public accountancy firm of Christen, Brown, and Rufer. *The Public Papers of Governor Louie B. Nunn, 1967–1971*, ed. Robert F. Sexton (Lexington, Ky., 1975), p. 235.

3. Raymond D. Overstreet (1942–　　), Republican from Liberty; elected to Kentucky House of Representatives in 1972. *Kentucky General Assembly 1974* (Frankfort, n.d.), p. 25.

4. Marlow Webster Cook (1926–　　), Republican from Louisville; attorney; member of Kentucky House of Representatives (1958–1960); Jefferson County judge (1961–1968); United States Senator (1968–1974). *The Public Papers of Governor Louie B. Nunn*, p. 185.

REORGANIZATION

REMOVAL OF POLITICAL PATRONAGE
Frankfort / December 18, 1971

THE decision to remove political patronage matters from the Governor's Office is strictly mine! It is my decision to place this necessary function under the administration of State Democratic Headquarters. I feel very strongly about the need to build the Democratic party. The way to do this is to have a well-organized, well-financed party at both the state and local levels. When the people see our party serving their needs, they will recognize our energies and concerns.

There is a right way, and a wrong way, to operate state government in the interest of Kentucky and in the interest of the Democratic party. The wrong way is to distribute patronage from the various departments of government. The right way to operate government is to have these departments carrying on those services needed and expected by all Kentuckians, without political interference. This we shall do. Every commissioner will run his own department. Every commissioner will appoint the deputies and directors needed to render the services I have mentioned.

You helped elect me. You believed in what I said during the campaign, and I want and need your help and patience. Where services are needed, jobs will be filled. But we have a lot of jobs today that will not be there six months from now. I can recall hearing you, on many occasions, complain that in your own counties there were jobs strictly for the sake of putting someone on the payroll. You said the jobs should not exist. Those who are on the payroll, but do not function in the interest of Kentucky, will not remain. You asked for this during the campaign. People are sick and tired of seeing state positions filled where there is no performance. This is not good for Kentucky. This practice would not be good for the Democratic party.

Where patronage is available, politics will get you a job, if you are qualified. But politics will not keep any job. Good government is good politics. This will be our mission. Let me remind you that I have instructed every commissioner, that in any patronage job, if the person is not fulfilling a maximum work load, that person is to be fired. The operation of patronage, therefore, is the party's business. The operation of state government is the people's business, and I intend to see that we achieve great heights in both areas for the sake of our Commonwealth, and the sake of our party.

KENTUCKY CHAMBER OF COMMERCE
Lexington / January 12, 1972

Your schedule of activities calls for remarks from the Governor, and one definition of remarks is "passing observations or comments." To follow your direction, I have a few passing observations and comments about the first weeks of a new administration. I believe we're off to a fine start, but I don't want the ultimate results to be like a story someone told me recently. A woman walked into the drugstore to buy a mudpack. Later, the druggist who sold her the preparation asked her husband if the mud improved his wife's appearance. "It did for a couple of days," the husband replied, "but then it wore off." I have no intention of letting our positive beginning wear off.

In my message to the General Assembly, several steps taken within various departments of state government which were in the best interest of the people were announced. These are initial measures to put state government on a sound business basis. As predicted in that address, some scoffed, saying state government cannot be compared to other businesses, that government is not designed to return a profit. No, but it would be nice to wind up each year with a surplus. Our ability to successfully handle state government programs on a businesslike basis means instilling the same philosophy in Frankfort as you do in your own operations.

The very nature of government breeds waste. The very theme of a businesslike approach is to eliminate as much waste as possible. Time is an example. Tighter control of employee time can result in dollars saved. To use a round figure, if there are 30,000 state employees, and each wastes only ten minutes a day, in a year's time, 1.25 million manhours will have gone down the drain. At $3.00 an hour, this represents a loss of $4 million annually. A small hole can sink a large ship.

I am aware of other areas of waste—in materials and supplies. There are those who believe the state has a perpetual warehouse where supplies and other items are always available, no matter the quantity used. The same holds true for waste of effort. The quality of one's work is directly proportional to the results taxpayers receive for their dollars paid in. You have no patience with those in your own firms who constantly display inferior standards; neither does Wendell Ford.

This brings me to another area of government, political patronage. By removing patronage from the buildings of state government, we are stressing the true mission granted us by the people of Kentucky. I believe the party in power has the right and obligation to place in available jobs those persons who have been supporters of the party. However, performance, not politics, will determine whether or not those jobs are kept. And the same holds true for any other individual working in state government.

We have approached this administration in a careful, responsible manner. Our first endeavor has been to analyze each department, to effect new procedures which will bring about their full justification for existence through service to you. I proved my determination for this by sending inflated budget requests back to the Council on Public Higher Education, with a directive to show greater responsibility in the area of budgetary recommendations. My determination has shown through the abolishment of the State Curator's position, a last-minute appointment before inauguration day, dictating expenditures of money which should have been allocated elsewhere, especially in view of human needs. Little time was required to understand that the Citizens Commission on Consumer Affairs had failed to justify its existence, and corrective action was taken. Our next endeavor is to provide legislative recommendations and leadership which will guarantee Kentuckians a more promising future.

Already, two major campaign pledges have received impetus from the Governor's Office through introduced legislation—consumer protection, and restructuring and strengthening the Council on Public Higher Education. The Assembly has just begun, and we are prepared to work with all members in seeing that this Assembly departs with the admiration and respect of our citizens. Our course is set. Through the orderly and progressive measures to bring a sound, businesslike atmosphere to state government, through a legislative package based on enhancing the living and working conditions throughout Kentucky, and right into the reorganization of state government which comes immediately after the General Assembly, we are accomplishing the goals called for through last November's mandate of the people.

You, who are present tonight, are echoing that government can be operated as I have indicated. The last item of your four-point purposes of the legislative conference printed in your program says: "to develop understanding of business policies conducive to sound business principles."

The invitation for my appearance enables me to communicate what can be accomplished, and what I know you want from state government. You have every reason to expect this attitude to prevail during the next four years. Yes, there are doubting Thomases, but to them I say: you believe easily that which you hope for earnestly.

LOUISVILLE AREA CHAMBER OF
COMMERCE CONGRESSIONAL FORUM
Louisville / January 14, 1972

SHORTLY after November 2, a reporter asked me to reveal a specific accomplishment which I would want recognized at the termination of my four years as Governor. Quickly I replied, "the successful reorganization of state government." That desire will not diminish, nor will my intensity of purpose decline. As the early days of this new administration pass, as I review in depth the operation of state government, and as I analyze what should be the true role of government, there appears to be no limitation to the positive effects of reorganization.

Before reorganization, however, I have an obligation to improve the current standards of governmental procedure. Some of you were in the audience, less than two days ago, when I commented on the practicality of a more businesslike approach to state government. While I have no intention of repeating those observations, the natural kinship of essential business principles and a reorganizational concept definitely exists. Reorganization cannot be successful unless we penetrate every department and agency with a business philosophy that is wise, alert, and responsive. The subsequent results of reorganization will weigh heavily on how well each employee adopts this philosophy.

Some contend that substantial reorganization is impossible. They point to the deep entrenchment of various power structures within state government and say the status quo can't be shaken. Status quo government is in fact regressive government. And to Wendell Ford, there is but one direction, forward! Obviously, I am inviting a greater degree of decision-making on my own part, I am aware that the results of decision-making prompt, in some quarters, strong opposition. This, however, is a risk one must accept, otherwise you would have a status quo Governor. The necessary exercise of leadership often comes without benefit of deliberation, and at times without benefit of desired counsel. For there are immediate decisions a Governor must make strictly by himself. This is one of the lonely periods of office. Ron Mazzoli[1] has felt such a weight, but he has demonstrated courage of conviction. Any lesser quality brands those of us in public office as unfit for service. We must assume our roles in public life with a backbone rather than a wishbone. We must govern by hopes rather than fears. Something less is criminal.

If my appearance today calls for the entertainment of questions from the floor, I deem it proper to preface the question-and-answer session with these thoughts. As each day passes, the demands by others on a Governor increase. Right now, the Governor's Office is receiving, on a daily basis, over 1,000 pieces of communication from the public. A quick check this week shows that we are averaging nearly 500 phone calls a day, over 300 letters, and about 200 visitors. To each individual who writes, telephones, or comes in, their reason is important. The subject matter is endless, though all of it is funneled into a single purpose—to provide Kentuckians a better opportunity in life. That is what they want; that is what we want. I am committed to doing the best job humanly possible which means I am committed to the realization that my decisions must be based on what is best for all Kentucky.

Our state has emerged as a land of dramatic contrast and contradiction. Changes within our society must be predicated on this realization, for even though we are all Kentuckians, we have distinctive differences in our culture, our geography, our economy, our abilities, and our motivations. Yet it is my duty to serve our more than 3 million people as equally and fairly as if they were of one culture, one idealism, and one family. I am encouraged by your demonstrated interest today. You are here to listen, question, and, I am sure, judge. Your presence sets the example for others. One-way government, where citizen awareness of the factual issues is alarmingly incomplete, only restricts progress. You are interested. You can help stimulate the sincere interests of others. You can perform a vital function by encouraging others to become more knowledgeable in what the real issues are, and in what the logical alternatives are, alternatives those of us elected by you must pass final judgment on, alternatives that ultimately bring about the lonely periods for those of us who must decide.

---

1. Romano Louis Mazzoli (1932–   ), Democrat from Louisville; attorney; member of Kentucky Senate (1967–1970); United States House of Representatives (1971–   ). *Who's Who in America, 1974–1975* (Chicago, 1975), 2:2039.

KENTUCKY MUNICIPAL LEAGUE
Cadiz / September 28, 1972

WHOEVER said, "few things in the world are more spacious than the room we have for improvement," must have been involved with municipal problems! We who are charged with the responsibilities of public matters face a never-ending task of improvement. We face obstacles of insufficient funds, personnel shortages, the burdens of excessive demands, and quite often we suffer from a lack of coordination between agencies. Throughout my years in public office, it has become increasingly apparent that these obstacles, plus others, result in a widening of the space between the state and local governments. This is exactly opposite of what we need. I said during my campaign for Governor that reorganization could help solve this dilemma.

In approximately thirty days, I will announce the first step in our total reorganization process. While the precise makeup of this phase hasn't been polished, I want you to know that we are well-on-the-road with a blueprint for an executive-policy unit which will be directly attached to the Governor's Office. Within the framework of this section will be budget functions, planning functions, fiscal management functions, federal relations functions, and local government functions.

To be very explicit, this will not be a large bureaucracy, which is exactly what we are striving to eliminate in reorganization. Instead, this will be a high-level assistance staff, responsive to the Governor and to local governments. After all, local government is where you find the people. In addition, there will be a Governor's representative in the various regions of the state to work with local governments. Also, every department of state government will designate a local affairs officer from the existing staff. The function of these individuals will be to deal directly with the local government representatives from my office. You will find our new approach, coming soon, a revelation.

But we need to do something right now with revenue-sharing. Counties and cities are looking for two-thirds of the $87 million coming from Congress and the U.S. Treasury. I know there isn't any pass-through with the state on this money, and rightfully so. But we're all involved. I sincerely believe the state is in position to render immediate help to most local governments. This we offer. I have arranged for an immediate joint effort to provide all the technical advice we have at the state level to make revenue-sharing an orderly transition for you. Our Department of Finance, Kentucky Program Development Office, and the University of Kentucky will make a concerted effort to provide whatever assistance you deem necessary. I might mention one particular item, the matter of federal accounting and auditing requirements under the new law. I am going to ask the County Judges' Association and your municipal league to sponsor meetings all over the state for the purpose of conferring with the technical advisors we will provide. Together we can make rapid progress in this entirely new program.

I have studied the implications and potentials of revenue-sharing for a long time. My research brought forth specific needs, and I saw the probability of a federal revenue-sharing effort. Yet it was not my intention to wait on someone else. Because I felt revenue-sharing principles offered practical solutions, I made commitments as a candidate, and fulfilled them shortly after becoming Governor. Kentucky is implementing its own revenue-sharing programs, and we have done so on our own.

I made other commitments. Major legislation benefiting cities and counties and local-government units is reality. Many of the procedures you have sought, for so many years, have finally been realized, and I am especially proud that this administration, with leadership from men like Dee Huddleston,[1] made this possible. I made the people of Kentucky a promise on home rule. We carried it out. I made the people of Kentucky a promise on state revenue-sharing. We carried it out. I made the people of Kentucky a promise that state government would be properly reorganized. We are carrying this out.

I listened and the people spoke. They spoke of their frustrations and their hopes. They spoke of their inability to get action from the county seat, from Frankfort, and from Washington. They spoke of the continued, and widening, alienation of the people from their government and of their feeling that programs were being run not with them and their needs in mind, but seemingly for the convenience of the people who ran the programs. They spoke of delay. They spoke of coming to government with one problem and of being shunted from one agency to another, from one level of government to another.

I made a major commitment to these 3.25 million Kentuckians. I pledged that state government would be organized to serve the people, that overlapping and duplication would be done away with, that like programs would be placed in one agency, that unnecessary functions would be cut, that necessary programs would be strengthened, that local government would be strengthened, that delivery of services would be brought closer to the people served. I intend to see that these things are done.

Let me offer a word of caution on federal revenue-sharing. This is not a horn of plenty, and I am glad to see so many local government leaders saying they are taking a wait-and-see attitude. In the first year, let's don't build in ever-increasing and never-ending costs.

There is no guarantee that this will be continued, and you deserve an example as to why. There is one man running for United States Senator from Kentucky[2] who has publicly stated he believes revenue-sharing should be "only temporary." He has also demonstrated his prior opposition to state revenue-sharing because you could have received its benefits during the past four years, and didn't. I'm not talking about Dee Huddleston, who strongly supported what is new lifeblood to your communities—the revenue-sharing plan we adopted in 1972.

But I am saying without reservation that there are forces trying to minimize the positive values of revenue-sharing. This philosophy in Washington will only make your job, and the future of our people, much worse. We have tried to loosen the reins of state government on the cities and counties so we can work in a true partnership. This is the only way we can get the job done for the people.

---

1. Walter Darlington Huddleston (1926–   ), Democrat from Elizabethtown; member of Kentucky Senate (1966–1972), majority leader (1970–1972); United States Senator (1973–   ). *Who's Who in America, 1974–1975* (Chicago, 1975), 1:1510.

2. Dee Huddleston's Republican opponent was Louie Nunn, former Governor.

REORGANIZATION (1)
Frankfort / November 28, 1972

EARLY in my campaign, I raised the issue of state government reorganization.[1] An interested public responded, making this one of the key topics in my bid to become Governor. Kentuckians have every right to expect improved government services. There is a widespread belief that we can slow down the rapid growth of state government and do more with the tax dollars now being spent. I join in this belief and feel reorganization will bring about a closer relationship between the public and their state government.

My commitment came from contact with tens of thousands of Kentuckians who recognized the need to improve government efficiency. They spoke of frustration. They spoke of delay in services. They didn't like the widening gap which has taken place over the years between government and the individual. Citizens complained about coming to Frankfort with a problem and being sent from one agency to another, from one level of government to another, without any results, except disgust.

My promise was to see that reorganization produced results in order that overlapping and duplication not continue, like programs be placed in one agency, unnecessary functions be abolished, necessary programs be strengthened, delivery of services be brought closer to the people in a quicker manner, and the tax dollar go further.

Insufficient planning compounds the difficulty of achievement. The growing number of various departments, agencies, and other units of government has brought about disorder in what should be a most orderly process with the result often becoming "make-work activities." Every Governor must set executive policy, plan for the future of Kentucky, and ensure accomplishment within the context of the powers and responsibilities given him by the Constitution and General Assembly.

My concept of government is that it exists to serve people. Our government needs to be oriented in purpose—to serve. Our organizations should be based on the end product of services to the people. We intend to make the organizations of this government fit that mold. This occasion brings us to the first step in a series of reorganizational steps. In the information packet we have provided, you will find references to the authority for reorganization and the work we have done since early July. You will also note my firm intention of keeping our legislative committees advised of all executive reorganization orders to facilitate interim and 1974 considerations. I want to emphasize this as only the beginning step. While we have no intention of wasting time, neither do we intend to deviate from the orderly process which must be followed. Kentuckians have waited thirty-six years for reorganization. I trust you realize the complexities involved which demand time.

In my opinion, this announcement sets the framework to achieve that orderly process so necessary if reorganization is to be as fully effective as it must. A prime consideration has been to prevent disruption of continuing services, as well as any needless expenses. We have accomplished both. We also expect this task to be a product of all government agencies concerned, plus the input of people knowledgeable about the organization and delivery of services. I might add that we have received extensive assistance from people and agencies outside Kentucky state government.

Let me be very candid. When a Governor decides to undertake reorganization, he must work with what currently exists. What do I have right now?

1. No single agency for long-range or short-range planning of statewide programs.

2. No single agency for planning and management of the financial affairs of state government.

3. No single agency to deal effectively with the needs of local government.

4. No single agency to adequately handle the state's relations with the federal government.

5. No single agency to execute and direct the programs encompassed in the executive budget and mandated by the General Assembly.

In other words, today we have a hodgepodge of activities. I also have a cabinet made up of administrative bodies, departments, agencies, and commissions with no functional relationship to each other, or to the Governor who must direct them.[2] Let me stress the following points as I conclude.

Before we developed any meaningful reorganization on an overall departmental and agency basis, there first had to be the basic foundations which I have discussed. This enables us to move immediately into further reorganization with the six areas of mutual interest and application. The ultimate goal is more and better services to the people of Kentucky for the tax dollars they are now spending. This becomes more practical with a coordinated effort in long- and short-range planning and financing.

A Governor has no opportunity or ability to begin effective elimination of duplication and overlapping in the service agencies until he has the management capabilities of an organization as reflected in the new Executive Department of Finance and Administration. Therefore, we are stressing programs, delivery of services, and functions as they relate to individual areas of need in Kentucky. We are stressing the improvement of management and planning capabilities through integration of planning and budgeting. We are stressing a new cabinet philosophy.

This philosophy will enhance the management and planning capabilities to carry out those programs beneficial to the future of our state. I will begin preparing executive orders to see that these first steps will be operational on January 1, 1973.

I. INTRODUCTION

The last major reorganization of Kentucky state government occurred in the mid-1930s.[3] Before then, more than fifty independent administrative agencies had been created. It was 1936 when those units were compressed into ten statutory departments reporting to the Governor. Today, some thirty-six years later, there are now more than sixty departments and administrative agencies providing public services and reporting to the Governor.

A recent Legislative Research Commission report makes this valid point: "The Reorganization Act of 1936 was in line with the best thinking of the time, but the opposite is true of the proliferation of departments that has taken place since 1936. No one can coordinate, supervise, and lead, in a truly adequate way, as many department heads as the Governor of Kentucky must deal with."

The creation of new agencies has been in response to the demands for services. As the demands for new services became effective in the Commonwealth, new agencies were added to the executive branch of the government without integrating them in the administrative structure of providing for their direct responsibility to the chief executive. As a consequence, the executive branch of the government became a hodgepodge of boards, commissions, and other independent agencies as state revenue collections rose from $11.5 million going into 1936, to $357 million in 1963, to $845 million last year. The impact of federal programs is evident in the fact that we had no significant federal grants in the mid-1930s, and last year they represented nearly $550 million in a total state budget of $1.8 billion.

The magnitude and complexity of present-day government overwhelms the traditional structures and methods for conducting the people's business. In the past decade, we have witnessed untold expansion of public services and governmental programs and with each expansion the interrelationship of separate programs becomes more apparent. Program interests spill over traditional departmental jurisdictions, efficiency in operations becomes more difficult, coordination becomes equally more necessary and elusive, policy determinations become more clouded as authority and responsibility become more diluted. All these difficulties are mirrored at the point where the public expects efficient and timely services from their public agencies and institutions. This compounds the dilemma which confronts program administrators as well as elected representatives. It is equally the source of much of the frustration which confuses the citizen; it is the problem which our reorganization effort addresses.

I pledged that government would be organized to serve the people, that overlapping and duplication would be done away with, that like programs would be placed in one agency, that unnecessary functions would be cut, that necessary programs would be strengthened, that local government would be strengthened, that delivery of services would be brought closer to the people served. I intend to see that these things are done. Today, we are taking the initial major steps in the fulfillment of this commitment and mandate.

II. BACKGROUND

A. Legal Setting

"The supreme executive power of the Commonwealth shall be vested in a Chief Magistrate, who shall be styled the 'Governor of the Commonwealth of Kentucky' " (Kentucky Constitution, Section 69). This has not been the practical result of executive department organization. Responsibility is, and has been, the Governor's. But authority has become diffused in a confederation of over sixty departments and administrative agencies and some 210 boards, commissions, and committees.

No Governor can administer in detail the day-to-day operations of state government. But every Governor must set executive policy and plan for the future of Kentucky within the context of the powers and responsibilities given him by the Constitution and the General Assembly. The people demand it. The Constitution requires it.

The reorganization plan announced today is the first phase in a restructuring of Kentucky state government to the simple yet fundamental end that "He (the Governor) shall take care that the laws be faithfully executed." (Kentucky Constitution, Section 81.)

The 1962 General Assembly (in KRS Chapter 12) at the request of Governor Bert Combs[4] gave the chief executive authority to reorganize the administrative structure to effect the fundamental constitutional requirement. The General Assembly authorized executive action for the following reasons, "Recognizing the necessity for grouping certain related functions of departments and administrative bodies in order to promote greater economy, efficiency and improved administration in establishing more effective organizational patterns and also recognizing the fact that such groupings and revisions in the general organizational structure need to be made as rapidly as possible when administrative functions change and the needs of government dictate." (KRS 12.025[1]).

I propose to carry out this legislative mandate because the needs of government do so dictate, the needs of the people of Kentucky do so dictate. Changes effected under executive order will be submitted to the 1974 General Assembly for confirmation. In the meanwhile, legislative committees will be advised of all executive reorganization orders to facilitate interim and 1974 consideration.

B. Work to Date

We began our systematic work on reorganization at the July 3 cabinet meeting. As a result of that meeting, every agency head provided my office with the data necessary for decisions and consultation. The reorganization staff has been constantly studying the mass of information and has been in continuing contact with agency heads. We have also been examining the state and federal law and regulations that act either to facilitate or constrain reorganization. We have studied the organization of every other state government in the nation and have been meeting with federal and other states' officials.

I realize that this work has been going on with a lack of attendant publicity. For that I am grateful because the relation of government to the people it is organized to serve is a sensitive subject matter. A prime consideration has been that reorganization must not disrupt government services nor incur needless expenses. Reorganization also must be a product of all the agencies concerned, as far as possible. For these reasons, I have elected to approach reorganization on a logical step-by-step, program-by-program basis. This decision is mandated also because the present state government structure has been busy in absorbing the great amount of new programs and expanded programs enacted by the 1972 General Assembly, in absorbing new federal programs and changes in existing federal programs, in absorbing organizational changes made by the 1972 General Assembly, in making appointments in some sixty agencies, and filling vacancies on over 210 boards, commissions, and committees.

C. Today's Announcement

Today's first announcement deals with a) the creation of a strong, viable program cabinet system; b) a new position of Chief Cabinet Officer; and c) the consolidation of central policy and executive support agencies that service the entire government. This first step is the beginning of the hard work of combining administrative units, of developing better and more responsive delivery systems for government services. Our emphasis is on setting a framework of government that can be managed, that is responsive to the needs of the people, that is fully accountable to the people's elected representatives, and that is sufficiently flexible to adapt to new needs in future years.

My concept of government is that it exists to serve people. Our government needs to be oriented in purpose—to serve. Our organizations should be based on the end product—of services to the people. We intend to make the organizations of this government fit that mold.

In the next several weeks, I will issue executive orders to put these changes into effect as of January 1, 1973. This will permit an orderly transition.

III. THE CABINET

A. Program Cabinet Structure

The cabinet, as the critical and unifying element of the entire governmental structure, is being organized into functional and workable "program cabinets" capable of dealing with the broad program interests which are not confined to a single departmental jurisdiction.

The cabinet is being structured into six program cabinets which will provide an effective focus and forum for immediate attention to questions of organizational streamlining as well as directing sustained attention to comprehensive planning, management improvements, coordination in program development, and the delivery of services. The six program cabinets are Human Resources, Consumer Protection and Regulation, Safety and Justice, Development, Transportation, Education and the Arts.

All departments excepting the central support agencies, including those headed by elected officials, and the new Department of Environmental Protection will be grouped among the various program cabinets, as will the various smaller units comprising the many boards and commissions. Chart I sets forth the various agencies constituting the program cabinets.[5]

One of the initial charges to the program cabinets will be the development of recommendations for further organizational streamlining and unification of common services. We are determined that internal restructuring within the functional service areas will represent sizable and significant contributions from the agency heads, the state employees involved in the day-to-day delivery of services, and knowledgeable persons outside the government. This is not to suggest that each program cabinet will reorganize itself, but it does mean that each program cabinet will first be directed to systematically suggest thoughtful and relevant proposals for consideration by the reorganization staff. The organization of these program cabinets does not imply a commitment to eventual establishment of a few giant super agencies within the government.

B. Chief Cabinet Officer

I am establishing the Office of Secretary of the Governor's Cabinet. The secretary will hold the dual assignment of Commissioner of the Executive Department of Finance and Administration, and will serve as the Chief Cabinet Officer in the area of governmental operations.

IV. CONSOLIDATION OF DEPARTMENT OF FINANCE AND KENTUCKY PROGRAM DEVELOPMENT OFFICE

A. Purpose

We are consolidating and unifying in the Executive Department of Finance and Administration all central service and policy responsibilities with the exception of those relating to personnel, revenue, and public information matters. This new department will take over all the functions now in the Department of Finance and most of the functions now in the Kentucky Program Development Office. These functions are not going to be merely rearranged. They are going to be restructured, completely restructured as they relate to policy, planning, and local government.

Professor James W. Martin,[6] a major force in the 1936 reorganization, in a recent treatise on *An Executive Office of the Governor for Kentucky* has set forth some major aims of state government which I believe state well the purpose of the new Executive Department of Finance and Administration.

1. The administration will implement the service programs for which the state makes legal and financial provision in such a way as to procure continuously the maximum product for each dollar expended.

2. The administration must have comprehensive long-range policy analysis and program evaluation in order to lay the groundwork for the Governor's leadership toward constructive legislation, including priority determinations.

3. The efficient operation of the state government calls for the constant harmony of political and administrative decision-making.

4. The conduct of state government must meet exacting social and ethical standards.

5. Kentucky will provide frequently revised and manageable state administrative organization.

6. The objective of adequate financial management is often undersold by the very group of people whom the state makes responsible for fiscal administration.

7. The number and complexity of state ties with its local governments, with other states, and with the United States dictate a means of

defining and maintaining consistent intergovernmental relationships.

8. The existing urgent Kentucky need for top, uninterrupted coordination is acute. It exists within and among major functions and perhaps even more insistently among overall agencies such as the Department of Finance, the several planning agencies, and the Department of Public Information.

B. Elements of the Department

We are establishing an Office of Policy and Management which will combine the basic responsibilities involved in budgeting and state planning.

This was a consensus proposed by a study team appointed by my predecessor which said: "We think that the requisite coordination of long-range planning and budgeting can best be achieved by assigning the two functions to a single division within the Department of Finance and Administration. This integration will facilitate communication between planners and budget personnel and will bring planning closer to the reality of operations."

State government, for too long, has needed a high-level, high-competence, professionally staffed and managed capability that might act as a "Policy Planning Unit," whose mission would be to perceive and define problems as well as solving them, and to evaluate various strategies to achieve various public purposes, as well as suggesting them. Such a unit is visualized as working in conjunction with relevant levels of decision-making throughout the state and to engage in anticipatory planning activities that would result in a unified perspective regarding the political, social, and economic development of Kentucky. This we attempt to achieve in the structuring of the new department's Office of Policy and Management.

The present system of financial management needs to be retained and strengthened in the new department. The new department will focus both on fiscal management and accountability in terms of state policy and planning. The new department also recognizes the close relationship of local government and state government. We are establishing a new Office of Local Government which will be the central focal point for the mobilization of all service resources in the executive branch to provide technical assistance and support to the units of local government, our counties, and our cities.

The General Assembly, with the recent enactment of the "Home Rule" legislation, tried to loosen the reins upon local government so that we could all work in a true partnership. To provide local government with help in developing their own programs to serve the people, this new state office will get close to the problems with which local officials are concerned. It will be in a position to place at the disposal of local government a cadre of knowledgeable technicians who are capable of helping put together feasible programs that will answer the needs of people. The need for an Office of Local Government is underscored by the advent of both the state and the federal revenue-sharing legislation, as well as other recent programs such as the new Pollution Abatement and Housing Authorities.

The remaining service and control functions of the existing Department of Finance will be regrouped to unify their capabilities. Kentucky Program Development Office programs that have an operational flavor will be relocated in various program agencies which have similar service responsibilities and missions.

The functions to be administered by the Executive Department of Finance and Administration are set forth in the following list, as is the disposition of the functions now performed by the Department of Finance and the Kentucky Program Development Office.

A. Executive Department of Finance and Administration

Office of the Commissioner

General Counsel
Staff support for his office (including debt and investment)
Authorities and Corporations (Turnpike, Property & Buildings, Housing, Savings Bond, Water Abatement, Capital Plaza)
State Planning Committee of the Cabinet/Urban Affairs Council

Office of Policy and Management

Budgeting
State Planning
Federal Aid Coordination
Organization and Procedures
Issue Analysis and Forecasts
State Plan Review (A–95)

Office of Local Government

Local Finance
Revenue-Sharing
Local Assistance
Development Districts
Local Plan and Project Review (A–95)

Bureau of Finance

Accounting
Purchasing
Engineering

Bureau of Services
   Data Processing
   Building Services
   Mechanical Systems
   Properties
   Communications
   Records and Archives
   Printing

B. REORGANIZATIONAL ASSIGNMENT OF KPDO PROGRAMS

To Office of Local Government
   Urban Affairs
   Community Planning and Development
   Housing Assistance
   Model Cities
   Development Districts

To Office of Policy and Management
   Appalachia Program
   Federal Aid Coordination
   Research and Analysis
   State Comprehensive Planning
   A–95 Review

To Program Cabinets
   Comprehensive Health Planning
   Human Resources Coordinating Commission
   Office of Economic Opportunity

To Department of Parks
   Outdoor Recreation

To Department of Commerce
   Economic Development Administration

---

1. Press conference; this was the first of ten major announcements on state government reorganization. The reference to the number of this reorganization announcement is made because this particular reorganization was hereafter usually referred to by number in Governor Ford's public statements. The other major reorganization announcements are as follows: Reorganization 2, Department for Natural Resources and Environmental Protection, January 3, 1973; Reorganization 3, Naming of Secretary of Human Resources, March 2, 1973; Reorganization 4, Department of Transportation, March 16, 1973; Reorganization 5, Computer Operations (Finance), April 25, 1973; Reorganization 6, Department of Human Resources, August 29, 1973; Reorganization 7, Department of Justice, September 11, 1973; Re-

organization 8, Development and Education and the Arts Cabinets, September 13, 1973; Reorganization 10, Department of Public Information, October 15, 1973; Reorganization 12, Consumer Protection and Regulation Cabinet, January 2, 1974.

2. The Governor used charts extensively in illustrating his reorganization designs. The specific charts for reorganization of the cabinet responsibilities are not reproduced in this volume. For a general overview see Appendix 2.

3. The latter detailed portions of this press conference were distributed in written form but are combined here with the oral statement made by the Governor.

4. Bert Thomas Combs (1911–   ), Democrat presently of Louisville; attorney; judge, Kentucky Court of Appeals (1951–1955); Governor of Kentucky (1959–1963); gubernatorial candidate (1955, 1959, 1971); judge, United States Court of Appeals, Sixth Circuit (1967–1970). *Who's Who in America, 1974–1975* (Chicago, 1975), 1:620.

5. See Appendix 2 for a general overview.

6. James Walter Martin (1893–   ), Lexington; professor of economics at the University of Kentucky (1928–1948), distinguished professor (1948–1964), emeritus distinguished professor (1964–   ); commissioner of revenue, Kentucky (1936–1939); commissioner of finance, Kentucky (1955–1957); commissioner of highways, Kentucky (1957–1958). *American Men of Science: The Social and Behavioral Sciences,* 11th ed. (New York, 1968), p. 1056.

CAPITAL CHAPTER OF
NATIONAL SECRETARIES ASSOCIATION
Frankfort / December 5, 1972

DAY after tomorrow marks the first anniversary of this administration. The press has requested a review of my initial twelve months as Governor, and on Thursday one of the topics I plan to mention is reorganization.

The fact we now have a handle on reorganization of state government is very pleasing to me. For thirty-six years there has been no major restructuring of a rapidly expanding system which affects the lives of every Kentuckian. Now, there will be. Last week I announced the first in a series of steps we are taking to reorganize government. I want to briefly touch on several points regarding this subject.

If you in this room who are secretaries, businessmen, professionals, farmers, or housewives failed to alter the procedures and mechanics of your work within a thirty-six year period, what degree of efficiency would prevail? How productive would you be? How much control on your budget would you have?

As a secretary, what if each time you filed a new report, you simply opened a new drawer? Before long, you would be scrambling all over the office trying to assemble your work. As a wife and mother, what if your homemaking chores had not been improved by the advancements of new methods, techniques, and supplies? Compare the efficiency of today and yesterday. And, of course, to you in the businesses and professions, how many companies succeed when management refuses to constantly seek improved standards, quality control, and closer coordination made increasingly more necessary through growth?

State government faces the same dilemmas. Today, there are more than sixty departments and administrative agencies reporting to the Governor. There are in excess of 200 boards and commissions. Response to growing demands for services and increases in funding, both from the state and federal levels, has brought about a many-headed animal with arms and legs going in every direction. It's my responsibility to offer a new plan for government's ability to serve people.

You can't properly determine programs and program financing unless there is a bridge between state and federal funding and statewide planning. In the past, these were separate operations. Now they will be together. You can't reach areas of need as quickly nor as completely as desired unless departments and agencies with corresponding concerns are more closely allied. Through our new cabinet concept, we can achieve this.

I believe, however, that my message tonight should be this. Reorganization of state government is a complex, time-consuming, detailed task. It is designed to bring a greater degree of professionalism to those who are employed, to eliminate duplication, to generate a stronger delivery of services to the citizens of Kentucky, and to provide more for the tax dollar being spent now. Reorganization must be an orderly process, built upon the input of many: my staff responsible for reorganization, knowledgeable individuals outside government, other states, and groups such as the Council of State Governments, and most assuredly department and agency heads. With such a vast array of information, the proper course can be charted.

We haven't called in expensive consulting firms as has been the case elsewhere. There are perceptive minds right here in Kentucky who know the needs of both the people and state government.

We are not making speed our top priority. We plan to proceed as rapidly as possible, but our first consideration is to the people of Kentucky to see that existing programs are not interrupted during this reorganizational period. After all, aren't each of us, no matter our livelihood, most interested in the orderly process of activities? As an illustration of my intent to secure departmental input, we are this week holding a series of program cabinet meetings to discuss future steps which should be taken toward total reorganization.

So what I am saying is that while we do have a handle, we have much more to accomplish. It would be inappropriate for anyone to say now, "this is the final plan." Yet, before any final plan can be drafted, there had to be the changes I announced last week. These are the foundations for further reorganization. As a further illustration of enlisting input, I will by open letter in the state employee newspaper invite suggestions from all employees. In many cases, those on the front lines have sound ideas as to how their own activities can better serve the public. This is necessary for a meaningful reorganization.

You in NSA have a slogan: "Better secretaries mean better business." This is the philosophy I want instilled in state government—something better, far better, for the benefit of all Kentuckians. I want to congratulate you in NSA for your attitude of self-improvement, for your willingness to help others prepare for a vitally important profession. Our jobs are made easier by efficient secretaries and especially those whose determinations are in behalf of self-improvement. No matter our course of life, we can't accept the status quo. This is the enlightening attitude of NSA and does much to make our office procedures better. I think your ranks will grow as more and more secretaries learn of NSA's values.

REORGANIZATION:
DEPARTMENT FOR NATURAL RESOURCES
AND ENVIRONMENTAL PROTECTION
Frankfort / January 3, 1973

RAPID changes have occurred within the past year, and certainly within the past six months, in the regulation and protection of the environment.[1] The nature of environmental decisions, the impact of federal Environmental Protection Agency regulations, and adequate governmental services to the citizens of Kentucky demand a state agency with flexibility and broad authority for the protection and preservation of our land, air, and water resources. This is of the highest priority now, and will be so in the future.

House Bill 3, enacted by the first extraordinary session of the 1972 General Assembly, created a Department of Environmental Protection, effective January 1, 1973. That environmental statute authorized the Governor, where necessary and appropriate, to undertake reorganization measures in the regulation of the quality of the natural environment. Recognizing that the authority and responsibility for many programs necessary for a healthful environment for all Kentuckians would otherwise remain in several state government agencies, I have today signed Executive Order 73–1, pursuant to KRS Chapter 12, which includes the following changes.

All functions, authority, and responsibility now vested in the Departments of Natural Resources and Environmental Protection are merged and consolidated within the Department for Natural Resources and Environmental Protection (successor agency of natural resources). In addition, functions, authority, and responsibility of certain other programs, found in the Departments of Health and Agriculture, have been brought into the successor agency. This agency has also been organized to encompass other functions which had not previously been included as you will note on the following charts.[2]

I believe a comparison of the organizational charts gives a visual understanding as to the use of the Kentucky Revised Statutes. Chart 1 shows the organization of several departments of state government relating to environmental protection before the first extraordinary session. Chart 2 illustrates the organization and functions of the Department of Environmental Protection as created by the 1972 General Assembly at its first extraordinary session.[3] It is important to remember that at this point, two departments exist—Natural Resources and Environmental Protection. In the natural course of our total reorganization a sound framework for further consolidation was established to accomplish those goals I have mentioned previously: better delivery of services to eliminate duplication and to develop the closest possible coordination. Chart 3, therefore, shows the organization and functions of the Department for Natural Resources and Environmental Protection established today as one of the seven program cabinets. In addition to merging the divisions of solid waste, air pollution, water pollution, and reclamation into the successor agency, the order also merges the divisions of forestry, soil and water conservation, and flood control and water resources from the Department of Natural Resources into its successor agency—Department for Natural Resources and Environmental Protection.

Furthermore, this reorganization measure has authorized this successor agency to implement a series of special programs including pesticides (from the Department of Agriculture), noise (from the Department of Health), wild rivers, orphan land and revolving fund, and beautification programs.

---

1. Press conference; this statement was read by the Governor.
2. These charts are not reproduced in this volume.
3. See Executive Order 72–1174.

NATIONAL ASSOCIATION OF REGIONAL COUNCILS
Minneapolis, Minnesota / February 25, 1973

I AM pleased that you asked me to address the opening session of your conference because the goals of this organization indicate a sharing with me of the same determinations in making government at all levels more efficient and more responsive to the people. Many of you perhaps know that Kentucky is in the middle of its first complete reorganization of state government in thirty-six years. I made this one of the main commitments of my campaign for Governor, and it is one of the priority thrusts of my administration. When I came into office, I inherited

a hodgepodge of departments, agencies, boards, and commissions—
almost 300 in all.

Partly this mix of bureaucratic sprawl was due to increased demands
for new services, but mainly it was a typical result of new money and
programs from Washington and Frankfort. In other words, every time
new money became available, the practice was to create a new agency.
Common sense fell to the usual bureaucratic assumption that it has
always been done this way! The results of this approach are painfully
evident in our state, extensive overlapping and duplication of services,
lack of coordinated planning and program implementation, complex
lines of communication where short circuits seem the rule rather than
the exception, and, most importantly, an alienation of people from a
government that seems aloof and unresponsive to their needs.

One area where alienation has been manifested is in the relationship
of local governments to each other, and to the state. Here is where the
system of regional councils has become most helpful. In Kentucky, we
call these regional councils Area Development Districts. With 120 counties, more than 350 municipalities, and over 270 special districts in
Kentucky, we have an obvious need for cooperation and coordinated
planning. Kentucky's fifteen Area Development Districts, or ADDs,
became a framework for interlocal planning and development, enhancing cooperation in many programs. The Area Development Districts
enable local officials and citizens to identify regional needs and establish regional priorities. The federal regulation requiring regional review
of most federal grant applications strengthens the regional planning
concept.

Two areas in which regional development is particularly helpful are
the maximum utilization of area resources and technical assistance in
planning and development, including help in general government
matters. One good example of local cooperation to utilize regional
resources is the district development fund initiated locally by banks in
the Kentucky River ADD. After granting a charter to this group for
the fund, ten banks in the eight-county area jointly contributed $50,000
to the development fund which was then matched by federal dollars.
Any community or industrial group in the ADD area is eligible for
financial assistance from this fund.

In the area of technical assistance to local government, one of our
ADDs has hired a city planner to work with local governments on fiscal
and managerial problems. Such technical staff assistance will gradually
increase throughout the state so that the interlocal partnership will
become stronger. As this partnership becomes stronger, I think it will
become increasingly more important that we avoid what has happened

to state government in the past. If a new planning board has to be set up for each new program affecting area development, we are going to increase the communication problems and reduce coordination of the total scope of services at all levels of government.

Our main objective in district development is to establish lines of communication between local officials and the state. If representatives of local government in each ADD district have to attend several board meetings to deal with the development of services in their area, we are going to lose the important input they can give regional development. These officials simply don't have the time to go to planning meetings for each new program. You know, it's ironic that all of our productivity seems to be absorbed by time-consuming meetings. I am one who believes we ought to spend 90 percent of our time doing and 10 percent talking, rather than 90 percent talking and having only 10 percent left for doing!

The budding of new regional planning bodies, whether for land use, rural development, or water quality, will only contribute to further restriction of the planning process. We must make use of existing planning bodies to encourage greater local participation. The creation of numerous planning bodies reduces the opportunity for local involvement and creates barriers between services to people. You cannot separate water quality from land use, land use from recreation, recreation from health, mental health from physical health, and so forth. With single planning bodies looking at all of these interrelated areas with a functional total-service concept in mind, planning and development will be better coordinated locally and at the state level. This can be done in the framework of regional councils.

Now, let's go one step further. Kentucky's Area Development Districts have strengthened the lines of communication between local governments and the state. Yet, we realize that the complexity of service needs for many governmental units in the state cannot be totally solved on the regional level. There will still be many problems to deal with on an individual basis.

The way we are going to assure individual treatment in our state is through the Office for Local Government which was one of the initial programs in our reorganization of state government. For the first time, county and municipal governments in the Commonwealth have direct access to the executive branch of state government. There are three basic functions served by the Office for Local Government: as a contact point to hear about local problems, as an identifier and expediter of the types of state assistance that can help address local problems, as coordinator of the state's resources to help serve the people of Kentucky through their local governments. This office works closely with our fifteen ADD districts in channeling state assistance to local governments. In fact, the advent of revenue-sharing has already proved the value of this relationship.

When my Office for Local Government became aware that all tax revenues were not being credited to local units of government in the state, they went through the ADDs to secure more complete data. It is critical to make sure that each unit of government gets full credit for all the revenues collected, because this affects the amount they receive from revenue-sharing and affects the amount the state government obtains. When the survey was completed, it was found that a number of local governmental units were not getting their full entitlements due to incomplete data. In the county data alone, we uncovered $16 million of unreported taxes. This would have been lost if it had not been for the cooperation of state and local officials through these new lines of communication and assistance.

The Office for Local Government has also initiated a process of evaluation to assist the district decision-making bodies in defining their own roles and to measure the effectiveness of regional planning and technical assistance. These evaluations will continue on an annual basis. They will help us make sure that our fifteen districts maintain the capability and support needed for them to realize the full potential of regional development and to provide the necessary technical assistance to local governments.

The governmental structures I have mentioned today give us the mechanism for more efficient and responsive government at all levels. They are designed to improve lines of communication between the people and their government. They should help bring local officials more into the mainstream of regional and state decision-making. They can help cut down the expensive and unnecessary duplication of services. I have also alluded to problems which we and some of you have already faced, but which others could later face. Hopefully, you who haven't, might benefit from the often unpleasant experience.

Four of the major areas receiving attention in the future from our fifteen ADDs will be manpower development planning, health planning, water quality management, and implementation of the Rural Development Act. As a final point, our total state reorganization will focus on seven cabinet program areas: environmental protection and natural resources, human resources, transportation, safety and justice, development, education and the arts, and consumer protection and regulations. There will be a new and improved relationship between these program cabinets and the ADD districts, and, of course, our Department of Administration and Finance Office of Local Government will coordinate that relationship. We are really talking about an orderly process of improvement. This is being achieved in Kentucky with one thought in mind—improving the delivery of service to all the citizens of our state.

REORGANIZATION: HUMAN RESOURCES
Frankfort / March 2, 1973

THE purpose of this announcement is to take another step in the reorganization of state government and in the restructuring of delivery of services as they pertain to the area of human resources.[1] My objective is the better delivery of services to the people and the better utilization of those tax dollars now being spent on human resource needs. This I intend to do in the most orderly fashion possible. And this I intend to do without disturbing or disrupting needed services now going to the people of Kentucky.

The human resources area is of critical importance. Here is where government actually touches the lives of those individuals I believe government should and can help: the sick, the aged, the handicapped, and those least able to help themselves. I want to emphasize right now that what we will do in the days ahead can be classified this way: increasing the strengths of our programs and eliminating the weaknesses in any programs found lagging. This endeavor will definitely improve the quality of life in our great state.

In order to accomplish these objectives, I am announcing the appointment of a Secretary for Human Resources, Laurel True.[2] As my chief assistant and main advisor in the total field of human resources, Mr. True has received from me several mandates. The secretary, after working directly with the reorganization staff and every agency lodged in the Human Resources Program Cabinet, will make final recommendations to me for actual restructuring that will affect these agencies and will direct the implementation of those decisions. In addition, the secretary will be primarily responsible for involving citizen participation in this new program area.

The secretary will activate and direct long-term comprehensive planning and oversee the preparation of realistic and unified budgets which will require the agencies to better concentrate on the major priorities of human needs. I am most interested in consolidated planning to shape a framework for long-term responsibilities rather than continuing a fragmented approach we now find because there is an absence of coordination in this area.

The Secretary for Human Resources will be responsible for overall direction and coordination of relations between the Kentucky government and the federal agencies that involve the departments in the Human Resources Cabinet. The reason for this is especially clear: we must avoid just being in the position of only reacting to the multitude of federal guidelines and directives in these program areas. Additionally, I am in this order directing that comprehensive health planning and the state Office of Economic Opportunity be directly attached to the office of the secretary and that the secretary provide for the administration of human resource programs not presently assigned to a single agency of the Human Resource Cabinet. I am abolishing the Human Resources Coordinating Commission, and its personnel, funds, and other resources are being transferred to the Secretary for Human Resources.

These are the priorities I am placing on this position, and this is what I expect to accomplish in a very short time. It is a tough assignment, and the secretary will need the cooperation, help, and patience of all Kentuckians who share our determination to make state government more responsive to the needs of people. Mr. True has repeatedly demonstrated his unusual capabilities and concerns in the broad spectrum of human resources. The complexities of this program cabinet are numerous, so it is vitally important that the Governor appoint someone in whom he has an abiding faith. This is why I am delighted that Mr. True has accepted the position. I have great confidence in Laurel True, as I do in the department heads with whom he will be working. Mr. True has my unqualified support and expectation that he, along with all involved in this program cabinet area, will get the job done without delay.

---

1. Press conference.

2. Laurel True (1933–   ), Frankfort; career public servant; first served in the Department of Health; during Governor Ford's administration he was director of the Kentucky Development Office and then became the first secretary of the Department for Human Resources; he served Governor Ford's

successor as special assistant for planning and is currently the first director of the Kentucky Health Systems Agency—West. Interview with True on August 19, 1976.

REORGANIZATION: TRANSPORTATION
Frankfort / March 16, 1973

SEVERAL months ago, our first major reorganizational announcement pertained to the program cabinet concept. From there we moved into the new Executive Department for Finance and Administration to establish a bridge between statewide planning and state and federal financing of projects. Next came the Department for Natural Resources and Environmental Protection and later the reorganization for Human Resources.

In what I have insisted will always be an orderly procedure, the continuing reorganizational process, we are now prepared to announce the new program concept of the Department of Transportation.

You have a more lengthy report in the form of a statement from me. On pages one and two, you will note the rationale behind this agency, as well as the input we declared necessary in arriving at the present level of agency involvement.[1]

In view of the transportation picture which has prevailed in Kentucky, a number of obvious governmental deficiencies were found. We have found that:

1. The present structure encourages promotion of individual transportation interests rather than the transportation needs of the state as a whole.

2. The present structure encourages a piecemeal approach to development of transportation facilities that will ultimately accelerate the problems created by urban and industrial development.

3. There is no single mechanism or system to deal with the comprehensive transportation problems that face our state and to recommend, based on sound planning, state transportation policy.

4. There is no single state agency that can relate to the U.S. Department of Transportation on all programs dealing with air, water, highway, and rail transportation.

5. There is not a centralized management point for planning, budgeting, coordinating, controlling, and implementing all modes of transportation programs including rail, air, water, and highway.

6. There is a need for a single organizational unit that will provide staff services and administrative support to a single transportation agency rather than a duplication of administrative support services to several transportation-related agencies.

7. There is a need to have a system or mechanism that more adequately involves local elected officials and private citizens in the transportation development process and is more responsive to the needs of the citizens of the Commonwealth.

As a result of this intensive study and in recognition of our responsibility for an efficient and effective transportation system for all Kentuckians, I have today signed Executive Order 73–288, pursuant to KRS Chapter 12, which establishes a Department of Transportation. All functions, authority, and responsibility now vested in the Departments of Highways, Motor Transportation, and Aeronautics, as well as certain other programs found in the Departments of Public Safety and Revenue, are hereby merged and consolidated within the new Department of Transportation. This order creates within the Department of Transportation an Office of Transportation Planning and a Transportation Planning Committee.

The Transportation Planning Committee will consist of the Commissioners of the Bureaus of Highways and Vehicle Regulations, Executive Director of the Office of Transportation Planning, and any others named by the Secretary of Transportation. They shall advise the secretary on transportation policies and directions for departmental long-range planning regarding all forms of transportation including highways, air, water, and rail modes.

The Office of Transportation Planning will be the heart or key to the effectiveness of a Department of Transportation. This office will consist of the Divisions of Planning, Mass Transit, Airports, and Environmental Systems. They will be responsible for developing and recommending to the secretary policies and procedures for the full spectrum of comprehensive transportation planning and development activities. The secretary, through his Office of Transportation Planning, will be responsible for coordinating the transportation planning functions of the Commonwealth so as to improve the quality of transportation services, promote comprehensive transportation planning, and provide consistency for transportation program plans at the state and regional level utilizing the input of local units of government. This office will formulate a comprehensive statewide facility and service-needs study and a long-range development plan intended to achieve balanced development and coordination of transportation activities.

Additional responsibilities will include evaluating and studying the impact of transportation facilities on the environment and airport activities as set out in KRS Chapter 183. One of the more important functions of this office is to address the public transit needs of the citizens of the Commonwealth. They will monitor developments in the public transit field and provide liaison, coordination, and assistance to appropriate federal, state, regional, and local groups concerning the mass transit mode of transportation.

This order also creates the Divisions of Budget, Public Affairs, and Audit Review, as well as the Safety Coordinator, which are support units for the secretary's office. The primary support unit for all of the Department of Transportation will be the Executive Office of Staff Services which will include offices for Personnel Management, Administration and Operations, General Counsel, and Computer Services. I have created a Bureau of Vehicle Regulations and a Bureau of Highways as the major operating entities within the Department of Transportation.

The single state agency for transportation, therefore, will, in my opinion, eliminate the minuses and offer any number of pluses in our ability to improve the delivery of services as they pertain to this program area. The single state agency for transportation will allow us to:

1) integrate transportation planning at the state and multicounty level in order to meet the increasing transportation demands and to achieve a balanced development of facilities and services;

2) more actively involve the citizens of the Commonwealth and local elected officials in the transportation development process;

3) have a consolidated planning program with long-term, comprehensive, statewide planning and a realistic and unified budget which will enable the state to better concentrate on the major priorities of transportation needs;

4) consider all modes of transport (air, rail, water, and highway) and all efforts (public and private) within the same organizational unit and in a consistent, coordinated, comprehensive, and continuing manner;

5) establish statewide comprehensive goals and objectives for the development of transportation facilities and the delivery of transportation services;

6) broaden the role of state government to deal more effectively in the federal system with national and local governments;

7) through improved management and by avoiding duplication help

reduce transportation costs and provide for a more efficient expenditure of funds;

8) help local communities define their transportation requirements and encourage the development of new transportation systems.

Again, what we are really talking about, as I have stressed in other reorganization announcements, is that we are striving to attain maximum efficiency through a businesslike, common sense approach to public problems which have intensified because of an increasingly complex society.

Let's take a hypothetical case. County "X" has transportation needs. Officials in the past have been forced to deal with various agencies where there has been no coordination. In 1973 and beyond, transportation is no longer a single unit issue. Counties have to look at the entire structure—roads, airports, mass transportation, river transportation, safety, and regulations. Also, a multicounty relationship becomes increasingly more important. Any two or three or more of these areas must have a coordinated direction. This, for the first time in Kentucky's history, is made possible.

---

1. Some of the detailed portions of this conference were in written form but are combined here with the oral statement by the Governor.

ANNUAL MEETING OF KENTUCKY ASSOCIATION OF HIGHWAY ENGINEERS
Lexington / March 24, 1973

I AM happy to be here. But more significantly, I think, it is important that I be here today. After last week's announcement of the creation of the Department of Transportation and the reorganization of the part of state government affecting the highway program, I realize how important it is that I discuss with you what has been done, why I have done it, and what role I expect highway engineers to play in the new department.

I think you are all aware of the broad outlines under which I am reorganizing state government. Programs have been consolidated in the areas of human resources, natural resources and the environment, education, development, consumer protection and regulation, safety, and transportation. In January, we created the Department for Natural Resources and Environmental Protection. This agency probably does not yet have all the functions that will be assigned to it. The first total reorganization, including not only the consolidation of agencies, but the establishment of a complete internal structure, is the Department of Transportation.

Why did I choose to begin at this point? One reason is that I saw in the Department of Highways a cadre of experienced and dedicated professionals which I thought could best set an example for all state employees as we work together to make reorganization successful. State government has many professionals, but nowhere else do you find the number of professionals united in a single program as they were in the Department of Highways. I think it is appropriate that you have dedicated your annual meeting to the theme of professionalism because, as I see it, your association most completely exemplifies the professional in state government. I rely on your professionalism in the necessary transition which must be made as we alter the structure and direction of government, not only in your area of responsibility, but in all of state government.

Old ways are always comfortable. They may not be the best way of doing things, but they are definitely the easiest. This was certainly true of old arrangements in Frankfort. Unfortunately, state government in the Commonwealth was not very efficient. Not only Governors and other elected state officials saw it. The public, long before politicians and professionals, recognized the difficulty of getting answers to specific questions. To the private citizen in need of help from Frankfort, state government was a maze in which he was more apt to get lost than reach his goal.

Your Governor was probably the most concerned of all by the disarray of state government. During the campaign I pledged to the people of Kentucky, and myself, that I would do something about it. Reorganization is my response to that pledge.

I want you to understand that the decisions I have made, particularly the creation of the Department of Transportation with a completed internal structure, were not made in a vacuum. My decision was made only after long and careful study by professionals whose judgment I trust, just as I trust yours in dealing with highway problems. My staff compiled information and made recommendations in the same way you would work in developing a highway project. Data was accumulated.

The experience of other states was evaluated. Finally, many alternatives were reviewed. To give you an idea of how many, the chart showing the organization of the new department was the fourteenth draft that had been made.

Out of all this planning has come, among other things, the Department of Transportation and within it the Bureau of Highways. Let me assure you now, the mission of the bureau remains unchanged. You are to operate a system of highways that will best serve the needs of the people of the Commonwealth.

I see two specific benefits for the engineering profession in the structure of the department. For one thing, by creating a separate office of staff services, I believe we have clarified the role that professional engineers will play in the highway program. At the same time, we have created specific areas outside the bureau in which the input of the professional highway engineers will be available. The Office of Transportation Planning will include highway engineers. In addition, we intend to assign a highway engineer to the staff of the Commissioner of Finance and Administration.

When I spoke to the Kentucky Society of Professional Engineers in Ashland in April 1971, I said that this decade would require the professional and technical talents of engineers if we are to solve the problems of urban transportation and the environment. I am more than ever convinced that this is true. The new organization presents an opportunity for your talents to be utilized in state government on a broader scope.

Perhaps you noticed a story in the *Courier-Journal* this week that summarized the accomplishments of the highway program to date. The headline spoke of the "End of an Era." I will not try to characterize that headline. I will say that the announcement of the new Department of Transportation might very well have been headlined as the "Beginning of an Era." New problems call for new answers. The Department of Transportation provides new means of seeking answers. But we must remember that not all the old problems have been solved. Kentucky still has many, many road needs.

In 1971, you and I discussed our highway program. I wrote, "I will support and enforce the Kentucky merit system law and the laws set forth in the Federal Hatch Act relating to political activities." And I assured you that "you would, . . . not be forced to contribute to political campaigns under threat of losing your job, being transferred to 'Siberia,' or losing of deserved merit pay increments." I have kept that pledge, not only to your society and profession, but to all state employees.

I told you that your salaries should be improved. As a result of the raises you received in September last year, engineers' wages have come from the lowest point—as compared to the adjoining states—to a median point. I promised you a Commissioner of Highways capable of administering the road programs. You read the many compliments that were paid to Charlie Pryor[1] last week. I believe that Lige Hogge and Jim Gray[2] will earn many more by their conduct in the offices I have assigned to them. You will remember too I promised the whole engineering profession that every appointment to the state Board of Registration for Professional Engineers and Land Surveyors would be made from a list of nominees submitted by the Kentucky Society of Professional Engineers. That provision was included in Senate Bill 280 which I signed.[3]

In closing, let me return to the theme which you have chosen for your meeting—professionalism. I respect all professionals for the contribution they can make to the lives of the people of the Commonwealth, particularly those who have chosen to contribute through the operations of state government. I respect the professional engineers who have committed their careers to the highway program. I recognize what you have done. I see the tremendous challenges you will face in the future and I rely on your competence and dedication to solve the problems that face us.

---

1. Charles Pryor, Jr. (1921–   ), Sturgis; banker; held numerous positions in Governor Ford's administration, among them secretary of highways (1971–1972), secretary of the cabinet and secretary for finance and administration (1972–1974). Interview with Pryor's secretary, October 22, 1976.

2. Elijah M. Hogge (1917–   ), Morehead; attorney; served as Rowan County attorney (1942–1953) and as county attorney for the Twenty-first District; served as secretary of transportation beginning March 1973; prior to this he was commissioner of motor transportation. James E. Gray (1929–   ), Frankfort; campaign coordinator of Governor Ford's primary and general election campaigns; past president of the Frankfort Jaycees. Biographical sketches from Governor Ford's office.

3. See an act "relating to registration for professional engineers and land surveyors," which was approved on March 27, 1972. *Acts of the General Assembly of the Commonwealth of Kentucky, 1972*, Chapter 148 (S.B. 280), pp. 634–47.

REORGANIZATION:
COMPUTER OPERATIONS
Frankfort / April 25, 1973

THIS morning's press conference is another in a series relating to reorganization of state government. What will be explained through statements and a slide presentation can be boiled down this way: we will improve efficiency and spend fewer dollars. The direct dollar savings is significant, and will come because we are doing what others merely talked about for years.

This particular reorganization plan will merge seven computer facilities into a single center. A centralized facility will increase the productivity of computer operations, cost less than we are now paying, and curtail the rapidly spiraling expenses demanded by the present system. Through this change we will achieve a direct cost savings of $2,400,000 a year, and avoid costs of $3,120,000 for a total savings of $5,520,000 per year.

Through the recently created Executive Department for Finance and Administration, we will offer computer power to the various state agencies much as an electric firm offers electricity to the individual consumer. In the process of centralization, we will also standardize the development of information systems in the various agencies. This will allow us to integrate information from various sources to produce proper management information. The long-term benefits from more effective management of our government programs will yield dividends for many years to come.

I have directed the Department for Finance and Administration to take immediate steps toward consolidating the state's computing power on the fourteenth floor of the Capital Plaza Office Building. I will, tomorrow, file an executive order combining the computer operations of that department and the Department of Transportation into one unit for administrative purposes.[1] By August 1, 1973, the computer hardware of this new organization will be physically moved into the Capital Plaza. By August 1, 1974, the seven individual agencies will be converted for computer operations under our single source plan.

The plan we have presented this morning is important for two reasons. First, we will save over $5.5 million annually through a reduction in existing data-processing facilities and because expansion under the current practices will not be necessary. Second, we are increasing the potential value of the computer in both decision-making and program management. Let me reemphasize a statement already made. We have arrived at this point without the expense of outside consultants, thereby taking advantage of the talents within state government to achieve a more businesslike posture. With these benefits, the direct savings will have an immediate impact on budgets. The indirect value on programs, however, will prove even more valuable through a better delivery of services to the people.

What has just been presented is a cure for the waste of tax dollars which has occurred in the past, and the prevention of future waste. This action proves that government can indeed do more at less cost whenever officials put the welfare of the public above all else. It is a program that makes sense, one much needed, long overdue, and one I am pleased to initiate.

---

1. See Executive Order 73–425 (August 26, 1973).

INTERNAL REORGANIZATION OF DEPARTMENT FOR FINANCE AND ADMINISTRATION
Frankfort / April 26, 1973

INTRODUCTION

In Reorganization Report No. 1, which I issued on November 28, 1972, the purposes and broad framework of our effort to reorganize state government were set forth. At that time, I announced three key steps in the reorganization: a) the creation of a strong, viable program cabinet system; b) a new position of Secretary of the Cabinet, and c) the consolidation of central policy and executive support agencies that service the entire government. I established the Office of Secretary of the Cabinet and combined that post with the position of Commissioner of the redesignated Executive Department for Finance and Administration. The functions of the Kentucky Program Development Office were merged into the Executive Department for Finance and Administration. The Office for Policy and Management and the Office for Local Government were created within the Executive Department for Finance and

Administration to provide additional capability to accomplish the department's broad-ranging responsibilities.

As we have proceeded with our reorganization program in the areas of natural resources and environmental protection, human resources and transportation, and as we study further the structure of the program cabinet areas of development, safety and justice, education and the arts, and consumer protection and regulation, the central role of the Executive Department for Finance and Administration has become increasingly clear.

OVERALL STRUCTURE OF DEPARTMENT

The Executive Department for Finance and Administration will include four offices: Office of the Commissioner, Office for Policy and Management, Office for Local Government, and Office for Administration and Operations. The Office of the Commissioner is, of course, inherent in the structure of the department, and the Office for Policy and Management and the Office for Local Government were described in Reorganization Report No. 1 and officially established by Executive Order 72–1168. The Office for Administration and Operations is a new organizational structure within the Executive Department for Finance and Administration, and the purpose of this change is to place greater emphasis upon improvement in the management of functions grouped under this office. Moreover, the broad responsibilities of the Commissioner of the Executive Department for Finance and Administration dictate that adequate provision be made for delegation of responsibility for supervision and coordination of the numerous state service functions of the department.

OFFICE FOR POLICY AND MANAGEMENT

The scope of functions of the Office for Policy and Management was set forth in Reorganization Report No. 1 and Executive Order No. 72–1168. The new organization establishes two staff positions in the office: a deputy for state budgeting and a deputy for policy and planning. An Information Systems staff has also been added. It will have broad responsibility for review and study of the utilization of computing equipment in the various state agencies and institutions. The staff will advise on all requests from agencies and institutions for the acquisition or rental of computing equipment.

The position of state Budget Director will be abolished and the Executive Director of the Office for Policy and Management will be the chief state budget officer to assure that the important function of budgeting is emphasized in administering the office. The Office for Policy and Management is not being structured into divisions or formal sub-units. The reasons are that the functions of planning and budgeting should be integrated. These and the other functions of the office argue for maximum flexibility in the assignment of the limited number of staff. Senior members of the staff will be designated as Policy Advisers, and each Policy Adviser will be responsible for planning and budgeting activities for a program cabinet.

OFFICE FOR LOCAL GOVERNMENT

The Office for Local Government will have two deputy directors and three operating divisions. One deputy director will be responsible for liaison with local governments, and the other will provide liaison with the Area Development Districts.

The Division of State-Local Program Coordination will be responsible for technical assistance in the planning of community development projects and programs, coordination of state activities relating to federal aid for local projects and programs, and the state clearinghouse function under the U.S. Office of Management and Budget, Memorandum A–95.

The Division of Local Management Assistance and Training will provide the staff resources needed to discharge the responsibilities of the State-Local Finance Office which is attached to the Office for Local Government, and the State-Local Finance Officer appointed by the Commissioner shall also serve as Manager of the Division. This division will also seek to develop programs aimed at strengthening the managerial resources of local government, especially with regard to compliance with federal program requirements, such as revenue-sharing.

The Division of Information Services will regularly disseminate information to local governments on federal and state programs and will respond to inquiries from local governments about such programs. We believe that the Office for Local Government has been structured to be responsive to the needs of local governments and to provide the communication and liaison needed for more effective coordination of state and local programs.

OFFICE FOR ADMINISTRATION AND OPERATIONS

The Executive Department for Finance and Administration is engaged in a number of activities essential to the operation of all agencies of state government. It is important that these activities be well managed, to provide a framework wherein accountability and responsibility can be more clearly defined. Related functions have been grouped under the Office for Administration and Operations. Within this office, there will be four bureaus.

The Bureau of Financial Management Systems will include the Division of Accounts, Division of Debt and Investment Management, Division of Management Information Systems, and the Division of Archives and Records. The Division of Accounts and Division of Archives and Records are existing units. The Division of Debt and Investment Management is a redesignation of the Fiscal Management Office, which has operated as an adjunct to the Office of the Commissioner. Administrative relocation of this function to the Bureau of Financial Management Systems is for the purpose of effecting greater delegation of responsibility for day-to-day operations. The Division of Management Information Systems is a new unit for the purpose of improving the production of information required for planning and decision-making. This division will serve not only the Executive Department for Finance and Administration but also the other agencies of state government. A major assignment of the Bureau of Financial Management Systems will be the modernization of the state's accounting and financial reporting system as well as the development of a practical, efficient management-information system.

The Bureau of State Purchases will include three divisions. The Division of Purchases will handle the functions of the present Division of Purchases with additional emphasis on the responsibility for review of personal service contracts. The Division of Communications and the Division of Central Stores and Printing also reflect internal reorganization of existing functions.

The Bureau of Facilities Management is a grouping of five currently existing divisions: Engineering, Properties, Mechanical Maintenance, Building Services, and Security. There are, however, two changes in functions. Engineering will be directly responsible for construction-contract procurement, and Properties will have statewide responsibility for coordinating procurement of real property for use by state agencies.

The Bureau of Computer Services is a major change in structure. This bureau will be responsible for managing a central-computing center which will ultimately serve all state agencies. The first step toward centralization will be the merging of the computer operations of the Executive Department for Finance and Administration and the Department of Transportation. This consolidation for administrative purposes is effective immediately and represents the first of several moves over the next year to eighteen months which will save the state approximately $2.4 million dollars and will avoid increases in computer expenses which would amount to as much as $5.5 million over the next fifteen months.

The Bureau of Computer Services is a dramatic illustration of the savings that can be realized through more efficient management. We are confident that the other changes being made in the structure of the Executive Department for Finance and Administration will facilitate further economies and will contribute toward improved management techniques to curb the growth in costs of government generally, and better plan and manage the expenditure of available tax dollars for the benefit of all Kentuckians. The centralization will be phased to permit an orderly transition. No program will be interrupted nor disrupted in this merger.

COMMISSION ON WOMEN
Frankfort / May 8, 1973

THERE is a lot of talent in this room today—leadership ability, knowledge of many vocations, initiative, and proven ability to be of service to others.[1] You represent many different fields of endeavor and interest. You were selected for the Commission on Women because of the descriptions I have just offered, and because I am convinced you want to be far more than a member of a commission in name only. Success requires a lot of work. Your qualities and represented professions indicate to me that you are the persons needed to get the work done— to ensure the success of the commission at the state level—and the success of its goals at the national level. And you, in being sworn in as a member of this commission, are accepting a responsibility to represent the hundreds of thousands of women like yourselves throughout the state.

Your duties are not concisely defined. Each of you will be given a copy of the statute outlining the commission's functions.[2] Listed there are four broad areas of concern: volunteer community improvement, programs educating the public about the problems of women, working with government on matters pertaining to women, and participating with other states on women-related programs. There's a lot of room for action within these points. But by no means are you limited to these four.

Let me suggest that your activities focus on three additional areas that I think valuable. First, investigate employment opportunities in government, education, and business. I'm going to stop here to emphasize that women do have a place in government. Three of my key commissioners (Gail Huecker, Department of Economic Security; Cattie Lou Miller, Personnel; and Margaret Willis, Libraries[3]) are women. But what is more important, they are exceptionally qualified women handling areas of big responsibility.

Second, develop a system for soliciting and maintaining a women's talent bank for use in appointments to boards and commissions. Again, since I took office, I have appointed forty-one women to various boards and commissions, and, again, these persons, like yourselves, were appointed for their qualifications—and not discriminated against because of their sex. Third (and this has been a national complaint for years), look into the extent of credit discrimination. These are only suggestions. The doorway is open. Your passing through that door and choosing paths of action will determine what progress will be gained for women. I want to leave you with a challenge. I challenge you to reactivate the commission, to carry out its goals, and to do something for women, and in doing something for women improving the lot of mankind.[4]

---

1. Press conference.

2. See an act "relating to civil rights," which was approved on March 24, 1972. *Acts of the General Assembly of the Commonwealth of Kentucky, 1972,* Chapter 255 (H.B. 430), pp. 1065–76; another related item is a joint resolution "directing the Legislative Research Commission to undertake a comprehensive study of Kentucky laws with regard to sex discrimination," which was approved on March 27, 1972. *Acts of the General Assembly of the Commonwealth of Kentucky, 1972,* Chapter 381 (H.R. 90), pp. 1648–49.

3. Gail Shannon Huecker (1928–   ), Louisville; social worker; commissioner of economic security from July 1972 until this unit became part of Human Resources; commissioner of the Bureau for Social Insurance (1973–   ); in Jefferson County before her current state service she was director of the Metropolitan Social Services Department. Cattie Lou Miller (1923–   ); secretary to Governor Earle C. Clements (1947–1950); secretary to Governor's Cabinet (1947–1955); clerk of Kentucky Board of Registration and Purgation (1947–1955); secretary to Governor Lawrence W. Wetherby (1950–1955); executive assistant to Governor Bert T. Combs (1959–1960); commissioner, Department of Public Information (1960–1967); chief

administrative assistant to Governor Edward T. Breathitt (1966–1967); executive assistant to Lieutenant Governor Wendell Ford (1967–1971); administrative assistant to Governor Ford (1971–1972); commissioner, Department of Personnel (1972–1975); chief of personnel auditing, Kentucky (January–August 1976); executive director, Kentucky Crime Victims Compensation Board (August 1976–   ). Margaret F. Willis (1906–   ), Frankfort; state librarian (1957–1976); coordinator of the Library Extension Division [changed to Department of Libraries and in 1973 became part of Department of Libraries and Archives] (1955–1957); head of circulation, Louisville Free Public Library (1944–1955).

4. The persons named in Executive Order 73–461 were Mrs. Marie Abrams, Mrs. June Rollings, Mrs. Otis Singletary, Mrs. William S. Gibson, Mrs. Buster Phillips, Mrs. James Golladay Baker, Mrs. Martha Layne Collins, Mrs. James Rosenblum, Miss Betty Hinz, Mrs. Harold Mullins, Mrs. Delores Delehanty, Mrs. Dolly McNutt, Mrs. Betty Justice, Mrs. Jo Crass, Mrs. Jackie Whalen, Mrs. Oteria O'Rear, Mrs. Harold Cowley, Mrs. Jack Neel, Mrs. Phillip Harrison, Mrs. Stella Demaree, Dr. Judy Daniels, Mrs. Mary Snorton, Miss Mary Hunter, Mrs. Thelma Stovall.

MERIT SYSTEM EXPANSION
Frankfort / August 6, 1973

THIS news conference is to announce what I believe will be a substantial improvement in the State Employee Merit System. In order to place relevant matters in the proper perspective, the following facts should be reviewed in a systematic way.

When the merit system was created in Kentucky state government, I was associated with the formal planning as a member of the Governor's staff. The same is true of the person who is my Commissioner of Personnel. Immediately after becoming Governor, I announced that job patronage matters would be handled by State Democratic Headquarters in order to eliminate that cost from the taxpayers, and to minimize the distractions historically created in the Governor's Office because of patronage. I also wanted to determine the effect of the patronage system, and in cooperation with our party chairman, we made an extensive evaluation of the system's impact on the overall operation of state government. As you know, there was no bloodbath when this administration succeeded the Republican party, nor was there anything to even remotely resemble the mass firings by my predecessor which cost the taxpayers approximately $1 million.

We proved that a Governor of one party can succeed a Governor of the opposite party and be considerate of the principles inherent in the merit system. During the first twelve months of the Nunn administration, 1,474 merit employees were dismissed. From December 1971 to date (twenty months) only 335 merit employees have been dismissed. Hearings are now promptly scheduled. There are presently only eleven appeals to be heard, and they are scheduled for review between now and September 6. Thirteen cases have been heard and are awaiting a decision by the full board. No others are pending. In contrast, there were 400 appeals pending at this point in the last administration.

My office has in no way interfered with the Personnel Department, allowing that agency to approve or disapprove requests for personnel action in strict accord with personnel laws and rules. I did not make a mission of ousting holdover members of the Personnel Board, nor did I move the administration into high-gear dismissals when normal succession finally brought a Democratic majority to the board. Only forty-eight merit system employees have been dismissed in the seven months my appointees have had majority membership on the board. In short, we have proven that the merit system can work, to the benefit of the taxpayers and state employees as relates to the 80 percent of state workers which the 1960 law contemplated would be covered.

More should, can, and will be done. Today, I am signing an executive order to bring some 4,200 additional state government positions under merit system protection.[1] This represents an additional 13 percent of the permanent work force. I will ask the next session of the General Assembly to amend the law that presently excludes those positions from the merit system, so as to accomplish in law what I am, by this executive order, accomplishing in fact.

The juggling of human lives in job patronage is not conducive to the dignity of man to which I think he is entitled. These 4,200 employees are entitled to the dignity of knowing that if they do good work in their jobs, it's appreciated, just as is the case with those who have performed well and have been under the merit system. In the mutual best interest of both the employee and the citizens of Kentucky, there must be certain checks and balances because the merit system should be used to guarantee the continuity and longevity of state employees. It should not be abused by hiding and protecting incompetent or nonproductive employees.

I believe the Kentucky taxpayer will reap good results from the step-up in worker morale, just as employee morale heightened when we stopped the widespread solicitation of state workers for the purpose of political donations, an act that is old and, in fact, improper. I believe the taxpayer will be spared the substantial cost involved in termination pay and spared the huge administrative expense that is part of dismissing several thousand people and hiring several thousand new ones after each inauguration. I have made this decision on a personal conviction that it is a right decision, and trust the course we have followed since December 1971 strengthens that posture which has been assumed.

---

1. See Executive Order 73–709 (August 7, 1973).

PROGRAM BUDGET PILOT EFFORT
Frankfort / August 27, 1973

THE 1972 General Assembly was presented a single program budget, that of the Commission for Handicapped Children, and an extensive examination of that pilot effort, including its reception by the Assembly, has been made.[1] That examination, in conjunction with a continuing review of the budget process by the executive branch, has resulted in the determination that the program budget concept can significantly improve the decision-making of state government. Thus, Governor Wendell Ford has announced that for the first time in history, Kentucky's governmental budget, taking a new and different approach, is being prepared on a program basis instead of the traditional organizational basis. Ford said that final instructions for preparation of the executive budget for the 1974–1976 biennium have been distributed to all state agencies. The budget will be presented to the 1974 session of the General Assembly.

Just what were some of the findings of that pilot program budget that encouraged a total program budget for state government? The pilot budget provided the Commission for Handicapped Children with a number of firsts including the ability to predict in advance the direction of a specific program and make decisions as to any changes that needed to be made in that program's direction, plus the establishment of a systematic method whereby the agency managers could analyze the ongoing programs and their operations. This systematic evaluation enabled the agency to identify potential problem areas and deal with those problems prior to their becoming uncontrollable; it provided the means to identify the actual cost of providing a specific service in any given program within the agency as well as having specific information about those costs that enables them to tell why the costs are what they are; and it gave the ability to compare the cost of delivering services with alternative methods of delivery and make decisions on the most efficient method of delivery.

The Governor contends these are results which can benefit all of state government. Since its inception, the executive budget has related expenditure of state tax dollars to the purchase of specific objects, such as equipment and salaries for support of organizational units, i.e., departments and divisions. However, the program budget for the Commission for Handicapped Children presented to the 1972 Legislature detailed the services which the state intended to provide, e.g., outpatient treatment for a specific number of children suffering from cerebral palsy. "This new method of preparing a budget places major emphasis on end results, rather than the means. It also is concerned with options and alternatives of delivering the best services to the most people at the lowest cost," Ford explained.

The Governor stressed that the program budget will increase agency responsibilities and accountability. It also permits and enhances program evaluation so results can be determined. With this budget, the emphasis will be defining programs, identifying who and how many (levels of service) are to be served (called beneficiaries), and what implementation.

Program budgets represent the second major step in the Governor's efforts to improve the delivery of service. The first step was reorganization around program cabinet areas. Under this reorganization plan, related programs were grouped under the direction of a secretary except for general governmental agencies. This action reduces the number of programs that cut across agency lines. Both stress the importance of results.

Ford said that as a former Senator, Lieutenant Governor, and now as Governor, he found a need to determine results. What did the taxpayer receive for his taxes? The answer must be clear and it must withstand objective evaluation and public scrutiny. Program budgets will be an effective tool toward that objective. The Governor also said he is providing $6,900 from his contingency fund to pay one-half the cost to conduct a seminar on the new budget concept for members of the General Assembly. LRC is to match the $6,900. Ford said, "Program budgeting will mean major changes in the executive budget format and the Appropriation Act. The changes need to be explained to members of the General Assembly in advance in order that they fully understand the value and the meaning of program budgets." Without the seminar, said Ford, there is likely to be confusion, misunderstanding, and disagreements in consideration of the budget.

The Governor noted that the staff of executive agencies need to be oriented to program budgeting, and the Commissioner of the Executive Department for Finance and Administration is to conduct seminars for all agencies in state government August 29 and 30. Presently, the Governor, by the nature of the traditional budget, is limited in reviewing agency budget requests. However, the program budget gives the Governor more ability to evaluate programs because goals and objectives of programs are an integral part of the newly designed budget. If, after implementation, a specific program doesn't meet its defined objective adequately or efficiently, then the program can be revised or eliminated.

Even though some programs cross agency lines, the Governor and others can quickly and accurately determine the total funds required to implement this objective. For example, both the Bureau of Highways and the Department of Public Safety are involved with traffic safety (the service). By checking the money spent in each department for delivery of the service, the Governor will readily be able to obtain total cost for that one program, even though it is divided between two agencies. Program budgets will require major changes in emphasis. The concept departs from just cost of salaries, current expenses, and current outlay, and emphasizes the total cost of a program. It is new in Kentucky and will mean major changes in budget preparation and review. Ford explained that the new concept will provide the General Assembly, agency program managers, and him with an overall view of individual programs, and allow him a determination of which alternative will best achieve the end result or purpose of a particular program. The establishment of priorities will be an essential part of budget preparation.

He stressed that if it encourages the establishment of priorities and analysis of results, such action will better assure that the people of Kentucky are receiving the best use of their tax dollars. Governor Ford said that no longer was it possible to justify next year's budget on how much was spent last year. Budgets must be based upon results to be accomplished. What is the objective in traffic safety, employment, economic development, returning the mentally ill to society, preventing disease, or protection of the consumer? With specific objectives established, beneficiaries identified, and the measurements defined, the Governor, the General Assembly, and the public can determine the extent the objectives are met and decide the level of services and priorities each program is to be given.

The change will also be accompanied by new terminology in the budget process. Terms such as major program areas, programs, subprograms, elements, subelements, goals, objectives, input, and beneficiaries will be used often. Initially, only programs and subprograms will be shown in the budget document. In a prior memo to all agency heads outlining instructions for preparing the budget, Charles Pryor, Jr., Commissioner of the Executive Department for Finance and Administration, defined several program budgeting terms. A "major program area" is the grouping of programs which are directed toward accomplishing different aspects of a governmental function. Each major program area is a component of a function. For example, the major program area "health services" may be considered part of the human resources function.

A set of related services directed toward the achievement of a specific objective with a clearly identifiable group of beneficiaries is a "program." For example, "communicable diseases" may be considered a program in the major program area of health services. A "subprogram" is a group of discrete related activities aimed at producing the designed output stated in the program objectives. For example, "venereal disease" may be considered a subprogram in the communicable disease program.

The "objective" is a short-range end product toward which program activities are directed. Objectives must be quantified within a specific time-frame. Program objectives should be consistent with the broad goals of the major program areas. In contrast, a "goal" is a long-range target toward which a major program area is directed. Quantification is not necessary for a goal statement. "Inputs" denote the resources employed in the accomplishment of objectives, and "outputs" are the products of a program's attempts to accomplish objectives. "Beneficiaries" are the recipients of the services to be rendered (who they are, how many there are, and where they are located).

When program budgeting is fully implemented, the various programs will be subdivided. The breakdown will, for some programs, be four or five levels. An example is transportation—highways will be a major program area; construction will be a program. The class of roads (i.e., interstate, primary, secondary, etc.) will be a subprogram. Highway numbers (i.e., I-64, U.S. 68, Ky. 80) within a class will be an element. Within a highway number, costs such as right-of-way, design, and construction will be a subelement.

1. Press release. This release is included because of its essential elaboration of the program budget concept frequently referred to by Governor Ford.

See an act "relating to the composition of the membership of the Commission for Handicapped Children," which was approved on March 25, 1972. *Acts of the General Assembly of the Commonwealth of Kentucky, 1972,* Chapter 152 (S.B. 290), p. 661. See also an act "relating to appropriations for the operation, maintenance, support and functioning of the government of the Commonwealth of Kentucky and its various officers, departments, boards, commissions, institutions, subdivisions, agencies, and other state supported activities," which was approved on March 15, 1972. *Acts of the General Assembly of the Commonwealth of Kentucky, 1972,* Chapter 60 (H.B. 335), pp. 183–228.

BUDGET SEMINAR
Frankfort / August 29, 1973

As I look out over this large group of commissioners, fiscal officers, and program managers here to discuss the 1974–1975 budget, I'm beginning to think that I should have brought a few extra troopers with me to ensure that I get out of this room with a few dollars left. These two days of meetings on program budgeting are quite unusual for state government, but I firmly believe these sessions will be highly beneficial to all of us who are involved in the "budget process."

Recently, I made the decision that we would implement a new budgeting system for state government. This is a decision that has a major impact on all of us in this room. The preparation of the next budget is the most crucial task that you face in the next few months. The decisions that are made during this period will affect the lives of every Kentuckian and will involve the expenditure of billions of our tax dollars. This is serious business, and we must take it seriously.

Since we have been working on the next budget for a few weeks, I'm sure most of you will recognize that the budget process is being changed considerably. In the past, we have primarily been concerned with what we are buying, how much we are buying, and how much it will cost the various state agencies and divisions to buy goods and to employ certain people for the two-year budget period. Very seldom have we looked at the services we are providing, the need for the services, and to whom we are providing the services. Very seldom have we had clearly stated objectives of what we intend to provide to the public during the execution of the budget. Very seldom is not often enough. Implementation of program budgeting in all state agencies will provide the process and the information whereby we will look at our public needs, our public services, and our alternatives to provide the services.

Notice that I said program budgeting will provide the process and the "output" oriented information for making decisions. Program budgeting, or any other kind of budgeting or management process, will not make decisions. Operating decisions will still have to be made by those of us in this room. I will still make policy recommendations to the General Assembly, which will have to make the final budget decisions in the form of an enacted appropriation bill. The people will still be making the decisions. In many instances, decisions, although facilitated by a more logical process and better information, may be more difficult to make since the benefits and the consequences, in terms of public services and public needs, will be much more apparent than in the past.

A minute ago, I said that meetings as we are having today are rather unusual for state government—why? Because we are bringing together virtually everyone involved in the budget process to explain and to discuss improving the process. By meeting together we are recognizing that our problems span agency and even program cabinet lines; and we are recognizing that the budget process is a joint effort involving both the executive and legislative branches of government. The presence of members of the joint Senate-House Committee on Appropriations and Revenue and staff members of the Legislative Research Commission signifies their interest in this budgeting concept. Later today we will have a chance to hear their views and to participate in discussions with them concerning this effort. Obviously, I do not believe that the executive and legislative branches of government will, or even should, agree on all policy decisions. Yet the presence of both the legislative and executive branches here today demonstrates the common interest and concern we all have for making government more efficient and effective by instituting more "businesslike" management processes.

I cannot overemphasize the importance of the task in which we are all involved. Secretary Pryor, Jim King, and staff members of the Office for Policy and Management are available to assist you in this undertaking and other management and policy matters.[1] I expect each of you to cooperate fully with them.

1. Charles Pryor, Jr., for more information see speech from March 24, 1973, in this section, p. 125. James King (1930–   ), Fayette County; government administrator; held several positions with Governor Ford, among them executive director of the Office of Policy and Management, secretary of the Executive Cabinet, and commissioner of finance; prior to serving Governor Ford he had held several positions in the Department of Parks; currently he is administrative assistant to Senator Ford in his Washington office. Senator Ford's Louisville office, October 22, 1976.

HUMAN RESOURCES CABINET ANNOUNCEMENT
Frankfort / August 29, 1973

I HAVE a very strong and deep feeling about today's announcement because I believe that this is the most important day in terms of service delivery by state government since I assumed office as Governor. What I have said throughout my public life in regard to the purpose of government becomes even more visible through today's announcement.[1] The new human resources concept is not a shifting or a grouping of old departments. It is a complete realignment and creation of a new system of service delivery directly to hundreds of thousands of Kentuckians and indirectly to all Kentuckians.

To repeat, I cannot overemphasize the importance of this occasion. Never in the history of our Commonwealth, I believe, have so many devoted so much time, study, work, and deliberation in order to conceive a single program cabinet. The inauguration of the Human Resources Cabinet is a major event now, but the positive impact will increase as months pass. That impact will ultimately be found in our encouragement, development, and protection of the personal independence, dignity, growth, and economic self-sufficiency of Kentucky's citizens. But above all as in other phases of reorganization, we are prepared to operate in program concert rather than reacting "after the fact" to critical issues of the period.

Following my brief remarks here, a detailed explanation of the Human Resources Cabinet structure will be made. What we shall unveil is a comprehensive and involved program, designed as a vast improvement over past activities, with much greater efficiency in providing the type of help Kentuckians deserve. Today's announcement actually began sprouting roots the second year I was Lieutenant Governor. From that period I had an opportunity to see how inadequate the old system was, and how it continued to remain so. I recall numerous sessions Bill Wester, Jim Fleming, and I had on this very subject when we analyzed the total human resources opportunities for years to come and made this a key platform in my campaign.[2] As time passed, and we began considering reorganization, the human resources aspect loomed as the most pressing need among many serious problems of government responsiveness.

One of the clear-cut facts which emerged during that era centers on how state government efforts have been dissipated over the years. Confusion has grown and duplication has, too. Costs versus results were found inappropriate. Uncontrolled growth, frequently due to new federal programs, prompted less than a coordinated and integrated approach to helping the greatest resource we have, the people of Kentucky.

State government reorganization as already announced and defined is successfully working. Yet no single cabinet will touch more Kentuckians, individually, than the one we are presenting this afternoon. I hope the briefing, and subsequent sessions if desired, prove valuable to you, since public understanding is of paramount importance if our citizens are to fully benefit from the services and delivery this cabinet can provide.

Three months after I created the Human Resources Cabinet, in December 1972, I established the Office of the Secretary. That order directed him to make a detailed analysis and develop specific recommendations for restructuring the agencies within the cabinet. Input was extensive from within state government, from the federal government, and by public interest groups who have contributed immeasurably in guiding this reorganization. But most certainly, the heavy burden has fallen on Secretary Laurel True, Jim Fleming, and Donna Smith to be the guiding principals in this endeavor.[3] And they have performed impressively!

You will, for instance, note a new unit, that of the ombudsman. In recent sessions where my office has been located in northern Kentucky and the State Fair at Louisville, time and again I saw the frustration of people who did not know where to get an answer, whether that answer should come from city government, county government, state government, federal government, or a private source. As the Human Resources Cabinet touches so many thousands, the ombudsman will become a vital link in tying service to need. Government must become more personal!

In this concept being announced, you will also note extensive consolidation of departments and commissions to reinforce the state's ability to deliver services efficiently and effectively. I estimate that $5 million will be saved annually in administrative costs alone, because of the new plan. This is money which can now go to service. I think it is important that you be given a step-by-step introduction to the cabinet structure. I am convinced that after an orderly overview you will attach the same significance as I to a major new direction in state government that will have a profound impact on persons living in every county in this state.

In December 1972, I created the Human Resources Cabinet and called for recommendations from all agency heads within that cabinet on programs and organizational structure.[4] In March 1973, I established the Office of the Secretary for Human Resources. That order establishing the secretary directed him to make a detailed analysis and develop specific recommendations for restructuring the agencies within the Human Resources Cabinet.

Since that appointment, the secretary and his staff have met repeatedly with Human Resources Cabinet members and other agency officials, both individually and collectively, to develop a philosophy of program operation and delivery of service that would provide the greatest possible benefit to the people of this Commonwealth.

Based upon a review of these recommendations, the secretary prepared a draft of "principles" to guide the reorganization. These principles were submitted to public interest groups, professional organizations, officials from other states, and federal officials for review and recommendation. Using these principles as a foundation, the secretary then spent long hours with me and my reorganization staff developing concepts for the Human Resources reorganization.

During these meetings, I reached the following conclusions regarding state-provided human resources services:

1. Under the present structure, state services tend to "categorize" the recipient and deal only with separate elements of his problem. This often inhibits the full correction of problems that do not lie exclusively within one agency. Effective human services result from the comprehensive range of services delivered in a coordinated and integrated manner.

2. The present mix of government services and regulatory programs is confusing. The citizen is expected to diagnose his own problems, identify the appropriate state agency, and schedule his receipt of services. Coordination of state services is the state's responsibility.

3. Human development services should be provided in a manner that recognizes the family unit and strengthens family ties.

4. A compassionate and realistic determination of need and an accurate assessment of the potential for solving problems should be the basis for determination of eligibility for service.

5. Publicly provided services should be accessible to citizens wherever they live in the Commonwealth, and emergency services should be available on an around-the-clock basis.

6. Elected officials, recipients, and the public-at-large should participate in the planning, policy formulation, and evaluation of the human resource programs and services.

7. All public officials must be accountable for the quality, quantity, and the effectiveness of services provided. Both program audits and fiscal audits must be an integral part of management to assure that all expenditures are proper and that maximum benefit is derived from each tax dollar.

8. The Commonwealth provides only a portion of the total human resource services within Kentucky. Voluntary organizations, nonprofit corporations, private agencies and individuals, local public agencies, and others provide essential elements of the total system. State government programs, therefore, should be organized to cooperate with and encourage the development and utilization of these nonstate resources.

I am now announcing what I believe to be a major progressive step in our effort to provide the kind and quality of services we need to build a better future for all the people of Kentucky. My overall goal is to encourage, develop, and protect the personal independence, dignity, growth, and economic self-sufficiency of Kentucky's citizens. We will more quickly realize this goal by implementing an organizational structure which coordinates the full range of publicly provided human-development services and delivers them in an integrated manner.

The plan I announce today is based on recommendations resulting from the work of my reorganization staff and representatives of the Commission on Aging, the Commission on Children and Youth, the Department of Child Welfare, the Department of Labor, the Department of Education, the Department of Economic Security, the Commission for Handicapped Children, the Department of Health, the Department of Mental Health, the Bureau of Veterans Affairs, the Commission on Women, the Comprehensive Health Planning Commission, the Office of Economic Opportunity, and the Office of Youth Affairs.

To implement these principles of service, I have today signed and filed an Executive Order pursuant to KRS Chapter 12, and have established a new Department for Human Resources.[5] The Secretary for

Human Resources will head the department, and will report to me. He will be Kentucky's highest appointed official responsible for directing the operation of all human resource programs and services provided by the Commonwealth. The main organizational units within the department are four program bureaus, three staff officers, and a Bureau for Administration and Operation. All program activities of the formerly separate human resources agencies are consolidated into four bureaus: a Bureau for Social Insurance, a Bureau for Social Services, a Bureau for Health Services, and a Bureau for Manpower Services.

The Bureau for Social Insurance will operate all income maintenance and all income supplementation programs of the Department for Human Resources. That is, it will issue financial support to the poor, unemployed, and needy, and will issue food stamps and pay for medical assistance. The Bureau for Social Services will provide child welfare services, foster care, adoptions, family services, and all other general counseling in support of families and individuals who require assistance for successful and adequate human development. The Bureau for Health Services will operate all programs of the department that provide health service including all physical and mental health programs. This bureau will take over the functions of the Department of Health, the Department of Mental Health, and the Commission for Handicapped Children. The Bureau for Manpower Services will operate all manpower development and job-placement programs of the department, including all job recruitment and business liaison functions, job training, and worker-readiness functions, and job counseling and placement. The consolidation of the separate departments and commissions into four program bureaus will reenforce the state's ability to deliver services effectively and efficiently. Relieving program managers of administrative detail and combining administrative operations will increase the quality of service delivery, and will eliminate costly duplication. I estimate that it will save between $4.5 and $5 million annually in administrative costs which can then be used for services.

The Office for Policy and Budget will provide staff support to the secretary and the program bureaus in overall planning, budgeting, program audits, and policy analysis for the department, and will be particularly concerned with issues that involve two or more bureaus. The Office of the Counsel will provide legal advice to the secretary and other officials of the department, and will represent the department in legal proceedings.

The Office of the Ombudsman is an entirely new unit. By creating this office, this administration has established a precedent significant to every Kentuckian. The ombudsman, whom I appoint on the advice of the secretary, will receive and investigate complaints by citizens with regard to services rendered by the Department for Human Resources. The Bureau for Administration and Operations will consolidate numerous support services now furnished by nineteen separate units, such as preaudits, accounting, data processing, purchasing, and duplicating, for all the department.

In a final word about this organizational plan, I call your attention to the Human Resources Advisory Councils and Human Resources Regulatory Boards. As you know, this administration is committed to bringing government to the people, and people to the government. In this reorganization, the many citizen advisory groups have been collected together and elevated to an important relationship directly with the secretary. In this order, I have instructed the secretary to call joint meetings for the citizen groups concerned with common problems so that the state may benefit from a comprehensive review of the issues.

This reorganization holds much promise for the people of Kentucky in improved service and improved economy, but I think it is important to point out that fulfillment of this promise is dependent upon the continued efforts of thousands of dedicated state employees. I am confident they will work diligently to meet these promises. In closing, let me emphasize that this reorganization, and the subsequent internal organizational structure that must be established within units I have created here, are all designed to enable the Commonwealth to encourage, develop, and protect the personal independence, dignity, growth, and economic self-sufficiency of Kentucky's citizens. I have concluded that establishing a single Department for Human Resources will best serve this end.

---

1. Press conference; here the oral and written statements of the Governor are combined.

2. William Wester (1921–   ), Fayette County; he was Governor Ford's chief administrative assistant and is currently serving on Senator Ford's Washington staff; for his official appointment to the Governor's staff, see Executive Order 71-2 (December 7, 1971). James Fleming (1922–   ), Franklin County; he was a special assistant to Governor Ford for research and is presently serving on Senator Ford's Washington staff; for his official appointment to the Governor's staff, see Executive Order 72-468 (May 30, 1972). Senator Ford's Louisville office, August 10, 1976.

3. Laurel True, for more information see speech from March 2, 1973, in this section, pp. 117–19. Donna Smith (1939–   ), Harlan County; she was administrative assistant to Governor Ford; for her official appointment to the

Governor's staff, see Executive Order 72–470 (May 30, 1972). Senator Ford's Louisville office, August 10, 1976.

4. See Executive Order 72–1167 (December 22, 1972).

5. See Executive Order 73–777.

REORGANIZATION:
DEPARTMENT OF JUSTICE
Frankfort / September 11, 1973

IN the orderly process of reorganization which we are following, major changes have already taken place.[1] The stage has been set for many other long-term improvements, and we now see the coming together of a total package. We established the program cabinet concept, brought forth the new Executive Department for Finance and Administration to coordinate statewide planning as well as both state and federal financing, and have reorganized in the areas of environmental protection, human resources, and transportation. Today, I am announcing the Department of Justice.

Each cabinet, in my opinion, offers a special approach to vastly improved state services. The Justice Department Plan, as reviewed and evaluated by federal officials, promises to be a model throughout the nation, for it is unique among our sister states. In the field of criminal justice for the adult offender, we have produced one agency to deal with the individual from the time of investigation through the release back into society.

Since taking office in December of 1971, I have committed myself and my administration to the improvement of Kentucky's criminal justice system. It was, and is, my belief that we can improve the quality of life for our citizens through the reduction of our crime rate and the continuing improvement of our justice agencies.

We already have made substantial progress. Last year, Kentucky's crime rate was reduced by 8 percent, the largest decrease in the United States. Kentucky has begun a 15 percent salary incentive program that will assure minimum education and train students for local police. Patronage has been removed from our probation and parole system. A professional parole board has been appointed. A public defender sys-

tem was initiated for the first time in 1972. A new Penal Code was prepared as passed by the General Assembly to take effect in July 1974.
The 1972 budget for agencies in the law enforcement and corrections
field represented a 25 percent increase over previous years. As Lieutenant Governor, I led the fight to include $2 million in new money for
the Kentucky Crime Commission. This made it possible to attract an
additional $3 million in federal funds for both local and state law en-
forcement agencies. As Governor, I then earmarked almost $7 million
for the Kentucky Crime Commission and, right now, that is bringing
in about $21 million in new money to Kentucky's justice system. More
recently, Kentucky has received over $2 million in federal grants for
crime-control projects and to upgrade our corrections program. This is
an unprecedented accomplishment, a national recognition of Kentucky's
recent achievements in criminal justice.

Today, I am announcing another major step in my effort to provide
Kentuckians with the best possible system of justice, one that will
continue to reduce our crime while assuring justice to all our citizens.
The right to justice is perhaps as compelling as any other right democratic government can ensure. It is central to the quality of life in our
state. My goal is to enhance our system of justice through a reordering
of the justice system in the Commonwealth. The gathering together
and coordination of essential elements in the justice system can provide
for a better allocation of resources by avoiding overlaps, enabling a
unified planning and budgeting operation, and recognizing the inter-
relationships among all essential elements of the criminal justice system.

For some time, members of my reorganization staff and representatives of the Departments of Public Safety and Corrections, the Crime
Commission, the Kentucky Law Enforcement Council, and the Office
of the Public Defender have been studying our present efforts in the
criminal justice area. They have made recommendations based on their
study and have determined that:

1. The present system is really no system at all. It is too fragmented
with each agency covering only a single or limited aspects of an individual's involvement in the justice system.

2. The present structure encourages the pursuit of individual departmental interests in the justice area, without regard for the totality
of the justice system.

3. There is no single mechanism for providing a comprehensive,
coordinated program for meeting the challenge of too high crime rates,
too many criminal repeaters, and too little effective rehabilitation of
offenders.

4. Every aspect of the justice system, including police, corrections, the judiciary, and most especially the people of the Commonwealth who come in contact with that system could profit from a continuing, high-quality justice training program.

5. There is currently no centralized management point for planning, budgeting, informing, coordinating, directing, and implementing the various aspects of the criminal justice system.

6. There is a clear need for a central organizational unit to provide staff services and administrative support to a single justice agency rather than the diffuse and inefficient duplication of these services existing today.

7. There is a need for a more effective justice system, one geared to best serve the citizens of the Commonwealth wherever they are affected by our system of criminal justice.

As a result of this intensive study and in recognition of our responsibility for an effective and efficient criminal justice system for all Kentuckians, I have today signed the Executive Order, pursuant to KRS Chapter 12, establishing a Department of Justice. All functions, authority, and responsibility now vested in the Departments of Public Safety and Corrections and the Crime Commission, and specified functions, authority, and responsibility of the Kentucky Law Enforcement Council and the Office of the Public Defender are merged and consolidated within the new Department of Justice. The Secretary of Justice will head the department, with overall responsibility for providing a unified direction to the Commonwealth's justice system. As chairman of the Crime Commission, the secretary will receive the advice and recommendations of the commission on the full range of criminal justice problems and needs. The Executive Office of Staff Services, headed by an administrator responsible to the secretary, will be the department's vehicle for overall planning and unified budgeting. It will enable the secretary to set and peruse departmentwide priorities. It is through the Executive Office of Staff Services that the secretary will be able to eliminate costly duplication and red tape and can streamline the delivery of needed services.

The Office of the Public Defender for administrative purposes is attached directly to the Office of the Secretary. The legal counsel for the department is in the Office of the Secretary. Three bureaus are created within the Department of Justice. The State Police will be elevated to become the Bureau of State Police and will be the law enforcement arm of the department, free to concentrate specifically on police operations and criminal investigations. The Bureau of Corrections will have a twofold responsibility: institutions and community service. This includes all adult correction institutions from maximum to minimum security, prison farms and industries, and the community-related parole and probation services. The Parole Board is attached for administrative purposes to the Office of Commissioner of Corrections. The creation of a Bureau of Training provides the secretary with the tools to upgrade the capabilities of the police, corrections, and judicial elements of the justice system. The Commissioner of Training will have the expert assistance of the Kentucky Law Enforcement Council for police training, the existing Commission on Corrections and Community Service for corrections personnel, and the existing Judicial Council for appropriate judicial training programs.

There must be no weak links in Kentucky's criminal justice system if the thrust is truly to be justice and quality. The creation of this single state agency for the broad aspects of the criminal justice system will enable us to integrate criminal justice planning and budgeting at the state level best to meet the complex problems of crime and effective administration of justice, develop a statewide priority system for the justice area, more comprehensive than is possible within the context of a narrow-directed agency, provide a focal point for citizen reaction to the criminal justice system, provide a single unit with a single priority evaluation for dealing with federal, local, and other state agencies, train department personnel in the best techniques and professional standards in all aspects of the criminal justice system, and provide effective management tools for the Secretary of Justice to ensure intradepartmental efficiency and accessibility to pertinent information.

The purpose of this entire reorganization effort has been to better serve the people, to make state government more responsive to their desires, and to help solve the problems we all face. These concerns are nowhere more important than in the protection of citizens from crime and in the fair administration of justice. My expectation is that establishing this Department of Justice will better accomplish these ends.

I think it is important to look at reorganization in three stages. First, where was the Commonwealth of Kentucky heading before reorganization? The answer is obvious to anyone who understands the complexities of government, the increased demands of society, and the growth factor which has often produced a tail-wagging-the-dog effect. In cold, hard facts, it was heading out of control—out of control of the Governor, the Legislature, and the citizens. Second, what should be expected of government, where can improvements be anticipated, and does our rationale for change carry with it logic, innovation, and vision? Third, an analysis of reorganization is never ceasing. As I have said before, improvements do not come overnight, especially since Kentucky state government has, for the most part, been operating the same since the late thirties.

But now, as we are close to wrapping up reorganization for the 1974 General Assembly's action, all Kentuckians will have the opportunity to see and feel the positive effect of reorganization as reflected in our budgeting by objectives. For we have done one thing that very few, and possibly no other, states have accomplished. We have joined a new organization with budgeting by programs. In no small measure, reorganization will have its new meaning in the budget. The new budget approach would not have been possible without reorganization.

I now want to announce the man who will make the Justice Department work, Henri Mangeot,[2] an attorney with impressive experience in administration at all levels of government—local, state, and federal. By assuming the office of Secretary to the Justice Department, he brings a keen understanding of how there must be not only coordination among agencies, but coordination among different levels of government. The key to this understanding is not just a realization of coordinating needs; rather, it is an insight into the ultimate effects of coordination years from now. Crime is a heavy financial burden on mankind. The reduction of crime eases that burden not in the mechanics of a system designed to fight crime, but in the saving of life, property, and personal liberty. I feel confident that we now, for the first time, have the single mechanism whereby a profound impact will be felt on Kentucky's future—one that bodes well.

---

1. Press conference; here the oral and written statements of the Governor are combined.

2. Henri L. Mangeot (1928–   ), Louisville; attorney; administrative assistant to Congressman Frank Burke (1959–1963); Attorney General's Office, deputy (1963–1969); executive assistant to the mayor of Louisville (1969–1973). Biographical sketch from Governor Ford's office.

REORGANIZATION:
CABINET FOR DEVELOPMENT AND CABINET FOR EDUCATION AND THE ARTS
Frankfort / September 13, 1973

TODAY's announcement brings us the sixth and seventh program areas of reorganization, taking us another step closer to putting the entire package together.[1] In our first reorganization report last year, we identified the program cabinet structure for state government. At that time, we outlined the areas to be included in the Development Cabinet and the Cabinet for Education and the Arts. Since then, we have worked out the detailed responsibilities to be delegated to each of these program areas. And today, by Executive Order, I am establishing the positions of the Office of the Secretary for Development and the Office of the Secretary for Education and the Arts.[2]

I am also announcing the persons who have accepted the challenge of two extremely important posts. The Office of the Secretary for Development will give the state a single head to guide and promote agricultural, industrial, and recreational programs, administered by the organizational units that compose the Development Cabinet. The Departments of Agriculture, Commerce, Parks, and Fish and Wildlife Resources, the Bicentennial Commission, the State Fair Board, and the Geological Survey now will be able to work more closely with one another in strengthening the state's economy and enhancing individual opportunity. The end product by grouping these individual agencies into a family unit offers an improved delivery of services as they relate to Kentucky's economic environment. In these two areas, I have chosen the cabinet structure rather than a single department. Constitutional and statutory limitations prevent a departmental structure.

The anticipated success of development will affect our state's economic growth and therefore the economic improvement of all Kentuckians. The Development Cabinet programs touch the lives of all our citizens, affecting our working life as well as our leisure. I am appointing Dr. Charles F. Haywood[3] as the Secretary of the Development Cabinet. He holds outstanding credentials for meeting the responsibilities assigned to this office. He is an economist, knows economic development, and will set forth policy direction in a coordinated approach to the economic issues facing this state now and in the future.

First, let me discuss the Office of the Secretary for Development. This action means that the state will have a single head to guide and promote the state's agricultural, industrial, and recreational programs that are administered by the organizational units that make up the Development Cabinet. My objective in making this appointment is to improve the delivery of these developmental services as they relate to the state's economic environment.

The expansion and growth of the state's economy is a most important area of concern to me. The success of development, more than any other area, will affect our economic growth and the economic improvement of all Kentuckians. The creation of jobs through our industrial promotion, the attraction of tourists by our park system, and the selling of Kentucky's products through agricultural promotion are all developmental programs which strengthen the state's economy and enhance individual opportunity. The Development Cabinet is an area that touches a vast majority of our citizens. It touches the businessman, the farmer, the skilled factory workers, and the service worker. It touches both our working life and our leisure life.

The Secretary of the Development Cabinet will act as the liaison between the Governor, the departments within the cabinet, and with citizens concerned with the economic development of the state. In this capacity he will expedite matters and will monitor the economic impact of the state's physical development. He will coordinate and assist all Development departmental heads in further refining the agricultural, industrial, and recreational objectives of the state government. Especially, I will urge the secretary to work closely with the Department of Transportation and the Department of Natural Resources and Environmental Protection to coordinate all facets of the state's development effort.

The secretary will direct long-term developmental policies by focusing upon the state's total agricultural, industrial, and recreational potential that can be gained by stimulating the development of the state's physical resources. He will recommend to me the desired reorganization of agencies within the cabinet, and he will advise me on executive actions, legislative measures, and other steps that may be thought desirable to assure that the people of Kentucky will be well served by the Development programs. He will evaluate and act upon all budget requests originated by the agencies included in the cabinet and will represent the cabinet in the budget and legislative review process.

And additionally, so that all developmental activities can be coordinated by a single office, I am assigning the secretary the responsibility of coordinating the Appalachian Regional Development programs. The responsibility for directing these programs will provide for a more comprehensive approach to stimulating the economic development of the Appalachian counties. I am also transferring the responsibility for administering the Economic Development Administration programs now assigned to the Department of Commerce to the Office of the Secretary.

In establishing the Education and Arts Cabinet, we have built the foundation to oversee an orderly program of growth. Secondly, I have approved the following changes and assigned the following units to the Education and Arts Cabinet. The teachers' retirement system is transferred from the Education and the Arts Cabinet and will be an independent support agency under, and reporting directly to, the Secretary of the Cabinet; the Council on Public Higher Education in Kentucky is transferred from the Education and the Arts Cabinet and will be an independent agency under, and reporting directly to, the Governor. The Council on Public Higher Education was reorganized on my recommendation by the 1972 General Assembly. The council has set a new direction and has been given new authority by the legislation. The council is the coordinating mechanism for the programs of our state institutions of higher learning. In itself it is not a program agency. For this reason, it has been transferred from the program cabinet. The Division of Archives and Records is transferred from the Executive Department for Finance and Administration to the Department of Libraries.

The Office of Secretary of the Education and Arts Cabinet is established and assigned the following responsibilities. He will recommend desired reorganization affecting agencies in the Education and the Arts Cabinet and will advise me on executive actions, legislative measures, and other steps that may be thought desirable to assure that the people of Kentucky will be well served by the Education and Arts programs. He will perform such tasks as may be assigned incidental to the Governor's powers and responsibilities with respect to the agencies included in the Education and Arts Cabinet, and the secretary is to establish procedures for the study and evaluation of programs and activities and their management. The secretary will develop long-range plans covering the agencies in the cabinet to assure orderly program growth through priorities, fulfillment of state needs, and economy and efficiency.

You will notice that the Council on Public Higher Education is transferred from the Education and Arts Cabinet to serve as an independent agency under, and reporting directly to, the Governor. The Council on Public Higher Education was reorganized on my recommendation by the 1972 General Assembly. The council has set a new direction in progress and has been given new and additional authority by the legislature. As you are aware, the council is the coordinating mechanism for programs of our state institutions of higher learning, rather than a program agency, and for this reason it has been moved out of a program cabinet.

I am naming Dr. Lyman Ginger as Secretary of the Education and Arts Cabinet. Dr. Ginger has demonstrated an exceptional understanding of the needs of education and also fosters a great appreciation for the arts.[4] He can fully relate the various functions assigned to this cabinet and develop policies to best assure orderly program growth in the units assigned to the cabinet. Dr. Ginger will be charged with the responsibility of recommending desired reorganization affecting agencies in this cabinet, as well as advising me on executive actions, legislative measures, and other steps that may be considered desirable to ensure that the people of Kentucky are well served by the Education and Arts program. You probably have questions about each area, and at this time, I want to call on Dr. Ginger and Dr. Haywood to both comment and respond to your questions.

---

1. Press conference; here the oral and written statements of the Governor are combined.

2. See Executive Orders 73–819 and 73–820.

3. Charles F. Haywood, Lexington; former director of economic research for the Bank of America; dean of the University of Kentucky College of Business and Economics (1965–1975), professor of economics (1965–   ); director of the Office of Policy and Management (Feb. 1973–Aug. 1973); secretary for development (1973–1974). Biographical sketch from Governor Ford's office.

4. Lyman V. Ginger, Lexington; dean of the College of Adult and Extension Education at the University of Kentucky (1954–1956); dean of the College of Education at UK (1956–1966); state superintendent of public instruction (1972–1976). Biographical sketch from Governor Ford's office.

REORGANIZATION:
DEPARTMENT OF PUBLIC INFORMATION
Frankfort / October 15, 1973

UNDER the reorganizational concept we are applying to state government, consideration has been given to certain "service agencies" which perform a wide variety of tasks both for the general public and state government as a whole. The Department of Public Information fits this category and therefore shall operate separate and independent from any of the program cabinets, responsible to the Governor's Office through the Secretary of the Cabinet, and be headed by a commissioner. However, a close working relationship between the department and each of the program cabinets shall be established to effect the most comprehensive coordination possible in the dissemination of information.

Although prior to this order affecting the Department of Public Information, state government did indeed have a similar agency. There also were numerous subunits established within departments and agencies not aligned with the Department of Public Information which performed essentially the same functions as did the Department of Public Information. As years passed, the growth of these subunits attenuated any coordinated informational and communications program, and often the result was duplication of time, money, and effort. Under the new order, no informational activity as assigned to the Department of Public Information shall be carried out except by the Department of Public Information. The exceptions to this will be Fish and Wildlife and Military Affairs.

The Department of Public Information shall be divided into four divisions: Administrative Services, Information and Communications, News, and Advertising and Promotion.

The involvement of the Department of Public Information is often underestimated. In many instances one might consider the Department of Public Information as an agency that reports news of state government, when actually this is a minor part of the total picture. For clarification, the following activities should be enumerated to show how responsive this type service agency must be to the public and to enhance other operations of state government.

The Travel and Promotion Division of the Department of Public Information is charged with promoting the state's tourism industry and the Department of Parks. The division also creates educational and informational pamphlets, brochures, posters, and cards for the many agencies of state government. These materials are designed to inform taxpayers of services available to them. The division has the responsibility of coordinating the construction of informational booths for use at fairs and trade shows. In addition to answering as many as 1,400 tourism and travel-oriented requests per day during certain periods of the year, the division answers inquiries from school children and other individuals interested in Kentucky's livability. One of the division's prime missions now is supporting the Bicentennial Commission with no increase in budget.

The Information and Communication Division disseminates news of government, and produces and supplies travel films to schools, civic organizations, and TV stations. Through the division's photographic section, audio-visual materials and photographs are supplied for in-house use, to private enterprise and organizations for use in literature for programs that advertise Kentucky.

The Department of Public Information's news section releases informative stories to the daily and community newspapers which do not have Capital bureaus or access to wire services. These news releases supplement materials published by the private sector news services, thus providing the taxpayers with additional information of new and diversified services being made available to them by their state government. Surveys by the section's research and clipping service reveal that these releases are being published. Similar informational materials are prepared specifically for the state's radio and television stations. The radio-TV section's daily newsliner, which can be reached by a toll-free WATS number, averages more than 1,000 calls weekly from radio and television outlets.

Well over one-half of the department's budget is earmarked for the promotion of Kentucky and tourism. These efforts in turn generate dollars, and create jobs for Kentuckians. Last year tourists and travelers spent $635 million in Kentucky. In tax revenue alone, this meant $50 million flowed into the treasury. Therefore, the Department of Public Information is one of the few agencies of government actually responsible for creating business for the state's second largest industry, tourism. Of the department's budget, $156,000 is appropriated to the Matching Funds program. This program exemplifies this administration's philosophy of returning government to the people. The money is invested in fifteen regional tourism programs. Citizens' groups and organizations within each region have virtual autonomy in deciding on advertising and the preparation of literature to sustain these programs.

In respect to personnel, reorganization and centralization of the information programs of state government enables the Department of Public Information to pare the number of publicity, informational, photograph, and support positions scattered throughout state government by nearly 25 percent, from 222 to 169. Of this, thirty-four positions are tour guides and promotion assistants in Public Information's nine information centers. In fact, many of the 169 are support personnel. If it were not for the centralized and professional care of information specialists, government would find it necessary to contract costly public relations and advertising agencies to administer the necessary informational programs which have become a vital function for people to communicate in our complex, public-relations oriented society.

APPROPRIATION AND REVENUE BUDGET SEMINAR
Louisville / November 13, 1973

THIS seminar represents a new spirit of cooperation between the executive branch and General Assembly by attempting to better understand the budget process and the role of each. As a Senator and Lieutenant Governor, I recognized a need for a better understanding of the budget, and was willing to fund one-half the cost of this conference because it is an important seminar.

As most of you know, I have asked the Executive Department for Finance and Administration to prepare the budget in a program format which is entirely new to all of us. That decision was based upon the General Assembly's request for fifteen agencies to have program formats in the 1974–1975 budget and my belief that a change in emphasis is needed. While I was campaigning, the people of Kentucky voiced their desire for improved delivery of service. This was a commitment, and reorganization and program budgets are directed toward that objective. Program budgets are result-oriented. Measurement of result is an integral part of the process.

When Charlie Pryor and his staff were asked to prepare program budgets, we recognized, and I hope you recognize, the problems involved.[1] We have been involved in reorganization. Historical costs for neither the programs nor new agencies are available. Needs, goals, and objectives are essential parts of program budgets. The Office of Policy and Management is working closely with the various agency personnel, but there will be shortcomings. In some areas neither you nor I will be satisfied. But we need to recognize the time involved. The change has been made in less than six months. The procedure is entirely new, yet the change is to emphasize and improve results. Some may find the change confusing. Remember, it is different and does not lend itself to comparison to past years.

Implementation of program budgeting in all state agencies will provide the process and information whereby we will look at our public needs, our public services, and our alternatives to provide the services. Program budgeting will provide the process and the "output" oriented information for making decisions. Program budgeting, or any other kind of budgeting or management process, will not make decisions. Operating decisions will still have to be made by those of us in this room. I will still make policy recommendations to the General Assembly, which will then make the final budget decisions in the form of an enacted appropriation bill.

In years gone by, state agencies have primarily been concerned with what they were buying, how much they were buying, and what it would cost to buy goods and employ certain people for the two-year budget period. Very seldom has anyone looked at the services being provided, the need for the services, and who really receives the services. Very seldom were there clear objectives of what state government intended to provide the public during the execution of a budget.

We are bringing together virtually everyone involved in the budget process to explain and to discuss improving the process. By meeting together we are recognizing that our problems span agency and even program cabinet lines, and we are recognizing that the budget process is a joint effort involving both the executive and legislative branches of government. Even with cooperation throughout, measurements will have to be refined. The true rewards will be our ability to evaluate results at the end of a budget period.

Do not forget the change in emphasis. Program budgets will emphasize results rather than salaries, current expenses, and capital outlay. Hence, we are setting the stage for effective program evaluation. Emphasis should be placed on results anticipated and program objectives. Alternatives are important and I assure you that we are weighing alternatives throughout our consideration of the budget. When reviewing budgets with the cabinet secretaries and their staffs, please consider these factors, which I have just mentioned.

The spirit of cooperation is more than holding a seminar. It is the full cooperation in budget evaluation. I have given Representative Joe Clarke[2] my assurance of cooperation. Cabinet secretaries and their staffs will work with the Revenue and Appropriation Committee to explain budget requests. Copies of the budget requests have been forwarded to LRC, but meetings will permit detailed evaluation and answers not obvious in the requests. I do ask you to work through the cabinet secretaries in arranging and holding all meetings you may wish to schedule.

The budget will reflect both accountability and responsibility. To do this, programs will be related to organizations. Also, the accounting system will be revised to record program costs, and we will strengthen our allotment process. Program budgets have another important value —involvement of all managers. Budgets in the future will be built from the lowest unit in an organization. By the time the budget recommendation is presented to the General Assembly, it will be thoroughly evaluated and will represent the top priority needs of the people. That involvement will better assure that each manager knows what results are expected. Follow-up and evaluation will then determine the degree to which a manager and staff have fulfilled those expectations.

That is the crux of program budgets. It tells what is being done, who is being served, and how good the service is. We know the need and what portion of that need will be met within funds provided. It is a contract of sorts. You will appropriate funds for us to meet a certain level of need. Each manager knows what is expected of him. Evaluation will tell us the results. I hope that you will concentrate on results expected. I pledge to you that I will concentrate on meeting those expectations.

---

1. Charles Pryor, for more information see speech from March 24, 1973, in this section, p. 125.

2. Joseph P. Clarke, Jr. (1933–   ), Democrat from Danville; attorney; elected to the Kentucky House of Representatives in 1970; chairman, Southern Conference, Council on State Governmental Environmental Quality Committee (1972–1973); chairman, National Legislative Conference Committee on Ethics and Campaign Financing (1974–1975); secretary of Danville-Boyle County Industrial Foundation; board of directors of the Ephraim McDowell Memorial Hospital. *Kentucky General Assembly, 1976* (Frankfort, 1976), p. 21.

STATEMENT RE:
CONSUMER PROTECTION AND
REGULATION CABINET
Frankfort / January 2, 1974

I AM announcing two secretarial posts, Secretary for the Consumer Protection and Regulation Cabinet, and Secretary for the Department of Transportation.

As you know, in completing our reorganization of state government, only the Consumer Protection and Regulation Cabinet secretary position remains open. Today, I am appointing Elijah M. Hogge to that position.[1]

Mr. Hogge is currently the Secretary of Transportation and has served as commissioner of the old Department of Motor Transportation. He has performed with exceptional ability in both capacities, and with his legal training and experience, plus his administrative knowledge, I believe he is the one individual to assume this new responsibility. In many respects, Secretary Hogge has been a jack-of-all-trades as well as master of many and it is good that a Governor has this type of individual resource to call upon at any time when a particular task must be undertaken.

I make this point as the highest compliment to Secretary Hogge. He has approached various duties in state government with a keen business philosophy and at the same time has recognized the importance of improved delivery of services to the people of Kentucky. As Secretary for Consumer Protection and Regulation, he accepts another major challenge, especially in regard to the vital area of personal protection. I want to express my sincere appreciation for his willingness to take on another tough job. This cabinet post also carries with it great responsibility in the energy field—Public Service Commission and the Department of Mines and Minerals. He will play an important and, I know, effective role in gasification and liquefaction of coal.

To fill the vacancy created by Secretary Hogge, I am also today appointing James E. Gray Secretary of Transportation.[2] I do so with the utmost confidence in his outstanding administrative capacities, his quick grasp of problems and common sense approach to solutions. Mr. Gray will in addition to becoming secretary, continue to assume the responsibilities which he had as Commissioner of the Bureau of Highways. In this period of budget preparation, the energy crisis, and as we approach our second Session of the General Assembly, it is important to maintain the continuity of the Bureau of Highways through Mr. Gray's grasp of the agency and his planning for the future.

---

1. Elijah M. Hogge, for more information see speech from March 24, 1973, in this section, p. 125.

2. James E. Gray, for more information see speech from March 24, 1973, in this section, p. 125.

STATE OFFICE BUILDING DEDICATION
Owensboro / February 19, 1974

THE arms of state government reach out in all directions to help the people of the Owensboro-Daviess County area. As services increased through the years though, these arms have been stretched too many ways, creating unnecessary hardships on people, and reducing the ability of government to meet your needs in the best manner possible. You know the problems—endless miles of red tape, being shuffled from door to door and office to office. You travel to one side of town for the answer to a question. Then you have to go back across the city for a solution to another problem.

No longer will that be the case here. The new State Office Building we are dedicating today will take care of that. Eight different agencies of state government which provide a wide variety of services to the people of this area finally have been brought together where they belong—under the same roof. Whether it's social services or health services you're looking for, it's here. If you need rehabilitation or comprehensive care assistance, it's here. Or if it's information about air-pollution control or revenue you are seeking, the answers all can be found right here—at the corner of Second and Frederica streets. What this will mean, in simplest terms, is increased efficiency and improved delivery of services from your state government to you.

There are many reasons we all can be proud of this building, which is one of the most attractive and impressive state government centers in the Commonwealth. High on the list is the fact that we were able to make it a reality, from ground breaking to the final brick, in less than two years. Normal construction time for a building of this dimension is a minimum of two years, often longer. However, a pilot project—a construction management service—was utilized and this building was ready for occupancy on December 15, 1973, a year and nine days after ground was broken for it. In addition, by using this method, reliable estimates show that we saved at least $500,000 in construction costs, and that's a bargain by anyone's figuring!

I am particularly pleased that this administration brought the building to you. It is yet another example of how state government has been able to respond to the needs of Owensboro and Daviess County in the spirit of cooperation and helping others. There are many examples of state government playing an expanded role in this area—examples too often overlooked or forgotten. My first biennial budget is proof of the increased attention which has been given to this area.

The budget now before the General Assembly offers the same considerations. It does so in education, protection of life and property, and services to the blind, disabled, and handicapped. It does so in transportation, street and road repairs, and economic development. It does so in a way that touches the lives of each and every resident of Owensboro, Daviess County, and all of Kentucky. We have heard much about a juvenile diagnostic center for this area. We had it once, but the Republicans struck out by trying to force it on people who did not want it, and we lost it. I now have placed the funds for that center in this budget. I trust that reason will prevail and we can locate that valuable center to help children in this area.

The Hearing Defect Center at Brescia College, which is doing such a wonderful job, was due funds from the Office of Management and Budget, but these funds were impounded by the present administration in Washington. I have been working hard toward the release of these funds, and they are now available. My staff is working with this group to update their application, and I am hopeful this application will receive approval. This is another area in which we are dedicating ourselves to help those who are less fortunate.

No one can understand the curtailment of funds for libraries across this state and nation. I have included several millions of dollars in this budget to see that we continue to offer this valuable resource to our people. In fact, just recently I gave to the local library here some $15,000 to make up for the loss of funds. The attitude of helping people must prevail with all decisions made here and in Washington.

So you can see that the seemingly endless needs of this community, this area, and this state are continually challenged. It is a challenge I firmly believe we are meeting and I know we will continue to do so. I will continue to dedicate my efforts to helping the people not only of Kentucky, but particularly my hometown.

HEALTH AND WELFARE

COMMENT ON INSURANCE COMPANY SEIZURE
Frankfort / February 16, 1972

AN extremely serious matter has been brought to my attention by the Commissioner of Insurance, Harold B. McGuffey,[1] pertaining to certain irregularities and alleged violations of Kentucky Statutes in the conduct and operation of three domestic life insurance companies located in Louisville. If allowed to continue, these irregularities could have an adverse affect on the companies' policyholders, creditors, public stockholders, and the general public. Therefore I have directed Mr. McGuffey to take every legal step necessary in this matter to protect the companies' policyholders, public stockholders, creditors, and the general public.

Today Mr. McGuffey has requested, and has obtained, from the Franklin Circuit Court an order seizing the three domestic life insurers, namely Teachers' National Life Insurance Company, American Businessmen's Life Insurance Company, and Western Pioneer Life Insurance Company. These insurance companies are controlled by American Pyramid Companies, Inc., through its controlled affiliate TSI, Inc., both holding companies located in Louisville.

Under the seizure order, the commissioner as rehabilitator will take possession and control of all of the property, books, accounts, documents, and other records of the companies as prescribed by law. Commissioner McGuffey will take such future actions as he deems necessary, or expedient, to reform and revitalize the companies. He has informed me that he has appointed an able and competent staff to administer the operations of the companies. I can assure you that every effort will be taken to see that the insurance policies of the seized insurers, which have been issued principally to policyholders in this state, will be protected.

Within a short time Mr. McGuffey will be in touch with segments of our domestic industry for assistance in this matter. I want to emphasize that I have the greatest confidence in the integrity and ability of our domestic industry, and that this action taken today constitutes a regrettable exception to the good reputation that Kentucky's insurance industry enjoys nationwide.

---

1. Harold Bowen McGuffey (1920–   ), Smiths Grove; teacher and in-

surance agent; commissioner of insurance, Commonwealth of Kentucky (1971–   ). *Who's Who in Kentucky, 1974* (Atlanta, Ga., 1974), p. 417.

POST WHITE HOUSE CONFERENCE ON AGING
Louisville / May 30, 1972

> Age is a quality of mind;
> If you've left your dreams behind,
> If hope is cold,
> If you no longer look ahead,
> If your ambitious fires are dead . . .
> Then, you are old!

THE author of that poem escaped identification. But far more important than a name is the message given in a very few words. Age is indeed a quality of mind. Bernard Baruch[1] frequently said and I quote: "To me, old age is always fifteen years older than I am!" This is a wonderful philosophy of life. Those who look at age as did Mr. Baruch certainly are unlike the description of the poem I read as an introduction to this address. An increasing number of senior citizens are not leaving their dreams behind. To many, hope is warm, rather than cold. They look ahead with ambitious fires which are very much alive. They are not old! Such individuals, along in years, have before them one of the greatest challenges ever, to gather other senior citizens into a vibrant, effective group in order to perform a multitude of services.

The theme of senior citizens month is "Action Now." I believe that theme is double-barreled, as it calls for action from two sides: Kentucky's 476,200 citizens who are sixty years of age or older and a state administration which is responsive to your needs. Let me first talk about the role you can play. Have you stopped to consider the real impact nearly one-half million persons can have on society when they decide to work in harmony for the betterment of that society? To some, the answer will be yes, but that's not good enough. Kentucky's senior citizens have a selling job to do, stimulating the interest, enthusiasm, and cooperation of others who are in the same category.

Life expectancy is moving higher and higher. Because your numbers are increasing annually, so does the potential for your services. What does this mean? It means you have time to give others. I can think of community after community in desperate need every month for persons to assume leadership roles in civic projects. It means your counsel in matters relating to your past experiences is valuable. Only the foolish refuse to consider the voice of experience. It means you can give more of yourself to your political party or to the actual functions of government at all levels. It means you can make life better for yourself now, as well as for those who will reach your plateau in life at a later date. You can contribute to the establishment of continuing education. You can ease the transition for others from the hectic to a more leisurely life. You can lend others the profits of your mistakes and encourage them with the successes of your endeavors. These, and other "real necessities," are not platitudes, nor are they shallow dreams. They are real bonuses, and only you can offer them if you decide to do so.

Equally as vital are the contributions you can make to other senior citizens, persons less fortunate than you, persons who look to their peers and their government for solace, hope, and, yes, inspiration. No one understands the needs of senior citizens as do those who experience day by day the pressing needs. As your Governor, I wrestle with such problems constantly and will do so until proper solutions are found. To that end I pledge to you, and we have already made substantial starts in several areas, an administration which is compassionate, but even more realistically, one which is determined to establish a positive record in this regard. Our new directions include the provision of housing for senior citizens and tax reform to accommodate those least able to pay. This administration has taken first steps through legislation in both areas. Because of tax reform, you will now receive far more services from state government while paying less individual taxes. This is an undisputed fact.

In the field of health care, no area of my new state reorganization will receive stronger emphasis from the Governor's office. At the same time, you will find more and more impetus on the part of my office, and I believe other Governors' offices, in persuading the federal government to abandon its ineffective health and welfare practices of the thirties and formulate more logical programs which will truly reach those in need, and with impact. Your leisure time is another concern. State government is gearing up to provide variety in its offerings to those seeking cultural, recreational, and educational opportunities.

Nothing, however, can be done without proper direction. One month to the day after I was inaugurated as Governor, I appointed former state Senator Henry Beach[2] as Executive Director of the Kentucky

Commission on Aging. He has plunged into this new role with as much aggressiveness as anyone possibly could, and we maintain close communication on the subject of his responsibilities. To provide even closer support from my office, I have also assigned a person on my staff to serve as liaison to assist the executive director in expediting a growing program designed to improve the quality of your life.

I think we are entering an era without precedent. I base this on legislation already passed, the early progress made by our Commission on Aging, the growth of its support to your needs through districts, the attention you are receiving directly from the Governor's office, and most assuredly do I base this on your own activities. They say when a person has "clout," he gets things done. Kentucky's senior citizens can have as much clout as any group in our great Commonwealth. I expect it as I see you growing daily, not just in numbers, but rather in the activities of your numbers. I expect it because we are in harmony as we seek to conquer the ills which have for too long beset senior citizens.

I predict you will be pleased with the attitude of this administration as you find it more of a neighbor rather than a simple acquaintance. I do so because of other things which we already have accomplished: a generic drug bill; implementation of the Homestead Amendment and language in that bill permitting exemption to those who rent out part of the dwelling in which they live; and the vehicle for state participation in any federal program under the Older American Act. You will see this in the Department of Economic Security through the implementation of new and more far-reaching programs and by my latest commissioner appointee. You will see this all the way through state government in libraries, parks, health, education, safety, and other departments. With three and a half years remaining in this administration, we will have many opportunities to meet together. If our first theme is "Action Now," let us join in force so that as I leave office you will say we did have action, but more importantly, it brought results![3]

---

1. Bernard Mannes Baruch (1870–1965), American financier; adviser to United States presidents beginning with Woodrow Wilson; United States representative on United Nations Atomic Energy Commission (1946). *Who Was Who in America with World Notables, 1961–1968* (Chicago, 1968), 4:62; *Collier's Encyclopedia*, s.v. "Baruch, Bernard Mannes."

2. Henry Beach (1915–   ), Democrat from Louisville; Baptist minister; member of Kentucky Senate (1968–1972); chairman, Billy Graham Crusade (1957); group leader, Jefferson County Democratic Organization. *Kentucky General Assembly 1970* (Frankfort, n.d.), p. 11.

3. On August 7, 1974, Governor Ford gave a similar speech at the Camp-

bell County Senior Citizens Picnic at Green Meadows in Melbourne. This speech is not included in this volume.

SOUTHERN GOVERNORS' CONFERENCE
Hilton Head, South Carolina / September 5, 1972

OUR states and the nation face a massive crisis in health care. Report after report isolates such problems as rapidly rising costs, inadequate facilities, personnel shortages, ineffective planning of facilities and services, fragmentation of health services, and too little emphasis on preventive services. The list could go on almost without end. The problems are epitomized in Kentucky as I am sure you experience them. For our state, the lack of planning and management in health services resulted in a disjointed approach that we knew had to be corrected as soon as possible.

While in the Kentucky Senate and Lieutenant Governor's office, these shortcomings became increasingly evident to me. The proliferation of agencies bothered me. I saw the harmful effects caused by a void in the proper distribution and utilization of manpower and facilities. Thus, as a very practical matter, we embarked on an aggressive program where innovation and coordination will no more be shackled.

We recognized that the vast majority of these difficulties related to disorganization and lack of design and structure of our health care system. This, being a legitimate responsibility of the state, dictated what we feel is the most significant piece of health legislation in our Commonwealth's history. It's called the Kentucky Certificate of Need, Licensure, and Regulations Act of 1972 and has three major provisions: an authoritative base for planning and development of health services and facilities under comprehensive health planning; a single board responsible for licensure and regulation of health services and facilities; and a vital linkage between the planning function and the licensure-regulatory function.

Let me emphasize that this legislation relates to planning and regulating services as well as facilities. Kentucky now stands among only two or three states in the nation in combining health facilities and health services, and I suspect that many governors are examining the feasibility of merging these arms just as we found so necessary. There must be correlation between the public and private sectors of health care. This is now provided. In the past, public care was at a distinct disadvantage financially, in staffing, and in the ability to render competent service. In our case there had to be a centralization of licensure bodies. Previously, ours were scattered in all directions.

Though we implemented comprehensive health planning in 1967, our success had been less than satisfactory. Too much emphasis was placed on organization of committees with inadequate attention to the rational development of a statewide health care system responsive to the needs of the people. The licensure-regulatory process link with planning, by a state authority, has much logic. It puts teeth into comprehensive health planning and gives much greater coordination to the entire picture of health care and services than before. Our certificate of need board will consist of fifteen members representing the hospital association, medical association, nursing home association, nurses association, dental association, and consumers. Our commissioners of health and mental health work in an advisory capacity.

For the first time we will be able to look at the total health care picture and have regulatory power in doing so. The ultimate goal cannot help but put this entire matter on a much more sound businesslike basis with the needs of all the citizens as first priority.

KENTUCKY WELFARE ASSOCIATION
Louisville / October 13, 1972

SOME expected me to say something about the recent federal legislation affecting your work and the impact it will have on the delivery of human services in Kentucky. Obviously you are very much interested in this, but there are others well qualified and informed on the new legislation to do this. Anyway, you will probably get a couple of hundred memorandums on this subject in the next few weeks, so I don't want to spoil your fun in reading them!

It is more important that you understand what the Ford administration position is with regard to the work you are doing. I also want to tell you what I expect from each and every one of you, because the success of our welfare program in Kentucky stands or falls on the kind of job you perform out in the field. Welfare is an emotional issue. It should not be. Rather welfare should be approached in a compassionate, businesslike manner where the dignity of man is foremost. The blind, disabled, and aged deserve dignity. Helpless children, no matter their origin, must not be treated in a callous way. Our aim must be to reduce swelling welfare rolls through productive measures which achieve goals too many politicians and officials have talked about while actually running from the solutions.

We have welfare problems in Kentucky and in every state of the nation, but where there is a problem, there also is a solution. You are part of that solution. We must humanize, modernize, and increase the efficiency of our welfare system in Kentucky in order to help those less fortunate become healthy, productive citizens. As long as we allow benign neglect to push those who have been denied opportunities into the corner of apathy, we will always have a swollen welfare roster.

During this conference, you have heard references to welfare myths. There is no doubt that such misunderstanding retards our progress in human resources work. I want to expand what was said to you as the myths pertain to Kentucky. Here are five of the more persistent misconceptions which plague you. Let's dispel them with facts.

Myth: The welfare rolls are full of able-bodied loafers.

Fact: In Kentucky only 8.3 percent of the total adult population on welfare is considered employable or trainable. These are mothers of dependent children. National figures show less than 1 percent are able-bodied fathers.

Myth: Once on welfare, always on welfare.

Fact: In Kentucky the average length of time a family stays on welfare is 2.3 years.

Myth: Welfare families have lots of kids, then have more to get more money.

Fact: In Kentucky, the average welfare family has 2.5 children and this average figure is dropping. New cases show 2 or less, while the latest census shows the average family in Kentucky as having 2.3 children.

Myth: Most welfare families are black.

Fact: In Kentucky only 32 percent of the AFDC[1] families are black. National averages are only slightly higher due to the large urban centers.

Myth: Welfare people cheat to get more money.

Fact: Our monitoring systems show less than 1 percent guilty of fraud or misrepresentation.

I want to assure you today that the Ford administration is not lead-

ing from these kinds of misconceptions. I know there are problems in
our welfare system, but I intend to approach these problems in a positive, constructive manner. During the course of my campaign, and
throughout these first few months of my administration, I listened to
the frustrations of many people. They spoke of their inability to get
action from the county seat, from Frankfort, from Washington. They
spoke of the continued and widening alienation of the people from
their government; of their feeling that programs were being run not
with them and their needs in mind, but seemingly for the convenience
of the people who ran the programs. They spoke of delay. They spoke
of coming to government with one problem and of being shunted from
one agency to another, from one level of government to another. With
these thoughts in mind, we have set ourselves to the task of reorganizing state government to better meet the needs of people.

The Department of Economic Security has already begun internal
reorganization, and Gail Huecker[2] has shown nerve and dedication to
this task that bodes well for the area of human resources. Gail is stressing a modernization that will get services to your clients in the quickest,
most effective manner. This kind of philosophy will, over the long run,
tend to humanize social services. People will no longer be shuffled from
pillar to post in order to receive the kind of services they need. Another
positive approach Commissioner Huecker is taking in reorganization is
attention to the flexibility of federal guidelines in social legislation.
Rather than being intimidated by federal legislation and begging off
that our problems come from Washington, Commissioner Huecker
is working positively to tailor Kentucky's welfare program to the needs
of Kentuckians.

I want to mention just a few improvements that have already begun
under the new reorganization of the Department of Economic Security.
Coordination of complementary services is first. There are many agencies which provide overlapping and duplicating services. These are now
being coordinated to eliminate this kind of waste. The $120,000 grant
of $30,000 local and $90,000 DES funds announced at Wednesday's
Jefferson County Fiscal Court meeting is an example of the effort being
made to control the duplication and fragmentation of overlapping services. Computerization and decentralization of the food stamp program
is second. This $80 million program was being handled manually, caus-
ing delays and tying up needed personnel. Making food stamps available through the Post Office gets the service to the people where it is
more effectively handled. This will also free-up the central staff for
more pressing problems.

Regionalization of case work is a third improvement. This allows the case worker to learn more about the local community, to become personally involved in the community, to see more cases per day, and avoid chasing all over the city or the mountains to see clients. Redefining of job responsibilities is fourth. By making greater use of paraprofessionals and by redefining what various jobs need to be achieving, our limited staff should be able to make greater use of manhours spent with clients in meeting their needs.

These and other programs are all designed to upgrade our welfare system, but in the end, it is up to you, the people who work directly with the clients, whether or not we are to have a successful welfare program in Kentucky. I challenge you today to take up this positive approach in improving our welfare system and take it to the people. We are dependent on your input for planning and your personal commitment in carrying out the programs to bring proper welfare services to Kentucky. I know there are many frustrations involved in reorganization. But if you can be positive and look to the challenge ahead, Kentucky will show the nation how to produce a human resources delivery system geared to meeting real, human needs.

We will try to relieve you from the paper thicket through computerization of necessary functions in order to give you more time with clients. We will do all we can to help you. But we expect you to prove to the people that government can and will serve them. We want to change Kentucky's welfare system for the better and you can do it. A change for the better is the hope for every citizen, taxpayer, and welfare recipient. A change for the better is an absolute necessity, because only then will welfare be the proper tool of mankind it was intended. I pledge my administration's support in the work you are doing. You will not hear from my administration any of the negative rhetoric that has plagued you so long. I will work with you, and I expect you to work for the ultimate goal of reform.[3]

---

1. AFDC, Aid to Families with Dependent Children.

2. Gail Huecker, for more information see speech from May 8, 1973, in the Reorganization section, p. 132.

3. On May 12, 1974, Governor Ford also made the following statement regarding welfare: "Too often the word 'welfare' becomes misused. Those who drafted the Constitution suggested that the new government would serve, rather than suppress, the people. If we promote the general welfare we do make life easier, ease individual burdens, and accomplish an act of Christianity, an act of brotherhood, and in one real sense help to ensure domestic tranquillity and establish justice. There are always, unfortunately, those who through no fault of their own have honest needs which they can-

not provide. When others respond, I consider it a decency of government or a decency of individual or group." This statement is not included in this volume.

KENTUCKY OCCUPATIONAL
HEALTH AND SAFETY
Louisville / October 18, 1972

I'LL take my cue from the note on your announcement, "It's all business—no luncheon is involved," and get to the point in a hurry so you can go to work. I want to explain what I see in the philosophy and intent of occupational health and safety legislation. I also want to mention the steps we will be taking to implement the legislation.

We have come a long way in the area of industrial health and safety since the impact of the industrial revolution in the latter half of the eighteenth century. The worker in England's industrial plant of that period was completely neglected. He was considered of much less importance than machinery and industrial production. In this country, it wasn't really until after the Civil War that the industrial revolution had its impact. We have all the sweat shops and horrible working conditions of that time represented in our history books.

Through groups representing the worker, government involvement, the leadership of progressive conscientious employers, and improved technology, we have made great inroads in assuring safer working conditions. Yet we still see unfavorable statistics each year which indicate there is much room for improvement. In Kentucky alone, there were some two hundred lives lost in industrial accidents during 1971. In this same period, some 22,000 persons were injured on the job. The human misery and suffering reflected by these statistics are appalling, not to mention the economic loss to individuals, families, industry, labor, and to the economy of the Commonwealth. We can't blame this loss of life and loss of man-hours on any one group. There are several parties responsible for improving occupational health and safety. State government has its own responsibility, and the legislation you will discuss today is an attempt to meet this responsibility with positive action.

As is often the case, such significant and far-reaching legislation brings about apprehension and concern among many people. While my administration is firm in its devotion to safety and health for our citizens, we are also aware of the feelings of all sectors of our citizenry in this matter. If we are to realize a safer and more healthful working environment in Kentucky, then all of us—management, labor, government, and professionals—must work together as a team. Only in this way, with all parties becoming involved, can we initiate the kind of positive action Kentucky needs in industrial health and safety.

At this point, I want to mention what has been done so far. This may help give you a framework to consider for the remainder of this session. As a first step, we enacted the law and amended it in the extraordinary session.[1] We also designated the Kentucky Department of Labor as the state agency responsible for the program. Last June I appointed a Kentucky Occupational Safety and Health Standards Board composed of twelve persons. Equally represented are labor, industry, agriculture, and the safety and health professions. Commissioner Yocom,[2] by virtue of his office, is chairman of the board. These individuals are working to develop new safety and health standards through the professional staff of the Department of Labor. These standards will be in your hands by the end of 1972. The new standards and regulations are of direct importance to you because they will serve as reference guides as you develop your own safety and health programs.

As we went about the task of developing a plan and new safety and health standards, we also began structuring an organization which would implement our plan. This organization, we concluded, should fit our basic idea of a plan which was both developmental and voluntary in nature. Federal guidelines require a compliance factor as part of the implementing organization, but have left the education and training factor optional. We included education and training whereas many states have not chosen to do so. We did this because we believe that if voluntary compliance is to succeed, education and training in both management and labor are absolutely necessary. Commissioner Yocom has recommended entirely new qualifications for compliance and training officers, required by the state plan. He is presently recruiting and training this staff and you will soon be working with more qualified and trained individuals than in the past.

I believe you can see that while this administration is firm in our approach to the safety and health of our citizens, we have taken a route suited to the best interests of all. We are prepared to do away with hazardous conditions where we find them while educating and training all concerned to our new standards. Very shortly, I will appoint a three-man panel provided by the act. Officially, this panel will be called the Kentucky Occupational Safety and Health Review Commission. The primary duty of this commission will be to hear appeals concerning portions of this program which certain parties may consider unfair. In order that all our citizens may enjoy the benefits of increased safety and health, I have, during this past week, issued an executive order whereby state government employees are included in the coverage of the act.[3] Provisions are also included in the act which cover city and county workers of the Commonwealth.

This act of safety and health is, on the one hand, designed to offer to Kentucky citizens a new concern for their physical well-being and, on the other hand, it offers to industry a reduction in the many problems resulting from injured or physically ill workers. It is, above all, designed for a team effort, an effort by management, labor, and government. The dreary statistics can be greatly reduced. I ask your help in seeing this come about.

---

1. See an act "relating to the safety and health of workers employed within the Commonwealth of Kentucky," which was approved without the Governor's signature on June 27, 1972. *Acts of the General Assembly First Extra Session 1972*, Chapter 7 (S.B. 5), pp. 101–3.

2. James Yocom (1928–   ), Democrat from Shively; electrician; member of the Kentucky House of Representatives (1970–1972); past president of the Shively Democrat Club; resigned from the House of Representatives in the spring of 1972 to become commissioner of labor. *Kentucky General Assembly 1972* (Frankfort, n.d.), p. 23.

3. See Executive Order 72–868 (September 15, 1972).

PUBLIC ASSISTANCE ADJUSTMENTS
Frankfort / November 3, 1972

ON October 13 I said welfare "should be approached in a compassionate, businesslike manner where the dignity of man is foremost."[1] I also said this administration would not lead from misconceptions based on the many "welfare myths" that plague us. There is the myth of "Why work when you can live it up on welfare?" But the fact is that welfare payments are so low they could hardly be considered an attractive alternative to working for a salary. The average grant to AFDC families in Kentucky is $119 per month.

The significant error of this kind of misconception, however, affects the people who fall in the class of aid to the aged, blind, and disabled. In Kentucky, cash grants to these people fall somewhere in the range of $61 to $102 a month for single individuals. It would take a callous and sinister person to say we ought to deny support to the blind and disabled, and there is no justification at all for denying support to those who have given the greater part of their lives in making this country what it is.

In the past, whenever there has been an increase in Social Security payments, the state has had to reduce public assistance grants to senior citizens receiving both Social Security and Public Assistance. The intent of this federal regulation was to achieve equity between those receiving both Social Security and Public Assistance and those receiving only Public Assistance. Unfortunately, this federal requirement has served to penalize many of our people in the aged, blind, and disabled category. With the 20 percent increase in Social Security recently signed into federal law, we were faced with a decision in readjusting Public Assistance to achieve the equity required by Washington. If we stayed with the procedure followed in the past, we would have been forced to reduce Public Assistance to 40,000 Kentuckians. I decided that this kind of procedure needed to be changed.

This morning I am directing Commissioner Huecker[2] to release funds from the Department of Economic Security budget to prevent the reduction that would have resulted from the recent Social Security increases. With $2.3 million of state funds, we will purchase $3.9 million of federal money for a total of $6.2 million to be used to offset the increases. In addition, these funds will make possible a $15 increase in the agency's standard used to compute grants to the aged, blind, and disabled.

The effect of this major change in policy will be to raise Public Assistance grants going to those not receiving Social Security in order to achieve the equity required by federal law. This action assures that the 40,000 in the aged, blind, and disabled category will not be penalized by the new Social Security bill. And 62,000, or 95 percent of this category, will get an increase in their Public Assistance checks.

Funds for this change will come from existing appropriations to the Department of Economic Security. Prudent management has proven beneficial! Provisions of the recently enacted Social Security Law will federalize the aid to the aged, blind, and disabled category on January 1, 1974. Our budget does not expire until June 30, 1974. I am therefore authorizing the department to use funds which will accrue as a result of the federalization for this purpose and through monetary savings from the prudent management I mentioned.

The changes I have outlined are effective with the grant payments to be made for January. Until that time, I have directed that the Social Security increases which were received beginning with October checks be disregarded by the Department of Economic Security in computing Public Assistance grants until this order is effective. This will ensure the availability of these funds to the aged, blind, and disabled.

---

1. This is a quote from a speech which Governor Ford delivered to the Kentucky Welfare Association at the Seelbach Hotel in Louisville, on October 13, 1972. That speech is included in this section, pp. 172–75. This speech was given during a press conference.

2. Gail Huecker, commissioner of the Department of Economic Security, for more information see speech from May 8, 1973, in the Reorganization section, p. 132.

KENTUCKY OCCUPATIONAL PROGRAM KICKOFF
Frankfort / January 16, 1973

It is perhaps fitting that I have been given the opportunity to announce our new Kentucky Occupational Program tonight. As Chief Executive of the largest employer in the state, I think it is obvious that all of Kentucky can gain from this new program. Since this is the first formal announcement of the program, it might be helpful to provide some background information.

We in Kentucky, like every other state in the Union, have the problem of troubled employees. This individual might be suffering from alcoholism, drug abuse, or any one of several emotional handicaps such as marital, legal, or financial difficulties. To understand the significance of this problem, the general figure for troubled employees is alarming, about 10 percent of the entire work force. Since there are about 1.2 million employees in Kentucky, this would indicate that

120,000 are disturbed in one of several ways. Three thousand of these would be in state government.

Obviously, the troubled employee is not able to perform his job as efficiently as desired. Estimates for an average cost of this serious problem run at about 25 percent of the employee's salary. In Kentucky we are talking about something in the neighborhood of $140 million, an economic loss of staggering proportions. This reflects merely the cost in salaries, not the money that may be lost by the effect of the troubled employee in the way he does business. One prominent doctor in the area of alcohol research stated, "When you have a problem drinker who signs contracts or makes investments, he can lose 1 million dollars in five minutes."

Alcohol actually is the worst culprit in the case of the troubled employee. At least half of the employees in the troubled category in Kentucky are there because of alcohol-related problems. I quoted some figures that show how employees with these kinds of problems can cost the employer, but this is obviously not the real impact of the troubled employee. It is the tragedy and suffering that he and his family must go through until the problem is solved. So possibly what we can do will be even more meaningful to thousands of innocent victims. There have been several attempts to get to what really is an ancient problem. The difference in the program that I am announcing tonight, however, is in the approach to the problem and the statewide system of comprehensive care centers that can now provide treatment.

In the past, the focus mainly has been on those labeled as the visible drunks. These are problem drinkers who can no longer conceal their illness, people who file through the courts, who fill jails, and account for over 50 percent of the policeman's time. We must continue to try to cure these people. However, the visible drunk makes up only about 5 percent of the alcoholic population. Also, because of the unfortunate progressive nature of their illness, by the time one is in this category, rehabilitation becomes more difficult. It is estimated that only about 15 percent of the alcoholics in this category show improvement under treatment, and that is on a very relative basis. The other 95 percent of those touched by this illness are still functioning on the job, are still with their families, and probably lead a respected life in their communities. These are the people this new program can help. These are the people we need to reach before they slide into the nearly unreachable visible drunk category.

What we are launching is designed to get to these people at the earliest possible stage of their illness. The recovery rate for this kind of program is estimated at about 60 to 70 percent with some estimates running as high as 80 percent. The main thrust of this program is accurate identification of the troubled employee through job performance. This is case finding and differs from the old technique. Under the former method of identifying the troubled employee, a supervisor would look for the symptoms of drinking, drug abuse, or emotional disturbances. By now using case identification, the supervisor can see when there has been a change in the employee's job performance and can professionally and diplomatically suggest counseling as a possible remedy. In the past, this type of system even if desired has not been possible. Today, Kentucky is ready for such a program.

We have spent nearly eight years developing a network of comprehensive care centers throughout Kentucky. The availability of these centers to the citizens of the Commonwealth is perhaps the best in the country. In each of these centers, there will be competent personnel to work with business, industry, and local government agencies in their region. There will be a new Office of Occupational Programs established in the Department of Mental Health. The Division of Alcohol and Drug Abuse will include occupational programs. The new office will also assist state agencies in helping them develop their programs. In short, this is intended to be a widespread endeavor. The goals are ones that we all can identify with and work toward achieving together.

The main burden would seem to be borne by you in the comprehensive care centers throughout Kentucky, but I wonder if this is in fact true? Tonight, I want to ask the agency heads out there, how many hours are you losing from your staff because of the troubled employee problem? Have you been able to do anything about it before now? Think about it, then recognize the new steps being taken and awaiting your participation. This is an effort that we must all work together on. In the end, it affects us all. In the end, it can substantially serve all Kentucky.

OWENSBORO COUNCIL FOR
RETARDED CHILDREN
Owensboro / March 12, 1973

I WAS asked to direct my comments tonight to the hope for the mentally retarded. Probably the most important thing that I could say is, look around you. This is the hope for the mentally retarded, just like it is the hope for most of the needed services in Kentucky. Concerned citizens, involved businesses, and dedicated workers have come together for the purpose of meeting a common goal. Without this coalition of concern and involvement very little would be done in communities throughout the Commonwealth. Successful programs can only be achieved through this kind of partnership.

There is only so much that state government or any government for that matter can do in trying to serve the needs of the people. We are constantly coming head-on with the dilemma of trying to meet unlimited needs with limited resources. We also face the frustration of bringing our available expertise and manpower to bear on problems needing solutions only to see them fail because of lack of interest in the communities where the problems exist. This has not been the case with our statewide programs in the area of mental retardation, and the Owensboro Council for Retarded Children is a prime example of how it can be done. You have developed an outstanding, coordinated effort to help those with a problem which has been dealt with historically in an unfeeling, antisocial manner. The mentally retarded have been subject too often to a hopeless institutional treatment more designed to get them out of the eye of society than to integrate them into society. The national conscience has been stirred with disclosures of crowded and understaffed institutions where maintenance of the population has been the basic concern.

You who have worked with the problem of mental retardation in Owensboro have played an important role in changing the direction of solving this problem. Working closely with the Green River Comprehensive Care Center, you have instituted a system of ongoing care and rehabilitation which gives great hope indeed to those with the problem and their families. What we are seeing emerge is a coordinated effort which begins with day care for the preschool children. The child then can be integrated into the public school system and the cycle for hope is begun at an early age. As the individual with the retardation problem grows, he can work into sheltered workshops and eventually adult activities to further the process of rehabilitation. The group home provides a homelike atmosphere for the learning process, and the individual can work out in the community or in the sheltered workshop for the personal gain that gives a sense of pride and achievement.

I know that everyone here knows of the many accomplishments of jobs which not only give satisfaction to those who do the work but provide an income for them as well. It sometimes seems that progress in rehabilitation is at a snail's pace, but little accomplishments like this are the foundation upon which great successes are accomplished. We are trying to make inroads on the state system for serving the needs of the mentally retarded by improved programs and better equipped and run facilities. The basic philosophy for this statewide development is to provide inpatient services at our institutions and to work for community-based programs where those with a problem can receive attention regardless of where they are.

The new $14-million Oakwood facility is now open, and we will have over 400 new beds when it is completed. This may well be the finest facility of its kind in the country. We have put $1.5 million into the expansion at Hazelwood. When the facilities are all completed, we will have about 1,000 beds in our institutional facilities for the mentally retarded. We also have twenty-three comprehensive care centers throughout the state which are working with local communities to bring new hope to the mentally retarded. They are providing the same kind of services as you have here, but I know that these people would be the first to admit that they would not be as far along as they are without the help and involvement of organizations such as the Councils for Retarded Children throughout Kentucky.

We are opening the window for the mentally retarded in our state. No longer will we tolerate the treatment of this problem by burying it in the recesses of antiquated facilities or the philosophy that it is a hopeless problem to be hidden from society. I think that there is more hope for the mentally retarded today than there ever has been. Partially this is due to a new concern of government at all levels, but mainly it is the efforts of concerned groups like yours. You have pressured and badgered officials to recognize the urgency of the problem. You have worked with the planning bodies dealing with the problem. You have given time and money to the realization of the new direction in dealing with the mentally retarded, but most of all, you have cared. I congratulate you on the success you have already achieved here, and I join you in the new hope that we all have for our mentally retarded. With such a coalition of concern, the future is brighter for them than ever before. You can be sure that you will have the support of my administration as you continue the slow process of rehabilitating those individuals who in the past had been swept into the corner of hopelessness by a society which didn't care.

BROWN CHALLENGE GIFT
Frankfort / March 15, 1973

DOING things differently to improve life for others is a never-ending task which I hope will be visible throughout my administration as Governor. As we search for new ideas, as we strive to accomplish the goal of human betterment, it is comforting to know there are individuals willing to join in this crusade.[1] Today I am especially pleased to announce a proposal based on a most generous challenge gift, which can initiate a unique dimension in health research. This proposal will be brought before the 1974 Kentucky General Assembly with the full endorsement and support of the Governor's office.

Briefly the plan involves a grant relationship between state government and the Eleanor and John Young Brown, Jr. Foundation. Mr. and Mrs. Brown have offered a challenge gift of $1 million toward the establishment of a research center on aging.[2] Their gift is contingent upon the Commonwealth of Kentucky matching that amount and earmarking it for this particular project. I will propose that the state appropriate $1 million and provide enabling legislation for the center when I deliver the next budget message. This ongoing project will be designed for the benefit of every Kentuckian as well as older people throughout America. Mr. Brown has designated the University of Kentucky Medical School as the center's permanent location and has the concurrence of President Singletary.[3]

This is an exciting opportunity for Kentucky with unlimited potential in behalf of an increased quality of life for the aged. Kentucky can eventually become a world leader in this research field whereby the results will be measured in numerous ways. Although America is the richest nation in the world and the number of persons over sixty-five grows each year, research pertaining to the aging process with emphasis on the extension of one's physical and mental qualities has received practically no consideration. Kentucky can make one of the most significant contributions in the history of medical science by probing for a breakthrough on the question of why man grows old and what can be done to extend one's productive lifespan.

---

1. Press conference.

2. John Y. Brown, Jr., Louisville; president, Kentucky Fried Chicken to 1971, chairman of the board (1971–1974); owner, Lums Restaurants; director, Kentucky Colonels professional basketball team (1973–1976); national chairman of National Young Leadership Council; vice-chairman, Democratic National Telethon (1973); member, state Democratic executive committee. *Who's Who in America, 1974–1975* (Chicago, 1975), 1:399. Eleanor Brown (1940–   ), Louisville; chairman of the board, Kentucky Colonels professional basketball team (1973–1976). Telephone interview, *Courier-Journal* and *Louisville Times*, readers information bureau, June 29, 1976; telephone interview, Kentucky Colonels team office, June 30, 1976.

3. Otis Arnold Singletary, Jr. (1921–   ), Lexington; president, University of Kentucky (1969–   ). *Who's Who in America, 1974* (St. Louis, 1974), 2:2845.

AMBULANCE REGULATIONS
Frankfort / March 26, 1973

THERE has been considerable discussion during the past few weeks over ambulance services regulations adopted recently by the Kentucky Certificate of Need and Licensure Board. As I review the pros and cons of the matter, I have two major concerns. First, I am concerned that the state not take action that will place an undue hardship on current providers of ambulance services and ultimately affect the availability of services to people. Also, I am concerned that some parties are suggesting that the state has far exceeded its authority and should withdraw from this matter and do nothing with regard to the regulations and improvement of ambulance services. The problem of emergency medical services is a highly complex as well as emotional one. It is not a problem unique to Kentucky.

The national Congress has legislation before both the House and Senate pertaining to emergency medical services. A major provision of these legislative proposals is the development of emergency medical transportation systems. The magnitude of the problem is becoming increasingly apparent to every citizen. As we see demands for emergency services increasing, we see little progress being made to improve the system. The National Academy of Science has termed emergency care as that weakest link in our health care system. National studies indicate that up to 20 percent of accidental highway deaths could be avoided if we had an effective emergency medical services system. The importance of transportation services to the emergency service system is clearly demonstrated by data from the American Heart Association. They estimate that over 10 percent of the 275,000 coronary deaths each year could be prevented if proper emergency care were rendered at the scene or on the way to emergency facilities.

I believe that any problem of this magnitude is an appropriate concern of government at all levels. State government is deeply committed to the solution of this problem and is currently involved in three major areas: first is the area of training and technical assistance. Over 400 emergency medical technicians were trained during 1972 in a cooperative program involving the State Health Department, Department of Public Safety, colleges, universities, vocational school and health resources throughout the state. Our goal is to train over 400 additional technicians this year in twenty-four courses offered at sixteen locations throughout Kentucky. Regional Comprehensive Health Planning Councils throughout Kentucky are currently involved in an intensive effort to plan and develop areawide systems of emergency services including transportation, communications, and facility components. Due to the nature of the problem (and especially the operational expense of a high quality service), increasing emphasis is being placed upon the need for a multicounty approach to services. Proper organization of services appears to be the key to success.

Purchase of services and equipment is our next concern. Effective July 1, 1972, ambulance services were included for the first time as an eligible benefit for reimbursement under the Medicaid program. This action enables payment for emergency ambulance services provided to over 320,000 elderly and disadvantaged Kentuckians. I feel this represents a significant step toward development of a viable financing base for emergency medical transportation services. Utilizing various federal grant programs, Kentucky has secured funds and assisted local governments and other groups in the purchase of forty-two modern, fully equipped ambulances to serve twenty-six counties. Approximately fifteen additional ambulances will be purchased this year. Two-way radio communication is a key element in the emergency services system. The state has again utilized a host of federal funding sources to develop areawide communication systems that are in place in sixteen counties with an additional twenty-two counties to be completed in late summer.

Licensure and regulation is a third area of state concern. This area of responsibility is the current focus of attention. I will not debate whether or not the regulations adopted by the board are appropriate, but I will defend state government's responsibility to assure to the citizens of the Commonwealth that ambulance services meet the necessary minimum standards to assure an acceptable quality of care. My concern is, and I believe state government's role should be, to work toward the highest possible quality and availability of emergency services for all Kentuckians. As the facts indicate, we can and should do better in this most important area of our medical care system.

I believe the regulations established by the Certificate of Need and Licensure Board are realistic goals and represent a quality of emergency medical transportation service that every Kentuckian deserves to have available. It would be unwise and inappropriate, however, if in pursuit of this goal, we disrupted existing services to the people or cause undue hardships on current providers, that have rendered invaluable services for many years and under most circumstances at no charge to the patient.

In order to stabilize this situation and return us to a path of constructive development, I have instructed the Secretary of Human Resources to meet with the board at its regular meeting in early April. He will explore with the board the feasibility of developing a phased plan that provides for levels of services. This will continue to move us toward our ultimate goal of quality emergency medical services, but will also maintain the availability of existing resources.

RIVER REGION
MENTAL HEALTH-MENTAL RETARDATION
BOARD
Louisville / April 4, 1973

So many efforts of the River Region Mental Health-Mental Retardation Board, and other such groups across the state in our twenty-two comprehensive mental health centers, deserve public applause. You work hard without pay and with no other reward than the fact that you are sincerely doing your part to help other people. This knowledge of helping others is, I am sure, personally gratifying. The success that our mental health program has had is, to a large extent, due to this degree of community involvement. Without the awareness and compassion you have shown, the best laid plans from our Mental Health Department would have been stifled.

Kentucky was the first state in the country to establish a total statewide system of comprehensive community mental health centers. The advantage of this early organization is coming to light. With the current freeze on federal funding, many states are now scrambling to open their centers. Most who aren't as far down the road as Kentucky will find huge gaps in their mental health program that will take time to fill—perhaps a dangerously long time.

I am also proud of the leadership coming from our Department of Mental Health in getting us to our present stage of development. Two early decisions in the system of implementation of a statewide mental health program gave the program real impetus for development. One decision was to concentrate more on the staffing of our community centers than on facility construction. This decision was based on the belief that we could use existing facilities to house the staff and concentrate on services. The second decision was to make citizen boards the mental health and mental retardation authorities in each area instead of simply having them act as advisory bodies. The product and responsibility of the local board becomes quite clear. Civic pride and a feeling of contribution to home communities has helped our program immensely, as is evident in the River Region Program.

With an equally strong commitment, we in Frankfort are trying to match your efforts by developing an effective delivery system for services to the people. It is only through this kind of team approach that we can realistically meet the needs of the people. One of the most impressive features of the improved mental health program in Kentucky is the information-screening-referral system at each center. In my opinion, this referral service lies at the heart of each center's basic program. No matter what problem a person may bring to the center, there is a system for putting that person in touch with an appropriate resource to solve the problem. This illustrates what I am talking about when I speak of the need for reorganization of state government so that people won't be pitched from pillar to post when they seek help.

Our reorganization will complement your programs and utilize your experiences in the total context of a statewide system for delivering services to the people. Since our announcement of reorganization of the new Human Resources Cabinet, Secretary Laurel True[1] is finding the initial steps very encouraging. Last month he met with commissioners of the departments which fall under this program area to establish a defined plan for further and complete reorganization. I want you to be aware of our procedures because you are vital to the input which guides reorganization.

Since the first meeting of the cabinet, Secretary True and his staff have been working with commissioners of the various agencies in the human resources area to seek common ground. They have also examined other states' approaches to human resources. This phase has turned up several areas of concern which many of the involved agencies believed warranted attention. Time does not permit me to go into great detail on these concerns, but two central themes emerged. One point bothering agencies is the need for a clear understanding that service systems must be advocates for the user. Too often service systems are found to be advocates only for themselves. This indicates how we must coordinate the referral patterns within the human resources agencies, and it means looking at your information-screening-referral system as it might be incorporated into interagency functions. Another common area of concern is the matter of a unified records and management system. So you can see the mechanics of reorganization, if done properly, becomes a complex undertaking.

At yesterday's meeting of the Human Resources Cabinet, a set of "guiding principles" for reorganization was drafted by agency personnel and the secretary's staff. These guiding principles are consensus statements, derived from their search for common and unique philosophies, objectives, and problems. We want reactions to this document. Here you come into the picture. All of the regional mental health-mental retardation boards will be asked for input. When you look at the guiding principles which should be sent to you in about a week, reflect on them with the same sincerity that you have shown in administering the program here. It is important to have your counsel as we move down the road to reorganization.

With the growing understanding of needs generated by your reactions and other investigations, the cabinet will be looking at the kind of resources each agency has to effectively meet Kentucky's human resources needs. At this point, we will be looking for duplication, as well as gaps, in the services system. The result of all this will be an improved plan for a human resources delivery system. It will utilize existing resources, yet be flexible enough to accommodate future resources and programs in order that the people of Kentucky are properly served.

You have done a fine job in the River Region. In providing the degree of community mental health system that the people of this area enjoy, you have already contributed to our reorganization efforts. To those who administer these programs, the purpose and objectives are quite understandable. You, as individuals committed to the betterment of others, have an intelligent grasp of the desired goals.

But beyond this comes the layman, the citizen who is touched by our efforts, the taxpayer who financially supports our endeavors, the man on the street who finds government confusing and impersonal. I don't want government to be impersonal. Our success can be measured several ways. One of the most important ways is in our ability to reach the layman, the citizen, and the taxpayer, and prove to him that we are on the right road to a far more efficient delivery of services, whereby people are helped through government. This is my desire and, I am convinced, your desire. By working together we will meet the needs of today and lay a strong foundation for the future. The area of human resources touches more Kentuckians than any other program cabinet. So the responsibility is awesome and far-reaching. Yet I welcome the challenge of total reorganization because I see from it the true purpose of government serving people.

---

1. Laurel True, for more information see speech from March 2, 1973, in the Reorganization section, pp. 117–19.

COMMISSION ON ALCOHOL
AND DRUG PROBLEMS
Frankfort / April 13, 1973

IT is a personal pleasure to be with you this morning to express my sincere appreciation for your having agreed to serve on the Commission on Alcohol and Drug Problems.[1] The widespread abuse of alcohol and drugs has created a serious threat to many Kentuckians. Therefore, your duties as members of this commission are more extensive and encompassing than those required of members of the first Commission on Alcoholism established by the legislature in 1952. I hope that among other things, you will stimulate community interest in alcohol- and drug-related problems through such means as encouraging education programs for children and adults; activating programs in and for industry; encouraging awareness activities through churches, schools, and community centers; and utilizing the news media to reach the state's smallest areas as well as the largest cities. As an advisory board, your responsibilities will include advising the Department of Mental Health on matters relating to alcohol and drug problems and assisting that department, the Interagency Council on Alcohol and Drug Problems, and the Division of Alcohol and Drug Abuses with their comprehensive regional and occupational programs.

I am extremely proud that each of you has accepted the appointment to serve on this vital commission. Despite your qualifications and your genuine interest, your job will not be simple. But then, helping people is not always an easy task. Your duties will require time, and they will demand much of your patience, but above all they will require wisdom. You have indicated a willingness to work. I welcome this attitude because to be effective you must work hard, and I expect this to be an effective body. During my campaign for Governor, I pledged that my administration would concentrate on the reduction of alcohol and drug abuse.

In the past sixteen months, federal and state grants have provided money to step up the State Police investigation of drug violators and to allow the State Police to hire additional officers to be assigned to the drug enforcement program which we have done. Drug arrests by State Police during the first year of my administration increased 63 percent over the previous year. Last night, as a matter of fact, State Police carried out a coordinated series of raids at Bowling Green, Ashland, and Owensboro, which resulted in the arrest of twenty-one persons on charges of sale and possession of drugs. As a part of that operation, additional arrests are expected in two other cities within a very short period of time. These arrests will affect three states. This was the culmination of several months of intensive investigation by special units. Their efforts will, in my opinion, be a determined threat against the pusher in particular.

Alcohol problems also have received the attention of this administration. During my first year in office, the Kentucky Department of Mental Health received a one-half million dollar grant for alcohol abuse and addiction, and the Office of Occupational Programs was established in the Mental Health Department to aid troubled employees. You probably won't be receiving public recognition for what you are about to do, but you will reap much self-satisfaction in knowing that you are working to make the Commonwealth of Kentucky a better place in which to live. For this I thank you and pledge my full cooperation.

---

1. See Executive Order 73–274 (March 14, 1973), formation of Kentucky Commission on Drug Problems.

PRESIDENT'S LUNCHEON OF THE KENTUCKY HOSPITAL ASSOCIATION
Louisville / April 17, 1973

To understand the enormous dimensions of health care throughout the country, including Kentucky, a "big business" label is easily drawn from the following: in manpower, the health industry ranks as one of our three largest employers in America; general hospital expenditures, just in Kentucky, run over $300 million; approximately 35,000 persons are part of a $200 million payroll in Kentucky general hospitals. Obviously these data only skim the surface as one considers the magnitude of your profession, and just as obvious is the realization that you do have problems equal in proportion to the size of your industry. These can be divided into two categories—in-shop concerns, and the broader area of statewide and nationwide considerations.

In-shop matters are not unique to a single institution. Rising costs, retention of qualified personnel, the constant demand for more sophisticated equipment, and general management difficulties are no strangers to any of you. They are, nevertheless, becoming more perplexing as time passes. So it is with the development of statewide health care systems. We seem to be in the position of always searching for solutions which will benefit all who look to your institutions for help.

The Kentucky Hospital Association has demonstrated positive leadership through professional input, as we work toward developing a comprehensive health care system for the Commonwealth. Without this attitude, state government would be seriously handicapped as it attempts measures designed to attain health care goals. We are partners in a compassionate cause, dependent upon each other to a great extent.

You participate in self-analysis and examination to measure your own effectiveness, your own responsibilities, and your own contributions. Let us, therefore, examine four general areas of involvement in which the state must act, in my opinion, in developing a comprehensive health care system. First, we must assure that health services and facilities evolve in the context of statewide planning and distribution. I believe Kentucky merits a high grade on its report card because of Regional Health Planning Councils and their degree of involvement at the local level. They are "people-based," which means consumer representation is extensive. Health needs generated from these regional councils are fed to the State Comprehensive Health Planning Council, chaired by a member of your organization. Here the need for health care services and facilities can be coordinated on a statewide level to allow for more efficient and effective distribution.

Comprehensive planning, however, is only good if followed by implementation. The second area of state responsibility, then, is in assuring that the people of Kentucky receive quality health care through the process of licensure. Your organization was a guiding force behind the establishment of the Certificate of Need Board in the last legislature. Kentucky stands among only a few other states combining the planning and regulation of services as well as facilities. This capacity ties together many loose ends which have caused problems in the past. A lack of management-directed planning and of coordination between public and private sectors in health care facilities and services have handicapped Kentucky in prior years. Hopefully, we have stepped upon a higher plateau where vision is not restricted when the care of our fellowman is at stake.

A third area of responsibility of state government in health care is the coordination of medical/health sciences manpower training and education. The Health Sciences Committee of our Council on Public Higher Education is beginning an exhaustive study of the entire medical/health education field in Kentucky. The results of this study should give us the framework of an educational system which will match our immediate and projected manpower needs with a statewide education system to satisfy these needs.

One major phase of this deliberation is the University of Louisville report to be transmitted to the Council Committee. As an integral part of the statewide study, it would be inappropriate for anyone to speculate on it without having all facets of the study, which won't be available until the fall. What we're doing here is a first for Kentucky, and I am confident that we are now doing what is proper and best for all Kentucky. I know that you are as anxious as I am to see what this study turns up. In any case, the movement to coordinate health education in a statewide system based on a need is overdue. I am firm in my commitment to this as a major priority of our state education and health services program.[1]

Finally, the state has an obligation to purchase health care services for certain segments of our society who couldn't otherwise afford them. The best health services and facilities in the world are of no use at all if the doors are open only to a select segment of society. Constant attention to the improvement of our Medicaid program enables government to really begin fulfilling its obligation. Rather than becoming merely a regulatory, impersonal entity—somewhere distant from people—government should provide the life-saving and life-giving services to individuals who, through no fault of their own, cannot adequately care for themselves.

When I see mankind as the recipient of a concerned government, then this office I hold does have meaning and purpose. In all of these areas of responsibility, I see the state as a working partner with groups such as yours. Without a partnership, we risk surrender to a system of health care that would be unrealistic and inefficient. To borrow an old expression, we can boil down the attitude, which I contend we must have, into three brief ideals: "Coming together is a beginning; keeping together is progress; working together is success."

---

1. On May 11, 1974, Governor Ford spoke at the dedication of the Family Practice/Student Health Service Building at the University of Kentucky. In his remarks he stated that this facility and its programs would produce "more effective academic programs and better preparation of students, improvements in the distribution and effectiveness of health manpower in the

state; and improvements in Kentucky's overall health care delivery system." Later the same day Governor Ford spoke in Louisville at the dedication of Norton-Children's Hospital. In his remarks he stated, "It [Norton-Children's Hospital] promises to improve the delivery of service, not to mention reducing the potential for various problems which have threatened the quality of health care across the nation—problems such as rising costs, inadequate facilities, personnel shortages, and fragmentation of services. Thousands of children, not only within the Falls Region Planning Council boundaries, but from the entire state, will benefit from this new facility and especially those professionals who now have the working conditions and tools to provide the highest quality care." "And soon this complex will be joined by the new U of L Teaching Hospital, a significant addition to the medical center." Neither of these speeches appears in this volume.

AMERICAN PUBLIC HEALTH ASSOCIATION SOUTHERN BRANCH AND KENTUCKY PUBLIC HEALTH ASSOCIATION
Louisville / May 11, 1973

BY this point in your conference, you have probably heard so much about accountability that it is coming out of your ears. I hope that my comments today will not come under the classification of overkill. My charge is to tell you something about what legislative bodies expect in public health accountability. As a former state senator, and because the Kentucky State Budget is an executive budget, I believe that I have a feeling for what this aspect of accountability means to you. In effect, of course, you are ultimately accountable to the people. So am I, and so are your legislators. In reality, however, this accountability is achieved through a chain of command to which you have to appeal for approval and funding of your projects.

Let's talk for a minute about how this works. Although we generally refer to our form of government as a democracy, it is, in fact, functionally a republic. That is to say, people don't participate directly in the process of public decision-making, but they "hire" representatives to make critical decisions for the masses. These "managers," then, employ people and arrange resources to deliver the services which they were elected to perform. Periodically, the people evaluate these "managers" to see if the bureaucracy has delivered the services they expect from their government. If it has not, new managers are hired! It is my opinion, then, that public health services are accountable to the people, but through the normal political and governmental channels. I am sure that you have heard something like this in the many sessions you have had in this conference, but I think it is important to emphasize the point.

Elected officials, "hired" by the people, have to look closely at the situation of limited resources and unlimited needs to determine just what kind of a mix of services they want to buy for the people. In the past, public health, like other public services, has been operating pretty much on the basis of a line-item approach to fund programs. With the pressure of more and more to be done, and fewer resources with which to do them, the people making decisions are asking, and rightly so, these questions: What needs to be done? How will you do it? How much will it cost? And will the job be properly accomplished? Line-item budgeting only tells us what it costs to run an agency, not what it costs to solve a problem or the cost-benefit relationship of running a program. In buying the best mix of services to meet the needs of the people, we can no longer rely on line-item decision-making.

So, what is it, then, that your legislative bodies expect in public health program accountability? First, they expect you to have a good network of intelligence to identify and locate public health problems. Obviously, if they don't know what the problems are, how serious they are, and where they are, they can't be expected to fund program solutions. Secondly, they expect you to have considered as many alternative solutions as possible in your program design. In every problem, there is more than one way to get from point a to point b, and your legislative bodies are going to want to know why you have chosen the solution you did. You in the public health profession should be very much aware of alternatives. We generally look at health services in terms of treatment and maintenance, but you have been very successful in selling the preventative approach as a viable alternative.

Thirdly, your legislators are going to ask you what difference it will make to the health of the people if they buy your program. They are going to want to see measurable objectives, and they are more interested in measuring incidence of disease than they are in measuring the number of inoculations. They want to know what the real program impact will mean to achieving a healthy society. Finally, they are going to expect you to present your programs in a language they can understand. We in state government are often accused of using a bureaucratic language which confuses the public. I am sure that there is a language unique to your profession too, but you have to realize that legislators are generally not going to be familiar with it. Communication is central to understanding and if we can't understand what it is that you are trying to do, we will have a more difficult time deciding what services we select.

We all share the same goal, achieving a healthy society, but you must realize that it is only with the correct mix of services that we can achieve the goal. Legislative bodies are going to be more discreet in the future when they buy services to meet the people's needs. They are going to look for crossovers in services and levels of responsibility for meeting health needs. You have to keep in mind that they must consider their own alternatives in choosing the optimum mix of services for the people to whom they are accountable. It becomes your task, then, to present to these people programs which will be defensible in light of their accountability to the people. You are in a competitive partnership with elected officials to prove that what you do really does make a difference to the health of our society. This kind of relationship will create a better system for public health services in the future.

BLACK LUNG BENEFITS
Frankfort / May 21, 1973

On February 15 of this year, I requested of Labor Commissioner James R. Yocom[1] a full analysis, including recommendations for action, of the black lung benefit program. That report was submitted to me on April 16, and this administration has been at work on acting on and implementing its recommendations. Newspaper articles and editorials, as well as items from a report of the Legislative Research Commission, have given rise to a good deal of speculation with respect to filings by black lung claimants.

A series of actions are now in process. First, meetings are being held with representatives of Kentucky's underground coal mine operators. They are for the purpose of emphasizing the importance of having miners file black lung claims with the federal government prior to July 1, 1973, which is the deadline of Part B of the Federal Coal Mine Health and Safety Act. Such claims, if awarded by the federal government, will be paid from general U.S. Treasury funds. For claims filed after July 1, awards at the federal level will be charged back directly to the responsible mine operator. Therefore, this is one obligation which the operators must assume for their own protection. The state and the United Mine Workers will cooperate in this most important effort. Second, we are arranging for conferences with representatives of the states of Pennsylvania and West Virginia for the purpose of identifying common interests in a problem which is before these three largest coal-mining states.

Third, a process of negotiating with the federal government on a variety of interrelated functions and responsibilities regarding black lung has begun. These meetings will deal with dust-level standards for control of black lung and the need to have those standards accepted as a defense in black lung claims; a more thorough data exchange system on claimants to avoid administrative duplication; and the federal standards for states' reassumption of full responsibility in this area. Fourth, the Commissioner of Labor has been instructed to create a task force for coordinating all of Kentucky's activities in this area.

The problem here does not lend itself to simplistic solutions. We are not the only people who face it, nor are we the only ones who have studied it. In the surrounding states and in Washington much effort has been spent on understanding and resolving the enormous social and economic impact of black lung. The LRC proposal examines one aspect of the problem. Unfortunately, the proposal as the news accounts have represented it is not likely to be the complete solution for claims filed. It is true that black lung benefits can be "absorbed" by Social Security Disability Benefits, but only if the claimant meets the stringent disability standards of the Social Security Administration. And very few do.

Under the black lung workmen's compensation disability test, a miner is judged disabled if he is unable "to compete to obtain the kind of work [he] is customarily able to do, in the area where he lives, taking into consideration his age, occupation, education, effect upon [his] general health of continuing in the kind of work he is customarily able to do." Under Social Security, however, the test is whether or not a man is unable to work at all, without regard to geographic inconvenience or even a shortage of employment opportunities. Therefore, the typical black lung beneficiary will not be eligible for Social Security disability. Some will, and in those cases, we will take full advantage of that opportunity. Coal is vital to Kentucky. It means jobs, taxes, and a sound economy. It is not just the province or the responsibility of a few, and this view will guide our actions in the coming months.

1. Press release. James R. Yocom, for more information see speech from October 18, 1972, in this section, pp. 177–78.

CAMPBELL COUNTY
SENIOR CITIZENS ANNUAL PICNIC
Melbourne / August 1, 1973

Two years ago, I stood before you as a candidate for Governor. On that occasion, which I remember well—a senior citizens picnic as we are again enjoying—I outlined programs which would be implemented if the people elected me. This afternoon I return, prepared to report that what once were promises offered are now promises kept.

I came to you in 1971 for political support. You responded, not just at the polls but also in your willingness to lend wisdom to a cause which would benefit the senior citizens of our great state. Together we have taken more positive steps than ever before in programs now helping a major segment of our population that is growing in size—heading toward the 400,000 mark. I appreciate this invitation in order that you might be brought up-to-date in some straight talk where facts are facts and where the evidence of commitments which have been kept should be presented.

Kentuckians voted for the Homestead Exemption Amendment which I publicly supported, and during the 1972 General Assembly this amendment was implemented. The law provides for compensating tax rates to aid those sixty-five and older who own property.[1] But we wanted to do more as pledged, and we did more. We passed legislation setting up the Kentucky Housing Corporation to aid in financing, constructing, and rehabilitating residential housing for persons and families of limited incomes. Last October I announced the appointments to this important working body.[2]

One of the greatest areas of concern for all Americans, but especially for our elderly, is health care. We have made significant improvements in this crucial area. One landmark piece of legislation was the bill establishing our new health facilities and services Certificate of Need and Licensure Board. This bill provides for the orderly and systematic development of health facilities and services based on local needs, as interpreted by local citizens, consumers, and health personnel. It gives us the ability to assure that all facilities, present or planned, will be best suited to the needs of older Kentuckians by establishing reasonable standards for personal care facilities, intermediate care facilities, and mini-homes which had heretofore mushroomed without adequate inspection or supervision.[3]

The Drug Formulary Council established under our Generic Drug Law is preparing lists of drugs and pharmaceuticals with their generic names, equivalent to brand name drugs. This permits the pharmacist to substitute the less expensive generic drug for a brand name product. Many older Kentuckians and others have to pay a significant portion of their fixed incomes for drugs and pharmaceuticals, and this program will lighten the burden.[4] For the first time, there is state licensing and regulation of hearing aid dealers. Now we can prevent the fly-by-night dealers with selfish motives who prey on our people.[5]

Something I didn't promise the last time I spoke to you was the establishment of a Research Center on Aging at the University of Kentucky. This was not in the picture then. On March 15 of this year, I announced support of a proposal put to us by the Eleanor and John Young Brown, Jr. Foundation to establish such a center. They agreed to contribute $1 million toward the establishment of the center if the state would match this amount with state funds and provide enabling legislation. I have agreed to present this to the 1974 General Assembly with the strongest support possible from my office to see it funded. We have the chance to become a national leader in aging research. The benefits can be far-reaching.[6]

With the crunch of an inflationary economy and a fixed income, the elderly are finding themselves caught between a rock and a hard place. We have made some gains in easing this problem through the programs I have already mentioned. But more direct means have also been implemented. October 1 last year, we took the 5 percent sales tax off groceries as I pledged we would. We had already managed to remove this inequity from medicine in the 1970 session. But with the food tax removal the impact on those with a fixed income is obviously greater. With food prices skyrocketing, this is a significant benefit—if you had to pay 5 percent on the groceries you take home now, the bite would hurt a great deal more![7]

Two years ago I also touched upon inequities in the Social Security and Public Assistance regulations which particularly hurt older Kentuckians. The principal reasons for our concern were the regulations which affected people getting both Public Assistance and Social Security payments. Basically, the situation which existed forced a drop in Public Assistance payments at about the same rate as the increase in

Social Security. Last November I announced that we would use funds already existing in the Department of Economic Security which were freed up by a change in federal regulation and prudent fiscal management to remove the inequity in our payments.[8] Over 40,000 Kentuckians would have been penalized by the increased Social Security payments had we not used our money to bring up both those who were on Public Assistance and those who were not. We achieved the equity required by federal law without penalizing our people.

The Commission on Aging is launching the federal nutrition program for older Americans and should increase the scope of this program in the future. Today, for instance, we announced receipt of a $1.5 million federal grant which has been sought for a long time.

Whenever new directions are taken, snags develop, despite how hard one tries to prevent them. We have experienced snags, but we are going to reorganize the snags out! Another campaign commitment I want to add to this report deals with this very problem and falls under the heading "Reorganization." Reorganization of state government is progressing well. Within the next sixty days our package should be complete. Those phases of reorganization which are already in existence clearly indicate that government can be more responsible and responsive. In our planning for human resources, we have given, and will always give, the highest possible priority to expanded coordination to meet the present and future needs of senior citizens. Our intent is to have clear sailing, rather than snags, in all programs affecting senior citizens by giving older Kentuckians a chance for the quality of life they have earned. Every element of the program is designed to aid men and women like you who have spent a productive lifetime helping make our state and country the wonderful land it is today. The reorganization blueprint looks good. Our anticipation is high that government will become more personal than ever before because this is the primary thought in designing reorganization.

I honestly believe, just as you have witnessed our carrying out of those programs proposed two years ago, you will witness continuing vast improvements in the coordinated efforts to have the best program on aging in America. We are going to continue pushing for implementation of the programs I have already mentioned, as well as to seek workable solutions for other problems which are frustrating senior Kentuckians. I intend to have the Ford administration remembered for those things which were done, and not things which were only promised. And I believe the fruits of our labors are quite visible.

James Russell Lowell, the famous American statesman and writer, once said, "All the beautiful sentiments in the world weigh less than one single lovely action." With your help, we will make this the period in our state's development known as "the era of caring through action."[9] Older people throughout the state and country have worked hard to give younger generations the privileges and opportunities we have. It is only just that we work equally hard to see that these people who have done and are still doing so much for us are not neglected in the conduct of government.

---

1. See an act "proposing an amendment to Section 170 of the Constitution of Kentucky, relating to property exempt from taxation," which was approved March 30, 1970. *Acts of the General Assembly of the Commonwealth of Kentucky, 1970,* Chapter 186 (H.B. 147), pp. 682–83. See also an act "relating to revenue and taxation," which was approved March 27, 1972. *Acts of the General Assembly of the Commonwealth of Kentucky, 1972,* Chapter 285 (H.B. 162), pp. 1333–38.

2. See an act "relating to the financing of lower income housing and providing for the creation and establishment of the Kentucky Housing Corporation," which was approved March 16, 1972. *Acts of the General Assembly of the Commonwealth of Kentucky, 1972,* Chapter 70 (H.B. 27), pp. 266–87. The appointees mentioned here were named in Executive Order 72–1009 on October 30, 1972. They included Donald Bradshaw, Ed Hancock, Laurel True, John Ross, Damon Harrison, Al Brinkley, John Polk, James Shuck, Pat Gish, Ernest Pepples, Mrs. Hortense Young, Robert Hoff, and Mrs. Donald Ballusen.

3. See an act "creating a State Board of Medical Licensure and removing medical and osteopathic licensure from the Department of Health," which was approved March 25, 1972. *Acts of the General Assembly of the Commonwealth of Kentucky, 1972,* Chapter 218 (H.B. 244), pp. 900–918.

4. See an act "relating to the use of generic names for prescription drugs," which was approved March 27, 1972. *Acts of the General Assembly of the Commonwealth of Kentucky, 1972,* Chapter 126 (H.B. 427), pp. 558–62.

5. See an act "relating to hearing aid dealers and fitters," approved March 10, 1972. This act created the Board of Licensing Hearing Aid Dealers and Fitters. *Acts of the General Assembly of the Commonwealth of Kentucky, 1972,* Chapter 48 (H.B. 70), pp. 145–58.

6. For information on the Browns and their proposal, see the press conference from March 15, 1973, included in this section, pp. 185–86.

7. See an act "relating to revenue and taxation," which was approved March 15, 1972. *Acts of the General Assembly of the Commonwealth of Kentucky, 1972,* Chapter 62 (H.B. 337), pp. 241–55. Governor Ford clarified the provisions of this act in a statement on September 21, 1972, which is not included in this volume. He noted that prescription medicine and farm machinery would not carry sales tax.

8. This announcement was made by Governor Ford at a Frankfort press

conference on November 3, 1972, which is included in this section, pp. 178–80.

9. James Russell Lowell, (1819–1891), Cambridge, Mass.; author, educator, diplomat; editor of the *Pioneer* (1843); corresponding editor of the *National Anti-slavery Standard* (1848); editorial writer for *Pennsylvania Freeman*; professor at Smith and Harvard; editor of the *Atlantic Monthly* (1864–1872); United States Minister to Spain (1877–1880); United States Minister to the Court of St. James's (1880–1885); author of numerous works. *Who Was Who in America: Historical Volume, 1607–1896* (Chicago, 1967), p. 393.

LOUISVILLE CHAMBER OF COMMERCE
Louisville / November 27, 1973

ONE of the most refreshing and personally satisfying outcomes of my first two years as Governor has been the development of a new cooperative spirit among state government, your local governments, and the private sectors so important to this area. When, as a candidate in 1971, I said Louisville and Jefferson County could become a mecca of progress, I did so with the full realization that state government would have to demonstrate its commitment to this end. State government would have to perform, rather than delay. Pledges to the citizens of Louisville and Jefferson County would have to be more than idle political rhetoric. An attitude of concern would have to be real instead of window dressing.

If state government walked its half distance or three-quarters distance, I felt sure you would be there to meet us. Time and time again, this has been the case. On numerous occasions, the people of this area have benefited because a working partnership evolved. The end result has created a ripple effect throughout Kentucky, for as Louisville and Jefferson County experienced good fortunes, so did all Kentucky. As our largest metropolitan center, this area reaches out in service, in progress, and in stability, bringing rural and urban Kentucky closer together in a healthy atmosphere.

Let's continue our successful ventures with the same attitude that has prevailed over the past two years. There is more to accomplish, and by working in concert, the strides already taken can be maintained, perhaps even lengthened. Society's growth, its expectations, and its just needs serve as reminders of the responsibilities each of us in this room share. Now another opportunity presents itself. Health care, medical training, and adequate facilities for both have been registered in your minds and in mine for a long time. This issue is complex and doesn't lend itself to hasty action, shots from the hip, or isolated decision-making. Again, what we do or do not carry out in this area affects other portions of Kentucky. This is especially true with the topic of medical support.

Recognizing a need is secondary to adequately satisfying that need. I believe the course we are now taking together will satisfy a pressing need. In preparing for this action, we were careful. As a candidate for Governor, I promised the people of Louisville and Jefferson County and, in fact, all Kentuckians that I intended to find a way to build a regional teaching hospital facility—a facility that would not only serve a regional need but also provide a teaching hospital for the great University of Louisville Medical School which has served all Kentucky so well in the past.

When I took office, I directed the Council on Public Higher Education and the appropriate health planning bodies to evaluate the total health training and delivery system in our state. I asked them to recommend to me a course of action best for all Kentucky. Based on exhaustive studies and their recommendations, I am here to announce that I will include in the Governor's next biennial budget the sum of $31 million for a University of Louisville teaching hospital. I am also here to recognize the assurance given me by the judge of Jefferson County, Todd Hollenbach, the mayor of Louisville, Frank Burke, the mayor-elect, Dr. Harvey Sloane,[1] as well as community leaders, that shared financial and other support is guaranteed. The $6 million from each the city and county, the continuation of indigent care financing, and the transfer of property from the city add to this overall package.

The problem to which we have addressed ourselves has been a problem since the mid-fifties. But this is a symbol of what can be done when all of us work together in behalf of others. Good things can be accomplished for the benefit of people. I want to commend Judge Hollenbach and Dr. Sloane for their leadership in refraining from making this program a political issue during the recent campaigns. It was necessary that the council approach this question in an unbiased manner, totally free from any pressure, and this was the case.

---

1. Louis J. "Todd" Hollenbach III (1940–   ), Democrat from Jefferson County; attorney; elected Jefferson County Judge, 1969. Telephone interview

with James Smith, Office of the County Judge, June 29, 1976. Frank Welsh Burke (1920–   ), Democrat from Louisville; attorney; member of Kentucky House of Representatives, 1957; United States House of Representatives (1958–1962); mayor of Louisville (1969–1973). *Who's Who in America, 1974–1975* (Chicago, 1975), 1:438. Harvey Ingalls Sloane (1936–   ), Democrat from Louisville; physician; mayor of Louisville (1973–   ); director, Park DuValle Neighborhood Center, 1971. *Who's Who in Kentucky, 1974* (Atlanta, Ga., 1974), p. 476.

OUTWOOD REPLACEMENT
Frankfort / June 21, 1974

THE Commonwealth of Kentucky's responsibility to those less fortunate, who through no fault of their own must have special care and treatment, is a complex and ever-changing program of government.[1] Our primary concern must always be the individual, the person receiving competent professional service in an environment conducive to that service. Each is entitled to no less.

In Dawson Springs, the Outwood facility has been uppermost in the minds of many throughout the study,[2] review, and planning by me, the Department for Human Resources, and the General Assembly. There have been rumors and speculation during a lengthy period of intense deliberation, as we worked toward a final decision for the improvement of patient care. Certainly the community and area involved have been interested and concerned about the future of Outwood. I believe we now have the best solution: best for the mentally retarded residents there, best for the economic and employment base at Dawson Springs, best for the taxpayers who support such facilities, and best for the future direction of service to Kentuckians who utilize special care centers.

First, there will be no termination of mentally retarded facilities at Dawson Springs. There will, in fact, be vast improvements through third-party service by a professional organization specializing in the mentally retarded and mentally handicapped. The agency or provider selected will work in conjunction with the state and be supervised by our Department for Human Resources. Outwood's present facilities will continue for two years, with certain physical improvements. During the next two years, the state will continue whatever financial support is necessary for the Outwood patients because patient funding is in the executive budget. However, during that period, a planned replacement for Outwood, to be built on the present site, will become a reality. Let me emphasize one point here: this is a permanent program at Dawson Springs.

We, therefore, will have obtained the finest resources in terms of facilities and professional standards for the mentally retarded at Outwood. There are numerous advantages. Patients will receive better care in modern facilities through a private organization which will generate federal funds not available now. The new and improved program and facilities will make these funds possible, thereby expanding care advantages to the patients. Private capital will be used to replace the facility rather than taxpayer funds. Employees choosing to remain at Outwood will have minimal adjustments to make compared to closure of Outwood. Additionally, the potential now becomes much greater for employment opportunities and benefits. Volunteers in the Dawson Springs area, who are so important to this program, will be able to continue their valuable service to patients.

The state will seek proposals from qualified, proven, and interested organizations who provide this particular program. It is my intention to seek the advice of the Kentucky Association of Retarded Children and the Department of Human Resource's Institute for Children, and others, for the purpose of identifying potential service providers. The idea of third-party contracting is not new in matters pertaining to human resources. This approach has proven extremely beneficial to all involved—the patients, their families, the state, and the taxpayers. I spoke of this in my budget message to the General Assembly. Certainly this solution is in compliance with legislative recommendations, and I am pleased that we are prepared to move forward very rapidly in behalf of others.

---

1. Press conference.

2. On October 1, 1973, Governor Ford issued a statement announcing a study to "determine the best procedure to incorporate superior medical care for patients" at the Outwood and Western State Hospital facilities. The Governor also stated "that Outwood is an institution in need of extensive, and expensive, repairs; the facility is far inferior to Western." This statement is not included in this volume.

UNITED AUTOMOBILE WORKERS
RETIREES PICNIC
Louisville / September 23, 1974

I APPRECIATE this invitation today which gives me the opportunity to talk straight with you about this state's efforts to bring about a better life for our senior Kentuckians; where facts are facts, and the evidence of commitments that have been kept should be presented. As a candidate for Governor in 1971, I outlined programs which would be implemented if the people so desired. Today, some thirty-two months later, I can report that what once were pledges offered are now pledges kept. Together, we have taken more positive steps than ever before in programs now helping a major and very important segment of our population. Let's take a look at what we—you and I—have been able to accomplish.

The Homestead Exemption Amendment, which I publicly supported when it was before the people for a vote and helped in its implementation by the 1972 General Assembly, provides for compensating tax rates to aid those sixty-five and older who own property. The 1974 Legislature strengthened this act by prohibiting increases of assessments on homestead-exempt property. We established the Kentucky Housing Authority to aid in the financing, construction, and rehabilitation of residential housing for persons and families of limited incomes.

One landmark piece of legislation was the bill establishing the new Health Certificate of Need and Licensure Board. This has given us the ability to assure that all facilities, present or planned, will be best suited to the needs of older Kentuckians by setting reasonable standards for personal care facilities, intermediate care facilities, and mini-homes, which had heretofore mushroomed without adequate inspection or supervision. Legislation was enacted establishing a Generic Drug Law. Pharmacists are now permitted to substitute the less expensive generic drug for a brand name product. Many older Kentuckians and others have to pay a significant portion of their fixed incomes for drugs and pharmaceuticals, and this program will lighten the burden.

For the first time, there is state licensing and regulation of hearing aid dealers. Now we can prevent the fly-by-night operators with selfish motives who prey on our people. We took the 5 percent sales tax off groceries as promised. With food prices skyrocketing, think of the difference this has made.[1] We added $7.6 million each year in the

1974–1976 executive budget to support the 20 percent of Kentucky's aged, blind, and disabled who will no longer be eligible for federal aid.[2]

The budget also provides service to 8,000 more senior citizens. It responds to requests from small communities and rural areas for prevention of dental disorders. We are also willing to spend a quarter of a million dollars more to assist our elderly citizens at home rather than put them in institutions. I know how very much our libraries mean to you and all other Kentuckians. This is why my executive budget for the next biennium contained $11.7 million so that Kentucky's stature in library services could continue to grow. A great portion of this appropriation was to replace lost federal funds. And $1 million in matching funds was provided for the establishment of a research center for the aging at the University of Kentucky. We have a chance to become a national leader in researching the biological aspects of aging, and the benefits can be far-reaching.[3]

We have attacked some of the problems which are frustrating senior Kentuckians and found workable solutions. I believe the fruit of our labors are quite visible. Yet we all realize more needs to be done, especially at the federal level where your voice is not being heard. Since I want to be your United States Senator, you deserve to know what some of my priorities for older Americans will be. No single group is feeling the crunch of double-digit inflation harder than you. This is of foremost concern to me, and the first step that must be taken is tax relief and tax reform. We have to lift the burden off the retired, low and middle income taxpayers, and plug the tax loopholes of the rich and huge corporations, just as we have done in Kentucky.

Social Security benefits should reflect the country's rising cost of living. Obviously those of you who receive $146 a month know it doesn't. We need to look at the benefit level and we need to look at raising the amount of money that a person can earn and still not have to take a cut in benefits. In addition, there is an urgent need for strengthening the administration of the Social Security system because it is the economic mainstay of the majority of older Americans. Another high priority of yours, which I support, is federal funding for transportation subsidies for elderly riders. A lack of transportation deprives many elderly citizens of shopping for food or clothing or the ability to seek employment and medical care.

I am aware of plans to phase out all Title III programs and place them under Title VI of Social Security. This would mean the termination of many programs which are very important to you and replacing them with a cash increase in Social Security payments. Like you, I desire a flexibility in these services, where you have the option of an increase in payments or taking advantage of the programs offered. If elected, I will work toward this end.

I, for one, believe older people throughout the state and country have worked hard to give younger generations the privileges and opportunities they have. It is only right that we work equally as hard to see that these people who have done and are still doing so much are not neglected by their government. This has been the basis of our relationship in the past. And I pledge this is the way it will continue to be when I am in the United States Senate.[4]

---

1. For further details on the Homestead Amendment, the Kentucky Housing Authority, the Health Certificate of Need and Licensure Board, the Hearing Aid Dealer licensing and regulation, and the removal of sales tax, see speech from August 1, 1973, to the Campbell County Senior Citizens Annual Picnic in this section, pp. 200–204.

2. For further information see Governor Ford's speech at a Frankfort press conference on Public Assistance Adjustments on November 3, 1972, included in this section, pp. 178–80.

3. More details on the Research Center for the Aging can be found in a statement issued by Governor Ford on March 15, 1973, included in this section, pp. 185–86.

4. Governor Ford's opponent in the 1974 Senate race was incumbent Senator Marlow W. Cook.

EDUCATION

KENTUCKY EDUCATION ASSOCIATION
Louisville / April 14, 1972

WHEN any school term concludes, there is an evaluation process by teachers, relative to the achievements of students. I have frequently heard educators remark about this most difficult period, because they are conscious of a duty which involves their appraisal of a total performance. Anything less is not ethical, and I say without reservation, it is easy for a Governor to find empathy with such a task.

As Chief Executive, it falls my lot to weigh carefully the total budgetary and legislative programs, both of which have tremendous impact on our entire society. Every citizen deserves equal consideration from a responsible Governor, whether he or she be lawyer or laborer, truck driver or teacher, personnel clerk or pupil. Therefore my job prompts occasions for others to sit in judgment. Yet there is, I firmly believe, only one logical, proper, and intelligent approach. That is, I must do as you do in the classroom, which is to determine one's grade on the basis of every factor.

While campaigning for Governor, I submitted to the teachers and school administrators in Kentucky an outline of priorities I believed, and you said you believed, would be necessary for the public elementary and secondary education system. In our first session of the General Assembly, all but two of these priorities were realized. One of the two was partially attained. In this address, I want to mention several subjects vitally important to the education of our children. Again, referring to the campaign, I stated numerous times that several different groups, all of them citizens of Kentucky, were interested in professional negotiations. I also stated that when the committees which represent these groups join in basic agreement on the content and process of such a professional negotiations bill, its passage would have my full support.

Not only did most of the superintendents, principals, and school board members disagree with the classroom teachers as to the content and procedure for implementing the bill but also a large number of teachers throughout Kentucky expressed disapproval. Since there was a polarization involving the various segments of education, it became obvious that the conditions of my campaign promise had not been met. Since this was the situation during and immediately after the General Assembly, I decided that the profession, and those who must always be given first consideration—the children—would be better served if the bill were vetoed. I stand by my campaign commitment. When you, in concert, resolve the issue, I will act accordingly. It has become even more obvious, since the veto, that there indeed is a wide range of philosophical differences about professional negotiations. My mail, and other forms of personal communication, emphatically reflect this atmosphere.

Between twenty and thirty large school systems now have professional negotiations planned and worked out at the local level. If professional negotiations are as desirable as some claim, and if it will improve schools as some advocate, I strongly recommend that superintendents, school boards, and teachers at the local level begin immediately to make arrangements for a correctly structured professional negotiations bill, which could be acted upon under conditions conducive to favorable action. Since there is widespread disagreement, it seems that the affirmative response will come only after teachers and administrators, at the local level, join to decide how they would work together, the conditions of their negotiations, and the general overall recommendations for implementation.

In the very early days of a new administration, we do find substantial attention given to your profession. The taxpayers of Kentucky, in supporting education, ask that the wisest application of funds possible be guaranteed. In line with my campaign commitments, and those needs reflecting the direction of education in Kentucky, the new biennial budget merits recognition. Approximately 90 million additional dollars, all state money, is provided in this budget. The preparation of any budget for the Commonwealth dictates an understanding of what monies will be available, and how these dollars are to be distributed, in consideration of the many services state government must provide all its people.

Education fared well! I want to illustrate with eleven of the many reasons why this is the case. First, the foundation program law has been continued and expanded. This law is worded in such a way that normal, natural growth occurs each year. Implementation of this regular growth for the next two years will cost the state $5,888,000 the first year and $7.6 million the second for a total of approximately 13.5 million additional dollars. This money is for expansion alone. Second, the cost of $3,000 life insurance for every certified member of the teaching profession will be 2.5 million additional dollars for the coming biennium, another pledge kept. Third, the 6 percent increase in salaries for each staff member, allotted under the minimum foundation program law, means we must provide $12.7 million additional over the natural and normal growth the first year, and 26.5 million additional dollars the second year for a total of 39.2 million additional dollars in salary increases alone.

Next, the increase of 6 percent for current expenses for each unit in the foundation program will be $2.5 million the coming year, almost $5.5 million the following, for a total of 7.9 million additional dollars in the biennium. Fifth, capital outlay of $100 for each allowable unit will cost 3.1 million additional dollars the first year, and 6.4 million additional dollars the second. This totals $9.5 million over the past biennial budget. Also, the cost of added units for vocational education and classrooms for exceptional children will be $2.8 million the first year, and $6.8 million for the second, a total of over 9.5 million additional dollars in the two-year period.

One of the principal programs to which I have been committed, and my seventh point, is vocational education. In order to take care of an emergency item for the current year, $600,000 was added to the budget for beginning construction of a vocational-technical institute in Louisville. Additional funds will be secured when needed to pay for equipment for buildings already under way. Eighth, approximately $6.8 million has been added to the budget for schools for the deaf, the blind, and for financing the new school for the mentally retarded.

My ninth point is implementation of kindergartens—again a campaign promise. To finance a task force conducting intensive study and planning for the kindergarten programs, $50,000 has been allocated for the first year. One hundred units in kindergarten have been allocated for the second year, at a cost of $1 million. Tenth, approximately $25 million will be spent each year to provide for the free lunch program. Federal requirements were changed last year. Now we must place approximately one million additional matching dollars every year in the budget to secure federal funds.

Last, approximately $1.5 million has been placed in the teacher retirement system to pay for prior services; $1.9 million was added for salaries of teachers already retired; and $6.9 million was budgeted in current matching programs for the two years of the biennium. Our records show that this is the largest appropriation to the retirement system ever given. This is the partial attainment to which I have previously referred, and the more than $10 million for retirement is a strong indicator of what can come in the future.

I have offered many figures. Yet they represent the multiple efforts of state government in behalf of your profession, and certainly in behalf of children. Looking at our total effort, we have moved aggressively forward in many areas long neglected and in others with much more substance than before. The emphasis in my first budget shifted to elementary and secondary education which I believe has been on the short end for many years. Looking at the total picture, more than fifty bills received the necessary support you wished. This is further proof of responsiveness. If you add all of the gains, you will recognize that pronounced advancements are now under way. I see no reason why we can't continue this thrust on the total front.

In conclusion, I want to emphasize two sets of figures. The first is Kentucky's tax effort to elementary and secondary public education. In the first biennium it amounts to $610 million. This is general fund money alone! Adding other funding, you are receiving $818 million in the next two years. But even more important, it is the undisputed fact that this administration went much further—by $90 million—to do more for teachers, students, and the entire system than in the last two years of the previous administration. There were many strong demands for this $90 million extra, and I made a value judgment that it should go to you. The benefits of this new money can be far-reaching; I trust you will help guarantee its impressive potential.

KENTUCKY WESLEYAN COLLEGE
Owensboro / May 13, 1972

SOME of you who will leave today perhaps are thinking, "Well, it's all over now. We've studied, we've done our classwork. We've written our papers and passed our examinations. Now let's accept our diplomas and go." This is fine, of course, but you might think a bit more, and say, "Well, it's all over now, but what really did all of this mean?" With enrollments up 98 percent in Kentucky colleges and universities since 1961, and with 43 percent of last year's high school graduates in the state going on to college, this becomes an important question for all Kentuckians. Just what impact does this college experience have on an individual?

One of Mark Twain's characters had an opinion worth mentioning. "Training is everything," he said. "The peach was once a bitter almond; cauliflower is nothing but cabbage with a college education." Training does mean a great deal. Few would dispute the impact of a college education. But it isn't everything. The day you stop learning, you stop living! A serious scholar of American higher education described the major benefit of a college education as the "ultimate improvement in occupational and intellectual life, resulting from changes in skills, knowledge, and attitudes." To see what these changes might be, we must use the social scientist's microscope. We must accept the dangers of generalization and analyze the impact of a college education by looking at general characteristics of college graduates, as opposed to those who have not had the college experience.

A very recent publication by the Carnegie Commission on Higher Education indicates that individuals with college degrees do indeed differ in many respects. They point out that college is but one influence on an individual's life. But that survey indicates it is a significant influence. One of the most obvious areas where your college education will show its impact is in your occupational outlook. Here are some findings which may be of interest. How will you fit in the next several years?

You will tend to be more satisfied with your job, more highly paid, and less subject to unemployment. In fact, you stand to earn over $230,000 more in your lifetime than will a high school graduate and over $390,000 more than the person who dropped out before the eighth grade. Males, twenty-five years old, with four years or more of college make about $4,000 more annually than high school graduates and over $8,000 more annually than those who didn't finish the eighth grade. This difference can only become greater with the increase in college graduates entering the job market. Nearly 60 percent of the men will hold white-collar jobs, and nearly 78 percent of the women who enter the employment market will select white-collar opportunities. There are indications that your college experience will also show an impact on your family life.

One very interesting statistic indicates that only 13 to 16 percent of the men with college degrees never get married. You girls run a little faster, and only 12 percent will miss the altar. Women with college degrees tend to work and have fewer children. It might be interesting to note here that the balance between men and women graduates is changing significantly. In 1960 only 34 percent of the graduates were women. In 1970 this increased to 40 percent and the percentage will increase more. You will tend to be better consumers and family managers because of the college experience. You will have happier marriages and be generally more optimistic about the future. College graduates tend to see a more realistic relationship between the bad and good aspects of life, where nongraduates concentrate on the stresses of life. College graduates also have different attitudes toward reading and television than do those who did not graduate from college.

You will probably watch fifty-nine minutes of television each day as opposed to the ninety-five minutes a day by nongraduates. When you entered college, the favorite three TV programs for male college graduates were "Laugh-in," "NFL Football," and "Mission Impossible." The nongraduates liked "Bonanza," "Gunsmoke," and Dean Martin. The college women liked "Laugh-in," Dean Martin, and "Family Affair," while their nongraduate counterparts liked "Bonanza," "Family Affair," and "Laugh-in." Would "All in the Family" replace at least one of these programs for both groups today?

You will probably read forty-one minutes a day of all types of materials as opposed to twenty-four minutes a day by nongraduates. Your favorite commentary magazine will probably be the *New York Times Magazine,* your favorite news magazine will probably be *Time,* your favorite general interest magazine will probably be *Reader's Digest,* your favorite man's magazine will probably be *Playboy* and your favorite woman's magazine will probably be *McCall's.* That is, if you fit the norm.

Four years of college may also have an impact on your health. You will use health services more than nongraduates. You will also tend to have less psychological distress than the nongraduate, but you will suffer more nervousness. Don't worry about the nervousness, though. You will also have fewer breakdowns. Many might question this, since the business/executive world is ulcer prone.

Your personal life will show impact from four years of college. You will be more likely to attend church than the nongraduate. Approximately 83 percent of the college graduates are churchgoers, as compared to 81 percent of the high school graduates and 73 percent of the dropout population. You will be more active in community activities than the nongraduate. You will probably be more liberal and tolerant in your attitudes toward, and in your relations with, other individuals and groups than will the nongraduate. I hope all of us become more tolerant in the future, except in the case of our own lives. Tolerance with personal complacency will offer society only a bad check! You will tend to show less prejudice, although you may feel it the same as the nongraduate, because you are more receptive to changing values and beliefs. You should also show greater rationality in your values.

Finally, your experience with college will make an impact on your political attitudes and activities. Recent surveys indicate that over 90 percent of the political elite on all levels are college graduates. Every once in a while, though, a poor, country boy from Yellow Creek slips by. That's the danger in generalizing! You will also tend to be more active in your support of political candidates. A significant majority of the college graduates will vote in national elections except during off-year congressional elections. I sincerely hope that you will take an active interest in politics, because only through greater involvement of all the people can politics truly serve the people.

I have generalized a great deal today about what changes the impact of a college education may have on you. I think, however, that time will show that there has been a great impact on your life because of your college experience, and that your life experiences will be changed, at least a little, because of it. A final point—there are exceptions to the averages. Men and women rise up every day in this world, overcoming adversity, kicking out the obstacles of misfortune, and proving to themselves, as well as others, that self-determination is a product of man rather than society. This class will become part of a future study, as will others graduating in 1972. While I wonder what the subsequent results might be, I have no fear of them. I congratulate you for the effort which has brought you here today. I especially want to congratulate those who have helped you along the way, because you were helped, even by many you will never see or know. Do the same for others, even those you may never see or know.

COOPERATIVE OFFICE PRACTICE
PROGRAM LUNCHEON
Frankfort / May 25, 1972

THERE is an old proverb which says that the sound of one hand clapping produces no noise; a good statement to consider when weighing the value of any cooperative venture. Many hands must have come together in the organization and development of your Cooperative Office Practice Program because it has been heard. You probably know that I have had a working experience with the program and still do. Betty Lee began working for me when I was Lieutenant Governor and came with us to the Governor's Office. Then she changed her name to Betty

McDonald. Donna Clark is currently helping my secretary, Helen Price, with dictation, transcription, and general office work.[1]

I believe that other supervisors in the Cooperative Office Practice Program will back me up when I say that there is very little risk in accepting a student from this program. You are fine workers and quick learners. The great thing about this cooperative program is that all participants benefit from it. The employer not only gets good help and a chance for a good full-time employee when the student graduates, but he also has the opportunity of making a positive contribution to the educative process. The school gets expertise from the employer in designing a realistic classroom curriculum, which helps eliminate a cause for school dropouts and for a lack of interest and motivation in the student. You, of course, stand to gain the most from this cooperative program. You receive an excellent combination of classroom training and on-the-job training as well as an excellent opportunity for employment after school. We have several state employees who are graduates from the Cooperative Office Practice Program.

Perhaps the most important aspect of your program is that it puts vocational education in the proper perspective. Our society has a tendency to overemphasize the value of everybody's having a college education. I think college is important, and it can be a fine experience for the right individual. The point is, however, that vocational education is equally important and should be so recognized. No organization can function efficiently without highly trained people at all levels. You should be aware that your vocational training will be a great boon to advancement in your permanent jobs after graduation. Advancement is not automatic, of course, but you have an advantage over those who haven't had the training which you just completed.

---

1. Betty Lee McDonald (1952–   ), Franklin County; member of secretarial staff when Ford was Lieutenant Governor and Governor; participated in Cooperative Office Practice Program. Donna Clark (1953–   ), participated in Cooperative Office Practice Program and assisted Helen Price; has since moved to Denver, Colorado. Helen Price (1931–   ), Franklin County; executive secretary to Governor Ford; for official appointment see Executive Order 71–14 (December 8, 1971). Information obtained from Senator Ford's Louisville and Washington offices, August 10, 1976.

LINCOLN FOUNDATION, INC.
Frankfort / August 28, 1972

I AM pleased to announce this afternoon that the Commonwealth of Kentucky is transferring the Lincoln Institute property in Shelby County back to the Lincoln Foundation, Inc., at no cost to the foundation. The property originally was deeded to the state in 1947 by the institute, for the use and benefit of the state Board of Education. Until July 1, 1971, the institute was operated and maintained as a state educational institution. In 1971 the Commonwealth leased the buildings to the Louisville Board of Education and the United States of America for the establishment and operation of the Residential Manpower Center.

Anytime government can exercise a civic-minded philosophy, which is in the best interest of the Commonwealth and its people, it should be willing to take appropriate action. Because the Lincoln Institute no longer serves its original educational purpose to the state, I feel that it is only fair and reasonable that the property be reconveyed to the foundation.

According to the transaction, the foundation will maintain and operate the Whitney M. Young, Jr., Birthplace Memorial House as a museum, library, and shrine to the memory of the late Whitney M. Young, Jr.[1] The foundation also agrees to obtain and preserve on the premises for the accessibility of the general public for viewing the publications, artifacts, and other items of the late Mr. Young. At this time, I am very happy to return the land to the foundation.

---

1. Whitney Moore Young, Jr. (1921–1971), social work administrator; dean of the School of Social Work, Atlanta University (1954–1960); executive director, National Urban League, New York (1961–1971). *Who Was Who in America with World Notables, 1969–1973* (Chicago, n.d.), 5:805.

CHAMBER OF COMMERCE
GOVERNOR'S TOUR
Lexington / October 5, 1972

KENTUCKY today has many opportunities as well as many problems. Problem-solving is a major priority of the Governor's Office, as well as of all state government. It is essential that we use all of the resources available to us in solving the perplexities that affect Kentucky's present and future. The intellectual depositories of our universities must be brought to bear in this direction. Government at the state and local level needs the knowledge and perspective of these institutions, as a basis for decision-making and control.

The extent of the involvement of the University of Kentucky, in activities that affect state government, is already considerable. This is gratifying and encouraging. Staff support for the Governor's Council of Economic Advisors is furnished by the Office of Business Development and Government Services of the College of Business and Economics. A new master's in public administration program will provide graduates with know-how in government. The Bureau of Government Services is expanding its range of assistance to local governments. Basic information for planning, decision-making, and management control is being produced. Employment and personal-income projections, an input-output model, are prime ingredients of this support.

The College of Engineering is researching methods to remove sulfur and methods best fitted to gasification and liquefaction of Kentucky coal. The Kentucky Geological Survey produces water resources, minerals, geological mapping, and topographical data used by many state departments. The Water Resources Institute is a key part of our total water-resources planning and development effort. The role of the College of Agriculture and the Cooperative Extension Service in improving farming methods is well known. Best known is the valuable assistance given to communities in their development programs by extension resource specialists. The farmer, we must realize, is a businessman too. Since he is faced with the unfortunate situation of buying on an open market and selling on a closed market, he needs expert help to maintain a livable margin between investment and profit.

These are but a few of the areas in which the university, state government, and the business community are working in close partnership. The list should and will grow to the benefit of all. Yet, in my opinion, we have only begun to take full advantage of the wealth of talent and resources available through our state universities. This is especially true here at the University of Kentucky. I also want to point out that nothing much will happen if state government, the business community, and the academic community are not working together in a cooperative partnership.

As a businessman who has become involved in state government, I am well aware of the importance of government programs realistically fitting the needs of the business. We can't sit in our offices in Frankfort and dream up programs that we think are needed. We have to plan on the basis of research done by the university and problems posed by industry. You will recall that we have, on this tour, heard of industrial problems, just as we have seen industrial growth. We are all responsible parties in this partnership. Government, business, and higher education have to work in concert or our best hopes will be nil. If the universities don't involve the business community in research and curriculum design, they may not get the expertise necessary for a progressive operation, and they may have to face future manpower problems that could have been averted.

If the state doesn't involve both of these groups in planning government programs related to business and industry, they risk an oppressive rule that will benefit nobody. Both the university and business community have much to gain from involvement with state government. This is not only true with research and development, but in the area of services as well. So let us today not merely applaude the achievements we have made to date, but let's look to the challenge ahead. We must all face up to our responsibilities in this partnership to make Kentucky an attractive place to do business and an economically healthy place to live.

INTRODUCTION OF ADOLPH RUPP
Louisville / November 20, 1972

WHILE thinking about the accomplishments of our honored guest, one fact emerged which deserves consideration. We aren't paying tribute just to a basketball coach. Adolph Rupp[1] has excelled in a variety of endeavors. Had he chosen to pursue another career, I honestly believe his friends and peers would have extended acclaim equal to the purpose of tonight's affair. What if Adolph had decided to stick solely with a business career? My gosh, as a part-time farmer-businessman, he has demonstrated an uncanny knack for achievement in the economic arena. Who knows how much wealthier he could have become? Or what if he had gone on stage as a comedian? Surely he would have rivaled Bob Hope, Jack Benny, Jackie Gleason, and the other truly great funny men of our time.

I can see Adolph as Dr. Rupp, the world-famous psychologist, on par with Sigmund Freud! I can see Adolph as General Rupp. Any man who developed the offense he did on the basketball court would have been a perfect counterpart to Patton's thrust through Germany! And, let's put a minister's robe on this man. He has preached so many effective half-time sermons during his career that there's no question about his ability to bring out the best in all of us.

Few individuals have been blessed with so many sons. Even fewer have seen those young men achieve so much glory during college, as well as beyond. Yes, in theory, Adolph has successfully practiced the arts of business, psychology, humor, farming, journalism, politics— and the list is almost endless—in addition to coaching and teaching. It would be redundant if I recounted the athletic accomplishments of this man. Yet, in my opinion, it would be inappropriate if I did not briefly dwell on his many other contributions to mankind and mankind's society.

Adolph didn't teach only shooting, defense, ball-handling, and physical conditioning. These lessons were temporary in view of the ultimate standards he wanted others to attain in life. Rather, he taught self-control, motivation, courage, responsibility, dependability, and the value of inner toughness. He taught the true meaning of victory, of free enterprise, and of unselfishness. He taught this so well that generations to follow will profit from his works.

When Adolph Rupp proved to the world that in basketball nothing good comes without personal sacrifice, he left a legacy for men and women to follow. In other words, he rekindled the pioneer spirit and applied it to a sport in desperate need of his early mastery. The Rupp message was simple and direct: "I'll show you how it's done if you want to succeed." He did; they followed; and basketball's greatness in America and the world today attest to his philosophy. It is a distinct pleasure for me to introduce our guest of honor, a man of a million capabilities, not the least of which is delighting any audience with his wit and wisdom. Coach Rupp, it's now your turn to speak. There have been a lot of comments already, but judging from the comments in your behalf, I'm sure you haven't minded waiting.

---

1. Adolph Frederick Rupp (1901–   ), Lexington; head basketball coach at the University of Kentucky (1931–1972); named Southeastern Conference Coach of the Year (1963–1966, 1968–1972); National Coach of the Year, UPI, AP (1951, 1959, 1966). *Who's Who in America, 1976–1977* (Chicago, 1976), 2:2714.

KENTUCKY ASSOCIATION OF SCHOOL ADMINISTRATORS
Louisville / December 11, 1972

To most people, education is only visible in the classroom. As administrators, you know the vast superstructure that functions behind the scenes to help the classroom teacher accomplish his or her job in the best possible way. Integral to this superstructure is the partnership that exists between state government and the school systems throughout Kentucky. I know you are interested in what we are doing in Frankfort as it relates to your situation as school administrators. I will attempt today to cover several issues over which many of you and your fellow educators in the state have expressed some concern.

First, on the issue of revenue-sharing, we are not planning a special session of the Legislature to allocate the state's share of federal revenue-sharing funds coming to Kentucky. As I have said before, the dispersal of these funds will be made on the basis of statewide needs, in the context of Kentucky's total financial resources and demands for services. If a special session were called at this time, our legislators would be expected to allocate this new money without an opportunity to study its best use. I think any commitments from me at this time would be premature.

I want to assure you, however, that I do appreciate the importance of education to the future of the Commonwealth. Dr. Ginger[1] will be working closely with us in developing the 1974 to 1976 education priorities, and I feel sure we can provide improvements in the areas which are of concern to you. A good example of what coordinated planning across disciplines can do is the State Comprehensive Occupational Information System and the development of a statewide total system for vocational education. The information system will provide a data bank of information on Kentucky's manpower demands, present manpower supply, and educational resources which will help in annual and long-range planning at the local educational agency level.

What this amounts to is a supply-demand inventory of all persons trained or educated within the state of Kentucky, matched to available and projected employment in the public and private sectors of the state. This kind of information has to be gathered and coordinated from many sources. It serves as a good example of what can be done when coordinated planning is applied to a particular problem—that of manpower and education. With the information provided by this system, vocational education in Kentucky can be built in a total concept of facility construction and curriculum planning that will be tailored to real needs. It will provide the concrete facts on which to base decisions for future directions of education in the Commonwealth. Even though the occupational information system is compiled on a statewide basis, its real use will be at the local level. It will allow the development of a total system from training to placement through the allocations of resources to meet local needs. The basic unit in this system is the county.

The impact of vocational education on the future of our state is impossible to overestimate. A reliable study has indicated that by 1975, 81 percent of all jobs in the country will require a vocational education type of skill. This may come as a shock to a society where the majority of people think of education as one through twelve and possibly four years of college. We are a college degree-oriented society. But if we are aware of the trends to vocational skills, we can prepare for an educational system that will meet realistically the needs of employment opportunities. Without your cooperation and assistance in the development of these two types of vocational schools in the state, however, we will not be able to put together a statewide program that is needed to give Kentucky a truly progressive education system. We desperately need your help because we are not financially able to put one of these schools in every county of the state.

Vocational education can also have an impact on other state programs. One example is in helping reduce the welfare rolls in Kentucky. If we are to make any significant inroads on reducing these welfare rolls, we must provide training opportunities for employable skills. Through our vocational education program, we have the ability to do this. There will be no hope for offering the people now on welfare the dignity of gainful employment until they are trained in a skill.

Another way educators have shown the effectiveness of coordinated planning and program development is in career education. Through this conceptual approach to education, curricula can be planned in a system that combines the student's awareness of his capabilities and interests with a realistic understanding of the work environment he will face after school. Kentucky presently has several career education projects funded under the vocational education act, but it will be a while before this is a statewide involvement. I am convinced that career education is the way of the future, because it produces graduates who enter the work world with a realistic expectation of what they will be doing and equipped with the kind of training that will benefit them best.

Speaking of career education, I am sure that you here this morning are also concerned about those who have made education their careers. These are the teachers who have given many years of service to the Commonwealth and have reached the age of retirement. Briefly, I want to mention three areas of teachers' retirement in which we have made improvements during this first year of my administration. We are aware that there needs to be an equity of benefits between all retirement systems for public employees in Kentucky, and we expect to work toward this goal.

First, $1.5 million were appropriated during the last Legislature to keep the teachers' retirement system sound and to assure that the system can properly provide all currently authorized benefits. Second, nearly $2 million were appropriated to cover a 5 percent cost-of-living increase for all retired teachers. This money will be expended over the present biennium. Third, we increased the minimum annuity to assure all retired teachers $5.00 for each year of service. This will affect several thousand retired teachers who were getting less than the $5.00 minimum annuity payment before we made the change. Finally, let there be no question, I am committed to the thirty-year retirement provision brought up during the last General Assembly. I intend to support the funding needs to make this provision a reality, and I will do all I can to see that equity is reached in this area of teachers' retirement.

All of the topics that I touched upon today are part of the structure I mentioned at the beginning of my remarks. If we are to assure our citizens the best possible educational system, we must see that this structure is sound and productive. I hope that all of you will help us at the state level to see that we meet our education responsibilities in a coordinated effort, that will give our people the kind of schools they need.[2]

---

1. Lyman Ginger, for more information see speech from September 13, 1973, in the Reorganization section, p. 155.

2. Governor Ford also addressed the Kentucky Association of School Administrators on August 5, 1974. This speech is not included in this volume, but much of the same data is in his speech from February 9, 1974, which is included in this section, pp. 242–45.

COMMENTS TO KENTUCKY
CONGRESSIONAL DELEGATION
Washington, D.C. / February 21, 1973

I'M glad that we can all get together this morning to discuss the President's proposed budget as it affects Kentucky's educational programs. My concern is that we do not permit changes in program funding based upon false assumptions, the assumption that local governments can pick up the slack with general revenue-sharing money and the assumption that major federal programs can be abruptly terminated without having serious program effects on state and local governments. The gentlemen who are with me will provide specific program comments.

As we are all aware by now, the proposed federal budget outlines a radical and important change in federal-state-local financing for the delivery of public services. The federal government, like any other government or business, must (indeed should) change its programs as the needs of the public shift. Of course, these changes may occasionally mean that programs which are not effectively operating must be reduced or totally eliminated. However, we must be extremely careful that in drastically altering federal programs, the state and local governments are provided with adequate alternatives for meeting public needs. Major changes in funding, and major restructuring of public delivery systems, cannot be accomplished overnight and certainly cannot be accomplished by impounding current year funds appropriated by the Congress.

In providing for changes in the financing of programs, we must not act so hastily and haphazardly that adequate alternative funding sources are not immediately available to provide for essential services. When categorical grant programs are abolished in favor of special revenue-sharing, we must be sure that enough time is provided for an orderly period of transition. Changes in the funding of programs must not be allowed to cause needless breakdowns in services to the public, simply to ensure an arbitrary spending ceiling by a specific date.

However, there are other areas of concern besides the time factor, specifically education. It is impossible to assess the total effects of the President's proposed changes in education, and the impact of special education revenue-sharing on the reduced or terminated programs, since the draft of the law has not been released. We do know several important programs in Kentucky will be drastically affected, or terminated, even with special revenue-sharing. The three program proposals which best illustrate our concern are 1) the termination of all federal aid for public, local school, and college libraries; 2) the abolishment of EDA;[1] 3) the failure to provide adequate support for student loan programs.

The elimination of categorical aid programs for public libraries evidently rests upon the assumption that all community library programs will be continued with general revenue-sharing. State and local officials across the country were told by Mr. Nixon's administration that general revenue-sharing was being provided to relieve the fiscal crisis which state and local governments have been facing. We were told that general revenue-sharing was not to replace existing categorical aid programs. Yet all library aid has been terminated, since libraries are permissible areas of expenditures under general revenue-sharing. Local public libraries could conceivably be funded, but most cities and counties have already committed their general revenue-sharing funds for drastically needed improvements in other essential governmental services. They had no advance warning that library aid would be eliminated. Additionally, we have been told that local governments may not use any of their general revenue-sharing funds for educational operating and maintenance expenses. Where does this leave Kentucky's local school libraries, since they will lose $1.4 million? Why have the library aid programs not been combined into the special education revenue-sharing proposal, with adequate funding provided?

An abrupt abolishment of EDA will have a severe impact upon Kentucky's ability to construct vocational education facilities. It was anticipated that Kentucky would receive approximately $9 million over the next two fiscal years for state and local vocational facilities. If EDA is not phased out in an orderly process, the facilities which we expect to construct this year and next year will possibly be delayed for another two to three years. We are aware that the budget proposes to shift EDA-type funding to rural development and urban development programs; however, it must also be recognized that the delay in creating new programs and the establishment of administrative mechanisms could require as much as two years.

I approve of, and appreciate, the President's support in requesting the full authorization of $959 million for fiscal 1974 and a supplemental appropriation of $622 million for fiscal 1973 to fund the basic opportunity grants program authorized by the education amendments of 1972. I feel that the full funding of the basic opportunity grants program is a step in the right direction toward assisting the needy students of our state to attain a college education. However, it appears that along with the recommendation of full funding for the basic opportunity grants, the President has disregarded a provision of the act which barred the awarding of these grants in any fiscal year, if the appropriations for supplemental educational grants, work-study payments, and direct student loans were less than specified by law.

The President's proposed budget for 1974 does not satisfy these minimums. Although the basic opportunity grants program is laudable, Kentucky will take a step backwards without support of the companion programs. With no money available to supplement the basic opportunity grants from the scrapped National Defense Student Loan Program and the Educational Opportunity Grant Program, many students may be left marooned with only half the aid they need to attend college—and no way of raising the balance.

---

1. "The Economic Development Administration (EDA) was established September 1, 1965, by the Secretary of Commerce to carry out most of the provisions of the Public Works and Economic Development Act of 1965 (79 Stat. 552; U.S.C.), as amended. . . . The primary function of EDA is the long-range economic development of areas with severe unemployment and low family income problems. It aids the development of public facilities and private enterprise to help create new, permanent jobs." *United States Government Manual 1973/74* (Washington, D.C., 1973), p. 130.

ANNUAL CONVENTION OF THE KENTUCKY SCHOOL BOARDS ASSOCIATION
Louisville / March 13, 1973

PROBABLY by now your heads are swimming because of the many speeches, discussions, and interchanges of ideas which have come from this conference. Well, misery loves company, so I join you in wonderment over so many words, since there seem to be none left for me! Such a situation helps a speaker adhere to the proven rule—be brief and be seated.

This wrap-up session does provide us with the unusual situation of a common relationship between the person up here and you in the audience. We have all had the experience of putting our names on the ballot to seek approval from the citizens. The people have said yes, and we now find ourselves in the position of returning their confidence by administering for the benefit of others. Perhaps the greatest temptation of any officeholder is concentrating on short-range gains that generate immediate attention and bring political rewards before we leave office. This is the easy route and it often reaps the most applause for our ears, but it is not the correct way to meet our obligation to those who have given us the opportunity to govern. Obviously, we do have immediate and ongoing needs that must be attended to if we maintain continuity in the areas we govern. Yet I am convinced that if we don't keep one eye on the future, our decisions eventually shortchange the governed. This is the relationship of mutual responsibility that we must consider in the context of down-the-road activities.

In your school systems next fall, a new group of young boys and girls will begin their formal education. They will be excited, anxious, scared, inquisitive, mischievous, and energetic. They will be products of rich homes and poor homes, fast learners and slow learners. They will be healthy, and some will not be healthy. They will come to school with full stomachs and empty stomachs. Some will have advanced preparation, others will enter a totally different environment. These are your children; they are my children.

When they leave the systems you are governing now, it will be 1985. Think of it! Twelve years from now, these young people who are being placed in our trust will step onto another plateau of the world— the world of 1985—one year beyond the fictional world George Orwell created in his novel *1984*. Let us hope the world he imagined does not result, but we can do more than hope. We have an opportunity to help ensure against this and, at the same time, create a better opportunity for them if we properly plan ahead. What will their world be like a dozen years from now? What can you do to prepare the child for it who enters your system next year?

One of the first considerations is the job market. We have seen that as early as 1975, over 80 percent of the jobs in Kentucky will require some vocational education type of training. This means long-range planning of facilities and curricula to meet this situation. In Kentucky we are trying to meet this need with new facilities, both for high school and beyond. One goal is to establish institutions that are within a reasonable distance of every citizen of the Commonwealth. The para-medical vocational education center planned for Louisville has long-term implications, both through the training of young men and women and through the results of that training which will benefit others of all ages. We are also trying to plan for the types of vocational programs needed in the state through a statewide information system for vocational education. This system will provide the data necessary to match programs with manpower demands.

Another inroad is the career education program. This system combines the student's awareness of his capabilities and interests with a realistic understanding of the work environment he will face after leaving school. There are other job-related factors to consider. In the last ten years the increase of women workers has exceeded the increase of male workers. Although the trend is leveling off, we are now more aware than ever before of the impact women have on occupations.

Again looking to the future, we must also face the challenge of preparing our charges for the greater amount of free time that will confront them. With the experiments of a four-day workweek, common sense dictates attention to the threat of idleness. In short, it becomes critical that students seek individual fulfillment, and this will be taught in our schools as well as in our homes. The self-realization of each student in his or her role as a contributor to the wealth and life of society becomes another growing responsibility of education, especially as we view the years ahead.

Society is becoming more complex. It is increasingly difficult to forecast the future, due to the rapid changes affecting our lives. Not until 1901 did Marconi send a weak radio signal—the letter "s"—from Cornwall, England, to Newfoundland. Today, we send clear pictures and voices through outer space and think nothing of it. In 1903 aviation history was made at Kitty Hawk. Before that, man had attempted to fly like the birds and had failed. Just look at what has been accomplished since he finally succeeded. Look also at our attitude toward change, toward advancement, toward technology. We began sending men to the moon, and in a very few years this feat has moved to the inside pages of our newspapers. In one sense, we're so used to change, we consider it matter-of-fact. In another sense, there is so much change it does astound us. There is additional change occurring every hour on the hour it seems. How does all of this affect the student leaving your institution in 1985?

First, new methods to prepare that student for change are mandatory. At the same time, schools must be capable of offering that preparation, and this means anticipating the needs of tomorrow, a most difficult task. Schools must equip their students just now beginning an education to adjust to rapid advancement while at the same time not forgetting the basic foundations which have always led to knowledge. We must concentrate on the caliber of teachers who will take the six-year-old, turn him over to another, and another, until that individual is transported through an educational process of stability and excellence—an educational process that should undergo the impact of change as much as any other facet in life.

As we look to curricula and what to do with our responsibilities in education, the most important point to remember is that we are not only preparing future jobholders, but we are preparing young people who will live in a much closer society. While we are shrinking the physical distances between people through technology, communication, and transportation, the critical interdependence between individuals is increasing. The number of international conferences held in 1900 was slightly over 1,000. That figure will increase at least nine times by 1975. What will it be in 1985? Obviously, our youth must be able to cope with the problems of living as a world community and not as an isolated community. This, in itself, poses serious considerations as to future plans for education. If we are to live in a world of peace, in a society free of prejudice, ignorance, and fear, there is only one hope— we must educate future generations to live together in an environment of mutual acceptance and cooperation. Your position of leadership is where it must begin. As the governing body of our school systems, you have to look to the future and what you can do to prepare the graduate of 1985 for the world of 1985.

The people have spoken through the ballot. They have entrusted us with the responsibility to ensure a climate of peace, harmony, and economic stability in which they, and future generations, may live and grow. At a time when the distance between the governed and the governing has created a severe credibility problem, it is even more critical that we prove to the people that their trust in us is warranted. We can do this if we set aside the temptation to build early monuments to our administrations and instead carefully lay the foundation for a better future for generations to come. We have to do this with the trust that those who follow our administrations will do the same, so that we can stop playing catch-up, a game we seem to perpetuate by short-range goals. Let's return the public trust with an eye on the present to take care of immediate needs, but let's also keep the other eye on the future. Remember: The future of the present is in the past—that the future of the future is in the present.

NATIONAL ELEMENTARY SCHOOL GUIDANCE CONFERENCE
Louisville / March 29, 1973

It is always easy for me to welcome people to Kentucky. I am proud of this state. Its Indian name translates "land of tomorrow," and one fictional character in an early novel said that heaven must be a Kentucky of a place. Even though it was land of tomorrow to the Indians, it is a land rich with history today and a land of extreme promise for tomorrow. Often referred to as "daughter of the East, and mother of the West," Kentucky played a key role in the development of our country.

This role yielded many firsts for our state. The first suspension bridge in America spanned the Ohio River from Covington to Cincinnati in 1887 and served as the model for the Brooklyn Bridge. The first Trappist monastery in America was founded at Gethsemani in 1848. The first permanent non-Indian settlement west of the Alleghenies was at Harrodsburg. One of the leading Protestant denominations in the country, the Disciples of Christ (or Christian Church), was formed near Paris. The first packaging of garden seeds and the invention of the broad broom came from the Shakers at Pleasant Hill, and the first public gathering to be illuminated by electricity was in Louisville during 1883. Even the first telegram sent by Alfred Vail to Samuel Morse was related to Kentucky; it announced the candidacy of Kentuckian Henry Clay for the presidential election.

As educators, you might be interested to know that Kentucky's

Legislature was the first in the nation to authorize a system of free public schools, in 1794, and William Holmes McGuffey began writing his famous readers while teaching at Paris. Even though it is interesting to talk of past accomplishments, and it's normal to brag when you get the chance, I know that it is the future to which we owe our time and efforts. For it is the future that our children and their children will inherit. If we don't keep this in mind and plan far ahead, we will have failed our duty as administrators and educators.

The elementary school counselor team plays a key role in performing this duty. You are the first professional group to bring the child into his educational experience and to begin the foundation that will determine what kind of future the child will have. Approaches to child guidance may differ from state to state, but we all have the same goals: to help our children grow through a better understanding of themselves and the world in which they live, to a productive and rewarding future as adults. This is an awesome responsibility. Each one of us has to realize that we are not going to do it all on our own.

Cooperation is the keystone of success in every goal-directed professional program. I referred to the elementary school counselor team earlier because it is just that—a team effort. There are many members of this team—counselors, counseling educators, state and local guidance supervisors, professional education associations, school administrators, government agencies, teachers, and parents. Each has his or her own role, but all are interdependent in giving the child the kind of educational experience that is necessary for development. I am not leaving elected officials out of this team either. It is the responsibility of the governing officials in this country to provide leadership, encouragement, and lines of communication for this and other team efforts in our conduct of offices. We have to look beyond the term of our administrations, just as you look beyond the time you personally work with a child, in making the kind of decisions that will have lasting impacts. Ours is not the task of telling you what to do, any more than yours is the task of telling the child what to do. We, rather, can only help create the machinery that will enhance your performance in the best manner possible. Just as you are trying to open the doors that will allow a child to pass into other years unafraid and prepared, governing officials should be opening avenues for the professional, parent, and teacher to give the child a continuity of training in his development.

I am proud that it was in this administration that the Kentucky pupil guidance services were funded by the state for the first time. This seems even more important in the face of what is happening in Washington, for if we had not taken this step it is quite possible that we may have lost this program. It has been said many times that children are our most important resource, and as such, they are our most important responsibility. Yet the impact of our responsibility comes to the front in later years. If we give children quality guidance now, we should expect quality adults later.

I hope this conference is a success, and I hope you enjoy your stay in Kentucky. Although I realize that this kind of meeting doesn't allow much time to visit the many historic sites and areas of natural beauty Kentucky has to offer, I urge you to return when you can stay longer. We are observing the state's bicentennial celebration in 1974, and, if you can't come this year, you won't want to miss our two-hundredth year festivities. You will always find a warm welcome in every region of Kentucky.

MURRAY STATE UNIVERSITY COMMENCEMENT
Murray / May 4, 1973

FOR at least sixteen years, and longer for some who are graduating today, words of wisdom have rained upon you—at times like a gentle shower, and at other times in torrents! By tradition, your last official role in this university is the participation in an exercise where there is one more lecture. I promise a brief address![1]

Thinking about your classroom experiences, you will recall that to reach this plateau, this conferring of a degree, you had to be on target. Right answers on examinations, the proper response to questions in class, and the ability to convey your correct procedures to those judging you indicated achievement. Yet there is another dimension to individual accomplishment which is often restrained by the fear of failure. So if I could pass along one piece of advice, it would be this: Don't be afraid of making mistakes. You're going to be wrong many times between now and the day you die. You're going to make mistakes. If you don't, your existence will have no purpose, no meaning, no promise, for you will have no initiative, no enterprise, no interests. One's errors are the portals of discovery. Refusing to try something new, or different, is shutting the door to success, to progress, and to revelation.

What is most important is your attitude toward mistakes. Let them be honest. Let them be sincere. Let them be worthy of the goals you strive to attain. If these conditions prevail, then it will be unnecessary to seek excuses for your mistakes. Logic finds an inherent danger in accepting human error as "one of those things that's bound to happen." Errors are bound to happen, yes, but what of the individual who has no spirit to challenge his committed faults? In my opinion, the right to stumble is matched by the responsibility to recover. There is no immunity to personal error. There is only the obligation to profit from error. History teaches us that great men and women refuse to falter because of their mistakes. Henry Ford forgot to put a reverse gear in his first automobile. Thomas Edison once spent over $2 million on an invention that proved of little value. A writer once penned, "He who makes no mistakes lacks boldness and the spirit of adventure. He is the one who never tries anything new. He is the brake on the wheels of progress." However, you will never succeed beyond the mistake to which you are willing to surrender. Only when nothing is done to prevent, or correct, your mistake does it become a serious, unjustified blunder.

In this nation are many freedoms—even the freedom to go broke. There is the freedom to be wrong, so long as the end does indeed justify the means. Whatever your future profession might be—science, education, engineering, business, agriculture, or any of the others—remember those who have preceded you and succeeded did not succumb to the fear of making a mistake. On the contrary, they drove on, recognizing the eventuality of error and at the same time with the realization that discovery or success comes only when one freely pursues it.

Hopefully, my admonition is clear. By cautioning you against a reluctance of doing something for fear of mistake, I do not want to leave the impression that mistakes can be accepted as commonplace. Hermann Goering, in his instructions to the Prussian Police, said in 1933: "Shoot first and inquire afterwards, and if you make mistakes, I will protect you." Such instructions have no foundation of decency. But if you set your sights on what is honorable, you will overcome mistakes through personal advancement and triumph. The weak, and meek, take one of two routes. They live in horror of mistakes, thereby permitting a useless life, or they cling to fragile excuses for their mistakes. The bold, and energetic, have a singular maturity about mistakes. They recognize the probability of many and benefit from the few which do occur. You are in one of those categories right now.

---

1. Governor Ford gave similar commencement speeches on the following occasions: May 12, 1973, Western Kentucky University; May 13, 1973,

Eastern Kentucky University; June 6, 1974, Owensboro High School. These speeches are not included in this volume.

INSTALLATION
OF DR. JAMES G. MILLER
Louisville / October 5, 1973

IT is a privilege to be part of this historic occasion. Dr. James Grier Miller[1] is eminently qualified for the responsibilities and challenges of his new position. He is a graduate of Harvard University, the Harvard Medical School, and holds a Ph.D. in psychology. His career has touched many corners of life: author, editor, educator, psychologist, psychiatrist, social scientist. In every area, his record has been one of excellence.

He comes to the University of Louisville at a most important time in the school's proud history. U of L, founded in 1798 as the first municipal university in the nation, is old and rich in tradition. Like so many other institutions of higher learning, U of L must cope with a rapidly changing period, dictated by society's anxiousness, ambitions, and aggressiveness. Three years ago we welcomed the university into the state system of higher education, opening the door for greater opportunities which can meet the increasing needs of preparing men and women for what I believe will be an exciting future. Many of our state's doctors, dentists, social workers, engineers, lawyers, business leaders, public officials, teachers, and other professionals owe a large debt of gratitude to U of L for offering them an educational opportunity.[2]

In recent years, the school has emerged as a major regional center for scholarship and research, yet has continued to fulfill its responsibility to our state's largest community, retaining its involvement in public service. New areas of academic study, campus expansion, and increased enrollment are healthy indicators of the University of Louisville's past and present growth. Since we are observing the celebration of the university's one hundred and seventy-fifth anniversary this year, it is both fitting and proper to reflect with considerable pride on the accomplishments of the past. It is also a time to recognize the increasingly important role U of L can play in meeting higher education needs of the future.

I am confident that U of L will continue to progress in many directions under the leadership of Dr. Miller, just as it did under his two immediate predecessors, Dr. Woodrow Strickler and Dr. William Ekstrom.[3] He has already demonstrated a personal concern for the welfare of the university and its students. He understands the dual role he can play in shaping the university's growth as both administrator and educator. He made this clear when he said, "I was unwilling to become president unless . . . I was acceptable as professor." We are fortunate that he did accept. And now it is my personal pleasure to introduce the sixteenth president and newest professor of the University of Louisville, Dr. James G. Miller.

---

1. James Grier Miller (1916–   ), Louisville; president of the University of Louisville (1973–   ); numerous other positions at other universities. *Leaders in Education*, 5th ed. (New York, 1974), p. 753.

2. On June 9, 1972, at a press conference, Governor Ford stated, "Seventeen million dollars more in state support from the administration will go to U of L these next two years, to properly give the institution its rightful place in our system of public higher education." Then on February 6, 1974, at another press conference, Governor Ford made the following statement, "Beginning with the 1970 budget on which I fought to increase general fund support for the University of Louisville, the state has provided over $44 million, and I have recommended another $73.3 million for the next two years—a total of over $117 million the city and county would have to pay. They chose to terminate $1.8 million provided each year of the next biennium. Someone has to assume fiscal responsibility to assure that service at the University of Louisville can be maintained at the level recommended by the Council on Public Higher Education. I accept that responsibility." Neither of these press releases are included in this volume.

3. Woodrow Mann Strickler (1912–   ), Louisville; president of the University of Louisville (1968–1973); numerous other positions within the University of Louisville. *Leaders in Education*, 5th ed. (New York, 1974), p. 1057. William Ferdinand Ekstrom (1912–   ); acting president of the University of Louisville (1972–1973). *Directory of American Scholars*, 6th ed. (New York, 1974), 2:177.

MADISONVILLE COMMUNITY COLLEGE DEDICATION
Madisonville / October 18, 1973

KENTUCKY's community college system has covered many miles of progress since its creation eleven years ago. Time has proven the wisdom of the 1962 Legislature, which abandoned the extension center philosophy in favor of the community college network. The number of community colleges in Kentucky has grown from five to thirteen in the last ten years.

Though we are here today to formally dedicate the youngest member of the system, we are doing much more than christening a new campus. We are witnessing the renewal of a partnership between a community and a college that serves it. Already the college has demonstrated a genuine spirit of community awareness through the service-oriented programs introduced to its curriculum. Interest in mining engineering and reclamation technology is particularly keen, since Madisonville is one of the state's leading coal-producing areas. The need for expanded programs in these fields will be given high priority in future consideration. Community requirements for trained health personnel to serve your hospital, clinics, and nursing facilities also are great—here is another way the college becomes a sound investment.

The college is presently engaged in joint planning and programming with the Madisonville area vocational school to achieve better utilization of facilities. Gratifying progress has been noted in offering special student services, such as a special admissions counselor to aid disadvantaged and minority students, a program to aid in the education of handicapped students, and a learning lab with specialists in individual instruction to assist disadvantaged students.

The community has been given a voice in program planning. Specialized advisory groups in business, industry, mining and reclamation, the arts, and allied health assist the advisory board in determining the program priorities. All the ingredients for a successful partnership are here: community interest, a well-equipped campus, a broad range of programs, and dedicated leadership. Working together, no problem will be insurmountable, no goal will be out of reach. Working together, you will grow together—college and community alike—and all of Madisonville and this area will be the better for it.

INSTALLATION
OF DR. DENO CURRIS
Murray / November 12, 1973

IN 1943 the president of Harvard University described his purpose in appointing a university committee on the objectives of a general education in a free society. I believe what he included in a report that January 11, nearly thirty-one years ago, offers an appropriate introduction to this particular day for Murray State University. Here is what he said: "The primary concern of American education . . . is not the development of the appreciation of the good life. . . . Our purpose is to cultivate in the largest possible number of our future citizens an appreciation of both the responsibilities and the benefits which come to them because they are Americans and are free."

Therefore, I say to you this hour, Murray is not entering its second half-century to develop an appreciation of the good life. Rather Murray is in a new era to continue cultivating an appreciation of both the responsibilities and the benefits which come to students and others, because they are Americans and are free. The man who has accepted not this particular charge but, I believe, one which parallels it is Dr. Constantine William Curris.[1] The responsibilities and benefits which have come to Murray's new president in a short span of time do indeed reflect an appreciation, because his accomplishments illustrate a growing reputation as an educator, administrator, and leader.

As Murray's sixth president, Dr. Curris accepts greater responsibility than ever before, for himself due to his position and for this institution due to the era and demands of society. With such responsibility can come new benefits. The guidance of Dr. Curris will be cherished by the students and the region affected by Murray University's new direction.[2] Every man's work becomes a self-portrait. Murray reflects the character of those who preceded Dr. Curris, just as it will someday reflect his character. He has indicated his desire to see this university known for its high quality of purpose and programs. He can help create a theory that the seventies must become known as a decade of refinement in higher education. Certainly the opportunities are abundant.

I look forward to working with Dr. Curris, who can draw on his experiences as a faculty dean, as a vice president for student affairs, and as a director of educational programs. I look forward to working with him because of his enthusiasm, his maturity, and his understanding that service from Murray offers resources of development for a state and its people who deserve nothing less than the best. It is my pleasure to extend a personal welcome to the man who will chart Murray's new directions as he assumes the presidency of Murray State University.

---

1. Constantine William (Deno) Curris (1940–   ), Murray; vice president of Midway Junior College, Midway, Kentucky (1965–1968); director of educational programs for West Virginia Office of Higher Education (1968–1973); president of Murray University (1973–   ). *Who's Who in American College and University Administration, 1970–1971* (n.p., 1970), p. 115.

2. On August 26, 1974, Governor Ford also spoke at the ground breaking ceremony for the Livestock Exposition Center to be located at Murray State University. In his remarks he stated, "Not only is agriculture this Commonwealth's number one industry, it is also the one resource of which this country does not have a shortage. And it is the only major, positive factor in our international balance of trade. . . . Shows and expositions, which serve as both educational and promotional purposes for the livestock industry, can be held here. It is a fact that much of the recent advancement of America's livestock industry can be attributed to the many outstanding shows and expositions throughout the country." This speech is not included in this volume.

LOUISVILLE PUBLIC SCHOOLS ASSEMBLY INAUGURAL
Louisville / February 9, 1974

CONSIDERABLE confusion exists about the status of education in Kentucky today. You see in one place that the state is sliding from forty-seventh to forty-ninth among the other states in per-pupil spending in public education. Then you watch a television editorial blistering various special interest groups for releasing misleading statistics. A newspaper editorial talks about the continuing failure of state government to come to grips with the worst deficiencies and inequities in public education. But a newspaper columnist arrives at the conclusion that it's hard to make a case that the state is failing the public schools. You hear a legislator claim that the Governor passed up a "golden opportunity" to help education in his budget recommendations. Then you read that the Kentucky Education Association has called the Governor "sympathetic to the needs of education." Just what are you to believe?

Education has been under a microscope since the beginning of public schools. It receives the lion's share of state tax money; sixty-five cents of every general fund dollar is earmarked for education. Yet many continue to criticize state government and the Legislature for failing to meet the problem head-on. Exactly where does the amount of money the General Assembly appropriates for elementary and secondary education stand among the fifty states? The answer was ninth best in the nation last year, and it should very easily be higher this year.

When I presented my executive budget recommendations for the next biennium to the General Assembly, again I stressed my determination to provide a quality education for our children. This we are accomplishing and this is what I believe. Two years ago, when Kentucky had no public kindergarten, we started one. Two years ago, when special education was minimal at best, we prescribed a shot in the arm. When the teachers' retirement system prior-service deficit had been overlooked for years, we cut a small slice from the total amount. And when the state needed 2,600 new classroom units, we made construction a reality.

My recommendations for the next biennium not only guarantee continued massive support but go above and beyond what even I think the most optimistic might have expected by providing tools which stress quality. Let's look at some of the significant contents of our educational package for the next biennium. I have recommended an $85.7 million increase for the minimum foundation program which, among other provisions, will increase teacher salary allotments by 7 percent in fiscal year 1974–1975 and by an additional 9 percent in fiscal year 1975–1976, increase current expense allotments by 7 percent in fiscal year 1974–1975 and by 9 percent the next year, increase capital outlay allotment by $150 per unit during the biennium; provide 100 additional kindergarten units, provide 450 additional vocational education units to serve 13,500 more students, and provide 1,100 more special education classroom units, by far the greatest advancement this Commonwealth has ever made in this very important area. Prior to 1972 only 1,030 special education units had been funded throughout the state's history!

In addition, we have provided monies for other programs, which touch the daily lives of students in all corners of the Commonwealth. These additions include $964,000 additional state matching funds, so we can take full advantage of federal school-lunch funds. A hungry child is a handicapped child. The state's efforts to eliminate this disgraceful fact of life amounted to thirty-two million free meals and 600,000 reduced-cost meals during the last two school sessions. May we never again find a hungry child in any of our schools! For operating new and expanded vocational facilities, which will open during the biennium, and to meet safety and health standards in existing schools, $1.8 million has been requested in addition to $13.4 million for construction of vocational education facilities to serve 19,500 students. A total of 32,000 new opportunities will be made possible for students in this area during the biennium. To expand our regional education offices to fifteen will require $1.3 million and $500,000 will be used for the production of both mathematics and science television series for junior high students. I ask you: Is this merely "brick and mortar" money, these funds that will erect the buildings to put hands and minds to work?

Would you like to hear what two of our state's school administrators thought about the budget? Let me share with you two letters that recently have come across my desk. One letter from the vice chairman of a northern Kentucky school board said, "I am particularly pleased that you are so aware of the tremendous needs in the area of education. . . . with your kind of understanding, Kentucky's elementary and secondary schools shall not remain on the bottom rung of the education ladder any longer!" Another, from a school superintendent in western Kentucky, expressed this opinion: "On behalf of my school system, I wish to commend you for the interest and action in your proposed budget for funding of elementary and secondary education in Kentucky. In the eyes of school people, you will be remembered as a Governor who was a friend to the boys and girls of the State of Kentucky." I can assure you these letters weren't from relatives or in-laws! I do not use these letters for any self-serving purpose. They illustrate the validity of the point I am trying to make: that the state is doing right by the public schools. I offer my proposed budget for elementary and secondary education, an increase of $120.4 million over the present biennium, as proof. I also want to pay tribute to past Legislatures and Governors. They have been responsive, often without due recognition.

Still, the state cannot carry the burden alone. Let's be honest and frank in assessing the major problem public education faces in Kentucky. As far as funding goes, local efforts are as different as apples and oranges. Some communities have gladly accepted their responsibility to create a high standard of education for their children and proceeded to build schools, improve and expand programs, and employ the needed personnel. Others have not. As a result, there's pressure for more money at the state level. Yet there is a reluctance on the part of many legislators to find ways for additional money when they know their school systems back home have made an all-out effort to support the system at the local level, while others have not. That's why Kentucky's community support for elementary and secondary education ranks forty-second in the nation, even though there are legal and constitutional steps available to any community willing to expand its own effort for education.

You know what I'm talking about. You realize that it's important—essential—that a community becomes involved and takes an interest in its schools. The public awareness which the neighborhood school boards in Louisville have created has gained national attention. More important it has stimulated community action, which can serve to strengthen the foundation of your public school system. I want to congratulate you for your participation in the educational process. Public school accountability can be increased through citizen involvement. Increased citizen support at the community level is the only way the statewide image of Kentucky education will be improved.

LOUISVILLE VOCATIONAL-TECHNICAL INSTITUTE GROUND BREAKING
Louisville / April 3, 1974

THIS ground breaking is a good illustration of how a state-federal project for people suddenly became the full responsibility of the state. More than two years have passed since we first announced plans to develop a postsecondary vocational-technical institute in Louisville. Certainly there has been cause to wonder if the project had been placed aside, or even forgotten. I'm here today to tell you it wasn't, and hopefully you'll understand the circumstances after I tell you a story about how the best laid plans can go astray in the Frankfort-to-Washington shuffle.

Let's go back to January 1972, when the General Assembly in response to my request for funds to construct this school appropriated $5 million to be matched with federal funds. The next step was to outline the need for additional employment opportunities in Louisville, so that the city could be designated a special impact area and eligible for federal assistance from the Economic Development Authority for this project. Preliminary groundwork was completed in May. In June the University of Kentucky committed $2 million of its bonding capacity to the project, bringing to $7 million the amount of state funding available.

Then in November we ran into a roadblock. The President had declared a moratorium on all EDA projects. All the progress we had made thus far came to a grinding halt.

We found ourselves right back where we started, even though only months before I had personally received verbal assurance of support from federal officials both in Washington and Atlanta. Every effort to change Washington's mind fell on deaf ears. The state was left to shoulder the project alone. This we have done, not because of a commitment to make this school a reality, but because it is needed, because it will serve Kentucky, and because it moves into many occupations, especially health-related ones, which are so necessary to improve our quality of life. Despite a disappointing turn of events by the federal government, this two-year period has not been a waste of time. It has been utilized to plan the school's curriculum, to design the structure, to acquire the land, and to prepare for immediate construction.

This community is Kentucky's largest industrial center, and one of the largest in the South. It has the largest market in the state. It is our major transportation network. But like many other large cities across the country, Louisville has faced the possibility of a threatening crisis, the decline of urban life. Such an occurrence would not only have severe implications for those living and working in the metropolitan area but on the entire state. A healthy Louisville is essential for a healthy Kentucky. The new vocational-technical institute can be a major contributor to the revitalization of this urban area. Let's look briefly at what the school can do for Louisville, Jefferson County, and all of Kentucky. It brings another institution into our system of higher education, for all programs will be administered through the University of Kentucky Community College system.[1] It is designed to complement the new teaching hospital at the University of Louisville. It will provide new vocational training opportunities for all Kentuckians. Already plans are being made to expand the school's curriculum, even though it is not scheduled to be opened until the fall of 1975. Construction of this school creates a new service industry for Louisville through staff positions and other employment in the management and operation of the institute. Also its central location will be an asset to downtown Louisville, serving to head off out-migration of both workers and industry.

Beyond what it produces, the school will benefit every county in the state through trained competent personnel in many fields of endeavor. The many civic-minded groups and interested individuals who labored so diligently in behalf of this project are to be congratulated. The state is proud to have been a partner in helping you realize another vision you hold for this great community.

---

1. On August 13, 1974, Governor Ford also spoke at the ground breaking ceremony for the $1.1 million Jefferson Community College Learning Resources Center in Louisville. This speech is not included in this volume.

BRESCIA COLLEGE COMMENCEMENT
Owensboro / May 12, 1974

ONE hundred and eighty-seven years ago, in the same month that you are graduating, the Constitutional Convention opened in Philadelphia. Actually, the stated purpose was to revise the Articles of Confederation. In recalling history, many of you will remember that such a revision didn't materialize. Instead, after lengthy, often stormy, deliberations which produced many compromises, a new document emerged—one which has withstood innumerable tests since it became effective on March 5, 1789. I want to briefly discuss one aspect of the Constitution, the preamble, because those who framed this statement of ideals offered a purpose of responsibility which must be rekindled today, especially at all levels of government.[1]

No matter the course one pursues in life, if there is a fundamental creed, appropriate to each individual in my opinion, it is summarized in the preamble. "We the People of the United States." Listen to these first three words, "We the People." The authors gave full recognition to the people as a whole, rather than any select body. It doesn't say we the liberals, we the conservatives, we the editorial writers, we the rich, we the firstborn, we the Republicans, or we the Democrats. It says, we the people. And this in itself is what the government is all about—

responding to people, serving them, and recognizing that the people do indeed have the last word. Support of a better community calls for a direction of energies to the betterment of people. Already we see the preamble guiding our energies in a single direction, whether we are an elected representative of the people or a volunteer servant for the people.

"In Order to form a more perfect Union." In this phrase, the founding fathers expressed hope that the new national government would be an improvement over the previous loose union of states. Improvement! Together we must seek improvement, through your own resources, and as administrations conduct the affairs of others. Often, joy is found in success, just as we find regret in failure. Yet our efforts, both collectively and individually, have the greatest promise when we remember that the goal is a "more perfect union."

"Establish Justice." This means a guarantee of individual rights, the integrity of our court system, and the recognition that fairness to all is something held as sacred in a society where there are differences. The establishment of justice dictates an obligation on each of us which is sometimes difficult, sometimes pleasant. The issuance of reward or punishment, the deciding of controversies, and the actual carrying out of specific laws frequently test our true character. But with the privilege of being a citizen in this greatest of all nations goes our acceptance of this duty, if we ourselves have any right to the establishment of justice.

"Insure domestic Tranquillity." Time changes certain concepts of the preamble, but not the basic intent. When the Constitution was being adopted, domestic tranquillity referred to disputes between or among states. As the nation has grown, so have the domestic responsibilities of government, to a point where domestic programs are today uppermost in our minds. Our way of life is determined by whether or not there is domestic tranquillity. Domestic unrest is an illness where cures are still to be found.

"Provide for the common defense." This requires little explanation. Properly, there is no reference to offense. A strong nation is one, in part, where others refrain from infringing on its territories, or if they do, the common defense ensures there will be adequate protection of our citizens and property. It is an important segment in the preamble, which has changed in the last 187 years only from defense against bows and arrows to defense against nuclear attacks.

"Promote the general Welfare." Here again, we find close comparisons of government and personal citizenship. Our programs, our aims, our intentions are to promote the general welfare. And we need never apologize for helping others less fortunate! Too often the word "welfare" becomes misused. Those who drafted the Constitution suggested that the new government would serve, rather than suppress, the people. If we promote the general welfare we do make life easier, ease individual burdens, and accomplish an act of Christianity, an act of brotherhood, and in one real sense help to ensure domestic tranquillity and establish justice. There are always, unfortunately, those who through no fault of their own have honest needs which they cannot provide. When others respond, I consider it a decency of government or a decency of individual or group.

Let me digress for a moment. The burdens placed on many students to achieve an education continue to mount. Student assistance, help for those in need and who want a college education, is a good investment for the future. For those who will follow you at Brescia, we enter a new era of support to independent colleges. I have authorized the Higher Education Assistance Authority to submit an application under the State Student Incentive Program which will make $620,000 available to Kentucky college students beginning next fall. State government will place $310,000 of surplus funds into a matching program with the federal government. For the first time in the history of Kentucky, students attending independent colleges can qualify by need for direct gains. These funds will enable many students to continue their education despite the rising costs, and I am convinced this is the proper and necessary approach government should be taking. We are confident that state revenue will exceed our estimates, and by submitting the application now, we fully expect the federal government to match our share.

"And secure the Blessings of Liberty to ourselves and our Posterity." Liberty is a blessing. Anyone who has been denied liberty without recourse can recount the horror, the sadness, and the loneliness of such a circumstance. Yet the preamble does not speak only of our liberties; it illustrates the call for liberty to others who will follow us. It therefore says that each of us in our own time has an obligation to make sure that life for our children and our children's children is a little better than we found it. Once more, I ask you: Isn't this your goal? And once more I suggest to you that this is the goal of any who are elected to office.

"Do ordain and establish this Constitution for the United States of America." To me, the preamble says much in few words. High ideals are embodied in the framework of our government. They are considered fundamental to our American way of life. Our actions, yours and mine, no matter what mechanism we use, should be directed toward promoting these ideals, nothing less. The preamble understands that we are involved in the unending search for better government. It sets forth the objectives for which the Constitution was written. While it grants no powers, it is powerful. The preamble and Constitution is our guide for political, governmental and civic life.

Read it again: "We the People of the United States, in Order to form a more perfect Union, establish Justice, insure domestic Tranquillity, provide for the common defense, promote the general Welfare, and secure the Blessings of Liberty to ourselves and our Posterity, do ordain and establish this Constitution for the United States of America."

If, in a real sense, each of us is placed on this earth for something more than individual existence, the preamble is a source of great inspiration. A free society offers a rather brisk trade in ideas. Yet stability of government is necessary for stability of society. Our nation has survived numerous traumatic experiences. The Constitution, and preamble, offers strength in adversity and direction when the route is unclear. No matter our method of service, we can all learn from the preamble, and, in my opinion, do a little better job.

---

1. This was a favorite theme of Governor Ford and was used frequently.

MOREHEAD STATE UNIVERSITY
SUMMER COMMENCEMENT
Morehead / August 1, 1974

IN reading commencement addresses given by others, there seems to be no limit to the variety of topics. Perhaps what I want to discuss will appear unusual at first, but it shouldn't be. An academic setting provides the atmosphere for open, frank, and candid discussion. I want to talk about politics, a subject that demands open, frank, and candid discussion.

While observing various graduating classes, one thought keeps running through my mind. That thought bears on future responsibility to be accepted, in whatever vocation or avocation you choose. I have profound respect for what you want out of life, just as I know the contributions you can make to society in return, if you so desire. We hear and read much about distrust, declining credibility, scandal, dirty tricks, and other improper acts which too often overshadow the quantity of good throughout this country. Because politics and government fall under the magnifying glass of press observation far more than any other element of society, attention becomes greater with reflection on these two areas.

Yet all is not perfect with the press. Where editors and opinion-writers decry the faults of others, neither are they without fault. Where reporters claim unbias, this very quality often is a glaring omission in their stories. What I am saying is this: Whatever your vocation or avocation, no one has a corner on perfection. There isn't a rightful hold above all others on integrity. There are bad apples in any barrel. Such a fact should not be interpreted as an excuse. On the contrary, such a fact should stimulate our collective energies toward improving this situation. We have every right to recognize, however, that there are many more good apples, whether the barrel represents the press, politics, government, private enterprise, or whatever.

Most involved persons, I believe, take their responsibilities seriously. Yes, mistakes are made, but the great majority are proven to be mistakes of the mind rather than the heart. On the other hand, in all professions, we find some who bypass responsibility, and too often their own profession is painted with a broad brush. You are graduating in an era where public attention toward politics has never been more extensive, where public attention is in danger of becoming public apathy, but where public attention, properly directed, can strengthen our political system. How can this strengthening come about?

First, let's return to the preamble to the Constitution. Three words, "We the People," set the tone for tomorrow, if you are willing to listen and respond. Three words, "We the People," admonish all of us in politics that in some way the credibility of this profession will be restored, because the people, not the politicians, have the final say. Now if both groups come together, people and politicians, remembering the real power rests with the public, the people's attention has once more been properly directed. The constructive approach is an effort by all responsible men and women in and out of the political arena to correct any ills which besiege us. No political process operates within a vacuum; therefore, you are affected whether you participate directly or not. How you are affected depends on the degree of your participation.

I believe the conduct of political activity must be your business and you must make it your business. Wrongdoing by design harms the public on a permanent basis. Wrongdoing through human error, and none of us are immune, can be corrected for the benefit of the public.

Yet while the conduct of political activity must be your business, all of us who are in politics have to demonstrate political morality and repudiate anything less. Otherwise, we don't deserve your support, nor do we truly honor a profession which must have honor. The political system we have has been the major force in keeping our country strong, viable, and able to accept change.

Logic finds an inherent danger in accepting human error as "one of those things that's bound to happen." Errors are bound to happen, yes, but what of the individual who has no spirit to challenge his committed faults? In my opinion, the right to stumble is matched by the responsibility to recover. There is no immunity to personal error. There is only the obligation to profit from error. History teaches us that great men and women refuse to falter because of their mistakes. Anything less in the field of politics is an affront to the people of the United States!

This is how I feel, and, as I said earlier, the subject deserves frank, open, and candid discussion. If our political system is to be stronger and regain lost credibility, all of us in the system must correct our errors, take steps to see they never occur again, and thus set personal standards which others will follow in the future. I hope you will demand accountability by demonstrating responsibility through participation in politics and government. I don't say this for any political party, nor do I say this for any particular candidate. I say it for Kentucky and America.

MORGAN COUNTY
SCHOOL DEDICATION
West Liberty / August 31, 1974

EARLIER this week a dream which the people of Morgan County have had for many years came true with the opening of this new school. While I deeply appreciate Senator Stacy's[1] kind words about the state's role in bringing this about, I think the real credit must go where it rightfully belongs, to you and all Morgan Countians. You are the ones who saw the need for a larger facility, which would accommodate twice as many pupils. You are the ones who saw the need for a more modern structure to replace one which had served out its usefulness. You are the ones who accepted the responsibility for financing the new school through the sale of bonds. What we have accomplished together has been for the same purpose: the benefit of our children and our children's children.

Later this afternoon, we will break ground for a new vocational school which, like the new high school, will have a positive impact on your community. It will triple the vocational education opportunities through an increased enrollment capacity. The primary emphasis will be placed on industrial education, so that the graduates can find jobs right here in eastern Kentucky. In years past, many of our young people have been traveling in various directions, often long distances, to find work. But we're now bringing this out-migration to an end. The way to do it is to offer the training for the kind of skills which are needed by Kentucky industries. We want to keep Kentuckians in Kentucky. This is what is happening in Kentucky; families are more able to remain close to home.

Your friend and mine, Carl Perkins,[2] shares this belief, and he's personally seen to it that much Appalachian Regional Commission money has found its way back to this area where it can be put to good use. Carl Perkins is "Mr. Education" in Washington. Beyond this title of respect, he is recognized in numerous other leadership roles as having a positive impact on this area. I consider it a privilege to have the opportunity to join with him in many people-projects, especially when the fruits of labor become obvious like new education facilities. This is a happy occasion for all of us, and I thank you for asking me here to be with you.

---

1. Joe D. Stacy (1925–), Democrat from West Liberty; farmer, banker, insurance agent; past commander of Holly Coffey American Legion Post; director of Licking Valley Rural Electric Cooperative Corporation; chairman of Morgan County Democratic executive committee (1956–1969); member of Kentucky Senate (1968–1975). *Kentucky General Assembly 1974* (Frankfort, n.d.), p. 8.

2. Carl D. Perkins, for more information see speech from October 7, 1972, in the Democratic Party Leadership section, p. 588.

SOUTHERN REGIONAL
EDUCATION BOARD
Lexington / October 8, 1974

THE decade of the sixties was a period of rapid growth in the state-supported institutions of higher education in Kentucky, similar to conditions in states which you represent. During the period 1960–1970, revenue from legislative appropriations in Kentucky increased over five and a half times. Full-time enrollments were growing over two and a half times. Earned degrees virtually doubled. The state-supported system expanded from six to eight senior institutions during the period, with the addition of the University of Louisville and Northern Kentucky State College. The University of Kentucky Community College system increased from five extension centers to fourteen community colleges.

The problem of meeting the requirements of an expanded state system, coupled with rapidly rising costs while at the same time maintaining certain traditional standards, has been the challenge of the seventies. Thus, the sixties were known for growth. The seventies have, by necessity, focused on refinement. The 1970 Kentucky General Assembly, recognizing rapid expansion in higher education and sensing a multitude of new problems, directed the Council on Public Higher Education to prepare a role-and-scope study of the state system of higher education. While the study was prepared by the council staff at that time, it had input from state institutions as well as the nine member legislative Interim Study Commission on Higher Education, which had the responsibility of receiving the study and recommending statutory changes as it saw fit to the General Assembly and Governor.

As Lieutenant Governor in 1970, I was able to see the need for a more effective coordinating structure in Kentucky. Even before, as a state senator in the mid-1960s and as an administrative assistant to Governor Bert Combs in the early 1960s, I had observed firsthand the rapid growth and development of higher education. The study conducted by the council was completed in early 1971 and coincided with my campaign for Governor. The major recommendations were later incorporated into my education platform and ultimately were incorporated into Senate Bill 54[1] of the 1972 General Assembly. This legislation had my complete support as well as that of most members of the General Assembly. Basically, it provided that ten lay members be appointed by the Governor as the voting members of the council, plus the chief executive officer of each institution as a nonvoting member. Also it provided for increased council review and approval of programs, specifically in the area of graduate and professional degree offerings, along with increased council involvement in the budgetary recommendation and review process, including required council review and approval of all capital construction projects in excess of $100,000. Finally, Senate Bill 54 provided for the recognition of the council as a part of the executive branch of government for coordination purposes. Senate Bill 54 was passed by the General Assembly and I signed it into law on March 8, 1972.

In separate legislation, approved by the General Assembly, I recommended and supported the concept that the Governor be removed as the chairman of the Governing Board of the state university. This role placed Governors in dual positions, especially with budgeting. The Carnegie Commission, a few months previously, had recommended that Governors not serve in this role. I believed the recommendation to be sound and acted in accordance with it. Because of my association with state government and studies by the Carnegie Commission and others, I was, and am, quite aware of the potential influence of a Governor over public higher education in his state. The power of budget decisions, appointments to governing boards of the institutions, sponsoring, signing or vetoing legislation, and the affecting of public attitudes all serve to place the Governor in a role which can profoundly affect, positively or negatively, higher education in the state. In exercising my role in higher education, I have looked to the council and the institutions working through the council for leadership in the field of education. While I recognize my responsibility as the chief executive, the real work and achievement of coordination has been made possible by the council, the institutions, and the General Assembly pulling together to resolve issues in higher education.

The term coordination implies the existence of separate units each with some freedom to control its own operations and thus the need for a mechanism to work in concert toward those purposes that cannot be achieved by isolated, individual actions. In such a mechanism, the requisites for success are the ability of the coordinating agency to be persuasive and the willingness of the units to subordinate their individual interests to common goals. The Council on Public Higher Education, through restructuring, has worked to carry out the mandate of the 1972 General Assembly. The purposes of coordination have and are being achieved through the cooperation of the council and the individual institutions.

Many of you have had similar experiences in higher education in your state. With your permission I would like to cite some of the achievements of our council over the past two and a half years as well as current issues being studied. It has developed a comprehensive plan for higher education in Kentucky to be completed before the next session of the General Assembly. They enforced the development of a management information system to provide compatible information for planning and information purposes, and they developed criteria for evaluating new graduate and professional programs. Further refinement of the budget-request format assisted their work. Task groups have been formed in medicine, dentistry, nursing, pharmacy, and allied health. An area health-education system has been developed and initiated. Two of nine proposed areas have been selected and are in operation. Additional studies have been undertaken in law, manpower needs, continuing education, tuition levels, and consideration of problems, associated with students transferring from one school to another.

Examples of interinstitutional cooperation have been identified through the establishment of the Northern Kentucky Consortia and the Owensboro Consortia. Expanded opportunities for students in special fields of study have been expanded with the assistance of the Southern Regional Education Board and other interested agencies. These are but some of the examples of coordination in Kentucky. I want to thank each of you for coming to Kentucky for this annual meeting of the SREB. We in Kentucky are proud to be a part of the SREB and will continue to look forward to working with each member state in the future.

---

1. See an act "relating to higher education and making an appropriation," which was approved on March 8, 1972. *Acts of the General Assembly of the Commonwealth of Kentucky, 1972,* Chapter 39 (S.B. 54), pp. 129–35.

PUBLIC SAFETY

THOSE in attendance today reflect a theme I am interested in conveying throughout my administration—a theme of cooperation for the public good. When various groups work together, positive accomplishment becomes a possibility, rather than a probability. In this room are local officials, members of the legislative branch and the executive branch. Our purpose is a united effort to upgrade the criminal justice system in this state's largest metropolitan area. It is my pleasure to announce several grants from the Kentucky Crime Commission to Louisville and Jefferson County for this expressed purpose. These grants total nearly a quarter of a million dollars and will provide a public defender system, a court administrator, a court study, and full time prosecutors in the Commonwealth Attorney's Office.

This money, together with the work of local officials, will give a substantial boost to the overhaul of an antiquated law enforcement system. The mayor and county judge[1] announced last Thursday steps to merge the city and county police, thus providing a unified umbrella of police protection for the entire county. On Saturday they announced a new jail and courts complex, with centralized booking-and-holding facilities. These facilities should relieve the certain obvious problems in our courts and correctional institutions.

We have therefore an example of people working together on a project beneficial to others. As Governor, I am working on a daily basis with local officials to help solve local problems, just as I am working with the General Assembly to help solve statewide problems. In this spirit, we must not only continue, but we must demonstrate our increased willingness to put together all the pieces of a giant puzzle. It is my hope, and intention, that this grant of $105,000 plus $15,000 of state matching funds and $15,000 of local matching funds for the establishment of a public defender system in Jefferson County will provide this needed service. I am particularly pleased that the vehicle chosen is nonpartisan, being a nonstock, nonprofit, private corporation, which will give insulation from any political influence.

The grants of $50,000 to the county for full-time prosecutors in the Commonwealth Attorney's Office should be of special benefit, with the expectation that those hired will be selected on the basis of ability rather than politics. I have asked the State Crime Commission to monitor the program to ensure that the money is applied in the best interest of law enforcement. The remaining grants of $32,250 and $20,000 for a court study and court administrator respectively can add immeasurably to this judicial process. This will help speed the time from arrest to trial.

I have also today asked the State Crime Commission to set aside $200,000 for Jefferson county. This money would relieve the county jail from overpopulation by utilizing the city jail until a new cooperative facility is built. In addition, these dollars would help facilitate centralized booking procedures and the functional merger of the city and county police departments.

---

1. Mayor Harvey I. Sloane and Judge Louis J. "Todd" Hollenbach. For more information, see November 27, 1973, in the Health and Welfare section, pp. 205–6.

SUPERVISORY PERSONNEL OF STATE POLICE
Frankfort / March 27, 1972

THIS occasion dictates not a lengthy speech from your Governor; rather it commands public attention for a small group of men who have earned far more recognition than they will ever receive. In these very brief remarks, I want to address the citizens of Kentucky in behalf of those to be honored[1] and in behalf of the organization they represent. We can all take great pride in knowing that there are among us men who are willing, if necessary, to risk their lives in order that the rest of us may have peace in ours. Express that pride to the next police officer you see!

We sometimes must be reminded that today's law-enforcement official faces greater frustrations, more problems, mental and physical abuse, and a loneliness few will accept in whatever their vocation might be. Remember this the next time you see one of these men on duty! Perhaps there is a definite absence of understanding among all of us as to the increased educational, technical, and psychological demands placed on our policemen as the years have passed by. Think hard about this in days to come! Sacrifices such as we have seen from these men and others merit the response and support of a citizenry sufficiently aroused to assume an active role in the enforcement of our laws. Without our participation, the laws of any democratic system will not withstand the tests to which they are being put.

And now, directing myself to you who are being honored, let me reiterate my appreciation, my respect, and my solid stand behind the Kentucky State Police and all other law enforcement agencies in this state who work so diligently for the safety of others. William Penn[2] once said: "Justice is the insurance we have on our lives and property. Obedience is the premium we pay for it." I would add that your acts of unselfish service and heroism are the dividends which we, the public, receive.

This is a special day, not just for the recipients of today's awards, but for each Kentuckian who must surely feel the good fortune of a highly professional agency whose single dedication is your security, and mine.

---

1. Governor Ford honored the following individuals with awards at this ceremony: Troopers Thomas Collins, Ray Morris, Henry Shipp, former Trooper D. K. Atcher, Detectives Edwin Ballard, Ralph Ross, David White-house, Marion Campbell, and Detective Sergeant Richard McQuown.

2. William Penn (1644–1718), colonizer; founder of Pennsylvania colony and its proprietary governor (1682–1692, 1694–1718). *Who Was Who in America: Historical Volume, 1607–1896* (Chicago, 1967), p. 475.

CRIME COMMISSION GRANTS
Frankfort / April 12, 1972

WHEN addressing the Legislature in my State of the Commonwealth report, I indicated that changes in Kentucky's criminal justice system were long overdue. It was my intention to see these reforms undertaken. I also pledged support to the Kentucky Crime Commission for substantial funding to see that the needs of Kentucky's law enforcement community would be met. Later, in my budget message to the General

Assembly, I asked for $6.7 million over the next two years to guarantee approximately $19 million in Federal Safe Streets Act funds for Kentucky and committed this administration to broad changes in every component of the criminal justice system.

Legislation in this area was given strong support from the Governor's Office. The passage of specific measures, as shown on charts provided, marks the beginning of a determined effort to improve police, courts, and corrections—realizing that crime will only be reduced when we assure that our laws are intelligently enforced by trained and educated police, when trials are promptly held and accused offenders are properly represented by counsel, and when our jails and prisons begin to correct, rather than alienate, those in custody.

The Legislature demonstrated its discontent with the past and its willingness to boldly push ahead. Its members, both collectively and individually, are to be highly commended for their efforts. Also, the bipartisan Kentucky Crime Commission and its sixteen regional crime councils deserve recognition for their initiative and responsiveness in behalf of all Kentucky. Today I am announcing the largest number of Kentucky Crime Commission awards ever made. I have approved some $2.2 million in grants for criminal justice programs throughout the Commonwealth, some of which will go toward immediate implementation of the laws enacted by the 1972 General Assembly.

Of fifty-five awards, forty-five go to local units of government. The ten grants designated for state agencies are also designed to benefit local communities. A $450,000 grant to the Department of Corrections will begin the sweeping changes I deem necessary in our system of probation and parole. The parole division will be reorganized. Forty new probation and parole officers and ten administrative-level personnel will be added as soon as practicable, strictly on a merit basis. The existing patronage-riddled system from the past will be stopped. We will begin supervision of all felons, including those who are the most serious offenders not making parole, who are ordinarily released to our communities without supervision. The new staff will also make it possible for the department to offer state supervision to minor offenders sentenced in lower courts throughout the state—a new first for the Commonwealth.

Two awards totaling $262,000 will establish a statewide police radio communications system. With this implementation, every full-time police department will be able to communicate with every other full-time police agency in the state. Twelve additional cities will be supplied with terminals to the Frankfort Computerized Crime Information System. Information on stolen automobiles, stolen property, and wanted persons will be made available to their local police agencies within minutes.

Nine awards from the Crime Commission will allow increased usage of the State Police Crime Laboratory in Frankfort. It is a fact of life that many local police agencies make little or no use of physical evidence gathered at crime scenes because they simply don't have access to a modern crime laboratory. I want to make these services available throughout the state, beginning with areas experiencing the highest crime rates. Approximately $347,000 will provide nine localities with the men and equipment needed for special crime-investigation units that will collect, preserve, and transfer evidence to the state crime lab in Frankfort.

What has been said is frosting on the cake. Time does not permit detailed commentary. But every Kentuckian will become more secure through these grants, which, by the way, mark only a beginning in what I believe will be a criminal justice program of national significance. These awards provide for a variety of long-needed programs, only a few of which I have mentioned. The police-incentive plan provided for in our 1972–1973 budget is another example of the people-services which will come out of this administration. Hopefully, all of this, plus more in the wings, will be translated into a reduction of crime in our streets and into a system of fair and equal justice for all.

KENTUCKY FEDERATION
OF WOMEN'S CLUBS
Lexington / April 18, 1972

You probably have never had a guest speaker begin his remarks by passing along a telephone number. But this is exactly what I am going to do. You might want to write this down: 1–800–372–2960. What I have given you is the Consumer Protection Hotline, a telephone number that any Kentuckian can use whenever it is felt that consumer assistance is necessary from the Attorney General's Office. 1-800-372-2960 is a workable symbol of the direction state government is taking to protect you from fraud, deception, misleading advertising, or any other disreputable act presently being perpetrated on innocent citizens of Kentucky. It is a workable symbol in that it brings people much closer to those who can be of service. This telephone number is a distinguishing feature of new legislation which this administration said would be provided and did provide only weeks after assuming office.

Consumers face a variety of problems. The first, of course, is the dwindling purchasing power of dollars earned. The national economic picture is frightening, when we consider prices, frozen wages, unemployment, and other factors influencing our pocketbooks. But when consumers pay inflated prices for goods or services and then cannot be assured of what they purchased or cannot be comfortable with the financing agreements made, their problems intensify. Not only are fraudulent procedures a crime against the consumer, they are also a crime against the responsible businessman. Often a "black eye" is given to an entire business segment because of the unholy acts of a single person.

We have an ethical business community in our state. The great majority of those on whom you and I depend for services and goods are individuals of high principles, whose business codes offer us confidence. Unfortunately, however, there are the bad apples, and this is the title of a movie I hope each of you will see. The Bad Apple has been produced for the Attorney General's Office to alert citizens to the ever-present threat of consumer fraud. Now in final production, it will be available to organizations such as yours in the very near future.

In the 1970 General Assembly, separate packages of consumer-protection legislation were introduced. After much debate, the consumer was left in the same predicament as before. State government had failed to satisfy serious needs.

During my subsequent campaign for Governor, I pledged a forceful administration in behalf of the consumer. That campaign commitment has been kept. By placing the powers, duties, and functions of consumer protection in the Office of Attorney General, we have centralized this project. Investigative, educational, and legal services are guaranteed to the consumer.[1]

If you believe you have been victimized, you now have a source of help. Too, we will have a sixteen-member citizen advisory council to work with the Attorney General's consumer protection staff, thus giving us input from men and women who are conscious of the problems and willing to help offer solutions.

I want to signal this advancement by presenting some day-by-day situations confronting Kentuckians. In each case, our most recent session of the Legislature took positive action. We now have laws preventing these examples. You purchase a super-duper item costing $300. "Easy" and monthly payments of $10 for twenty-three months are agreed to, with a final payment of $60. This includes finance charges. You honor every payment but cannot make the large, final one. So the company repossesses the item you purchased. Now there's a law to make the so-called balloon payment less harsh on the consumer. If the last payment is more than twice the average of earlier ones, you can refinance without penalty.[2]

In another example, a high-pressure salesman comes to your home and through convincing language, you succumb to a sale. The next morning, after finally admitting to your husband that you saved him money by purchasing an item for $450 that really cost $500, there is a family discussion. Following negotiations, you agree with your husband that the contract should be canceled. Under a new law, you have three business days after a sale through home solicitation to cancel. This is known as the "cooling off period," and with the exception of sales under $25 or insurance, you now have consumer protection. There is a 5 percent, but not exceeding the down payment, cancelation charge allowed.[3]

A third example is, in his making a sale the salesman offers you a rebate if you will refer names of other customers. So you give him a list (which doesn't always set well with your friends!) and he allows you a rebate on each sale thereafter. This is now prohibited.[4]

And how about those out-of-town magazine hawks? The 1972 General Assembly said solicitors of various publications must now register with the local sheriff or local Chamber of Commerce.[5] The next time one of these strangers knocks on your door, ask for his local credentials.

As you can see, we are taking aggressive steps to protect you, the consumer. But we also need your help. When you detect something improper, alert the Attorney General's Office through the hotline. For we can only have complete consumer protection when the public does its part in ridding society of those who would do anything to make a dishonest dollar. False, misleading, or deceptive acts or practices in the conduct of any trade or commerce have been given a strong blow through legislation. State government responded to your call for consumer protection.

In conclusion, we have gratifying evidence that we are indeed now on the right track. Arizona has already considered what has been done here in the first 120 days and plans to pattern their consumer-protection efforts after those in Kentucky. This is another service to the people, as promised. And after all, government does exist to serve people.

1. See an act "relating to consumer protection," which was approved on February 17, 1972. *Acts of the General Assembly of the Commonwealth of Kentucky, 1972,* Chapter 4 (S.B. 52), pp. 4–15.

2. See an act "relating to restriction of consumer credit loans and payments," which was approved on March 6, 1972. Ibid., Chapter 34 (H.B. 174), p. 126.

3. See an act "relating to home solicitation sales," which was approved on March 2, 1972. Ibid., Chapter 29 (H.B. 176), pp. 119–22.

4. See an act "relating to referral selling and sales," which was approved on March 1, 1972. Ibid., Chapter 23 (H.B. 172), pp. 102–3.

5. See an act "relating to salesmen of printed material," which was approved on March 14, 1972. Ibid., Chapter 55 (H.B. 73), pp. 179–80.

FEDERAL REGULATION
OF THE OHIO
Frankfort / April 24, 1972

REPEATED incidents on the Ohio River, involving accidents by shipping concerns, have caused death, injury, property damage, inconvenience to citizens, and tremendous expenses heaped upon the individual taxpayer. The federal government has been lax in its regulations and surveillance of large inland-water traffic. There seems to be more intent in policing light pleasure crafts than in protecting us from the calamitous domination of heavy shipping. What must be demoralizing to many, and is totally astounding to me, is the federal reaction thus far displayed in these latest tragedies. I have found little, if any, real evidence of determination whereby we can expect relief from future threats to river safety and security.

Whether the occurrence be a chlorine-filled barge at McAlpine Dam, an explosion at Cannelton Dam, or a crash into the Big Four Railroad Bridge, there is at issue a growing menace the federal government must halt without delay. I am calling on the President to exercise firm leadership in prodding those who have the ultimate authority to help eliminate additional problems on the Ohio, as well as other navigable rivers.

Ohio River shipping tonnage approximates that which passes through the Panama Canal. We are expecting a substantial increase in this method of transportation, while recognizing the amount of dangerous cargo being pushed along our water routes. This is one more domestic issue that Washington must face rather than allowing its demise through continued inactivity. As Governor, it is perplexing that no legal authority is available to me whereby sufficient steps could be taken in the public interest. I can plead our case to Washington and will do so as often as necessary to gain relief. I call on others, including the editorial staffs of our media, to join me in urging the President and Congress to act promptly and forcefully in acquiring responsible measures relating to our growing river traffic conditions.

KENTUCKY COUNCIL ON CRIME
AND DELINQUENCY
Louisville / September 7, 1972

THE timing for this address could not have been better. Only yesterday at the Southern Governors' Conference, part of our morning business session was devoted to crime, corrections, and justice. Earlier in the conference we discussed a related matter—the control of hand guns. Revealing to me in all of this was the very fact that Governors are placing the highest priority ever on the problems that vitally concern you.

It became obvious during the conference that, as Commissioner Holmes[1] said in his introduction, this administration had indeed charted a new course, not only in corrections, but in all phases of the criminal justice puzzle. And it is a complex puzzle. Governor Hall of Oklahoma termed crime "the chief enemy of every governor." Governor Mandel of Maryland looked across the conference table at Governor George Wallace,[2] telling us of his experiences in the control of hand guns and how perhaps the Governor of Alabama might not have been crippled had his would-be assassin been a resident of Maryland and thereby subject to newly provided investigative procedures before buying and carrying a pistol.

I want to assure you here tonight that America's governors are giving much more than lip service to the dilemma of public safety. Legislatures are involved as never before, as well as independent organizations, such as the United States Chamber of Commerce when it recently underscored the critical need for reform in our corrections systems. Let's look at a difference in philosophy which has come about. Four years ago, in a speech before southern Governors, my predecessor took the conventional or easy way out in dealing with criminal justice in Kentucky. He blamed it on someone else, and I quote: "It is rooted in our court system and its coddling of criminals." This is where we disagree. Yes, there are huge gaps in our court system. Yes, there has been coddling of criminals. But the measure of one's posture in this is not rhetoric; it is action.

I have no intention of belaboring you with facts and figures. Yet you, and the public, deserve a full accounting of what we are doing in facing up to our responsibilities to stem the tide of crime. Our first budget offers a form of revenue-sharing to fund a 15 percent supplement to local police officers who qualify through self-improvement. Because of the President's wage-price freeze, we have thus far been denied approval in implementing this program. But I have communicated with the President, urging his approval, and am prepared to testify in Washington for our police officers before the Federal Pay Board. I firmly believe an exemption will be made in our behalf.

We also have increased the salaries of our State Police by 5 percent in addition to their annual increments. We have transferred thirty state policemen from the Division of Boating to more complex duties, in order to take full advantage of their training and experience. These individuals are being replaced with qualified men who have achieved water safety and patrol standards. Their appointments are based on merit to comply with state and federal regulations. In order to intensify our detective force, we are removing detectives from time-consuming arson-investigation activities and assigning ten fully trained members of the Fire Prevention Division to that task.

Overall, we have increased the budgetary allotment to public safety by $10 million in the first biennium. Kentucky now has seven new circuit judges to decrease heavily overburdened court dockets. To assure that everyone, regardless of his financial status, receives fair and just protection under the law, we are establishing the Office of Public Defender, a $2.6 million project guaranteeing constitutional rights of all accused.

No aspect of criminal justice in Kentucky was so in need of overhauling as was our corrections system. Our administration inherited a corrections system that was not only critically underfunded but was so riddled by patronage that it was on the verge of total collapse. Beginning at the top, Kentucky is fortunate to have one of the most progressive and firm-minded corrections reformers in the country. Commissioner Holmes comes to us with impressive credentials and a compassionate interest in people. He has reorganized the Corrections Department with genuine concern for a system which rehabilitates, rather than one which only punishes.

Don't think for a minute there will be coddling of criminals. I remind you of the tough stand taken during recent disturbances at our state penal institutions. I told the press we wouldn't stand for any foolishness and we didn't. Our new law governing the State Parole Board will help Commissioner Holmes carry out his reform of Kentucky's correctional system. We have not only assured professional competence of the appointees, but we have taken the board out of politics.

On the fiscal side, we have also made positive contributions to Kentucky's correctional system. We have increased state appropriations going to our corrections department by over 30 percent this biennium. We have increased our support to the Kentucky Crime Commission from $2.1 million to $6.7 million. This new money going to the Crime Commission can bring an additional $16 million of new federal dollars into the state over the biennium.

One visible component of the new direction in Kentucky's corrections system is the new Blackburn Correctional Complex near Lexington. This model facility, designed to help parolees adjust to life in the "outside world," could set the pace for correctional institutions of the future. We are not going to build any more giant facilities of the one-to two-thousand inmate category. These oversized, impersonal types of institutions only decrease the opportunities for correction and rehabilitation and increase the chance for trouble. The smaller, more manageable centers, well staffed with professional help are in our plans for a new Kentucky correctional system. We are building also a $4.9 million forensic psychiatry facility for mentally disturbed inmates now residing in our prisons. This is just another component of a Corrections System that believes in rehabilitation, as well as protection of law-abiding citizens.

A word of caution—money, bricks, mortar, and fancy charts give us no assurance of success unless they are properly used. I become irritated with government officials who try to convince us that everything will be fine and dandy just because there has been massive funding. The wise use of funding determines success or failure. In our case, there had to be massive funding in order that we might prevent the collapse of our correctional system, restore dignity and a sense of self-improvement to our police officials who have been bypassed for too many years, recognize that without proper compensation we will not have the quality we must have in our judges, and take advantage of federal funds available, yet not acquired.

In a large sense, the fifty states have been supported most effectively by the Safe Streets Act. As Governors, though, we are concerned and critical that the President of the United States seeks only 57 percent of the authorized funding for this activity. Crime is a 100 percent challenge and deserves total commitment. This total commitment is reflected in Kentucky's expanded approach.

You can see, I trust, the overall picture—from the policeman on the beat, through the courts, in corrections and probation and parole. All must work together if we are to substantially erase the threat of crime. Our police need the support of every decent citizen of this state. Our courts must have the ability to provide speedy trials while assuring everyone those protections granted by our Constitution. Our criminal population must realize we want them freed, but only after they are free of criminal behavior. Our institutions are wastes of money if they don't rehabilitate, and our parole system is inept unless those released have continuing professional guidance and supervision. Only when all of these factors come together in concert will we be able to say the war is being won.

I am practical enough to expect further difficulties. We cannot solve overnight the puzzle of crime and delinquency that has eluded us for decades. We cannot anticipate complete calmness in our overcrowded institutions when they have been hellholes for ages. But we have finally placed the pieces in proper position. We are beginning to fit each into the other. When this puzzle is completed, the picture will be one of more security than ever before for our families, our properties, and all which is so meaningful to the law-abiding citizens of this great state.

---

1. Charles J. Holmes (1933–   ); schoolteacher (1960–1962); Clark County, Indiana, Probation Officer (1962–1964); director of Indiana Department of Corrections Youth Camp Program (1964–1966); involved in a research project for Notre Dame University at the Indiana Department of Corrections (1966–1967); administrative assistant to the Indiana commissioner of corrections, Southeastern Indiana Criminal Justice Planning Agency (1969–1972); commissioner of corrections for Kentucky (February 1972–May 1976). Telephone interview, January 4, 1977.

2. David Hall (1930–   ), Oklahoma City; attorney; elected Governor of Oklahoma in 1971; law professor at the University of Tulsa Law School (1963–   ). Who's Who in America, 1974–1975 (Chicago, 1975), 1:1282.

Marvin Mandel (1920–   ), Annapolis; attorney; member of Maryland House of Delegates (1952–1959); elected Governor of Maryland in 1969; chairman of the Middle Atlantic States Governors' Conference (1970–1971), Caucus of Democratic Governors (1971–1972), National Governors' Conference (1972–1973). Who's Who in America, 1974–1975 (Chicago, 1975), 2:1979. George C. Wallace (1919–   ), Montgomery, Alabama; attorney; member of Alabama Legislature (1947–1953); Governor of Alabama (1963–1966, 1971–1974, 1975–   ); Candidate for President of the United States, American Independent party (1968). Who's Who in America, 1974–1975, (Chicago, 1975), 2:3198.

OFFICE OF PUBLIC DEFENDER
Louisville / October 17, 1972

SINCE the third century, governments have wrestled with the problem of providing representation for persons charged with a crime, but who could not afford it.[1] The Sixth Amendment to the Constitution of the United States assures that, "In all criminal prosecution the accused shall . . . have the assistance of counsel for his defense." The very essence of democracy is the concept of equal justice under law. Yet for most of our country's history, this right to counsel was applied only in federal prosecution. Only nine years ago did the highest court in the land rule that this applied in state criminal trials.[2]

We know the unhappy result of the law's failure to meet the just expectations of those governed by it. Law loses its stabilizing influence; at best the result is alienation and lack of trust in the legal system. At worst, there is unrest and violence. In America today four systems are used to provide counsel to indigent defendants: assigned counsel, public defender, private defender, and a mixed public-private defender. The oldest of these—and that which has been used in Kentucky—is assigned counsel. When a defendant in this state appeared before a judge without counsel and said he could not afford counsel, the judge appointed a lawyer to represent him. The selection was frequently limited to those lawyers present in the courtroom at the time. The lawyer was not paid a fee, nor was he reimbursed for any money he might have spent in preparing a defense. The result was too often inadequate preparation and as inexpensive a defense as possible. The system of assigned counsel was designed to fit a rural society. For many years it worked well in Kentucky. At a time when criminal justice was comparatively uncomplicated, and criminal case loads much lighter, counsel could afford to take the then rare assignments, at no fee.

This is no longer practical or proper. It has been increasingly difficult to assure just process of law with our growing population and crowded courts. Now Kentucky becomes one of the few states in the Union to meet realistically the intent of the Sixth Amendment and of Section II of our own state constitution. It has been said that the quality of a nation's civilization depends on the way it enforces its criminal laws. And there can be no civilized enforcement of criminal law without full legal assistance to the accused. This we shall have! I am today announcing a public defender program for the Commonwealth of Kentucky. I am also announcing the procedure to quickly implement the program.

Here is where the challenge lies. We have fifty-three judicial districts in Kentucky which will have to establish local public defender offices to carry out the intent of the new law. This must be done and approved before the $2.6 million appropriated for the program can be released. I am requesting this be done in ninety days!

In order to accomplish this challenging task, our Office of Public Defender will have to coordinate with each circuit court judge, the presidents of the respective bar associations, local fiscal court judges, and other concerned parties. These local groups will determine how this public defender program will be carried out. It will be the task of our public defender, his deputy, and assistants to make sure the letter and intent of the law is followed. The interest in our public defender program out in the state is considerable and we think we have the man to meet the challenge.

With this introduction and assuming he still wants the job, it gives me great pleasure to announce my appointment of Kentucky's first public defender: Mr. Anthony (Tony) M. Wilhoit. Mr. Wilhoit is a 1963 graduate of the University of Kentucky Law School. While a student at UK, he served as a legal aide in the Attorney General's Office. He has practiced law in Versailles since passing the State Law Board and served one year as police court judge. He has also served three years as city attorney. Mr. Wilhoit is presently serving in his fifth year as county attorney for Woodford County. We believe we have the right type of person in Tony Wilhoit to get the job done, and get it done right. Shortly, his deputy and assistant will be announced.

I want to publicly express my respect and appreciation for the service rendered in this important endeavor—the Kentucky Bar Association, the Circuit Judges Association, the County Judges Association, Skip Grafton of Louisville who worked diligently on the enabling legislation, and to my chief legal counsel, Larry Greathouse, who has been a vital link from my office with the groups mentioned.

---

1. Press conference.
2. *Gideon* v. *Wainwright*, 372 U.S. 335 (1963).

PRESENTATION BEFORE
THE PAY BOARD
Washington, D.C. / December 14, 1972

PLEASE accept my deep appreciation for this opportunity to bring our case before you. My mission is in behalf of over 2,600 officers in our state who have an opportunity to participate in the police training and Educational Incentive program, as well as Kentucky's 3.5 million citizens, vitally concerned with security of person and property.

Basically, we are attempting to upgrade the status of local law-enforcement officials through a plan which says, "If you become better qualified to do a more effective job, we will supplement your salary." Every individual who becomes eligible for the proposed 15 percent salary increase would be doing far more than merely obtaining a raise. He must successfully complete specific requirements to improve his status as a police officer. I suggest you equate this with being elevated within a business structure because of self-improvement, which enhances one's ability to assume more responsibility.

In the fight against crime, the single most important factor is the policeman. He makes the split-second decisions affecting the future freedom or even the future existence of other members of society. In this era of sophisticated crime-fighting equipment, training becomes paramount. Such specialized tools are totally ineffective until policemen are continuously taught to use properly what is now available and what will be available. The best way to improve immediately the educational levels of men entering police service, to improve the continuing education pursued by officers already in service, and to spur policemen to improve their own performance on the job by in-service and basic training is to establish a training and educational incentive program. Salary increases are payable only upon satisfactory achievement of mandatory training and educational requirements.

Last year, over 63,000 serious crimes were reported in the Commonwealth. Five years ago, only 38,000 such crimes were reported. Yet we aren't one of the nation's worst examples, and we don't want to be. Let's not be subjected to after-the-fact approaches in crime prevention! Despite this increase and despite the good intentions of many, neither the available revenues to improve police salaries nor the training necessary to implement modern crime-fighting techniques have been within the fiscal reach of local government. As a result, Kentucky's policemen continue to earn substantially lower wages than men in comparable cities.

The Police Training and Educational Incentive Act authorized by the 1972 General Assembly[1] was adopted unanimously by both houses of the Legislature and has been overwhelmingly endorsed by Kentucky's criminal justice community, the Kentucky Crime Commission, and the sixteen regional crime councils responsible for local planning under the Safe Streets Act. Passage of the police training act represented a significant milestone in the four-year struggle on the part of the Kentucky Crime Commission to achieve statewide minimum educational and training standards for police.

If the Pay Board turns down our request for a 15 percent increase to local policemen meeting the state incentive training and educational standards, we will be unable to implement these standards. On the other hand, if our request is granted, we expect that almost all local policemen in Kentucky will participate in a program setting minimum standards as follows: 1) That each officer receive a minimum salary of $4,350—in itself a pitifully low figure; 2) That each officer hired on or after July 1, 1972, have at least a high school degree or its equivalent as determined by the Kentucky Law Enforcement Council; 3) That each police officer hired on or after July 1, 1972, successfully complete a basic training course of at least 240 hours at a training school certified or recognized by the Kentucky Law Enforcement Council; 4) That every officer in a police department successfully complete at least forty hours of in-service training per year.

I think the issues are clear. The need for improved-quality law enforcement in Kentucky is undeniable. The mandate of the people of Kentucky instructing the state government to take action to rectify this situation is unquestionable. I implore that this board not deny the citizens of Kentucky the improvement in law enforcement services which the State Training and Educational Incentive Program for local police will achieve. Let us join together therefore to see that this type cover story becomes less and less necessary. If we are truly concerned with law and order, there is no better place to prove that interest than this room.

Even more far-reaching is that the Kentucky Plan is now being observed by other states. There is strong interest in our approach which means there is a broad interest in your decision. I would, therefore, ask that the Pay Board join with us in the nation's fight against crime and authorize the full implementation of the Kentucky Law Enforcement Foundation Program Fund.[2]

---

1. See an act "relating to police salaries," which was approved March 17, 1972. *Acts of the General Assembly of the Commonwealth of Kentucky, 1972,* Chapter 71 (H.B. 203), pp. 288–93.

2. On February 8, 1973, Governor Ford made another announcement which stated in part, "This all boils down to a ridiculous matter, embroiled in politics, where the Nixon administration takes a goal of law and order and then restricts a state like Kentucky that is actually doing something to reduce crime. All of this conflicting information tells me one thing: the Pay Board doesn't know what in the world they are doing.

"Now what is the Pay Board decision? Simply stated, they tell us that from July 1, 1972, to June 30, 1973, the state can implement the Educational-Salary Incentive Program at a 5.5 percent level, with the exception of Louisville and Jefferson County, though this is where we have 41 percent of the serious crimes in Kentucky!

"Beginning this next July 1 to June 30, 1974, the state will be permitted to proceed under Phase III, which means another 5.5 percent, but this time including Louisville and Jefferson County. There is also a provision for gross inequities, which we contend are obvious in this case, but no clarification of those provisions is provided at this time."

PUBLIC DEFENDERS
SEMINAR LUNCHEON
Lexington / May 11, 1973

Too often crime and criminal justice are used as vehicles to gain public office. Politicians playing on fear and images resort to negative sloganeering such as being "soft on crime" or accusing the courts of "coddling the criminal." I have pledged my administration to take a more positive approach to the critical need for action in criminal justice. Crime is a complex problem, and it can only be solved by an integrated strengthening of the entire criminal justice system, from the policeman on the beat to the parole officer.

Let me mention a few of the programs that have given Kentucky a reputation as being one of the most progressive states in the country in criminal justice: a 15 percent salary supplement for local police if standards are met; special units for organized crime and narcotics investigation; modernizing communication and information systems on a statewide basis and tying-in with the FBI in Washington; new crime lab facilities, from mobile units for on-the-scene investigation to sophisticated central labs for detailed work; seven new circuit court justices; a study of the entire court system to see where changes may be made—"justice delayed is justice denied"; a revision of the criminal code; a Prosecutor's Assistance Division in the Attorney General's Office to aid local prosecutors; and an upgraded standard for members of the State Parole Board to professionalize it; and new techniques in rehabilitation rather than simply punishment (smaller facilities like the Blackburn Correctional Complex, work release, shock probation, and the forensic center).

These and other programs are designed to fight a realistic war on crime, a war we think we can win. They are based on the belief that criminal justice is a system, not just a slogan. One of the most important ingredients in any criminal justice system is credibility. If the people don't believe that the system is capable of protecting their well-being, property, and rights, they are going to shrug it off and go their own way. We know the unhappy consequences of the law's failure to meet the just expectations of those governed by it. Law loses its stabilizing influence. At best, the results are alienation and lack of trust in the legal system. At worst, there is unrest and violence.

Charged with the responsibility of defending those who face prosecution, yet cannot afford an attorney, you and your colleagues must see to it that no person is denied his right to equal protection under the law and to due process simply because he is poor. Your job is not, as some mistakenly believe, to free the guilty, but rather it is to see that justice works the same for rich and poor alike. Let no one think that crime is found only among the poor. It can reach into the boardrooms of corporations and even into the White House itself. Still, under our system of law, the poorest and those least able to protect themselves must stand on equal legal footing with the corporate executive or the presidential advisor.

Your job, just as mine, is to serve the people. You must be prepared, and I know you will be, to champion the causes of many whose cases are not popular. You must be prepared to seek the truth wherever it takes you and to devote all of your professional skill and competence to your client. In terms of money, your rewards will not be great, though professionally, your rewards should be. You will know that you have lived up to those high standards long established by the legal profession.

You are all qualified to do a professional job in meeting the commitments of a public defender, but professional ability cannot alone achieve the kind of justice we are seeking. The best public defender system in the world is rendered useless if nobody knows about it. I wonder what the results would be if a poll were taken today, asking people what a public defender is or if they know whether there is one in their state? My question to you then is, "How are you going to make yourself visible to the public you serve?" Without the visibility, all of the good intentions we have will be in vain. We have the potential to show the nation how justice can and should work. The mechanism has been established, the program has been funded. Now it is up to you to see that it becomes a reality.

REMARKS TO KENTUCKY STATE POLICE
Frankfort / June 13, 1973

WITH the twenty-fifth anniversary of the Kentucky State Police near at hand, this is an appropriate time for me, as Governor, to talk to you about the future of the Kentucky State Police as this administration sees it. I would prefer to do this on a more personal basis. But, with the demands on your time and my time, it is impossible for all of us to be together. Because of this, I enthusiastically accepted the opportunity to speak to you by video tape.

The overwhelming need to do something concrete about the high rate of crime on our streets and traffic deaths on our highways has been a matter of grave and major concern to me. I wish we could make all the necessary changes overnight. But you and I both know we can't. We have to do things on the basis of priorities. I constantly underscore the urgent need to better the lot of the law-enforcement officer—by giving him the tools and the incentives to do a difficult job. I believe you men to be the single most important link in the entire criminal justice system. Where would the public be without the law-enforcement officer?

The courts can sentence the criminal. Our jails, prisons, reformatories, and other correctional facilities can hold and try to rehabilitate him. And the probation and parole officers are there, ready to work with him and keep him on the straight and narrow after he is released. But it is you, afoot in the alley or hollow, or alone on the highway, who must first find the man and bring him in—frequently at the risk of your own life—before those other links in our criminal justice system can be brought into play.

In some nineteen months since I took office as Governor of this state, three state policemen have died. Eight others have been shot and wounded. One of them was permanently disabled. With my support and encouragement, the commissioner and his staff are reviewing plans to assure that state policemen can provide their families and themselves with financial security if this supreme sacrifice is made for the safety of Kentuckians. We should do no less for you than this.

In my first budget message, delivered to the General Assembly in full Session shortly after becoming Governor, I warned that we would make no real headway in reducing the crime rate unless we were ready and willing to deal with every element, every problem, in the criminal justice system. In short—as I stated then and as I will again state to that same body when they return to Frankfort next January to consider our next budget recommendations—we have to put the money where heretofore there was a great deal of talk but little in the way of hard cash. I will have no patience with anything less.

For you—the State Police officer—the commitment already has led to some significant changes. More are yet to come. But first, let me review briefly what has already taken place since January 1972: an across-the-board 5 percent pay raise, effective July 1, 1972; a transfer of the boating patrol function to another agency, freeing some thirty additional State Police officers for full-time criminal and traffic enforcement duty;[1] and the elimination of a vehicle shortage, which has existed since 1970, by approving the purchase of 361 new cruisers, all of which should be on the road by this July. With my support and encouragement, Commissioner Ron Johnson[2] directed that all new cruisers be assigned to troopers patrolling our highways (canceling plans to purchase new cars for supervisors, including himself).

In addition, the commissioner has instituted a procedure in his office which allows you to have an input into planning for the acquisition of other new equipment. For example, some new and better radios have been purchased at your request. Also, as a result of your suggestions and requests, the commissioner has approved the purchase of fifty new electronic sirens, lights, and outside-car speakers for trial on heavily traveled, high-speed routes. Plans are being completed to buy some protective screens for cruisers as an experiment in trooper safety in remote areas.

Other changes include transferring all regulatory responsibilities out of the Department of Public Safety, thus recognizing that the State Police must function as a separate and independently operated law enforcement agency, as was the original intent of the bill creating the Kentucky State Police back in 1948;[3] elevating the officers of field and criminal investigations commanders to number two positions under the State Police director, thus shortening and improving lines of communications between headquarters and the working officer in the field; increasing funding and manpower for drug enforcement; and expanding the air patrol with the acquisition of four helicopters.

Now, let's talk just a bit about a few of the changes which lie ahead. Although some of our plans are still in the talking stages, there is one subject about which I can make a firm commitment. I know that some of you, perhaps even all of you, have been concerned because State Police were not included in the 15 percent pay subsidy which local officers are beginning to receive. However, State Police pay scales have been under study at my direction for some time now. Both Commissioner Johnson and I have agreed fully that something needs to be done, and done soon, to bring State Police pay into closer alignment with that paid some local departments, as well as the salaries of your counterparts in our neighboring states.

We have a two-part plan. Effective on July 1 of this year, every officer serving in the pay grade of "Trooper," with eight or more years of service—computed from the date on which he began cadet training—will receive an automatic 5 percent increase in pay and will be officially designated, on record, by the title of "Senior Trooper." For those who do not yet have eight years' service, this means that they can now look forward to the same automatic pay increase when they reach their eight-year service date. And for those of you who might be concerned that this increase would have the effect of changing your normal pay increment date, let me assure you that it will not. Your normal increment date will remain the same. Although the current State Police budget does not include sufficient funds to meet the costs of that July 1 increase, I have taken care of that by authorizing an expenditure of $90,000 from my contingency fund. That money will carry you through until July 1974. By then, we expect that the "Senior Trooper" pay allocation will be included as a regular item in the budget.

In addition, when I submit my budget to the General Assembly next January, it will include an appropriation request for another pay increase which will affect State Police personnel in all grades. You have my personal guarantee that I will remain fully committed to this plan as I have described it to you today and that my administration will communicate that commitment clearly and emphatically to the next General Assembly.

The Kentucky State Police, in my opinion, is the finest law enforcement agency in the United States. We want to keep it that way.[4] By introducing these incentives, it is my hope that they will help you to continue to attract the sort of men we need as officers in the years to come and by rewarding those who are making a career of it now. Thank you for allowing me to take this portion of your valuable time.

----

1. In January 1972 Governor Ford transferred the responsibility of patrolling Kentucky's waterways from the State Police to the newly created Water Safety Division of the Public Safety Department. Twenty-eight boating recruits began four weeks of intensive training for their new duties in March of that same year.

2. Ron Johnson (1940–   ), Frankfort; public relations and marketing consultant; assistant highway commissioner (1966–1967); assistant to the Kentucky Speaker of the House (1969–1970); assistant to the Lieutenant Governor (1970–1971); assistant to the Governor (1971–1973); commissioner of public safety, commissioner of the Bureau of State Police (1973–January 1975); Kentucky Jaycees Outstanding Young Man in 1974. Telephone interview with Johnson on January 5, 1977.

3. See an act "to provide for the public safety by creating a Department of Kentucky State Police," which was approved on March 18, 1948. *Acts of*

the General Assembly of the Commonwealth of Kentucky, 1948, Chapter 80 (H.B. 291), pp. 172–74.

4. The Governor noted his interest and concern for law-enforcement officials in an address before the State Police Cadets Class Number 44 on February 25, 1972. He said on that occasion, "Rest assured, as long as Wendell Ford is Governor, he will do everything in his power to help you maintain the highest standards of performance, dignity, and service. There will never be a compromise." This speech is not included in this volume.

KENTUCKY PEACE OFFICERS ASSOCIATION CONVENTION
Owensboro / June 27, 1973

CHILDREN have a way of simplifying those things which are often mystifying to the sophisticated and complex world of adults. To them, the entire problem of crime and the system of criminal justice is a matter of cops and robbers! I think you would agree that although this is not entirely accurate, there is a good deal of truth in it. In the war on crime, it is the police officer who stands first and foremost on the front lines. He remains the single most important individual in the criminal justice system's response to crime.

Like other citizens, I have long been concerned about the frightening increase in crime throughout the state and country. Here in Kentucky, we saw an average annual rate of increase in serious crimes during the years 1966 through 1970 of 13.4 percent. But here is a gratifying change. Last year, crime in our state was down 8 percent—the first reduction since World War II and an actual decrease of some 5,000 serious crimes! I think we are beginning to turn the corner on crime. A major reason, I sincerely believe, is the quality of police officers we have in the Commonwealth.

In Kentucky, as in other states throughout the country, the image of the policeman is improving daily. It is improving because today's policeman is better trained, better equipped, and better educated, and in Kentucky better paid. He is also more involved in his community, more aware of public relations, and more sophisticated in dealing with crime on the streets. It is largely through the policeman's own initiative and professional pride that these changes are occurring. He has had to fight bad stereotyping and citizen apathy in matters of crime and criminal justice. But times are changing. A perfect example is the enthusiasm you have shown in our efforts to upgrade police officers through the salary-incentive program. As you know, we fought a long and tough battle, and in the face of discouragement we finally won. This victory will help improve your image because you will be better police officers. One reason I am confident is that you have indicated the high degree of self-improvement you yourselves want.

Children playing cops and robbers see the policeman as the perpetual good guy. What young boy hasn't wanted to be a policeman when he grows up? Yet, when the child does grow up, he is often more quick to criticize than compliment the men who daily risk their lives to assure our safety. It seems that although everyone is for law and order, many people want law and order mainly to keep other people in line. If it inconveniences them personally, they are likely to turn with abuse against the policeman. The police officer has had to put up with a lot of verbal abuse in the pursuit of his duty. He has been called the "fuzz," the "bull," the "badge," and most recently, the "pig." A policeman has to be almost superhuman in the face of this, but he has an unusual occupation and self-control gets him through it.

I want to read you a passage from a recent novel which says pretty well what people seem to expect from every officer:

> One doesn't last a day in police work if one wears his heart on his sleeve; and the man who takes very little personally, who with mild eyes and a stern jaw accepts all abuse, threats, mockeries, with the indifference of a man born deaf and blind—who puts insult away as quickly and lightly as he drops his ball-point pen back into his pocket—that man grows tougher with experience. . . . The policeman learns such patience as would shame old Job. He learns to stand lightly in the present moment at once committed and detached, like a true philosopher or like an old-time Christian who knows this world is no home, but a wilderness.

Yet, when those who complain loudest about the police find themselves in trouble, they are quick to call for a policeman to help them safely through the wilderness. If we all expected as much from ourselves as we do from our police, we would have less need for them.

One of the problems with which you have had to deal is citizen apathy and the fear people have had of getting involved when they see others in trouble. But I think this is changing too. I saw a story in the paper which encouraged me about citizen involvement. It happened in the same city which only a few years ago produced the terrible story of a woman who was assaulted and killed while several people looked out of their apartment windows, afraid to get involved. The city is New York, but this time people were not afraid of involvement. Three men accosted a woman on the street and stole her handbag. When they jumped into a cab to make their getaway, fifty men surrounded the cab and refused to move until the policeman arrived to arrest the assailants. If this can happen in New York, it must be happening in many cities throughout the country.

We can be sure that crime will continue as long as there are people in the world who refuse to accept the integrity of life and property. If we are to continue the downward trend in crime which Kentucky showed last year, we are going to have to work together. We are going to have to continue the upgrading of professional police work like you are doing. As citizens we are going to have to accept more responsibility and get involved when others are in trouble.

I am convinced we can win the war on crime, if we take it on as a team effort. My administration is committed to be a strong partner in this effort and will do all we can to help you perform your duties. Our criminal justice legislative package from the last General Assembly has had its impact, but the real job has to be done in the communities. This is where we can really impact the problems of crimes and make our streets safe again.

It will also take cooperation between communities because crime knows no geographic or jurisdictional boundaries. We are looking with interest at the plans which Clinton, Pulaski, Wayne, and Russell counties are formulating to consolidate into a regional police agency. This will be the first multicounty regional police force in the country outside New York City. It could lead the way to strengthened law-enforcement capability in the state. I want to compliment you on the jobs you are doing. It is a source of pride to me and to every Kentuckian that we logged a decrease in major crimes last year, and you are the men who are mainly responsible. No matter what city or county you are from, we in Frankfort see you as "Kentucky's Finest."

KENTUCKY ASSOCIATION
OF CHIEFS OF POLICE
First Annual Conference
Lexington / August 9, 1973

It is a personal pleasure to be involved with the beginning of this new and needed coalition of police chiefs. As an administrator charged with serving the public interest myself, I know how useful it is to be able to get together with others in a similar position and discuss mutual problems. There are differences from state to state and from town to town, but we are all dealing with people problems, and these problems tend to be similar, in the same way as people are similar. Your new association can be an excellent forum for exchanging valuable information in the common purpose of public safety and welfare. I encourage you to make the best use possible of the opportunities presented by this new association to help you better serve the people of Kentucky.

You have already done an exemplary job in serving our people as evidenced by Kentucky's 8.1 percent reduction in the crime rate, compared to the 3 percent national average. This is the first state reduction in crime since World War II and represents an actual decrease of some 5,000 serious crimes. I'm proud of our law-enforcement agencies in compiling this record, and I think you and your men deserve public recognition for pursuing your responsibilities in law enforcement with such success.

Obviously, your main interest is the protection of life and property from those who haven't the moral fortitude and conviction to respect the rights of their fellow citizens. If you weren't so committed to this cause, you wouldn't be wearing the uniform which stands for law and order! Yet, in order to make the major gains in the war on crime that the reduction percentages indicate, there has to be a special effort on the part of all who are concerned with law enforcement. In Frankfort, we have committed state government to work more closely with local law-enforcement agencies as a responsible partner in the criminal justice system. Cooperation is essential if Kentucky is to continue its assault on those who are a threat to the lives and property of all Kentuckians.

One such example of our efforts to aid local police agencies is the nationally unique 15 percent pay-supplement program, which was finally instituted this summer after a long but victorious hassle with the so-called law and order administration in Washington. Now, many other states are looking with interest at Kentucky's program as well as the other major revisions we are making in the state's criminal justice system. I am convinced that this new direction of the state as a strong partner with local police agencies will be mutually beneficial to everyone concerned.

We are placing new emphasis on law-enforcement capabilities of the State Police. One major effort we are making in this area is our campaign against drug traffic in the state. The special narcotics unit in the State Police has been very effective in this area, showing a 187 percent increase in narcotics arrests since it was organized in 1970. We are proud of this record, and we know that it wouldn't have been possible if it were not for the outstanding cooperation we receive from local police agencies throughout the Commonwealth. Drug pushers, like other criminals, know no geographic or jurisdictional boundaries, and our narcotics unit works statewide with local police to combat this critical problem.

I believe that one of the best ways to fight the problem of drug trafficking is to cut down on the potential outlets for the dealers. You are probably aware that certain promoters of major rock festivals have been looking at Kentucky as an event site. I am alarmed at the possible consequences and believe you join me in this concern. We have learned from sad experience that literally millions of dollars in drugs have been traded and sold at various rock festivals, large and small, and I don't intend to allow Kentucky to become another mass market for narcotic trading, at festivals or anywhere else! Such events breed trouble from those who care more for their ill-gotten profits than the welfare and entertainment of our young people. Under our constitution, as Governor, I have the responsibility of protecting the health and welfare of all our citizens. Based on this responsibility, I have instructed my staff to investigate all legal remedies available to me to prevent the staging of any mass rock festivals, where widespread dope pushing is made easy, where sanitation problems are overwhelming, and where traffic congestion brings about disaster. The Attorney General[1] has offered the support of his office in this preventive measure, so the warning from me had better be understood by those promoters who are thinking about Kentucky.

I firmly believe the people of Kentucky have a right to be protected against any undue or unnecessary infringement upon their personal safety or dangers to their general health and welfare. In my opinion, festivals of the magnitude of those made infamous elsewhere would represent a very real danger to our citizens, and I do not intend to see it occur in Kentucky! As you know, hundreds of thousands of young people gather in a small area and become marks to those who use such festivals to sell their stores of hard drugs. If I can take whatever legal steps to prevent this, your jobs will be easier in the long run. If I didn't take this stand, some of you in this room would become involved in the awesome job of policing huge rock festivals in Kentucky, and you know it isn't a pleasant task by any means.

Let me make another point so there will be no misunderstanding. I am not opposing rock music or rock events. If legitimate promoters want to stage their productions in the proper facilities, under adequate supervision, and where there will be no problems as I have mentioned, I welcome this type of entertainment. If, for instance, a legitimate promoter wants to rent Freedom Hall or the Capital Plaza and treat the young people in the audience in their best interests, they will find a cooperative administration. But I draw the line against any who would promote something that is contrary to the security of our citizens. I hope you support me in this stand!

I also want to mention briefly another common goal. This is the prevention and reduction of traffic accidents. You have heard the screams, have seen the broken bodies and the property damage. Yet we continue to face more deaths and injuries on our highways. The answer hasn't been found, but together we can keep searching until the trend starts downward. We need your help, your ideas, and your constant efforts to educate the public on traffic safety. In this regard, we have just produced a new film about this subject. It is available to you because we want as many Kentuckians to see it as possible. If it can save one life, it's worth every penny of the cost.

We will work with local police agencies in as many ways as are necessary to continue the downward trend in crime. The war on crime is a tough one, but together we can win it. I am convinced of this, and I assure you that my administration is committed to this end. Conferences such as this, where law-enforcement officials from across the state can get together and seek out areas of mutual concern, can go a long way in winning this war on crime. I applaud your initiative in sponsoring this exchange of ideas, and I wish you the best of success in the association's meeting the needs for which it was designed.

---

1. Ed W. Hancock (1925–   ), attorney; attorney general of Kentucky (1972–1976). *Who's Who in America, 1974–1975* (Chicago, 1975), 1:1301.

KENTUCKY COUNCIL ON CRIME
AND DELINQUENCY CONFERENCE
Louisville / September 12, 1973

PRISONS across the country have experienced a long, tense summer. Rare was the week when you picked up a newspaper without reading about a disorder or rebellion at some correctional institution. In July, two men died, twenty more were injured, and the Oklahoma State Penitentiary at McAlester was nearly destroyed after a weekend riot, where twenty-three persons were held hostage. That same month closer to home two guards died as a result of a rebellion at the Southern Ohio Correctional Facility at Lucasville—victims of the inhumane, savage revenge of convicts. Two weeks ago in Michigan City, Indiana, insurgent inmates held three hostages at knife-point before releasing them forty-eight hours later. And just last week in Illinois, 270 prisoners seized eleven guards for a day at the Stateville Penitentiary.

Kentucky did not escape this wave of disorders. This summer inmates twice seized hostages at Eddyville. We were fortunate, however. No one was injured, no lives were lost, and no concessions were made! Whenever disruption occurs, there is no singular way to respond. Each situation dictates a particular action. Often immediate decisions are required, based on limited knowledge of what the troublemakers are going to do next. Personnel in the correctional field can't enjoy the luxury of the "Monday morning quarterbacks" or the second guessers! Still, this awesome responsibility calls for cool heads, rational thinking, and a special toughness.

When anyone yields to the demands of convicts who have created chaos, the door opens later to further disturbance. On the other hand, the management of prisons today must constantly strive to eliminate those conditions which spark uprisings. This is a tough job, in Kentucky and elsewhere, since society places a low priority on government expenditures and government's intensified efforts to improve correctional facilities.

In view of experiences around the country, I believe we have been fortunate, despite our own share of troubles at both Eddyville and LaGrange. But a feeling of being fortunate must not be interpreted as an attitude of satisfaction. To be perfectly blunt, who can predict what will happen tomorrow, or next week? We simply aren't in position to say there is no smoke, and consequently no fire. Yet, we are in position to say that we have made substantial progress, and in view of the conditions we were forced to assume, the word substantial can be underlined.

Our approach has been based on strength, no nonsense, and the realization that deficiencies which have existed for many years simply cannot be corrected in twelve or twenty-four months. On the other hand, we believe the potential for problems has been reduced, and this is seen in the daily routines of over 90 percent of those imprisoned.

Henry Cowen[1] put it well when he said, "There's no way I know to prevent the taking of hostages and other disturbances if you run a prison with rehabilitation programs and under the laws. The staff has to relate closely to the inmates and the inmates to them. The potential for seizing hostages, for killing, is always there. Changes for the betterment of the inmate and his future have been made, but you've always got that group that doesn't appreciate change." I would add that changes for the protection of society have also been made, despite the distance we still must travel.

No one wants to remedy continuing deficiencies more than I, more than Commissioner Holmes,[2] and more than those who are truly responsive to a modern correctional system. We are attempting to do this with a genuine concern for a system which rehabilitates—rather than one which only punishes—one which is fair and firm, without coddling. In doing so, we hope to eliminate the causes of discontent that lead to violence. Many innovative ideas and much long-needed overhauling in our corrections system have been put in motion during the last twenty months. Moves were taken not only to improve prison security, the obvious weakness that prompts notions of a revolt, but also to make life behind the walls more decent and humane.

There is a quiet revolution going on in Kentucky's penal system aimed at rehabilitation of prisoners, not just incarceration. Perhaps most of you in this room are aware of the progress, but let this be a forum to inform others. An improved treatment program, where group counseling is used, was introduced into every institution in the state. Prison regulations were clearly defined to inmates at Eddyville and LaGrange for the first time. Programs were introduced permitting prisoners who have good records in institutional adjustment to be visited by families and friends in a more relaxed atmosphere. Action has been taken to dry up the drug traffic that existed at both Eddyville and LaGrange, a difficult task at best. A matrix program, designed to provide self-help opportunities for twenty-eight inmates with drug problems, started in December at Eddyville. New and extensive training and orientation programs for probation, parole, and correctional officers were initiated.

Additionally, the state's public defender system was extended into the prisons for the first time. That office now receives ten to twelve requests for assistance each week from inmates. Funds were channeled through the Crime Commission enabling the Department of Corrections to implement several progressive and long-needed operations at Eddyville and LaGrange, including expanded industrial and educational programs, renovation of certain existing facilities, and increased security.

A monthly correctional co-op newspaper, composed by residents of all the state's felony correctional institutions, in addition to staff of the Department of Corrections, was started in December. This newspaper informs the residents about new laws, rulings, and opportunities available to them and is proving how inmates and administrators can work together. A revised admissions and orientation program, designed to give new prisoners a clear-cut idea of what to expect from their fellow inmates, correctional officers, and prisoners was implemented at Eddyville.

A security coordinator for all state prisons was hired. His job will be to review and update present security measures, not only providing greater assurance of safety to the public, but making life safer for the inmates. Medical service has been expanded and will be a continuing top priority.

We also opened the Blackburn Correctional Center and the Harlan County Forestry Camp. Both are small, community-based centers, designed to help prisoners adjust to life in the "outside world." Centers such as these could set the pace for correctional institutes of the future and can serve as incentive for good behavior to prisoners in other institutions who want to qualify for transfer to one of them. These changes and improvements are important to men who are confined. They are equally important outside the walls, since they reduce the threat of revolt.

People want us to do something to instill the proper behavior in a man in prison, so that when he is released he does not go back to prison; rather he lives a law-abiding life and becomes useful to himself and society. The community also demands a sense of security, and rightfully so. We must continue to ensure the minimum potential for rebellions and disorders. By showing concern for the prisoners, their food, medical attention, and other day-to-day routines, the atmosphere and morale becomes better. This helps prevent an Attica.[3] Experience shows we are not coddling prisoners; we are rehabilitating them. In the long run, rehabilitation of an inmate offers far greater security to society.

Unlike numerous other programs of state government, the correctional report card will not offer a true indication of progress for quite some time. Our patience, and persistence, can pay great dividends if all who are directly involved maintain the supreme degree of responsibility required and show by their individual actions that the course which has been set is right and proper. Adversity and frustration are the sands which tend to restrict the gears of correctional progress. But I think we have a pretty hefty oilcan in the leadership of people like Chuck Holmes, his staff, and interested citizens, who are determined to see the machine run smoothly.

---

1. Henry Cowen (1929–   ), Fulton; schoolteacher; school supervisor (1960–1964); deputy warden for custody (1964–1969) at Kentucky State Penitentiary; associate supervisor for custody at LaGrange Reformatory (1969–1972); superintendent at Kentucky State Penitentiary (1972–May 1976); presently at Iowa State Penitentiary in Fort Madison, Iowa. Telephone interview with Cowen on January 4, 1977.

2. Charles Holmes, for more information see speech from September 7, 1972, in this section, pp. 267–70.

3. On September 9, 1971, over 1,000 prisoners at Attica State Correctional Facility in New York seized thirty-two guards as hostages. *New York Times,* 10 September 1971, p. 1.

CRIMINAL JUSTICE SEMINAR
Atlanta, Georgia / November 16, 1973

If you follow the sweeping hand on your watch, you will see that thirteen seconds pass pretty fast. Just about the time it took me to make that statement. Based on 1972 figures from the FBI's Uniform Crime Report, a burglary occurred during that time. At least this was the average for last year. So we can say with some conclusion, that since I have begun the text of this address, at least one, and perhaps two incidents of burglary have taken place in the United States.

Last year a murder was committed every twenty-eight minutes, and a rape every eleven minutes. An aggravated assault happened every eighty-one seconds, while there was a robbery every eighty-four seconds. This is not a pleasant way to begin an address, but if we are to cope successfully with crime, we must face up to the unpleasant aspects of life in American society.

Possibly some of you in this room have been direct victims of criminal acts. There is no question whatsoever that everyone in this building has been indirectly harmed, because the expense of crime is a burden to every citizen in this country. Governors across the United States are placing higher and higher priorities on the subject of criminal justice, giving more of their time, energy, and resources to this end. Oklahoma Governor David Hall has termed crime "the chief enemy of every governor." In this state, Governor Jimmy Carter[1] has declared November as crime prevention month, and in an open letter to Georgia citizens he said in part, "Crime is an ugly business. And unfair though it is, we are all involved. Because if anything is going to slow down the tremendous progress and growth of our state, it's going to be the criminal element."

I use these examples, and there are countless others, to make a point. While words do little more than signify a recognition of the problem, Governors are backing their words with action. Governors are finding positive results of their new initiatives and are developing strong working relationships with individuals and agencies, such as George Murphy of the Law Enforcement Assistance Administration. Of course, there are different approaches from state to state and town to town, but we are all dealing with people issues—security of life, rights, and property.

This seminar has been designed to give you a strong forum for exchanging valuable information to better understand approaches which are working well in the field of criminal justice. As a prelude to our comprehensive day-and-a-half package, I want to offer some personal thoughts on what states can do and are doing about the spreading cancer of crime. Major crime is a wealthy industry, in many ways a sophisticated industry and in other ways an industry where its own warped intelligence creates great difficulty for those who must cope with the causation of crime. For too long, the ability to fund crime has been far greater than the willingness to fund crime-fighting. Therefore, it is incumbent on whomever has the power to piece together the various weapons in the battle against crime to allocate the many resources available in such a way as to guarantee a structured, unified approach.

Southern governors have taken fairly uniform positions on funding and program principles which we believed to be critical in turning the corner on crime in our respective states. Several of us testified or had testimony presented before congressional committees considering the future of the Safe Streets Act and criminal justice monies available to the states through LEAA. Our testimony supported the bloc-grant concept and systemwide planning at the state level. The bloc-grant concept embodied in the Safe Streets Act was not merely a forerunner of general revenue-sharing. It was also a gradual and orderly means of allocating the public resources to the entire problem of solving crime at the most effective level—the states.

Systemwide planning at the state level has proven to be a vital and effective element in the coordination of decision-making, resources allocation, and response to common problems. The problems of the criminal justice system are interdependent because crime is such a complex matter. It can only be solved by an integrated strengthening of the entire criminal justice system, from the policemen on the beat, through the courts, corrections, probation, and parole systems.

Program discretion by the states was challenged this year with proposed amendments which would have required a certain percentage of the money allocated to a state to be spent in a specified program area. Many of us again responded by working through our state's congressional delegations to delete these amendments. We were successfully persistent in this effort because of our belief in accountability at the state level. One of the most important ingredients in any criminal justice program is credibility. If the people don't believe that the system is capable of protecting their well-being, property, and rights, they are going to ignore it and go their own way. We know the unhappy consequences of the law's failure to meet the just expectations of those governed by it. Law loses its stabilizing influence. At best, the results are alienation and lack of trust in the legal system. At worst, there is violence and unrest.

Crime commissions, criminal justice planning agencies, and law-enforcement commissions in our respective states have been putting the money where crime must be fought. A review of fiscal years 1969 through 1972 indicates that state planning agencies have allocated almost 65 percent of all local funds to high crime areas. But additional action is necessary.

One way states can take the initiative is by grouping all criminal justice agencies into a central organizational unit. This creation provides a system that can plan and react to the criminal justice needs and problems of the state in the most efficient manner possible. Too often existing crime-fighting systems are really no systems at all! They are fragmented with individual departmental interests, with no integrated planning and budgeting machinery. A single, streamlined, state agency eliminates potential weak links. There are other areas where states can show initiative and originality.

Regional information systems with a statewide hookup and state-supported crime lab facilities can put the many arms of state law-enforcement agencies in concert, thus eliminating unnecessary time-consuming delays in the justice process. States can pump additional funds into their crime-fighting programs to generate additional federal dollars for prudent use in funding new projects. To assure that everyone has equal protection under the law, states can establish public defender programs. There can be no civilized enforcement of criminal law without full legal assistance to the accused. Corrections systems in many states need to be overhauled. Patronage must have no standing in the selection and retention of parole board members, as well as probation and parole officers. Corrections programs based on a genuine concern for rehabilitation, rather than only punishment, ones which are firm without coddling, can be implemented. By doing this, many of the causes of discontent, which have led to violence in our nation's prisons, can be eliminated.

Proper training of all individuals involved with enforcing and administering justice—the police, corrections officers, public defender staff members, jailers, sheriffs—must be given renewed emphasis. Training must be elevated to an equal footing with the operational basis and not treated as a subservient group.

We have all of these programs in Kentucky and there is real evidence to support what we are doing. Last year, crime in Kentucky was reduced by 8 percent, compared with a 3 percent decrease nationally. This was the first reduction in our crime rate since World War II, and there was an actual decrease of 5,000 serious crimes. Naturally, we aren't satisfied. We want to see more dents put in the machinery of crime, but I am pleased with the initiative shown in designing programs which can strengthen law enforcement. One additional program you might be interested in was a 15 percent salary-educational supplement for over 2,600 local policemen across the state. We presented a plan to the General Assembly and it was adopted.

I believe the police officer stands first and foremost on the front lines. He remains the single most important individual in the criminal justice response to crime. He makes the split-second decisions affecting the future freedom, or even the future existence, of other members of society. In this era of sophisticated crime-fighting, training at all levels becomes paramount. Specialized tools and equipment are totally ineffective unless policemen are regularly schooled to properly use what is now available and what will be available in the years to come. The best way to improve immediately the educational levels of men entering police service, to improve the continuing education of officers already in service, and to spur policemen to improve their performance on the job by in-service and basic training is through a training and educational incentive program.

We were drawn into a ten-month ordeal with the Federal Pay Board and Cost of Living Council before Kentucky was finally able to implement this program. Quite possibly the delay was compounded because our program was so unusual, so unique (to use the Cost of Living Council's description) that the Pay Board had no guidelines to follow in reaching their decision. They did not understand at first that ours was not a mere request for increased salaries. It was a different state response to the problem of crime and justice and represented, for Kentucky, a significant milestone in achieving statewide minimum educational standards for police.

A little more than a year ago, I told the Council of State Governments' legislative workshop in criminal justice that I would like to see the decade of the seventies, in contrast to the sixties, remembered for its intelligent response to the problems of crime and justice in society. Through the continued concern and cooperation of all of us here today—law-enforcement officials, administrators, local, state, and federal government leaders—this does not have to be simply a dream; it can become a reality.[2]

---

1. David Hall, for more information see speech from September 7, 1972, in this section, pp. 267–70. James Earl Carter, Jr. (1924–   ), Democrat from Plains, Georgia; peanut farmer and warehouseman; member of Georgia State Senate (1962–1966); Governor of Georgia (1971–1974); President of the United States (1977–   ). *Who's Who in American Politics, 1975–1976*, 5th ed. (New York, 1975), p. 150.

2. On November 21, 1973, Governor Ford gave the same speech at the Southern Police Institute graduation at the University of Louisville. This speech is not included in this volume.

TRUCKERS' STRIKE STATEMENTS
Frankfort / February 4 and 5, 1974

WE have just concluded a two-and-a-half-hour meeting on the trucking situation.[1] While there have been a few incidents of violence, and several others of personal intimidation, Kentucky thus far is not experiencing the serious problems found in certain other states. Nevertheless, I deem it necessary to take further steps to protect the welfare of all Kentuckians and to ensure the orderly shipment of essential supplies such as food, medicines, gasoline, and heating fuels.

For the last three days, the Kentucky State Police has increased its surveillance on major trucking routes. The State Police has responded to complaints and has investigated each. In the last twenty-four hours, there have been four episodes of violence reported to the State Police. There have been numerous rumors, found to be exactly that—rumors.

After reviewing intelligence reports and consulting with various officials who are directly involved in this matter, I am taking further steps to reach our objective of peace and calm. I have placed the Kentucky National Guard on standby alert. We have developed a contingency plan for the use of National Guard helicopters with the State Police for surveillance in whatever part of Kentucky is necessary. We are developing other plans of action which hopefully will not be necessary, but which can be immediately implemented if the situation demands it.

Included in the meeting, besides my staff, were the State Police, National Guard, and Bureau of Motor Transportation. The Attorney General's Office will be kept fully informed as each step progresses.

I fully sympathize with the plight of the truckers. They are caught in an economic crunch, not of their creation. Rather it's because of a complete lack of a national energy policy. However, my first interest must be the safety, health, and welfare of the people of Kentucky. I will not condone violence, intimidation, or any other act of disruption. Additionally I will not allow, within my ability to prevent it, people to be hungry, people to be cold, and people to be without essential items for everyday life.[2]

As you know, several steps have been taken in the last few days to increase our capacity of providing protection to the general public during the current trucking situation.[3] First, additional State Police units were placed on major trucking routes. Second, a thorough assessment of activities involving either violence or intimidation has been made on a continuing basis. Third, the Kentucky National Guard was placed on standby alert. Fourth, National Guard helicopters were ordered to active duty to conduct surveillance missions with the State Police. Fifth, a meeting of carriers (which included independent truck drivers) was held to further assess the problems involved in moving various items throughout Kentucky.

Based on all information available, the situation is critical. Communities are experiencing serious reductions in food, gasoline, heating fuels, and many other materials. Carriers have indicated they will move their cargo with a planned procedure of state protection. I am, therefore, taking the following steps. One thousand national guardsmen are immediately being activated. These men are being activated in all sections of the state. The Kentucky National Guard, in conjunction with the Kentucky State Police, will provide for the protection of life and property, and assist within all resources, the nonviolent movement of essential truck shipments. What I am talking about is a planned system of conveying trucks from one point to another in order to ensure the orderly movement of materials in Kentucky.

Anyone who has materials to move can contact either their local State Police post or nearest National Guard armory. The request will be processed to establish a protected convoy and the carrier will then be given a schedule of movement. We will conduct all operations during daylight hours as another safety precaution. Interested carriers can begin making calls for movement arrangements at 8 A.M. tomorrow.

Other activities by the State Police and National Guard include continued helicopter and light aircraft patrols, additional motorized highway patrols, and the guarding of essential public property as required; both the National Guard and State Police will be prepared to perform other missions as may be directed. Obviously, we are first concerned with vital items. Food, heating fuel, gasoline, and medicines must be provided, and I consider the transporting of such as a major public service on the part of truckers and carriers. As convoys are made up, however, other items will be moved along with the priority supplies.

I do not want either violence or intimidation. I fully recognize the critical problems being experienced by independent truckers. Just as I said yesterday, they didn't create them, Washington did. From reports, I am also convinced that many of the incidents reported are not the result of truckers but hoodlums who find this situation an opportunity to create unrest. This will not be tolerated. The safety and welfare of all Kentuckians is my first consideration! I have been in contact with other Governors. I am asking Governor Dan Evans[4] to call an emergency meeting of the Executive Committee of the National Governors'

Conference in Washington, D.C., tomorrow or no later than Thursday morning. The Governors of the Great Lakes Region will be meeting then.

---

1. Press conference on February 4.
2. On the same day Governor Ford also made a statement as chairman of the National Democratic Governors' Caucus. He said, "To imply the necessity of the federal government urging Governors to restore order and commerce is an insult to those of us nearest the situation. Had there not been the hodgepodge of federal fumbling in the Energy Crisis we wouldn't be in this position today. It is becoming a habit that when Washington creates domestic chaos, Washington then calls on the Governors to restore calm." This statement is not included in this volume.
3. Press conference on February 5.
4. Daniel Jackson Evans (1925–   ), Republican from Seattle, Washington; Washington State Representative (1956–1965); Governor of Washington (1965–   ); member of executive board of the National Governors' Conference (1966–1967, 1973–1975). *Who's Who in American Politics, 1975–1976*, 5th ed. (New York, 1975), p. 283.

APRIL TORNADO RELIEF
Frankfort / April 5, 1974

THE trauma of this disaster is too great for me to tell you that everything is fully under control.[1] I can state to you that the full powers of my office are being exerted to minimize the suffering and to expedite relief. We are still surveying the extent of the damage and seeking ways to begin rebuilding. I can assure you that we will do everything we can to find funds to restore these communities.

Let me recap where we are. My office, our Civil Defense Office, the National Guard, and many many other state agencies have been in operation day and night since the first disaster struck. We had not recovered from Campbellsburg before disaster struck again. We have eighty-seven deaths confirmed. I requested and the President has declared Kentucky a disaster area. This action will provide both emergency relief and financial assistance.[2] Procedures on how to apply for financial assistance will be described later. I have directed each state agency to cooperate in the rescue and cleanup to the full powers of their office. That effort has been under way from the initial impact.

I have asked Charlie Pryor,[3] the secretary of the executive cabinet, to review state financial assistance available. He informed me that the Kentucky Farm Development Authority has funds to guarantee loans for farmers and that the Kentucky Housing Authority has funds to lend to low-income families after July 1. Commitments could be made sooner. If adequate funds for low-income families are not available from other sources, the housing authority will issue the necessary revenue bonds to make the loans. In addition we have reviewed the availability of funds from federal agencies.

Trailers are available for locating on pads in trailer parks which are fully developed, but due to the magnitude of this disaster, we cannot assume the responsibility for site development. Our people will be working with each area to determine those sites which qualify. Procedures for obtaining these trailers must be coordinated with local officials. Also from the Farmers Home Administration, long-term loans at the rate of 5 percent interest are available. From HUD (Department of Housing and Urban Development) funds for low-cost housing are available; and from the Small Business Administration, long-term loans at the rate of 5 percent interest are available. Procedures on obtaining this assistance will be described by the responsible officials.[4]

---

1. A series of tornadoes caused heavy damage in various parts of Kentucky on April 3, 1974.

2. The counties approved by the White House were Anderson, Boone, Boyle, Breckinridge, Bullitt, Clark, Clinton, Cumberland, Franklin, Grayson, Green, Hardin, Harrison, Henry, Jefferson, Lincoln, McCreary, Madison, Meade, Nelson, Oldham, Rockcastle, Scott, Simpson, Taylor, Warren, Wayne, and Whitley.

3. Charles Pryor, for more information see speech from March 24, 1973, in the Reorganization section, p. 125.

4. On April 8 Governor Ford announced that eleven Federal Disaster Assistance Administration One-Stop Centers were to be located across the state to assist victims of the prior week's tornado disasters.

STATEMENT ON MINE PICKETING
Frankfort / July 22, 1974

I VERY much appreciate the opportunity of meeting with President Miller [1] today to sit down and discuss many matters of mutual interest. The meeting was productive, informative, and beneficial.

We have mutual concerns and will approach these concerns on a cooperative basis. The UMW is entitled to the full rights of peaceful picketing without interference. All sides are entitled to the protection of life and property. President Miller and I want a peaceful situation.

Therefore, I have agreed to remove the non-Harlan-based State Police from Harlan County and President Miller has agreed to limit the number of pickets at the Highsplint Mine to a reasonable number.

The State Police assigned to Highsplint Mine area will not convoy strikebreakers through the Highsplint picket line, nor cordon off the public highway, but will permit peaceful interchange between pickets and employees.

I also call on Duke Power to resume bargaining immediately and again reemphasize that the facilities and services of my office are available, just as they were made to the UMW today, and will continue to be available.[2]

---

1. Press conference. Arnold Ray Miller (1923–   ), president, United Mine Workers (1972–   ); coorganizer of Miners for Democracy (1969); president of Black Lung Association (1970–1972); vice president of special projects, Designs for Rural Action, Inc. (1970–1972); Board of Directors of Appalachian Research and Defense Fund (1970–1972); trustee of the United Mine Workers of America Welfare and Retirement Fund. *Who's Who in America, 1974–1975* (Chicago, 1975), 2:2149.

2. Relating to this matter Governor Ford made the following statement on August 30, 1974: "The formal signing of a contract between the United Mine Workers and Eastover Mining Company, a subsidiary of Duke Power Company, relating to the Brookside Mine is welcomed news.

"That, as reported, both sides alluded to concessions while pledging cooperation, gives cause to recognize the very strong potential for a bright future through joint efforts and constructive reasoning. I am personally grateful to everyone who participated in the proceedings which have brought a positive response.

"I do not like strife and discord. My office was made available to the principals with a good line of communications established to assist in maintaining as best as humanly possible the balance necessary in a period of deep concern, then hope. Because we were kept informed by all principals, for a lengthy period of time, they provided necessary help in our monitoring of the situation to its conclusion.

"My office will always be available for whatever assistance might be necessary, or desired, in negotiations or conferences between parties relative to the common good of the people of Kentucky." This statement does not appear in this volume.

KENTUCKY FIREMEN'S ASSOCIATION
Shively / August 13, 1974

At times we read or hear about an unusual feat, or heroic act, performed by firemen. But on as many, or probably more, occasions, we don't learn about them. They pass unnoticed to the great majority. Unfortunately, there is no accurate count of the number of people you right here in this room have helped, the personal sacrifices you have made, or the times you have gone beyond the role as fireman. No doubt each of you can recall significant episodes in your professional life. Whether the ultimate result was success or failure, there are incidents implanted very deeply in your minds.

Now let's turn this around a bit. Despite the achievements of fire fighters, the compassion often displayed, the personal satisfaction you feel for a job well done, are you being taken for granted? I wonder how many realize the degree and proficiency of training you must undergo? I wonder how many realize the sophisticated improvements in fire fighting which have come about over the last few years? I wonder how many realize the anguish your families experience? I wonder how many realize that the fireman in 1974 is far different from the fireman of 1954, and that the fireman ten years from now will again be a different type of public servant?

The cold, hard facts are that your profession has improved dramatically over the years. Old-timers can point to these advancements with pride. Young firemen recognize this trend is going to continue because fire fighting, lifesaving, disaster prevention, and all the other aspects of your profession will call on the best and take nothing less. Thank goodness there are so many who are willing to tackle tough, demanding, and often thankless jobs—persons who are meeting the day-to-day challenge of an uncommon task, with uncommon determination and ability! Your story deserves telling over and over again, for it's a positive story in behalf of others.

As a public official, I have heard your concerns, your desires, your problems, and your ideas. I've heard it because we've had an open line of communication. Your organization has been an exceptional group to work with in many endeavors. You have provided input and feedback, which is so essential if government is to truly serve. You've helped bring about an awareness of the recognition Kentucky's fire fighters are due for the many contributions they make to the people of this state. Because of your interest and cooperation, we have been able to be a partner in introducing and expanding a number of programs, which benefit both you and the public you serve.

In 1971 when I was campaigning for Governor, you let me know that fire fighters needed and deserved greater personal protection, both for yourselves and your dependents. You told me about a volunteer fireman in western Kentucky who lost his life while on duty. This man who died serving his community had no insurance and his family and friends were left to shoulder the responsibility of settling the estate alone. I promised you then that I would move to correct this inequity. As a result, we were able to expand the workmen's compensation program to include unlimited injury or sickness coverage, as well as greater death benefits and income protection for you. We were also able to enact legislation allowing part of the fire department aid funds to be put to use as an insurance program for you. This same legislation opened fire department assistance to all classes of fire departments.

You let me know of a need for more money in fire department aid. We were able to do something about it by raising the budget allocation from $100,000 a year to $300,000 in 1972–1973 and to $350,000 in 1974–1975. You voiced your concern for increasing the continuing training and educational opportunities. As a result, in 1972 we succeeded in establishing and funding the Commission on Firefighters Training and Educational Standards. This program was strengthened in 1974 by legislation to take advantage of federal funds. We reorganized the Fire Services Vocational Training Program, expanding it to include additional instructors and equipment. The State Fire Marshal's Office was reorganized, and we increased its operating budget by $500,000 to provide better and more efficient service to you and your communities. Also we haven't overlooked volunteer fire departments. A need existed for financial assistance, so we established a fund totaling $150,000 over the biennium to assist these units in acquiring equipment and training, especially to improve rescue operations. As you can see, your input has made a significant impact. We never seem to accomplish everything we want. But we have made unprecedented strides in your behalf during the past thirty months. The examples I have given only touch the surface.

I want to encourage you to continue to offer assistance, thoughts, and ideas. Advice from responsible groups such as yours is invaluable. You know better than anyone just what the problems and needs are at the local level. A first requirement of any person who holds public office is that he relate to, talk with, and seek to understand the public, the people who put him where he is. It is not enough that he do this only when he is running for office. More importantly, he must do this after he is in office. I have tried, as best I could, to keep an "open door" in Frankfort. I have tried, as best I could, to take state government out to the people. As long as I hold public office, my door is going to be open to you and to every other Kentuckian. You will never have to sit around my office (your office) waiting to get in. As in the past, you are going to be in on decisions from the beginning. We may differ on occasion, but you are going to know how I stand before I act, and you are going to have input.

A mutual spirit of cooperation has grown and prospered between state government and your organization during the past two and a half years. Your profession, similar to numerous other groups, is affected by a variety of conditions. Right now you are plagued by factors so powerful that only the federal government can cope with them. Thus far, the record is bleak. It can all be boiled down into a single word, shortages. I happen to know how severe the impact is on fire departments not only in Kentucky but throughout the United States. Communication supplies are almost impossible to acquire on schedule. An absence of raw materials curtails the production of essential fire-fighting equipment. You're even having difficulty buying uniforms! And of course inflation is tearing your budgets, professional as well as personal, to pieces.

Shortages and inflation have jumped on your backs like a wild bear in the wilderness. They haven't been shaken off, and it's going to take plenty of muscle to do so. Only at the federal level can you find relief that will be permanent and worthwhile. It bothers me, because I know what you mean to every community in Kentucky. Every day that goes by without an improvement means the problems are compounded. This is why public officials, and those who are affected by the actions of public officials, must always stay in touch. Anything less is not only undesirable, it is against all the principles of what our government is based upon.

STATEMENT ON THE DANIEL BOONE TREATMENT CENTER
Frankfort / August 23, 1974

SEVERAL days ago, I ordered a hold on the relocation of the residential and day treatment program now housed at the Daniel Boone Treatment Center pending a complete and comprehensive evaluation and review. I have received recommendations from my staff and have discussed the program with the chairman of the special legislative committee named to review the proposed relocation.

From these discussions and public expressions of interest by the northern Kentucky community, I have concluded that the Daniel Boone Treatment Center is not in the proper location to best meet the needs of the youthful offenders served there. The problems these children have experienced began in their homes and their respective communities, and this is where the problems must be resolved. We must work with the entire family where they live.

In order to benefit from the various resources the northern Kentucky community has to offer, the present program at Daniel Boone Treatment Center should be relocated from a rural setting to the urban area. The focus of the program and the real needs of the children are of primary concern, but these have become secondary to some of our critics. I have concluded that the controversy surrounding the proposed location will seriously hamper the future effectiveness of the program. Therefore, the day treatment program will not be located in the proposed facility at 423–425 Greenup Street, Covington, Kenton County, Kentucky. The portion of the proposed facility that was suggested for use of the Treatment Center is not, in my estimate, satisfactory for this purpose.

I have directed the following actions be taken by the appropriate officials:

1. There will be two program elements:
   A. Day Treatment, education-oriented program;
   B. Group Home program.
2. That alternative facilities be located in the urban area to house the program.
3. That the present program be continued at the Daniel Boone facility until all relocation plans are completed to ensure no disruption of services.

4. That alternative plans for the future use of the Daniel Boone property be completed.

5. That the terms of the proposed lease on the properties at 423–425 Greenup Street, Covington, be amended to reflect the changed use.

This puts us in position to deal directly with concerns expressed by members of the General Assembly and provides the best possible care for the children who need it most. I want to reemphasize my support of the efforts of the Department for Human Resources in moving away from the old-fashioned concept of banishing children from their communities. Whenever possible, community-based day treatment, group homes, and foster care will supplement, rather than supplant, expensive residential care in meeting the needs of Kentucky's children. This approach conforms with national trends in delinquency prevention and treatment, and it is the proper direction for us.

KENTUCKY NATIONAL GUARD DINING-IN
Louisville / October 5, 1974

GENERAL FRYMIRE, general officers, officers of the best National Guard in America![1] And you are the best! I hear praise from other states, just as I hear praise from Kentucky, and it makes me proud to be associated with you. It is a distinct pleasure to again participate in your Dining-In. Last year we had a great time, though I'm sure some of you don't remember a thing about it! This event is unique in America, in that it is the only dining-in where officers of both the Army National Guard and Air National Guard come together for an evening of service and social relaxation.

The evening in which we participate is important to an organization where esprit de corps is prominent, not by necessity, but rather because a spirit has been built from your own personalities and this spirit is felt by others. The National Guard in 1974 has the greatest responsibility ever accorded to a reserve component. You represent the primary back-up for the mobilization of our nation's active-duty forces. The emphasis accorded reserve components has increased each year since Secretary Laird[2] announced the total-force concept in 1970.

Today the National Guard is better manned, better trained, and better equipped than ever before. Yet we must always recognize there can never be complacency, even if new plateaus have finally been reached, because new challenges await you, just as demands for new initiatives will no doubt loom over the horizon. The responsibility of the Guard to our nation is greater than ever before. With a zero draft environment we have turned to an all-volunteer force. We recognize that on a national level there has been, in some instances, a lessening of the standards for entry into active force service, a fact that should cause concern. In contrast, the National Guard is an all-volunteer force, but there has been no lessening of standards among you, nor do I expect this to occur, especially in Kentucky.

I look to the citizen soldier as a mainstream for American integrity and strength, the stabilizing factor in our total defense force. Without your willingness to serve America, to leave your job and family in the face of emergency, this country and most certainly this state would be in jeopardy. On two occasions this year I have called you into the service of our state. Last February it was necessary to ensure the orderly movement of food, fuel, medicines, and other essential materials over our roadways. These were sensitive times when you provided escort service to trucks bearing those life-needs. Again, in April, when Kentucky was devastated by a series of tornadoes, you vaulted into action without hesitation to serve thousands who were victims of tragedy. You served your state and the people until heat was restored, until the injured and dead were accounted for, until shelter was found, until food was plentiful, and until order could be routinely maintained. Your presence on those dreary April days and during those long fateful nights was security to men and women of all ages. I can't recount how many times I heard compliments about the courteous, efficient, and professional manner in which you fulfilled your mission.

We in state government have recognized the value of the National Guard to the Commonwealth, and the 1974 General Assembly spotlighted this recognition through the enactment of legislation, and I am proud it was administrative legislation, calculated to benefit the guardsman and to encourage continued duty to our state and nation.[3] Together we have achieved much in a short period of time with the ultimate goal of building a National Guard of quality and quantity. Hopefully, what has been accomplished by working in concert will stimulate continued attention not only to your many values but also to your additional needs.

Good reports come from the Guard. The Air National Guard has announced its combat-ready status as C-1 and its strength at 104 percent. The Army National Guard attained 106 percent in April and received an additional 350 military spaces as a result of excellence. You received additional units into the state which enabled us to expand into three new communities. This is the first reorganization in my memory where Kentucky received strength instead of losing it and was able to expand into communities rather than withdrawing from them. I congratulate you for your positive action.

Another good report, and I don't know how many of you are aware of this, is that in September the pistol team recently won a national competition. Those who participated are from Bowling Green, Paducah, Broadhead, Lexington, and Louisville (and if I have left someone out, I'll probably get shot!). They scored highest in the Winston P. Wilson Rifle and Pistol Championship, a prestigious event. As your Governor, I have enjoyed working with you. I don't mind saying that I'm a guardsman at heart, and always will be, carrying the concern and importance of the citizen soldier with me as days pass and years follow. This has been another fine evening and I thank you for giving me the privilege of sharing it with you. It is a privilege, because of who you are and what you stand for.[4]

---

1. Richard L. Frymire (1931–   ), Madisonville; attorney; member of the Kentucky House of Representatives (1962–1965), majority leader (1968–1969); named adjutant general of Kentucky National Guard in 1971. *Who's Who in American Politics, 1975–1976*, 5th ed. (New York, 1975), p. 323.

2. Melvin R. Laird (1922–   ), Republican from Wisconsin; member of Wisconsin State Senate (1952–1956); chairman of various areas of the platform committee, Republican National Convention (1964); chairman of Republican Conference, 89th and 90th congresses; secretary of defense (1969–1972); domestic adviser to President Nixon (1973–1974). *Who's Who in America, 1974–1975* (Chicago, 1975), 2:1786.

3. These benefits included a five-point preference when applying for state employment; dependents of a guardsman killed while on active duty can attend a state university tuition free; active-duty pay was increased to twenty-five dollars per day; and a state income-tax credit was created for Guard members. This comes from a speech given by Governor Ford on June 7, 1974, and is not included in this volume.

4. On October 17, 1974, Governor Ford dedicated the Boone Armory in Frankfort. This speech is not included in this volume.

STATEMENT ON LEAA GRANTS
Frankfort / December 2, 1974

You have been given a complete summary of the various programs which were approved for funding as a result of the $1.6 million Law Enforcement Administration grant we are announcing today.[1] In order to conserve time, I will not go into all the details, but there are several points I want to emphasize.

Many of you will recall the landmark legislation enacted by the 1974 General Assembly, Senate Bill 334,[2] which reaffirmed Kentucky's intent to develop a model court system. This bill provided for the enactment of a number of novel steps to unify and expand state financial support to our courts and the offices of commonwealth attorneys. The act set July 1, 1976, as the effective date of implementation of the many, far-reaching reforms—unless earlier funding became available.

Now, as a result of this grant, we will be able to implement several of the programs ahead of schedule. Specifically, funding is now available for immediate commencement of the full-time and part-time assistant commonwealth attorneys program in all of the state's fifty-five judicial districts as well as implementation of the judicial expense-allowance category on January 1, 1975. Full- and part-time assistants for commonwealth attorneys received the major share of the grant, $715,068, while $79,452 was provided to meet expenses for judges during the first half of 1975.

Several other innovative programs also received funding, including one which will provide expanded judicial training and continuing education for statewide criminal justice personnel through our Justice Department's Bureau of Training and the State Judicial Training Council. Each of these programs represents a major step forward in our ongoing efforts to create a modern and efficient judicial system.

What is most significant, however, is that the LEAA[3] recognized Kentucky as the first state in the nation to develop a comprehensive program of improvements of courts and related activities and gave encouragement to continue our efforts by awarding this grant. While some other states are involved on a piecemeal basis through their own programs with LEAA grants, Kentucky's plan is that of a total concept, which makes us unique and I believe ahead of the game. It will require a cooperative effort from all levels of government if we are to reach our goal. The grant being announced today reflects that effort, of which all Kentuckians can be proud.

1. Press conference.

2. See an act "relating to the financing of a unified state court system," which was approved on March 29, 1974. *Acts of the General Assembly of the Commonwealth of Kentucky, 1974*, Chapter 369 (S.B. 334), pp. 714–16.

3. The Law Enforcement Assistance Administration was established June 19, 1968, by the Omnibus Crime Control and Safe Streets Act of 1968 (Stat. 197, as amended by 84 Stat. 1880; 42 U.S.C. 3701). The purpose of LEAA is to assist state and local governments to reduce crime. Block-planning funds are granted to each state to finance development of an annual comprehensive law-enforcement plan. *United States Government Manual 1973/74* (Washington, D.C., 1973), p. 293.

ENERGY AND ENVIRONMENT

COAL SEVERANCE TAX DISPOSITION
Frankfort / December 31, 1971

ONE of the critical issues confronting the 1972 General Assembly will be the question of what becomes of the money to be raised through a severance tax on coal. As things now stand, it would appear that all of this money is to be placed in the General Fund where, if the past is any guide, it will become lost in general government. None of it, in other words, will be used to do anything other than to finance the routine and daily demands of government. The reason I have called this press conference today is to propose that at least one-third of the amount to be derived from a severance tax on coal be earmarked for the financing of a new authority which would address itself to providing the funds needed to finance an all-out attack on the environmental problems confronting Kentucky and assisting local cities and counties in the coalfields and elsewhere in solving financial problems.

Unless we address ourselves now to helping the cities and counties of the coalfields to prepare for the future, to prepare for the day when there is no longer any coal to be mined, we are going to be left with ghost towns of the type to be found throughout the western half of the U.S. This has been the pattern of mining communities in the past. But it need not be the pattern for mining communities of the future under the proposal I am making here today. Unless we also address ourselves to the environmental degradation of the past and take steps to correct it now, future generations will be forever asking why we failed to act.

Let me say first that I personally believe that any severance tax enacted by Kentucky should be on all minerals, as is the case in most of the other states with severance taxes, or as they ought to be known, special taxes. This would be much fairer to the people of Kentucky and would greatly help ease their tax burden. Nevertheless, it appears that this is not to be! Additionally, I feel that given the ideal situation it ought to be possible to return a portion or all of any severance tax to the cities and counties where the mineral was extracted. This it would appear, however, is prohibited by the Constitution of Kentucky. In view of these circumstances, I am therefore proposing that at least one-third of the revenue to be derived from a severance tax on coal be earmarked for use by a new public authority, which will be known as the Kentucky Environmental and Local Development Authority.

This proposed authority would be similar to the Kentucky Turnpike

Authority. Under my proposal it would receive approximately $10 million annually. It would be authorized to issue bonds, to provide seed and grant money to assist local counties and cities in financing public improvements, and, of the greatest importance to Kentucky, it would have the authority and funds to correct the abuses of the past that have damaged our landscape, our water, and our air. This $10 million state tax money could generate, through federal matching funds, as much as $30 million more for the authority. Assuming federal matching funds remain available, the authority could expect to have up to $400 million to spend over the next ten years on its projects, programs, and proposals.

What would this money be used for? Under the proposal I am outlining today it would be used for the following purposes:

1. To reclaim the orphan strip mines—the pre-1966 lands, those lands who no one has the legal responsibility to reclaim—to higher land uses, including industrial sites, residential sites, and including sites for low-cost housing, for recreation, including parklands, lakes, hiking, riding, and cycling trails, and primitive camping.

2. For the installation and maintenance of treatment devices in eastern and western Kentucky to purify the acid mine water.

3. To provide loan and grant money to Kentucky cities and counties to assist them in financing municipal improvements, including sewer plants, water plants, sanitary land disposal centers, and solid waste collection systems, and other public facilities. The grant money would be available on a matching basis to assure a local initiative.

4. For the restoration and reclamation of orphan slate dumps, particularly those that are now burning and releasing unhealthy and noxious fumes into the air; and for the closing of those abandoned underground mines which are possible health and safety hazards.

5. For the reclamation of streams damaged by sedimentation from surface mining, farming, and construction.

6. For financing, through the state universities, Spindletop Research, Inc., the University of Kentucky, the Kentucky Coal Research Board, and the University of Louisville, of research which addresses itself to Kentucky's environmental problems. Work now under way at these institutions suggests that they, in cooperation with industry, have the talents to help solve many of our environmental problems.

These are not small problems of which I speak. It will take years to solve and correct them, but given a state commitment of the type I propose today, given the federal matching funds and hopefully in the future greater federal funds for environmental restoration, they can be solved. Consider, for instance, Inez in Martin County, Kentucky—

a community with insufficient funds to finance municipal improvement but a community, nevertheless, that is destined to become one of the great mining towns of this state. Funds available through the authority could help this community provide itself with the amenities it needs to attract new industry, to serve as a center for the coming mining industry, and to prepare itself for the day when there is no longer any coal.

The most significant feature of this proposal, however, is that it permits the state, the legislature, and the Governor to take constructive action this year which offers the promise to Kentucky to solve many of its environmental problems within the next ten years. This proposal represents concrete, constructive action, backed by the funds and the organization to get about the task of cleaning up our environment.[1]

---

1. See an act "relating to revenue and taxation," which was approved on March 15, 1972. *Acts of the General Assembly of the Commonwealth of Kentucky, 1972*, Chapter 62 (H.B. 337), pp. 241–55.

SEVERANCE TAX STATEMENT
Frankfort / February 21, 1972

I HAVE followed hearings by the Joint Appropriations and Revenue Committee of the General Assembly with deep respect for its thoughtful and serious study of my budget and revenue proposals.[1] Testimony during these proceedings, as well as other information brought forth, indicate the superior performances Kentuckians have received from the Departments of Revenue and Finance as they diligently helped prepare my budget. There has been, and rightfully so, a great deal of attention paid to the coal industry, to a severance tax, and the effects of both on the overall future of our state. General agreement is that a moderate severance tax will not harm the coal industry. I agree.

One question, however, has emerged which demonstrates the necessity and propriety of the Joint Appropriations and Revenue Committee hearings. In discussions regarding a severance tax, there is some disagreement as to whether or not a shifting from deep mining by small operators to surface mining might occur. I do not think there will be. But if there is any doubt, my determination is to erase it. I do not want there to be any possibility of our driving out of business the small, deep operator who exists on a narrow profit margin. I do not want there to be any possibility of our encouraging an increase in strip mining which some say might occur if small, deep activities diminish. Therefore, I am recommending an amended severance tax, dropping the percentage rate from five to four. The thirty cents per ton tax item would still apply. This is an ecological decision! I want to wipe out any thought of altering mining practices which would not be in the best interest of Kentucky, and my consideration is the protection of the environment.

The Ford administration will improve the quality of our environment in every way possible. The Joint Committee has shown its similar interest by posing this question. I want to publicly thank Representative Clarke and Senator Downing[2] and all members who have performed so capably in this regard. For without their wisdom this issue might have escaped all of us. I am especially pleased to recognize the depth of the Joint Committee's study, for without such interest and examination, there could never be the full analysis which a budget and revenue proposal deserves from an independent body.

In preparation of the budget and revenue proposals, the Departments of Finance and Revenue have strictly an economic responsibility. In this role they have served us well. But as Governor, I have other responsibilities. Among many considerations is protection of the environment. We are, then, proceeding to accomplish this objective, to eliminate any possibility of changing mining operations where emphasis transfers from deep areas to stripping. This preserves the integrity of small business and retains jobs. The Revenue Department does not anticipate a reduction in our very conservative revenue estimates. We could lose a maximum of $3 million annually.

Because this is a new tax, the Revenue Department established its estimates in the most conservative manner possible. The department feels that even with this alteration, its estimates will stand. I am of the same opinion, but in order to be very prudent, I want to reduce my budget by $3 million per year. This would satisfy any remote chance of a revenue loss. We can accomplish this by reducing capital construction $1 million annually, the contingency fund by $1 million annually and taking $1 million annually from budgeted surplus. This move saves the marginal deep miner an estimated seven and a half cents per ton on his operation. More importantly it strengthens our dedication to the environment by eliminating any possibility of a rush on stripping operations.

---

1. On February 18 Governor Ford had issued a statement on the testimony of several professors on the future demand for coal and the ability of the economy to absorb a severance tax. He stated that the professors had "concluded that the Department of Revenue has proceeded properly and accurately in its recommendations, that economic conditions point very favorably to the severance tax, that delivery costs do not impose an undue burden, and that demand for Kentucky coal has never been brighter."

2. Joseph P. Clarke, Jr., for more information see speech from November 13, 1973, in the Reorganization section, p. 160. C. Gibson Downing (1929–   ), Democrat from Lexington; lawyer; member of the Kentucky Senate (1966–1973). *Kentucky General Assembly 1972* (Frankfort, n.d.), p. 5.

INTERLAKE INCORPORATED
Newport / May 31, 1972

MANY people, on both sides of the Ohio River, have realized the significance of Interlake. As the largest industrial employer in northern Kentucky, Interlake's 1,300 people represent a significant economic thrust to this great area. However, also on both sides of the river, many people have been aware of the ecological impact of large industry. The dark clouds of particulate emissions have been a visible evidence of this cost. But many of these clouds are disappearing thanks to Interlake. We have heard today how, through the "bag house" facility, 9,800 tons of particulate matter will be annually filtered out of the northern Kentucky and southern Ohio air.

We have to be impressed at the technology which can take 99.3 percent of the particulate matter out of the emissions from the furnaces here. We have to be more impressed, however, that this has been done in a fully operational plant. Interlake has shown that it can provide for economic growth and still protect the health and welfare of both the people and the environment. This company has indeed shown that, in order not to be part of the pollution, you have to be part of the solution. Being part of the solution is not cheap. I have known of the tremendous expense involved and I commend you on your willingness to go the whole route. Yet, with these large expenditures in controlling the pollutants, Interlake ranks highly as an industrial manufacturer. How, then, did they manage to assure the economic growth they offer without going out of business trying to pay for it?

Let's look at the example of Interlake and see how a partnership developed, which will set precedent for similar arrangements in other industrial facilities. The partnership was begun by Interlake in the process of financing construction of this facility we view today. In order to raise the necessary funds for capital outlay, the company went to Campbell County to secure monies through the sale of industrial building revenue bonds. Management at Interlake saw the opportunity of using a 1969 amendment to the Federal Tax Reform Law to acquire tax-free revenue bonds. This was due to the nature of their application. An amendment to Chapter 103 of the federal regulations allowed exempt status for the revenue from such bonds if first a federal, local, or state agency would certify that the purpose of the facility was to control atmospheric pollutants, or second if the facility were to be designed to meet or exceed federal, state, or local pollution requirements.

This precedent-setting decision on the part of Interlake management then activated the other partners: the Commonwealth of Kentucky and Campbell County. The state was able to certify that the facility we see here today would indeed meet the appropriate standards and the bonds would qualify as tax exempt. Finally, it came time for the third partner to enter this innovative relationship. It is to the credit of the people and officials of Campbell County that the sale of these industrial building revenue bonds was so successful. They played an important part in helping Interlake become a good neighbor and citizen of their community. What an example you in northern Kentucky have set for the rest of the state to follow! Everyone involved has ample reason to be proud.

This is the time of year when schools are graduating those completing various phases of their education. Each time I stand before high school or college seniors, the question crosses my mind: will commencement speakers who address the children of those seniors I am facing still have to talk about pollution? I do not want this to be the case. I want the speakers who address our children's children to point with pride at the accomplishments of our generation. An occasion such as today lends more than hope to this prospect. Interlake has shown the kind of leadership and innovation it requires to resolve the industrial-ecological conflict. State government during the next three and a half years will show a similar leadership.

As you have no doubt heard, because of the Supreme Court ruling in the Tennessee voter-residency requirement question, Kentucky must have a Special Session of the General Assembly, which I have called for June 8, to bring our one-year voter-residency law into line with the federal court's thinking. I have not formally announced all of the subjects to be considered during this brief Special Session. But to-day I am formally announcing that we will include the establishment of my Environmental Quality Control Commission to the agenda. This is the lost House Bill 294 which had passed both chambers in regular session but failed to reach the Governor's desk for signature due to a clerical error.[1] The importance of such a commission whereby protection of the environment rests squarely on the Governor's shoulders cannot be measured today or six months from now. But it will be measured as my time in office passes. That yardstick will show that rational men can work out proper and logical solutions which benefit both industry and the environment. It will show that Kentucky can indeed have clean air, clean water, and a countryside in which all of us can once more be proud.

Pride in accomplishment is one of the highest compensations a public official can receive. Pride in accomplishment is sought by responsible industry. We see this hour why all associated with Interlake have just reason to be proud. I predict this hour a growing sense of pride throughout Kentucky as we move to accomplish once and for all what needs to be done in order to restore the endangered ecological balance of nature. Please accept my most sincere congratulations for a job magnificently done. You deserve the applause of all citizens for demonstrating an effective "solution for pollution."

---

1. On March 20 Governor Ford had issued a statement on the "Lost House Bill 294." "House Bill 294 is a key to our reorganizational plans and has been one of the very important pieces of legislation to this administration. Its intent was a major plank in my environmental platform and I am not only distressed at the failure of this document to be enrolled, I am very much put out. . . . Since there was a total of 119 bills engrossed on that last hectic day, it was necessary to utilize clerical help outside the actual clerks office. . . . The error is regretted by all concerned. . . . In the last-minute rush of the legislative sessions, there is always a danger of this type of incident. Safe-guards will be recommended for the future to avoid a recurrence of this nature."

THE STATES' ROLE IN THE ENERGY CRISIS VERSUS ENVIRONMENTAL QUALITY
Bismarck, North Dakota / June 26, 1972

THE states' role in the energy-environmental crisis promises to be a restricted one, if the present pattern of federal-state programs persists. If so, we need to face up to the fact and gear our state to administering policy decision. Or, we must take the initiative by having a substantial input into national legislation in the formative stages.[1] If not, we must accept ever-shifting federal decisions at the regional, state, and even local levels.

States, and particularly governors, must assume more initiative and begin to make solid policy proposals. If not, we are consigning ourselves to a role of reaction and to the somewhat thankless role of enforcers of the decisions of the federal godfather.

At a minimum, we must ensure that federal energy and environment programs are flexible enough to interpret and administer in light of state conditions. Recent federal legislation, and bureaucratic interpretations, have not tended to grant states this necessary flexibility in seeking environmental quality. That is one reason why we have been adjusting, then readjusting, state programs, administrative procedures, and machinery. States have not been able to ensure that necessary element of government—a degree of certainty in objectives, a degree of certainty in administration.

However, pending federal legislation offers a hope that the Congress and the President are recognizing what De Tocqueville recognized long ago, that the United States can be governed from Washington, but the United States cannot be administered from Washington. For example, states, through governors, must work to see that land-use legislation is flexible enough for the states to have a role greater than just a ministerial function. We need to know the broad outlines of what to do, not the detailed prescriptions to how to do it. The people through their national government can set the objectives. The people through their state governments can set the administration.

The energy-environmental quality problem may well be at the crisis stage, as many believe, and as our panel subject indicates. If not, it is at least a real dilemma. For two basic facts will govern any government— set objective or administration regarding the subject. We are going to have more energy and we are going to have a cleaner environment. The people demand both. The role of government, as I see it, is to balance these two certainties. The role will not be easy to carry out. But the voters are going to judge every president, every governor, every administration on the basis of this issue as much as they are on any issue in the coming years.

The states are going to have to meet air standards, water standards, solid waste requirements and meet them soon. At the same time the states are going to have to make an input into policy decisions and their administration with respect to utilities on a scale never seen before. Energy consumption will go up 50 percent by 1980; an additional 1,200 billion kilowatts is expected to be installed by 1990, requiring an additional 1,000 generating units of the present maximum capacity, on 300 different additional sites. Capital requirements will be some $400 billion. By 1980 nuclear energy will have expanded fortyfold since 1970, to close to 10 percent of total energy consumption. Coal consumption will have increased from 800 million tons. Domestic natural gas and oil supplies will be extremely limited.

We can see that the time span for the closing of the two-pronged dilemma is short. This nation needs an energy policy. This nation needs a land-use policy. Both need to be flexible enough to give the states a real role not only in administration but in decision-making. I have hopes that the peculiarities in the two areas will give us this flexibility. The federal government probably is going to leave rate-making to the states, if for no other reason than it is a detailed and thankless job with no political gain. The details of land-use planning and zoning likewise probably will be the role of the states. The states' base power in any role they play is going to be valid and acceptable land use. State utility regulation is going to have a new dimension of responsibility. Every energy decision will have to be balanced by an environmental impact decision. How well the states handle these decisions in the short run will determine our role in the long run.

Now I would like to bring my discussion closer to home. In Kentucky, we have vast coal reserves. We have vast water resources. Both are necessary in the production of electricity. Thus we have a considerable amount of electrical generation going on in our state. Much of the electricity used in midwestern and northern cities is generated in Kentucky—and the potential is there for a marked increase. Since 1965 we have exported energy on an ever-increasing scale. As I see it, electricity has one advantage over other forms of energy now available to us. Most, if not all other, forms of energy have an impact on the environment both in production and in their use. Electricity has a major impact on the environment in production, but virtually no impact in use.

In Kentucky we see five major areas of impact on the environment from the production of electricity: 1) Coal-ash from generating plants; 2) sulfur dioxide emission from generating plants using high-sulfur coal; 3) use of land for transmission lines and related equipment; 4) thermal pollution of water; 5) effects of coal mining on land, air, water.

A substitute for electrical energy will be a long time coming. A substitute for coal, a major fuel for production of electricity, will be a long time coming. Coal is now used to produce 51 percent of the nation's electrical power. Eighty-one percent of the coal consumed in Kentucky is for the production of electricity. We can eliminate 99 percent of the coal ash with today's technology. We can control thermal pollution of water with cooling towers. We can have better land use by planning. We can control the effects of mining by enforcing good reclamation laws. In Kentucky we are preparing to do a better job of all these steps by the recent creation of the Department of Environmental Protection.[2]

However, there is no technology available to effectively remove sulfur dioxide from emission from coal-burning generation plants. Kentucky has a vital interest in solving this problem, since our large western Kentucky coalfields produce a high-sulfur coal. Our 1972 General Assembly appropriated $390,000 for research into this problem by our state university.

This is a national problem, however. I believe it is in the nation's interests of utilities to find an answer. A leader in electrical generation in Kentucky has proposed, since the early 1960s, that utilities express their interest and concern. He has proposed—and I endorse his proposal— that action be taken at the federal level to have utilities assess themselves a reasonable rate per kilowatt hour to create a research fund. If answers are not found, we soon will be faced with a critical decision— do we take a vast amount of the nation's coalfield out of production, or do we continue the pollution of the air? It will not be an easy answer. We must act while we still have an alternative. (Rate-payers are going to have to pay more than the absurdly low $50 million a year for research and development or we will have no clean environment.)

In our state, we feel we have a strong reclamation law to curtail the effects of strip mining of coal. Strip mining is a much cheaper way to mine coal and, in many cases, the only way to reach vast resources. Yet it has the most far-reaching effect on our environment. We admit we are not positive our law will work because it has never been enforced as the General Assembly intended. We are going to enforce it. It adds expenses to the miner's operation, thus adding to the cost of electrical power. Yet, if we do not prove it will work, public sentiment will force strip mining out of existence. If so, the cost of production of available coal will increase even more. The cost of generating power will increase, and the cost of electricity to consumers will increase—if it is available.

Strip mining, because it is less expensive, faster, and safer, has become the major method in the production of coal. Almost half of the nation's production is by strip mining. Kentucky produces about one-sixth of the nation's coal supplies, and more than one-half of our production is by strip mining. As energy needs increase, more and more states will be required to face the environmental problems associated with strip mining. In Kentucky we believe that the harmful effects that accompany surface mining have been tolerated long enough, and we are putting forth an all-out effort in solving the dilemma that exists between environmental protection and the demand for energy resources.[3]

In March of this year, Kentucky put into force a new regulation that will assure the protection of our water resources from the adverse effects from surface mining. The surface mine operator is now required to bring all waters leaving his operation to acceptable minimum standards. In addition, Kentucky is formulating through research many other positive measures to reduce the environmental impacts from surface mining. It is very important for a state to have good laws and regulations, but it is just as important to see that these laws are enforced. I have made sure that the Division of Reclamation, the agency charged with the enforcement of Kentucky's surface mine laws and regulations, will be equipped with the qualified personnel to ensure that the coal operators are in 100 percent compliance with all surface mining laws and regulations. To implement this policy, I have authorized the hiring of thirty-three new persons. These will include water quality specialists, engineers, agronomists, and additional reclamation inspectors.

As all of us here know, however, regulation is only part of the solution to the problem of bringing surface mining into agreement with true conservation principles. Another part of the solution, and perhaps the greatest part, lies in greatly expanded research. In the past, no one took the time or effort to survey and analyze the problems related to surface mining. Today, the Commonwealth of Kentucky is actively cooperating with the Appalachian Regional Commission and the Environmental Protection Agency in conducting research and demonstration projects on such problem areas as revegetation, sediment control, water quality, slope stability, and control of acid mine drainage. We feel that the results of these research and demonstration projects will be of tremendous benefit to Kentucky and other states when additional legislation on strip mining is needed. We have taken the lead in formation of the Interstate Mining Compact to jointly seek answers to these problems.

We also recently enacted legislation to create a $500,000 revolving fund to match federal funds to reclaim "orphan banks" or spoiled areas left prior to our current reclamation laws.[4]

What have we said? We have three alternatives. We can cripple this country by eliminating use of energy which pollutes the environment. We can have the energy and continue to damage our environment. Or we can provide ways to produce and use energy that do not have such adverse effects on environment. Both the applications of known answers and the search for new answers will cost money. Who will pay the bills? The fuel producers and the energy producers must pay their share. But the consumer will bear a heavy portion of the burden.

We must come to the realization that the cost of keeping a quality environment is a legitimate cost of producing power. To what extent and to whom go the bills, we must determine. We also must have planning. We need at least a five-year lead-time on plans of utilities for increased generation capacity and distribution capabilities.

How do we make these decisions? In Kentucky, our new Department of Environmental Protection is charged with regulation and planning for environmental impact. Our enlarged and strengthened Public Service Commission is charged with regulation of rates and planning for increased public utilities needs. We are providing for a close working relationship between these agencies. One cannot make decisions without input from the other. We believe we can have the necessary electrical power and we can have environmental quality. It is the state's role to determine where, when, and how much each need must bend to accommodate the three. We think we are preparing to fill that role.

---

1. Delivered at the Midwestern Governors' Conference.

2. See an act "relating to environmental protection," which became law without the Governor's signature on June 27, 1972. *Acts of the General Assembly First Extra Session 1972*, Chapter 3 (H.B. 3), pp. 5–65.

3. In a press conference on August 1, 1972, Governor Ford said: "The poor conservation practices of the past are going to end now. I have repeatedly said the errors have been in those officials who winked at the law, who refused to enforce the law, and who failed to provide the strong leadership necessary to protect our environment." The speech is not included in this volume.

4. See an act "relating to strip mining," which was approved on March 27, 1972. *Acts of the General Assembly of the Commonwealth of Kentucky, 1972,* Chapter 270 (H.B. 47), pp. 1172–78.

INTERIM REPORT ON STRIP MINING
Frankfort / August 30, 1972

WHILE campaigning for Governor, I repeatedly warned the people of Kentucky against elected officials and irresponsible operators who were wantonly disregarding the strip mining laws of our state.[1] One of the pledges I made during that period was a commitment to enforce strictly the strip mining laws, and we're doing so. Less than three months ago the man I felt best qualified to serve as Commissioner of the Department of Natural Resources assumed that responsibility. He agreed with my mandate of strict enforcement, of the need to protect our natural resources, and of my determination to crack down hard, and fast, on those who would ravage our land—either the operator or anyone else involved.

You have already seen evidence of his responsiveness in new approaches to reclamation and siltation control. He said there would be more information in the near future. Today, Commissioner Harris[2] has more.

Last week, Commissioner Harris took one of many personal strip-mine inspection trips he has planned. The results and reports which he passed along to me are the most disgusting and appalling revelations I have ever witnessed during my public life. Often you have heard the phrase "the rape of our mountains." That phrase, in my judgment, isn't strong enough to describe what Commissioner Harris has found.

He is here today to show the people of Kentucky what has happened when there is a combination of irresponsible strip operators and irresponsible public officials. His report is a stinging indictment of callous disregard of Kentucky law, Kentucky's mountains, and the citizens of Kentucky by those who held public trust and responsibility during the past four years. There is every reason to call this an indictment, for those who permitted the ravages and destruction of our land should have to face the jury of Kentucky.

Based on the commissioner's report—still to be completed because of the magnitude of his findings—I have ordered seven strip mining permits suspended and four suits to be filed in cases known to this date and have requested the full legal investigation by the state Reclamation Commission of this pillage which has taken place over the past several years. As Governor, I intend to use every legal weapon available to halt what has happened and expose for proper action those who were involved in any way.

---

1. Press conference.
2. Thomas O. Harris, commissioner of natural resources, for more information see speech from February 7, 1973, in the Agriculture section, p. 367.

REVOLVING FUND TO RECLAIM ORPHAN STRIP MINE BANKS
Morganfield / October 26, 1972

SEVERAL weeks ago, one of the television networks devoted a lengthy amount of prime news time to an incident that I think spotlights this occasion.[1] The program dealt with a beautiful forest preserve located in another section of the United States and the fears and regrets of the area citizens that the preserve was in danger of being lost because of population expansion. The thrust of the television commentary was that throughout America land is becoming more and more scarce. All indicators point to an increase in this dilemma.

Therefore, the thrust of our announcement is a reverse attitude we are maintaining for Kentucky. Today we begin restoring and returning land rather than writing off this acreage as having fulfilled its usefulness. Our approach is a simple one. But you know, history records many simple processes which have generated a better life, and we are convinced this program will do exactly that.

Man's concern for the environment is worthless unless man does more than fret and fume. This year, during my budget message to the Kentucky General Assembly, it became evident that activity would replace fretting and fuming. We had an idea which resulted in a plan. We funded the program and are ready to begin working.

That idea was born of concern, concern for the thousands upon thousands of acres of orphan banks the result of surface mining—abandoned land, stripped land, seemingly useless land, and most certainly unsightly land. But it doesn't have to be this way. The state can buy it, reclaim it, sell it . . . buy more, reclaim more, and sell more. The ultimate result is apparent. I therefore recommended a program to the General Assembly which provides a revolving fund to reclaim orphan strip mine banks. In our first biennium we provided one-half million dollars which will generate federal matching funds. Our next step zeroed in on land which could be purchased for reclamation.

There are two sites in this area which we have entered into agreements for, and with the added bonus of Job Corps support, approximately 670 acres will be reclaimed in our first venture. These projects in Muhlenberg and Hopkins counties will do even more. With Job Corps students actually performing the reclamation work, skills will be taught in heavy equipment operation, equipment repair, cooking, carpentry, and electrical installation. This comes through the construction of an on-site facility, and the educational and training programs offered through the Graflex Division of the Singer Company which has contracted with the Department of Labor. The 260-acre Muhlenberg site is being obtained from Peabody Coal Company, and the 410-acre Hopkins site from Island Creek.[2] Work begins immediately. We plan to restore this land to greater value and usefulness as quickly as possible.

This is a perfect example of cooperation among several groups—state government conceiving and developing the program, providing the money and engineering, the private sector willing to sell land it has used, the federal government funding and implementing a new job-skills program specifically for this need, and the Singer Company establishing the training and guidance to carry on the work. This marks a new approach in America to bring old land back to life. I predict other states will follow our example. But even more important, I see a solution to waste, a solution benefiting communities throughout Kentucky, and perhaps countless other states.

---

1. Press conference.

2. The Muhlenberg County site is located off KY 181 near the Western Kentucky Parkway, about eight miles from Central City. The Hopkins County site is near Earlington, east of Madisonville, off old highway 41.

GOVERNOR'S ANNUAL
CONSERVATION ACHIEVEMENT
AWARD DINNER
Louisville / November 11, 1972

CONCERN for our environment is more widespread today than it ever has been before. For sportsmen and conservationists, however, this concern has been around for many years. I doubt if this widespread public awareness of our natural resources will be a short-lived fad. It is enough to say that if we do not implement our concern for the environment with positive actions, we will be endangering life itself. Yet we must also realize the intangible values that nature has afforded us that are sometimes overlooked. Through nature we are allowed the opportunity to rejuvenate ourselves to become closer to the meaning of life and to increase the understanding of ourselves. Ralph Waldo Emerson said, "It is in the woods we return to reason and faith."[1] What a simple, basic truth!

I know that everyone at this dinner shares in a mutual concern for the environment. The League of Kentucky Sportsmen is the oldest and largest conservation group in the state. Sportsmen are in a very real sense the pioneers of environmental involvement. At first this involvement was to foster fish and game management that would ensure continuation of hunting and fishing sports. The basic concept was to put a stop to the killer complex that led to pillage of our fish and game populations without adding to them.

In Kentucky we have a unique relationship between sportsmen and state government. The Department of Fish and Wildlife is an autonomous agency, solely supported by revenue from hunting and fishing licenses and federal matching funds coming from excise tax on sporting goods. Our nine-member Fish and Wildlife Resources Commission is appointed by the Governor but from names submitted by the state's sportsmen. The League of Kentucky Sportsmen is the third party in this cooperative relationship and it represents lay membership throughout the state. Unlike in other states, the league does not play a watchdog function, but rather, it takes an active role in fish and game management and conservation programs. This three-pronged approach to wildlife management allows for a balance unavailable in other states. As Governor, I intend to assure this autonomous relationship, and we will work with you as closely as possible.

We have heard some outcries against hunting in recent years. Many of the complainants are speaking with genuine concern for our wildlife, but I want to take a moment to respond to these complaints. Hunting and fishing enthusiasts form the only group that puts money into wildlife management practices. The fact that this represents more than self-serving involvement is well illustrated throughout our thirty-seven wildlife management areas. I can't speak for every one of these areas, although I am sure the same would hold true in each, but I know there are many nonhunters who profit from the Ballard County wildlife management area. I have hunted there, but it is interesting to note that of the 41,000 visitors last year, nearly 27,000 came for nonsporting purposes. These were bird-watchers, hikers, horticulturists, and many people just wanting to get away from it all.[2]

We have almost 200,000 acres in Kentucky like this. And the sportsman is not the only one to benefit from the pleasures of nature they provide. As a sportsman, and as a citizen of the Commonwealth, I too share the concern for our environment. I spoke of this concern during my campaign, and I have followed up with actions to illustrate this concern. During the last session of the General Assembly, we passed two key bills that will have future importance for our natural resources. These are the Wild Rivers bill and the Endangered Species Act.[3] We made the Endangered Species Act flexible enough to cover Kentucky species not on the federal list of endangered species. I know many of you were instrumental in formulating these bills, and in their passage, and I appreciate your support.

This administration has taken a strong stand on strip mining. Callousness in mining and reclamation methods has had a devastating effect on game and fish populations as well as the land areas. It can mean destruction of wildlife habitats with far-reaching consequences as well as pollution of our streams with acid and silt. Perhaps the most important bill to be passed was our Environmental Protection Act,[4] which allows for coordination of activities now spread throughout different agencies of state government. These agencies are now working out the transfer of duties that will be coordinated in the Environmental Protection Commission. An announcement on this will come before the first of the year.

We are in communication with Washington in the implementation here in Kentucky of the Federal Water Pollution Control Act. Our planning is being geared to Kentucky's needs, and we will take advantage of any guidelines that will improve our chances for grants. I have to report that the situation is not good with regard to federal money available under this act. In fact, we are not only going to be short of what we were originally told we would get, but we will be getting less than we presently receive. There are thirty-four other states caught in this squeeze by Washington, and we plan on joining with them to apply some pressure in securing our money. We are also adjusting our state plan for air pollution control to meet the requirements of the changes in the 1972 federal act.

In short, this administration intends to do all it can to assure a healthy and stable environment. We will do this with conviction, but in a rational manner to assure the best long-range results. All state programs which might have an environmental impact will be planned with the long-range consequences in mind. We don't want today's solution to become tomorrow's pollution. I hope that the League of Kentucky Sportsmen will continue its positive contributions to the conservation of our natural resources. I want to leave you with one suggestion, however, as a way that we could get even more support for our conservation program. In 1971 we sold 545,000 fishing licenses and 270,000 hunting licenses, but league membership stands at 30,000. If we could exploit this potential market for new members, we could enrich our efforts to get the conservation message to the people.

---

1. Ralph Waldo Emerson (1803–1882), Massachusetts; essayist, intellectual, poet; leader in the American transcendentalist movement. *Concise Dictionary of American Biography* (New York, 1964), pp. 271–73.

2. Governor Ford elaborated on this theme in an address at this dinner on November 10, 1973. His remarks stressed the many benefits of nature and the responsibilities of all citizens in efforts of conservation. The speech is not included in this volume.

3. See an act "relating to the establishment of a Wild Rivers System," which was approved on March 23, 1972. The act guaranteed environmental security for sections of the Cumberland, Red, Rockcastle, and Green rivers. *Acts of the General Assembly of the Commonwealth of Kentucky, 1972,* Chapter 117 (S.B. 138), pp. 525–33. See also an act "relating to the protection of wildlife," approved on March 9, 1972. Ibid., Chapter 40 (S.B. 49), pp. 135–36.

4. See an act "relating to environmental protection," which became law without the Governor's signature on June 27, 1972. *Acts of the General Assembly First Extra Session 1972,* Chapter 3 (H.B. 3), pp. 5–65.

STATEMENT TO U.S. SENATE COMMITTEE
ON INTERIOR AND INSULAR AFFAIRS
Washington, D.C. / February 6, 1973

SENATOR JACKSON[1] and distinguished members of this committee. I appreciate the opportunity to discuss land-use planning with you, a subject of far-reaching and critical implications. Perhaps no other topic affects every citizen more than the use of our land. I appear before this hearing as Governor of Kentucky. I believe that many of my fellow governors share my feelings, and I serve as vice-chairman of the Natural Resources and Environmental Management Committee of the National Governors' Conference. However, I do not speak for anyone this afternoon, other than the citizens of Kentucky.

The concept of land-use planning is not new. Historically, individual agencies responsible for specific projects or programs have planned the use of land. Cities have had land-use ordinances, and counties are developing countywide plans for land use. Farm organizations have been involved in this subject since the late 1930s. In the last session of the Congress, the Senate passed legislation dealing with land-use planning. The President has stated that such legislation should be given high priority in the current Congress. I trust this attitude will prevail through the necessary allocation of funds; otherwise whatever is accomplished becomes a futile exercise in academics.

Land-use planning is an area of governmental intervention which many of us wish was unnecessary. Yet we have come to the conclusion that it is necessary. Pessimists say civilization is doomed already by our greedy consumption of the earth's resources and the resulting impact on the environment. Optimists picture a much better world based on technological development. I prefer to side with the optimists. But if we are to benefit from technological gains, there must be an orderly process in which to apply new ideas, techniques, and knowledge. Actually, we aren't addressing ourselves to the present. Whatever action is taken must assure that our children and their children enjoy the heritage of open spaces, natural beauty, and a clean environment. We must assure a harmonious development, a balanced economy, even food to eat for those for whom we hold this country in trust. As a people, we have come to the conclusion that this is the only way we can have a balance between development and protection of our environment.

We are actually a hybrid society—part free enterprise, part government controlled. Let us, in this endeavor, permit the full input of all concerned, rather than assigning land use solely to federal dictation. I support S.268 because it recognizes a need, yet gives states the opportunity to move first. In my opinion, this is the proper course, since states are in the best position to reflect the individual citizen's urgency and desires. States can assure local government and citizen input, and this is deserved as programs are contemplated in a matter as far-reaching as this.

Therefore, I am convinced we all would prefer that states have the opportunity to develop land-use plans before the federal government is forced by necessity to assume the entire responsibility. If states, with congressional encouragement and assistance, can provide and implement their own programs, the question of constitutionality of federal policing powers will not have to be resolved. In Kentucky, I classify land-use planning as a "preventive" measure. Fortunately, we are not in the undesirable position of having to act through crisis, where often even greater instability is created. We still have open spaces we can protect, natural resources we can conserve, natural beauty we can preserve, and a natural heritage we can maintain to pass on to our children. With planning, we can continue economic development which does not conflict with environmental and ecological priorities. With planning, we can guarantee the reservation of agricultural lands to assure adequate production of food and fiber. With a land-use system in operation, all users of the land can be confident that their needs will be protected, an orderly development in the use of land can proceed, and the disorganized abuse of land can be prohibited.

I support S.268 because I feel strongly that states should be granted flexibility in developing their own land-use plans. Not only does each state have its individual geophysical makeup, but some such as Kentucky have many varying geophysical regions within their own borders. Each state may have widely varying existing mechanisms for assimilating the necessary data on which to base a plan. For example, we in Kentucky have 121 water and soil conservancy districts which already have begun gathering the type of data necessary to implement land-use planning. These districts each have their own full-time staff and engineer. Kentucky, as other states, is entering into use of the National Aeronautics and Space Agency's remote sensing abilities to help inventory, then monitor, the state's existing and potential land uses.

I am convinced some method of agreement between states for contiguous areas of like geophysical characteristics is necessary. The provision for compacts would provide this method. I am opposed to sanctions being imposed on other federally funded programs. However, I believe it will be Congress's responsibility to provide a mechanism to assure that one state's land-use plan is not jeopardized by the failure of other states to comply. This mechanism should be provided for use if states do not show acceptable progress in the funding period of S.268. Permission to enter into compacts and assurances of a good faith effort by all states are important to states like Kentucky. We share borders, most of them river-basin borders, with more states than any other, with the exception of our neighbor Tennessee. Yet, I am hopeful that cooperation among states can be accomplished without federal government intervention.

Kentucky has been anticipating and preparing for this day. As a candidate for Governor, I recognized that some planning action was necessary. During my first fourteen months in office, much has been accomplished to gather geophysical baseline data. Our 121 conservation districts are within two months of completing an inventory of present land use, land-use capabilities, water resources, and mineral resources. We have gathered information on population and growth patterns and transportation systems. Our cost breakout for this basic data gathering is about $750,000 per year. In addition, our initial efforts to utilize NASA's remote sensing capability will cost some $275,000. I anticipate that the continuing cost of updating information will remain about the same, since it will require continued on-site inspections and could cost more as more detailed information is necessary.

We anticipate a greater expenditure in obtaining more qualified personnel to assemble this information, to gather local government and public input, and then to implement the plan. In other words, good land-use planning will not come cheaply. States are now faced with ever-increasing demands for services and limited resources with which to provide them.

I urge adoption of an allocation formula which takes into consideration the varied geophysical makeup of states such as Kentucky. We have some 1,400 miles of navigable waters, plus many hundreds of miles of smaller streams. These waters and their basin areas will be critical in terms of planning priority. I would prefer to see the percentage of federal participation as originally proposed by Senator Jackson and his colleagues, and I would hope the funding will be increased. I believe the actual cost of this joint effort will depend upon what the federal government is going to require of the states. I hope we don't get into another impoundment mess where requirements are legislated by Congress but the funds to meet the requirements are withheld by the executive.

Clean water legislation is an excellent example. In the amendments of 1972 to the Clean Water Act, the formula for allocation of funds was changed from population and mileage of waterways bases to a "needs" base, penalizing states such as Kentucky because we had been working at meeting our needs. Although dropping from 1.6 percent of funds appropriated to 0.6 percent, we weren't hurting too badly, because Congress had appropriated more funds. What really hurt was the President's impounding of more than one-half the funds appropriated.

In Kentucky, federal participation for construction of sewerage facilities has dropped from $75 million to $33 million over the biennium. At the same time, the federal government is telling us that we have less time than before to meet clean water guidelines. Federal legislation tells us we must have all streams clean enough for all uses by 1983. To provide the sewage treatment facilities to make this possible will take about $2.5 billion or $250 million per year. The new federal participation is supposed to be 75 percent, which would be some $187 million per year. Yet we have been cut to only $33 million over the current biennium. I cite this point to emphasize what I fear can happen to good and much-needed legislation such as this you are considering. I hope you will keep this in mind as you finalize the bill.

In closing, I support S.268 because it recognizes the national concern and the need for land-use planning. Yet it recognizes that we must achieve a balance between land as a resource and land as a commodity. S.268 recognizes that we must achieve a balance in which our concerns for the environment, which is essential to life, and our concerns for the social climate, which is essential to stability, do not infringe upon our right to property, which is essential to liberty. S.268 recognizes that it is the state, working through local governments, which can best assure this balance. This philosophy must be maintained. Thank you.

---

1. Governor Ford was testifying in regard to S.268—Land Use Policy and Planning Assistance Act of 1973. Henry Martin "Scoop" Jackson (1912–   ), Everett, Washington; United States House of Representatives (1947–1953); United States Senator (1953–   ); chairman, Senate Committee on Interior and Insular Affairs; chairman, Democratic National Committee (1960–1961). *Who's Who in America, 1974–1975* (Chicago, 1975), 1:1560.

ENVIRONMENTAL QUALITY COMMISSION
Frankfort / March 12, 1973

WITH the announcement of a seven-member Kentucky Environmental Commission, we are taking another positive step in an area that has experienced continuous attention from this administration. I am well satisfied with the advancements we are making in the protection of our environment. It is a lengthy process, but one where results are already apparent. I am also aware of the many miles remaining in this critical venture and therefore applaud the willingness and enthusiasm pledged by the seven who are being appointed today.

A dual function as advisors directly to the Governor and as an advisory body to the Commissioner for Natural Resources and Environmental Protection is a most desirable feature of this commission. Each member helps bring balance to the job, along with a level-headed approach whereby environmental improvements and economic growth can be totally compatible. Their credentials are highlighted by a proven track record of nonemotional, practical experience in matters which have previously benefited Kentucky. A variety of interests will be represented within this commission—the interests of sportsmen, conservationists, education, and the business community.

As an indication of the commission's initial responsibilities, I want to call your attention to a day-long program to be cosponsored with the Kentucky Federation of Women's Clubs on April 3. This will be an Environmental Awareness Conference, held in Frankfort, and highlighted by both state and federal officials. Full details will be forthcoming.[1]

---

1. After this speech, Governor Ford introduced the new members of the commission. They were E. T. Sauer (Louisville), Mrs. Jackie Swigert (Louisville), William Gorman (Hazard), Sterling Crawford (Hopkinsville), T. K. Stone (Elizabethtown), Oscar H. Geralds, Jr. (Lexington), and Ted R. Richardson (Independence).

ENVIRONMENTAL PROTECTION
AGENCY MEETING
Washington, D.C. / May 9, 1973

I AM here today to discuss and explore with you, and to seek advice on, particular energy problems facing Kentuckians. Present projections show that Kentucky will be doubling its energy needs every six years. Reliable performance twenty-four hours per day, day after day, of electrical energy to Kentucky consumers is essential to the health and public safety of every Kentuckian. All of us recall the "brownouts" and "blackouts" experienced by our large urban centers due to power drains on existing energy supplies. Besides our own energy drain, we have routed Kentucky energy to New York for the last two summers, and trends indicate that this kind of pooling of energy resources will continue in the future.

We are aware of the national energy policy as set forth by the President. We in Kentucky are moving forward. Our policy is one of responsible growth. Kentucky's 1972 industrial activity has proven that strong growth and environmental protection can exist side by side. I also recognize the seriousness of the energy crisis facing Kentucky and the nation and believe there is an answer for both. We must meet the challenge of the energy crisis with new power supplies and yet avoid overburdening our air and water with pollutants. We in Kentucky have made progress in the reclamation of surface mined land. We have made progress in the reclaiming of orphan banks. We are testing new concepts of reclaiming strip mined land for use as pasture. The University of Kentucky College of Engineering is moving ahead with research into which processes for liquefaction and gasification best fit Kentucky coals and also into the problem of sulfur content of certain coal. This effort is funded by an appropriation, requested by me, from the 1972 Kentucky General Assembly. The long-range implications of this work for both usable supplies and resource conservation are obvious.

Of the three major energy sources—natural gas, coal, and petroleum—consumed in the United States today, Kentucky, during 1972, produced over 120 million tons of coal. Of this total, some 52 million tons were high-sulfur coal. This energy source in particular poses tremendous capital investment and technical problems in the effective reduction of sulfur dioxide emission. This energy challenge is one of the great opportunities for Kentuckians. We have already begun to meet that challenge. But we have a long way to go, and we know it.

We are aware of the five-year research program presently supported by EPA to determine the local extent and effects of power plant emissions from tall stacks (large power plant effluent study). We are equally aware, moreover, that commercial availability of proven industrial scale acceptability of an SO_2 emission removal process is not yet ready to be constructed and put on the line of electric utility plants.

We in Kentucky are urgently seeking proven methods for reduction of SO_2 emission in order that the orderly growth patterns we have established in Kentucky may continue. I urge and propose that Kentucky's Department for Natural Resources and Environmental Protection undertake a joint effort with the Environmental Protection Agency to search for proven SO_2 emission reduction hardware across this country or elsewhere for utilization in Kentucky. For the maintenance of the health and public safety of Kentuckians, we must begin these kinds of efforts now. I believe that we must meet this energy challenge through innovative and cooperative approaches.

Years of ecological problems are not corrected overnight. What is significant, however, is the record of early accomplishments, the innovative programs being carried out, and the progressive attitude instilled within Kentucky state government. What is also significant is the attitude we are finding throughout Kentucky—a growing sense of responsibility on the part of industry, a willingness to take the initiative, and a full understanding that government and the private sectors can work together for the common good. Your sincerity and assistance are equally important.

KENTUCKY GAS ASSOCIATION
Lexington / June 22, 1973

YOUR invitation provides me an opportunity to discuss one of the most critical issues currently facing Kentucky and the nation. As representatives of the Kentucky Gas Association, you are directly involved in what has become a well-used public term—"the energy crisis." While it would be somewhat redundant for me to stand here and inform you about the problems of your particular industry, I feel it is important to discuss the general subject—that of an energy crisis—and tell you where state government stands in facing this complex subject.

It becomes routine for individuals to ask, "Do you really believe there is an energy crisis, a true gasoline shortage, a threat to fuel consumption?" And I answer, "Yes." The next question is more difficult. "Why the shortage? Why has this suddenly confronted the people of America?" Whatever the reasons, and there are obviously many, hindsight serves little purpose. How serious the crunch becomes will depend upon the action all of us take—the citizens, their governments, and the fuel industries. It would be impossible to give you, in the time permitted, a comprehensive report on the energy crisis. For several months my staff and I have been putting together the many pieces that make up this puzzle, in order that a clear picture might emerge. Our contacts have been numerous, with key personnel in the oil, gas, coal, and power industries. I have held serious discussions with consumers, have exchanged information with other governors, have reviewed specific items with federal officials, and have compiled volumes on the subject.

Let's look, therefore, at a few of the unpleasant facts facing us. At present, there is a 35 percent dependence on out-of-country oil and a day-by-day charge on this supply. By 1980 our dependence will soar to 60 percent. Yet we still cannot secure the Alaskan Pipeline. We are now living under a five-day strategic oil reserve, an alarming figure which should be improved to ninety days. Great Britain has a ninety-day strategic supply while the world's most viable nation does not. There is an air of uncertainty surrounding the gasoline shortage. Last fall, when only a handful were suggesting the prospects of shortages, official denials were prompt and unhesitating. When the Interior Committee held oil import hearings in January, the picture had changed somewhat, but the outlook was for "isolated spot shortages" at worst. I am sure most of you have noted earlier closings of service stations, with some being closed altogether on Sundays. Others of you may have been limited to ten gallons at other stations.

Nuclear power is not in the immediate future. There is a misconception, that because we have harnessed the atom, we can quickly develop nuclear power plants. It will come, though not soon. Solar energy is also years away. Skylab does prove solar energy value and indicates a practical application in the future. Coal is in abundance. The country is estimated to have 500 years' supply, and the demand will increase dramatically in the very near future. But with this blessing comes additional problems, environmental problems. Somewhere we must find the acceptable balance between environmental considerations and our ability to provide coal for energy. Which leads me into a matter all of us should carefully weigh.

This nation desperately needs and must now establish a comprehensive, high-priority energy research and development program. And while this is primarily a federal matter, states such as Kentucky must become an advocate. You possibly remember that during the 1972 session of the Kentucky General Assembly, I proposed, and the legislature approved, funds for coal research. We are the first state, I believe, to enter into this crucial field. I consider energy research, with emphasis on coal gasification and liquefaction, a matter of utmost importance for the 1974 General Assembly and will have a significant proposal on this for the legislature.

Fuel shortages are not caused by a lack of domestic energy resources. There are adequate domestic supplies of energy to meet all of our requirements for the foreseeable future. In addition to the coal reserves, the oil shale deposits in the western United States are an untapped energy resource of great potential. Geothermal power, the heat contained in the earth, could be a major supplier of energy. There are large volumes of oil and gas yet to be discovered on the outer continental shelf and in the U.S. The shortages we are experiencing, and others projected, are the direct result of the nation's failure to anticipate the problems and to develop policies to deal with them. This is especially true in the area of energy research and development.

Senator Henry Jackson[1] has proposed an energy research and development program with a clear objective, "to provide the United States, by 1983, with the capability to be self-sufficient in environmentally acceptable sources." His efforts merit our full consideration. But what about today, next week, next month, and next year? In Kentucky, as elsewhere, we will have to show responsible action. Today, I am announcing a series of steps your state government is taking in this regard.

By executive order, I have established a Kentucky Energy Council, to be composed of the Commissioner of Commerce, the Commissioner of Mines and Minerals, the Commissioner of Natural Resources and Environmental Protection, the Secretary of the Transportation Department, and the Chairman of the Public Service Commission.[2] In that order, I gave the council eleven responsibilities. Without mentioning all, here are three specific ones: To prepare an inventory of energy needs for the Commonwealth and contingency plans for meeting such needs; to develop major programs to educate the public on energy conservation practices; to recommend research and development efforts which will contribute to the integrity and adequacy of Kentucky's energy resources. Right now, this council is in Arkansas meeting with representatives of other states on the energy crisis. So you can see they have wasted no time in going to work!

I am also today officially asking the citizens of Kentucky to begin a most serious and concentrated energy conservation program. Suggestions will be forthcoming. But in the area of gasoline, I am requesting that Kentuckians voluntarily reduce their driving speed by ten miles an hour. Some consideration has been given to mandatory speed reductions to conserve motor fuels. I prefer the voluntary route. This will indicate how meaningful the gasoline shortage is to the citizens, for if the people are truly concerned, we will find a substantial reduction in traffic speed. Reducing speed from sixty to fifty miles an hour will conserve gasoline by 11 percent. I hope and pray there will be another benefit—the reduction of traffic deaths and injuries. To lead in this effort, I am ordering all state agencies to reduce the speed of state vehicles by ten miles an hour in sixty- and seventy-mile zones, with the exception of emergency vehicles on emergency runs. I am also directing all agency heads to initiate a gasoline conservation plan and reduce the use of state vehicles.

In addition, and this does not directly deal with the fuel shortage, I am directing all agencies to immediately review vehicle use to ensure that vehicles are being operated strictly on state business. There is a tendency in state government, as in private business where cars and trucks are provided for work, for some individuals to become lax in operation of vehicles. I will not tolerate this and any abuse reported to me and found true will be dealt with in a most severe manner.

Gasoline shortages can have two detrimental effects on Kentucky. Our great tourist industry can suffer. Last year out-of-state travelers alone drove over 5.3 billion miles on our highways. Shortages can also reduce the income which goes into our road program, and this is something we must follow very closely in preparing our budget for the next two years. As members of the Kentucky Gas Association, I enlist your support. I need your advice, your input, and your help. You know better than most that the energy crisis is not a cry of wolf. I know that we must join together to turn this dilemma around for the benefit of all citizens whose lives are touched hourly by energy.

Yesterday you heard about synthetic natural gas, a promising element of relief, but due to production requirements, an item which is probably seven years away. This information supports my theory of the necessity for an interim period of conservation, but even more so my contention that research and development must become a crash program. Also the warning that any coal gasification timetable is tight, and any problems in developing the process will bring delays, should be another incentive for both government and industry to push on in a cooperative venture. Certainly public education—to make others fully aware of not just the crisis but the subsequent effects it can have on us all—is a corresponding role we must assume now. Your invitation is appreciated. You provided a forum whereby these announcements could be publicly made. And while you are not a gasoline association or involved in certain other energy categories, you are a vital part of this state and nation and have much at stake as we pursue a topic which should furrow the brows of us all.

---

1. Henry Jackson, for more information see speech from February 6, 1973, in this section, pp. 329 and 332.
2. See Executive Order 73–868 (June 22, 1973).

ACREAGE FEES FOR STRIP MINING AND DISASTER CHECKS
Frankfort / September 10, 1973

THIS afternoon's press conference allows me a dual pleasure—the opportunity to present checks in payment for one-half of the permit and acreage fees collected for strip mining in fiscal year 1972–1973 and disaster checks to three counties and two cities for reimbursement of expenditures made to repair public damages.

During the 1972 meeting of the General Assembly, the strip mining law was revised to provide for the sharing of revenues received from strip mining fees.[1] The state of Kentucky is authorized to distribute 50 percent of all strip mining fees to the fiscal court of the county in which the permitted operation is located. Kentucky state law prescribes a $150 permit fee for each permit plus a $35 acreage fee for each acre of disturbance permitted. During the fiscal year ending June 30, 1973, there were 20,760 acres permitted by the Division of Reclamation which is a decrease of 6,102 acres as compared to the preceding fiscal year total of 26,862. The number of permits have also decreased from 871 permits in fiscal 1971 to 633 permits in fiscal 1972. The computation of your share was calculated by taking one-half of the permit fee of $150 (a $100 increase above last year) for each permit issued, plus one-half the acreage fees at $35 per acre (a $10 increase above last year) minus credit for undisturbed acreage on previous permits. The increases in acreage fees account for the additional money even though we had less acres disturbed this year.

This is the second time that the state of Kentucky has returned to your respective counties a portion of the money collected by the state to be used by the fiscal courts. A total of $431,263.50 was collected as the county share in thirty-seven counties for the fiscal year ending June 30, 1973. This is $75,348.50 more than the amount returned to the counties a year ago. The two largest checks to be distributed are to Muhlenberg County in the amount of $69,511 and Pike County in the amount of $43,697.50. Next, I shall present the disaster checks totaling $52,427.87 to various Kentucky communities. The money was obtained by a disaster declaration under Public Law 91–606.[2] All of the checks are for reimbursement of April 1972 flood damages, except Jefferson County, which is being reimbursed for the chlorine barge incident of March 1972.

I have another announcement to share with you this afternoon. I am providing $123,500, through my contingency fund, to the Department of Banking and Securities for the implementation of a much-needed program to upgrade personnel and operations within that department. For a long time, there has been a need to rectify some areas within the department, and the current budget doesn't provide funds to improve these situations. The money from this grant will allow the start of a program to include the hiring of additional bank examiners, two attorneys, an accountant, a trust examiner, and an economic analysis unit by personal service contract, upgrade three senior bank examiners, and to increase the enforcement budget for the Division of Securities. The intent of this decision is improved consumer protection and a more professional approach to the state's role as it relates to banking and securities regulations.

---

1. See an act "relating to strip mining," which was approved March 27, 1972. *Acts of the General Assembly of the Commonwealth of Kentucky, 1972,* Chapter 270 (H.B. 47), pp. 1172–78.

2. See an act "to revise and expand Federal programs for relief from the effects of major disasters and other purposes," the Disaster Relief Act of 1970, which was approved December 31, 1970. *Public Laws and Administrative Material,* Public Law 91–606 (S.B. 19), pp. 1890–905.

KENTUCKY MUNICIPAL
LEAGUE BANQUET
Louisville / September 21, 1973

LAST Wednesday the White House held a special meeting to focus on immediate energy problems facing our country. Eleven governors were invited, and I would like to report on the two-hour session, because this topic affects every community in Kentucky. As you are aware, the energy shortage hit all of us in a rather sudden fashion. Because it did, there were skeptics, and rightfully so. For the logical question to be asked was, "How in the world could a nation so technically advanced, and a federal government which should maintain a preventive eye on matters of universal concern, allow this to happen?" But asking the question now does not solve our dilemma. Hindsight may keep similar situations from occurring again, but hindsight should be placed aside so we can get on with the issue at hand.

President Nixon gave us an overview of what he said should not be put in crisis terms. I'm not sure I can agree with his refusal to use the word crisis. Nevertheless, in discussing where America is today with energy, the President was right when he warned: "There is no easy solution"; "The demands for energy are bigger than the supply"; "For a short term, it's going to be tough"; "A philosophical conflict must be dealt with." Let me take each of these four comments and elaborate.

First, the serious problem is identified in our projected shortages of distillate fuel oil for the coming winter. A projection of a 10.4 percent increase in usage over last winter has been made. If we have a very severe winter, the national problem will increase. While Kentucky appears right now to be more fortunate than many other states, we still must exercise caution. We do recognize that national gas production has ceased to increase, thereby creating more of a demand for fuel oil. What we weren't given in the energy meeting was a winter climate forecast from the U.S. Weather Service, but apparently some do feel this winter could be much colder than the last one.

Rising distillate fuel needs cannot be met from U.S. refineries which are bothered by both limited refinery capacity and limited quantities of acceptable quality crude oil. Increasing gasoline requirements compete with distillate fuel for a portion of this limited refinery output. So our situation is this: America could wind up short from 150,000 to 350,000 barrels of crude oil per day, depending upon the weather and the availability of imports. The answer may rest in several actions. Mandatory fuel allocations may be imposed: we were told this decision is due in a few days. The use of a higher sulfur oil may become necessary; though, during the meeting the Nixon administration addressed itself to easing air quality standards in a pretty confused way. Prior to the meeting, the President called for variances to enable big fuel users to utilize coal or high-sulfur oil. Yet during the meeting, Russell Train, new head of the Environmental Protection Agency,[1] appeared to take a different stance.

The confusion which resulted only compounded difficulties which governors face. Will there or will there not be variances granted by EPA? The only commitment EPA offered was an attempt to shorten the hearing period for those states asking for variances. And the question to which I could not find an answer was, if we do face an impossible situation, why not establish minimum variances now in order that states might automatically conform with the revised standards until the acute problem subsides? Possibly you now can see that our meeting failed to produce firm directions. It did serve to lay out the immediate obstacles ahead, but only hinted at ways to overcome them.

I have concluded that we must continue the actions Kentucky has been pursuing for months. We cannot cry wolf. If so, many will refuse to believe it's true when a serious disruption occurs. We must monitor our fuel supplies and understand that to some degree there will indeed be a shortage. We must offer programs of fuel conservation and move into a public education approach for these programs. Certainly, we need voluntary restrictions from all of our citizens. And we must continue to press our demands on the federal government that it expedite action, make firm decisions, and not delay in preparing for whatever lurks around the corner. In addition, every step possible must be taken to minimize any damage to the environment while improving the immediate energy problem.

The immediate consideration is, however, only one of three levels we have to climb. After this winter, all energy solutions will not be at hand. You simply do not gain an adequate fuel or energy reserve by flipping a switch. Our shortages will be with us the following winter and very likely another. This, then, is the second level to overcome. The third is long-range activity to ensure America against another energy shortage. Energy resources in the U.S. and the world are plentiful. It just takes time to acquire the reserves and apply the technology. As I mentioned previously, this winter our demand for clean oil from other countries won't be met. The substitute will be higher sulfur oil and this affects the environment. Every effort will be made to shift supplies in order to use low sulfur fuel in areas where air pollution is greater and the higher sulfur fuels in areas where the atmosphere can better accommodate it. Naturally this isn't the ultimate desired, but given two bad situations—no energy for heating or power, and the need to relax air standards temporarily—one reluctantly accepts the reality of variances.

So it is incumbent on us to push forward in energy research and development. I took first steps in the 1972 budget and have advocated a joint effort among states, the federal government, and industry to solve this problem. Kentucky is a natural for this type of research and development. My emphasis will be on seeking those resources which can place Kentucky in a position of leadership for a cause to benefit all mankind.

---

1. Russell Errol Train (1920–   ), Washington, D.C.; attorney and government official; judge, United States Tax Court (1957–1965); president, Conservation Foundation (1965–1969); undersecretary, United States Department of the Interior (1969–1970); chairman, Council on Environmental Quality (1970–1973); administrator, Environmental Protection Agency (1973–1977). Who's Who in America, 1974–1975 (Chicago, 1975), 2:3101.

KENTUCKY COAL ASSOCIATION
ANNUAL MEETING
Lexington / October 12, 1973

No longer should there be any doubt that serious energy problems do exist. There are natural gas, oil, shale oil, and even uranium shortages. Gas stations across the country are reducing hours of operation. Propane gas, diesel fuel, kerosene, and jet fuel are under a federal government allocation program. There is no natural gas available in many locations, even in Kentucky, for new homes and industry. But we are not running out of coal! As more people turn to electricity to meet their energy needs, the importance of coal is magnified as the one answer to coping with the energy crisis.

Of the nation's potential ground energy sources, 4 percent is in oil, 3 percent in natural gas, and 91 percent in coal. Studies show the

United States has almost one-half of the coal reserves in the world. U.S. reserves are estimated at 1.5 trillion tons, according to a U.S. geological survey report more than enough to last through the year 2400. Since Kentucky is back on top as the country's chief coal-producing state, already nearly 10 million tons ahead of its nearest rival, West Virginia, there is no need for me to tell you what a great challenge and opportunity exists for our state and its coal industry. The challenge is twofold. We must meet the energy crisis with new power supplies and still maintain a sound ecological climate.

Coal, in particular, has come under environmentalist fire for its noxious by-products of nitrogen oxides, sulfur dioxide, and flyash, as well as through strip mining. People seem to be saying, "Assure us of uninterrupted power—don't let us freeze, and at the same time protect our environment." It's a big order, but the goals can be accomplished. Easing this tug-of-war between environment and economic develop-ment—between the natural environment and that which is man-made—is no simple task.

The seriousness of this subject dictates a rational, calm, and sound approach if we are to fulfill our responsibilities in a positive manner. It also demands cooperation on both the part of government and the private sectors in working to achieve a proper balance between that which is needed and how to meet such requirements. This is the atti-tude we want to see throughout Kentucky—one of working together for the common good. Certainly Kentucky, through the cooperation of both state government and the coal industry, has made progress in the reclamation of surface mined land in the reclaiming of orphan banks which were a blight on our countryside years before the 1966 strip mine law.[1] We are also testing new concepts of reclaiming strip mined land for use as pasture.

The 1972 General Assembly, upon my recommendation, established a revolving fund to reclaim orphan strip mined banks. In our first biennium we provided one-half million dollars which will also generate federal matching funds for this purpose. Last spring the state, through the fund, purchased 670 acres in Hopkins and Muhlenberg counties for reclamation. More is in the mill.[2]

There are other examples of what Kentuckians are doing to restore life to strip mined land. You see prime examples in Pulaski and Breathitt counties. Flying over east Kentucky, you can see hundreds of acres of "new green." Beyond this, we find a pressing need for energy research and development. Kentucky, in my opinion, is the ideal state for such scientific works. In 1972 we got the jump on others by budgeting for coal research to increase Kentucky's position in advancing gasification and liquefaction projects into the state. Today, I want to report on the studies.

The research was undertaken by the Institute for Mining and Minerals Research at the University of Kentucky in July 1972. Recently the institute submitted its annual report for the first year. Much preliminary groundwork has been laid. Since this project is of such great and immediate concern to the coal industry, let me relate ten significant accomplishments the institute made in one year. Kentucky coal was tested in the U.S. Bureau of Mines' low BTU gasifier in Morgantown, West Virginia, and the U.S. Bureau of Mines' synthane process at Pittsburgh. The objective was to establish characteristics of Kentucky coal so the state can compete for plant locations for various processes. An evaluation of various processes to produce low BTU gas, high BTU gas, and liquids from coal has been completed. Available data on coal reserves and an evaluation of this data have been compiled. Potential sites for the location of gasification and liquefaction plants in Kentucky have been identified and evaluated. Discussions have been held with a number of plants about locating a facility in Kentucky.

Data was collected on oil pipelines, gas pipelines, water availability, rail systems, and other details applicable to a coal-utilization industry. The purpose of this study was to provide information necessary for plant site selection. Experimental work was started on a high-temperature sulfur-removal system. Removing the sulfur at high temperatures from low BTU gas is one of the major technological problems involved in low BTU gasification today. The potential of various coal-cleaning procedures for the removal of organic and inorganic sulfur from coal has been evaluated. A blending study has been initiated to meet short-term problems for high-sulfur coal usage. Encouraging results have been obtained in an experimental program to determine the effects of alkaline washing on the swelling index of Kentucky coals. A study of the caking characteristics of Kentucky coal is being continued. An experimental apparatus to study the hydrodesulfurization of coal has been constructed and operated. Data on various Kentucky coals has been collected and will be published this year.

Last, a proposal to undertake research in the area of production of synthetic crude oil from coal was submitted to the National Science Foundation. I have just been informed that the proposal has been approved. You are the first to know that the National Science Foundation has given the go-ahead on a two-year, $780,671 "Synthetic Oil from Coal Research" program. The project will focus on the cost-controlling processing stages in the liquefaction of coal and should have far-reaching, positive implications for the coal industry. The program would not have been possible without an aggressive state proposal which the National Science Foundation liked and approved. Just as important is the joint financial support the project received. The National Science Foundation is contributing $480,671 to the study, while the state and a private industry, Ashland Oil, are contributing $150,000 each.

This is an example of the new movement to propel Kentucky to the front in the field of energy research. This is also the kind of cooperation I believe in, where government and private industry share talent and resources for the common good. I feel sure we will see more examples of this new thrust in the months ahead. Much has been done, but there still is more to do. Only through research and development will the future be strong. Our intent is to move ahead now, just as Kentucky gained an advantage nearly two years ago by starting a program of coal research. R & D will be a major priority of my next budget proposal because of the positive impact it can have not only on your industry and all Kentuckians, but on the nation as a whole. It is also my contention that there must be a joint venture among state government, the federal government, and the private sector to fully implement a massive R & D program which can solve our energy problems, protect the environment, and ease the burdens we now experience. Kentucky is the ideal location for a cooperative effort and I am working to bring this about. It can have a fantastic impact on your industry because you have the reserves needed to give America energy.

In essence, my position is based on the theory that coal's future rests with what we do now to see that long-range use of coal and its by-products activates the industry more and more each year. Research is the key. Research will enable us to protect the environment. Research will solve the energy crisis. Research will find greater uses for coal. Research will give your industry more growth, greater security, and the first-class status you deserve. Our 88 million-plus tons thus far put us way ahead of West Virginia, and there is every indication that the boom is loud. I'll tell you one thing: With the emphasis on research and development, the demand for coal, and the responsible attitude of your industry, that loud boom today will sound like a wet firecracker later on, because we have the resources to serve this country through your industry, and it's going to happen.

When Kentucky's coal industry shows a sharp increase in production and record levels of employment, we have to be doing things right. And this is exactly the situation which means the economic factors are indicators of good times. Through September of this year employment is beating the significant gains recorded in 1972, and I might also add that September employment was the highest on record, 28,700. Through September 15, Kentucky had already produced over 3 million tons more than the same period last year, even though the number of mines licensed, including strip and auger-strip, has decreased.

---

1. See an act "relating to the regulation and control of strip mining and providing for the administration thereof, the enactment of an Interstate Mining Compact, and providing for the reclamation of orphan soil banks," which was approved on January 28, 1966. *Acts of the General Assembly of the Commonwealth of Kentucky, 1966,* Chapter 4 (H.B. 36), pp. 63–96.

2. See an act "relating to strip mining," which was approved on March 27, 1972. *Acts of the General Assembly of the Commonwealth of Kentucky, 1972,* Chapter 270 (H.B. 47), pp. 1172–78.

ENERGY CONSERVATION ACTION PLAN
Frankfort / March 4, 1974

IF Kentuckians are feeling discomfort, sacrifice, and other unpleasant aspects of an energy shortage, Americans elsewhere are finding the pain much more acute.[1] We are, in fact, better off than others. Let me give you some examples. Residents of many states, including Washington, D.C., fight the frustration of odd-even days when they can purchase limited amounts of gasoline. They wait in long lines, sometimes over three hours. They drive from gas station to gas station in a costly effort to acquire a few gallons at each. In areas of Florida, you buy gas only after making a reservation.

Elsewhere, with winter much colder, even the price of firewood costs two and three times what we pay in Kentucky. West Virginia coal miners went on strike because they couldn't drive to work. We averted a possible shutdown situation by careful allocation of emergency fuel. Heavily industrialized regions are experiencing mass layoffs. Even the trucking situation was more severe in other states than Kentucky. I could give you more examples, but the point to be made is offered with mixed emotions. First, I'm glad the people of Kentucky aren't being as adversely affected as citizens in other states. Yet I have deep sympathy for those who live beyond our borders as they try to cope with the

energy crisis. Second, even though we are much better off, I wonder
how long we can maintain our relatively good position among others,
how long we can successfully shift fuel here and there, how long we
can hold down unemployment, and how long we can prevent serious
hardships directly caused by this national dilemma.

By viewing conditions in other areas of the country, I see the perplexing problems which haven't yet rained down upon us. I can say our
allocation staff is doing a bang-up job, that state government is responding to the maximum, even with normal shortcomings, and that
Kentuckians are cooperating in this trying period. Still, the threat of
worse times remains. That threat is compounded in Washington when
the national administration confuses everyone with conflicting stories,
false promises, and no single direction of attack against the energy
crisis. The threat is compounded when the executive branch and Congress are at odds at a time when the welfare of people is at stake, and
their welfare is being shoved aside by the inability of both branches to
work in unity. And that threat is compounded by a President whose
closest advisors publicly are at odds in approaches to energy shortages.
This is not just Wendell Ford's observation. It smacks governors, both
Democrats and Republicans, right in the face. I've heard their an-
guished pleas for some positive response, then seen them leave bitterly
disappointed to go home and try to make the best of it on a state-by-
state effort.

Here in Kentucky, state government has taken many steps to reduce
energy consumption in an attempt to lessen the severity of the crisis. We
created the Kentucky Energy Council to prepare an inventory of the
state's energy resources and needs. We opened the Office for Mandatory
Allocation to assist Kentuckians who were unable, or finding it difficult, to obtain fuel and home heating oil. A directive was issued last
year to all state agencies reducing the speed limit for all state vehicles.
A thorough review of vehicle usage by each agency was ordered, and a
plan to reduce state government's gasoline consumption by approximately 10 percent was introduced. We called for voluntary reduction of
fuel usage in the state and Kentuckians responded in an admirable
fashion. A publicity campaign was initiated by the Department of
Public Information, with the cooperation of private industry and the
Department of Commerce, for radio, television, and newspapers, inspiring people to conserve energy. And within the past few months, we
have conferred with federal energy officials about alleviating problems
facing this state.[2]

As part of a continuing energy conservation effort, today we are
proposing that local communities across Kentucky develop and imple-

ment a two-step transportation energy conservation action plan. Toward this end, we are requesting that each major urban area develop a plan oriented to increasing the people-carrying capacity of existing systems through additional occupancy of transit facilities and private automobiles and increasing existing highway capacities through short-range, low-cost capital improvement projects which will encourage car pooling and use of public transportation.

One of the undeveloped resources available for reducing fuel consumption is the use of commuter car pools. If widely adopted, this method can have a significant impact on saving gasoline, be implemented quickly, and it requires little or no capital outlay. As will be discussed later in this meeting, a number of computer programs are available for automated matching of car pool passengers. Several such programs have been introduced in the state, including one here in Frankfort for state and federal employees.[3] We are enthusiastic about the success of our program. In the first two weeks, more than 100 car pools were registered, representing 400 employees. This program can work in your communities, too. However, for it to be most effective, it needs your leadership and support.

State government stands behind this program and is ready to provide you with experienced technical advice and financial aid. Secretary Gray[4] and his staff will explain what assistance is available. With your support, this program can be a success.

---

1. Press conference.

2. One example of cooperation between the state government and the federal energy officials was an agreement on diesel fuel allocations. On March 6, 1972, Governor Ford announced, in remarks not included in this volume, that the Federal Energy Office had agreed to make 4.4 million gallons of diesel fuel available to halt the shortages in the production of Kentucky coal.

3. Participants in the conference received two lengthy memoranda entitled "Kentucky Transportation Energy Conservation Action Plan" and "Organization for Carpooling." These detailed the rationale behind car pooling and the means of implementing car pooling on a massive scale.

4. James Gray, for more information see speech from March 24, 1973, in the Reorganization section, p. 125.

RED RIVER PROJECT
Frankfort / April 24, 1974

IN expressing a position on various issues, I must consider every side without any personal emotion and weigh carefully the ultimate results as they affect all citizens and all sections of Kentucky. This is my first responsibility as Governor. The Red River project reflects such a posture. Any decision by the Governor, for or against, must be made in light of the overall best interest of the Commonwealth with future needs being fully analyzed. Whenever there are differing opinions, each side should respect the other if indeed each side is willing to listen to every possible feature. After that, when a decision must be made, you base your expressions on the total aspect.

I have the highest respect for those who exercise their citizenship in the Red River matter, whether they be for it or opposed to it. But those of us in positions of leadership are duty-bound to be decisive, realizing the difficulties involved and even more so, realizing in any controversial issue you cannot please everyone.[1] The Red River project is of long standing. It should be settled once and for all and after reviewing every fact available, I am convinced it is in the best interest of Kentucky's future that the project proceed.

I have heard some say that in an election year I should oppose it. I disagree. Such decisions for political expediency are irresponsible. My opponent, Mr. Cook, has on this date finally taken a stand on a federal project that has been under the jurisdiction of his office the entire time, over five years, he has been in the Senate. Perhaps he can now be against the Red River project because it is an election year, but this is not the way I believe public officials should react. Because it has been, and still is, a federal project, directed and funded by the Congress, Senator Cook has had ample opportunity before now to oppose it.[2]

In looking at the overall benefits of the Red River project, I must consider the present and future needs of Kentucky and Kentuckians. Support of this project is based on my firm conclusions that water supply and flood control are mandatory. The downstream shift of the dam site at an increased cost of several million dollars was only for the preservation of natural features pointed out by ecological interests and I fully agree with this method of preserving the environment.

There is no question about the impending lack of clean, sufficient drinking water for areas and communities below the dam. We must think of the future and act now to ensure that the future will not find insufficient water supplies. We must think of protecting property and lives from flooding and stop flooding which this project will do. We must think of uncontrolled development in the area and uncontrolled activity which could simultaneously destroy the values project opponents want to protect. So do I. This lake will not destroy the Red River Gorge.

I agree fully with the Sierra Club in their letter of March 6, 1968, which states: "We believe that the vital objectives of the Red River Reservoir project can be achieved by a dam at the downstream site, with a seasonal pool level of 700–710 feet. If the seasonal pool is kept within these limits, many of the important scenic and recreational features of the Gorge can be preserved, as well as most of its value as an outdoor biological laboratory." This statement by the Sierra Club coincides with my feelings. This position can be achieved with the project.

---

1. The proposed Red River Dam was designed by the Army Corps of Engineers to provide an adequate supply of water to the Red River valley and to prevent the flooding which had damaged Powell County for over twenty years. The site originally chosen for the dam was vetoed in favor of a location which might better preserve the natural beauty of the area. Many environmentalists, however, continued to oppose the erection of the dam, which would necessarily flood a portion of the gorge area to create a lake.

2. On August 29, 1974, Governor Ford attacked Senator Marlow Cook's position on the dam. He said: "Of course, even though my opponent was for the dam at the high site in 1968, and as mentioned, voted twice this year to hold down interest rates charged on Corps of Engineers' projects, he now wants to make a political issue out of his change in position. This has never been a partisan political matter before." The speech is not included in this volume.

CUMBERLAND FALLS CHAIRLIFT
Frankfort / May 28, 1974

IN 1972 one of the priority legislative items of this administration was the Wild Rivers bill,[1] the first ever to be passed in Kentucky and signed by the Governor. During the last session of the General Assembly we strengthened and extended that act. Our successes were the result of a cooperative effort from conservation interests and this administration, for which I am very grateful.

The principles and purpose of the Wild Rivers bill have been applied by me in regard to the Cumberland Falls chairlift. I have instructed the Secretary of the Cabinet, Secretary for Natural Resources and Environmental Protection, and Commissioner of Parks[2] to cancel immediately the Cumberland Falls chairlift project. Even though land uses permitted within the exterior boundaries of a designated stream are severely restricted, our efforts, and the responsible approach, have been to thoroughly research our legal position in this particular matter, a time-consuming endeavor which has been under way in order that we could be in full legal accord with the bill's intent. All salient facts as applied to the statutes to the area involved and to the project itself were concluded during this past weekend, and therefore the project is null and void.

As the statutes so state, and as the General Assembly envisioned, boundary determinations would understandably be a lengthy process because of physical mapping and charting of protected specific areas. The act established a deadline of June 16, 1974, but in this case we have accelerated these determinations. On countless occasions, I have said that mistakes can be made by government, but they should be recognized and corrective action should be forthcoming. I have, therefore, taken those steps to maintain the integrity of the Wild Rivers bill and will move at once to see that the cut portion at Cumberland Falls is adequately restored.[3]

---

1. See an act "relating to the establishment of a Wild Rivers System," which was approved on March 23, 1972. *Acts of the General Assembly of the Commonwealth of Kentucky, 1972,* Chapter 117 (S.B. 138), pp. 525–33.

2. Charles Pryor, Jr., Thomas O. Harris, and Ewart Johnson.

3. The controversy over the Cumberland Falls chairlift did not stem only from a disputed interpretation of the Wild Rivers bill. Questions were also raised regarding a sixty-year lease granted in February 1974 by the state

government to the Cumberland Falls Chairlift, Inc., for the operation of the lift. State Senator Tom Ward, a Democrat from Versailles, was a leading opponent of the lift and termed the contract "a giveaway to friends of the Parks Department." Ward claimed the state had been cheated before by this same company in its operation of the chairlift at Natural Bridge State Park and would be subject to even greater frauds at Cumberland Falls, a much larger resort. Frankfort *Kentucky Post*, May 23, 1974, and *Lexington Leader*, May 23, 1974.

SECOND AREA MEETING OF THE KENTUCKY ASSOCIATION OF CONSERVATION DISTRICTS
Henderson / July 31, 1974

I APPRECIATE the opportunity to appear before you today. We in Kentucky are fortunate to have developed an outstanding working relationship of state government with our 121 Soil Conservation Districts. This is the way it should be. You and I share the same objectives and are committed to the same goal—the conservation of our natural resources and the protection of our environment. This relationship has been to Kentucky's benefit. One example of how we have been able to work together for the common good is through the Watershed Development Program. I want to commend you for the role you have played in making the second area's watershed program second to none in Kentucky.

Not only do watersheds guarantee flood protection to the people of your area, but they also provide countless other benefits. Look at what the Mud River watershed has meant to this area. It has given you the Lake Malone recreational area, which attracts thousands of visitors. It provides the municipal water supply for the city of Lewisburg, and it serves as a campground for the Audubon Boy Scouts Council at Russellville. I know the watershed program in all areas is not without some controversy. I am studying the situation and have the Department for Natural Resources and Environmental Protection under instructions to do everything it can to help. I want to do what I can to resolve it, whether it takes legislation on the state level or federal level.

Another example of how state government and our Soil Conservation

Districts are pulling together in the same direction is the Sediment and Erosion Control Program which was funded by the 1974 General Assembly.[1] We are going to initiate this program by working through your districts with other local units of government on the same cooperative basis that you have proven to be so successful. Right now our Division of Conservation in the Department for Natural Resources and Environmental Protection is working on an agreement with the Soil Conservation Service to intensify the soil survey effort in Kentucky. As you know, it is difficult to make wise decisions concerning land use, erosion control, or land capabilities without a detailed soil survey.

Soil surveys have been helpful not only to individual landowners, but to all levels of government in their land-use planning. And, speaking of land-use planning, you're probably wondering just what our situation is, since the subject holds such far-reaching and critical implications for all of us. In Kentucky, I classify land-use planning in the short run as a preventive measure. Fortunately, we are not in the undesirable position of having to act through crisis, where often even greater instability is created. We still have open spaces we can protect, natural resources we can conserve, natural beauty we can preserve, and a natural heritage we can maintain to pass on to our children. We can continue economic development which does not conflict with environmental and ecological priorities. We can guarantee the preservation of agricultural lands to assure adequate production of food and fiber.

However, in order to see this come about, we can no longer depend on short-term, knee-jerk, or selfish decision-making in the land-use arena. I'm talking about a federal land-use policy. The nation needs it, and Kentucky needs it. With a land-use system in operation, all users of the land can rest confident that their needs will be protected, an orderly development in the use of land can proceed, and the disorganized abuse of land can be prohibited. I have some definite thoughts as to what a federal bill should and should not contain. It should not call for federal zoning. It should not permit an increase in federal authority over state and local decisions concerning the use of state and local lands. It should be an enabling act, where the federal government focuses its review on the procedures to develop and the state's ability to implement the state land-use programs, and not on the substance of those programs.

A federal land-use act should not require state planning over all land within the state. It should not mandate state zoning, but reassert local zoning powers; nor should it tell a state how much or what specific land should be included in the state land-use program.

Such an act should not alter any landowner's rights to seek judicial redress for what he regards as a taking. Private property rights must not be altered at all. It should require state governments to develop a process which achieves a balance between concerns for the environment and concerns for the social climate. The federal government should provide the states with wide latitude in determining methods of implementing the act. Finally, such legislation should endorse the concept that local land-use decisions should be made by those decision-makers closest to the people—local governments.

Actually, we aren't addressing ourselves to the present. Whatever actions are taken must assure that our children and their children's children enjoy a heritage of open spaces, natural beauty, and a clean environment. As a people we have come to the conclusion that this is the only way we can have a balance between development and protection of our environment and resources.

You who have been entrusted with the responsibility of conserving our soil know better than anyone that a sound land-use policy is necessary to the protection of this country's agricultural base. And it must be protected! Agriculture is one resource of which we do not have a shortage, and it is the only major positive factor in our international balance of trade. That's why what you are doing is important, essential to the national well-being. That's why it is imperative that people in the cities and suburbs recognize that the U.S. is the Saudi Arabia of agriculture. Farmers are the backbone of this nation's economy. Shortages come down to resources and commodities, and they are all tied directly to the land. From here on out, the strength of every nation's monetary unit, the strength of the dollar, will relate not to manufactured items, but will relate to resource units—to food, to minerals—and only that.

I promise you this: any land-use legislation I have anything to do with, you will be asked for input to it, and from the beginning! You won't have to wait five and a half years before you hear anything from me about it. Your input and feedback is going to be a vital part of a land-use program, because it affects you, your life, and your livelihood. Your input has already been most helpful. Last year when I appeared before a Senate committee in regard to Senator Jackson's land-use bill,[2] the committee was quite impressed when I told them Kentucky's Soil Conservation Districts had already started a county-by-county natural-resource inventory. And just last month at the National Governors' Conference in Seattle, I said that when a national land-use bill is passed, its success will rely heavily upon the input and cooperation of our conservation districts. There is a mutual spirit of cooperation between state government and you. I propose, I more than propose, I pledge that this same spirit of cooperation will be the basis of our relationship when I am in the United States Senate. You deserve attention, not an isolated, impersonal federal bureaucracy. You deserve attention, not a closed door.[3]

---

1. See an act "relating to the election of the boards of supervisors of conservation districts," which was approved on March 27, 1974. *Acts of the General Assembly of the Commonwealth of Kentucky, 1974,* Chapter 151 (H.B. 49), pp. 331–33.

2. See speech from February 6, 1973, in this section, pp. 329–32.

3. Governor Ford spoke on a similar subject to the third meeting of the Kentucky Association of Conservation Districts on October 3, 1974. The address is not included in this volume.

AGRICULTURE

KENTUCKY COUNCIL OF
COOPERATIVES LUNCHEON
Louisville / January 20, 1972

WHEN I received an invitation to speak here today, some asked me to discuss my plans for state action in the area of farm and rural development. Most of you have heard me discuss these ideas before, hopes I have for rural Kentucky. As a candidate I could only advance proposals for your consideration. As your Governor, I can act in your best interest.

History offers a very significant bench mark for the Democratic party on farm and rural development. The party I represent has traditionally served this segment of our society well. You saw a vast difference in the thrust given agriculture and rural subjects during the general election campaign. Rural Kentucky responded in my behalf because rural Kentucky believed that the attitude I projected was sincere, as contrasted to the silence of my opposition. Now, I expect to prove my sincerity—as you should expect me to. I plan to follow a course which reflects your own contributions to mankind. That is a course of hard work, a course of dedication, a course of frugal management.

Those of you who may have heard me talk of hopes and plans may have noticed one thing. I often stated that the realization of these hopes and plans depends upon a spirit of cooperation—the very spirit which brought about this Council of Cooperatives. Each organization in this council is primarily concerned with specific topics. Yet you share a common goal, the continued good fortune of rural Kentucky. Your goal is the same as mine and I am going to see that state government does its part. As we embark on what can become an era of unequaled development for rural Kentucky, I ask for your help, your support, and your advice. I ask also that you remember one reality: in the end, only the Governor can make certain final decisions. This is the lonely period I have mentioned so often. This is the time I solicit your trust and faith, for my ultimate desire is to have your respect.

As I pledged during my campaign for Governor, I am going to replace the defunct Governor's Commission on Agriculture with the Governor's Council on Agriculture. I plan to create the Kentucky Farmers' Advocate Office. The head of that office will be accountable to me and serve as the chief administrative officer of the council. In other words, government in Kentucky will once more be working for you, and with you! As Governor, I intend to serve as chairman of the

Council on Agriculture. This will be a working body of qualified representatives of you and the farmers of our state.

This council will be charged primarily with assistance in the administration of an agriculture program called "new farms." We have selected this title because the immediate aim will be to rebuild the family farm as a profitable institution in Kentucky. Our program's ultimate quest will be to develop rural Kentucky as an attractive alternate to urban life, to slow the departure from the farm, and to encourage our young citizens to make the family farm a way of pleasant living again.

Why are the number of family farms declining? You recognize the increasing difficulty of earning enough money to support a family on the farm. The Ford administration is keenly aware of this illness. We are aware that conveniences still aren't available, at any price. Water and sewer lines are good examples. My administration will assist in every way possible to remove this economic barrier.

We are now working with the Public Service Commission and other authorities to develop necessary legislation and processes to strengthen the fiscal and administrative operations of water districts. Within a short time, we will be introducing in the General Assembly legislation creating a Kentucky Sewer and Water Authority, as I pledged, to make available to rural communities the ability to construct sewer and water systems at great savings to users.

The farmer needs credit at reasonable rates. More than that he needs the ability to retire his obligations and still realize an acceptable return on his investment and time. The farmer needs expertise to help him increase production. Even more, he needs the ability to market his product for a realistic return. The key to development of rural Kentucky is a strengthened farm economy. If Kentucky's farmers are able to remain on the farm or return to the family farm by earning a comfortable living, we have a solid foundation on which to build.

We know what the problems are. We know the direction we need to take. We can accomplish our goal only if we all move in the same direction. If all of us, individuals, elected officials, and organizations committed to the development of rural Kentucky, are communicating and are in concert with our efforts, we can achieve maximum results earlier. This is what I plan; this is what I hope. This is what I know our Council on Agriculture and our Farmers' Advocate Office can provide.

I have pledged the cooperation and efforts of my administration and I am keeping my pledges. The Kentucky Farm Development Authority must sufficiently help farmers in securing funds for investment in farm operations. We will support legislation to permit cooperatives greater accessibility to credit in order to serve your members. Also having administration support, as I pledged, is a low income housing bill which I believe will help stimulate rural community development. These are just a few of the steps, both direct and indirect, we plan to take.

You represent an effort by Kentucky's rural citizens to help themselves. It is state government's responsibility to help any of our citizens achieve what they cannot achieve for themselves. State government during the Ford administration stands willing to help you, help your members. We are ready to do those things that only state government can do for rural Kentuckians. Our actions in ensuing days will prove our intent. But we need your advice, your assistance, and your cooperation in effecting our program. I ask you to call on us, as I ask you to respond to our call to you.

KENTUCKY STATE FAIR
Louisville / August 17, 1972

ON my way here this evening, I thought of other trips to the State Fair and recalled the excitement those trips stirred in me. Being raised on a farm and continuing my farming interests through 4H work, I always looked forward to fair season in Kentucky. The county fairs and the friendly competition among our neighbors was something that was eagerly anticipated. But the State Fair has always been a major event for me. It is an event to look forward to, and an event to be remembered over the long winter months.

Look around and you can see an island full of delights for every member of the family. The carnival excitement of the midway lures the young at heart. The exciting stage shows offer a variety to please all tastes in entertainment. Competition in the many horse show events always brings a thrill to our many horse lovers, and the old west comes alive at the rodeo. The real pleasure of this great event, however, is nowhere more obvious than throughout the exhibit areas. It is here, where we can see the products of family farming in Kentucky. It is here, where we can all experience the rewards of rural life and realize that the State Fair is above all a family fair.

For those of you who have never had the rich experience of growing up on a family farm, here is your opportunity to share the experiences of those who know what it means. For those of us who have had to leave our farms, the exhibits and livestock bring back a nostalgia for the good life of family farming. I know the farm as a place where a family can work together with a common purpose, building a bond not easily built elsewhere. I know the family farm as a place where children can learn a sense of responsibility and independence. I also know that the family farm has become endangered. It faces major problems that threaten its very existence, and I intend to use the influence of my office to preserve this essential American life-style. I have pledged my administration to save the family farm in Kentucky, and we have started activities to accomplish this.

It was with this purpose in mind that I asked the General Assembly to give me the responsibility and the authority to help save our rural way of life. The result was our new Governor's Council on Agriculture and a truly representative voice for the farmer in the Kentucky Farmers' Advocate Office.[1] We frankly admit that we don't have all the answers for the problems plaguing the small farmer. We do not have any mystical "game plan." We do know that the Council on Agriculture will set itself to the task of meeting the problems facing Kentucky's farmers. We have designed a vehicle for planning that includes a majority of full-time farmers who have a real feel for these problems.

We know that we must increase the net income potential of the family farm. We must find a sensible solution to farm ecology without putting all of the economic burdens on the family farmer. We will promote Kentucky farm products and find new farm markets for Kentucky farmers. We will also see that the family farm is provided with a chance for a quality of life which will make it a more attractive place to live. This means good rural roads, water and sewage systems, electricity and gas, and whatever else it takes to make farm life as comfortable as life in the city.

As chairman of the Council on Agriculture, and having direct administrative control over the Farmers' Advocate Office, I can assure the farmer that he will have a strong voice in solving his problems. I intend to make that voice heard in Washington as well as in Frankfort.

This is my first fair as Governor of the Commonwealth, and it gives me a real feeling of pride to officially open this event. I hope that future fairs will be as great as this one and that I will be able to tell you that the family farm is well on its way to recovery. We are already looking forward to the upcoming bicentennial celebration in 1974. The State Fair of that year should be a historic event in its own right by being a major attraction in the bicentennial year with its theme as Kentucky's two hundredth birthday. The bicentennial fair will reflect Kentucky's rich history as an integral part of our yearlong celebration. Fairs in the Commonwealth have come a long way since the annual sheepshearing began on the William Story farm near Georgetown in 1782. I invite you now to join me in this celebration of rural life. Come to the fair and see for yourself why this is indeed the wonderful world of Kentucky.

---

1. See an act "relating to the development and promotion of agriculture," which was approved on March 13, 1972. This act created both the Governor's Council on Agriculture and the Kentucky Farmers' Advocate Office. *Acts of the General Assembly of the Commonwealth of Kentucky, 1972*, Chapter 53 (S.B. 125), pp. 174–78.

COUNCIL ON AGRICULTURE
Frankfort / February 7, 1973

As one who was reared on a farm in Kentucky and who recognizes the intangible benefits of farm living, I am deeply disturbed by adverse developments in recent years. Years ago, the farmer was largely self-sufficient. He grew or raised what he needed for his family, and sold or traded any excess for pocket money or staples. When times were real hard, such as they were during the Great Depression of the thirties, if he could hold on to his land he was usually better off than the general public. In those days, neighbors cooperated and families worked together in a common purpose. The family farm was a place where children could learn a sense of responsibility and independence.

Today, with sophisticated equipment, high-powered fertilizers, pesticides, and concentrated feeds, the farmer can produce crop yields and livestock gains which just a few years ago would have been beyond comprehension. REA[1] cooperatives and various credit agencies have produced a better standard of living on the farm. However, the tremendous required investment, brought about by spiraling costs of land and machinery and the relatively small capital turnover on the average farm, have now placed agriculture in a noncompetitive position with industry for available loans and qualified labor. Moreover, the quality of rural living in terms of material benefits, that is, in available services and cultural opportunities, though greatly improved, has not kept pace with that of urban and suburban living.

The net result, as you know, has been mass exodus from the farms to the nation's already congested cities. Whereas approximately 30.5 million Americans lived on farms in 1930, in 1970 only 9.7 million lived on farms. In the last decade alone, rural population in Kentucky declined by 45 percent. Although the number of acres farmed has not changed significantly, the number of farms has decreased drastically. Those who remained in farming have been forced to borrow heavily in order to enlarge their operations in an effort to build or maintain their profit margins.

I am concerned about the fact that the average age of the farmer in this country is steadily rising. Young qualified people who would like to get into farming are unable to do so because of the prohibitive costs of land and equipment. A young man starting from scratch—if he goes into farming on the size and scale necessary to make a decent living—cannot expect to get out of debt until he is an old man. In short, the family farm generally is no longer a profitable enterprise.

At one time in the nation's history, it was considered progress for agriculture to become so efficient as to enable surplus farm labor to fill jobs in industry and elsewhere. Today, however, these good jobs are no longer available in the numbers that they once were. Further migration from rural areas will only contribute to the already critical housing and unemployment problems of the cities. I do not advocate that all these people return to the farm. But I do believe that many people living in our cities would prefer to live in rural towns and communities if the opportunities were there. In order to make this possible, we must improve rural schools and roads, provide good clean water and recreational facilities, and make available more and better jobs. We can accomplish the latter by attracting industry to rural areas that is compatible with agriculture and the environment. In short, we must provide an attractive alternate to urban life, and I am firmly convinced that the first step toward achieving this goal is improving the condition of the farmer by making the family farm a profitable institution once again. By putting more money in the farmers' pockets, we can improve the general economy of rural areas and thus make all the other things possible.

Due to the nature of farm problems today, many of the answers will have to come at the federal level. Consequently, I have pledged myself and my office to be the number one state government advocate of Kentucky farmers in Washington. I am relying on this council to keep me informed on federal legislation and administrative programs of interest to Kentucky farmers. Decreased farm population should not be a green light for politicians and bureaucrats to lower priority of farm problems, as obviously is happening in the federal executive branch.

There are also some specific actions we can take on the state level to promote the welfare of the entire farm community in Kentucky. For example, as Lieutenant Governor, I worked closely with men like Tom Harris and Mack Walters[2] in creating and funding the Kentucky Tobacco Research Board. I supported the constitutional amendment which requires that farmland be assessed for agricultural purposes rather than potential use. And, although I believe the sales and use tax should be broad based, equity and fairness dictated to me the advisability of exempting farm machinery. As Governor, I recommended that the legislature also exempt groceries. During the regular session of the 1972 General Assembly, I supported many other bills in the interest of Kentucky farmers, ranging from environmental protection measures to animal disease control laws to increasing the credit available to farmers through the Kentucky Farm Development Authority. I asked the legislature to create this council to replace the defunct Agricultural Development Commission.

I mention these things only to underscore my concern for the problems and challenges facing Kentucky's number one industry. I intend to chair the council personally, and I have selected as members you who represent a broad spectrum of Kentucky agriculture. Bankers, educators, and administrators of farm programs are all represented on the council. But the membership is primarily composed of full-time farmers—both large and small, of diverse backgrounds and ages—representing practically every agricultural commodity produced and marketed in Kentucky. Who should know better the problems and needs of Kentucky farmers than Kentucky farmers themselves? Who is better able to point out the urgency for specific research and for new and improved markets and marketing methods?

Now I know you are concerned about our duties and functions, other than those set forth in the broad and general terms of the act creating the council. The old Commission on Agriculture had as its principal objective a $1 billion gross income from agriculture in Kentucky. This was a worthy objective. Certainly increasing agricultural production should not be neglected by this group, but I think it is time we turned our attention toward seeking ways of increasing the net income of Kentucky farmers. Overproduction of many commodities is a problem in itself; however, I am convinced that Kentucky farmers are also underproducing in many areas in which they could be competitive. We must concentrate our efforts on finding ways to put more money in the farmers' pockets. This may involve the introduction of foreign crops to Kentucky soil. It may mean developing new strains and hybrids of domestic crops and livestock. It will probably mean locating new markets for our old products. It will certainly mean finding new ways to increase efficiency of production on the farm and more profitable methods of marketing at home and abroad.

What we attempt is largely up to you. There is nothing we can do about the rising price of land. And, obviously, there is nothing we can do about the weather, although I am sure there were a great many soybean farmers who wished we could last fall! Beyond that, however, our opportunities for identifying problems, initiating research, promoting and coordinating agricultural programs, sponsoring legislation, and making recommendations to farmers whenever we deem appropriate are very great indeed.

One of the first things you may want to undertake is updating the potential study made by the old commission. You may also desire to appoint various committees and subcommittees to study the problems connected with each commodity grown or produced in Kentucky. Committees and subcommittees could be formed to investigate the potential of new products and new markets. The expertise of marketing and product specialists could be utilized effectively, and we should explore how best to gain this expertise. You may also want to investigate the feasibility of a leasing pool for farm machinery and heavy equipment as a way to overcome the initial investment prohibitions.

Another idea which you may spend some time studying is further encouragement of commodity cooperatives, in which a portion of the producer's income is used to find new markets and promote and advertise his product. It has been suggested that this council might have a profound influence in the area of consumer education. Both you and I know that the farmer receives the lamb's share of the consumer's dollar and the middleman gets the lion's share for processing, packaging, and distributing the finished product. But the average consumer is only concerned about what it costs to feed his family. Even though the farmer has a long way to go to achieve parity with the middleman, rising prices for farm products—while other goods have been under price control supervision—is rapidly making the farmer the scapegoat of many consumers.

You may wish to establish a pilot project in which all of the now fragmented governmental and private efforts to help farmers would be brought together into one coordinated effort. Such a project would be a control situation in which each program could be tested for its relative value and worth. With local, state, and federal governments working in concert with private organizations, hopefully some solid answers could be obtained that are not now evident in the prevailing patchwork method of combating farm problems.

Assisting you in whatever you may attempt will be a full-time staff appointed by me with your approval. Our first staff member has been named. Others may be added as needs dictate and budget permits. I appreciate your attendance today and look forward to an association with you which will result in some concrete advancement of the financial opportunities for Kentucky farmers.

---

1. Rural Electrification Administration, created by presidential Executive Order 7037, 1935; currently operates under Rural Electrification Act of 1936 (49 Stat. 1363; 7 U.S.C. 901 et seq.). "REA does not own or operate rural electric or telephone facilities. Its function is to lend money and to assure its repayment and to provide management and technical assistance to achieve program objectives." *United States Governmental Manual 1973/74* (Washington, D.C., 1973), pp. 98–99.

2. Thomas O. Harris (1918–), Democrat from Worthville; banker and farmer; member of Kentucky Senate (1968–1974); past board director of America's Jersey Cattle Club; past director of Carroll County Industrial Development Foundation; chairman of the board and director of First National Bank of Carrollton; vice president of International Dairy Show of Chicago. *Kentucky General Assembly 1972* (Frankfort, n.d.), p. 8. Mack Walters (1916–), Democrat from Shelbyville; farmer and tobacco warehouseman; member of Kentucky Senate (1970–1974). *Kentucky General Assembly 1972* (Frankfort, n.d.), p. 7.

JUNE DAIRY MONTH
KICKOFF LUNCHEON
Lexington / June 1, 1973

By now, almost everyone knows that "you can never outgrow your need for milk," that "you can find a new you the Grade A way!" The reason for this understanding is the most successful farm commodity promotional effort in the world. Since the American Dairy Association began under the sponsorship of the Farm Bureau in 1945, it has grown into a strong and effective voice for the dairyman. As the pioneer in nonbrand farm commodity advertisement, it has consistently promoted the interests of the dairy farmer and the dairy industry by telling their story. As a former farmer (that's as bad as a Hereford heifer!) I want to participate in telling the story of the American dairyman today, because there should be a better understanding between the consumer and the farmer.

If we are ever in agreement, I imagine it would be our desire for reasonable prices on those items we buy, as well as our desire to make a reasonable profit in our businesses. Unfortunately, the dilemma of prices and profits is a most difficult matter in today's life. The dairy industry ranks third in Kentucky's agricultural income with about 14 percent of the total. Our milch cow herd is the twelfth largest in the country, and even though we are seeing a decrease in the size of this herd, milk production is going up. With 6,000 fewer cows in 1972 than the previous year, our approximately 19,000 dairy farmers still produced 50 million more pounds of milk! This upgrading of dairy herds is continuing. Although we have fewer cows this April than last year, production is up twenty-five pounds per cow. I think you can see that dairy farmers are not standing still. They are continually upgrading their stock to produce greater yields. Yet with all this growth and productivity, all is not rosy. Even with milk bringing the highest price ever, the dairy farmer operates on a pretty slim margin of profit.

Senator Herman E. Talmadge,[1] chairman of the Senate Agriculture Committee, touched on this very point in his home state of Georgia. "The difference of costs over profits," he said, "has, unfortunately, taken its toll on many of our dairymen—in Georgia, in the southeast, and throughout the country. A full 2 percent of the dairymen have gone out of business since January of this year." Simply stated, dairymen are struggling with a profit squeeze of considerable proportions while they continue to protect the consumers' interest with one of the best product bargains available today. Some who have closely studied this matter say that if the figures of the number of dairy farmers affected by production difficulties continue at the present rates they could reach a crisis point by the end of this decade. This is not alarmist thinking. I remind you of the present crisis in the motor fuel industry. We should have learned by now that to say "it can't happen here" is to beg for a crisis situation.

Let's take a minute to look at some of the reasons for the squeeze on our dairy industry. The U.S. Department of Agriculture has selected a few categories of prices paid by the farmer which show substantial increases from the base year of 1967 through March of this year. Feeder livestock is up 93 percent, interest paid by the farmer is up 65 percent, taxes are up 61 percent, wages are up 46 percent, feed is up 44 percent, machinery is up 39 percent, and family living items are up 32 percent. Inflation is real, and the dairy farmer has to cope with this reality.

To give the consumer one of the most nutritional products on the market, the dairy farmer adds protein supplement to his feed and the cost for this supplement has tripled in the last year. Yet the U.S. Department of Commerce shows that dairy products have not increased in costs as much as other goods and services bought by the consumer. Perhaps these few figures will illustrate my point: public transportation is up 43.4 percent, shelter 34.5 percent, all services are up 33.4 percent, medical care is up 32.5 percent, food is up 23.5 percent, apparel and upkeep is up 22.3 percent. Dairy products, including milk, are up 17.1 percent.

The dairy farmer is also a consumer and has to face rising costs like the rest of us. The facts are plain. The dairyman is not seeing much profit between meeting production costs and selling his product in comparison with other industries. The American Dairy Association is doing a lot to tell the story of milk and the dairy industry. Marketing cooperatives such as Dairymen, Inc., are helping sell dairy products. But I think it is important that the dilemma I have described is understood by us all. Understanding is important.

What is most important though is our ability to resolve, in the interest of both the consumer and the seller, the complexities of continued rising costs in order to curtail this spiral which plagues us all. Certainly the Governor's Council on Agriculture is deeply involved in this and other cost areas. But getting to the heart of the problem and then developing workable solutions will demand cooperation from the states, the federal government, and the agriculture community. To this end the Governor's Council has pledged itself.

I appreciate your invitation and am glad to offer these observations. Hopefully, Dairy Month in Kentucky will enable others to become more informed about this vital industry. No doubt you were aware of some of the figures I offered, but what seems necessary is public understanding through open discussion of issues affecting so many Kentuckians. Your industry is much a part of our way of life. After all, who ever heard of motherhood and apple pie without a scoop of ice cream, a slice of cheese, and a glass of cold milk?

---

1. Herman Eugene Talmadge (1913–   ), Democrat from Lovejoy, Geor-

gia; attorney; Governor of Georgia (1948–1954); United States Senator (1957–   ). *1976 Congressional Directory, 94th Congress, 2nd Session* (Washington, D.C., n.d.), p. 41.

NORTH AMERICAN LIVESTOCK
SHOW AND EXPOSITION
Louisville / June 21, 1973

TODAY I am announcing the first step in a major livestock exposition for the state of Kentucky.[1] We will take this step with a show in November 1974 of the beef division, and plans are being made to bring in the swine, sheep, and possibly dairy divisions in the future. The event, to be named the North American Livestock Exposition, will be held at the Kentucky Fair and Exposition Center November 17–24. In addition to the show activities, two breed organizations, the National Angus and the National Polled Hereford, will hold meetings in conjunction with the show.

Kentucky already has a national reputation for staging shows and expositions, and I am confident that this major undertaking will be a success. Our state Department of Agriculture, which will direct this new exposition, already conducts one of the nation's more unique programs of purebred cattle shows and sales. Also the Louisville Barrow Show has grown to be one of the nation's top swine events. Consideration has been given to merging the Louisville Steer Show with the new exposition to make it a complete show for beef cattle.

The objectives of a national livestock exposition have a direct bearing on the future of our livestock industry. We know the demand for meat products will continue in the years ahead; predictions indicate a needed increase of 7 billion pounds by 1980 and that beef producers will face strong consumer demands. Shows and expositions will help meet these demands because they are both educational and promotional. In fact, much of the advancement of America's livestock industry can be attributed to the many outstanding shows and expositions throughout the country.

Louisville is a natural for an undertaking of this magnitude. Besides the accessibility and outstanding facilities at the Fair and Exposition Center, Louisville is the hub of major transportation links. It is also in a relatively close proximity to the major livestock-producing states.

I am pleased that Kentucky's livestock interests have been able to join with others throughout the nation to initiate this new livestock exposition. We have sought such a program for a long time. The national agricultural spotlight will be focused on Kentucky, the participants will benefit our economy, and we have every reason to feel pride that Kentucky has been recognized as a capable host for this significant event. We also have hopes that the livestock exposition may someday be the largest in the nation.

---

1. Press conference.

GOVERNOR'S COUNCIL ON AGRICULTURE COMMITTEES
Frankfort / July 24, 1973

It's good to see you this morning. I want to express my sincere appreciation to each of you for consenting to serve on one of the fourteen committees of the Council on Agriculture. You have demonstrated a genuine interest in Kentucky's number one industry by leaving your farms and businesses to come to Frankfort, at your own expense.

I am not going to stand up here today and talk about the problems and challenges facing agriculture and rural development in Kentucky. Neither am I going to tell you about the great potential our state has in these areas. You know better than I what these problems are. You know that Kentucky has the natural resources, the human resources, and the geographical location to resolve these problems and to become a leader among her sister states in the development of her God-given attributes. What we need is long-range planning with proper leadership. I believe the nucleus of that leadership is within the confines of these walls. You represent both the expertise and the experience in your respective fields of endeavor. I do not believe we could have searched longer or more diligently and found a better cross section of talent and experience for the task at hand.

I am concerned with finding ways to increase the net income of our farmers, and of making our rural areas better places to live, work, and rear our families. I am firmly convinced that the success of the latter depends to a large degree upon the success of the former. Our ability to enhance educational and cultural opportunities, to provide clean water, sewers, to make available new recreational and health facilities, and to improve rural roads and highways will depend to a great extent upon our ability to elevate the general economy of Kentucky's rural areas. By attracting industry that is compatible with agriculture and the environment to rural areas, we can make available more and better jobs. But just as important, and perhaps even more important, to the rural economy we will be putting more money in the farmers' pockets.

Specifically what we attempt is largely up to you. There are obviously areas in which we can do very little. Due to the nature of farm-rural problems, many of the answers will have to come at the federal level. Certainly we should make every effort to make our views known in Washington and to assist in molding the decisions made there which affect our daily existence. This is important today, perhaps more than any time in history.

There is also much that can be done on the state and local levels that will promote the welfare of the entire farm community in Kentucky. For example, putting more money in our farmers' pockets may involve the introduction of foreign crops to Kentucky soil. It may mean developing new strains and hybrids of domestic crops and livestock. It will mean locating new markets for our traditional products, an effort which has been under way from my office as well as the Department of Commerce for months. It will certainly mean finding new ways to increase efficiency of production on the farm and more profitable methods of marketing at home and abroad.

Without elaborating, I will simply say that our opportunities for identifying problems, initiating research, promoting and coordinating agricultural programs, sponsoring legislation, and making recommendations to farmers whenever we deem appropriate are very great indeed. You, of course, are aware that unfortunately the Commonwealth of Kentucky has limited financial resources and faces seemingly unlimited needs. There are other segments of our society with problems just as real and needs just as legitimate. Before letting you begin working on this comprehensive program, I have three announcements to make which are of major importance to the agricultural sector.

First, I am immediately activating the Kentucky Farm Development Authority. Although we may yet have to have a test case to determine the constitutionality of this agency, I am today appointing Walter Meng, Jr., of Bourbon County and R. O. Wilson, Jr.,[1] of Livingston County to serve on that body along with the Commissioner of Agriculture, the Commissioner of Banking and Securities, the State Treasurer, and the chairmen of the House and Senate Committees on Agriculture and Natural Resources. The purpose of this agency is to "guarantee loans for the purchase of farm land and buildings thereon, or for buildings to be erected thereon." It is designed to assist those people who want to go into farming or who want to expand their farming operation, but are unable to get the necessary credit without such a guarantee. I believe this agency affords us an excellent opportunity to do something about involving more young people in agriculture in Kentucky. Since the trend today for young farmers who do not have family farms is to rent land and use their available capital for operating purposes, I want the appropriate committee or committees of the council to study the advisability of asking the General Assembly to extend the purpose for which a guarantee may be made to include farm machinery as well as land.

Second, I am also immediately activating the Kentucky Farmers' Advocate Office and naming Bill Burnette[2] to head that office in addition to his duties as executive director of the Governor's Council on Agriculture. As set forth in the same act which created the council, the duties and responsibilities of that office are to keep the Governor and the council informed on current agricultural and agribusiness developments and problems; to carry out such directions as the Governor and council may issue; to advocate and promote programs for the advancement and promotion of agriculture and agribusiness; to make the facilities of the office available to farmers and to serve as a forum to which farmers may direct questions and problems; to serve farmers as a source of information on federal and state agricultural programs; and to make available to farmers such other information and services as the facilities of the office afford.

Third, I will have in the next executive budget provisions for a new facility at Spindletop Farm which will be utilized by the agricultural experiment station's Foundation Seed Project. When completed, the new structure will contain offices, cold rooms, modern cleaning and processing equipment, and adequate dry storage facilities. As you know, the purpose of the Foundation Seed Project has been to increase supplies of superior varieties of seed of known genetic origin, in order to meet the needs of commercial farmers in Kentucky, and at the same time to maintain both the genetic and physical purity of that seed. Their efforts have been seriously hampered in the past due to lack of space and adequate processing equipment. They have been forced to contract with commercial seed dealers around the state for a large part of these services. These firms neither had the time nor the facilities to adhere to the strict handling requirements of the Foundation Seed Project. This new structure, however, will better enable the project to accomplish its objectives, and greater yields of improved varieties of grasses and feed grains should contribute markedly to an expanding livestock industry in Kentucky.

I appreciate your attendance today and look forward to an association with you which I am confident will result in some concrete advancement of the financial opportunities for Kentucky farmers.

---

1. Walter Meng, Jr. (1913–   ), North Middleton; farmer and farm credit official, Kentucky Farm Development Authority; past director, Bourbon County Farm Bureau Federation; past director, Bourbon County Livestock Improvement Association; currently with the Central Kentucky Production Credit Association in Paris, Kentucky. Provided by Meng, January 5, 1977. R. O. Wilson, Jr. (1928–   ), Iuka; farmer; member, Kentucky Farm Development Authority; former member, Livingston County Fiscal Court; member, Kentucky Farm Bureau Mutual Insurance board; member, Kentucky Farm Bureau Board of Directors; member, Livingston County Fair Association; chairman, Livingston County Farm Bureau. Provided by Wilson, January 4, 1977.

2. William E. Burnette (1943–   ), Frankfort; instructor, Murray State University (1968–1972); partner, Kentucky Reprint Company (1970–1973); executive director of the Governor's Council on Agriculture and head of Kentucky Farmers' Advocate Office (1973–1975); deputy commissioner, Kentucky Department of Agriculture (1976–   ); member of the Governor's Task Force on Agriculture; organized the farm and agribusiness community during Governor Ford's campaign for the United States Senate (1974), also for Julian M. Carroll in 1975 and Jimmy Carter in 1976. From résumé from Burnette, January 4, 1977.

STULL'S SEED FIELD DAY LUNCH
Sebree / September 21, 1973

You asked me here today to speculate on the farm outlook in Kentucky, a subject traditionally so complex and unpredictable that even the *Farmer's Almanac* dares not risk an opinion on it. Today the future looks very good, perhaps better than ever before. But can we say the same about tomorrow? Never before have farm prices been more turbulent, unpredictable, and dependent on the whims of weather, demand, and the federal government. Today we are witnessing record prices and record farm production at the same time—an unprecedented event.

Whether good or bad, depending on your point of view, the federal government is gradually beginning to disengage itself from commercial agriculture. Mandatory production controls, while they will remain on certain commodities for some time, are on the way out. Price supports and direct payments are losing favor with an increasingly urban, consumer-oriented Congress. The prevailing opinion, of course, is that farmers are becoming efficient and flexible enough to return to free enterprise and that commodity prices should be allowed to seek their own levels based on supply and demand.

Deemphasis on government controls and subsidies will undoubtedly mean less stability in both commodity supplies and prices received. Agriculture will be more prone to temporary shortages and surpluses and to fluctuating prices. Farm cooperatives and trade associations will likely assume a greater role in production planning, as well as marketing and pricing. Unstable prices and reduced subsidies, along with rising costs, will combine to force more marginal farmers out of business. The trend toward larger, more efficient, family operated commercial farms will probably continue. Those who remain in farming will be more business-oriented, quick to adopt new innovations and labor-saving practices, and wiser in the ways of the marketplace.

In the short-run at least, the prospects for agriculture never looked better. Prices will undoubtedly fluctuate in the months ahead and will probably stabilize below current levels, at least for a while. Prices may never again reach the peaks of the past summer, but they will continue to be strong, as domestic demand is great and foreign buyers continue to bid against domestic buyers for the nation's raw agricultural products. Yet farmers are approaching these facts with cautious optimism.

Production costs are at an all-time high. Dairy, livestock, and poultry producers are extremely hesitant about expanding due to high costs of feed, land, and equipment. Grain farmers are disturbed about anticipated critical shortages in transportation, fertilizers, and propane gas. Increased production of all commodities is being hampered by high interest rates. There remains the overhanging possibility of export controls and the reinstatement of price freezes by the federal government.

Kentucky farmers are experiencing the same problems and challenges facing farmers across the country. But you know that Kentucky has the natural resources, the human resources, and the geographical location to resolve these problems and become a leader among her sister states in the development of her God-given attributes. Last year, cash farm receipts exceeded $1 billion for the first time in our state's history. However, Kentucky farmers still trail far behind the rest of the population in disposable income. I am concerned with finding new and additional ways to increase the net income of our farmers and of making our rural areas better places to live, work, and rear our children.

Positive steps have been taken in that direction the last twenty months in Frankfort. We established the Council on Agriculture, a broadly representative group that will help determine what actions can be taken on the state level to promote the well-being of our farming community. We activated the Kentucky Farm Development Authority, which will assist those people who want to go into farming or who want to expand their farming operation, but are unable to get the necessary credit. We activated the Kentucky Farmers' Advocate Office, which gives you the farmer a direct line to Frankfort.

We will make provisions in the next executive budget for a new facility at Spindletop Farm in Lexington, which will be utilized by the Agriculture Experimental Station's Foundation Seed Program. This structure will better enable the project to accomplish its objectives, and greater yields of improved varieties of grasses and feed grains should contribute markedly to an expanding livestock industry in Kentucky.

As chairman of the Council on Agriculture, I requested that a study be conducted by the University of Kentucky on our state's agriculture potential. The study is nearly finished, but the complete results will not be ready until next month. However, I have been told the results will be startling to the people of Kentucky, farmers and consumers alike.

I want to assure you that you can consider state government a committed partner in overcoming many of the problems facing agriculture and agribusiness today. I invite you to bring your concerns to Frankfort when you think we are not doing an adequate job. To be aware of what other people are up against in meeting the challenges that face them each day is the beginning of understanding. From understanding, we can work toward problem solving, which, in the end, will result in a better quality of life for everyone.

BURLEY AND DARK LEAF
TOBACCO EXPORT ASSOCIATION
CONVENTION LUNCHEON
Louisville / October 15, 1973

IT is a pleasure to welcome you here today. We are proud to host such a distinguished group in Kentucky. I want to tell you about a new cigarette that has been developed in our state. You won't find it in the tobacco stores or in a cigarette machine, but more than ten million have been produced. Right now the only place you'll find this particular cigarette is in laboratories of more than 500 scientists and investigators throughout the world. They are performing tests on what has become known as a "reference cigarette" which was developed by the Tobacco and Health Research Institute at the University of Kentucky. When perfected, it could be a most significant boost for the tobacco industry.

Both you and I know that the tobacco industry has trod perilous ground in recent years. There were the Surgeon General's Report, advertising bans, warning labels on packs and in advertising, assaults from the front and rear by the Senator "who gathers no moss"[1] from Utah, and the recent legislation enacted in Arizona banning public smoking.

Last year, Kentucky marketed more than 413 million pounds of tobacco, 70 percent of the nation's burley product. Tobacco is our state's leading single money-producing product. There is hardly a farm family in the Commonwealth that doesn't receive a portion of its cash income from tobacco. I'm not giving you these facts and figures to impress you. You, better than anyone else, realize what Kentucky means to the tobacco industry. What I'm telling you is that I am aware of the tobacco industry's tremendous impact on Kentucky.

What I also want to tell you is that we are concerned about the problems threatening the entire tobacco industry. And here in Kentucky, we are doing something about it. Because elements in our society began to raise questions about the implications of smoking to human health, we decided Kentucky could and should play a leadership role in providing some responsible answers—answers which reflect concern for the well-being of our fellowman, answers which reflect our desire that the tobacco industry not suffer from unwarranted and unsubstantiated attack, answers which substitute truth for suppositions and scientific fact for emotional suspicions.

Three years ago the Kentucky legislature enacted a bill creating the

Kentucky Tobacco Research Board and authorizing the University of Kentucky's Tobacco and Health Research Institute to begin an intensive research program. The legislation specified the research effort be directed toward "proving or disproving questions of health hazards to tobacco users and toward preserving and strengthening the tobacco industry in Kentucky."[2]

A tax of half a cent per pack was placed on all cigarettes sold in Kentucky to provide funds for the research. This has resulted in an income of approximately $3.4 million a year, administered by the board which includes representatives of the tobacco interests of the state. As Lieutenant Governor this was one of my pet projects, and I have always been proud to have helped lead the fight to begin this program. As Governor, I continue to support this research because Kentucky and the nation need these answers.

This program is the only such effort in the world which provides the opportunity, under one administrative structure, for the full scope of the problem to be studied. It represents a cooperative venture between the state and two of the university's highly respected colleges, Agriculture and Medicine. Now in its third year of operation, the program has gained national stature and has been visited during the past year by scientists from all over the world. A recent study conducted by the National Clearinghouse for Smoking and Health revealed that 20 percent of the world's research in this area is being conducted by the University of Kentucky institute.

The "reference cigarette" now being analyzed is only one of the institute's major discoveries. Because their work could have a profound impact on the tobacco industry, let me briefly share with you some of the institute's other important contributions. The College of Agriculture believes it is possible to control genetically the nicotine level of burley and flue-cured tobacco. Commercially acceptable varieties have been developed and are being used to determine the biological aspects of nicotine. Studies have shown that the characteristics of smoke chemistry and the biological activity of cigarettes can be modified by certain factors. Investigators using the smoke from experimental cigarettes have established that every adverse biological activity studied to date can be minimized. There is evidence that people differ in their reaction to the effects of smoke and that many medical problems may be associated with only a certain group of individuals. Smoking machines have been developed to duplicate the full range of human smoking behavior and are being used to determine the effects of smoke on experimental animals. Procedures for determining how, and how much, people smoke have been established and are being used in continuing research.

The institute has tackled the problems head-on. Continued research is imperative if the tobacco industry is to continue to survive and still meet an obligation to the American public to provide a product that has no adverse consequences to health. I hope this report is as encouraging to you as it is to me. We are proud of the work being accomplished by the institute. More important to all who are concerned with the life of the tobacco industry and the well-being of mankind is the accumulation of evidence which has led the institute to predict that someday it will be possible to produce a cigarette that the Surgeon General will not label "Dangerous to your health."

---

1. Frank Edward Moss (1911–   ), Democrat from Salt Lake City, Utah; attorney; president of Utah State Association of County Officials; two terms as president of National Association of District Attorneys; United States Senator (1959–   ). *1976 Congressional Directory, 94th Congress, 2nd Session* (Washington, D.C., n.d.), p. 179.

2. See an act "relating to taxation of Cigarettes and prescribing purpose and use of revenues collected," which was approved on March 30, 1970. This act created the Kentucky Tobacco Research Board. *Acts of the General Assembly of the Commonwealth of Kentucky, 1970*, Chapter 255 (H.B. 466), pp. 880–86.

FARM TOUR DINNER
Owensboro / October 18, 1973

IT would be hard for me to mask my enthusiasm over what I have to tell you because the information is based on the potential strength of agriculture in Kentucky. Hopefully you will share in this optimism which is based not on a pipe dream, but on reality through strong leadership from individuals such as you.

Let me borrow your imagination for a few minutes. Would you believe that corn production in the state can be more than tripled, that five times as many soybeans can be produced, and that Kentucky's alfalfa production could grow to sixteen times what it is today? Think what would happen if our land was devoted to crops with the greatest potential, and the forage and grain were used to feed livestock. Kentucky farmers could triple their livestock income above feed costs! And can you imagine Kentucky's agricultural resources when used at their maximum capabilities, generating an annual gross farm income of $2.7 billion?

This may sound fantastic, but the opportunity is here now. These projections are not the idle speculation of someone. They represent conclusions reached through a detailed study of Kentucky's agricultural potentials by a special committee of the University of Kentucky's College of Agriculture. This is the study that, as chairman of the Governor's Council on Agriculture, I asked the university to make, beginning last spring. It is needed because Kentucky's economic progress depends to a great extent on future developments in agriculture.

Just completed, the detailed analysis says to you and me that Kentucky can do far more in establishing itself as a national leader in agriculture. The gains we are experiencing today can't compare to the dramatic advances we can achieve tomorrow. Time doesn't allow elaboration in any great detail, but I expect the Council on Agriculture to hold a statewide seminar soon, where our potentials study will be the major subject of discussion.

In arriving at estimates of Kentucky's agriculture potentials, the committee presumed that all human, natural, and man-made resources with which Kentucky has been blessed would be used at their maximum capacity. At the same time, the committee noted that due to the average age of farm operators, customs, lack of capital, and the reluctance by many to make radical changes, full capability may never be realized. The point is, though, how close are we willing to come in reaching full capability. In calculating the gross farm income that maximum production would yield, average prices prevailing in 1971 were used. Since no effort was made to forecast future prices, the value figures in the study reflect real potential growth, rather than inflation.

Now, what must we first consider? Kentucky's greatest agricultural potential lies in using our land resources at total capability. For instance, Kentucky farmers are now harvesting cultivated crops from only 2.3 million acres, cutting hay from 1.5 million acres, and using 5.4 million acres for permanent pasture—a total of 9.2 million acres. With proper management, Kentucky has 14.9 million acres capable of producing crops: 5.9 million acres are suitable for cultivation, 5.5 million could be used for hay and meadows, and only 3.5 million acres should be in permanent pasture.

Based on these facts, as well as historical data, and considering how new varieties and new technology will result in increased yields and greater efficiency, the potentials committee assigned the most productive soils to crops that yield the highest return per acre and arrived at the following conclusions. Total grain production could be increased 75 million bushels by 1980! If maximum capability can be achieved an additional 200-plus million bushels could be produced at some future date. The total value of all crops including tobacco, soybeans, and seed crops could be raised from approximately $767 million to more than $1 billion in 1980. The long-run projection here is $1.86 billion. Total income from all livestock and livestock products could be increased from $507.9 million to $723.4 million in 1980. The maximum potential is more than $1.1 billion, with beef cattle, hogs, and broilers making the most striking gains. Livestock value above feed costs shows a gain of $438.6 million by 1980 and $750.9 million eventually.

Thus the total gross farm income including horticultural crops and forestry products could increase to $1.6 billion by 1980. A potential annual gross farm income of $2.7 billion could be achieved at some future date, if maximum capability is realized. It becomes apparent that a potential annual net farm income of $1 billion is possible. It may not happen in our lifetime, but it is possible.

I have given you quite a few figures, and they may stagger the imagination. I must emphasize these potentials are not predictions or goals. They are possibilities and should be considered only as such. But why shouldn't we set our sights high and go after the rewards? Attainment depends on a number of factors. It hinges on farmers being able to secure adequate amounts of fertilizer, fuel, machinery, credit, and good hands. Currently the demand for all of these is great and supplies will have to loosen if farmers are encouraged to expand their operations.

The potentials study also points out that a lack of marketing facilities currently is restricting expansion in some areas. This supports a contention I have expressed previously. I have, therefore, appointed a committee consisting of John Koon, Dr. Harold Love, and Bill Balden[1] to solicit and screen applications for a marketing specialist to work out of my office with the following duties and responsibilities: to work with any farm group seeking to improve its marketing position, to keep abreast of the procurement needs of all processors of Kentucky agriculture products in the Kentucky marketing area, and to work closely with the Industrial Committee and the Department of Commerce in attracting manufacturers of agricultural products into the state. You're going to be hearing a great deal more about this study, for it is designed as a tool, not as just another report which will gather dust on someone's shelf.

What we're really talking about is money in the pockets of farmers, money in the pockets of those whose businesses serve farmers, and money in the pockets of countless others who benefit indirectly from a strong farm economy. I think it's safe to say that agriculture has received more working attention from this administration than ever before and the pieces are falling into place—pieces which are producing a sound, comprehensive picture that is bright, that is logical, and that will be viewed with envy by others from beyond our borders.

———————

1. John W. Koon (1914–   ), Louisville; served on the Kentucky Vocational Educational Council and the Kentucky Comprehensive Health Planning Council; currently executive secretary of the Kentucky Farm Bureau Federation. Provided by Koon's office on January 4, 1977. Harold Love (1918–   ), Lexington; university professor; member of Governor's Council for Agriculture and adviser to its subcommittee on marketing; extension professor of agricultural economics and specialist in agricultural marketing firms. Provided by Love on January 4, 1977. William H. Balden (1921–   ), Danville; farmer; director of the Council for Burley Tobacco; served on Governor's Council for Agriculture; past president, Blue Grass State Sheep Association; currently first vice president, Kentucky Farm Bureau Federation. Provided by Farm Bureau office on January 4, 1977.

KENTUCKY FARM BUREAU
Louisville / December 4, 1973

You've probably heard someone say: "I have both good and bad news for you. First the good news." In some respects, my remarks this morning can be identified with that expression.

Last October, we announced the results of an agricultural potentials study for Kentucky.[1] The news was good, because it represented an exciting and positive future for your industry and the industry that affects the lives of all Americans. The potentials study is something you will learn more and more about. It is designed as a helpful tool for agriculture, rather than just another report which gathers dust on someone's shelf. Now in the planning stage is a statewide seminar to better acquaint farmers with the study. As chairman of the Governor's Council on Agriculture, I asked the University of Kentucky to prepare this document, and those who worked on it have brought forth what

I believe will be an invaluable document for the future of Kentucky farming. Although many of the projections sound astounding, they are realistic under the proper circumstances.

The study's conclusions give cause for enthusiasm. The University of Kentucky College of Agriculture's special committee working on this project admittedly found the brightest possible results under ideal conditions. Yet even if maximum achievements are never reached, where we stand today and where we can be tomorrow is highly significant. It bodes well for much greater economic gains, a direction surely each of you want to pursue.

To help ensure an organized and coordinated pattern in reaching this growth, the council plans to organize committees on the county level to help implement potential studies for each county. I might announce that the University of Kentucky is now going further by preparing individual county potentials reports. I want to encourage all of you here today to participate and work with these committees so that each county can see its potential realized.

The study also pointed out that a lack of marketing facilities currently restricts expansion in certain areas, supporting a contention I expressed previously. As a result, I have appointed a committee that is now seeking applicants for a marketing specialist position. This specialist will have the following duties and responsibilities: to work with any farm group seeking to improve its marketing position, to keep abreast of the procurement needs of all processors of Kentucky agriculture products in our state's marketing area, and to work closely with the Industrial Committee and the Department of Commerce in attracting manufacturers of agricultural products into the state.

If this news is so good, and I believe it is, there has to be a note of caution. Changing conditions prompt an understanding that problems can exist to turn good news to bad, unless we are prepared to solve those problems. Today, I cannot hide my concern about the gravity of a crisis which threatens to unfavorably impact the potentials study, at least temporarily. This is the energy crisis. But let me quickly add that our energy crisis does not have to adversely affect Kentucky's farm future forever. For this reason we must drive on in our use of the study.

For the time being, however, we must be realistic about an energy shortage. Without fuel, tractors and other equipment become lifeless. Transportation will be restricted, land will be left unattended, and processing will slow to a dangerous pace. Farm homes will also feel the crunch. A shortage of propane and heating oil will get worse before it gets better. While the implications are disturbing in the rural community just as in urban areas, we cannot throw up our hands in surrender. This is not the American tradition. Our heritage is based on our abilities to cope with adversity, grow stronger because of it, and then move on to the next job which might await. I am confident this same attitude will prevail in the energy crisis.

Immediate relief can only be accomplished through wise and prudent conservation of existing fuel supplies. State government is a dedicated partner in helping the farmer and all Kentuckians through this difficult period of uncertainty. The Farmers' Advocate Office, your direct line to the Capitol, and the State Mandatory Allocation Office are working hand-in-hand to assist farmers who are experiencing problems. Since November 1, when the office opened, more than 800 farmers have received direct help.

A major obstacle centers around unclear and constant revision of *Federal Register* regulations. Many producers and distributors are confused by the regulations and turn people away by mistake. Another administrative nightmare is determining allocations based on what the farmer used the same month the previous year. All of you know what a wet fall we experienced in 1972, while conditions this year have been much more conducive to fall harvesting. Since the energy crisis is national in scope, the federal government must move without delay to eliminate confusion, establish further priorities, and give the leadership we need to become self-sufficient with our energy in the shortest possible time. Kentucky can, as I have said before, play a major role through liquefaction and gasification of coal to produce energy by-products. To this end of research and development, my office is working night and day.

Nevertheless, getting through this winter is not going to be our only hurdle. Life-styles and working-styles will be altered beyond the winter, and I say this because we have to face reality. How each of us copes with the situation will determine the extent of the difficulties. This means cooperation in conserving fuel, eliminating wasted effort, and encouraging both Congress and the White House to provide the national direction necessary in solving the present crisis, as well as ensuring such a blight will never hit us again. So our mission is twofold: get through the energy crisis and make the potentials study a reality. I have every faith in our ability to do both.

---

1. See speech from October 18, 1973, in this section, pp. 379–82.

COUNCIL ON AGRICULTURE SYMPOSIUM
Louisville / February 13, 1974

SIGNIFICANT progress has been made in Kentucky agriculture during the past two years. And if one unique aspect in this new direction has emerged, it has been the spirit of cooperation found in all segments of the agricultural community. I believe state government has rekindled that spirit by charting a new course for those Kentuckians entrusted with bringing life to our land. Where before there was no working Council on Agriculture, there is today. Where before there was no Farmers' Advocate Office linked directly to the Governor, there is today. Where before there was no increased emphasis on marketing, there is today. Where before there was no true billion dollar farm economy, there is by a quarter billion more today. And where before there was no true outline of Kentucky's agricultural potentials, you have one today.

Credit for these steps forward belongs to you. You expected a new direction and you have responded to our challenges in an overwhelming fashion, taking the initiative to provide the leadership which can only bode well for Kentucky's agricultural future. The theme of this seminar, "More in '74," is not mere idle chatter. There was more in 1972, more in 1973, and there can be more in 1974.

Since last October when we announced the agriculture potentials study for Kentucky, I have spoken a great deal about this Commonwealth's agricultural capabilities. I have noted the long-term potential of a $2.7 billion annual gross farm income. My principal interest, as the farmer is concerned, is helping him realize a fair and reasonable return on his investment and labors. Net income is what I am talking about—money the farmer can spend as he sees fit, whether it be for living expenses, a new tractor, to pay off a mortgage, send his children to college, or take his family on a vacation.

If this means increased production of certain commodities, we want to help. If it means finding new markets, we want to help. If it means developing new and improved marketing methods or establishing new marketing facilities, we want to help. If it means an educational program that can change or alter outdated customs or habits, or if it means working on all of these areas at the same time, we are ready to help. Our objective, our programs, and our energies will be directed to this end in the coming months and years. This is what "More in '74" is all about.

Secretary Butz[1] will indicate this in his address. He is a man with a difficult job and has already experienced some very trying times. His task is to be the farmers' spokesman in Washington. He was a farmer, former Dean of Agriculture at Purdue University in our neighboring state of Indiana, Assistant Secretary of Agriculture under President Eisenhower, and author of countless agricultural articles. Mr. Butz has been the President's Secretary of Agriculture since December 1971 and is recipient of the American Farm Bureau Federation's Award for distinguished service to agriculture in 1972.

Last year Secretary Butz asked a farmer if he handled a lot of money since prices were climbing so high. The farmer replied, "Yes, but I'm not stopping any of it!" This response shows the age-old farm dilemma—a quick pass-through of dollars where few remain in the farmer's pocket. "More in '74" attacks such a problem, a national problem as well as a state problem. To offer Washington's viewpoint, I now present Secretary of Agriculture Earl L. Butz.[2]

---

1. Earl Butz (1909–   ), Republican from Indiana; instructor of agricultural economics at Purdue University (1937–1946), head of department (1946–1953), dean of the School of Agriculture (1957–1968); dean of Continuing Education (1968–1971); vice president of Purdue Research Foundation (1968–1971); assistant secretary of the United States Department of Agriculture (1954–1957), secretary (1971–1976). Who's Who in America, 1976–1977 (Chicago, 1976), 1:470.

2. Governor Ford noted on his delivery copy, "We have one thing in common—we offer the president advice and he usually doesn't take it."

KENTUCKY AGRICULTURAL EXPORT CONFERENCE LUNCHEON
Louisville / July 17, 1974

Much has been said and written about this Commonwealth's agricultural capabilities since we announced the potentials study last October. We have noted the long-term potential for a $2.7 billion gross farm income. My principal interest, as far as the farmer is concerned, remains helping him realize a fair and reasonable return on his investment and labors. I'm talking about net income. In the last two-and-one-half years, we have explored new ways state government can help bring this about: by increasing production of certain commodities, by finding new markets, by developing new and improved marketing methods, or by establishing new marketing facilities. One area never before pursued deals with expanding Kentucky's role in trade with foreign countries and that's what I want to talk to you about today.

The importance of agricultural exports to the national trade balance cannot be overemphasized. Farm product exports for fiscal 1974 are expected to total around $21 billion, nearly $8 billion more than the previous year. With exports far exceeding imports, agriculture's contribution to the United States trade balance will increase to a record $11.5 billion, more than doubling last year's effort. All this will help to offset the rising costs of nonfarm products which the U.S. imports; products like petroleum, the cost of which is expected to reach $25–30 billion by 1985. Sizable exports of some type will be required to offset this. Since this country holds an advantage in production and export of farm products, a principal beneficiary would be U.S. farmers.

So the question I want to put to you today is this, "Are we in Kentucky reaching our greatest potential in this area?" I, for one, don't think so and hope a better understanding of the opportunity that awaits us will result from this conference. We have set two goals for this meeting: to bring together producers and processors who are intimately involved with production and marketing and to study the mechanics of foreign trade.

Of all the agricultural products in Kentucky only one, tobacco, plays a significant part in our country's export programs. In 1973, 60 million pounds of Kentucky burley, valued at $75 million, ended up on foreign markets. An additional 35 million pounds of burley, in the form of manufactured products, also were exported. Altogether agriculture accounted for less than a third of the total products exported from Kentucky in 1972, the latest year where figures are available. These figures may be two years old, but they tell me one thing. We can do more! We know Kentucky has the capacity to produce many times more than it is now.

To help draw a more realistic picture of the potentially feasible changes that can occur in Kentucky, based on today's conditions, the UK College of Agriculture is preparing a new marketing study. I requested this study upon the recommendation of the Council on Agriculture. The potentials study gave us an indication of just how much we can produce. The marketing study will determine the maximum marketing potentials. Though the study is not finished, I've been given a preview that reveals wide differences between Kentucky's historical share of the domestic and world markets, and what our farmers could be producing.

Kentucky has the resources and manpower to produce a much larger share of the world's need for food, feed, and fiber. If our farmers are to increase their production and income, a greater share of the domestic and export market needs to be theirs. The latest study determines a potential for marketing three times as many soybeans, four times as much corn, five times as much wheat, twice as much milk, and three times the present number of feeder calves. This shows we have the capacity to produce more than we can consume. So what do you do then? You look for a market elsewhere, and for this is what we want to be prepared.

You can see the opportunity for the future which is presenting itself. You can see the challenge which Kentucky farmers and government must have the foresight to recognize. For farmers, the challenge is to increase efficiency and productivity, thus gaining a larger share of the export market. For government, it means giving more attention to promoting and merchandising agricultural products. Reaching Kentucky's fullest production and marketing potential is what our programs and energies will continue to be directed toward in the coming months and years. There can be more in '74 and beyond!

Now is the time to map a course for the future, because if Kentucky doesn't capture its share of the world market, somebody else will. This is the decision we must consider and the challenge we must accept. What we're talking about can have many lasting benefits for Kentucky's agricultural community. As long as the United States is dependent on foreign nations for such essential nonfarm products as petroleum, agricultural exports will assume a greater load in retaining a favorable balance of trade. When this country is once again producing more than it can consume, we must have ways to market the surplus—and markets abroad are the logical answer. Kentucky does have the potential to produce and market more, much more, agricultural commodities, which can have a positive impact on both the farmers' net income and the state's economy. Finally, the idea of increasing Kentucky's contribution to the export market has never before received any great emphasis. Unless we do consider it and are ready to grasp the opportunity when supply again exceeds demand, this Commonwealth's agricultural capabilities will not realize their greatest potential.

ALL-KENTUCKY PRODUCTS BREAKFAST
Louisville / September 13, 1974

In the course of the past two days, you've had the opportunity to take a firsthand look at what goes into and stands behind Kentucky's agricultural products. You've seen our poultry, grain, beef, swine, and tobacco operations. You've seen how these products are readied on the farm for market. Hopefully you also saw something else—the pride our farmers and producers take in what they are doing. I can tell you it's there. And this morning I want to talk to you about what is being done to keep that pride alive and help this Commonwealth's agricultural capabilities realize their greatest potential.

For those of you who are from out-of-state, let me digress just a minute. Your host for these tours was the Governor's Council on Agriculture, which we created through the 1972 General Assembly. The council was formed to develop and promote a statewide agricultural and agribusiness program to stimulate the growth of the state's agricultural economy. When members began their work, they decided the first logical step in developing an overall program was to determine the state's capacity to produce. This was accomplished through a production potential study, completed last October. This study indicated, among other things, that Kentucky could generate an annual gross farm income of $2.7 billion—if land and other resources were utilized to their maximum capabilities.

However, this was only the beginning. After the potentials study was completed, the next logical step was to determine how much Kentucky farmers could expect to market profitably over the short term and long run. So the University of Kentucky was asked to conduct a marketing study which would accomplish four objectives: to project the needed output of major agricultural commodities produced in Kentucky for 1980 and beyond; to project Kentucky's share of domestic and foreign markets in 1980 and beyond; to appraise the adequacy of marketing and transportation facilities in Kentucky and nearby areas; and to estimate the amount and adequacy of on-farm storage facilities for grain in 1980 and beyond. Just completed this week, the study says to you and me that Kentucky has the resources and manpower to produce and market a much larger share of the world's need for food, feed, and fiber. Time doesn't allow elaboration in any great detail, but I do want to touch on several points and conclusions which the study made.

If Kentucky is to capture more than its historic share of the domestic and world markets, the study says that now is the time for producers, handlers, and processors to make a vigorous and determined effort toward this end. Some specific examples can be given. Currently some Kentucky packers are purchasing from 50 to 60 percent of their slaughter hogs from out-of-state. Unless Kentucky increases pork production, possibly by using a larger percentage of its corn as hog feed, the current situation will continue to exist. Most of the states south and east of Kentucky are grain-deficit states. Thus it appears here is where Kentuckians should strive to increase corn sales. In addition, new and efficient grain handling should bring about a higher usage of Kentucky-grown corn, and possibly a decline in importations. More on-farm grain storage facilities in both the cash-grain areas and the grain-deficit areas of Kentucky should increase the movement of grain within the state, expanding the growers' market. More grain and soybean buying stations or elevators are needed in central Kentucky. There is also an equally urgent need for more on-farm drying and storage facilities. Farmers with these facilities will have the opportunity to obtain a larger share of the demand for feed grains at local feed mills.

When possible and feasible producers should consider contracting a portion of their annual production in order to obtain a larger share of the market. The study recommends that Kentucky's research and educational marketing programs be expanded and that producers work to increase the quality of their product. Increasing the demand for the Commonwealth's agricultural products will benefit all involved handlers and processors, as well as producers. Future programs aimed at gaining a larger share of the market should be developed with the cooperation of all groups concerned.

The report takes a hard and thorough look at the future marketing needs for tobacco, cattle, pork, milk, and grain. Especially optimistic forecasts are made for beef, pork, corn, soybeans, and wheat. It found that our milk-marketing facilities, which compare favorably with those found in the rest of the South, should have more than adequate capacity in the future. Primary emphasis is given to the commodities which represent 95 percent of the state's gross farm receipts, but several other interesting points were made about the poultry, timber, lamb, fruit, and vegetable markets. For example, whether Kentucky can capture a larger share of the broiler and egg market depends to a great extent upon production costs here and in the current major broiler- and egg-producing areas. The availability of a year-round supply of locally produced grain should provide a more competitive climate for Kentucky poultrymen.

Gross receipts from timber and primary wood products can be enhanced. As opportunities present themselves, Kentuckians should strive to obtain industries that process lumber into high-value products. Such a move would enrich the state's entire wood industry. Should the demand for lamb and mutton strengthen, Kentucky can again have its historic share of the market. Present marketing facilities are adequate. Kentucky's closeness to major metropolitan areas presents the opportunity to capture a larger share of the nation's fruit and vegetable market. Mechanical harvesting and suitable varieties are the keys to expansion in this area.

It is my hope that this study will stimulate an awareness of what can be accomplished in Kentucky. Certainly it gives our agricultural industry something on which to build and grow. From this independent evaluation, I have emphasized some of the positive aspects to show what the council can do to develop a comprehensive program which will lead to an increase in the net profit for Kentucky's farmers.

Those areas where problems are indicated will require evaluation and, I am sure, much deliberation. As you know, there hasn't been a study made where 100 percent agreement was found, and I imagine the same will hold true in the council's latest endeavor. But dialogue and constructive exchange can be healthy for our agricultural communities, because I am sure there is one point of agreement. That point is let's keep working together for the full benefit of this vitally significant industry where all who are involved are equally important, to Kentucky and to each other. One final note. We have provided many tools to help agriculture. I also am funding the compilation of a buyers' guide which should be welcomed. It will contain a listing of the producers and processors in the state and the commodities in which they deal. This guide will be supplied to you as soon as it is finished.

ECONOMIC AND INDUSTRIAL
DEVELOPMENT

BOWLING GREEN-WARREN COUNTY
CHAMBER OF COMMERCE
Bowling Green / January 7, 1972

THE other day, I ran across a code of conduct, written in 1815 for the four employees of Carson, Pirie and Company, now Carson, Pirie, Scott of Chicago. The owners had set forth these rules: "Store must be open from 6 A.M. to 9 P.M. the year round; store must be swept; counter base and showcases dusted; lamps trimmed, filled and chimneys cleaned; pens made; doors and windows opened; a pail of water, also a bucket of coal brought in before breakfast (if there is time to do so and attend to customers who call)." The rules went on. "Store must not be opened on the sabbath, unless necessary to do, and then only for a few minutes; the employee who is in the habit of smoking Spanish cigars, being shaved at the barber shop, going to dances and other places of amusement, will surely give his employer reason to be suspicious of his integrity, and honesty; each employee must pay not less than five dollars per year to the church, and must attend Sunday school regularly. Men employees are given one evening a week for courting, and two if they go to prayer meeting. After fourteen hours of work in the store, the leisure hours should be spent mostly in reading."

I use this to illustrate how times have changed. If you imposed such a code today, how long would it take your employees to leave? Yet, even though we find this more-than-a-century-old order to employees somewhat amusing, remember that in 1972 Carson, Pirie, Scott is a magnificent American enterprise. Obviously, that firm's management kept pace with the times. As employment practices continue to take on a fresh look, so do management attitudes relating to all phases of business and industry. So it is with industrial promotion. Too often our failures in securing needed economic growth through acquisition of new firms is the result of three ills.

The first ill is shown in our refusal to try new approaches, to come up with new ideas, and to present imaginative programs that spark the interest of prospective industry. This is why, during the next four years, Kentucky will develop more sophisticated marketing techniques to sell our state and our communities to the nation's increasingly sophisticated businesses. There are countless untried methods of attraction. All it takes is innovation, from both a state and local effort.

The second ill, opposite from the first, stems from our refusal to rely on certain time-tested approaches, frequently unintentional, but nevertheless a grim fact of life. We have several pluses in Kentucky. One is a willing, trainable work force. Next, we have the atmosphere of warmth, pride, and helpfulness which can entice those looking for new locations. This, in my opinion, is a very special attribute. Then there is the geographical pattern of Kentucky, along with our state's position in relation to the industrial, business, and financial centers of America. Within our borders is a unique combination of regional settings attractive to a variety of business. Nature has been good to us. We must never forget to emphasize these attributes.

The third failure is sometimes in leadership. Moderate success often prompts complacency. The unwillingness to share responsibility, and thus discourage new blood, new enthusiasm, can only be harmful. While leadership essentials dwindle from the top, the fault does not entirely rest at this plateau. All of us are affected by both success and failure in our economic programs. Therefore, when leadership doesn't measure up, the problem becomes a universal burden. Limited involvement obviously is not the answer. It takes a total push, from the man who needs work right up through the man who secures that opportunity for work. This is why I want to become Kentucky's number one salesman, as Governor. I would be remiss in having any other philosophy. There are, by the very nature of the office, special opportunities for any Governor of Kentucky who is sincerely concerned with the economic stimulation of his state. I am concerned!

This is why, in the first days of my administration, even as the General Assembly convenes, and during the most demanding period where time is scarce, I am nevertheless anxious to visit groups such as yours to reaffirm my intention of working for you. It is especially gratifying to recognize the abilities and energies of the Bowling Green-Warren County Chamber of Commerce. Your newsletters, brochures, continuing programs, and obvious effectiveness are a source of inspiration. The progress you have made, the potential you project, and my desire to work hand in hand prompts me to predict a rewarding future. There won't be lip service from either side; there's going to be a lot of action.

There will be action in seeking the highest quality industries for Kentucky. There will be action in promoting the need for new businesses offering half-shift employment opportunities, so vital for instance in areas such as this where students can find jobs. There will be action in providing training for the unskilled and the semiskilled, through an expanded vocational education program, one based on the training demands of today and tomorrow, rather than yesterday. There will be action in community planning, whereby federal and private funds can be secured to meet the housing needs of our people and invigorate our entire housing industry. This will open thousands of jobs in the building trades and increase the market for building materials, appliances, and other necessary products. There will be action in the protection of our environment, a factor to make our communities better places to live, which will help sell our communities to others.

These are but a few of the basic components of my jobs-for-Kentuckians program. They are commonsense approaches. If I sound optimistic, it's because I am! It's because I know you are willing to become a partner in this economic alliance, and I am straining at the bit to establish a sound track record for Kentucky. For these reasons the Department of Commerce is already planning, working, and moving. New emphasis is being placed on commercial development with particular attention to landing regional offices for industry, commerce, finance, and private recreational facilities. A coherent promotional strategy will be formulated, based on research and relating to industry's requirements to Kentucky's resources and taking into full account environmental implications.

A comprehensive, long-range industrial and commercial site overview has been started. This will be the basis for a coordinated program of site development as contrasted to the current scattered effort. Attention is also being given to the implications of science and technology for Kentucky's economic growth, with careful scrutiny of the possibilities from coal gasification and liquefaction. Here alone is an unlimited, probable boon. I guess we can sum it all up by using the title to a recent popular song, "We've Only Just Begun."

JOBS FOR VETERANS PROGRAM
Louisville / January 18, 1972

A few months ago, as I traveled about out the state discussing various problems which face Kentuckians and the solutions available, one problem stood out. It remains with us today. Many fine young men, after serving our state and nation in the armed forces, are returning home to become full-time citizens. Too many are frustrated, however, by the lack of a most important ingredient—a good job. Many people—people like you—have started providing some solutions. Yet, despite the best efforts to date, job supply has not kept pace with job demand. Unemployment among returning veterans is continuing to rise.

As your Governor, I want to express my personal appreciation to your employers, assembled here today, pledging your cooperation in providing available jobs to veterans. It is this spirit of cooperation and mutual concern that I want to expand, to reach employers all across Kentucky. What you do here today for the Vietnam era veteran will be seen as concern put into action by industrial Kentucky. During my campaign, I made some proposals for attacking this problem. I felt then, and I feel now, that state government, especially the Governor, should take a leadership role in trying to assure that work is available to veterans and that veterans' skills are matched with available jobs. I promised action within sixty days after I assumed the office of Governor. Today, we are ahead of schedule in fulfilling that commitment.

One of the first steps I am taking is the dissolution of the existing Governor's Task Force for Jobs for Veterans. In its place, I am creating the Kentucky Veterans' Jobs-Skills Force.[1] The Jobs-Skills Force will be composed primarily of people like you from across the state, leaders in business and industry who understand job needs and know where jobs are. Our Jobs-Skills Force will involve other business leaders in a statewide effort to make jobs available to veterans. The president of the Kentucky Chamber of Commerce, William Neal of Owensboro, has agreed to be on this force. The president of the Kentucky Jaycees, James Vernon of Corbin, has agreed to serve, along with John B. Clarke[2] of General Electric's Appliance Park here in Louisville. This force also will be a communications link between employers, veterans representatives, and agencies concerned both with providing jobs for veterans and placing veterans in those jobs. With this in mind, I also plan to appoint representatives of our veterans' organizations, governmental, and independent citizen groups concerned with the problem. Vic Priebe,[3] known to all of you as a guiding force in this field, has agreed to serve.

An initial responsibility of the state Jobs-Skills Force will be to organize area Jobs-Skills Forces. They will be set up in each of twenty-six areas served by our State Employment Services' regional offices. Each of these offices has a veterans' employment representative and each office is required to give veterans priority in job placement. They have plenty of applicants now. But they need opportunities to offer the veterans. Knowledge of job opportunities is what our Area Jobs-Skills Forces will provide, in addition to assuring that veterans are given the opportunity to match their skills with any available position.

We understand that there are employers, as many of you may be, who do not ordinarily list job openings with State Employment Services. Those employers will be asked, as you have been, to commit a number of available positions to veterans so that our Area Jobs-Skills Forces can work with local Employment Services offices. This will assure veterans applying for jobs the opportunity to match their skills with the openings employers make available.

We plan to take an idea which has begun here and spread it statewide. The success of this effort depends upon the success we have in involving our business and industrial employers, as the success depends on the commitment of this administration to assume its responsibility.

Through funds available to us, we are appointing a director and three staff members to work full time with our statewide Jobs-Skills Force, to carry out my directives and the task set before them. Initially, some of these staff members will be assigned to work in the Jefferson County area in a cooperative venture with the local segment of the National Alliance of Businessmen and the local Chamber of Commerce. A staff will be assembled, and work will begin before the end of my first sixty days in office, as I pledged. I earnestly solicit your support and interest. I do not intend that this be a token effort. I do not intend for state government's obligations, or my obligation, to end with these words.

There are guidelines that I will ask our Jobs-Skills Force to follow. There are goals I will ask our Force to strive for. I anticipate that people of the caliber sought as members of this Jobs-Skills Force will find this only a beginning. I pledge the efforts of state government to achieve this end.

I would not come before you today to give a pep talk and ask you to do anything in which the Ford administration is not prepared to lead. As you may know, we now require our Personnel Department to give veterans extra consideration for placement in state employment. Today, the Ford administration goes one step farther. As I began speaking to you, a member of my staff entered in the office of the Secretary of State in Frankfort, with an executive order signed by me.[4] Fulfilling another commitment I made to the people of Kentucky, I am ordering all departments of state government to require employers receiving state contracts to list with the Employment Services any jobs which must be filled to fulfill the state contract, so that veterans can be given priorities under existing requirements.[5]

---

1. See Executive Order 72–51 (January 18, 1972).
2. William Harry Neal, Jr. (1925–   ), Owensboro; Natural Gas Utility

executive. *Who's Who in Kentucky, 1974* (Atlanta, Ga., n.d.), p. 429. James Vernon (1941–   ), owner of radio station WYGO in Corbin, Kentucky; served on Governor Breathitt's Advising for Young Kentuckians Committee, Governors Nunn's and Ford's veterans jobs forces, Governor Ford's Land Use Council, and Governor Carroll's Historical Events Commission and Film Commission; commissioner of public information (1975–   ); president of Kentucky Jaycees (1971–1972); vice president of National Jaycees (1972–1973). Telephone interview with Vernon on January 4, 1977. John Baldwin Clarke (1927–   ), Prospect; company executive. *Who's Who in Kentucky, 1974* (Atlanta, Ga., n.d.), p. 42.

3. Vic Priebe (1929–   ), Louisville; doctor of theology; associated with Jobs Now since 1968; executive director of Action Now; metro director of National Association of Broadcasters. Telephone interview with Priebe's secretary on January 4, 1977.

4. See Executive Order 72–51 (January 18, 1972).

5. On April 10, 1973, Governor Ford welcomed home to Kentucky four former prisoners of war. In his remarks he stated, "I believe you have re-awakened many of us to past conflicts and the horrors of prison camps in other wars as well as the death, destruction, and wounding. If our memories won't fade again maybe, just maybe, there can be a universal realization that these men being honored today will set an example for others. And we'll try harder in the future to give the world peace rather than problems, our energies rather than our shortcomings, our love rather than our hate." In the same speech Governor Ford also stated," I oppose the rebuilding of North Vietnam with our tax dollars and welcome the addition of other voices as I raise mine in sincere disagreement to a philosophy which is difficult to even consider." This speech is not included in this volume.

OFFICE OF MINORITY BUSINESS ENTERPRISES
Frankfort / March 17, 1972

I AM signing an Executive Order today creating a Kentucky Office of Minority Business Enterprise in the state Department of Commerce.[1] In signing this order, an innovative and far-reaching program is established—one to meet the needs of many Kentuckians, not just a select few. I am pleased to announce that the Office of Minority Business Enterprise is a national pathfinder.

During my campaign, I promised to help the people of this great state. I promised to aid them economically and socially; by creating this new office, another commitment is being fulfilled. This program stipulates that the Office of Minority Business Enterprise coordinates state minority enterprise activities and utilizes the resources of the state administrative structure to encourage and improve minority firms. A two-year grant from the Office of Minority Business Enterprise of the U.S. Department of Commerce is providing three-fourths of the program's financing.[2]

---

1. See Executive Order 72–214 (March 14, 1972).

2. In a related press release the following elaboration was made: "Kentucky has received a $150,000 grant from the federal Office of Minority Business Enterprise to help implement a Kentucky office. Governor Wendell Ford and John Jenkins, director of the federal OMBE, jointly made the announcement May 10. Kentucky became the first state south of the Mason-Dixon line to establish a state office of minority enterprise when Governor Ford created the Kentucky office in the state Department of Commerce by Executive Order on March 14.

"John Jenkins complimented Governor Ford on his forward-looking action and pledged full cooperation and support from the federal agency.

"Governor Ford termed this innovative program 'far-reaching—a plan to meet the needs of many Kentuckians, not just a select few.

" 'The Department of Commerce has been directed to move rapidly to put the program into effect,' continued the Governor. 'And they will make every effort to fully cooperate and coordinate with local programs under way or planned in Louisville. It is absolutely essential that this be a real team effort if we are to be successful.

" 'We cannot expect overnight miracles,' added Governor Ford. 'But we can take positive and productive steps to improve the economic chances of Kentucky's minority groups and this is an important step both economically and morally.

" 'We want to assist existing minority owned firms to expand and to help get new business ventures started on a sound basis. I want to make it clear that this is a business program,' continued the Governor."

INDUSTRY APPRECIATION LUNCHEON
Louisville / May 18, 1972

It is altogether fitting that we have set aside this week to honor Kentucky's 2,900 industrial firms. These firms directly provide more than 250,000 jobs and pay close to $2 billion annually in wages. The multiplier effect of this activity spreads across our entire economy and is the primary building block for a state personal income in excess of $10 billion.

Kentucky state government is vitally interested in the profit picture of every sector of the state's economy. Agriculture, construction, mining, trade and services, finance, manufacturing, etc., are all of great significance to Kentucky's progress. We want the programs of government to stimulate growth in every economic category. Yet, hard economic facts say clearly that growth in manufacturing jobs and income has been the prime stimulant to Kentucky's economy over the past decade. Continued manufacturing growth is essential to our future prosperity. Some 80,000 manufacturing jobs were added to the Kentucky economy between 1960 and 1970. This was the primary kicker in the generation of 160,000 other nonfarm jobs during this period. And the addition of $5.1 billion more in personal income—more than double the 1960 figure—is attributable in large part to industrial growth.

However, Kentucky continues to have a significant deficit in jobs and income when compared to the national ratios. In terms of nonagricultural jobs, we are something like 200,000 short. In terms of personal income we are $2.7 billion light. These deficiencies must be corrected before Kentucky is truly in the nation's economic mainstream. Creating additional jobs is the basic answer to Kentucky's problems of unemployment, underemployment, and the economically underprivileged.

I am firmly committed to programs and policies of state government that will stimulate growth in jobs and in personal income. I am determined to have growth in each and every sector of this state's economy. It is clear that new directions must be charted if our programs for industrial development continue to be successful. Change has presented us with new opportunities as well as new problems. Our programs must respond to the changing requirements of industry, the problems of ecology, the need for greater skills in our work force. Fortunately, the Kentucky Department of Commerce is forward-thinking and is in tune with the need to fit the programs to the times. A few new program directions or refinements of particular importance at the present time need special enumeration.

It is imperative that the fullest cooperation and coordination exist between all development groups in Kentucky. The increasingly complex locational problems of industry and commerce dictate this. We must work as a team and bring all of our talents to bear both on opportunities and problems. I have asked the Department of Commerce to maintain close contact with all development organizations and with every business organization in the state. The channels of communication must be kept open between us. A second point is that development programs must be broadened in scope to reflect the opportunities of the 1970s. Strong emphasis on industrial development must continue, but programs to stimulate growth in the commercial sector must be added (10 million jobs are expected to be added nationally in trade, services, and finance during the next ten years. Programs to encourage existing industry to expand must be pursued. The Department of Commerce has already put into action a small commercial development program emphasizing the attraction of regional offices and investment in private recreational facilities. Early signs are encouraging.

Our industrial development effort must be modernized and is a third area of concern. A research-based overall strategy must be, and is being, developed for promoting the location and expansion of industries best suited to Kentucky's resources. The time has come to emphasize selectivity and quality in our development programs. Our merchandising of Kentucky's resources, the promotional advertising, and the salesmanship are being fitted into an overall strategy. The hit-or-miss approach just doesn't work anymore.

Fourth, an adequate supply of quality sites must be available for industry. These sites must have adequate water and sewerage facilities and they must meet environmental quality standards. This is a critical and tough problem. The solution in the final analysis must be worked out locally, but state government has an urgent obligation to help out. The Department of Commerce is putting together a site development plan for Kentucky. For the first time we will have an overview of the site situation. This will enable communities, Area Development Districts, and state agencies to set rational priorities for developing sites based on facts. In this way we can make sense out of the problem. Federal agencies who can provide financing assistance are enthusiastic about Kentucky's approach and progress. We're doing a few other things to correct this situation. For example, $600,000 in new funds were appropriated to the Kentucky Industrial Development Finance Authority for the next biennium. It is my thinking that first priority in the use of these loan funds should go to site development. Two million dollars were made available to local port authorities in the budget.

Substantial portions of these funds will be used for river-related site development. Also, legislation to expedite the construction of local sewerage systems was enacted.

The conflict between economic growth and environmental quality is a fifth concern and must be resolved in a rational manner. Environmental pollution control is a major issue facing the entire nation today, and we are all aware that it is a complex problem complicated by emotional overtones. We are facing up to this problem in Kentucky. Our air and water pollution control commissions know where they are and where they are going. Industry can now get a firm answer in Kentucky.

But there have been problems of the lack of adequate coordination because of diffused authority among agencies. This cannot and will not be allowed to continue. Legislation was passed consolidating all environmental pollution control functions in a Department of Environmental Quality. A single advisory commission will advise the department regarding its programs. The responsibility for environmental pollution control is placed squarely on the shoulders of the commissioner and the Governor. This, in my judgment, is where it belongs.

Kentucky's environmental pollution control regulations are strict and in line with federal standards. They are also fair. Strictness and fairness will continue to be the case. We fully intend to adequately protect the health and welfare of our citizens. Every responsible business feels the same obligation. But our regulations will also be reasonable; they will take into account the economic impact, and they will allow for continued economic growth. I firmly believe that rational men can provide for both acceptable environmental quality and needed economic growth. But decisions must be based on reason rather than emotion.

A good climate for doing business must be maintained. I am committed to this and I intend to keep this commitment. The Commissioner of Commerce[1] tells me that in his judgment Kentucky's competitive position is sound. Full facts are being developed in cooperation with the University of Kentucky and will soon be available. We intend to digest thoroughly this latest study and make it work for your betterment as well as ours.

Now in conclusion let me touch on the management of state government for a minute. State government is a big and expensive business. We have an obligation to operate state government as efficiently and as economically as possible. The objectives of private industry and state government are in many ways parallel. However, we can and must apply the same sound principles and techniques of management to state government as you apply to the management and service units of your firm. I am determined that Kentucky government will match the efficiency of comparable office and service operations of industry.

---

1. Damon W. Harrison (1918–   ), Frankfort; director of research and industrial planning, Louisville Chamber of Commerce (1957–1960); director of research and planning, executive assistant, Kentucky Department of Commerce (1960–1971); commissioner, Kentucky Department of Commerce (1971–1975); presently commissioner, Kentucky Department of Energy. Biographical sketch received from Harrison's office.

INDUSTRIAL RESOURCES REVIEW
Prestonsburg / September 27, 1972

IT is an unusual opportunity to meet with a mixture of professional developers, major industrial firms, and interested eastern Kentuckians representing communities with untapped resources for growth. You have already visited and heard facts about our important northern Kentucky area which is Kentucky's second-largest urban concentration.[1] You have seen a slide presentation pointing out Kentucky's advantages as a place of production and distribution.

Kentucky is a great place for business to operate at a profit. We intend to make it even better! Programs to improve our highways, water and sewerage systems, industrial sites, education, and recreation are rapidly moving ahead. Our excellent business climate will be maintained. Our tax system is, and will continue to be, equitable, balanced, and competitive. Regulations on industry and commerce will be fair, but they must adequately protect the public's interest and protect the health and welfare of Kentuckians.

Tonight I want to touch specifically on some of the opportunities and problems of eastern Kentucky and what we are doing about them. Kentucky's Appalachia is intriguing. You are seeing its magnificent early fall beauty. But there have been perplexing economic and social problems going back to the late 1940s. Coal mining employment began to slump and unemployment began to skyrocket. Welfare rolls mushroomed and the out-migration of people swelled in volume and totaled 322,000 during the 1950s. The decade of the 1950s saw a cloud of gloom hanging over the economic future of eastern Kentucky. Many simply wrote it off as an impossible solution. But there were also those who believed, and despite out-migration, a core of tough leadership remained.

Positive action began in the early 1960s. The area's roads, education, water, sewerage, health, and recreation facilities were dramatically improved through governmental programs specifically designed to stimulate development. Eastern Kentucky now has good highway access in large part; five state vocational-technical schools and thirty-nine extension centers are located here which is the heaviest concentration on this type of training in Kentucky. Nine major state parks are in the area. A renewed spirit touched the mountains. Things began to happen, per-capita income increased, out-migration slowed, manufacturing jobs grew, and new firms opened.

This was important progress, yes, but far from satisfactory. Eastern Kentucky still has the tough problems of too few jobs, income far too low, and too much of the population depending on welfare. But let's not wring our hands; let's tackle these problems. My administration will make a determined and sustained effort to stimulate the creation of more jobs in Appalachia. The Department of Commerce is attacking the job picture on several fronts. We are pushing for more private recreational facilities, for more supportive industries, and, of course, for more manufacturing. Additional manufacturing jobs and wages are particularly important because of their multiplier effect across the local economy. This is what makes this Industrial Resources Review Project of particular importance.

You have been shown the industrial resources of a number of eastern Kentucky communities this afternoon, and you will learn more during your visits. This is concrete evidence that we have cities ready for industry right now. Many parts of eastern Kentucky, however, are lacking suitable developed industrial sites. A realistic appraisal leads to the conclusion that some communities in eastern Kentucky simply do not have a site and utility-potential adequate to support a major plant. We therefore cannot expect to locate a sizable factory in every community. However, I am confident that we can, by an all-out effort, develop sites and locate major plants within commuting distance of every eastern Kentuckian. Our road network now makes this feasible. Employment opportunities within commuting distance of every qualified eastern Kentucky worker is a prime objective of my administration.

The Department of Commerce is putting together the first Kentucky site plan. This will allow us to channel our site-development efforts in a rational effective manner. A key element in this plan is the identification and evaluation of large sites and areas capable of serving several counties and communities. This will be a top-priority effort. A particularly promising situation at the London-Corbin growth center is being explored as a pilot effort. Very soon a corollary site-identification-and-evaluation project focusing on the Appalachian development highway corridor will start. This project will be involved not only with industrial but commercial sites as well. I will insist that new site possibilities created by the Hazard-Henderson Parkway be included in this project. This two-pronged attack on the site problem will provide the facts needed for action.

The efforts by state government in eastern Kentucky as well as in other slow-growing areas have been entirely too piecemeal. Each agency has too often done its own thing, without coordinating with the activities of others. A fragmented approach is not fully effective. I intend to correct this not only for eastern Kentucky but also for other parts of Kentucky having a sluggish growth history.

A "Governor's Task Force for Slow Growth Counties" will be formed. Membership will include the commissioners of Commerce, Highways, Parks, Natural Resources, Economic Security, Labor, Finance, and the administrator of the Kentucky Program Development Office. The Governor's Office will be directly involved in all proceedings. The Commissioner of Commerce will be directed to analyze problems and opportunities as a basis of action by the task force. The task force will be directed to formulate an action plan bringing to bear their full resources on the problems of slow-growth counties.

Time does not permit telling every industrial success story in eastern Kentucky. Three of these make the point and particularly intrigue me because the cities in which they operate were long considered a lost cause for growth. Control Data Corporation is employing 145 people in Campton (population 419) on component parts for computers. Productivity and quality of work has exceeded the company's most optimistic expectations. Continental Conveyor and Equipment Company at Salyersville (population 1,196) just a few miles down the road from here makes conveyor belts; sixty-five are employed and expansion is planned. High productivity and good labor relations are reported. Etowah Manufacturing Company came to Manchester (population 1,664) four years ago with about 15,000 square feet of plant. Today 190 people are employed in 81,000 square feet of plant space. Employment is expected to increase next year. Metal items are produced. The record speaks. Industry is successful in eastern Kentucky.

Let me close with what I hope is an omen. Our latest figures indicate a decline in unemployment in many parts of eastern Kentucky, just as we are seeing throughout the Commonwealth. Unemployment in Kentucky now stands at 4.5 percent, which is 1.3 percent below August of 1971, and that is a significant decrease and we are proud of it. There is no reason for the dark clouds I mentioned earlier. By taking the right steps, we can proceed now in gaining the advantage of renewed emphasis on economic growth for this area. After all, what is government all about? It should be service to people, to our children's future, and to the future of their children. Every degree of service possible will be made available to you by the Ford administration, today, next week, next month, and next year.

---

1. On June 16, 1972, Governor Ford announced a $40 million expansion project for the Greater Cincinnati Airport, located in Boone County. This speech is not included in this volume.

GOVERNOR'S PRESIDENTIAL CONFERENCE ON EXPORTING AND EXPORT FINANCING
Louisville / October 26, 1972

WHY would so many key Kentucky businessmen and chambers of commerce representatives come together to discuss export trade? What possible interest could these individuals from this inland state, in the middle of America, have in discussing foreign markets? Logical questions? No doubt to many, they are. I think you can answer these questions with one word, "profit."

When it comes to seeking out areas for greater Kentucky profits, there is every reason to escape from the past and set new sights. If any of you doubt this, you should lose these doubts by the end of this landmark conference. Greater profits for Kentucky's business and financial firms mean more money in your pockets, more jobs for Kentuckians, more revenue for public services, and a sounder economic base for the state as a whole. To assure that the Commonwealth expands its profit potentials, we have to think big, think profit, and think world market.

All you have to do is pick up a newspaper, a weekly news magazine or turn on the news to realize the world we live in is a world of shorter distances. One principal reason for the shrinking world is our constant pursuit for economic markets where we can sell or trade our goods and services. During the early period of our country's expansion into foreign markets, we were virtually unchallenged as an economic power. Historians point to the fact that the American flag followed the American dollar into many foreign countries. This was a period of dollar diplomacy, when we saw our economic and political influence spreading at an unprecedented rate. The results were often one-sided and not always good in the long run. The international economic picture has changed a great deal, but the value of finding foreign markets for American goods and services remains a vital and essential part of our national involvement in a world community.

The world marketplace has become much more competitive and sophisticated. Our economic power has received challenges abroad from such economic coalitions as the European Economic Community, the European Free Trade Association, and massive Soviet Union trade. Now we are seeing the emergence of Asian economic influence with the growing world-trade involvement of the People's Republic of China and the very powerful Japanese economic community. Competition in the world market has become fierce and severe. There are many people who think that the third world war will not be a military confrontation, but rather one of economic confrontation.

What does all this mean for Kentucky? It means that world trade is where the action is, and we need a bigger piece of the action. Kentucky exports of manufactured goods, agricultural products, and coal obviously have added to the employment and income of many Kentuckians. It has added needed profits to many of our business firms. But we can do far better. A major priority of my administration is economic growth —to increase jobs, wages, and profits. We have a good climate in Kentucky for doing business at a profit and we intend to keep it that way. Even more, we intend to improve it.

Experience and results show that our basic development programs are sound and effective. We have committed $2 million to our Port and River Development Commission. We are expanding our already extensive highway systems to make it easier and cheaper to transport Kentucky's products. We plan to adjust programs which benefit our business and financial communities and add new ones to meet the changing economic conditions at home and abroad. I intend to see that Kentucky has a sound and improved program to assist you in world-trade activities. The Commissioner of Commerce[1] has been directed to provide recommendations to achieve this. This meeting should become a think-tank for implementation of new ideas. Yet, in order to be successful, we must have your full cooperation as well as the help of our federal partners. I am confident that we can be successful and increase your sales and profit opportunities in this important sector of economic activity. Let's not assume for a minute that world trade is somebody else's business. We must make it our business!

I realize there is a minimum of conversation around Kentucky about our role in world trade. But we can open a whole new package of business potentials if we set our minds to it. You will hear success stories today, stories which really say, "It can be done in Kentucky on a much greater scale." This approach to economic gain offers a chain linkage effect to revenue growth. Expanded world trade stimulates new business development in the state. It broadens sales opportunities for existing firms. Supportive agencies and businesses can expect more demands for their services. A larger variety of requirements is always presented when there is an expanded world-trade effort.

Since I began my remarks today with questions, I shall end with questions. One, what type of trade missions would be most practical and have the greatest promise for Kentucky firms? Two, how can we focus our port development programs to facilitate world trade? Three, what are your specific needs from state government to increase your opportunities for world trade? Four, can you rechannel your own operative methods to become more involved in the export business? Five, how deeply should we become involved in attracting "reverse investment"? This exciting field of commerce has soared in some other states, having a direct bearing on the local economic climate. Six, if reverse investment is a necessary ingredient to future economic growth in Kentucky, how should we go about contacting foreign prospects with a good potential for Kentucky?

I present these as food for thought. Numerous others will surface before this conference is over. And it wouldn't surprise me at all if in this room there aren't creative answers which will have a very positive touch on Kentucky's future. If so, that positive touch will also be in your future. State government is willing to go all out to help its people through you.

---

1. Commissioner of commerce, Damon W. Harrison, for more information see speech from May 18, 1972, in this section, p. 405.

CHARLESTON BOTTOMS POWER
GENERATING STATION GROUND BREAKING
Maysville / November 1, 1972

My back must be getting better because the doctor who has been treating me has given me approval to do some spade work this week. The facility we are breaking ground for today represents a major contribution to this area and to the state. The economic potentials of the Charleston Bottoms station are significant, but the more essential contribution will be the electric power it will generate.

The seriousness of the energy crisis facing Kentucky and the rest of the nation is alarming. Most of you will recall the "brownouts" and "blackouts" recently experienced by our large urban centers due to power drains on existing energy supplies. These problems have spread in recent years, and forecasts indicate they will continue to occur unless our ability to generate new energy increases substantially. In the past, national consumption of energy has doubled every ten years. Present projections show that the doubling will occur every seven to eight years and Kentucky will be doubling its energy needs every six years. In 1970 the United States consumed 67.8 thousand trillion British thermal units of energy. By 1980 this will be in excess of 100 thousand trillion BTUs, and by 1985 the U.S. will need 125 thousand trillion BTUs of energy. If you don't think these weird sounding statistics affect Kentucky, you are mistaken. Besides our own energy drain, we have routed Kentucky energy to New York for the last two summers, and trends indicate that this kind of pooling of energy resources will continue in the future. We are, in fact, headed for national energy policies and controls that will involve every state in the country.

To realize the impact of our declining energy resources, you don't have to look any further than your own area. For the past two years, there have been no additional industrial or commercial tap-ons allowed for the use of natural gas in this area. Recently, the Public Service Commission approved a request by Columbia Gas to refuse any additional residential tap-ons. This is a startling example of the energy crisis: you cannot use natural gas for any additional energy needs in this area. I think you can see why we all need to be concerned. We must find other sources for energy. This means primarily coal and fuel oil with the slowly emerging development of nuclear energy. Nationally, the projections show a growing reliance on coal and potential nuclear energy resources as well as imports of oil and liquid gas. This means more facilities such as the one we are breaking ground for today.

The significance of this $125 million power generating station to this area should be obvious. Without it, you would be severely limited in attracting new business and industry to your area. Residential power would be limited to existing electrical power service, fuel oil, and propane gas. With this new facility, you have enormous opportunities for expanding economic development as well as greater energy resources for residential use. There will be approximately 1,200 construction jobs needed through the duration of this project; over 400 of these will be local residents. The gross income to the local economy from the building stage is estimated at from 10 to 12.5 million new dollars. When completed, the potential for attracting new industry will generate 2,000 new jobs at the industrial park. Some believe this may be a conservative estimate. Local tax revenue should increase by more than $200,000, including some $90,000 for the school system.

With all of the positive and progressive aspects of this facility, I am well aware of the element of controversy involved here. It is an inescapable fact that power generating stations in the past have had an impact on the environment. I know that many of you have been concerned about how the Charleston Bottoms plant will affect ecology in this area. I think that you can take encouragement from the fact that management at Eastern Kentucky Power Cooperative is committed to all that is possible, at any cost, to assure adequate pollution controls. Over $10 million has been allocated for the purpose of installing the most efficient pollution control devices available at this facility. All existing and newly adapted standards for anti-pollution control have been met, and the commitment is here to do anything necessary to minimize pollution. My administration has been and will remain committed to a clean and healthy environment. I also realize the seriousness of the energy crisis facing Kentucky and the nation. There is an answer for both. We must meet the challenge of the energy crisis with new power supplies, yet we must avoid overburdening our air and water with pollutants. This can be done with the kind of positive attitudes shown by all of the individuals and groups involved in this project.

MEETING OF STATE MANPOWER COUNCIL
Frankfort / March 30, 1973

TODAY I am announcing the establishment of the Kentucky Manpower Council. This council shall advise on the development, implementation, and operation of a statewide manpower planning program.[1] I expect this body to assure the maximum return from the public dollar spent to meet Kentucky's manpower needs. Every Kentuckian has an obligation to be a productive and useful citizen. At the same time, government must be aware of every Kentuckian's birthright to an opportunity, whereby one can participate to the fullest measure of one's ability. This means providing the access to basic education, social, and occupational training necessary for a satisfying employment so essential for a full life. Equally as important, it means working toward full employment as opposed to sanctioning an unnecessary percentage of idle hands and minds, at the expense of those who do work.

Kentucky has experienced shifts in the employment structure during the economic boom of the early and mid–1960s and also during the high unemployment period brought on by the recession. Along with an increase in workers, there has been a demand for changing occupational patterns and increased job skills. Presently, only one job in ten calls for unskilled labor. Yet in the near future, approximately 80 percent of the jobs will not require a college degree. But they will require specific training.

Thousands of Kentuckians have benefited over the years from a vast array of federal, categorical manpower programs, which were created to increase skill, employability, and income. However, federal programs haven't always matched local conditions. In Kentucky for instance, our rural areas are handicapped since the majority of these federal manpower programs are designed for more densely populated communities. I am convinced that we in Kentucky better understand our own problems and can solve them more effectively at less cost. A council such as this can be an important catalyst. It brings together program sponsors, clients, business, industry, and local government representatives under an umbrella of a concerned state administration. This council will be instrumental in developing and implementing appropriate action to improve our manpower delivery systems.

---

1. See Executive Order 73–277 (March 14, 1973).

OWENSBORO-DAVIESS COUNTY
INDUSTRIAL FOUNDATION LUNCHEON
Owensboro / April 4, 1973

I'M going to make a prediction. During the next two years, local industrial promoters will become more involved and concentrate their
efforts with greater zeal than ever before. I say this while recognizing
the activities of yesterday, a demonstration of successful hard work,
careful planning, and tough selling of their communities to prospective
companies by citizens who wanted new economic life for their home-
towns. But let's look at this prediction in light of what's going on
throughout America.

At one period in our recent history, when industrial promotion by
the smaller and medium-sized communities began, there was an advantage quite evident in specific regions. This came from groups who
were "firstus with the mostus" and from groups who "got the jump
on others" because they had the foresight to recognize how anxious industry was to expand, to relocate, to diversify. These organizations developed sites, raised local funds, and were ready to provide necessities
such as water, sewerage, and electricity. They went after prospective
industry, exercised good public relations, and in a cohesive body offered an attractiveness that management desired. But time has narrowed the advantage gaps which once existed. Nearly everyone began
getting into the act, so competition grew stronger. New ideas became
routine.

Today, states all have the tools in their industrial promotion chests
and most are the same. Likewise, communities have geared up in similar
fashion just to stay in the race. The construction of interstates, parkways, airports, and other transportation resources has slowed down.
Does this, therefore, mean that acquisition of new and expanded firms
will slow down? No. It means that a different picture is emerging.

First, communities and states have become ecology-minded. The
blue-ribbon industries are those which have also become responsible
environmentally. Hence, there will be more selectivity than ever before
in the type of industries sought because citizens will demand it. So, combining an almost universal effort by communities with their desire to
land only the best industries, matters are going to become pretty tight.
Success on the local level will, by necessity, depend on greater involvement and concentration, and this is why I make my prediction.

When my Commissioner of Commerce[1] learned about this meeting, he sent word to me that the presentation made to your last industrial prospect was one of the most impressive he has ever seen. I know you are recognizing the growing competition and the increased difficulties of acquisition, and I applaud your joint effort by so many concerned people. The best way to put it is that the "right people" were out there battling—government leaders, bankers, businessmen, professionals, and labor. I know you well enough to be assured that you handled the situation efficiently and will continue to do so. This is important, your having all the answers, the enthusiasm, and the attitude prospects are looking for. This type of effort must be kept up if we are to succeed. Remember: "business is never so healthy as when, like a chicken, it can stop scratching for what it gets." You must do more and keep working on the selection of a new industrial park site. You will need the additional expansion space.

My administration is working night and day to assist local efforts through activities of the Department of Commerce and other agencies including the Governor's office. Commerce is continually trying to promote Kentucky as an attractive place to locate. We are trying things differently. Note the New York trip and the emphasis others placed on our livability. Friday I will address the Governor's Industrial Appreciation Banquet, honoring new and expanded firms which made Kentucky grow in 1972. It was a good year and 1973 should be even better.

A broad scope of government programs and services interrelate to the attractiveness of the state for industrial promotion. While it might not be readily apparent, one such effort in this direction is the Kentucky Manpower Council I named last Friday. We have to be aware of our obligation to provide equal access to basic education, social, and occupational training for a rewarding life from gainful employment. We must take into account the changing trends of occupational patterns and job skills and the need to match training opportunities to changes in the future. Federal programs haven't always been effective in meeting local needs; there has been a tendency to tailor them to urban programs and Kentucky has many rural needs for such training.

We cannot accept a situation of less than full employment. If we do, we will be aiming too low. The council will serve as a catalyst to bring together sponsors, clients, business, industry, and representatives of local government under an umbrella of a concerned state administration. Council members carefully selected to be representatives of the agencies involved, clients from the manpower program, representatives of business, labor, and local government groups. It is only through cooperative efforts that we can truly progress.

1. Commissioner of commerce, Damon W. Harrison, for more information see speech from May 18, 1972, in this section, p. 405.

INDUSTRY APPRECIATION WEEK
ANNUAL LUNCHEON
Louisville / April 6, 1973

INCREASED industrial activity has been the foundation of Kentucky's strong economic surge. Increased jobs and wages provided by manufacturing plants have stimulated our entire economy and improved the quality of life for hundreds of thousands of Kentuckians. This makes it entirely fitting that we set aside a week each year to honor our almost 3,000 manufacturing plants providing employment for more than 260,000 Kentuckians and providing $2.2 billion annually in wages.

Today we offer a special thanks to the seventy-five manufacturing firms who announced new Kentucky locations in 1972 and the 125 expansions by existing industries.

This new industrial activity was diversified in terms of product as well as in geographical location. The products announced fit well into Kentucky's existing, sound industrial mix. And the fact that new plants were announced for fifty-eight different communities underscores the widespread geographical scope of our industrial resources and activity. The decision to announce these seventy-five facilities in Kentucky indicated that our business climate, resources, and attitude toward industry was found to be more than good. The announcement of 125 plant expansions last year also indicated satisfaction with Kentucky's business climate and faith in our future by firms already here. This is gratifying.

Two hundred announcements of new and expanded manufacturing activity to employ 12,800 workers and invest $195 million represented a good year. But these figures do not tell the full story. This activity has an important multiplier effect. A total of 33,000 additional jobs will eventually be created in Kentucky by these actions if the computer at the University of Kentucky Office of Business Development and Government Services is right.

Our policy is one for responsible growth. We intend to maintain a good climate for production. Our tax base will be fair. Our regulations will be reasonable. Solid industrial activity in 1972 points out that strong growth and environmental protection can exist side by side. We don't hide the fact that Kentucky's air and water pollution control regulations are pretty tough. But at the same time, we know they are reasonable and fair. We also know that responsible industry wants this attitude; they portray it themselves. Industry, which as I say also wants environmental quality, has worked in close partnership with state government and many problems have been satisfactorily resolved.

We have carefully analyzed Kentucky's tax situation in relation to competitive states. We looked at changes made by the 1972 General Assembly. The Department of Commerce asked the University of Kentucky College of Business and Economics to compare Kentucky's taxes on industry with four locations, in each of nine other states. The results showed conclusively that Kentucky's state and local taxes are in a very favorable position. The business of economic development is undergoing rapid and great change. New opportunities and problems call for new approaches if we are to keep pace. I want to touch briefly on what we are doing about a few of these.

There is an energy problem in this country and it is for real. Wishful thinking won't make it go away. It is obvious that shortages of energy create unique problems for economic growth not only in Kentucky but throughout the nation. It is equally obvious that a rational national energy policy is required for a full solution to the problem. Unfortunately, this has been delayed all too long. But I want Kentucky industry to know that I am acutely aware of the problem as it affects our state. My ability to correct the situation is, of course, limited. But there are some things which are being done to alleviate the problem. The University of Kentucky College of Engineering is moving ahead with research into which processes for liquefaction and gasification best fit Kentucky coals, and also research into the problem of the sulfur content of certain coal. This effort is funded by an appropriation, requested by me, from the 1972 General Assembly. The long-range implications of this work for both usable energy supplies and the Kentucky coal industry are obvious.

Today I am designating the Kentucky Economic Development Commission as the agency to keep me informed about the energy situation as it affects this state and to recommend appropriate action. This broad-based commission which represents the entire business community can effectively do this. The Kentucky Department of Commerce is the operating arm of the commission for this assignment. Close coordination

will be maintained with all appropriate private and public organizations. Even with this announcement, I want to add that we're already
on the move to find out what the situation in Kentucky really is.

The Department of Commerce has mailed questionnaires to 913
manufacturers with fifty or more employees as a starter; replies thus
far being received from 466. I urge all others to cooperate! For the first
time, we have specific information about industry's problems, and we
want more. Seventy-four fuel suppliers have been asked to provide
monthly information about the energy situation. An energy information
clearinghouse will be created to help Kentucky firms find sources of
energy. Assistance will also be provided about alternate fuels which
can be used. Yes, we are concerned with the energy problem, and I
am convinced that these steps being taken are positive and useful.

On another matter, the lack of an adequate supply of developed,
environmentally adequate industrial sites continues to be a major
problem which must be solved if we continue to grow. During the
past year the Department of Commerce has given close attention to this
limitation. Sites, ready to sell now, have been identified and special
promotional brochures developed for these. Sites with good potential,
but needing improvements, have been isolated, and communities are
being urged and given assistance to bring these to a ready status. Large
site areas with a potential for providing jobs for several counties have
been found. Initial plans for development are being formulated for the
most promising of these. For the first time, we have a comprehensive
statewide site inventory and a site development plan. But site development is costly and financing must basically come from local sources.

The problem is complicated because the new federal budget has for-
saken grants for sewers and water lines for the specific purpose of
creating jobs. Kentucky, up to now, has made good use of grants from
the economic development administration. People have benefited. The
development of salable sites in a number of rural communities was
possible only because of these grants. This is a serious blow to rural
development although Washington rhetoric would have us believe that
all is well. Nevertheless, we intend to counteract in the best way
possible this negative action through positive actions of our own.[1]

While this is not the appropriate time to formally discuss the next
budget, we are, by necessity, examining future priorities. One aspect
of this examination is a substantial appropriation for the Kentucky
Industrial Development Authority—money earmarked for industrial
site development. That consideration must be made in view of federal
decisions which have put more of the burden on our backs, and it must
also be made in view of the anticipated resources and other needs in

Kentucky. But a revolving investment can stimulate site development, and I will carefully consider this accelerated approach.

Perhaps human nature causes industry—both old and new—to be taken for granted. In our fast-paced society, we move from one subject to another without retaining sufficient time to reflect on our blessings. Today is a reflection on our good fortune, brought to Kentucky by both existing and new industries. This reflection reminds me of a creed my administration offers: that "coming together is a beginning, keeping together is progress; and working together is success." If all of us follow such a creed, Kentucky can accomplish whatever goals are necessary and desired. This occasion is a perfect example of coming together, keeping together, and working together, and look, my friends, at what we have truly accomplished!

---

1. On May 9, 1973, Governor Ford made a statement to the HUD meeting in Washington, D.C., expressing his dissatisfaction with proposals in the 1974 federal budget to abolish the Economic Development Administration. Without EDA funds Kentucky would face unnecessary delays in new projects for economic development and manpower training, and Louisville would not be able to build its already planned Vocational-Technical Institute. This statement is not included in this volume.

TWENTY-FIFTH ANNIVERSARY OF THE
KENTUCKY DEPARTMENT OF COMMERCE
Frankfort / July 2, 1973

TWENTY-FIVE years of progress has made it possible for people to live better in Kentucky. This is what economic development is all about. Tonight we gather to reflect and also to look beyond this occasion. We can reflect with pride, and we can look into the future with optimism. We can, and we should, reflect on the farsighted action by a man for whom I have the utmost respect, Earle C. Clements,[1] who began a foundation of economic growth in Kentucky that today sparks our optimism, stimulates our enthusiasm about the years ahead, and gives us a legacy in which to mold the patterns of tomorrow. The well-being of people is the true objective of programs for growth, particularly those having governmental sponsorship. Governor Clements not only recognized this a quarter of a century ago, he put the philosophy into action.

Economic growth became a prime objective of Kentucky state government with the creation of the agriculture and industrial development board in 1948. Governor Clements understood the seriousness of our economic status, especially in comparison with other states. His response was brief and to the point, more jobs and higher incomes for Kentuckians. A two-edged sword existed with the need for employment and income growth. It was apparent that necessary governmental services could not be provided by the inadequate revenue base of the era. A better life, therefore, would enhance government's ability to serve.

Just a few figures underscore what has taken place since 1948. Personal income of Kentuckians increased from $2.3 billion to $11.8 billion. But more importantly, personal income per Kentuckian jumped from 65 to 80 percent of the national average. Kentucky has been steadily narrowing this critical gap. Of significance, I believe, is that Kentucky has done so during periods of strong national growth which means that competition was even tougher on states like Kentucky which lagged behind the national average. An agricultural state, Kentucky suffered too from the decrease in farm employment caused by greater mechanization and larger farm units. So nonagricultural wage and salary jobs—458,000 of them—were added during this period and became the basis for our state's income gains. An obvious advantage of manufacturing jobs was the multiplier effect they had on other jobs and income. The dollar began circulating in more places, and today we find this effect a key to our overall economy.

I could list at length the advance Kentucky has experienced during this period, especially in view of the distance we had to travel. But figures tend to be dry, and this occasion prompts a look at the future as well as the present. Progress breeds problems, more so in a growing society where technological change is rapid, where public attention to conflicting factors often borders on the impatient, and where intellect must commingle with common sense. A favorite expression not so long ago was "a happening." Last year Kentucky experienced many "happenings" under a variety of headings and they were good. They were good for people and they were good for the development of this state. These happenings are continuing into 1973 and most certainly our economic status is worthy of enthusiasm, particularly as we analyze 1972.

Over the next ten years we project an additional 350,000 nonagricultural jobs for Kentucky; 100,000 or so will be in manufacturing. This magnitude of growth will bring Kentucky close to parity with the average state. But it's not enough. Our goals for the next quarter of a century should be for job and income levels that rival those of the most affluent states, and I firmly contend we can meet the challenge.

Our efforts must emphasize balanced growth. Manufacturing over the next decade will continue to be the key to economic expansion, but greater attention must and will be given to increasing the tempo in the commercial sector. At the same time we must ensure that the many facets of life in Kentucky are met by industrial compatibility. Without question, Kentucky has a serious responsibility in the maintenance of its livability. Our outstanding quality of life is a positive force which acts as a magnet in attracting others. I think we have to be very selective as we entice others into Kentucky in order that our livability is never jeopardized. Our potential for growth is well known from the standpoint of geography, transportation, natural resources, tax structure, potential energy supplies, and personal productivity. Turning our potential into accountable reality means governmental leadership under a variety of headings.

The quality of the Kentucky work force will be the key factor in Kentucky's economic growth. Our training and educational system must be adequate to produce top caliber employees at all levels. This is particularly true of vocational-technical education where the real action will be. Steps are now under way to develop an Occupational Training Information System as a basis for shaping courses that meet the needs of industry and commerce. I have appointed a Kentucky Manpower Planning Council[2] to coordinate training programs for maximum impact.

Quality must be stressed in our industrial promotional efforts. New industry must be compatible with our environmental objectives, and I am pleased to observe that this is already being achieved through close cooperation between new industry, the Department of Commerce, and the Department for Natural Resources and Environmental Protection.

Let's become more alert to new opportunities for growth. Increased effort is being placed on speeding up commercial growth by the Department of Commerce. Particular emphasis is being placed on acquainting private recreational industry with the opportunities along our interstate corridors and lakes. We are also pushing strongly to bring company headquarters, regional offices, and distribution centers to Kentucky.

In looking for new approaches to economic growth, a term has emerged which I predict you will add to your vocabulary because it will be as familiar in the next few years as "industrial promotion." The term is reverse investment. Nearly a year ago I first talked about the established values of reverse investment. The Department of Commerce began pursuing the concept of foreign firms establishing high-quality operations in Kentucky, and you can expect to see beneficial results in the near future. Strangely enough, reverse investment has received scant mention thus far, an unfortunate situation since it is an extremely important part of the changing activities of economic development. It translates into programs that encourage foreign-based firms to invest their capital and produce their products in the United States. Both the company involved and the state profit from this program, which is actually the reverse of the traditional situation—that of U.S. plants expanding overseas.

The idea behind reverse investment is to improve the balance-of-trade situation for our country. It provides jobs for Americans, helping to counteract the unemployment created when U.S. plants have relocated in another country. And it circulates new dollars to assist the multiplier effect I mentioned earlier. Economists see the approach as a highly competitive venture in the future. I can tell you tonight that Kentucky is on the ground floor and thus will have a more advantageous position to entice the cream of foreign industry which is seeking expansion. As our Department of Commerce enters the next quarter of a century, it is even more significant, in my opinion, that something new has appeared on the horizon. So I commend to you a subject just in the formative stages, yet a subject which twenty-five years from now will be "old hat." Reverse investment will have a desirable impact on Kentucky if our planning is appropriate, if our efforts are sufficiently widespread, and if both government and the financial sectors work in concert to get out in front before the rest of the field starts moving. This is my charge to state government.

The future also holds responsibilities above our heads in various other areas. We are committed to doing everything possible which will ensure adequate supplies of energy. And I cannot overemphasize the importance of energy research and development, another subject which will gain added attention when the 1974 General Assembly meets. Since economic growth occurs mainly in attractive communities with adequate supporting facilities, another dimension to the new Office of Local Government emerges, a dimension giving communities the expertise in becoming business and industrial attractions. It's a large and encompassing package. There are so many variables in economic development, yes variables as changeable as the weather. The next twenty-five years will be measured by how well we cope with the variables.

Because of the firm grip we now have, supported by facts, and because we are Kentuckians, I am optimistic!

---

1. Earle C. Clements (1896–   ), Morganfield; Union County judge (1934–1942); Kentucky Senate (1941–1944); United States House of Representatives (1945–1947); Governor of Kentucky (1948–1950); resigned as Governor to complete the unexpired term of United States Senator Alben W. Barkley and in January 1951 he began a full term which expired in January 1957. *The National Encyclopedia of American Biography, 1953–1959* (New York, 1960), 1:130.

2. Executive Order 73-277 (March 14, 1973). The Kentucky Manpower Planning Council was replaced by the Kentucky Manpower Council.

ECONOMIC FACTORS
AND BUDGET SURPLUS
Frankfort / August 3, 1973

JUST last Tuesday, I released a report on Kentucky's unprecedented growth over the past eighteen months.[1] Unfortunately, the public has been shielded from the subject, because in many instances the story as it finally appeared was minimized. Before any of you jump to conclusions, let me use a famous expression and make one thing perfectly clear.[2] I am not fussing at you as reporters. But I am discouraged at the play these significant and positive revelations received. I believe it is front-page news, or a worthy lead to radio and television broadcasts, when a state economy overwhelms the national trend, when Kentucky has reduced unemployment three times faster than has this country, when Kentucky tops forty-seven other states in personal income growth, and when we double the national increase in nonagricultural employment.[3]

I believe every Kentuckian can be proud of these and other economic factors which heretofore have never blessed our state. These comments are made to reinforce my satisfaction in what has occurred since the end of 1971 and are made as a preamble to the subject of government funds. Revised revenue estimates for fiscal 1973–1974 reflect the healthy economy we have experienced in the last eighteen months.

They also reflect uncontrolled inflation. The revised figures are $775 million for the General Fund against a previous estimate of $751 million. No change was made in the $251 million road fund estimate. In addition, we maintained a net $30 million surplus at the beginning of fiscal 1973–1974. By the time our next biennial budget goes into operation, we expect approximately $86 million in federal revenue-sharing will be available. Therefore, as we begin planning the next budget, you can see we must consider a surplus of $140 million—the $30 million, plus the revised $24 million, plus the $86 million.

I am proud that we have operated state government in the black, which figures, even beyond inflation, clearly indicate. I intend to continue operating state government with a surplus in order to cover unexpected events which might demand certain resources. Prudent financial stability in these times is absolutely essential. However, the surplus we are now facing as budget preparations are initiated places us in a unique position. Someone said we would have more problems with a large surplus than if we didn't have a surplus at all! Possibly so, but it is comforting to have the nest egg. What this person is warning is that there are those who would urge the Governor to recklessly jump into the surplus without considering what might be down the road. You can count on my receiving far more suggestions on how the money should be spent than how much we will have to spend. Which brings me to the emphasis of one word—responsibility.

No matter how bright conditions are at this hour, and they are bright indeed, situations can change. In five months I will present my budget message to the General Assembly. Between now and that date we will prepare for any eventuality, good or bad. To be responsible, one must consider the following facts. And I think it is important that those who might advocate spending understand this. First, what is Washington doing to state programs? We still don't know. This compounds the difficulty of budget planning. How many million dollars in federal funds will be cut or impounded under the so-called New Federalism of the Nixon administration? In all candor, we must expect reductions which directly affect services to our people. In turn, we have to think about plugging the holes.

Second, can we expect the same rate of general fund increase next year? This is doubtful. Inflation must be brought under control at the national level, and at the same time Kentucky cannot be expected to sustain its fantastic margin of state growth versus national growth as we have experienced the last year and a half. Economists look for a breathing spell.

Third, what about the energy crisis? The road fund reflects the present energy crisis and the complexities of forecasting its effect. The supply and price of gasoline and their effects on the purchase of new vehicles simply cannot be determined at this time.

Fourth, we must consider federal regulation on strip mining which might well substantially reduce our severance tax income. The proposed twenty-degree-slope regulation would curtail activities in eastern Kentucky, and even with an increase in the volume of underground mining, there would be an adjustment during a specified period.

Fifth, and this is highly important, we must remember that the surplus portion from federal revenue-sharing represents nonrecurring money. When I mention responsibility, it would be totally irresponsible to saddle the people of Kentucky with burdens created by appropriating revenue-sharing funds on programs having recurring expenses.

Sixth, increased future income will have to go to increased costs for existing programs because of inflation. Our only flexibility will be real growth. My Council of Economic Advisors has indicated that there is a concensus on a slower real growth in late 1974 and early 1975.

Now, returning to use of the surplus: Only one satisfactory option exists for nonrecurring type expenditures. To commit these funds to recurring costs means a tax increase in either fiscal 1975–1976 or 1976–1977. I will not propose any action that causes a tax increase now or in the future, and that is final! To summarize, the outlook on state revenue is good, but could be misleading. Many variables lurk outside, interest rates, federal legislation, the national economy, energy, and so on. The continuation of existing programs will require most of the "inflation" funds to offset increases in commodities and services. Yes, the state economy is healthy, but we have our work cut out for us in making absolutely sure that where our large surplus goes will be marked with responsibility and will be a help rather than a hindrance to Kentuckians now and in the future.

---

1. Press conference. The report Governor Ford is referring to was released on July 31, 1973, and is not included in this volume.

2. At this point in time President Nixon, in many of his speeches, used the phrase, "I want to make one thing perfectly clear."

3. "The last eighteen months are without precedent in Kentucky. Our economic growth is far exceeding the national averages in various categories. In fact, we called for a second review of facts and figures before making this announcement, because the results are so startling. Last year the state's nonagricultural work force grew by 54,700, or a 5.9 percent increase over 1971. But an even more impressive figure is that we almost doubled the national rate. In unemployment, which is declining steadily, Kentucky did

three times better than the rest of the country, and for the first four months of 1973, personal income for Kentuckians showed gains better than forty-seven other states in the Union." From a note attached to this speech.

KENTUCKY CHAMBER OF COMMERCE
STATE FAIR LUNCHEON
Louisville / August 21, 1973

DURING the past few weeks, information pertaining to Kentucky's economic and quality-of-life status has been released for public consumption. There is some confusion resulting from the data offered, and today I want to clarify the picture. One report which received rather prominent play in some of the press originated from an organization called the Midwest Research Institute (MRI). It was bad at first glance, since Kentucky ranked forty-seventh from the top in quality of life in the United States. Another report, which becomes part of a federal economic record, did not receive the prominence given the MRI report although this one was good about Kentucky. In fact, it was so good, we called for a review to make sure there were no mistakes.[1]

First, however, let's look briefly at the Midwest Research findings. Interestingly enough, even though it was just released, it covered only one period of time—the year 1970. It did not go beyond that date. Frankly, Kentucky didn't do too well in its quality of life when MRI tabulated the number of telephones per 100 people, or the cloudless days and the humidity, supposedly relevant indicators as this study would propose. Now maybe we don't have as many telephones per 100 residents as New York, but did you ever try to place a series of calls in New York City and keep any kind of schedule? I am not going to make a verbal assault on the MRI's findings. My concern is to point out that what was in 1970 isn't necessarily so in 1973.

In 1970 Kentucky's crime index was 10.4 compared to the national index of 7.2. Yet in 1972 Kentucky recorded an 8 percent plus decrease in crime while the national average showed only a 2 percent drop. In 1970 Kentucky was behind the nation in the number of homes with plumbing. Last year, we moved to correct this age-old deficiency with a comprehensive regional program for the development of water and sewer needs throughout the Commonwealth. In 1970 Kentucky was ranked very low by MRI on the quality of local and state governments. In 1973 we are well into total reorganization of state government and, through our Office of Local Government, have moved aggressively to provide governmental services second to no state in the country.

The alleged quality-of-life study often confused quality with quantity. For example, the report stated that Kentucky's parks are behind other states in the number of acres. Now you tell me what is better—a thousand acres of cactus around a dry gulch or 500 acres of recreation where the bass hit, the flowers bloom, and thousands of families come to have the time of their lives! You and I know the status of our parks system and are aware that other states pattern their own systems after Kentucky. MRI really missed the boat on this one, as it did in many other classifications.

But what is more significant is the realization that a three-year-old report which suddenly gets a headline showing Kentucky ranked forty-seventh is in numerous ways a distortion and should be repulsive to all Kentuckians, especially this group. Let me turn now to highlights of the second report I previously mentioned which covered eighteen months from January 1972 to June 1973: Kentucky doubled the national rate in nonagricultural employee growth; Kentucky tripled the national rate of decline in unemployment; Kentucky leads forty-seven other states in 1973 in personal income growth. At no time since the beginning of World War II, and in many cases at no time ever, has our state's economic advancements of the last year and a half been matched. And the point to remember is that we went far beyond the national scope.

As a companion situation, three days after our economic survey was released, I announced that in preparation for the next biennial budget, we would have a $140 million surplus to consider. If you examine these figures, you will find that, eliminating revenue-sharing, our general fund will wind up with a $50 million-plus surplus. I was criticized in 1972 when I said we would have a surplus, even though we eliminated the sales tax from food and restructured other aspects of our tax system. I believe a few doubting thomases said we were "juggling state revenue estimates." There were those who also said we would never reduce the percentage of cost in operating state government as we outlined in our first biennial budget. Today I can tell you we not only budgeted a smaller percentage, we went beyond, because in the first year we spent $12 million less than was budgeted.

The economic revelations demonstrate the success of new directions being taken by state government in its own operation, but to a much greater degree, in stimulating economic growth through a viable atmosphere for success in the private sectors. You are responsible for the viable atmosphere. In this room, executive talent abounds, and the directions you and other business leaders like you have charted bring us to the high point we enjoy today. With the 1972 nonagricultural wage and salary employment being the largest gain ever recorded in the Commonwealth, both manufacturing and nonmanufacturing contributed to the new era, with the same upward movement being felt in 1973. New industrial activity has continued briskly during the first six months of this year, unemployment registers lower figures than the previous months, and money is circulating vigorously because of unprecedented income gains.

With this overview, still there are problems. We recognize the work ahead in certain sections of Kentucky and are on top of the situations which demand continuing action from state government. We recognize also that there must be a breathing period. We can expect a leveling off at certain stages during the next two years. And we also recognize that our surplus must be approached with caution, with prudent decision-making, and with the understanding that nonrecurring factors dictate how this money should be spent.

I'm proud of Kentucky's present position. I'm proud of it especially in view of the discouraging national economic news, the plight of a surging food commodity price figure, the weakening U.S. dollar, and many less-than-desirable corporate reports. We must recognize that national problems which haven't been improved by Phases One, Two, Three, Three and a half, and Four will have a bearing on Kentucky.[2] Yet we can, in my opinion, stand tall among other states by maintaining this successful working relationship between state government and the private sectors.

Someone said the other day that a solution to our national economic headache is simple. We sold all of our wheat to Russia and the wheat price doubled. We sold all of our soybeans to Russia and soybean prices doubled. Now we just need to sell all of our stocks to Russia! You and I know it isn't that simple. We have reached our own plateau through cooperation, and if there are bouquets to pass out, let me hand them to you. Your own leadership, your own energies, and your own good citizenship have brought about many of the conditions which made our economic report so impressive. Kentuckians produce. Kentuckians have a unique ability to overcome hardship. And Kentuckians have a pride in whatever task is assigned. That production, that extra burst of initiative, and that pride meshed with the gears of state government brought about a fantastic eighteen months.

Our progress speaks for itself, much louder and with much more authority than a report that has aged for three years. Our state is healthy, its quality of life has improved greatly in three years, but we must keep working together if this trend is maintained. There is no doubt in my mind that each of you will be leaders in this endeavor, and I pledge without reservation the businesslike responsiveness of a state government where the primary objective is delivery of services no matter how small or how large the responsibility.

---

1. See note 3 of August 3, 1973, in this section, pp. 425–26.
2. President Nixon referred to his economic programs as "phases," changing the number as each new program was presented.

KENTUCKY ENERGY CONSERVATION CONFERENCE
Louisville / April 24, 1974

THIS conference is designed to stress our concern for the well-being of Kentucky industry and commerce. One of the very highest priorities of this administration continues to be the maintenance of a climate conducive to economic stimulation and growth. A state's health cannot be accurately gauged by any single factor. Many must be considered. However, a state's health is determined in great part by the number of people who work, by work output, by business expansion and acquisition, by personal income growth, and by the circulation of consumer dollars.

Kentucky's track record during the last twenty-seven months offers conclusive evidence that a state can overcome national adversity and exceed national averages which relate to the economic structure. During the past two years, we added 106,000 nonagricultural jobs, a record unprecedented in our history. Employment remains at a high level as we turn into 1974.

Kentucky has exceeded the nation in decline of unemployment, in increase of new jobs, and in per capita income growth. We have done so in the face of adversity, which tells all of us something very gratifying about the spirit and determination of Kentuckians!

While this total subject is complex and diverse, today's conference stresses energy conservation, another national dilemma which has altered the lives, both personal and business, of millions. Yet, again, Kentucky trudged through the fall, winter, and early spring crunch with less difficulty than elsewhere.

Energy! Energy shortages, energy crisis, energy problems! How familiar these terms have become in a brief period, and at the same time how controversial they have become.

Over the weekend, during the National Democratic Governors' Conference, we listened to four respected pollsters discuss the attitudes of Americans toward the term "Energy Crisis." Their conclusions were unanimous. Attitudes are skeptical at best.

In my address to the 1974 General Assembly on energy, I made the following statement: "Like others interested and concerned, you have no doubt asked, how genuine, how legitimate, is the energy crisis? Many have placed blame on the huge oil companies, believing some joined in an effort to make excessive profits out of a crisis situation. Nevertheless, whether the charges are true or not, those most knowledgeable, and who have been most critical, take pains to admit that a crisis does exist, no matter where the fault is."[1]

People do have reason to be curious and upset. The last issue of *Fortune* magazine said our domestic oil reserves are much larger than we think. But in a Sunday *Courier-Journal* article a noted geologist predicted a worldwide shortage of oil. The *Courier* also reported that John Weber of the Federal Energy Office said gasoline will be adequate this summer. But in the same edition, the American Association for the Advancement of Science conjectured that in two years our oil problem will be worse than during the embargo. People tell me they can't understand how gasoline can be so limited during specific months, then when the price goes up, there seems to be plenty. Even different federal agencies give different reports on the same days!

Given the understanding that there is confusion, and the public viewing all of this with a raised eyebrow, let's consider other matters where logic prevails. Good business practice involves conservation. Waste is costly, and I might add that conservation at today's prices makes waste a sin of both omission and commission! We have had an energy conservation program in state government for quite some time, saving tax dollars without altering services. We will continue to improve our efforts. I am convinced that the rational and prudent course to follow is uninterrupted planning, management, and conservation. I am convinced of its importance to the livelihood of all in Kentucky. For you, this is the surest way to have energy for business expansion. If, indeed, we are approaching an even tighter period than already experienced, the more we collectively do now, the better prepared we are for the future.

There is always the fear, backed up by analysis, surveys, and technical studies, that at present we are in limbo, with declining reserves a serious problem to be faced until alternate sources of energy become reality. And I might mention that Kentucky is working night and day to lead this nation in alternate sources through research and development in the field of coal liquefaction and gasification, the production of clean fuel.

We want the continuation of strong economic growth sufficient to absorb a growing labor force and keep unemployment at acceptable levels. We want to become relatively self-sufficient in our domestic capability to produce energy some time around the 1980s. Our dependence on foreign supplies must be less than in the preembargo days.

The consumption of energy in this country will about double over the next fifteen years if we consume at the same rate as during the three or four years prior to the embargo. It is impossible to double our domestic production in this period of time. There are limits which must be placed on imports because of foreign policy implications and the hazards of massive balance of payment deficits. Conservation and improved energy management, therefore, become the order of the day.

It may be wise to develop concurrently standby regulations to become effective if the situation again becomes critical. Time is available, hopefully, to pursue this in a thoughtful, orderly, and coordinated fashion. This conference is our first formal action in a broader conservation program. The case for conservation can be made. Our intention is to catch the attention of the business decision-makers in Kentucky. We will follow with a series of regional energy conservation seminars directed toward the technicians and engineers who actually put together plans at the plant level. Later, there will be a broad-based effort aimed at the public in general.

We are moving ahead in our energy conservation planning: An evaluation of the impact of varying levels of energy shortage on Kentucky industry is getting under way in cooperation with our universities. All major employers will be contacted during the summer about their energy outlook and ways to avert problems. Long-range energy requirements of Kentucky industry are being projected as a basis for long-range planning.

State government has been in the thick of the energy dilemma, trying to be responsive and responsible in making life better for those we serve. Our allocation office performed with distinction, under pressure, under the cloud of federal indecision and contradicting directions, and in a time where delay could bring undue hardship to the thousands of Kentuckians who asked for response.

Kentucky government has a responsibility to provide leadership in this problem area. We will meet that responsibility. However, we intend to approach this on a basis of full cooperation with industry and commerce.[2] And our overriding goal is to keep Kentucky's economy on the move.

───────────────

1. This is a quote from a speech Governor Ford delivered to the General Assembly in January 1974, which is included in this volume in the Legislative Messages and Statements section, p. 57.

2. On December 14, 1973, at a press conference Governor Ford presented "The Kentucky Plan" as his proposal to handle the energy crisis. The plan was twofold, first to continue on a much larger scale Kentucky's own research and development with coal and second to work with private enterprise and the federal government to build a demonstration plant in gasification and a pilot plant for liquefaction. This press conference is not included in this volume.

INDUSTRIAL COAL CONFERENCE
Lexington / April 25, 1974

THIS country in recent months has been made painfully aware of a shortage of energy sources, such as natural gas, oil, and even uranium. We are running short of everything—everything but coal. As America turns to coal to find an answer to its energy needs, Kentucky, probably more than any other state, has the greatest responsibility and opportunity in providing direction which will be felt throughout the United States, as well as in all parts of Kentucky.

My contention is based on several factors—Kentucky's vast coal reserves; Kentucky's potential for economic growth beyond any measure ever achieved; proven technology which can produce clean fuel from coal; and Kentucky's obligation to respond with aggressiveness and vision, whenever our future is threatened by adversity. Coal is the most practical and timely solution to America's energy crisis. It isn't simple, nor is it inexpensive, but what we have to offer on balance is the most logical and economical idea yet to come down the pike. We have made significant decisions in Kentucky which await federal judgment. These decisions will feasibly convert coal into clean, synthetic gas and oil and, I am convinced, can make a substantial contribution to national self-sufficiency in energy by 1980. Federal action would dovetail with state and private enterprise, promoting a joint venture among all three parties to help correct our country's latest dilemma.

And let me emphasize one point. The direction I propose for Kentucky will not deter us from improved environmental qualities, whether it be in air emissions or land reclamation. The program I propose is designed to produce clean fuel, to stimulate deep mining, and enhance environmental quality and safety standards through research. There are ways to change coal into high British thermal unit gas, as well as low BTU gas. There are ways to change coal into clean oil. And there are other opportunities for coal conversion. Countless by-products can result from coal. Since early 1972, scientists here at the University of Kentucky Institute for Mining and Mineral Research have been quietly pursuing energy research and development, as it pertains to coal. Liquefaction and gasification will work.

Sufficient technology now exists to prove it, through the construction of pilot and demonstration plants. Here again, Kentucky steps to the forefront in site locations, our extensive water supplies needed for conversion techniques, ongoing research and development, a productive labor force, transportation networks, and mining capabilities attuned to environmental protection. In order to keep Kentucky's position the most promising, the most logical, the most realistic, we must accelerate our research, thus assuring that certain types of Kentucky coal remain competitive over the coming decade. We mean business about putting our program into high gear. Just this past Monday, UK engineering officials received a proposal to construct a $3.6 million coal gasification plant on the UK campus.

Obviously, federal funding is vital for continued research and development, as well as the construction of pilot and demonstration plants. But Kentucky is willing to offer a program of financing, just as two Kentucky industries are willing to put up their own dollars. Each gives hope to the future. Last month, the Kentucky General Assembly approved my request for a $57.7 million energy program. One recommendation was that $3.7 million be appropriated for an expansion of our Kentucky Energy Resource Utilization Program. Such expansion will not be limited to coal gasification and liquefaction research. They will include further mapping of Kentucky coals, research and demonstration of improvements in mining technology and techniques, support of education and training programs to increase the supply of trained manpower for mining, research on reclamation problems and techniques, and research on environmental effects of Kentucky coal.

In addition, I recommended the expenditure of $4 million to construct an energy research facility here in Fayette County. Laboratory research already conducted proves we need expanded facilities and clearly we should have one of the nation's major centers for energy research. A third action involved a state commitment of up to $50 million over the next three bienniums, enabling the Commonwealth to participate in the design, construction, and experimental operation of pilot and demonstration projects for coal gasification and liquefaction. Under such authority the Commonwealth will be a joint participant with the federal government and private enterprise in accelerating the work of bringing coal gasification and liquefaction processes to commercial feasibility.

Investment in these projects will help assure adequate energy supplies for Kentucky and the nation. Moreover, such investments resulting in adequate energy supplies will make our state more competitive for new and expanded industry. State support will be repaid manyfold in the future, through increased employment, production of coal, new sources of income for our citizens, and tax revenue growth for state and local governments. No one else has come forth with such a plan or an offer. Other potential energy sources—oil shale, solar, nuclear—can neither meet our timetable nor have the production capacities we can generate by the end of this decade. There is no question about liquefaction and gasification. It's going to be produced somewhere. It is feasible, economical, and acceptable. Our program is intended for immediate engineering design. An interesting aspect to the private endorsement is that upon commercial production, a buy-back clause would be instituted for that amount which has been expended by state and federal governments in construction. Hence, our funds will have gone only for research and development, accelerating the time when coal can become a clean fuel in the form of gas and oil.

We're ready! The spin-offs prompt reminding of what happened through National Aviation and Space Agency, where our quality of life has been improved in medicine, communications, resource surveying, and weather forecasting. When more is learned about coal, who knows the many benefits to society which are now dormant under the earth? Another point to remember is that in extraction, we will be employing the deep-mining process, rather than strip mining.

This is a once-in-a-century opportunity to advance the economic growth of Kentucky as it has never been advanced and, at the same time, to provide answers to such pressing problems as environmental standards, mining safety, mining technology, and a solution to the national energy problem. Kentucky coal is a product whose time has come, because the technology says go, the reserves say go, added requirements, both physical and otherwise, say go, and two of the three partners in this plan are ready to go. Is Washington? I am optimistic because I believe we have an appealing and convincing case, a case based on fact, on proven results, and on a state that doesn't believe all responsibilities should be left to the federal government.[1] Your theme of this conference is "back to coal." I would like to use the term "forward with coal."

---

1. Governor Ford delivered a very similar address to the Coal Utilization Conference in Louisville on July 10, 1974. This address is not included in this volume.

INDUSTRY APPRECIATION ANNUAL LUNCHEON
Louisville / May 8, 1974

Just last week another industry announced plans for a new plant in Kentucky. At that time, the company president paid our state a very high compliment.[1] He said, "We feel this is an attractive place for us to do business, because of the people, and because of Kentucky's growing importance as a transportation and economic center." Here is a company based in Greenwich, Connecticut, that saw something positive in Kentucky and didn't hesitate to publicly commend our people as well as the progress we are achieving.

Last year seventy-four new industries located in Kentucky, while another ninety-four firms already here announced expansions. Altogether this amounted to an investment of $339 million. They too recognized the potential here for good business. I want to extend a warm welcome to each of the new firms and offer my sincere appreciation to the organizations which expanded their operations. Certainly each has cast a vote of confidence in the future—Kentucky's future. As long as industrial leaders do have faith in Kentucky, plus state government's ability to conquer the problems we are facing, we will forge ahead even further. Every Kentuckian can take pride in what's happening in this state, for Kentuckians themselves provide the impetus for success.

The new plants which have come here—every one of them—will be good for the state. Their products are well diversified. They are compatible with our industrial resources. They share our environmental objectives. And they are located in fifty-two communities, spanning north, south, east, and west. The list of new firms includes two Japanese companies, indicating that the "Reverse Investment" program we introduced to Kentucky over a year ago is starting to return some dividends. I predict that the names of foreign-based firms will become more commonplace in the years ahead. They will be welcomed and given the same fair treatment we extend domestic firms interested in Kentucky.

Why are industries finding Kentucky a great place to do business? You know the answer to that question, as well as I do—our central location, our first-class system of highways, our labor supply, and our livability. State government is daily trying to make Kentucky's business climate even better. Our tax system is, and will continue to be, equitable, balanced, and competitive. Regulations on industry and commerce will be fair, but as I have said before, they must adequately protect the public's interest—protect the health and welfare of Kentuckians. For that reason, we have been selective in seeking new industries, rather than throwing the door open for anyone. There are far too many service-oriented businesses and industries, where management is progressive and considerate, where product integrity and financial stability are exceptional, for Kentucky to be satisfied with anything less than blue-chip firms.

We're proud, very proud, of the industries we have in our state. And it is fitting that we salute business during "Industry Appreciation Week" because of its importance to Kentucky's well-being. Kentucky's 3,000 firms employ more than 280,000 people and pay more than $2.5 billion in wages. The multiplier effect spreads widely, stimulating every sector of the state's economy. Because industry has been good for Kentucky, state government is determined to maintain a sound business climate. During the past two years, we have laid the foundation for a program approach that should meet the needs of the next several decades.

Increased emphasis has been placed on the production and use of developmental research, as location decisions require more hard facts than ever before. We are stressing the requirements of individual industries as they relate to Kentucky's resources. A small, but effective, commercial development program has been started, with emphasis on national and regional headquarters offices, private-recreation facilities, and distribution centers. This program was instrumental, for instance, in the location of the Island Creek Coal Company Headquarters at Lexington.

International trade has been brought to a front-line status, through a twofold approach. We are working to interest and assist firms in increasing exports, and we are presenting the Kentucky story to foreign-based firms. Exports in Kentucky total about $600 million—big business, which we hope to make even bigger. Presently, we are working with ten foreign-based firms. A Department of Commerce representative will be in Dusseldorf next week to participate in an "Invest in the USA" seminar, with more than 200 German companies represented.

We've added a Minority Business Enterprise Program to help minority firms participate more effectively in Kentucky's economic affairs. This program features business counseling, education, and assistance in loan packaging. We have high hopes for this venture. We have developed new ways to better match vocational training with the needs of Kentucky employers—a pioneer effort in this field. And I can't let this occasion pass without complimenting the 1974 General Assembly for its increasing vocational education by 25 percent.

If we are to experience continued economic growth, adequate energy must be available. This is of great concern to us. We have established a permanent energy management program, not just to work on allocation, but primarily to evaluate our requirement-supply situation and make sure that energy is available for growth in this state. Just recently an energy conservation program for industry was initiated by the Department of Commerce. The key to our development programs is that we have not just accounted for each year's problems and opportunities. We have laid a solid foundation for the future.

Of particular significance is Kentucky's emerging role in the field of research. Industry is especially interested in our new energy research and development program, because of its potential for industrial power —clean power. We are currently discussing low BTU gasification projects with several major industrial firms, and this one aspect bodes well for Kentucky's contribution to energy self-sufficiency.

Close cooperation between the Departments of Commerce and Labor, combined with far-sighted leadership in both labor and industry, is welding an unusual partnership for progress in Kentucky. I pledge a continuing interest in the welfare of these new firms. You won't be forgotten. Last year, staff members of the Department of Commerce visited 200 firms that located in the state during the past five years to offer any assistance state government could provide. We wanted you to locate here, but, more importantly, we want you to grow and prosper.

---

1. The Governor is referring to Ralph E. Ward, president of Ragú Foods, Inc., a subsidiary of Cheseborough-Ponds, Inc. Ragú announced its plans to build a plant in Daviess County on May 2, 1974. Ford's comments on that occasion are not included in this volume.

REVENUE AND APPROPRIATIONS REPORT
Frankfort / June 6, 1974

THE appropriation bill for the 1974–1976 biennium[1] authorized a revision of appropriations within priorities established by the General Assembly, if lapsed funds at the end of 1973–1974 plus estimated revenue for 1974–1975 is less than, or more than, $916,371,095. The Commissioner of Revenue[2] has submitted revised revenue estimates as of May 31. That revision increases the estimate for 1973–1974 to $715 million, or $25 million more than reflected in the executive budget, and for 1974–1975 to $900 million or $70 million more than reflected in that document. The $10 million lapse anticipated during budget reviews remains the same, despite inflation which is a credit to belt-tightening in the management function of departments and agencies.

A basic answer as to why the excess revenue is more than anticipated lies in five areas:

1. Kentucky's economy has remained stronger than the national economy. This can be attributed to several actions by this administration and the 1972 General Assembly.

2. The energy crisis has not affected Kentucky as severely as many other states. Furthermore the Mideast embargo was lifted sooner than predicted, and remember, these estimates were made in December 1973.

3. Kentucky and the nation have experienced unprecedented inflation. The same cause that increases revenue also affects buying power. It increases both income and cost.

4. For the third year in a row, state agencies will not spend all funds

appropriated. Prudent management has certainly contributed to the amount which will lapse.

5. When the revenue estimates were made, and as we expressed to the General Assembly, they were conservative by necessity. Anything else would have been totally irresponsible to abandon cautious and conservative practices today when uncertainties are even greater. Think what the impact would be today had we appropriated wildly and the state economy had not exceeded the national economy. I would be here announcing a deficit, and wrestling with the curtailment of needed services throughout the state.

I recommended to the General Assembly that priorities for allocation of excess funds be written into law, in the event we did have a surplus. This was adopted by that body. They were enumerated in the appropriation bill. The act gives the Governor the authority to allocate any excess funds within procedures established. I am complying with the spirit and intent of that act. Today I conferred with the chairmen of the House and Senate Committees on Appropriations and Revenue and minority chairman of the House Appropriations and Revenue Committee.[3] I believe that the intent of the General Assembly has been fulfilled and the committee leadership agrees. You have the rationale and procedure used for initial increases by priority.

Several words of caution exist. First, we are still faced by unprecedented inflation. We are faced with a national economic crisis where no relief is in sight. I know that many agencies will require additional money to cover increased costs. We have started an intensive review with the understanding that close monitoring of the economy and its effect on both revenue and costs is even more important today. In this review, I have two immediate considerations—textbooks for our school children and books for our library system which is an integral part of our public education system. I have asked the Secretary of the Education Cabinet[4] for a list of library facilities which need funding, as well as an analysis on the increased cost of textbooks which are provided our school children.

In addition, the threat of shortages in energy still looms. There are many labor negotiations under way. The international money market which directly touches our economy is more unstable than last year. Additional losses of federal funds continue to plague us. For instance, I have expressed my concern for our library system and the effect losses in federal dollars had on it, where we had to compensate with state funds. Another example: only last month we received notice of another cut in federal funds for Kentucky. The Department of Housing and Urban Development has reduced funds for our comprehensive planning assistance programs. This is very important to local governments throughout the state. I consider it vital to the management of our cities and counties and have recommended that the state replace those monies so we can continue these programs at the same level as last year.

Therefore, I am going to be as cautious, prudent, and conservative as in the past in order that we do not fall into a trap of overspending. As programs are fully reviewed, additional priorities will be given and supported by additional revenue forecast.

---

1. See an act "relating to appropriations for the operation, maintenance, support, and functioning of the government of the Commonwealth of Kentucky," which was approved on March 19, 1974. *Acts of the General Assembly of the Commonwealth of Kentucky, 1974*, Chapter 81 (H.B. 288), pp. 136–64; press conference.

2. John McDowell Ross (1932–   ), Ashland; with the Kentucky Department of Revenue in the 1950s and 1960s; Kentucky revenue commissioner (1971–1974); currently director of tax compliance for Ashland Oil, Inc. Telephone interview with Ross.

3. Michael R. Moloney (1941–   ), Democrat from Lexington; attorney; assistant commonwealth attorney (1970–1971); Kentucky Senate (1972, 1974, 1976); chairman, Kentucky Senate Committee on Appropriations and Revenue (1974). Joseph P. Clarke, Jr.; chairman, Kentucky House of Representatives Committee on Appropriations and Revenue (1974); for more information see speech from November 13, 1973, in the Reorganization section, p. 160. Edward L. Holloway (1937–   ), Republican from Middletown; insurance agency owner; vice president of Associates Industries of Kentucky; president of Kentucky Tax Association; secretary-treasurer of Kentucky Society of Association Executives; Kentucky House of Representatives (1970, 1972, 1974, 1976); minority chairman of the House Appropriations and Revenue Committee (1974). *Kentucky General Assembly 1974* (Frankfort, n.d.).

4. Lyman Ginger, for more information see speech from September 13, 1973, in the Reorganization section, p. 155.

FRANKFORT CIVIC CLUBS
JOINT MEETING
Frankfort / July 10, 1974

THE community organizations represented here today form a bedrock of service through active involvement by you, the members. In this room is a good cross section of civic interest where the themes, creeds, and philosophies of the various clubs offer a singular chord, "Find a need and fill it." State government should be no different. There are unlimited needs which call for never-ending approaches to solutions. I want to tell you about one approach—one more way your state government has been trying to help—in an area of service where the boundaries are pretty wide.

In hearing this announcement for the first time, and discussing its purposes, keep in mind that the degree of response received will determine whether it is a success or merely a lot of expended time and effort. I predict that the response, when others realize what is now available, will be extensive. For years, Kentucky has harbored a wealth of personal talent. Keen minds, accountable research, extensive study, and unusual qualities of a technical and scientific nature have been with us, though unfortunately too much in a dormant status. Communities, businesses, industries, governments, special groups, and other institutions have been surrounded by this expertise. But they haven't drawn from the pool of knowledge, because there was no known pool from which to draw! Now there is, and based on the best information available, no other state in the nation is offering the type of program I am announcing. This is, in fact, a three-part program, the product of a year-long undertaking.

First, a Kentucky Scientific Manpower Registry has been computerized for easy access. It includes the names of over 1,700 academic scientists and engineers from throughout Kentucky. Second, a computerized register of scientific dissertations and theses has been developed. This includes more than 5,000 papers representing years of study by individuals during their pursuits of master's and doctorate degrees. Third, a listing of all scientific and technical libraries in Kentucky has been assembled for the first time.

The Manpower Registry permits a rapid location of an expert, or experts, with any desired scientific or engineering skills. More than 250 specialities, representing forty-one disciplines are on the register. What's more, they are all in Kentucky! These are men and women waiting to be called upon. The three-pronged program is for the future development of this state—but, more importantly, a development from within. It utilizes Kentucky knowledge, expertise, intelligence, and resources in an unprecedented approach to fulfilling the greatest potential of Kentucky's scientific and technical manpower. Let me emphasize again, we simply have not been taking advantage of our potential, despite the willingness of these individuals to lend a hand.

Now you're probably wondering what this means to you, your club, or your community. Suppose a prospective industry needs technical advice. Management requires experts in a particular field. The computer responds with names because we have the experts. Then management is immediately ready to engage them. Perhaps a problem arises involving agriculture. Specialized help is required. The computer can find that help. There is no delay. Another "for instance": A group of businessmen want opinions on a new venture. The register searches, offers names, and gets the parties together.

There are countless examples of how local governments can find assistance, how organizations can receive directions, and how institutions—business, professional, financial, and others—can use this system to acquire special help for special jobs. The published materials alone are invaluable, again through elimination of wasted time, since the research is already completed, and dollars will be saved. While the three-stage Manpower Registry is a free service, the personnel who might be subsequently contacted will, of course, have fees. But they certainly won't approach costs normally anticipated. You might also ask, if this is so great, why haven't we had it before? I don't have an answer, unless it is that no one thought of it before. But we have it now, and who can put a price tag on the benefits this program holds? All we must do is publicize it and make sure it is used.

One certain spin-off will be the ability to attract more research and development money into the state and thus strengthen our economic base. The numerous skilled scientists and engineers on our university and college campuses have been shortchanged in the past primarily because few knew the magnitude of our collective brainpower. Now this should change. With a diversified group entering into more and more research and development programs, new jobs, new opportunities, and new achievements will result. I'm highly pleased to make this announcement. I'm proud, since it shows another way state government can be innovative, and Kentucky can be self-reliant.

This program is not a product of an out-of-state consulting firm. It is the product of Western Kentucky University's Ogden College of Science and Technology, the University of Kentucky, the State Department of Commerce, and the Kentucky Academy of Science. In view of the work involved, the time required, and the persons who participated, a conservative estimate of the project's true cost, if accomplished by other sources, would be $150,000. It cost us $15,000. The quality of this program, the detail, the new concepts advocated, speaks highly of those who put this package together. Most importantly, it serves notice that the tools are now available to make a more productive use of Kentucky's technical manpower. We do have a lot to offer, and we must see that this new service reaches its greatest potential.

ANNOUNCEMENT OF COAL GASIFICATION PLANT
Frankfort / July 13, 1974

THE Commonwealth of Kentucky is entering into a formal agreement with Texas Gas Transmission Corporation to begin immediately a coal gasification project.[1] This action results from several factors. The growth of America's energy demands is running ahead of expansion in domestic capacity. Thus our energy crisis is only beginning. To remain economically strong, to alleviate personal and other hardships, and to protect our state's future with energy reserves, Kentucky has an obligation toward energy self-sufficiency. New methods of obtaining energy are absolutely mandatory. Kentucky can offer to its own people, and others, the resources and ability to acquire new energy. A Kentucky-domiciled corporation has illustrated its leadership and its concern in this matter by pursuing a course whereby clean fuel can be produced from coal to correct the growing imbalance of supply and demand.

My energy research and development program which was approved by the 1974 General Assembly provides the state's mechanism and input for this agreement. Prior technology, attained both in Kentucky and through other scientific achievements, has brought us to where we are today. The realization that due to national security the U.S. cannot rely on foreign supplies of energy, the major priority to eliminate shortages, and the present effects an energy crisis is having on

America all prompt extensive federal participation in research and development.

It is imperative that we move ahead with all deliberate speed. This agreement is in two phases, allowing us to proceed now with phase one, while being prepared for phase two when federal participation is acquired. You have a copy of the agreement to be signed here today. Let me briefly comment on phase one. Emphasis has been placed on the environmental impact study to assure standards which must be maintained in demonstration and commercial applications of the coal gasification project. This will be a $1.1 million undertaking by itself. The whole thrust of this is to increase energy supplies compatible with the quality environment we must have in the future, through the use of coal. However, engineering, design, and testing must be accomplished first, in order that the study is properly carried out.

Now for comments on phase two. Here we enter into the demonstration aspects of a gasification plant to prove technical and economic feasibility. The state's commitment coincides with federal participation. Therefore, phases one and two commit the state up to $35 million. Texas Gas will, at a minimum, match the state's total. It is anticipated that the federal share of the total project would exceed $100 million. Testimony from the Office of Coal Research has indicated that the federal role in demonstration projects can be expected by the end of this year. While this is not a guarantee, we know the realities and national demands. Yet there is another aspect. Depending upon future conditions, shortages of natural gas, crude oil, and the increasing cost of both, private industry may decide to continue gasification projects alone, if federal participation does not materialize. I believe it is logical to recognize that Texas Gas, having already invested a substantial amount of money in this program and willing to invest millions more, is not entering into this project with any other intent except commercial feasibility. The best approach, for the public interest, is a joint venture among Kentucky, Texas Gas, and the federal government. This is the end we are aggressively pursuing.

Now what does all this mean? It means that Kentucky is preparing for the nation's first commercial gasification plant that will manufacture pipeline quality gas from high-sulfur bituminous coal. It means that when the economic and technical objectives are met, Texas Gas will expand the project into a commercial-size plant. The investment of Texas Gas in a commercial-size plant is projected to be in excess of $600 million in 1974. Such a gas-generation facility offers numerous benefits. It helps compensate for shortages of natural gas, thus contributing to energy self-sufficiency. It attracts new business and industry to Kentucky. It provides jobs, both directly and indirectly because of related effects. It utilizes our vast underground coal reserves in a manner which protects the environment. This will also set the stage for other high BTU gasification plants. We are talking about more energy from clean fuel: a boon to our economy, new jobs, a stronger tax base, increased deep mining, and the expected new discoveries through research.

In summary, this represents our attempt to open an entirely new era of energy resources. It represents a fantastic opportunity for economic growth throughout Kentucky. It represents the beginning of new technology where we will find corresponding assets for many years to come. States which have energy will prosper in the future. Those without will suffer. So today Kentucky is getting a program on the road in a similar fashion to a NASA project where the details are complex, the work to be done is very extensive, and the expected results are both exciting and absolutely necessary.

---

1. Press conference.

SEVERANCE TAX CONFERENCE
Frankfort / August 1, 1974

THROUGH the years, Kentucky's coal industry has demonstrated its importance to the state's economy in many ways: as an industry which provides jobs, as the nation's leading producer of an essential source of fuel, and as an important tax base. Yet the counties, both in eastern and western Kentucky where the coal is extracted, have traditionally received little in return. In the past two and a half years, we have tried to reverse that attitude. Those of us who have the responsibility of operating your government must look at every opportunity for economic growth within the territory where our authority extends and find new ways to improve the quality of life for people.

You will recall that some progress was made toward this end in 1972 when the General Assembly, with my support, acted to return half of the receipts derived from strip-mining fees and acreage permits back to local governments. Several counties received as much as $60,000 which went directly to the fiscal courts.[1] Since then, we have continued to explore ways to provide additional assistance. Last March we took another major step in that direction when the 1974 General Assembly, upon my recommendation, adopted Senate Bill 281.[2] This bill provided for the return of excess severance tax revenues to the coal-producing counties. Appropriations were to be based upon the severance tax collected, rather than the amount of coal mined. Thus, the dollar value of the coal produced was recognized, not the tonnage, assuring that eastern Kentucky would not be deprived of its fair share. The appropriations are based upon the difference between estimated taxes and the actual collection for the previous fiscal year. This lets us know at the beginning of the year how much money will be available, therefore, not building up any false hopes.

The legislation which created this program had my full support because of its three primary objectives: to return more decision-making power on community needs to the people closest to the problems, to eliminate any delay in your receiving the money for one year, and to provide for long-range community development, which would offset the depletion of coal in these counties. I want to reiterate that roads and bridges can be a part of your community development program. I have been assured by members of the advisory committee that such projects can be approved under the guidelines established. This afternoon I want to announce that $6,247,705 will be returning to our coal-producing counties this year. In order that county judges and fiscal courts could become better acquainted with the objectives and details of this program, we invited you here today, so that you could get projects started as soon as possible.

It is important that we recognize that members of the Legislative Advisory Committee are members of the General Assembly, appointed by both the Senate and House of Representatives. They are dedicated to seeing that the full intent of this program is fulfilled and want you to understand how it works. Some of you may question why the money cannot be returned directly to the counties for the fiscal courts to spend as they see fit. I basically agree with this concept, but a constitutional problem exists here, and we must take care to prevent a conflict which could jeopardize the whole program. Therefore, the entire appropriation was assigned to a single state agency, the Executive Department for Finance and Administration, which will allocate funds for projects as recommended by the fiscal courts and approved by the Legislative Advisory Committee. I thank you for your attendance today. In closing, I want to challenge you to make this program, which can mean so very much to the people of your counties, work, so that it can be extended and expanded by the 1976 General Assembly.

---

1. See an act "relating to strip mining," which was approved on March 17, 1972. *Acts of the General Assembly of the Commonwealth of Kentucky, 1972,* Chapter 270 (H.B. 47), pp. 1172–78. Governor Ford returned funds from the 1974 fees to forty counties on August 29, for example.

2. See an act "relating to appropriations and the disbursement of appropriations," which was approved on April 2, 1974. *Acts of the General Assembly of the Commonwealth of Kentucky, 1974,* Chapter 262 (S.B. 281), pp. 502–3.

BOWLING GREEN KIWANIS CLUB
Bowling Green / August 8, 1974

As businessmen, professionals, and civic leaders, you have multiple interests. I want to talk about what should be a universal interest—your money. How government, at any level, utilizes taxpayer funds is a topic commanding frank, open, and frequent attention. But if the question, "Do you really know the rationale behind fiscal management by government," is asked, most people would give a negative answer. The reasons for this dilemma, and it is a dilemma for both government and the people, center around failure of communications. Those who should communicate, those who have the vehicles for communications, and those who ought to receive the communications fail to communicate.

Two advertisements in yesterday's *Wall Street Journal* illustrate that this failure is not restricted only to government. National Steel hinted its concern for better identity by saying: "You may know about two of our good customers, cars and cans. We'd like you to know about 20,000 others." A second ad by a different firm was headlined this way: "A speciality metals company that nobody knows about." I could use both expressions for programs which we have under way. You may know about a few, but we'd like you to know about many others. Obviously time limits wide-ranging discussion, so I will touch on the matter of surplus.

Last December when we were preparing the biennial budget and trying to determine revenue estimates, both tasks were unusually difficult because of factors we could neither control nor predict—inflation, the oil embargo, shortages of essential supplies and materials, the energy crisis, an absence of national domestic policy, and the lack of an agricultural export policy. Each of these items created a domino effect; for instance, the unemployment situation, commerce, and trade which rely on heavy fuel reserves and state/local programs affected by federal decisions. The economic future was bleak at best. A conservative revenue estimate was the only responsible alternative. We followed this with continuing analysis, utilizing the best information possible and the best minds available. In essence, I publicly advised the General Assembly of our conservative approach and requested the Legislature's approval of established priorities—their priorities—if the estimates were either above or below what we anticipated. And, as you know, the economic picture remained strained, even with the embargo lifting. We hoped for a surplus and were prepared for something less, as monitoring of the economy continued.

One bright lining in a dark cloud did exist. Kentucky's economy held better than that of the nation's—our unemployment figures were better, our rate of new job growth exceeded the federal indicators, per capita income was growing above other states, and agriculture showed strength. Yet any violation of the conservative approach, in my opinion and in the opinion of our economic advisors during this period, was intolerable. One fiscal fact distinguishes Kentucky government from the federal government. The Kentucky Constitution forbids our state government from operating with a deficit budget. This is the bench mark from which we have to start.

The result developed into a surplus for Kentucky. That surplus is approximately $125 million. Despite persisting problems, we are able to meet priorities of need beyond the new biennial budget which is almost a billion dollars more for statewide services, with no tax increase. Don't let anyone misrepresent what has occurred. Revenue-sharing accounts for less than 4 percent of the new budget. We have had to supplement federally funded programs with state dollars due to impoundments, curtailments, and abandonment of programs.

Now there are those who, with 20–20 hindsight, say we should have expanded our revenue forecasts. Caution was dictated for the very reasons already mentioned. The point is that we do have a surplus rather than a deficit. We can provide services instead of being forced to restrict them. Let's look at where part of the surplus has been placed: industrial haul roads, state police, libraries, education, schools for the blind and deaf, revenue-sharing to communities, land reclamation, mental health, and the return of severance tax to coal-producing counties. These programs, and others, touch the lives of every Kentuckian in a positive, beneficial manner. With seemingly unlimited needs and limited resources, we have an obligation to expand Kentucky's future potential where life will be better.

There are capital construction projects in the surplus. Every month's delay means at least 1.5 percent more in cost because of inflation. We cannot in good conscience allow shrinkage of the dollar when we know there are facilities which must be built. Would you deprive the multiple-handicapped of a facility which will become only the sixth in the entire United States? Would you deprive both the disadvantaged and the exceptional elementary and secondary school students of Kentucky special educational facilities? Would you deprive preschoolers the opportunity for kindergarten? We have done much with this surplus, yet there remains approximately $51 million from it, so we're not playing Santa Claus; we're earmarking funds where they can do the most good.

Now how did the surplus originate? Inflation created a portion, so we must remember that inflation also takes away. Economic growth, quite different from the nation, has indeed continued in Kentucky. Reorganization and prudent use of allocated funds by state agencies brought us over $26 million which were either saved through new concepts or not needed because we have, with few exceptions, managed the agencies with a tight hand.

Any Governor is faced with tough decisions when he has extra money because the necessities of society are always greater than the resources. These are real necessities, just as you consider what is essential for your families. I sought to allocate funds which, if available last January, would have definitely been allocated. Then I sought solutions to those special problem areas that rank high with the public but could not be anticipated six or eight months ago. Some examples are a sub-library for the blind, increased cost of textbooks for children entering or going back to school this fall, an EPA requirement that we develop river basin plans in order to qualify for $65 million in water and sewer projects throughout the state, and accelerated energy research and development which is one of the most promising programs for our children and our children's children because of what it will mean to their lives in years to come. I don't have all the answers, and I hope that whenever I make a mistake I can be big enough to admit it. But in good conscience, I can report to you that the surplus procedure will stand any test. Your money is being put to maximum use.

ASHLAND OIL EXPANSION
Frankfort / September 4, 1974

As most of you know, Ashland Oil is the largest company with corporate headquarters in Kentucky. With me today are Robert E. Yancey, Ashland Oil president, Robert T. McCowan, president of Ashland's Petroleum Division, and John F. Boehm, a group vice president of the Petroleum Division and president of its Valvoline operations.[1] I'm sure you already are aware of the importance of Ashland's two refineries located within the Commonwealth. These gentlemen have joined me here today to make some important announcements about industrial expansion plans here in the state.

I'm very happy that Ashland has asked me to join with them. Industrial expansion, particularly environmentally sound expansion such as we will talk about today, is a good investment for all Kentuckians. Not only will there be more jobs, but the expansion will contribute to a better energy-production base and to cleaner fuels for our use. And I feel that Kentucky has much to offer industry.

If I may, I'll briefly make the announcement before turning the conference over to the Ashland Oil officials. Ashland Oil plans to begin construction in the near future on two projects at its Catlettsburg refining and petrochemical complex. The total new capital investment in the projects will be approximately $100 million and upon completion will add more than seventy-five new jobs in northeast Kentucky—not counting the hundreds of personnel required in the construction phases. Ashland Oil will build a plant capable of producing 5,000 barrels a day of lubricating oils. This is an important facility not only for Kentucky, but for the United States. There is a growing shortage of basic lubricating oil in the United States which is becoming more critical as we continue to increase our consumption. This new addition will go far toward making our country more self-sufficient in the production of these lubricating oils. Ashland will use the material from this plant in its Valvoline products.

Also, the company plans to construct desulfurization equipment at its Ashland refinery complex. One piece of this new equipment will reduce the sulfur content of the heating oil, diesel fuels, and kerosine produced by Ashland Oil. A second major unit will take sulfur out of the crude oil processed by the refinery. This in turn will allow Ashland to produce heavy oils with a lower sulfur content that are burned by industry. This project means that Kentuckians and Kentucky industry will have available to them cleaner energy for their use.

Today's announcement is indicative of the positive feeling industry has for Kentucky—a state where working together means progress. Ashland Oil would not have undertaken such costly and massive projects without having a strong faith in the course state government is pursuing for the Commonwealth's economic growth, and for this faith I thank them and congratulate them on behalf of all Kentuckians.

---

1. Robert Earl Yancey, Jr. (1921–   ), Ashland; oil company executive; technical service engineer (1969–1972); operating superintendent (1972–   ). *Who's Who in America, 1974–1975* (Chicago, 1975), 2:3385. Robert Taylor McCowan (1928–   ), Ashland; oil company executive; vice president of Ashland Oil, Inc. (1967–1970); administrative vice president (1968–1970); currently executive vice president of Ashland Petroleum Division. *Who's Who in America, 1974–1975* (Chicago, 1975), 2:2089. John F. Boehm (1926–   ), Ashland; oil company executive; president of Valvoline Division of Ashland Oil, Inc. Telephone interview with Boehm's secretary, July 19, 1976.

TOURISM

TRAVEL CONFERENCE
Louisville / April 14, 1972

WHAT'S good for the travel industry is good for Kentucky! I say this, realizing it is not at all a new statement. But I say this to emphasize my intention, as your Governor, to ensure the finest travel industry possible in Kentucky. You will note a similar attitude in the Department of Parks; you will note a similar attitude in the Department of Public Information. You will find a responsiveness from other agencies, which on judgment day will be found unparalleled in their efforts to stimulate our travel industry.

Consider these names: Peabody, Island Creek, U.S. Steel, and Bethlehem Steel. Now think of Seagram, Brown & Forman, Schenley and National Distillers, along with Philip Morris, American Tobacco, Brown & Williamson, R. J. Reynolds, and P. Lorillard. I'm not through. Add Ford Motor, International Harvester, Eaton, Yale & Towne, and Bendix-Westinghouse. What am I getting at? It's hard to believe, but you can lump all these industries together and their annual payrolls will total around $10 million less than the cash the travel industry brought into Kentucky last year!

I have always admired figures. How do these measurements strike you—426–35.1–46? In some respects they represent the curves of Miss U.S.A., which is the touring crowd this wonderful land we call America sends to Kentucky. The 426 figure is a dollar measurement. That's how many millions of dollars came into Kentucky last year by out-of-state visitors. The 35.1 represents how many millions of individuals spent the welcomed cash. And the number 46 is how many millions of dollars these guests poured directly into the state treasury in taxes.

The business that brings us together was worth more than half a billion dollars to Kentucky in 1971—$585 million, in fact. And $159 million of it was spent by Kentuckians. That, by the way, is $11 million more than our home folks spent traveling in Kentucky in 1970. These are figures from the brand new survey just completed by Dr. Lewis Copeland[1] for the year 1971. Most of you are probably familiar with Dr. Copeland's work. He is the acknowledged authority on the economics of the travel industry. This is the thirteenth annual survey that he has completed for Kentucky's Department of Public Information.

Let's see what these three figures mean to us here in this room and to the Commonwealth. The $426 million from out-of-state is far and away the biggest year the industry has yet enjoyed. It's $32 million more than those visitors spent with us in 1970. It amounts to $142 for each citizen in this state. It provided $149.5 million in personal income to Kentuckians in the form of wages and proprietors' profits. Dr. Copeland tells us that $15,000 in retail sales provides one full-time job. Therefore some 28,000 jobs were provided in Kentucky by the spending of our out-of-state guests. While the private sector enjoyed this business, the records of the Parks Department reflect a greater loss. I assure you this will be changed.

The 35.1 million visitors came from just about everywhere. That's a staggering number of people, really. It's almost 11¾ times our entire population. It's more than the combined populations of twenty-six of our fifty states, and it's over 1.5 million more than the previous year's visitors. The $46 million that out-of-state visitors left in the state treasury by way of taxes is money that is absolutely essential to the economic health of Kentucky. It comes out to $15.33 for every Kentuckian. Without this influx of tourist gold, each of us would have to ante up an extra $15.33 apiece in state taxes every year to make up the difference. In addition to that $46 million, by the way, our 1970 visitors kicked in around $10.75 million in local taxes. Dr. Copeland is a year behind in figuring local taxes.

Apart from the good old meat-and-potatoes cold cash that comes to us in taxes, the spending of out-of-state visitors is of great interest to all Kentuckians. People who don't have actual contact with our visitors often feel that tourists are fine for those who sell them something, but not particularly interesting to those who don't. These citizens need to know just how the tourist dollar works and how it is spent once the tourist parts with it. The man who rings it up retains about ten cents of it. The other ninety cents is paid out in wages, supplies, rents, utilities, taxes, and other operating expenses. About thirty-five cents of it goes to wholesalers and distributors for food, gasoline, and other supplies. Another thirty-five cents goes into personal income like wages. State and local taxes take about thirteen cents and the other seven cents goes for utilities and other services. The third generation pay-out distributes it much more widely, of course, into all the things that our wages buy: installment payments, medical bills, clothing, groceries, and so on. The wholesalers in turn pay their employees and their suppliers and that money goes into the economic stream. It is the same way with the utilities companies, the laundries, the printing and advertising media, and so on. This is known as the "multiplier effect," and it's wonderful how it works.

Your state government is determined to do everything in its power to encourage and boost the tourist travel business. Our state parks are designed to bring people here. We play up our parks because they are the expression of our God-given natural beauty and our historical heritage. They form the bedrock of our other efforts. We cannot directly publicize your particular fishing camp, your bowling alley, your campground, your beautiful cave, or your fine motel. It's against the law. But we can and will help you in every legal way through matching funds, promotional materials, travel expertise, photographs, and artwork. We will include you and involve you in travel shows, think conferences, and special events. In other words, you are important.

---

1. Lewis Campbell Copeland, Knoxville; associate professor of statistics, University of Tennessee (1953–   ); fields of specialty: statistics, business mathematics, and research methods; author of numerous works on tourism and the travel industry. *Faculty Personnel: American Association of Collegiate Schools of Business,* ed. Richard Weeks (St. Louis, 1965), p. 416.

THOROUGHBRED CLUB OF AMERICA
Lexington / April 19, 1972

I AM here to talk business. This is an attitude we are instilling within every department of state government, because if government truly exists to serve people, as I say it does, it can do so only on a serious, businesslike basis. Those of us who have the responsibility of operating your government must look at every opportunity for economic growth within the territory where our authority extends, and we must do more. We must give full consideration to every aspect of our citizens' welfare. This means how he can live comfortably, safely, and enjoyably.

For too long the equine industry in Kentucky has been in "matter-of-fact" status by state government. Yes, there has been token support, but the lip service this valuable resource has received by far outweighs any solid examples of determined assistance. You have fought competition alone. You have brought us an important financial stimulus. You have provided some of the most magnificent scenery in the world. You have been employer, tourist, promoter, entertainer, benefactor, and warm neighbor. The gift of your industry, and that of others in the related disciplines, has meant so much to Kentucky as well as this nation. I doubt if anyone this minute fully realizes the impact you have on our society, the favorable impact which has brought a rich tradition over many years to this state. I want this propelled into a new era whereby your industry and all Kentuckians will benefit. Together, this can happen; the potential is exciting.

In 1972 Kentucky expects to receive more than $426 million from out-of-state travelers, for this is the amount we garnered last year. We expect out-of-state visitors to drive well over 5 billion, yes billion, miles just in Kentucky this year and feel confident that the number of non-Kentucky tourists will be in excess of 35 million persons. Their contributions to the overall economy of Kentucky cannot be measured simply. Their spending touches, benevolently, every man, woman, and child who resides in the Commonwealth. In other words, we welcome these guests. We need them, and I am convinced they need Kentucky. They need Kentucky because of what we offer. Your profession is a primary element in that offering. State government is aggressively promoting the tourist business. We offer a vacation of value, and the "call of Kentucky's countless attractions" is our bonus for tomorrow.

You know, when you think of Kentucky, you think of horses, bourbon, tobacco, and beautiful women. And they're all habit-forming. Yes, Americans everywhere do think of horses when Kentucky is mentioned. You are responsible for this, and my administration wants to help you be even more responsible for the well-being of this state. I know many of you here tonight have heard a similar statement. Well, Wendell Ford doesn't believe in meaningless rhetoric, idle talk, or false hopes. There will be no, for convenience sake, encouraging nods, nice smiles, or pats on the back, and then disappearance. The best way I can put it to you is this: there is going to be action.

Do you realize that in all the state brochures, illustrating parks, shrines, events, and activities, there isn't even one on the subject of horses? Now there's no excuse for your being ignored. You can expect something better these next four years.[1] Many of you present, especially those from Kentucky, have heard talk, talk, talk about a horse park to be located in the Bluegrass. As president of the state Senate in 1970, I worked diligently with others to gain authorization for a Thoroughbred state park. I harbored a strong trust that our cause would not be diverted and that a recreational and educational facility serving both Kentuckians and the vast touring public would come into fruition. Equally emphatic was my conclusion that we should emphasize your industry.

A year ago the fourteenth of this month, studies were made available which could have been the starting bell for a prompt move in developing the park. Executive silence prevailed. I don't plan on this administration, or you, being left at the gate. In our first 120 days, we have picked up the pieces. I have directed my Commissioner of Parks to move immediately in behalf of a horse park that will not only inspire greater tourism, but add immensely to the distinguishing features of Kentucky's vast and magnificent parks system.[2]

We intend for this project to more than pay its own way. There will be no expense forced on the taxpayers of Kentucky. While we will incorporate many of the ideas advanced in previous research by Spindletop and reviewed by interested citizens (some of you who are here tonight) we have other approaches relating to the ultimate acquisition and refinement of such a needed facility. A businesslike attitude will prevail. I expect an early review of our plans, and I say to you, I want, as you want, this achievement for Kentucky and for your industry which merits our full cooperation now and in the future.[3]

Let me remind you of one vital point. The degree of excellence of this state attraction will depend upon those of you who are as sincere in this as am I. We must have your support, your input, your influence. Otherwise, we cannot, as one example, expect a truly characteristic museum absolutely necessary for the success of this undertaking. So I am extending the hand of a new administration, asking that you join in an enterprise justified by heritage, by common bond, and by plain old common sense.

There is another aspect to all this. Kentucky's participation in the national bicentennial year should be focused in part on one of its finest natural tourist attractions. As another example of our early efforts toward a Thoroughbred park, I have fully apprised the chairman of our bicentennial commission of our intentions. He, too, finds a direct correlation between such a venture and the period Kentucky can expect its greatest influx of tourists. Here then is the course we have set. It is in your best interest, and in Kentucky's best interest. Now let's get on with the work at hand.

---

1. In addressing the Thoroughbred Club's Annual Dinner Purse on April 18, 1973, and the National Turf Writers Annual Banquet on May 1, 1974, Governor Ford noted the efforts of his administration in behalf of the horse industry. These included the selection of the track bugler as the state symbol for national advertising, the introduction of a new model rulebook for the Racing Commission, and the appointment of Keene Dangerfield as senior

steward for the Commission. These speeches are not included in this volume.

2. At a press conference in the Lexington Springs Motel, on September 26, 1972, Governor Ford announced the state's purchase of the 963-acre Walnut Stud Farm for $2.7 million. The farm, situated between Ironworks Road and I-75, was chosen as the site for the Thoroughbred State Park. The remarks at the conference are not included in this volume.

3. Governor Ford reaffirmed his support of the horse park in a press conference on May 24, 1974, which is not included here. He announced that, despite the lack of supportive federal funds, construction would begin, financed by state revenue bonds. Plans for the park included a visitor activity complex, a model farm, a camping area, and an area reserved for the horse association headquarters.

GOBBLER'S KNOB
Gilbertsville / May 19, 1972

A LEASE agreement was entered into by the Commonwealth of Kentucky and a private corporation, Holiday Camp Grounds, Inc., for the private commercial development of campsites on an area known as Gobbler's Knob at Kentucky Dam Village State Resort Park (December 1, 1971). This eleventh-hour lease granted during the last days of the Nunn administration violates public policy of development of Kentucky's state park system. It will allow private developers to preempt a portion of the park system for their own profit.

This private commercial development contains plans for the construction of 200 campsites, including a sewage treatment plant and trailer waste disposal system. This will be built by the lake and will discharge into the lake. I am convinced this will be in direct violation of the public policy of Kentucky with regard to water pollution. In addition, the proposed sewage treatment plant outlet is approximately 3,500 feet from the beach area, thereby endangering human habitation and the peoples' right to enjoy their state park system. Our public policy is clear: "The purpose of water pollution control laws is to safeguard from pollution the uncontaminated waters of the Commonwealth, and to prevent the creation of any new pollution of the waters of the Commonwealth."

What is more appalling is that the grading of the Gobbler's Knob area was done with state equipment and state personnel at the expense of the taxpayers of the Commonwealth. With full knowledge of this, former Governor Nunn, at the State Property and Building Commission meeting on November 24, 1971, made the motion for approval of the leasing agreement to private interests. This agreement and plan for private commercial development is jeopardizing the future public development of Kentucky's great park system. It is a precedent which endangers the health of Kentuckians using the water resources of this park for recreation.

I am, today, requesting the Commissioner of the Department of Finance to give notice of a State Property and Building Commission meeting for Wednesday, May 31. The commission will review the critical nature of the environmental and park system development implications of this lease, and, if necessary, move that the commission rescind and void this lease which I believe endangers the future public development and the reputation of our entire park system in Kentucky.

NATURAL BRIDGE
STATE PARK ASSOCIATION
Slade / November 10, 1972

TOURISM is a big and growing business in Kentucky. Last year 585 million tourist dollars were spent in our state. Out-of-state visitors contributed $426 million of this to Kentucky's tourist trade while traveling over 5 billion miles on Kentucky highways. The impact of this out-of-state trade in the Commonwealth is significant. It means nearly $150 million in personal income to Kentuckians as well as $46 million in state tax revenue and nearly $11 million of tax revenue going to local governments.

Statistics from our Parks Department show that we are improving on this. These figures show that we had 25.5 million visitors at Kentucky state parks last year, and estimates for 1972 are running at 28 million. Estimates indicate Natural Bridge will experience a large increase this year, or about 1.25 million visitors. Already this year, over 1,150,000 visitors have come to Natural Bridge.

There are many reasons for our popularity as a tourist state. One survey to determine what it was that tourists wanted to see on their travels showed that over 80 percent were simply "sightseers"—out to personally view the many historic areas and the natural beauty. This group of sightseers was further broken down, and it was learned that 71 percent were out to see the scenery, 58 percent wanted to see a famous place, 53 percent wanted to see a historical sight, and 40 percent wanted to see some natural phenomenon. I think you understand what this means for your area. The visitor here cannot only walk trails that Daniel Boone once walked, but he can see some of the most spectacular scenery our state has to offer. In short, you have a very exploitable commodity in the natural resources and historical significance of this area. Tourism, of course, is the cleanest industry we can have in terms of ecology. All of the small businesses and services that benefit from tourism are also in the "clean" category.

State government has traditionally supported the tourist industry in Kentucky. We have done this through our highway program and by developing the finest state park system in the country. We are also doing our best to promote tourism, to make people want to come to our state and feel comfortable and welcome while they are here. We now do this by using a combination of methods. We stepped up our national promotional campaign through magazines and newspapers. We increased our fall advertising campaign by 50 percent. This included nineteen publications like *Better Homes and Gardens, Redbook, Southern Living, Ladies' Home Journal, Progressive Farmer, Good Housekeeping,* and other prominent magazines. The circulation from these publications is nearly 5 million. Our spring campaign will be up about 30 percent and should reach 50 million people. The newspaper advertising will go to seventy cities having the greatest potential attraction.

We are giving Kentucky more exposure as a tourist state in major cities such as Cleveland, Columbus, and Detroit by participation in sport and vacation shows and through personal contacts. In fact, we recently distributed 125,000 pieces of promotional literature at the Canadian National Exposition in Toronto; we have added five cities in this type of promotion. Kentucky is getting a major share of the growing Canadian tourist travel. We recently completed a seven-day tour with AAA counselors from fifteen states and Toronto. This familiarizes people who plan tours from other states into Kentucky. Emphasis is put on the resort parks, such as Natural Bridge, which stay open year-round. New promotional materials are being developed for distribution to more than 600 automobile clubs, as well as other travel organizations, and to send to travel writers now working on special articles.

One of the major promotional contributions on which our Department of Public Information is now working is a seventy-two-page book promoting Kentucky travel and attractions. This book will not cost the state any additional expense because it will incorporate many separate brochures now utilized but too often tossed aside. The book will be ready by spring and is being designed as a permanent guide for our visitors. We have also stepped up our production of audio-visual promotional materials. This includes a new mini-travel film program, prepared by our staff at a considerable savings over commercial contracts. We also receive over 2,000 inquiries per day from March through July on Kentucky vacation possibilities. Every one is answered.

While on the subject of what the state is doing to promote tourism in Kentucky, I want to emphasize we are at the same time making our park system more economically sound through prudent management. Labor costs statewide at our parks ran $6,342,000 in fiscal year 1971–1972 for the period of January through September. During this same period for 1972–1973, the costs were $6,006,000. The effect of this high cost of running a state park is reflected in the net loss Natural Bridge suffered last year, $104,000. We are estimating a net loss of only $25,000 this year, and we expect park management here to meet that goal. We are glad to promote the state through our programs and to see that our park system is managed properly. This is our obligation. Yet I also know that we have to have the cooperative partnership of local businesses and governments. It is to your advantage to join the effort to sell Kentucky. Many of you are dependent on tourist trade for maintaining the local economy.

The study I mentioned earlier pointed to one way of getting the sales pitch to people which remains the most successful. This is the word-of-mouth technique, the oldest and most reliable means of selling tourism. Obviously this is the main intent of our tour and travel shows, but it has much more significance to groups such as yours. Each time a tourist returns home from his travels, he is going to tell a lot of other people about his trip. If the traveler tells a good story, more families will return to the same spot to "see it for themselves." This is called the multiplier effect. More good stories mean more good tourists.

If you can give the visitors to this resort park a good story to take home with them, you will see them and their friends in future years. This kind of a multiplier effect means a healthy local economy. So let's remember that we all have a part to play in selling Kentucky. From the governor's office in Frankfort to the room clerk at this resort, we want people to take a favorable story back with them after their visit to the Commonwealth.

By the time of our 1974 bicentennial celebration, it is estimated that

102 million people, 46 percent of the total U.S. population, will be within a day-and-a-half drive of Kentucky. This is a pretty sizable market for tourism. I promise that state government will continue to do its part in promoting Kentucky. We also will continue our highway programs and facility development. If we work together, we can continue to accelerate tourism in the Commonwealth. Let's join in this effort with new conviction and dedication. Let's give our visitors a good story to take home with them.

OPENING OF THE PATTON MUSEUM
Fort Knox / November 11, 1972

I AM proud to be a part of these ceremonies today, not only because we are dedicating a monument to a great military leader but also because this tribute to him was inspired by citizens of Kentucky.[1] Six years ago the possibility of constructing a new building to house the Patton Museum was nothing more than an idea—a farfetched one at that. But a group of private Kentucky businessmen took it upon themselves to do something about it. They formed the Cavalry Armor Foundation, Inc., for the expressed purpose of raising enough money to make the project a reality. They launched an international fundraising drive, and with the help of many, finally succeeded.

Today, we admire part of the fruit of their labor. This building was constructed at a cost of $250,000, all from private contributions that the foundation raised. It is the first building of a four-phase museum complex that the foundation envisions. The museum is a living history of the United States Army's cavalry and armor branches. I am sure that after seeing the museum, you will agree that it is more than just a storehouse for military hardware or an educational site. It is a vivid memory of part of the price Americans have paid in order that we might live in a free country.

What also impresses me about this project is that everyone in the area, civilians and military alike, became involved. Cooperation pulled this project through, the same spirit of cooperation General Patton required for victory in battle, though I don't think he ever fought one that lasted six years, like this one did.

To the best of our knowledge this is the only military museum of its kind in the United States. Colonel Wendell Prince,[2] chief of plans and operations at the museum, has predicted that it will become one of the most popular tourist attractions in Kentucky. We hope the colonel is right. We will do all we can to help. Last year, more than 300,000 visitors from across the United States came to see the museum. A survey of this group showed that 60 percent came to Fort Knox solely to see the museum. It is anticipated that a half-million people will visit this new facility the first year. When these people come, they will also see Kentucky; therefore, all of Kentucky can benefit.

I know that patriotism and respect for General Patton were major factors in inspiring the Kentucky founders of the Cavalry Armor Foundation to undertake this project. I think the popularity of this museum is testimony that the same feeling is shared by many people across Kentucky and throughout America. So it is an honor for me to participate and a pleasure to help open what is really a memorial to democracy, to bravery, and to those ideals which have made America the greatest nation in the world—the ideals that tyranny, oppression, and ruthless world political desires will never overcome man's God-given right to be free.

---

1. George Smith Patton, Jr. (1885–1945), San Gabriel, California; army officer and expert on tanks during World Wars I and II; aide-de-camp to General J. J. Pershing in World War I; major assignments in World War II as commander of United States Armed Forces on Moroccan West Coast, commander of Third Army (August 1944), and commander of Fifteenth Army (October 1945); promoted to four-star general (1945); recipient of numerous military honors, including the Distinguished Service Medal, the Silver Star, the Purple Heart, and the Congressional Medal of Honor for Life Saving. *Who Was Who in America, 1943–1950* (Chicago, 1950), 2:416.

2. Wendell Prince was a career officer who was later transferred to other posts and is now retired.

ANNUAL GOVERNOR'S
CONFERENCE ON TOURISM
Lexington / February 7, 1973

TODAY, we are announcing the 1972 Copeland report on travel in Kentucky.[1] In addition, I want to offer you a general outline of travel characteristics which will affect Kentucky and briefly mention some steps we are taking to make future Copeland studies even more impressive. The 1972 survey is exactly that—impressive. Thirty-six million more dollars were spent here by out-of-state travelers during 1972 than the previous year. Sixteen million more dollars were spent by Kentuckians as they visited throughout the Commonwealth. This means that while we are showing a substantial growth factor from in-state travelers, the rich cream, so vital to our overall economy is dramatically increasing, because we are bringing non-Kentuckians to every region of our state. And they're spending money.

I don't intend to burden you with a long list of facts and figures; you have a copy of Dr. Copeland's report. Yet, it is important that the general public be aware of the industry you represent and one in which we are so involved. Last year, $49.5 million in state taxes resulted from tourism and travel. The increase over 1971 is twice the annual budget for our entire Department of Public Information. And local taxes collected from tourists rose $900,000 over the previous year. In 1972, of the $635 million spent in Kentucky by travelers, $462 million represents out-of-state contributions to our economy. This is an 8.5 percent jump beyond 1971. The impact of this out-of-state tourist expenditure is significant. To Kentuckians it meant over $162 million in personal income. What would be our status without this support? I'm sure you know the answer.

I recommend your careful attention to the Copeland analysis. I make this request because it is a success story of far-reaching implications, pertaining to a segment of our economy deserving full understanding. After all, how many businesses in Kentucky produced $634 million last year alone, with 72 percent of the gross income being derived from outside the borders of this great state?

The tourist business is competitive. The battle for vacationers and other travelers grows more intense every year. This is another reason why I point with pride to our 1972 accomplishments; it's getting a lot tougher just to stay in the ball game. If we don't meet the competition, the trade goes elsewhere. New, innovative promotional efforts on the part of both state government and the private sector are mandatory. However, no matter the brilliance of our promotions, no matter the wealth of our natural beauty and recreational opportunities, unless there is another element, we will be plowed under by competition. That other element is hospitality.

Certainly we must offer scenic attractions, historic points of interest, outstanding facilities, good food, and a variety of "fun things" to do. But the key is the waitress, the room clerk, the guide, the dock operator, the shopkeeper, the station attendant, and I could go on and on. Visitors, no matter the duration or purpose of their stay, want to be welcomed. They want to be special for a while, and they deserve to receive the warmest degree of hospitality possible. Let us practice it more than we traditionally preach it. Obviously we are practicing hospitality. Nevertheless, I go back to competition and the tendency to rest on laurels. Other states and foreign countries are after our $635 million—which brings me to another point.

Foreign countries are becoming our strongest competitors. Through such programs as group trips and tour packaging, the lure of travel beyond the U.S. is becoming more attractive and less expensive than ever before. Tomorrow will be too late to meet this challenge. We must plunge head-on into the problem today. We are also noticing the trend toward regional tours. Today, people are thinking less of just visiting one state or one area. Our thinking and planning has to reflect this. Another characteristic of travel is the surging convention market. Many fine cities in Kentucky can attract conventions of varying sizes. This is a lucrative market to go after. Also we must not minimize the interest in quickie vacations. Businessmen find the need to unwind for three or four days every other month, which means they are looking for favorite locations where distance isn't prohibitive. Our geographical status tells us to aggressively pursue such a market.

Now, what is state government doing? We have stepped up our national newspaper and magazine promotional campaigns. Although this was done to some extent in previous years, there has been no real consistency until now. In 1970 about $30,000 went to national print advertising and in 1971 only about $10,000. We expended nearly $120,000 in 1972 and included nineteen prominent national magazines. We were able to generate more public consumption by concentrating on in-house advertising design, thereby having more dollars available for space purchase. The circulation of these magazines will enable us to reach 50 million persons because of our spring campaign. Newspaper advertising will go to seventy cities having the greatest potential tourist market.

We are expanding our personal contacts, have fifteen tourist, sport, and vacation shows planned for 1973, and are placing specific emphasis on the rapidly growing Canadian market. We are expanding our ability to generate feature stories and photographic layouts in national and international publications, and our files are brimming with the results. You simply can't overemphasize the importance of this inexpensive medium of calling attention to Kentucky. We have found success in bringing various editors, travel agency representatives, and tour counselors to Kentucky to let them see for themselves what we want others to know.

Also we have our parks system maintaining the strongest fiscal integrity ever and at the same time have improved service. We set a goal of saving one million dollars between June 1972 and July 1973 through new management programs. That goal was achieved in the first six months. As a result, an additional million dollars has become available to upgrade park facilities—money ordinarily which we would never have seen.

Finally, we have stepped up our production of audio-visual materials. This includes new mini-travel films prepared by our own staff for television and other viewing. I might mention that only in the last few weeks, one of the films was requested by British television.

This is only part of the story. It says what we are doing will benefit you. Yet everybody will benefit even more if we continue to find new ways of working together in the common purpose of getting more people to answer the call of Kentucky. Even more important, we want them to answer the call many times. In order to do this, we must work together. We must organize to achieve our goal.

---

1. For more information see speech from April 14, 1972, in this section, pp. 455–57.

KENTUCKY THOROUGHBRED
BREEDERS ASSOCIATION
Louisville / May 3, 1973

THERE is nothing like it. Each year at this time, the excitement seems greater and the anticipation more intense. Whatever you call it, the Derby, the Run for the Roses, the first leg of the Triple Crown, the race, it is the only event of its kind in the world. You have probably all heard the statement our great humorist, Irvin S. Cobb, made about the Derby: "Until you go to Kentucky and with your own eyes behold a Derby, you ain't never been nowhere and you ain't seen nothin'."[1]

When the horses step onto the track Saturday and the band starts playing "My Old Kentucky Home," we are all going to feel the familiar chills run up our backs. It's the same every year, the spirit stirred by that emotion-packed moment works in everybody. Yet the Derby itself is never the same. Each race has its own personality and its own character. Maybe it is this blend of the familiar, the traditional, with the expectation of something new that has helped to make this event what it is today. Ever since the first Derby, the interest in Kentucky on that first Saturday in May has grown. It continues to build toward the one-hundredth running, which also coincides with our bicentennial celebration. What a year that will be.[2]

Kentucky and her Thoroughbred industry have given the world an event unparalleled in the sports world. It has been mutually rewarding to our state and to your industry, and it can only continue to perpetuate itself each year. If there were ever a Kentucky without a Derby, there would have to be a race without a horse. A man walking around Churchill Downs one Derby day noticed a box with an empty seat in it. He stopped and said to the little old lady sitting next to it, "This is the first empty seat I've seen today." She replied, "Well, it belonged to my husband, but he died." He said, "It seems a shame to let such a good seat go to waste. Why didn't you give it to one of your relatives?" She said, "I would have, but they're all at the funeral." Your industry means much to this state and to this country. You have international impact.

---

1. Irvin S. Cobb, as quoted in *The 1936 Kentucky Derby Program* (Louisville, 1936), p. 52. Irvin Shrewsbury Cobb (1876–1944), Santa Monica, California; Kentucky author and humorist; staff writer and editor for nu-

merous local and national newspapers and magazines; radio personality; playwright and screenwriter. *Who's Who in America, 1943–1950* (Chicago, 1950), 2:120.

2. The one-hundredth Kentucky Derby was held in May 1974.

KENTUCKY'S WESTERN WATERWAYS ANNUAL MEETING
Cadiz / May 21, 1973

In the tourist industry, as with any business, there is a success formula. You begin with a salable product, you find markets and design a plan for tapping those markets, and you advertise. You make every effort to satisfy each customer, in order that he or she return, and equally as important, in order that he or she will pass a favorable word along to others. To put it more bluntly: you deliver the good product you advertise.

What is that product in the Western Waterways? Every person in this room has the answer. The product, wrapped into a single package, is family fun, entertainment, relaxation, and satisfaction. We can take the first principle of this formula—a salable product—as absolute in Kentucky's tourist trade. No other state in the country, in my opinion, can match our attributes. Certainly this is true in the Western Waterways area.

Just as western Kentucky is blessed with natural scenery, recreational, educational, and historical attractions, it also offers a variety of activities, easy accessibility, and comfort for the traveler. One national publication recently showered high praise on your region with the following comment: "With more than 170,000 acres of land and more than 3,500 miles of shoreline, the Land Between the Lakes is rapidly becoming a mid-American classic." There is no need for any of us here this evening to rehash the physical attributes of the Western Waterways. We know the territory, respect it, and want others to enjoy it.

Tourism is your business. Tourism is also a major responsibility of state government. When $635 million can be generated for Kentucky through the tourist and travel industry, the spin-off reaches every man, woman, and child in every county of our state. This happened in 1972, representing a whopping 8 percent increase over the previous year. And it came about through a cooperative effort between the state and private sectors—here and in all parts of Kentucky. As Governor, I am not only interested in seeing this state-private relationship grow, I am determined to follow through in those efforts which we can assemble to guarantee that your industry is improved by state government. To this end, there are certain commitments from me to you.

The first is publicity and advertising. The film shown earlier is a somewhat new concept utilizing the short feature approach to a single subject. Produced entirely by our Department of Public Information, it is one of several either already prepared or in the process of being made. Western Waterways can use a similar film. We're going to provide you with completed films, just for your region, through our department's budget and trained personnel. Such mini-films have widespread distribution, to television stations, local organizations, travel shows, and even to foreign countries.

For the first time in our state's history, we are offering a comprehensive magazine highlighting Kentucky's tourist bonanza. This new seventy-two-page, four-color book, now on the presses, will contain one section devoted to Western Waterways. Between July and next May, we will distribute enough copies to be read by over two million prospective visitors.

Advertising is critical. In past years little money was spent by the state toward national advertising, which meant you lost potential customers. This has been turned around, and we're now telling others about Kentucky, through major newspapers and magazines throughout the United States and Canada.

We also are operating state parks in the most businesslike manner ever achieved, recognizing they can indeed be a magnet to increase your own sales. I have directed that at no time will any underpricing of our services be permitted which might be incompatible with your business. We are bringing more and more visiting writers to Kentucky, escorting them on extensive tours of the state and providing them with materials for articles which cannot be valued in dollars and cents. Only recently we have had writers not only from many parts of America but also from Spain, England, and Holland.

Twice I have mentioned foreign countries. I have done so for a purpose. You and I have strong competition as we strive to expand our tourist industry. Other states are doing more and more to snare the tourist dollar. This is especially evident in their construction of park facilities. Groups of states are joining in package tours to lure visitors into a single region. But perhaps an even greater threat is the challenge from beyond the borders of our country. Americans are being attracted to other lands, and we must work together in finding ways to diminish the impact on our own business. Here is where Kentucky hospitality can play the most significant role.

Finally there is another problem facing the tourist and travel industry. A gasoline shortage does exist. At this time, there is no firm measurement of the shortage. Yet I hear of more and more vacationers who say they will take limited trips this year. The shortage could hurt unless we use some common sense in conserving gasoline in order to balance out supply and demand. Facts prove that reducing automobile speed from sixty to fifty miles an hour will conserve 11 percent of the gasoline used. From the information we have gathered through meetings with the petroleum industry, with the federal government, and through an exchange of data among other Governors, we believe there is, and will be, a gas shortage less than 11 percent. Obviously, the American people can solve this problem through self-discipline. And obviously, it is to our benefit that we encourage conservation in order that our travel industry might continue to grow.

Cooperation is the key. For instance, you cooperate with us in travel shows, and without you I know our efforts would not be as successful. We cooperate with you in providing promotional funds and materials. This spirit of working together can be a plus for all concerned. When we have it, everybody benefits. A $635 million industry in Kentucky is of paramount importance. Let's shoot for a $700 million goal, because when we reach it, Western Waterways will derive additional benefits, and we'll all walk down the road with a thoroughly satisfied smile on our faces.

FESTIVAL OF AMERICAN FOLKLIFE
Frankfort / June 25, 1973

DURING the past few months, and especially last week, Kentucky's participation in the Smithsonian Institution's Festival of American Folklife has received attention by the press.[1] By their informing the public about our unique program in Washington on July 4–8, I have detected in our press people a strong sense of pride throughout the

Commonwealth. Indeed, we are proud to have been selected as the national showcase state. This event, and the tremendous amount of work which has gone into it already, illustrate a measure of state government effectiveness which frequently goes unnoticed.

As Governor, I want Kentucky to receive the favorable recognition of others because this state and her people have much to offer and deserve such recognition. I'm sure you realize the different ways various states are viewed from the outside. It has been our determination during these first eighteen months to revitalize Kentucky's image throughout the nation and to place the many good sides of her face before those who look at us. Such a theme has been adopted, for instance, by our Department of Public Information. Public Information was given the responsibility of coordinating the Smithsonian's Festival.

My fourth meeting with Smithsonian and National Parks Service officials was last week in Washington. After pegging some tobacco, I reviewed final plans for the festival. I'm enthused about the event. Over one million visitors from all over the world are expected to see Kentucky on display, and you can't fully measure the benefits and value in dollars and cents. The festival will accomplish many things for Kentucky and will correspondingly benefit countless Kentuckians. It will show our great heritage, folklore, culture, and traditions. It will provide a forum for Public Information to tell others about the state and her peoples through the hospitality center. It will encourage family tourism which is invaluable to our economy. It will be an educational program of large dimensions. It will give us an opportunity to extend our hospitality through the approximately two hundred participants who can all become ambassadors of goodwill. It will bring joy into the hearts of our guests and, I believe, leave them with a warm feeling about the Bluegrass state.

It will also generate invaluable national and international publicity about Kentucky. This has been a massive undertaking on the part of state government with little fanfare, which is how state government often functions—getting the job done for people in a quiet, efficient manner. We have had tremendous cooperation from the private sector, along with the Smithsonian and the National Parks Service. The state's investment in dollars is extremely small compared to the anticipated return—about $40,000. As of today, we have received in-kind and cash contributions from the private sector amounting to approximately $75,000. The Smithsonian and National Parks Service, in addition to providing the facilities, will spend from $80,000 to $100,000 just on the Kentucky portion of the festival.

This morning's occasion marks our move to the nation's capital and is designed to familiarize you with the event. A number of individuals who have worked hard and long on the festival are with me, along with others as interested citizens who have played a major role in assisting the Kentucky program. In addition, a small representative portion of the participants have joined us to perform as they will in Washington.[2]

Public Information Commissioner Tom Preston and deputy commissioner Bob Whitaker are available for any particular questions you may have regarding the folklife festival.[3]

---

1. Governor Ford announced at a press conference on December 7, 1972, that Kentucky had been selected as one of six states to be represented at the Smithsonian Festival. At that time he said the festival would be held along the Greensward of the Reflecting Pool, near the Lincoln Memorial.

2. At the end of the briefing Governor Ford introduced the following individuals, noted for their contributions to the festival: Bob Berryman, Frank Dailey, Dr. G. W. Stokes, Ted Atkinson, Dave Hooper, James Nance, Alfred Bailey, John Edmonds, the "Gospel Truth" Singers, Hobert Rogers, Buddy Thomas, Mrs. Gifford Lowe, and Mrs. Hazel Miracle.

3. Thomas L. Preston (1934–   ), Carrollton; publisher and owner of the Cynthiana Publishing Company, Inc. (1959–1968); owner, Thomas L. Preston Public Relations (1969–   ); special assistant to the Governor for Information and Communications (1971–1974); commissioner, Department of Public Information (1971–1973); administrative assistant to Senator Wendell H. Ford (1975). Telephone interview with Preston, September 28, 1977. Bob C. Whitaker (1936–   ), Bardstown; deputy commissioner of Kentucky Department of Public Information (1971–1973), commissioner (1973–1974); executive director, Kentucky Historical Events Celebration Commission (1975); associate director, University of Kentucky Alumni Association (1975–   ). Biographical sketch from Whitaker, September 1977.

KICKOFF PREVIEW FOR
THE KENTUCKY '74 CELEBRATION
Frankfort / July 26, 1973

FROM the presentation which has just been revealed, the answers to what has become a general question should emerge. That question has been: "What in the world are they doing about Kentucky's bicentennial?" Any undertaking of this scope requires months of advanced planning, countless meetings with interested citizens throughout Kentucky, and a coordinating effort where alterations and changes are routine. Obviously, until a package is assembled, there is little of substance to tell. That package is taking shape.[1]

Once again, Kentucky pioneers new frontiers. Once again, we have seized the opportunity to show America and the world the kind of pioneering effort and enthusiasm which is our heritage of greatness. Daughter of the East and mother of the West, Kentucky is the symbol of pioneer America. But as we look to the year ahead, let's remember those who have given us that status. It was people like you who are in this room today who made Kentucky what it was, and is.

Individual effort, community and civic pride, kinship ties—these add up to achievement and new frontiers. People with a sense of history and commitment working together for the advancement of their fellow Kentuckians reflect a wonderful legend. Now it is up to us, today's Kentuckians, to put forth that same individual effort, to rally that same community and civic pride, to open up our family tradition so we can show the nation how to celebrate a two-hundredth birthday.

State government is a partner in this celebration. We have helped in the planning and have provided funding. We will be sponsoring some statewide activities as you heard today. But if the bicentennial is to succeed in the way we hope it will, it will be up to you and the people of our state. Only through a grass-roots campaign will the true wealth of our state be recognized. I hope every county in the state becomes part of this great celebration. We are rich in history and and in natural beauty, but it is our people who will make the lasting impression on the many visitors expected for the bicentennial. When they come to the Commonwealth, we want the celebration they see to be a true celebration of Kentuckians. No matter where they chart their trips, there should be a reminder of the greatness that is Kentucky and a personal warmth from every door that opens to them.

We gave the country a pretty good sampling of what awaits the visitor to our state while we were in Washington for the Smithsonian Festival. A lot of people will be coming to Kentucky in 1974 to see more. They will be looking at our tobacco country, river towns, the rolling bluegrass, the rugged mountains, lake country, and city life. They will be listening to our music, visiting our shrines, applauding our drama, and watching us work. They will see past and present.

Kentuckians have never been shy about bragging on our state and our communities, and now is the time to put together a show which will be the model for America's two-hundredth birthday. We are making plans interlaced with America's bicentennial. But today shows that Kentucky can be ready. We have a couple of years on the other states, and our own celebration will be the proving ground to illustrate how it is done.

As you leave today, take this message back home with you and spread the word—we are going to throw a people's party and every Kentuckian will host the celebration! Kentucky pioneers new frontiers because Kentuckians have always cared for their state and country in a special way. Now we can show how.[2]

---

1. Kentucky's Bicentennial celebration commemorated the two-hundredth anniversary of the first serious attempt at settlement, near the present site of Harrodsburg, in 1774. This community, established by James Harrod, Isaac Hite, James Sandusky, and twenty-nine other men, lasted only several months. The first permanent settlement in Kentucky was begun by Harrod on March 15, 1775, at a nearby location. Statehood status was not given to the territory until June 1, 1792. Thomas D. Clark, *A History of Kentucky* (Lexington, 1960), pp. 36, 41, 91.

2. On August 5, 1974, Governor Ford delivered a similar address on the steps of the Old Capitol and raised the Bicentennial State Flag for the first time. This address is not included in this volume.

FORT BOONESBOROUGH
STATE PARK DEDICATION
Boonesboro / August 30, 1974

THEY tell me it only took Daniel Boone three months to build the original Fort Boonesborough. It took us a year to reconstruct it, but you have to remember we didn't have the Indians looking over our neck to inspire us. As we look around us, we can see it was well worth the wait. Daniel Boone would have been proud of what has been accomplished here. I only wish I could personally thank all of the individuals who had a part in making this fort a reality; time will not permit it. Before we officially dedicate the fort, a brief review of Fort Boonesborough's history is in order.

In April 1775 Daniel Boone built a small fort, made up of two cabins which was known as "Fort Boone." Colonel Richard Henderson, the head of the Transylvania Company which financed Boone's expedition, arrived some time later. He wasn't satisfied with the size and location of the fort and ordered a larger one built at a site further up the river. This fort, completed in 1776, was "Fort Boonesborough."

Every effort has been made in this reconstruction to preserve the natural setting and scenic beauty of the area. We wanted the fort to be situated in surroundings similar to what they might have been when Daniel Boone walked these woods 200 years ago. The fort itself was constructed as it might have been by Boone's party—except, of course, for the air conditioning and electricity. No nails were used. The logs are notched to hold themselves in place. The shingles are slabs of wood held in place by poles, and the basic structure is as close to the original as we were able to determine. This is fitting, since the fort is, after all, a monument to the brave men and women who settled this area 200 years ago. Despite the hardship of primitive living conditions, these hardy pioneers were able to carve a society out of the wilderness.

In Fort Boonesborough, we can get an idea of how the people lived. Craftsmen are located throughout the fort, making everything from pottery to quilts. A blacksmith shop is in the center of the fort, so you can see how the early settlers forged their tools. The setting is designed to present a realistic picture of pioneer life. The timing of the completion of the restoration is perfect, because this is the first year of Kentucky's 1974 to 1976 Bicentennial celebration. The early settlers of this area contributed much to the history of our state and country. This new fort will give us the opportunity to offer visitors another part of Kentucky's living history. As one of Kentucky's outstanding tourist attractions, this fort should also be a positive stimulus to this area's economy. Tourism is a big business in Kentucky—$699 million last year alone—and this area makes a major contribution to that total.

In closing, I want to extend my personal appreciation to the Fort Boonesborough Association, the historical societies of Clark, Madison, and Fayette counties, the chambers of commerce and bicentennial organizations in these counties, other civic clubs, and all the interested individuals who worked so hard in making this fort a reality. Their input and assistance were invaluable, and what we see here today is the fruit of their labor. The determination of these groups and local residents to keep our history alive is bound to ensure the successful future of this park, which represents such a great part of Kentucky's rich heritage.[1]

---

1. Governor Ford also spoke at the ground-breaking ceremonies for the park's reconstruction on June 28, 1973. This speech is not included in this volume.

DEDICATION OF
NEW WELCOME CENTER
I-65 at Kentucky-Tennessee Line / September 26, 1974

THIS particular occasion is significant because it brings to your attention a very important tool in our economic program of tourism and travel. Here is an investment in Simpson County of nearly a half-million dollars, a mini-agency if you prefer, designed to serve people and help stimulate our huge tourist business. We don't just have a building and rest area. We have an important facility, to be manned by competent and interested personnel, for the benefit of many. I cannot overemphasize the role this center will play in creating an atmosphere so necessary to the $700 million plus Kentucky tourist industry, our Commonwealth's second-leading industry. An information center is no better than the people who run it, and you in this area have a reputation for extending traditional, warm Kentucky hospitality.

Historically, Kentucky has been a leader in establishing rest areas and information centers. This center is a first. Its modern contemporary architecture contains twice the number of comfort stations, and the skylight design increases its lighting while saving energy. Plans have been made to build information centers at each port-of-entry into the state. During this administration, as promised, we will complete two of these centers—one here in Simpson County, and the other at Fulton. The Simpson County information center serves on the south-central port-of-entry into Kentucky. Tourists can travel to the scenic Cumberland Lakes and eastern Kentucky highlands by the nearby Cumberland Parkway; to Louisville, the Bluegrass, and to northern Kentucky by arteries off I-65; and to western Kentucky by the connecting Green River Parkway. Kentucky is one of the few states that offers our southern travelers a northbound "information center," since most states only serve people coming from the north, but we like our southern neighbors too.

Kentucky's rest and information centers are designed for the safety, comfort, and convenience of the traveling public. They operate to serve the public through a joint effort of the state Department of Public Information and Bureau of Highways. Some of the services this center will offer include a picnic area for family outings, the availability of information specialists on duty eight hours a day, seven days a week, twenty-four-hour-a-day rest-room service, and printed materials that will be available to help make the travelers' visit to Kentucky more meaningful and enjoyable. Five information specialists will be employed to maintain this center.

As you know, millions of dollars are spent each year to promote Kentucky, but the people of all areas are Kentucky's key salesmen. As "goodwill ambassadors" they determine the length of stay and how many dollars the traveler spends in our state. I want to point out our rest areas and information centers work for all people—the privately owned motels, hotels, restaurants, and fine attractions—by providing information not only on state parks and shrines but also supplying informative literature and telling the traveling public about all the fine accommodations and scenic attractions offered in this region. Every section of the state is depending on the personnel of this center— your cave region, Bardstown, Lexington, Lake Cumberland, Louisville, to name only a few—to sell tourists on Kentucky. Many tourist associations have already expressed great enthusiasm for this Simpson County center and have high expectations for it. Your center provides the means for attracting more tourists to your region and to all of Kentucky.

COMMUNITY DEVELOPMENT

LOUISVILLE AREA
CHAMBER OF COMMERCE LUNCHEON
Louisville / January 17, 1972

THE risk of one's wearing out his welcome is when he makes frequent appearances before the same organization. You were kind enough to have me on the program last week. Now I show up again. This occasion, however, is highlighted by the installation of a close friend as president of your Chamber of Commerce. Therefore, it becomes a special event, and I am honored to be selected for a return appearance on this particular day.

One of Wilson Wyatt's unsurpassed skills is that of a public speaker.[1] He has the very rare ability to hold any audience in the palm of his hand. His choice of words and God-given style of delivery are unique examples of beauty within the framework of public speaking. The opportunities he has to put this to use as president will bring lasting credit to the image of Louisville and Kentucky. Wilson Wyatt speaking out for his community, and for his state, is our good fortune. It has a value without limit.

I appear this noon as a former Lieutenant Governor in behalf of a former Lieutenant Governor. I appear as one who has assumed a new role of leadership in behalf of another who has assumed a new role of leadership. In many respects, our ambitions, goals, and responsibilities parallel.

Louisville's successes and failures have financial and social impact on people throughout the state. It is in Kentucky's best interest for Louisville and Jefferson County to succeed in efforts to improve its quality of life. Therefore, I find great comfort in the fact that Wilson Wyatt will become even more active in an area where 22 percent of all Kentuckians live, in an area he loves so dearly.

It is no secret that for some years I have been a "Louisville watcher." I want this city, like all our state, to meet its challenges. Yours are often unusual. Many times we don't recognize the singular problems of Louisville, because we are not residents and don't identify with the problems. I do not underestimate the size of the challenge you and I jointly face. I'm sharply aware that I took office as Governor when there were nearly 15,000 unemployed people in Jefferson County, over 55,000 persons living on welfare or public assistance, and even 29,000 more living on food stamps. I am sharply aware that Louisville can advance only through necessary legislation which gives impetus to the leadership you have, to a potential, waiting ignition.

The day I became Governor, I asked one of the very capable young men of this community to begin work in my office for the purpose of helping me help metropolitan areas such as yours. His is a new assignment. It is a Governor's office first. It is another step in the fulfillment of my campaign pledge to you. Where necessary, legislation is being drafted. Where practical, new ideas are being formulated. Where possible, funds are being secured.

With Wilson Wyatt in the president's chair here, I feel we have added momentum in Frankfort. He knows what you need and how to go about getting it. He is aware of my desire to create an Urban Affairs Agency with the purpose not being to help state government, rather it will be to help local government and urban communities. I'm going to ask the legislature to make home rule something more than a century-old campaign phrase. You know the ancient and ridiculous situation by which the elected government of your city and county must come to Frankfort and ask for a specific new law. This happens everytime you need anything done that hasn't been done before. It all goes back to a theme I have projected for quite some time: government exists to serve people. It does not exist to make life needlessly difficult.

Your new president has distinguished himself in obtaining new industry for Kentucky. The coming years call for this achievement to be excelled if your community and your state are to keep pace with the nation. As competition grows tougher each day, so must our ambitions and energies gain muscle. A key element of our drive will be the seeking of corporate headquarters, light industry, and service-oriented businesses in addition to heavy industry. You can expect a strong partnership between Frankfort and Louisville in this endeavor.

To show our determination of growth, there must be specific state interest to enhance this growth. The budget which I will soon present will, in part, give attention to a major vocational training facility to serve this metropolitan community; increased state financial support of the University of Louisville as a state university where tuitions should be reduced; the provision of added community college services to Southwest Jefferson County; and crime prevention and the drive against drug abuse. I offer these as some examples of our present consideration. I offer them as examples of our interest in you.

I share with you the excitement of seeing Louisville's skyline change for the better. As community leaders and as a Chamber of Commerce you want this area to prosper. You want to make Louisville a city where good living is the pattern, not the exception. You want improved education, the elimination of traffic jams, marked business growth, jobs for people, and safety in your homes and on your streets. I want the same thing, for you and for all Kentuckians. I am anxious, Wilson, to see how good a team two former Lieutenant Governors can be in working with the people in this room and throughout this area to help Louisville, and Kentucky, move forward. I extend to you my sincere best wishes and congratulations. I extend to this organization my compliments for a decision well made.

---

1. Wilson Watkins Wyatt (1905–   ), Democrat from Louisville; attorney; mayor of Louisville (1941–1945); Lieutenant Governor of Kentucky (1959–1963); member, Board of Trustees, University of Louisville (1950–1958), chairman (1951–1955); first president of the Young Democrats Club, Louisville-Jefferson County. *Who's Who in America, 1974–1975* (Chicago, 1975), 2:3380.

STATE PAYMENT
OF UTILITY RELOCATION
Frankfort / March 27, 1972

THE purpose of this announcement is to illustrate one more way state government can, and should, be responsive to the needs of people. It often becomes necessary to relocate utility fixtures which exist on public right-of-ways. These include wires, poles, towers, cables, pipes, mains, conduits, fireplugs, and other appliances belonging to a municipality or a municipally owned utility or water district. Such action, as the cost is borne by the utility or municipality, has resulted in higher rates or local taxes paid by individuals.

An excellent case in point is northern Kentucky. Many projects of an immediate nature, or scheduled for the near future, demand the relocating of utilities from public right-of-ways. Nearly $2 million in relocation expense for removal and relocation of utilities in that one section of the state is currently planned. Great concern has been expressed that the cost would have to be passed along to those citizens living in northern Kentucky because of the projects. But state government has a solution. And I am happy to announce the introduction of an administration bill, with bipartisanship sponsorship, to eliminate the burden on people.

With the passage of this act,[1] all costs will be assumed by the Kentucky Department of Highways and through the acquisition of federal funds, which we have been assured will become available to Kentucky. This prevents any pass-along expenses to the citizens. In simple terms, we have discovered a problem and have worked to remedy that problem in the best interest of all involved. This is what government is about, and I want all Kentuckians to know of our determination to improve their lot. In addition to the massive undertakings in Boone, Kenton, and Campbell counties, there are other planned projects throughout the Commonwealth whereby this bill will grant relief to the individual's pocketbook. For instance, there are planned utility relocations at Ashland, Louisville, Lexington, Frankfort, Harlan, Monticello, and numerous other communities where this will prove its profound value.

The act carries an emergency clause, and when signed by me, will cover relocation of facilities after January 1, 1972. I urge the General Assembly to give quick and positive attention to this measure and appreciate the interest expressed by the northern Kentucky delegation representing both our major political parties.

---

1. See an act "providing for payment by Department of Highways for the removal and relocation of facilities owned by a municipality or a municipally owned utility, or a Water District established pursuant to Chapter 74 or a Sanitation District established pursuant to Chapter 220 of the Kentucky Revised Statutes," which was approved on March 27, 1972. *Acts of the General Assembly of the Commonwealth of Kentucky, 1972,* Chapter 361 (H.B. 498), pp. 1603–4.

LEXINGTON KIWANIS CLUB
Lexington / April 25, 1972

THE other evening while speaking at Keeneland to the Thoroughbred Club of America, I announced our intention to build a new state park in Fayette County. Reaction has been enthusiastic. People had become somewhat frustrated after a series of promises, news stories, and studies relating to a Thoroughbred park. In fact, they waited in vain for positive action. You won't have a repeat performance. I have already directed my Commissioner of Parks to pursue this venture, and pursue it with dispatch. Our target date is the Kentucky bicentennial year, because I want this exciting educational, recreational facility to be prepared for the expected surge of tourists coming to Kentucky in 1974.

Such an undertaking will mean economic stimulation for this area in particular and Kentucky in general. I think it points out the attitude of a new administration. That attitude is simply "getting the job done for people through government service." You know, we haven't been on the scene for five months yet, but you can already mark our efforts, and I am proud of this activity, substance rather than words. The next biennial budget proves this. Recently enacted legislation proves this. Programs under way in the first 100 days prove this.

Now I want to make another announcement. One of the major themes of my budgetary and legislative package was substantial improvement of our entire criminal justice system, from the policeman on the beat right through probation and parole. Too often this subject receives little applause from the general public. Though when we consider the frightening cost of criminal justice when substandard programs are employed, we are not fulfilling our duties in the best interest of the general public. Repeated confinement is expensive, unnecessarily so when modern and proven programs can be initiated whereby the great majority of those incarcerated can be returned to society as productive citizens. We plan to initiate a series of proven programs.

One such program is in this community. No longer will the former Kentucky Village-Department of Child Welfare Facility be abandoned. As an essential element in the overall upgrading of Kentucky's correctional services, we will establish a multipurpose correctional center, housing approximately 200 inmates. This new center will involve essentially three priorities: the treatment and education of selected first offenders; the gradual prereleasing of those offenders normally returning to the general region surrounding Lexington; and a work and maintenance unit. This is a minimum security institution dictated by the type of persons chosen to live there. We must better define our classes of prisoners and manage them according to the nature of their offense, psychological adjustment, rehabilitative potential, and proven conduct.

Society does itself an injustice when it transforms the first offender or the individual who has every indication for quick rehabilitation into a hardened criminal because of his environment and absence of professional therapy. During this first period, the Department of Corrections plans to transfer a work detail to Kentucky Village for renovation. In other words, we will save money by doing the job ourselves. We have a Frankfort work detail, a prisoner-maintenance crew on duty in the Capitol and in state office buildings under the supervision of the Department of Finance. They now return to the correctional facility at LaGrange each evening.

After initial renovations have been completed, the prerelease and first offender groups will be included at the center, with full operations planned by March 1973. Treatment programs to be offered will involve the establishment of a therapeutic community, stressing the development of self-control. Education and vocational training will be provided to prepare the youths for a more successful experience in the community. Prerelease will generally involve only those who have families in, or would be normally returning to, the Bluegrass region. This new facility will attempt to alleviate partially two problems currently facing the Department of Corrections. As of April 14, the department's institutions were approximately 50 percent over their rated housing capacities. We are also committed to eliminating the shock involved in any sudden release of a man from within an institution back to the community. This prerelease will work and, in the long run, taxpayers won't be burdened with the added costs of repeated institutionalizing.

Here is but one step in our plan. I could talk to you about emphasis on a newly constituted probation and parole system, or on the accelerated funding of programs to combat crime, or the goals we have placed through revenue-sharing to improve the caliber of police officers, and so on. But briefly, let me conclude these remarks by offering other facts I believe you will be interested in as they pertain to state government's attention to Fayette County.

What has our first budget meant to you, in round figures? The past two years state government allocated $19.9 million to the foundation program for elementary and secondary schools. The new budget increase is over $4.25 million. At the University of Kentucky we provided $26.9 million more and provided over an 18 percent increase at the Lexington Technical Institute. The Louisville Technical Institute received $5 million the first two years, and this facility will be administered by the University of Kentucky. There are substantial increases in mental health services, public assistance, and funds for agricultural services. The new state revenue-sharing program to cities for street construction and maintenance means $721,752 to Lexington. Remember, this releases local funds for other needed projects ordinarily used for road building and repairs.

You also should be aware of this undisputed fact. Through our restructuring of the tax program, the individual Fayette Countian, just like the individual living elsewhere in Kentucky, will pay less state taxes and receive more services. This even takes into full consideration the two-cent gasoline tax state government must have to fulfill its obligation of bonded indebtedness and continue our highway construction and maintenance efforts, which must keep pace with tomorrow's demands for a traveling public.

I am sure many of you are interested in our plans for the Versailles Road, a dilemma of unusual magnitude considering all factors. The present width, volume of traffic, great number of entrances, and high accident rate all figure into the picture. The Highway Department is working toward a proper solution, but the department is also under no illusions that the remedy is simple. We canceled a previous contract for one reason; it did not solve anything. In fact, the canceled plan called for a third lane between Keeneland and the Bluegrass Field entrance. If anything, it only extended the problem and would have been money wasted. A median guard rail prompts critical analysis. Experts tell us that a rail between the narrow lanes will only cause more accidents, since inside lane drivers have a tendency to shy away from such rails. Perhaps the ultimate answer is extensive widening, a slow and expensive process because of the nature and location of this highway.

I am grateful for this opportunity to give you my first report. I trust it reflects a maximum of activity rather than a maximum of lip service. We plan to tell you what we are doing, rather than what we hope to do. As other examples, we have been successful in bringing the Interstate Mining Compact to Lexington where permanent headquarters are being established near Spindletop. Coal research, specifically to enhance the type mined in western Kentucky (presently being threatened due to its high-sulfur content), will be conducted at the University of Kentucky. We provided special funds for this purpose. Also at UK, we for the first time have funded in the School of Medicine a Department of Family Practice. Also I do not want to omit mentioning a new hearing clinic for Lexington, supported by the next budget.

This is what government is really all about—providing service instead of promises. I look forward to another date when I can again report further progress as it directly relates to your community.

LOUISVILLE CENTRAL AREA
Louisville / August 31, 1972

I UNDERSTAND the significance of this gathering tonight. The composition of this group serves to underscore the common purpose of a new urban partnership, and Wendell Ford wants to be a part of that partnership. You have shown how far-reaching the concern for your community is; it has stretched all the way to Frankfort on several occasions since I have been Governor! More important, you have shown how far-reaching the willingness to work for your community is, and I hope my remarks will illustrate an equal interest from the Ford administration.

Louisville and Jefferson County face a familiar urban crisis, one threatening cities across the country. We are at a crossroad. We can continue either the steady gains toward a higher quality of life for this community and the state or we must face the inevitable decay of urban life. The direction pursued in Louisville and Jefferson County has obvious implications for those living in this metropolitan area, but it also affects the health of our entire state. This community is Kentucky's largest industrial center, and one of the largest of the South. It has the largest market in the state and is our major transportation center. Louisville is one of the nation's largest rail, highway, and water terminals. It is also the financial center of the state. Because of these and other related factors, a huge portion of state revenues comes from Louisville and Jefferson County.

Urban areas have traditionally provided for the surplus of revenue that allows development of statewide programs. In turn, however, it is often statewide programs that attract people and businesses to our urban areas. This relationship is interdependent. We must work together to assure its survival and growth. My administration is acutely aware of the problems you face. We have noted the declining real estate values in downtown Louisville: a staggering loss of $16 million in the past ten years. We see the problems of pollution and the need for a rapid, mass transit system in the city. We see the same warning signs of urban decay that have grown to terrifying proportions in other cities across the country. While your need for urban services is growing at an accelerated rate, urban revenue is at the same time declining. Working with your delegation to the 1972 General Assembly and with help from many of you here tonight, this administration has begun a state commitment to urban Kentucky.

Our last General Assembly made Kentucky the first state to initiate a revenue-sharing program with its urban centers. Louisville and Jefferson County will realize nearly $3 million from this innovative program for street construction and repairs. A community college for southwestern Jefferson County was added to our state community college system and nearly a quarter of a million was added toward the development of its educational program. The Louisville and Jefferson County school systems will receive $19 million in additional state aid. A Louisville and Jefferson County Public Defender Corporation has been funded by the state at $224,000 annually. Also, to help ease the burden of litigation, two new judges were added to the Circuit Court system here. New facilities are to be added at Central State Hospital for the criminally insane and mentally disturbed at a cost to the state of $4.9 million. A $1.6 million renovation of the Fairgrounds Stadium and Freedom Hall is under way.[1]

In short, these and many other projects and programs coming out of my first biennial budget give Louisville and Jefferson County the largest amount of Kentucky's revenue in the state's history. On the legislative side, too, this was a good year for your greater metropolitan area. Kentucky is among the first states in the country to adopt an enlightened policy toward its cities by creating a home-rule relationship with the city of Louisville. Kentucky is the first state in the country to grant complete home rule to county residents. Even though we are going through a difficult period now of understanding just what home rule will mean to this area, I am sure all parties affected realize the great potential of this agreement.

Also the legislature enacted the Kentucky Low Income Housing Authority which will aid in providing low-income housing for many residents living in our urban communities. Before the Police Court Costs Bill was passed in the last General Assembly, the Louisville Police Court was the only such court in the state not authorized to levy court costs. The Jefferson County Improvement District legislation allowed sale of the bonds voted in 1970 and the Jefferson County Jail and Corrections Bill enables the county to build the new jail and create a Department of Corrections. By the way, nowhere has there been stronger emphasis and funding by the state than in helping your community fight crime and delinquency, again through an unprecedented legislative package.

I am, of course, proud of this administration's record with regard to its concern for urban problems. We have initiated more programs aimed at alleviating the crisis of our cities than has any other administration in the history of the Commonwealth. And let me say here and now, no one man could have accomplished all of this for you. Your senators and representatives deserve recognition as well as others in the General Assembly. The program movers we had, from Dee Huddleston in the Senate as majority floor leader and Norb Blume as Speaker of the House, were vitally important to you.[2] The hard facts are that without such leadership, Louisville and Jefferson County would not have fared as well, nor could I enumerate so many pluses for your community at this dinner. What I really feel in my heart is gratitude for the support so many have given my programs. Hundreds upon hundreds—and I wish I could introduce every one right now—played key roles in the success story we can present with pride.

You might recall that during my campaign for Governor I publicly presented a comprehensive program for 22 percent of Kentucky's people. This legislative packet was the product of a great number of individuals who joined me in designing a better life plan for this area. Then it was a campaign promise from Wendell Ford. But I intended to keep my word and this hour stand before you to review with confidence the results. If actions such as this will help restore credibility in government, then we have provided a bonus.

Our program for 22 percent of Kentucky's people dwelt on eleven specific topics. In the first eight months of this administration, we have already accomplished our goals in seven categories and either have partially accomplished or are now working toward ultimate accomplishment in the remaining four. I am equally pleased as a Kentuckian to see the efforts Louisvillians and Jefferson Countians have made with their own initiative, with their own money, and with their own hard work. State and federal governments can offer assistance to urban areas, but it is only through local drive and self-determination that the crisis of our cities can effectively be solved. You have shown these principles in many ways. Twice in the past four years the citizens of Jefferson County have voted to increase their own tax burden for the common purpose of improving their community. Throughout the state and nation similar referendums are failing for lack of local interest. The success in Jefferson County indicates a willingness of the people in this community to make the necessary sacrifices to build a better quality of life for future generations.

While on the subject of taxes, let there be no misunderstanding. Through our programs of tax reform, the individual Kentuckian will now pay less taxes and receive more services than before. The sales tax on food will be completely eliminated in thirty days. Throughout Kentucky this will have a healthy effect on our economy, and certainly on the pocketbooks of those least able to pay. Your city and county governments have also extended their financial resources to improve this community. The city of Louisville has pledged all of its parking-meter revenues for the next thirty years to build the Riverfront Parking Garage. This facility serves as the functional nucleus for one of the most exciting urban projects in the country. On top of the garage is the Galt House and the Louisville Trust Building. Jefferson County has recently announced plans to construct a $12–14 million jail and courthouse complex. The city of Louisville used urban renewal funds to clear the east urban renewal area where your magnificent $75 million medical center is now located.

Other improvements in health facilities for this area can be seen in the expansion at Jewish and Methodist hospitals, the new Dosker Manor, and Children's Norton Hospital, now under construction. A real barometer of confidence in the community is the investment of private capital. Here too we see the willingness of local groups to chance the future and invest in your growing urban partnership. The Citizens Fidelity and First National buildings represent approximately $70 million in new construction. Site clearance has begun for the construction of the $37 million Shippingport Square complex. Approximately equal bids have been received to build a $30 million apartment and office complex on one side of the Galt House. Immediately adjacent to this proposed construction, the American Life and Casualty Company building is growing. These projects represent almost $150 million of new capital-construction investment in the downtown area.

You have Village West, a model public-housing complex built at a cost of $12 million. Vermont-American, a national corporation, is building its new corporate headquarters in the downtown area. Mammoth Life Insurance Company has renovated its building. On Broadway we see a new Portland Federal building and Bank of Louisville building as well as this building. More toward the river there are three new homes for travelers away from home. Site clearance has begun for the Greater Louisville First Federal Savings and Loan building immediately adjacent to the First National building. You know, this sounds like I'm hired by the Chamber of Commerce!

Private capital has given this community many new and exciting cultural recreational opportunities as well. These investments include the new Actors' Theatre, McCauley Theatre, and began the Louisville Zoo project. Such contributions to Louisville and Jefferson County show a willingness to work together for a better community. They show that the people of this community have a real vision of what a modern urban center can be, a vision which the urban partnership, in cooperation with the state, will someday come to be a reality.[3]

I have been greatly impressed with the program of the Louisville Development Committee to promote and advertise this great city, both locally and nationally. This activity fits right into the program of our Department of Commerce to seek and attract national and regional corporate headquarters and bring industries to Kentucky. The tangible evidences of the success of the Louisville Development Committee's program are all around us. We in state government certainly hope this program will be continued in the future.

In 1969 you spent $300,000 of your own money for the far-reaching Gruen Associates Study of Downtown Louisville. In 1970 you followed by acting on the recommendations of that study with an unprecedented private and public financing of the $100 million Riverfront Project. Tonight we will together take one more step toward the realization of your vision. I am proud to be able to announce a major contribution to your community by state government. The state of Kentucky, in financial partnership with the city and county, will build an exhibition and and convention hall in downtown Louisville. This is not a statement of intent. It is an announcement of the project itself. This facility will have approximately 225,000 square feet of space, of which 100,000 will be devoted to a free-span exhibition area. It will have complete kitchen facilities, meeting rooms, corridors, storage areas, and perhaps the most modern service facility for convention and exhibitions in the United States.

This new facility will serve the medium-size convention trade, something which cannot currently be done either at Freedom Hall or Convention Center. The State Fair Board will operate this new hall in much the same manner it now operates the Fairgrounds, and on a sound, businesslike basis. The combination of these two facilities should bring a lucrative convention business to Kentucky. The new exhibition hall will generate an estimated 22.3 million new dollars annually to the state of Kentucky. Revenue from this new money will help pay for the cost of the facility. It is estimated that the exhibition hall will lure over $100 million of new construction in the downtown area. It is also estimated that the construction of this facility will create a demand for at least two major new hotels in the central city because of the need for 3,300 new hotel rooms projected by 1985. It should stimulate the development of new retailing in the heart of Louisville and will put Kentucky and Louisville in a unique position to attract not only convention business, but national headquarters also.

Louisville Central Area, Inc., in coordination with the City of Louisville and Jefferson County, several months ago employed Gruen Associates to help determine the site. This was the firm that did the original study of downtown Louisville in 1969 and seemed to be an appropriate neutral arbitrator to recommend a site. They have recommended that the exhibition hall be located on the entire block bounded by Jefferson, Market, Third, and Fourth streets because it is near the center of the downtown area with the maximum redevelopment potential on adjacent blocks. The project will include a high-rise parking garage between Liberty, Jefferson, Third, and Fourth. This garage will help alleviate the downtown parking problem and provide nearby parking for people using the exhibition hall. Total cost for this project should run in excess of $20 million. Financing will be by a state bond issue, and I have been assured by the Mayor and County Judge that their governments will help by contributing $150,000 each annually for thirty years toward retirement of the bonds. The remainder will be the responsibility of the state, but the dividends which all Kentucky, especially the Louisville area, should reap are fantastic.

I congratulate your great new urban partnership on a fine beginning and say again, it is with great pride that this administration offers itself as another partner. Together we will realize the vision you have for our "City of the Seventies" and assure that this community and the state will provide future generations with a better quality of life. Let's take this beginning and show the rest of the country what can be done to save our cities. Thank you and good night.

---

1. On September 17, 1973, Governor Ford announced further plans for a $14 million renovation of the Kentucky Fair and Exposition Center, which would include air conditioning in the East and West wings and the Pavilion, plus the addition of multipurpose annexes to the East and West wings. This speech is not included in this volume.

2. Walter D. Huddleston, for more information see speech from September 28, 1972, in the Reorganization section, p. 98. Norbert Blume (1922–   ), Democrat from Louisville; labor representative, president of Teamster Local 783; Speaker pro tem (1970), Speaker of the House (1972–1974); vice-chairman (1972–1974), cochairman (1975), Legislative Research Committee; elected to Kentucky House of Representatives 1964. *Kentucky General Assembly 1976* (Frankfort, n.d.), p. 18.

3. On October 3, 1972, Governor Ford announced, "I have nine Kentucky contracts for Bureau of Outdoor Recreation grants we have acquired for Louisville. These fit perfectly with the theme of livability, since they will provide additional recreation opportunities to the residents of this area. These projects total $146,630 and illustrate how local and state government can work together with federal agencies to serve people." This speech is not included in this volume.

CHAMBER OF COMMERCE
GOVERNOR'S TOUR
Covington / October 4, 1972

IT's good to be back in northern Kentucky again. Each visit here shows me that this important area is adding to the growth of the Commonwealth. The Ford administration is very much concerned with northern Kentucky. Only last week I met with twenty-five out-of-state industrialists who were touring this area and eastern Kentucky. From that group there are several keenly interested firms.

During the last session of the General Assembly, we worked closely with your representatives to improve existing programs and to sponsor new developments. We increased the foundations program to elementary and secondary schools in the three counties by $7.4 million during the 1972–1974 biennium. Under the new Urban Aid Road Program, our new revenue-sharing plan, the tri-county area will receive an additional $1.2 million for construction and maintenance of city streets and county roads. This represents an 80 percent increase in highway funds going to these counties. The state will expend an estimated $4.2 million more for providing assistance to the aged, blind, and disabled dependent children and medical recipients. This means that an estimated 2,000 more persons will benefit from this period over the biennium. The community Mental Health-Retardation Center in Covington serving the tri-county area will expend approximately $1.6 million more in these counties during the new biennium than was available in 1970–1972. The new Northern Kentucky Reception and Diagnostic Center in Kenton County will be operational during this biennium at a cost of $971,000. There will also be a 90 percent of $1.6 million increase in total expenditures for children's services in this area through the Department of Child Welfare.

There have been several other increases in state-assisted programs in northern Kentucky and we are looking forward to a future of greater involvement in this area. One important development that should be mentioned: Of interest to the participants on this Chamber of Commerce Tour is education. I say this because we have not yet met an equity in northern Kentucky between job training or higher education opportunities and a good job market. In the past, the relatively lucrative job market in this area has been a factor in holding down the percentage of students going to college. Yet we also know that this area needs college graduates. In short, there is tremendous potential for vocational training and higher education opportunities to develop in northern Kentucky.

Aid to higher education is coming to this area in unprecedented amounts. You are building Northern Kentucky State College from the ground floor. You have an opportunity few institutes of higher education ever have, and I am glad to be a part of this unprecedented growth. You have the opportunity to make each component of this new university an integral part of the program. You can plan physical plant facilities and educational programs in a model development that others can take great pride in. With the new construction started on the science building and a new library now under way, you are well on your way to developing just the kind of educational facility northern Kentucky needs.

Let me mention one more plus for this area, and it shows how each part of Kentucky is important to the other. Last week we announced the acquisition of a 963-acre farm in Fayette County. This site will become a major state park, devoted to the horse industry of our state. The park will complement Big Bone State Park, and Big Bone will complement the Horse Park. Their locations along I-75 offer easy accessibility to visitors. Tourists can go from one to the other in a short time. Both will be historical in nature. They are emphasizing family camping. Big Bone, therefore, must receive the full attention of all administrations just as the Horse Park must. Without this attitude everyone loses, and I don't intend to see this happen.

Sectionalism is bad for any state. Unity of areas is healthy and needed. My administration's purpose will be to erase any feeling of sectionalism, and those programs I have mentioned, along with others you have received, prove this intention. The advances or declines of any region touch all others. It is foolish for anyone to continue advocating sectionalism. This Chamber Tour can do much to pull all Kentucky together.

HOUSING CORPORATION
Louisville / October 31, 1972

I AM especially pleased to announce my appointments to the Kentucky Housing Corporation and thus begin a new chapter in service to others. As most of you remember, this corporation became possible through passage of House Bill 27[1] during the 1972 session of the General Assembly, a measure that had strong support from my office.

You often have heard me say that government exists to serve people. This philosophy is reflected through the intent of the bill to establish the Kentucky Housing Corporation. It was designed to aid in the financing, construction, and rehabilitation of residential housing for persons and families of lower incomes within the Commonwealth. Where funds are not available from private sources, the corporation can issue its revenue bonds to provide funds for financing of low-income housing developments. Two hundred million dollars in revenue bonds have been authorized by the General Assembly to be used for making federally insured construction loans and mortgage loans to qualified sponsors.

In areas where needed housing is not or cannot be offered by local sources, the authority may finance and operate residential low-income housing facilities. One of the primary benefits of the authority is that provision of low-income housing sponsors a central source of funds, especially during the recurring periods when interest rates are high and residential construction virtually grinds to a halt. The authority was established not only to increase low-income housing production in metropolitan areas but also to lend a hand to people in rural low-income areas and to those displaced by highway construction and small-town urban renewal. The Housing Authority's staff will be a source of technical assistance for sponsors who may lack the expertise to deal with the mechanics involved in initiating a housing development.

The legislature also authorized the corporation to issue up to $5 million in housing development fund notes (ten-year term) to provide persons applying for mortgages the money necessary for down payments and closing costs and to aid in development costs of sponsors. I am confident these people whom I am appointing to the authority will give the leadership and professional touch needed to ensure that a dream of adequate housing for all Kentuckians will become a reality.[2] People everywhere deserve no less and now, through the Housing Corporation, Kentuckians will receive no less.

This is essentially the same bill vetoed in 1970 by my predecessor. In his message then Governor Nunn said: "This bill extends the state into a field in which adequate federal programs are meeting the primary needs of the people." Nothing could be further from the truth, and I challenge this corporation to move quickly to make up lost time caused by the 1970 veto and to put in motion the machinery so desperately needed by those who can provide low-cost housing in a dignified and respectable manner.

---

1. See an act "relating to the financing of lower income housing and providing for the creation and establishment of the Kentucky Housing Corporation," which was approved on March 16, 1972. *Acts of the General Assembly of the Commonwealth of Kentucky, 1972*, Chapter 70 (H.B. 27), pp. 265–87.

2. The Governor announced the appointment of Donald Bradshaw, finance commissioner; Attorney General Ed Hancock; Laurel W. True, Kentucky Program Development Office administrator; Revenue Commissioner John McDowell Ross; Damon Harrison, commerce commissioner; Al Brinkley, Louisville; and John Wright Polk, Lexington, all appointed to four-year terms; James A. Shuck, Owensboro, and Ernest L. Pepples, Louisville, to serve for terms of three years; Pat Gish, Whitesburg, and Hortense Young, Louisville, appointed to two-year terms; Robert B. Hoff, Florence, and Mrs. Donald Ballusen, Louisville, to serve for a term of one year.

ANNUAL CHAMBER OF COMMERCE BANQUET
Lebanon / January 29, 1973

THERE are a few items of local interest that I want to mention before-I get into the main body of my remarks tonight. Highways are important to the development of your area. This administration is committed to the completion of that system of arterial highways which begins at Campbellsville and will eventually tie in with the Blue Grass Parkway. This is a good example of the feeder road, or the "get to it" road system I referred to in my campaign, and I plan to see the development of these kind of roads throughout the state.

We were moving along pretty well on this work until the impoundment of federal funds and the unexpected death of the federal highway bill last year. The tie-up of federal money has cost us at least a year on every highway project in the state. It has, therefore, affected you. I have talked to most of our congressmen about this problem, and I can assure you that there is a united front being used to free up the federal highway money. I feel confident that we will get our money, but it is sad that we will have to lose so much time.

Another project you are interested in is Ky. 49 from the southeast city limits of Lebanon extending southeast to Bradfordsville, including the improvement of four deficient bridges. Total length of the project is approximately 8.4 miles. It is estimated that the route study will be completed by July 1, 1973, and it is hoped that design can be authorized by the end of this calendar year.

Another item of interest to you is the status of the State Police barracks post here. I had planned to maintain the post, but when I assumed office, a great amount of money had already gone into the construction of the state-owned building to house the headquarters at Columbia. I can assure you of one thing, although the post will not be located here, we are putting into operation a plan which will maintain the same State Police strength here as there always has been. First of all, there is presently one State Police sergeant, one detective, and two troopers who reside in Marion County. When the present cadet class graduates this Friday, another trooper will be assigned here. The State Police will maintain a suboffice in the courthouse, but to give you immediate contact, we are setting up a cooperative arrangement with the Lebanon City Police, whereby they will have twenty-four-hour direct radio contact with the headquarters in Columbia. All anyone in Marion County will have to do is call the Lebanon City Police, who will radio the State Police, and a trooper will be available in a matter of minutes.

This system would have been available now, except for bad weather preventing construction of the Columbia radio tower. Radio contact is presently available, but it is through relay from Elizabethtown. We expect the tower to be ready in about two weeks. We plan to extend this communications network to other county seat cities served by the Columbia Post within the next three months. This will greatly extend the availability of State Police services to the citizen through his local police force.

I know that you have worked very hard on developing the new industrial park and that you have had considerable assistance from the Department of Commerce in site layout and development. As you may know, the Finance Authority has approved the $55,000 loan and is only waiting for the title insurance on the property to free the money. This loan will help, but the real proof of local initiative is shown by the three banks which loaned $10,000 each to finance the park and the $50,000 in private pledges and contributions being solicited locally. I understand that over $36,000 of the amount had been raised by December 28.

Another project which should help in the development of the industrial park is the improvement planned at the airport. Our people in aeronautics tell me that the Federal Aviation Authority airport master planning grant that you have requested should be coming within a few weeks. This is significant because it will allow for the development of a master plan to implement the state airport development system which can gain additional federal help in the future. The main advantages in meeting state plan requirements for your airport is that you will have lighted runways and you will eventually have extended runways which will be suited for all-weather use. This will mean that your airport can accommodate the corporate type of aircraft which should be an asset to the development of the industrial park.

WINCHESTER-CLARK COUNTY CHAMBER OF COMMERCE
Winchester / February 19, 1973

THEY say that the greatest cause of death for politicians is swallowing their own broken promises. You in Clark County ought to take this to mean that there are a lot of ailing politicians who have passed through here on the campaign trail. Before I began my campaign for Governor, I decided that the main effort of my years in Frankfort would be to keep those commitments made during the campaign. This allowed me to set priorities for my administration through the processes of campaigning; priorities which would reflect the people's true needs and desires.

During the campaign, I told you that our administration would not allow the development of Ky. 627 (formerly U.S. 227) from Winchester to the Kentucky River to become another neglected promise if we were successful. You had heard this promise from every gubernatorial candidate to win office in the last several campaigns. I know that you have yet to see the first spade of dirt turned to meet those commitments. I am pleased to say we are now in the right-of-way procurement phase of this project. Most of the deeds have been secured. We are going to advertise for bids in August, and I plan to get the spade out of mothballs so that I can personally begin this long-neglected construction.

There are a couple of other highway projects we have taken on here which will benefit your communities in Clark County. One is the bridge over the L & N railroad on Ky. 89. We are presently in the design phase for this project and will move through the respective phases required to get the job done. The grade crossing on the Winchester bypass has been a source of many accidents in recent years. I have been aware and concerned about this dangerous crossing, as I am sure all of you have been. We put a grade separation for this trouble spot in our five-year plan, but felt it necessary to take immediate steps to alleviate the problem. We have authorized the installment of new high-intensity warning lights at this crossing. These lights are the first of their kind in the state and are larger in diameter and three times brighter than what we have used in the past. The lights should be here in sixty days, and I hope and pray they will eliminate the accidents at the crossing.

You probably have heard of the problems we are having in Washington regarding highway funds. Since Congress failed to pass a highway bill last year, and the President has impounded federal highway funds, we are having to change our plans to cope with the situation. These kinds of frustrations make it extremely difficult to give our citizens the kind of services we would like to, but we are doing everything in our power to see that our state priorities are carried out. We don't want to pass the frustrations on to the people, so we are trying to fill the gaps with state resources and are trying to exert as much influence as possible in Washington to remedy the situation. I believe victory will occur.

Of course, the development on Ky. 627 will impact another project that I committed myself to during the campaign. This is the Fort Boonesborough State Park improvement. Travelers now diverted past the park and Winchester will have a new access when the highway is completed. This can only mean prosperity for your community and Fort Boonesborough State Park. For years, we have been getting millions of dollars of advertising about the fort which was not paid for by the state. The new highway will help us to capitalize on this as will the improvements at the park. When these projects are completed, we will have one of the finest outdoor camping facilities in the country. Fort Boonesborough is already one of the most heavily used parks in the state, and the improvements should bring more people to enjoy this fine facility. They will be an economic asset to this community.

One other project the state is cooperating with you on is the library demonstration which is in its first year. Last fall, we helped to renovate the church building to house the collection and staff. You now have a new $14,000 bookmobile to take this valuable service to county residents who might not be able to get into town, and all services of the State Library are available for the first time to Clark County residents.

Even though the state can help in these library projects, it is only through local initiative and drive that they can succeed in accomplishing their goals. It is a good example of the kind of state-local partnership needed to provide the people of Kentucky with services that improve the quality of life for all of our people. Washington has not been helpful in the library area. We are facing the grim prospect of a total elimination of all federal funds going to libraries, after suffering a 43 percent cut last year. I just can't see the logic in the President demanding more self-reliance and then eliminating public libraries from his budget.

Our public libraries have long been the primary institution in all communities, large or small, where anybody can have access to the kind of material and information basic to self-improvement. In fact, public libraries used to be referred to as the "people's university," because they are available to anyone for learning and self-education. I think we are hearing some more of the kind of political rhetoric that is only self-serving and not people-serving. I hope that we all can survive the politicians who carelessly promise the world when they themselves know that they won't even deliver a highway. I want to assure you that my administration is not going to try to fool you with false promises or empty rhetoric. We want to work with you to give generations to come the kind of Kentucky we will all be proud of—not just meaningless promises at campaign time.

GREEN RIVER AREA
DEVELOPMENT DISTRICT
Owensboro / April 25, 1973

WE are seeing a new surge of growth in this region which signals a very promising future. With this growth, there is the accompanying new need for various services. New jobs, new people, and new homes also create new conditions for government. Water and sewer lines must be expanded, energy problems must be solved; attention to the environment is important. There will be added needs for schools, police, fire, and health services. The list goes on and on. Growth demands more responsibility from government and more cooperation among people so that the growth can be well planned with orderly, long-range considerations.

Fortunately, you have an excellent means for doing this through the Green River Area Development District. Kentucky leads the nation in the statewide system of regional development, and if any of you were at Minneapolis last February, you probably are aware of how other states admire Kentucky for leadership in this development. Area Development Districts serve as vehicles for local officials and private citizens to identify needs and priorities on a regional basis. They have established new lines of communication between local governments and the people of each district. They have provided a mechanism for proper utilization of regional resources. They offer local governments technical assistance in planning and development.

In the matter of technical assistance, the Green River Area Development District has been a real leader. This is the first and, so far, the only district to hire a "floating" city manager to work with local governments on fiscal, managerial, and revenue-sharing problems. In this area of general-purpose staff assistance, we can concentrate more on local priorities than on meeting the program requirements coming from Washington. Too often, new programs coming from federal money sources have encouraged an unneeded growth of planning bodies out in the state. This causes several problems in getting services to the people and in meeting local needs. I want to mention four.

Unnecessary proliferation increases the administrative burden in meeting categorical program requirements. It decreases the input by local officials and citizens if they have to attend several meetings to deal with the many programs going on in their districts. It increases the boundaries between services which are in fact closely related.

Finally, it reduces communication between local governments and the state. Let us therefore work toward strengthening the existing planning bodies and general purpose staff to alleviate these problems. Your Area Development District has shown leadership in accomplishing this, especially in the merging of categorical grants. By combining federal monies through this approach, you achieve better coordination between planning areas and reduce the administrative drain needed to handle the separate grants coming from Washington.

The area of largest concern in this reorganization because of the number of people affected, and the amount of money involved, is human resources. Nearly one-third of the funds distributed through Area Development Districts are human resources funds.

Since the first meeting of the Human Resources Cabinet, Secretary True and his staff have been working with commissioners of the various agencies in this program area to find common ground.[1] They also examined how other states have approached services in human resources. The product of this investigation came from the last meeting of the cabinet in the form of a set of "guiding principles." These are "consensus statements," derived from agency personnel and the secretary's staff in their search for common and unique philosophies, objectives, and solutions to problems in the human resources area. Here is where you have the opportunity and responsibility to help us accomplish our goal for the reorganization of state government—to build a delivery system of people services that best meet their needs.

The guiding principles document will soon be sent to all of the Human Resources Councils and Area Development District Boards for reaction. When you receive this document, which should be in about one week, reflect on it with the same sincerity and care that has given you a state and national reputation for leadership in regional development. With the growing understanding of needs generated by your reactions and other investigations, the cabinet will be in much better position to effectively meet Kentucky's human resources needs. At this point, we will be looking for duplication as well as gaps in the services system.

The result of all this will be an improved state plan for human resources. It will utilize existing resources, yet be flexible enough to accommodate future resources and programs in order that the people of Kentucky are properly served. I can't overstress the importance of having your council's input in reorganization. You are close to the people. You have the understanding of local programs and you can offer valuable advice in how to meet these problems.

In the end analysis, we are going to stand, or fall, as we plan together, work together, and serve together. Already the Green River Area Development District has shown how this can be done on the regional level. Now we need to extend this to the state level. I congratulate you on the outstanding performance in behalf of the citizens of this district. From your efforts, and with your help, we will extend this very real service concept to all people of Kentucky. After all, isn't this what government should be about? Of course it is! An organization such as yours, the attitudes you exhibit, make me proud when I can say to other states, "Let me show you what is being done in Kentucky, by Kentuckians!"

---

1. Laurel W. True, for more information see speech from March 2, 1973, in the Reorganization section, pp. 117–19.

GOVERNOR'S DAY IN ASHLAND
Ashland / May 11, 1973

THERE is an old saying that the sound of only one hand clapping makes no noise. We don't hear a lot of noise from northeastern Kentucky. The reason is that hands have been too busy working on needed projects. The spirit of cooperation and civic involvement abounds here. But perhaps you should pause, because the applause of future generations will come as they see a brighter tomorrow.

    In order for any community to progress, there must be an active partnership between state and local government and strong community leadership. We have a good mix of this in the Ashland-Boyd County area. I want to take this time tonight to fill you in on just a few of the projects with which the state has been involved in serving you. One program, vital to any community in the state, is highways. Highways are paths to progress, because they grant better access for all. Evidence of our commitment to the road program in this area can be seen in bids awarded at the Bureau of Highways on April 26. Possibly you aren't aware of our latest activities.

    We had the signing of the I-64 project, which will complete the final link for your east/west access to Lexington and Louisville. If you will remember, this project was threatened by the loss of federal highway funds last year. In order not to lose a full year's construction season, I authorized prefinancing of the I-64 project with 100 percent state funds on the faith that we would be reimbursed by Washington, if and when the federal highway bill is passed. I knew there were some risks to this decision. But without taking a few calculated risks, progress would be improbable.

We are aware that you need north/south access, too, and another award made at the April 26 meeting was for the Greenup County project on U.S. 23. Although this only runs 2.6 miles, the nature of the project will cost over $5.5 million. This represents quite a commitment! We have entered into the design phase of U.S. 23 from the Lawrence County line to I-64 to continue this north/south access route. We expect to begin preliminary right-of-way acquisition by this fall. Some of you are also interested in the possibility of a new river crossing on U.S. 60 at Highland Avenue and Forty-seventh Street. We hope to initiate a planning study next January, which means that our highway people will be up to talk to you by then. An early coordination meeting with local officials was held at Catlettsburg on February 15.

There are several other highway projects in this area, but I want to call attention to July 1—an important date. At that time the first state-local revenue-sharing program for urban road construction and maintenance will begin, based on community sharing of the gasoline tax. In Boyd County three road programs benefit from an already proven state revenue-sharing effort, as well as the new July plan: The Rural Secondary Program, in which the Bureau of Highways will spend approximately $208,000; the County Road Aid Program, in which they will spend approximately $72,000; and the Municipal Aid Program, in which they will spend for Ashland city streets approximately $132,000. Catlettsburg will receive approximately $23,000. City streets not incorporated in Boyd County will receive about $15,000 in Bureau of Highways projects.

Most of us drive to get where we want to go, but roads are not the only area of transportation where the state-local partnership is at work. The Ashland-Boyd County Airport Expansion Project has been approved for plans and specifications. Advertisement for bids went out April 23, and we expect to open the bids the twenty-first of this month. If everything goes on schedule, work will begin by July 9. The project will add an extension of 600 feet to the 5,000-foot existing runway and provide a forty-foot parallel taxiway system of about 5,100 feet. There are other features of the project, but the main point is that you are getting long-needed airport improvements. This is a good example of how the local, state, and federal governments can work together in your behalf.

Kentucky is making great strides in vocational education and this area is no exception. State review and approval of the Boyd County Extension Center for the Ashland Area Vocational School is completed, and the Boyd County Board of Education is now able to let the contracts for its construction. The project will cost about $1.2 million and will offer a variety of courses in various vocational careers. This is important to you, because we have seen that by 1975, over 80 percent of all jobs in the country will require a vocational education type of skill.

I said early in my administration that we were not going to merely give lip service to law and order in Kentucky. At noon today, I spoke to a training seminar for Kentucky's first group of public defenders, and I told them of the important part they will play in the reorganization of our criminal justice system. We are strengthening and improving every area of criminal justice, because I feel that a piecemeal approach would seriously jeopardize the effectiveness of the system as a whole. Kentucky's innovations in criminal justice have already drawn much interest from other states. You are probably aware that we were successful in getting the Federal Cost of Living Council to override the Pay Board decision not to allow us our 15 percent salary supplement to local police officers who meet standards. I consider this a major victory for law and order in Kentucky.

Our latest Crime Commission grants to Ashland and Boyd County have totaled more than $112,000 to strengthen criminal justice here in many ways. Besides increased usage of the State Crime Lab, you are getting a local police photo lab and a new radio communications system, which will put all of the population in immediate access with regional and statewide police services through local police departments. Most of the equipment has arrived for the radio communications system which will provide both intercity tie-ins, as well as intraregional communications via the tower which will be built here in Ashland. This kind of communication has been needed for ages to fight crime which knows no jurisdictional boundaries. There are also three jail improvements and six courtroom improvement projects in this region which will be important additions to the criminal justice system here.

Many other developments we are seeing have come about because of the strong system of regional cooperation Kentucky has in her ADD districts. This basis for regional cooperation, in combination with the new office for local government, to field individual local government problems, has combined to serve you in a variety of ways. One of the most tangible results of this partnership so far relates to revenue-sharing from the federal government. When the State Office for Local Government was alerted to the fact that not all local tax revenue had been credited to local units of government, they called on the ADD people to study the situation. The result was a discovery that over $16 million in revenue had not been reported, over $400,000 in this region alone. Since local tax revenue is used in computing the amount of revenue-sharing money going to these units of government, this was an important disclosure. You were being shortchanged by Washington because of reporting errors. It is through partnerships like this that Kentucky can truly move ahead to meet the needs of all citizens.

Since coming into office, I have spent much time and effort in meeting my commitments to streamline state government and stop the spiraling costs of operating it. I have done this with the conviction that although what we are doing today may not be as visible today as tomorrow, we had to begin to lay the groundwork for efficient and effective government for future generations. Good beginnings toward improved service delivery by state government are worthwhile only when this degree of efficiency is continued. I say this in light of another fact affecting your community. Unemployment in Boyd County has dropped nearly two percentage points in the last year—a substantial reduction. Through an involvement among the state, the private sector, and your own local officials, we must strive to see this trend maintained.

One of the most rewarding experiences a Governor can have is an understanding with others, like you, that coming together is a beginning; keeping together is progress; and working together is success. I have sensed this feeling between my office and your community, and let me say how pleasant it is that we can be in concert in our attempts at solving problems. State government's track record in behalf of your concerns is good. There is no reason in the world why it shouldn't be improved even more, in view of the understanding you and I have.

OWENSBORO ROTARY CLUB
Owensboro / May 23, 1973

I AM especially happy to speak to groups like yours. It gives me a chance to tell communities what state government is doing for them through programs directly affecting their areas. Many are not visible to everyone, and I think it is appropriate to periodically report on how our activities relate to you. Let's look at some of our activities in Owensboro and Daviess County.

A main project is the $2.9 million State Office Building which will serve as a central housing facility for social service agencies. This is to be finished next January 1. Another project is the WIN[1] program, which has placed nearly seventy former welfare recipients in private industry. More have been placed in public jobs which helps decrease the welfare roll in this area. Judge Tanner[2] has gotten 100 jobs for summer employment through the Emergency Employment Act, and he was able to get an additional twenty-eight summer jobs through increased state support. These are for the handicapped, veterans, and so forth, in the fourteen- to twenty-two-year age group.

Child Welfare has implemented new programs in this area. Examples are the group home for mentally retarded predelinquent boys and the Mary Kendall Home for Girls, and the Levy Home for Boys to provide short-term emergency services for young people in trouble with the law, instead of putting them in jail. The department has also arranged for a local family home to provide temporary shelter for children who are in trouble with the law or for other reasons need a temporary place to stay.

The Department of Mental Health has doubled staffing at your comprehensive care center; this means more full-time professionals for the many mental health services in your area. This is reflected in the $300,000 increase we provided to support these activities. We have expanded the Alcohol and Drug Abuse Program in this community. Together with the Volunteers of America, we have initiated the Halfway House for people with alcohol problems. There is also an occupational alcohol advisor and staff to work with local industry to combat the problem of the troubled employee. This is a $25,000 program.

Our Health Department has also been active here. They cleared the way for the $4.5 million renovation of the Owensboro-Daviess County Hospital and assisted in a 100-bed intermediate care facility. The home-care system has a $37,000 program to provide visiting nurses for rural health care. In the past two years, $75,000 has gone to the local county health program for increased operational costs, not just special programs. The Health Department has expanded its contract with the pediatric clinic which allowed sixty-nine new cases in the first three quarters of this fiscal year. There has also been a 30 percent expansion in the heart clinics, and over 30 percent of the black population has been screened for sickle cell anemia.

We've also made improvements in the criminal justice system. By increasing state funds to the Crime Commission, we brought additional federal dollars into the state, and Owensboro and Daviess County receive more than $300,000 of this money directly. This includes the $121,000 Police Consolidation Program begun by this county. In this innovative program, the fiscal court contracts with the State Police to provide experienced officers to serve in the county areas. Other counties in the state may adopt a similar approach for professional police services in county areas. In addition, you will benefit from the $241,000 regional police communications network being established.

There has been a continuing development of transportation facilities. Highways, of course, receive the lion's share of funding. Work started or completed on county roads in the past seventeen months in Daviess County amounts to $6,346,736. In addition, you will receive through state-local revenue-sharing as of July 1, $141,725 for county-road aid and $406,859 in rural-secondary aid. Municipal aid for Owensboro will total $227,689, for Whitesville $3,402, and for parts of Daviess County not included in an incorporated area $9,283. The latter three are new programs.

We haven't neglected this community's airport development, and state funding presently totals $137,000 for such projects as land acquisition and site preparation for the instrument-landing system completed this year; preparation of an operations manual to meet certification requirements; safety and security measures including fire protection, security fencing, and communications equipment presently in progress; and aid in preparing a long-range master plan, already under way.

In addition to these projects which directly affect this area, we have been working on statewide programs which favorably touch all the citizens of the Commonwealth.[3] After today you will have a better feeling for what state government is doing for you and your fellow Kentuckians. Let me leave you with another fact of which I am proud. In 1971 the unemployment rate in Daviess County was 5.7. Last year that was reduced to 4.3—a whopping improvement!

1. WIN is a federally funded program that began in 1967 under Title 4 a & c of the Social Security Act. This is a work-incentive program organized at the federal level through the Departments of Labor and Health, Education, and Welfare; at the state level the program is run by the Bureau of Manpower Services and the program is still operating. Telephone interview on January 4, 1977, with Jack Thorpe in the Bureau of Manpower Services.

2. Pat Tanner, Owensboro; Daviess County judge. *Who's Who in Kentucky, 1974* (Atlanta, Ga., n.d.), p. 236.

3. The Governor listed many of the programs in education, criminal justice, and other areas mentioned in other speeches.

CONFERENCE ON
LOCAL GOVERNMENT PROBLEMS
Louisville / June 21, 1973

FOR openers, I first thought of telling you that only a few years ago, a conference like this would never have caught wind in its sails. Then I wondered about my choice of words and whether or not some jokester might attribute the expression "wind in its sails" to a conference filled with verbal breezes and little else! Looking over your schedule, the subject matter, speakers, and participants, you can expect to leave this series of meetings with substantial information which will complement the important role you have. Hopefully, my brief remarks will measure up to the quality program this entire occasion offers, for there is very real value in what you can achieve here.

Indeed, a few years ago such a conference would have been doubtful. A *de facto* separation of government at all levels spurred on by a huge federal bureaucracy isolated one government from another. In turn, people were often left out in the cold with the governed feeling a great distance from those who were governing. The climate hasn't improved much, but there are indications that it will.

The positive response to this conference indicates why I am optimistic. Yours is probably the most representative group of individuals to meet in the common cause of improving government responsiveness to the citizens. I believe we have, in state government, helped set the stage for this interest, through reorganization, through emphasis on grass-roots involvement and through our own conviction that the closer government and people can become, the better served citizens will be. I believe you are finding a new determination on the part of the nation's governors to participate more aggressively in national affairs, where governmental programs are being reviewed with a fine-tooth comb. I believe you sense, as do I, an inspired demand by citizens that government stop being impersonal, that the gap between the governed and the governing be narrowed, and that there is a necessity for improved communications if we are to have a more intelligent understanding of issues, policies, and programs.

You have heard Jack Floyd speak about the effects of federalism on the states, and throughout this event you will attend sessions on technical aspects of running government, regional approaches to problem solving, and the impact of federal and state legislation on local government. It's an impressive package, designed to bring governmental functions closer together. And this is important, for if governments do seek mutual cooperation, people benefit. What we can accomplish in Kentucky, between state and local units, is exactly what must be accomplished between the federal and state governments.

Certainly, over the years you have been frustrated in your attempts to deal effectively with state government. I sensed this as a State Senator and as Lieutenant Governor. This is why I made reorganization a priority issue. As Governor, I join my colleagues in feeling frustration with Washington. So many of our programs are determined by the decisions rendered in federal agencies, and each year there is increased pressure on the governors to spend more and more time in Washington because of federal decision-making. Anyone who thinks we favor this approach is wrong. I would much rather have the added responsibilities in Kentucky, so long as the federal government gave corresponding support to our state. And to this end, governors are working—trying to convince the federal power structure that we can most certainly conduct the affairs of people in a more orderly and less expensive manner. At the same time, you are finding that, like Kentucky, state governments elsewhere are recognizing the values of returning a greater portion of government to local units, where the rank and file are much closer to those who make decisions.

In his final report, outgoing chairman of the national governors conference, Marvin Mandel,[1] said earlier this month, "The executive committee has continued to emphasize this year that the governors are not content to just seek federal handouts. . . . The federal government must learn that nationally conceived programs simply will not work without the heavy involvement of the governors and the states we represent." You have heard the term "New Federalism." I suppose its interpretation depends upon the political party you represent. But placing politics aside, let me describe one aspect of new federalism which has many ramifications. I agree with the President's desire to hold the line on spending. I agree with the President's announced intention to return more of the current federal responsibilities to the states, and I welcome the challenge. But what is happening? In trying to reduce the federal deficit, money allocated by Congress and designated for critical programs is being impounded or delayed. This is false economics, since ultimately the damage to programs and costs will be extensive.

Another example can be seen with the return of certain programs to states. The federal government is asking the states to accomplish in four months what it took Washington forty years to accomplish, and this is found, for instance, in vital human resource programs. No consideration was given to an orderly, properly timed transition. Neither has sufficient consideration been given to federal assistance in funding. Look at federal revenue-sharing. Although good in concept, it has served to cloud the reality that we are losing more from cuts in categorical grant programs than we are gaining in revenue-sharing. So indecision spreads, and confusion which is quite obvious in Washington filters down into the states and local communities. If dealing with the federal bureaucracy at any time is frustrating, this particular period has compounded the feeling. Because Watergate has consumed so much public attention, there is an added burden.

I have stated previously, and still maintain, that Watergate is in the capable hands of the Senate and the courts. After this affair is settled, America and her problems will remain very much with us, and we must, as officials, direct our attention to those duties expected by the people who have granted them to us, rather than becoming distracted by Watergate. It is incumbent on those leaders in Washington to stop the paralysis creeping into the federal government in order that Kentucky and your communities can move forward in a progressive, businesslike approach to service. At the last published count I have seen, sixty key White House appointments remain vacant. While meeting with federal officials on state matters, we have found a void in decision-making. Individuals seem uncertain where they will be tomorrow, so key state programs as well as those matters relating to your communities gather dust. In the face of uncertainty and confusion in Washington, we cannot at this time count on assumed stability from the federal government. It is up to us, then, to stabilize our state and local governments by creating a mechanism flexible enough to cope with whatever Washington sends down the pipeline.

This is one of the major concerns of our reorganization of state government. By grouping our agencies, departments, and commissions into seven functional program cabinets, we will be more flexible and will establish better lines of communications within state government. The most important aspect of this reorganization, however, is the move to establish better state-local ties through the creation of the Office for Local Government. For the first time in the history of the Commonwealth, local officials have a direct access to the executive department in Frankfort and a strong voice in state government. We designed the Office for Local Government to serve the following functions: as a contact point to hear about local problems, as identifier and expediter of the types of state assistance that can help solve local problems, and as coordinator of the state's resources to help serve the people of Kentucky through their local governments.

I see this arrangement as the only way we are going to prevent the chaos in Washington from spreading to our cities and counties. If we make the most of the potential in this new state-local arrangement, we can make federalism a living reality in Kentucky. We want to know what the local needs are in shaping our plans for state government. We are reversing the planning process from the traditional scheme of planning from the top down, by involving local officials and local citizens in state planning. As we increase and improve communications between local and state governments, we will form a strong partnership which can best utilize our resources. Our resources go beyond authority. What this Office of Local Government is really all about should be fully understood. We, in Kentucky, are trying to reverse the trend that exists between the state and local governments, just as that same trend must be reversed for the states and federal governments.

Since 1935 we have witnessed a steady buildup of concentrated power, authority, and decision-making on the part of the state, with cities and counties being left out. Such has been the case in the last forty years on the federal level. By returning authority, planning, and decision-making to the cities and counties—yes, to the people—government becomes more personal, more responsive. Our Office of Local Government provides the tools, the technological abilities, the talents, the research, and other help which cities and counties need. Our attitude provides you and your people with a greater opportunity than ever before to determine the course you should take, without interference from the state. This we must have throughout all levels of government. Now, in my opinion, is our last chance, at least in this generation, to reverse the concentration of power at the top. If we fail, power at the highest level will accelerate, and once more the isolation of one government from another will haunt progress. In Kentucky we're not going to let this happen.[2]

---

1. Marvin Mandel, Governor of Maryland. For more information see speech from September 7, 1972, in the Public Safety section, p. 271.

2. Governor Ford delivered two other addresses on this same theme which are not included in this volume. These speeches were given at the Civic Luncheon in Hopkinsville on June 29, 1973, and at the Kentucky Magistrates and Commissioners Luncheon in Owensboro on July 27, 1973. Also on July 31, 1973, Governor Ford lodged a formal complaint with the Interstate Commerce Commission over Amtrak's decision to terminate the Floridian Chicago-Miami passenger service which goes through Louisville and Bowling Green. On August 31, 1973, Governor Ford announced Amtrak's withdrawal of its application to discontinue operation of the Floridian. Neither of these announcements is in this volume.

CHAMBER OF COMMERCE
GOVERNOR'S TOUR
Richmond / October 2, 1973

IT is good to be in Richmond as we begin the 1973 Kentucky Chamber of Commerce Governor's Tour. This year's tour will focus on eastern Kentucky, a region rich in the history of our great Commonwealth and an area ripe for growth and progress. It has been six years since the tour last visited this region, and I know my fellow tour participants will be impressed by the changes that have taken place.

On several occasions during these next three days, I am scheduled to speak. However, I assure you whatever I have to say will be in the form of brief reports in the areas we visit—not wordy, but to the point. I have no choice. We're scheduled to depart for Berea at 1:10 P.M., and the bus driver told me if I'm not finished by then, he's leaving without me!

Richmond is probably best known around the state for being the home of Eastern Kentucky University. We are proud of Eastern for the job it is doing to meet the needs of present-day society with a keen eye to the future. Last October we broke ground for the new $65 million law enforcement center. Now under construction, this center is destined to become a regional training ground for law enforcement officers and a strong asset to Kentucky's higher education system. The leadership and foresight of Eastern's president, Dr. Martin,[1] was the force that made this project possible. He deserves the gratitude of all Kentuckians for this.

Eastern has also taken giant strides forward in other directions. A 600-acre farm was purchased for expansion of the school's agricultural-technological programs. There has been expansion of the Richmond community colleges, which offer two-year programs that attract both young people and adults interested in continuing education. There has been a complete renovation of the University Center, not to mention enlargement and expansion of other campus facilities. A record $19.8 million in state aid was made available to Eastern. The theme we want to emphasize at each stop of this tour is one of progress and cooperation. Eastern Kentucky University is an outstanding example.

The progress of any community is shaped by the responsiveness of local and state government to the needs that exist. Sometimes the actions of state government go unnoticed, so today I want to give you a brief look at some of the returns Madison Countians are receiving for their tax dollars in my first fiscal year. More than $348,000 was funneled through our Department of Parks for the development of a state park at Fort Boonesborough and maintaining the White Hall Shrine. The Department of Mental Health had a total expenditure of $729,304, which was used for mental health and comprehensive care center services, mental retardation facility services, alcohol and drug facility services, and other programs that provide help to people who need it.

More than $2.4 million was spent in state road funds, constructing and improving major arteries and the all-important "get-to-it" roads— the roads that must be safe for the buses that take our children to school and for the trucks that transport our farmers' crops to market. State government's total expenditure for Madison County was over $27 million. I could go on, but I see my time has run out. In closing, I want to remind you that we want state government to be responsive to the needs of the people of Kentucky, but if we don't hear from you, we may miss some problems that are of immediate concern. So when you want to communicate, do so. Thank you for coming today, and please ask us back. It's always nice to visit your community.

---

1. Robert Richard Martin (1910–   ), Richmond; educator, teacher, and principal, Mason and Lee counties public schools (1935–1948); auditor, di-

rector of finance, and head of business administration and finance, Kentucky Department of Education (1948–1955); superintendent of public education (1955–1959); president of Eastern Kentucky University (1960–1976); president of American Association of State Colleges and Universities (1971–1972). *Leaders in Education, 1974* (New York, 1974), p. 724.

CHAMBER OF COMMERCE GOVERNOR'S TOUR
Pineville / October 2, 1973

We in Frankfort have observed with pride Bell Countians' successful efforts to add to the progressiveness of eastern Kentucky. I am personally grateful for the opportunity to see the results firsthand and can assure you that state government will continue to cooperate with your endeavors.

Upon assuming office, we set priorities to be followed in developing programs for all Kentucky. My opponents and the doubting-Thomases called me irresponsible, said our reforms and projected biennial surplus of more than $3 million wouldn't hold, and contended we could not fund an aggressive two-year program in the manner I chose to pursue. In the first eighteen months, we tripled the national rate of unemployment decline, doubled the national rate of increase in nonagricultural jobs, initiated a comprehensive agricultural plan which is already paying dividends—our first true billion-dollar year—and in the first quarter of this year, led forty-seven other states in increased per-capita income. Not since World War II, and in many instances never, has this happened in Kentucky. As for a surplus, we'll have at least $140 million—$54 million from growth, plus $86 million in revenue-sharing, on which we are drawing interest until our legislature meets. The $54 million is directly tied to our state's economic gains, plus over a $12 million saving in state government operating expenses.

Now, I'll be the first to admit that the picture of our state isn't entirely rosy. But when our state prospers, as it has during the past year and a half, every section of the state benefits, either directly or indirectly. You may be thinking that the figures I've presented are impressive and things sound great, but you may also be wondering how this affects your community. By approaching state government in a businesslike manner, we have been able to prudently use tax dollars for people projects, so that you can get the benefit of your money.

During the past fiscal year, $13.2 million was spent by state government in Bell County alone to help provide a cleaner, safer, more prosperous, and enjoyable environment in which to live and work. Of the total, approximately $5.6 million was spent for health and related services, including day care centers, facilities for the mentally retarded and persons with drug problems. Nearly $5 million was allocated for elementary and secondary education so your children can obtain a quality education. Your children deserve no less, and state government wants to guarantee that they receive no less. State road funds for Bell County totaled $1.5 million, and this money was spent on "get-to-it" roads to provide safer routes for everyday transportation.

You in Bell County are blessed with natural resources, friendly people, and an excellent work force, which these businessmen will agree are important to attracting industry. Time and again you have demonstrated that you want the best for your community and have strived diligently toward that goal. In doing so, you have set an example for other counties to follow, which I am certain will be relayed to other parts of the state by those of us on the Chamber Tour. Additionally, your initiative has indicated to me that we can expect even a brighter report in the coming months. I could not conclude my remarks today without urging my fellow tour members to attend the Mountain Laurel Festival.

CHAMBER OF COMMERCE
GOVERNOR'S TOUR
Breaks, Virginia / October 3, 1973

THIS afternoon's stop in Pikeville will make the seventh community we have visited during the first twenty-eight hours of the Annual Chamber of Commerce Tour. Throughout the tour, we've been impressed with the progress the people of eastern Kentucky have made, and we are aware that Pike Countians have contributed their share toward this success. As government and business representatives, we come here today primarily for one reason—to get to know you better. By accomplishing this goal, we can relate to others what your community can offer additional industries and businesses.

One thing in particular strikes me about this community, and that is your initiative. Let me illustrate my point. Since the Chamber Tour was last in this section of the state, the Pikeville College established a two-year coal mining technology program, one of the first of its kind in the nation. There is much significance in this display of foresight. By establishing this program, you have shown a genuine interest in one segment of the population that is living and working in your community. Often, businesses are attracted to a community because its leaders care for its citizens. But you are blessed with other attention-getters, including an abundance of natural resources and an abundant supply of human resources.

It is true that all of these factors are essential in attracting industry and business to a particular area, but when people move to a new town, they also consider things like the crime rate, education, health facilities, and the environment. And this is where state government has been and will continue to be a partner in your efforts toward a more prosperous economy. During fiscal year 1972–1973, state government poured over $29.5 million into Pike County to help provide a cleaner, safer, and more enjoyable area in which to work and live.

More than $13 million was allocated to insure that your roads are adequate; nearly $9 million was spent here on elementary and secondary education, so your children might have the opportunity to obtain a quality education; and approximately $5.3 million was spent to provide health, mental health, welfare, and related services to Pike Countians. There is a saying that I feel Pike Countians exemplify: "Coming together is a beginning, keeping together is progress, and working together is success." Keep up the good work and thank you for allowing me to chat with you today.

CHAMBER OF COMMERCE GOVERNOR'S TOUR
Paintsville / October 4, 1973

OUR visit to Paintsville couldn't have come at a better time, since today marks the start of the annual Johnson County Apple Festival. I want my fellow tour participants to know they're going to have a hard time getting me away from here. The thought of a weekend of apple pie, apple butter, applesauce, apple cookies, and Johnson Countians is too enticing to pass up.

The Apple Festival continues to grow in size each year and captures the fancy of all who come to Johnson County for it. But it's not just your apples who win the friends—it's your people, who do it by showing visitors that Kentucky hospitality is second to none. Community pride such as this is something we have seen in every stop we have made on this tour. This spirit of cooperation has impressed all of us greatly.

Paintsville has much to be proud of. The new vocational rehabilitation hospital and the Mayo Vocational School are examples of community assets and a source of civic pride. The spirit of cooperation to which I referred earlier is most evident in the programs in which the hospital and school have been able to join together, working together for the mutual benefit of both. I have an announcement to make today concerning the Vocational School. The Appalachian Regional Commission has approved a $650,000 project involving both state and federal funds that calls for the replacement of the old Sawtooth Building on the vocational school campus with a new structure. In addition, funds have also been made available for the purchase of additional acreage next to the campus for building-expansion and the construction of parking facilities.

These programs are people programs. We want state government to be responsive to the needs of the people of Kentucky. The primary reason we're here today is fact-finding. We want to learn more of your needs and your potentials. The Chamber of Commerce has shown its willingness to be a part of this venture by sponsoring this tour. With state government, private business, and industry working together, much can be done for all of Kentucky. I thank you for having us here—and I hope you will invite us back again.

DAVIESS COUNTY
STATE VOCATIONAL-TECHNICAL SCHOOL
DEDICATION
Owensboro / October 18, 1973

THERE are many reasons to be proud of the new Daviess County State Vocational-Technical School we are dedicating today. It is a large, impressive structure. It has the most modern classrooms, workshops, and equipment. It was constructed and equipped at a cost of nearly $2 million. But of more importance, it is a living investment in our future.

The impact of vocational education on the future of our state cannot be overestimated. A reliable study has indicated that by 1975, 81 percent of all jobs in the country will require a vocational-education type skill. This may come as a shock to a society where the majority of people think of education as grades one through twelve, then possibly four years of college. We are a college-degree oriented society, but if we are aware of the trends to vocational skills, we must prepare for an educational system that will realistically meet the needs of employment opportunities. Regional vocational schools are one answer to producing graduates who enter the work world with a realistic expectation of what they will be doing and equipped with the kind of training that will benefit them best. They are our answer to the job-requirement needs of the future. They are insurance against a manpower shortage.

A strong vocational-education program not only assures meeting the occupational needs of people in a region but also serves to stimulate economic prosperity. No doubt you are aware that much industrial progress, an indicator of the economic pulse, is being made in the seven-county Green River Region, which this school serves. Since 1972, nineteen new industries have located in the area and thirteen others expanded their existing operations. There is visible evidence that such industrial growth is directly related to the training and educational opportunities the companies know this area can offer.

Presently, fifteen programs of training are offered here in trade, technical, business, home economics, and distributive education areas. More than 700 students are now enrolled in these courses. In addition, evening classes are provided for adults who wish to upgrade existing skills and for businesses and industries to hold special programs for their employees. All these programs are relevant to the industrial needs of the region and are designed to attract new industry. Industries locating in the area can be assured their educational and training needs are well served, that there is no cause for concern of a manpower shortage.

So I say to all present this morning, let us mark this day as not merely another ceremony. Let us take note of the investment we are making in the future which can ensure a better life and create new prosperity for our community, region, and state.

ANNOUNCEMENT OF
LEXINGTON CIVIC CENTER
Lexington / November 10, 1973

FOR almost twenty months, a group of individuals representing various sectors of the Lexington-Fayette County community have been working, planning, studying, and consulting in behalf of a concept with many dimensions.[1] Their purpose was to move from a dream to reality in the pursuit of a multipurpose complex, designed for conventions, exhibitions, sports, entertainment, business, and the arts. Within this purpose was a philosophy of benefit and progress for Lexington, Fayette County, Central Kentucky, and, in many respects, all of Kentucky.

For some time, it has been obvious that if such a center could be constructed to meet the full and proper purposes of its existence and the needs of tomorrow, financial support from the Commonwealth of Kentucky would be a determining factor in the success of this plan. I want the Commonwealth of Kentucky to be a participant and therefore am today announcing the intention of this administration to acquire $4 million to make this worthy project work.

There are many reasons why we should become involved. And I want to enumerate several. We're talking about the creation of a new industry. We're talking about the creation of new jobs. We're talking about the creation of new opportunities to enhance the entertainment and cultural potentials for our citizens. We're talking about economic growth. We're talking about expanded convention and tourist opportunities for the Central Kentucky area, where a multiplier effect benefits society. Through a self-supporting concept, the return on our investment is significant, because when growth is created, all Kentucky prospers.

This complex will contain a convention-exhibition center with 80,000 square feet of meeting rooms, banquet, ballroom, and display space, a sports and entertainment arena to seat up to 22,600 spectators, a restored, historical opera house for the arts, a hotel, parking facilities, and 70,000 square feet of business space.

The University of Kentucky is joining others in cooperating toward this project and will make the arena the Wildcats' new home. It will be a definite asset to the university, and therefore the state's contribution will go through the university in the development of this structure. I would also add that with the state's lump-sum contribution, we have also assisted in reducing the overall cost, since our portion will eliminate a portion of the debt service by lowering the bonding requirements.

Local government is another partner in this cooperative venture, because local government recognizes, as do we, the great benefits to be derived from such an undertaking. So it is with a great deal of pleasure, with optimism and personal assurance that we are on the verge of a tremendous opportunity for our citizens, that I announce the inclusion of $4 million in the next budget for the center here in Lexington. With approval of the General Assembly, which convenes in January, work can begin at once, and Kentucky can expect completion in approximately thirty months after the first shovel is turned.

I want to compliment other partners in this endeavor—Lexington-Fayette County officials; the City-County Tourist, Recreation and Convention Commission; interested private citizens in this room today; and others whose vision will prove that by working together, progress can be made, and our citizens will reap the rewards.

---

1. Press conference.

BARREN RIVER AREA DEVELOPMENT DISTRICT
Lucas / April 23, 1974

WE are seeing a steady surge of growth, orderly growth, in this region which signals a very promising future. With this growth, there is the accompanying need for various services. New jobs, new people, and new homes create new conditions for government. Water and sewer lines must be expanded. Energy problems must be solved. The environment must be protected. There will be increased demand for schools, parks, police, fire, and health services. The list goes on and on. Growth demands more responsibility from government and more cooperation among people in order to ensure the proper long-range considerations.

You have an excellent means for doing this through the Barren River Area Development District. Kentucky leads the nation in the statewide system of regional development—a concept I have long endorsed because its end product results in more personalized government. Area Development Districts serve as vehicles for local officials and private citizens to identify needs and priorities on a regional basis. They have established new lines of communication between local governments and the people of each district. They have provided a mechanism for proper utilization of regional resources. They offer local governments technical assistance in planning and development. This is good business!

In the matter of technical assistance, the Barren River Area Development District has been a leader. You have shown foresight and originality in innovative programs, such as the workshop you held last January for newly elected mayors and county judges in your district. You have established a fuel-allocation information center to assist counties in coping with the energy crisis. You devised an emergency medical service plan which, among other concerns, informs city and county officials what alternatives are available should they lose local ambulance service. And when several counties in your district suffered damage from the tornadoes which swept across Kentucky three weeks ago, you were there. Working in cooperation with the State Civil Defense Agency and the Office for Local Government, you assisted mayors, county judges, and other local leaders in applying for state and federal disaster assistance.

I mention these facts with full knowledge that you are aware of them. But I do this to publicly recognize your excellence! Kentucky's Area

Development Districts are proving their worth daily, and local communities are the better for it. Here you have the opportunity and responsibility to help us accomplish our goal for the reorganization of state government—to build a delivery system of people services that best meets their needs. In an attempt to eliminate much of the red tape which districts encounter when seeking federal funds to support their services, our Office for Local Government has prepared an integrated grant application—a single application which merges all potential sources of funds for the district. If this proposal is approved by the federal authorities next month, we hope to implement it for fiscal year 1975. It could be one of the most important actions taken to help people.[1]

The public is best served when decision-makers are close to the people. This means personal government rather than impersonal government. This means government with eyes and ears to see and hear—not just a mouth which only speaks. I cannot overstress the importance of your council's input into the programs and services of state government. You are close to the grassroots. You have the understanding of local programs. You can offer valuable advice in how to meet the local problems and needs.

Years ago when I first became involved in government, one fact became quite obvious. The closer people are to officials making decisions, the more responsive government is. I have tried to maintain that philosophy during the twenty-nine months I have served in this office. State-local revenue-sharing is one example. Home-rule legislation is another example—giving local governments increased powers and strengthening their ability to manage public affairs, as expected by those for whom they directly serve. The Office for Local Government is just another example.

The responsibilities of our Area Development Districts were increased and centralized as a result of reorganization. Through the Office for Local Government, you have the opportunity to maintain and extend your contacts with other agencies, thus coordinating planning programs. You understand this region's opportunities and its needs better than anyone. Unless government at all levels recognizes the importance of local and regional input, the bureaucratic system overtakes the democratic system. If no one listens, government loses touch with people.

In the final analysis, whether we stand or fall is determined by how well we plan together, work together, and serve together. Already the Barren River Area Development District has shown how we can do this on the regional level. Now we are trying to extend this to the

state level. I congratulate you on the outstanding performance in behalf of the citizens of this region. An organization such as yours, the
attitudes you exhibit, make me proud when I can say to other states:
"Let me show you what is being done in Kentucky—by Kentuckians!"

---

1. On July 22, 1974, Governor Ford announced the federal government's
approval of the adoption of an Integrated Administration Program. This
program, designed to eliminate bureaucratic red tape, proposed to merge all
potential sources of funds for the ADDs. At the same time, Governor Ford
issued the first quarter federal allotment checks to the state's fifteen ADDs.
This address is not included in this volume.

KIWANIS CLUB
Ashland / June 12, 1974

THIS morning, as I met with residents of Ashland and the neighboring
communities, the prevailing attitude of this area came through loud
and clear. I found a wealth of energy, enthusiasm, initiative, and resourcefulness. And I found a lot of people who cared. They cared about
their schools, parks, and roads. They cared about the blind, the handicapped, and the elderly. They cared about their community.

As I travel across the state, one obvious fact is seen over and over
again. Community progress is nearly always directly related to the
responsiveness of local citizens who are willing to join together in a
cooperative venture. These are the people who don't mind rolling up
their sleeves to get a job done. This is what I see every time I come to
Ashland, Boyd County, and this area. The community you are building
didn't come about by accident. It resulted because many cared. The
results of this cooperation, this commitment to work in concert for the
community good, are beginning to show. Ashland is growing and ma-
turing, reaching an unprecedented standard, in terms of quality of life.
You who stand up with your community have reason to be proud,
knowing that you have had a part in making it a better home for your
families.

In order to have and to maintain a strong community, the public is
best served when decision-makers are close to the people. One of the

very honest fears I have about government is a total isolation from the people. We are seeing this problem in Washington, and because of it, people suffer. If government is to fully serve, there must be communication, contact, feedback, and input between elected officials and the people. It's wrong to operate in a vacuum. Government needs a partnership from those who hold an abiding interest in his or her community, for these are the individuals who stand tall in the arena of responsibility.

Civic-minded groups such as yours can be an integral part of solidifying this partnership. Through your interest in community affairs, you serve as a link which brings people and government together. Very briefly, I want to expand on the reasoning behind a philosophy that says the public is best served when decision-makers are close to the people. Kentucky's first revenue-sharing program for local communities, where part of the gasoline tax is sent back for street improvement projects, is an example. You know how to put these funds to work in your own community better than anyone. Home-rule legislation, giving local governments increased powers and responsibilities, means added responsiveness to those directly affected. The establishment of our Office for Local Government provides a direct line of communication from the community to the executive branch, bringing Frankfort closer to the cities, towns, and counties. The state is now picking up the cost for the operation of our circuit courts, freeing additional funds at the local level.

As many of you know, we were involved in a ten-month ordeal, and finally were successful, with the Federal Pay Board and Cost of Living Council to implement a 15 percent salary-educational incentive program for local policemen across the state. Despite a 38.6 percent reduction at the federal level, we have maintained the state's share of funding to local communities and Kentucky's fifteen Area Development Districts, as part of the comprehensive planning assistance program. Legislation was enacted returning up to one-half of the excess severance-tax revenues to the coal-producing counties. And just yesterday we announced the implementation of a new procedure where 100 percent of Kentucky's share of Bureau of Outdoor Recreation funds will be directed straight into local communities. We're talking about $2.9 million for the next fiscal year. Normally, only 40 percent of these funds would be designated for cities and counties. This new procedure means that our communities will now be able to develop recreational programs according to priorities determined at the local level.

What this all boils down to is that for every matter, Washington should not be the capitol of each state, just as Frankfort should not be the city hall for every Kentucky community. Washington must listen to the states, just as the states listen to the communities from within. If no one listens, government loses touch with people. And this is what has been happening for too many years. You understand your own conditions and needs better than anyone. Unless government at all levels recognizes this, the bureaucratic system overtakes the democratic system, and no one wins.

You may wonder why I have been taking this office out in the state since last summer. It allows people who are unable to come to Frankfort an opportunity to express their problems and concerns. It permits me and my staff to let them know that we in government do care. And it gives me the opportunity to find out firsthand the issues which are foremost in the minds of our citizens.[1] Let me relate two examples of how our desire to listen has resulted in state government being more responsive to your needs.

Last night, I met with representatives of the United Cerebral Palsy Agency of Eastern Kentucky and of the Landsdowne Comprehensive Care Center to review problems of continuation funding for the Cerebral Palsy School of Ashland. Today I am pleased to announce that arrangements have been worked out, which will not only assure continued funding for this program but also provide a more stable and expanding basis of support. The record this program has established for itself in this eleven-county area is impressive, and I want to commend the representatives of these local organizations for their interest and commitment to working out what appeared to be a financial crisis for the school. I have also authorized $2,500 in state funds for the program to assure the continuity in staff during this period of transition in funding. My staff will work during the ensuing weeks to ensure total funding is available when the new school year starts in September.

Another matter of much interest is the Hood's Creek Road—a project which many have been trying to get off the drawing board since 1940. Like others before me, I promised you this road, and I intend to see this one through personally. It's a big project—$450,000, and it's something that's been needed for a long time. The road is narrow and unsafe for those who must use it to travel to and from work and school. We have reached a solution on obtaining the final parcels of right-of-way. This should be completed within the near future.

---

1. Governor Ford gave a similar speech to the Local Government Issues Annual Conference in Louisville on June 13, 1974, and one in Middlesboro

on State Government Day, June 17, 1974. These two addresses are not included in this volume.

MADISONVILLE STATE GOVERNMENT DAY
Madisonville / July 30, 1974

TODAY I want to talk to you about some things we are doing to make state government responsive to your needs and thus improve the quality of life for this community and communities like yours across the state, especially with an emphasis on the future for our children. During the past two and one-half years, state government has channeled into this community $8.4 million for human resources services—services which help the blind, the handicapped, the sick, and the elderly; $6.7 million for education—through the Minimum Foundation Program; another $1.4 million for expanding vocational-technical education opportunities at your vocational school; nearly $3.5 million through our Transportation Department for your streets, roads, and highways; $2.9 million for higher education, (it's being put to good use at your community college); and $1.5 million for public protection and regulation services. I mention these facts and figures as examples to reaffirm our conviction to help make state government a commitment partner in your community's growth and prosperity.

Speaking of growth and prosperity—two weeks ago in Frankfort, we made an announcement of great interest and major significance to this area. We announced that the state entered into a formal agreement with Texas Gas to immediately begin a coal gasification project in western Kentucky. The exact site for the plant has not yet been determined, but will probably be located within thirty-five to forty miles of Texas Gas's Slaughters Compressor Station. As you know, Slaughters is a major control point on the company's pipeline system and controls access to its major underground gas storage fields.

We are moving ahead with all deliberate speed on the project. This agreement is in two phases, allowing us to proceed now with phase one, while being prepared for phase two when federal participation is acquired. We are emphasizing the environmental impact study to assure standards which must be maintained in demonstration and commercial applications of the coal gasification project. This will be a $1.1 million undertaking by itself. The whole thrust is to increase needed energy supplies compatible with a quality environment we must have in the future, through the use of converting high-sulfur coal into clean fuel. However, preliminary engineering, design, and testing must first be accomplished, in order that the study is properly carried out.

In phase two, we enter into the demonstration aspects of a gasification plant to prove technical and economic feasibility. The state's commitment coincides with federal participation. Therefore, phases one and two commit the state up to $35 million. Texas Gas, at a minimum, will match the state's total. It is anticipated that the federal share of the total project will exceed $100 million. I'm excited about this venture because of what it will mean for Kentucky, and western Kentucky in particular. It will be a boon to this area, in fact to all Kentucky. I'm talking about more energy from clean fuel, additional markets for western Kentucky coal, new jobs and industry, a stronger tax base, and increased deep mining. This is projected, ultimately, as a $600 million undertaking—over a half billion. The positive spin-offs are unlimited.[1]

Earlier I mentioned the necessity of communication—input and feedback—if government is to truly serve people. We've proved this philosophy does work right here in this community. I'm talking about the Outwood situation. Realizing the need to make major changes for patient benefit, we sought alternatives. Responsible citizens and community leaders asked us not to close Outwood. As a result of this feedback and input, we were able to develop a new health-care approach, retaining the Outwood programs, but offering new facilities and expanded care.

Presently we are preparing a bid proposal for the leasing of Outwood to be ready by August 15. We are reviewing it with the Kentucky Association of Mental Retardation and the National Association of Mental Deficiency. We are asking these groups to assist us in reviewing the standards of care to assure quality care in this institution. As soon as this review process is completed, we will be in the position to submit the proposals to prospective operators. The goal which will be reached gives patients and staff modern facilities, improves staff benefits, maintains the fine environment at Dawson Springs, and relieves taxpayers from additional dollars, because we will get federal funds which have never been available before. Kentucky has been contributing to these federal funds, but they were never being returned. Now we will share in them. This project shows how reasonable groups can get together for the public good in a cooperative venture. We will put this out on contract this year, with the contract requiring a new

facility on the present Outwood grounds.[2] Along that same line, before
we go back to work, I want to tell you about two other community
concerns.

I have been asked about the Madisonville TB Hospital. Approximately twenty patients are in the hospital. Thanks to medical advances,
hospital care of tuberculosis patients has rapidly declined. So we
must look for alternative uses of the existing facility, which can mean
additional health care here. As we decrease inpatient TB care, we certainly want to expand outpatient services which will utilize portions of
the existing facility. We are also expanding public health programs,
especially those serving the elderly, disabled, and homebound. In
addition, services in the area of mental health are now being expanded
where more housing will be needed, which points to this hospital. A
very important matter is health manpower training. When the federal
government decided not to go with this type program, I felt the people
of Kentucky needed it and included for each year of the next biennium
$2.5 million that will enable Kentucky to move ahead in the training of
health manpower. The Area Health Education System is designed to
deal with the problem of health manpower distribution. One of the
two initial sites selected was the Madisonville area. This program will
bring to this area full-time faculty and students from our two health
science centers for education and training. This program will require
part of the hospital space. So you can see that the TB Hospital will
become a much more active unit than in the past.

I can understand your impatience regarding highway 41-South. This
has been a long time coming, but under this administration the project
is moving. I am not pleased with the progress, but to be very honest,
our Transportation Department is moving as rapidly as possible when
all factors are considered. Since we began, two delays have been imposed on us, both by the federal government. Let's look at the Lake
Street-Country Club Lane section. One is the requirement for an environmental impact statement, a time-consuming undertaking. The
second is an air-quality analysis, also time-consuming. Neither were
required before I took office. Both have been completed, right-of-way
plans have been completed. We are in the right-of-way acquisition
stage and are pushing to get this out of the way. There are 164 parcels
and twenty-three relocations involved.

Now let's look at the Country Club Lane to Robinson Street in
Earlington Section. The design public hearing has been held. The environmental impact statement is being circulated to the various federal
agencies. We will start right-of-way acquisition within the next few
weeks. There are twenty-seven parcels, and this should move quickly.

I might also mention that on the Earlington Section to avoid further delay, we placed state funds into the project, rather than waiting on federal funds. Hopefully we will be reimbursed someday.

I don't know of any project receiving more attention or being shoved harder than these. Yet I share in your frustration, because without the new federal requirements, we would save time. The point is that we are spearheading both sections, and no one else has done that before. And a final point, right-of-way acquisition can be speeded up when both sides work together for the best and quickest solution. But this is a two-sided matter between the state and property owners, and I call this to your attention, hoping everyone will work to see that the parcels are secured in the shortest possible time.

---

1. For more information on the Texas Gas gasification-liquefaction plant, see press conference of July 13, 1974, in the Economic and Industrial Development section, pp. 443–45.

2. For more information on the Outwood facility, see the press conference of June 21, 1974, in the Health and Welfare section, pp. 206–7.

STATE GOVERNMENT DAY
Munfordville / August 19, 1974

As state government moves out into Kentucky's communities, I'm beginning to feel like George Gallup, Lou Harris,[1] and all the other pollsters wrapped up in one package. This feeling comes because people are talking, expressing their concerns, their opinions, and their complaints. They are appreciative for the consideration given them. They are a reservoir of energy, initiative, and resourcefulness. And because of this, my staff and I have a much better understanding, I believe, of the role state government must play and of the expectations from those served by state government, or for that matter, any level of government.

Let me digress just a moment and talk about what state government's commitment to your area has meant during the past thirty-two months. State government has channeled into this community $4.6

million for human resources services—services which help the blind, the handicapped, the sick, and the elderly; $2.3 million for education through the Minimum Foundation Program; nearly $2.4 million through our Transportation Department for your streets, roads, and highways; $686,000 for higher education; and $4.1 million for public protection and regulation services. I mention these facts and figures as examples to reaffirm our conviction to help make state government a committed partner in your community's growth and prosperity.

When people come and visit us, what are they looking for? One thread which has run through all of our sessions which we have been involved in for over a year can be summarized. People are looking for answers. They want to know where they can get answers not only to matters of state government but to matters of federal and local governments, as well as the private sector. People are looking for personal government. They want the barricades between the governed and the governing torn down. People are looking for proof that their investment in government is worthwhile. People are looking for reassurance, in a time of uncertainty, a time of worry, and a time of change.

I don't have all the answers. As we bring state government to the people, there are opportunities to help immediately, to help later on, and also instances when the answer must be no. I would rather never say no. But this isn't fair, nor is it honest. We have unlimited needs and limited resources. We try to accommodate the unlimited needs by every method at our disposal, but it simply isn't possible. This is where the energy, enthusiasm, initiative, and resourcefulness of a community comes in. It's evident in Munfordville; it's evident in all sections of Kentucky. Community progress is nearly always directly related to the responsiveness of local citizens who are willing to join together in a cooperative venture.[2] Community progress stands a better chance when more decision-making and more tools are given to those officials who are closest to the people being served. We have concentrated on this fact for the past two and a half years, because you know your needs better than Frankfort, just as Frankfort knows the needs of Kentucky much better than Washington.

Some may ask, "What do you hear from those who visit your portable office?" I hear about inflation, transportation needs, interest in playgrounds and recreational facilities. I hear from individuals who have specific problems relating to health, to adoptions, to care for the elderly and the less fortunate. I hear about drainage problems, flooding, and shortages of materials. Let me give you a couple of unique problems to illustrate the many different circumstances. A discharged soldier's furniture and personal belongings had been lost for a year.

This man didn't know where else to turn, since the army hadn't been able to locate the items. He heard we were in a community close to his home and came by. A week later his items were located. A lady with several children lived in the country near a creek that suddenly flooded without warning. For three years she had feared for her family's life, but didn't know what to do. She came by. The next day an engineer from the state began working on the matter. The cause was a culvert, installed years ago during a project conducted by both the state and the county in which she lived. It is being corrected.

Now we don't bat a thousand by any means. But I believe by going to the people, we can help in many cases, and this makes it very worthwhile, for this is exactly the reason for the existence of government at any level. I think you want and expect public officials to listen and respond whenever possible. From the turn-outs in all sections of Kentucky, I know people are anxious to be heard. And what each has to say is important.

---

1. George Horace Gallup (1901–), Princeton, New Jersey; public opinion statistician; former professor of journalism; editorial and advertising surveyor for magazines and newspapers; chairman of the board of Gallup Organization Inc.; marketing and attitude research author. Louis Harris (1921–), New York City; public opinion analyst and columnist; pollster for numerous newspapers and magazines; proprietor of Louis Harris and Associates Inc.; marketing and public opinion research author. *Who's Who in the World, 1974–1975* (Chicago, 1974), pp. 361, 428.

2. On August 16, 1974, Governor Ford spoke at the Banana Festival Luncheon in Fulton, Kentucky. He commented on the first festival twelve years earlier and complimented the community on its fine work and genuine Kentucky hospitality.

HIGHWAYS

KENTUCKY HIGHWAY CONFERENCE
Lexington / March 20, 1972

IT is a pleasure for me to be here today among so many friends—road builders, mayors, county officials, and university representatives. Collectively, we have something in common. We know we can't please all the people all of the time.

When it comes to making decisions on roads, we often find ourselves between a rock and a hard place. Now, however, we can make some people-oriented decisions, thanks to the responsibility shown by the Legislature in approving my recommendation for support of Kentucky's road construction and maintenance programs. It was not an easy decision for me to make; and the legislators who voted for it did so only after considering all the alternatives. Yet, as I'm sure you know, there was no other choice for responsible leadership to make. I do not believe Kentuckians favor postponement of the day of financial reckoning by going for another bond issue and thereby adding to the debt-retirement burden that is already heavy. I think our citizens want to pay as they go, whenever possible.

I am proud of our road system in Kentucky. It is one of the finest in the nation. But much more must be accomplished, especially in a rapidly changing society. I am pledged to the construction of a number of road projects that will meet real needs. I intend to keep those pledges. I want to help fill in the gaps by building what I call "get-to-it" roads, the secondary routes which carry much of our intrastate traffic. One of my goals is to give rural and small-town Kentucky new and improved people-roads that will serve areas bypassed by our superhighways to enable these forgotten Kentuckians to "get to" our superhighways quicker and with more safety.

The modern highways we have in mind for these bypassed areas will be more than a convenience. They will be a very real economic asset. Per-capita employment is 200 percent greater in places served by good highways. Thus we offer economic stimulus which cannot be obtained any other way. My program does not overlook our urban needs—not by any means. The new municipal-aid program is a major innovation in Kentucky road building. The approval of the two-cent revenue increase for the road fund makes possible, for the first time, revenue-sharing with our municipalities.[1] Remember, this is in addition to existing state-government support. There have been some remarks, for obvious political purposes, falsely describing our revenue-sharing program, and I want the facts known.

During the campaign last year, I promised state and local revenue-sharing, whether or not expanded federal revenue-sharing came to pass. The municipal-aid program is just that, and its creation is as important as the creation of the Rural Secondary Program of 1948—which, by the way, was the last time Kentucky's motor-fuel tax was raised.[2]

My hope is that Kentucky's road program will progress along a number of different lines. Our interstate system is nearly complete, and we are second in the nation in mileage of our parkways, although we are far from second in population. We are third in the nation in obligating interstate funds in relation to the apportionment of interstate money. In road building it is essential that we prepare for tomorrow's demands today. Our mission is not only to build new roads but to properly maintain those we've already built, and we must continue to whittle down the debt we incurred to build what we have. It is a big order. But we can meet it, and we will meet it. A reorganized Highway Department will help, by getting maximum benefits from the road dollar. You have heard this before. But let me say, come, take a look, for it is already happening. The new budget for the biennium will also help by providing nearly $8 million for road programs that otherwise would have been siphoned from the road fund to fund activities of other agencies of state government.

Never has it been more important to plan roads and highways in the context of sensible and defensible priorities. Never before has the whole concept of road building been under such challenge as it is today. Environmentalists are questioning the need for additional roads. Their voices are becoming more insistent and influential. So it behooves road planners to carefully consider the effect of their plans on the quality of the environment. Attention must be given to this consideration, and I do not mean a token nod in the direction of protecting the environment. Social engineering now must have a role along with civil engineering. After all, roads and highways are built, in the final analysis, to benefit the people of the Commonwealth. As long as they properly serve the users, the people will support the program.

Our task is not easy. Like so much else in our dynamic and rapidly changing society, road building is becoming an ever more complex undertaking. Nevertheless, I'm sure you are equal to the task, and working together we can improve the quality of life for all Kentuckians.

---

1. See an act "relating to the taxation of motor fuels and prescribing the purposes for which such taxes may be expended," which was approved

March 15, 1972. *Acts of the General Assembly of the Commonwealth of Kentucky, 1972*, Chapter 61 (H.B. 336), pp. 228–41.

2. See an act "relating to the manner and method for the expenditure of funds set apart for the construction, reconstruction, and maintenance of secondary and rural roads," approved February 6, 1948. *Acts of the General Assembly of the Commonwealth of Kentucky, 1948*, Chapter 46 (H.B. 196), pp. 93–95.

MARKLAND DAM HIGHWAY BRIDGE
Warsaw/ April 12, 1972

I AM signing a contract today which is a joint agreement with Kentucky, Indiana, and the U.S. government to construct a highway bridge over Markland Dam on the Ohio River near Warsaw. In signing this contract, long-recognized transportation needs of both Kentucky and Indiana will be met.

The Louisville District of the Corps of Engineers will be responsible for the design and construction of the bridge proper and the access roads. According to the contractual agreement, the states of Indiana and Kentucky will finance the construction of necessary approach roads to connect the bridge to existing public highways. Kentucky's funds for construction of the bridge proper are coming from the 1970 Highway Act—$3,761,000 of federal monies was appropriated for this specific purpose.

To finance approaches on Kentucky's side, the state will be required to provide half of approximately $963,000. Kentucky's half will be matched by federal aid from secondary-road funds. The construction of the bridge to link Kentucky and Indiana will boost the northern Kentucky economy by providing an easily accessible approach for Indiana farmers to northern Kentucky's burley markets. Also, the highway bridge will serve as a main artery to guide tourists into two northern Kentucky attractions, General Butler and Big Bone State parks.

KENTUCKY BROADCASTERS ASSOCIATION
Louisville / May 12, 1972

MANY speakers begin by saying, "It is a pleasure to be here." That statement properly expresses my feelings today. But unfortunately, I must add that part of what is contained in my brief remarks will not be pleasant. It is imperative, however, because of this occasion and your public service attitude in providing network facilities, that I take advantage of your time and the time of those listening to radio stations around Kentucky. Whether you, or our statewide audience, realize it or not, we face a crisis in this state—a crisis on highways, streets, yes even backroads. The early tragedies of 1972, of death, injury, and economic loss, are overwhelming our normal efforts toward traffic safety. We must do something different, now and even more on a continuing basis, or face possibly the most perilous year in our history of automotive travel.

Americans, not only in Kentucky but elsewhere, perhaps have become so accustomed to grim statistics that the impact of what is happening escapes them. But it does not escape me as Governor. It does not escape the Kentucky State Police or other law-enforcement officials who must notify next of kin, listen to the screams of those in pain, and view the needless waste of life, limb, and property. I have never been more serious than at this hour. The question is, "How can that seriousness be transferred to others?" Proven methods are few. We constantly seek ideas which work in our never-ending attempt to reduce highway slaughter. Somewhere there is an answer.

Last year 1,023 men, women, and children died because of Kentucky traffic accidents. As of this morning, the figure for 1972 stood at 359. If such a pace continues, 1972 will become a far more disastrous year than 1971. These are fatalities; injury is not included—nor is the tremendous cost to those both guilty and innocent. While we can never place a value on life, let me discuss injuries, an often-overlooked statistic. In 1971, 807 people were injured in McCracken County alone. In Jefferson County 6,746 were hurt in traffic accidents. In Boone, Campbell, and Kenton, 2,362 persons of all ages suffered injuries. Madison County's total was 536. There were 590 injuries in Pike, 402 in Laurel, 2,030 in Fayette, 448 in Franklin, and 511 in Boyd. These are only a few grim examples of what happened last year, of what is happening this year, and of what we must drastically reduce in the months ahead.

There seems to be a matter-of-fact attitude on the part of citizens when we talk about highway safety. My friends, let's not accept the premise that soaring death rates, injury counts, and higher financial losses are something that is bound to happen. It doesn't have to happen! We can, and must, work together to turn a terrible situation around. I can't do it alone as Governor, nor can the State Police. We need the active concern of every individual driver, the cooperation of the news media, just as we are receiving today from radio, and the never-ending determination of all Kentuckians who inwardly react with deep sorrow whenever they become aware of another accident.

Therefore, I have an important announcement. On May 22 I plan to illustrate as dramatically as possible this growing problem by holding a series of crisis conferences in seven sections of Kentucky.[1] Joining me with the press in each area will be members of the State Police —men who go through every hour of the day one of the most depressing experiences imaginable, that of working wrecks. The May 22 Traffic Safety Program will inaugurate the most comprehensive war against violence on our highways in Kentucky history. While I have this responsibility as Governor, I recognize my duty as a citizen. I implore everyone listening to join me as worried citizens who want to commit themselves personally in this assault on the waste of human resources. We will be contacting later civic clubs, fraternal organizations, schools, business, professional, and labor groups, as well as law-enforcement officers in all communities.

This administration has initiated many people-service programs in its first 150 days—programs for education, for consumer protection, for environmental control, for economic stimulation, and for new jobs. Let us be equally as conscious about saving lives. I hope I am wrong, but there are established odds that some of you listening right now will be victims of what we are trying to prevent. Some of you will be involved in a head-on collision; some will lose control of your vehicles; others will be pedestrian casualties, while more will fall prey to side-swiping, chain-reaction wrecks, drunk drivers, and of course the ever-present speeders.

If this reminder will make you stop and be more cautious, if this plea will create a sense of awareness, then we will have taken a first, big step. Ahead are such hazardous periods as Memorial Day weekend, the July 4 holiday, Labor Day, and other dates when highways are crowded with drivers in a hurry, tired, unalert, and yes, irritable. Whatever must be done is our single priority. May 22 is our opening round in this match against sadness and ruin. Many of our approaches will be unique; hopefully they will stick in the public's mind to help slow the present accident trend.

People can do anything they want to do. Here is a challenge of enormous dimension, one which has thus far not been met. I solicit your assistance, not for the benefit of declining death and injury rates but rather for the benefit of you and your family. You know, as I talk with citizens in all sections of Kentucky, I find them most agreeable with the direction this administration is taking, especially as they understand the facts.

I am proud that we have been able to reduce the individual tax burden, yet provide more people-services. I am proud of the emphasis we are placing on a better life for our farm families, for our elderly, and for our children, whether it be through new kindergarten programs, special education, or vocational training.

At the end of this administration, which is the only time when reasonable persons can make judgments, I want Kentucky to lead the nation in livability, economic growth, crime reduction, and in personal opportunity. At that time, I also want Kentucky to trail the nation in highway disasters. You are important. And whatever I can do these next forty-three months to keep you alive and well, I will do. You deserve no less. Your family deserves no less. Kentucky deserves no less.

There is something else Kentucky deserves, regarding a matter far different from what I have just discussed. Kentucky deserves an honorable and efficient state employee work force, as well as an administration that upholds the law of merit employment. In the past administration, the state merit system was a sham. Public records prove it. Qualified, hard-working employees were fired strictly for political purposes, and the taxpayers' pocketbooks suffered because of this disregard for the law. I promised to protect the merit system. I call your attention to public records which prove conclusively that this promise has been kept.

Here is a comparison taken from official documents. Since January 1, 1972, there have been only eighty-eight merit system appeals filed in state government. Already, thirty-four have been heard. Yet a mere three reinstatements have been ordered and only three others recommended. This is even more conclusive because the present personnel board is controlled by Nunn appointees. During the previous administration, there were 400 appeals pending. There was such a logjam because of machine-gun firing that the personnel board couldn't even get to the cases. So the delay cost even more in the long run when back pay was ordered.

It is very clear that this is a new day for Kentucky taxpayers now receiving protection of their monies, as intended by the original passage of the merit-system law. The law clearly intends that if there are public employees who won't work, they should be replaced. This I shall do. But the law also intends that merit employees doing a good job should have no fear of political harassment. The mass firings of the past, and the subsequent ordered reinstatements and pay of back wages, heavily burdened the innocent, including you who pay taxes. I am not going to let this happen. I invite the press to review and fully report the facts. The citizens deserve your findings.

---

1. These addresses are not included in this volume.

KENTUCKY TURNPIKE ANNOUNCEMENT
Louisville / August 9, 1972

EVERY effort is being made to secure congressional approval for the extension of toll collections on the Kentucky Turnpike in order to carry out my previously announced road-construction program in Jefferson County and along that Turnpike. Specifically, this means the planned segment of the Jefferson Freeway between Preston Street and Dixie Highway, an adequate connector between the Outer Loop interchange with the Kentucky Turnpike and Preston Street, and modernization of the Kentucky Turnpike. Without the support of our Kentucky delegation, and the ability to acquire funds, these desperately needed projects would not be possible for an estimated fifteen years.

Our success, however, in having Congress authorize this program will be based on retaining all existing toll facilities. It is their decision, and it must be our approach since we know this is the only system that can be implemented. The importance for immediate action on these construction projects is paramount, and both the mayor of Louisville and judge of Jefferson County have agreed with the format in view of the projects' high priority.

As soon as Congress acts, we will start engineering to provide for the upgrading of the Kentucky Turnpike to modern interstate standards and also begin the necessary plans for the construction of the Jefferson Freeway and Outer Loop connector. We will eliminate congestion on those ramps now causing delays to motorists which, along with the total project, will most assuredly meet with overwhelming approval from the public.

CHAMBER OF COMMERCE
GOVERNOR'S TOUR
Shively / October 3, 1972

IT is good to be in Shively this morning as we begin the 1972 Kentucky Chamber of Commerce Governor's tour. On several occasions during these next three days I am scheduled to speak. To my fellow tour participants this could prove brutal, hearing the same jokes over and over again, the same person time after time. So I'm going to make a promise, and I'm going to keep it. My addresses will be in the form of brief reports in the areas we visit, not wordy, but to the point in as short a manner as possible. As for jokes—I'm always in the market for some new ones!

There is keen interest in Shively about highway matters. There has been for years. In the way of a progress report, work on the Watterson Expressway cloverleaf interchange reached the 60 percent stage September 1. This indicates that we are on schedule and should meet the September 1973 deadline. Our project for widening Dixie Highway was 40 percent completed on September 1. This should be wrapped up also by September of next year. I hope then we can find reason to stop using the grim name of "Dixie Dieway" because of the improved road conditions.

While on this particular subject, I cannot omit a personal plea. No matter how many millions we spend on highways, no matter how hard our State Police work, no matter how mechanically perfect our cars are, there still will be tragedy on the highways. This is because one element tends to lose out; that's the element of personal attention. As you know, I have participated in a number of traffic-safety programs this year, trying to reduce the killing and injuring of hundreds upon hundreds. Our results are encouraging only during those periods of maximum publicity. Man forgets quickly, and disaster strikes as soon as his guard is let down.

I must constantly remind as many Kentuckians as possible and will keep doing so until we find the solution. We do plan additional programs to combat the rising death toll. Someday we will find the answer. Another project which I know is of interest to the Shively area is the Cane Run Road improvement. This is a reconstruction job involving approximately $5 million. We are now about 60 percent through with the final design phase, but cannot yet give a completion date for the project. When finished, however, this project will benefit the Shively area a great deal.

Second, in the way of a future projection, I want to remind you that your area will share in the urban-aid road program enacted by the last General Assembly. This innovative revenue-sharing program, the first of its kind in the country, will return gasoline revenue to local communities on a population-formula basis. We are projecting $9.3 million in new highway revenue for this program in its first year. This new revenue will be distributed to over 400 municipalities in Kentucky to help them with local road and street development. Based on the 1970 census figures for Shively, and figuring a per-capita return of $4.92 to each municipality receiving this new road money, you should be getting about $94,000 for road development in the Shively area. We will give local governments the broadest possible authority in using the shared revenue to benefit local road needs. Remember, this is 100 percent a state of Kentucky program and is not part of any federal plan.

On the issue of the Ninth Street Interchange, I am afraid I can't give you much good news. The federal funds designated to go to this project are still waiting on passage of the 1972 federal highway act. We can do nothing until Congress decides, but I can assure you we are using as much influence as we can to prod them along. This project not only affects your area, but it ties up the downtown Louisville development because of its impact on the Riverside Expressway. You may remember that one problem holding up the project was an opinion on the part of federal authorities that it would not be necessary to have underground heating coils this far south. We still anticipate that the heating coils will be included in the project, but we must wait on passage of the highway act.

We want state government to be responsive to the needs of the people of Kentucky, but if we don't hear from you, we may miss some problems that are of immediate concern to you. So when you want to communicate, do so. Thank you for coming today, and please visit us when you get to Frankfort.

GREEN RIVER PARKWAY DEDICATION
Green River Parkway / December 15, 1972

ALL along the motorcade route today, I could sense the optimism of the people who had come to witness the opening of the Green River Parkway.[1] They knew that a new chapter of prosperity and progress was opening for the development of western Kentucky. The very fact that we have had breakfast in Owensboro, stopped at two ceremonies along the way, and are lunching at Bowling Green is testimony of the new ties that can develop between parts of our state that have not been readily available before. With this new modern highway our neighborhoods have expanded across the state to bring people closer together and to provide the opportunity for more cooperation and harmony between the people of Kentucky.

I know that the people of Bowling Green are education-conscious with one of the state's fine universities located here. With Brescia College and Kentucky Wesleyan at one end of the parkway and Western Kentucky University at this end, the educational opportunities for this part of the state are greatly increased. The parkway will provide a speedier and safer access to Western Kentucky University for a total of 925 students from Daviess, Ohio, and Butler counties now attending Western. It likewise will help the 667 students from Henderson, Webster, McLean, Hopkins, and Muhlenberg counties west of the parkway now enrolled in Western and almost as many counties east of the parkway. And this does not take into account future students who will be attracted by the convenience of reaching the college via the parkway. Further benefits will be accorded teachers taking night and weekend classes at Western who are employed in the counties touched by the parkway or adjacent to it.

Remember, though, the educational opportunities opened by the Green River Parkway are but one aspect of this new highway. The economic impact will even be more significant to this area, because it opens up greater access to new sources of supply and new markets to bring business and industry. As the "anchor town" for this end of the parkway, Bowling Green will be in a position to attract the kind of economic development that can mean more growth. The impact this can have on your community is illustrated by other communities after they became a hub center of merging highways. They experienced great economic development, and a new feeling of civic pride bloomed.

Recreational opportunities are also more readily available now than ever before for the people of this area and the many tourists who visit Kentucky each year. We have many beautiful natural resources in our state, and we want to share this wealth with others. The Green River Parkway, and all of our highways, are carefully planned to protect the land through which they traverse. At the same time, they are designed to provide the best service possible where that service is needed. These goals have been accomplished in the construction of the Green River Parkway. Highway Department engineers selected an alignment that supplied the greatest level of service when considering all aspects of our community needs.

Today is a great day for all the communities that lie along the route of this great new modern highway.[2] With the opening of the Green River Parkway, a new era of progress and development begins in western Kentucky. It is impossible to overestimate the significance of this new highway. Not only the two great towns of Owensboro and Bowling Green which anchor the parkway, but many fine smaller communities like Hartford and Beaver Dam can look to a brighter future and an improved quality of life. No town is too small to cash in. Rockfield, Cromwell, Aberdeen, Dundee, and Rich Pond are directly connected to interchanges with the Green River Parkway.

Indeed, all the communities along this parkway will be able to look back on December 15, 1972, as a day that new prosperity came to town just as Elizabethtown now looks back to the mid-sixties when the Blue Grass and Western Kentucky parkways and I-65 were dedicated. These roads turned Elizabethtown into a thriving crossroads community. Civic pride is greater than ever; industry is profiting and sharing in community financing and progress. Madisonville, a crossroads town only three years old, is experiencing the delightful benefits associated with better highways. You've heard the slogan "highways help people." That you can be sure of, and you can count on this administration to pursue a program of dynamic progress in all areas of life vital to the Commonwealth.

Coupled with Kentucky's interstate program statewide and the Appalachian Highway System in the eastern section of the Commonwealth, Kentucky's highways will have an even finer reputation than they now enjoy among out-of-state guests, many of whom take the time to write back and tell us they were impressed. This toll road will prove itself to be one more bright star in Kentucky's constellation of parkways.

We have already had two ceremonies to open this great new highway, and the people at each one were enthusiastic over the future opportunities that the Green River Parkway would mean for them.[3] Morgantown is in an ideal location to benefit from the parkway. Not only do you have two entrances onto the highway we are opening today, but you are also connected to the Blue Grass and Western Kentucky parkways and I-65 to the south. What this can mean to Morgantown and the surrounding communities is unlimited in terms of a much brighter future. The Green River Parkway gives this area an additional link with the interstate system. This means greater access to supply sources and markets for business and industry looking for expansion sites. Because of Kentucky's advantageous location to national markets, highways have become central to our economic development. Morgantown is in an excellent position to cash in on this situation, as are the surrounding communities.

The new parkway will also bring this area tourist business from people coming to visit cave country and the many fine state parks in western Kentucky. For the people here, a weekend retreat is more available than ever before. Tourism is big business in the Commonwealth. Last year alone, 585 million tourist dollars were spent in the state. Out-of-state visitors contributed $426 million of this to our tourist trade while traveling over five billion miles on Kentucky highways. This can mean new business opportunities for the communities along these highways. The opportunities are waiting to be tapped. The success you make of these new opportunities will be determined by your willingness to cooperate and work with your neighbors in making the kind of progress that will benefit all of the people in this region.

So, today I want to share your enthusiasm and optimism in the opening of this parkway. I know that you will meet the challenges of working together to turn this into the beginning of an era of progress that will create a better quality of life for generations to come. I want to assure you that while you are working in your communities down here, my administration will continue its efforts from Frankfort to give you the kind of assistance you need in being part of a progressive and growing Kentucky.

It is appropriate that the new highway we dedicate should be named for the Green River.[4] This river has played an important part in the growth of Kentucky. During our early years, the Green River was a principal artery of transportation used to transport agricultural products and logs downstream to market. Coal was taken on barges to St. Louis, Memphis, and New Orleans. The river still plays an important part in the economy of Kentucky. Last year about 13,000 floating commercial vessels made the trip up and down the Green River. It has served as an open door to a larger world of both progress and development.

Now, another door will be open: the Green River Parkway. Supply-and-market accessibility will encourage new economic development. It will also provide better opportunities for educational and recreational activities which have been unavailable in the past. Generations to come will have the chance for a better quality of life. Many towns, no matter how small, will benefit. Rockfield, Cromwell, Aberdeen, Dundee, and Rich Pond are directly connected to interchanges with the Green River Parkway. Owensboro, of course, will anchor this end of the new route. The impact this can have on our community can be seen in the fantastic development witnessed at Elizabethtown after they became a hub center of merging highways.

With the Green River Parkway, neighbors in Hartford, Beaver Dam, Morgantown, and Bowling Green are easier to visit. The natural wonders of Mammoth Cave, Barren River, and Rough River State parks are closer than ever for weekend or one-day retreats. These tourist attractions and many more will not only be more available to you, but to our friends in Indiana as well. And we welcome out-of-state tourists. They help pay our taxes! Along with improved accessibility, we should find more visitors coming to our state contributing to the already flourishing tourist enterprise. We would be selfish not to share our natural wealth. Kentucky is rich in scenic beauty.

Kentucky herself is becoming a crossroads state. We are a bridge between the industrial Midwest and the markets of the South and East. Right now the Commonwealth is in the center of a twenty-eight-state distribution area which reaches the northern manufacturing belt, the eastern seaboard, and the southern gulf ports. This area contains 73 percent of the nation's population, 73 percent of its personal income, and 81 percent of its manufacturing employment. The Green River Parkway is one more top-notch, limited-access highway to strengthen Kentucky's position. Indiana and Illinois have been brought closer to Tennessee via a Kentucky highway.

Our parkway system, the finest in the nation, has filled in the gaps between interstates enabling Kentuckians to utilize these highways to the fullest. The parkway system has allowed us to open up areas of the Commonwealth once isolated and remote. Within the next three years, Kentucky will open an additional five hundred miles of limited-access highways, linking us even further to the North, South, East, and West. This, my friends, is what I have set out to do, to bring benefits of all types to Kentucky—financial, social, educational, and cultural so that we all might live better in comfort and harmony.

1. This is a compilation of the series of speeches made along the route of the parkway at Bowling Green, Hartford and Beaver Dam Interchange, Morgantown Interchange, and Owensboro.
2. This segment was given at Hartford and Beaver Dam Interchange.
3. This segment was given at the Morgantown Interchange.
4. This segment was given at Owensboro.

KENTUCKY HIGHWAY CONTRACTORS ASSOCIATION
Acapulco, Mexico / January 22, 1973

MANY questions have been asked about our highway construction program and how it affects your industry. What are our prospects for 1973? This is not an easy one to answer. The difficulty lies in Washington. Our 1973 planning depends on congressional action and the national administration's budgeting policies.

What I have to tell you today is based on the best advice available and my own appraisal of what we can expect from Washington. Surely everyone in this room knows the sad details regarding federal highway legislation last year. The President has even usurped our right to funds through impoundment. The product of months of congressional hearings and conferences on highway legislation turned out to be no highway legislation, as the federal support we were expecting failed to materialize.

Hopefully, the Ninety-Third Congress will soon be at work on a Federal Highway Act of 1973, though any talk of "quickie" legislation seems impractical. In all probability, the Congress will go through its usual procedure of investigation, discussion, and conferences before a bill finally passes.

Commissioner Pryor[1] and his staff are thinking in terms of midsummer. They are hopeful that the 1973 act will be passed and signed by that time. I am working toward spring. In the meantime, what can we do to keep Kentucky's highway program going forward? Particularly, what can we do about the pressing need to move ahead on several important interstate projects? We have decided to finance, with 100 percent state money, some of the most critical projects, anticipating that the federal government will follow through on the commitment made by former Secretary of Transportation John Volpe.[2] That is, we can recover the usual federal share of the cost of financing interstate construction as soon as federal funds are made available by congressional action—and the administration releases. Nevertheless, it is evident we still do not know when or how much federal aid we can count on.

There are interstate projects in Kentucky that simply must go ahead. Consequently, we must assume the inconvenience, if not the risk, that goes with our own financing. We are in the position of a small merchant with a millionaire customer. The customer wants to make a substantial purchase but will tell us only that he will pay "someday." We know his credit is good; we just don't know how far we can carry him!

The projects I am talking about you could probably name. There is the surfacing project on the Carter County section of Interstate 64, the "missing link" in this important regional highway east of Lexington. Another section of I-64 that demands action is the River Front Project between Seventh and Thirteenth streets in Louisville that includes the massive Ninth Street Interchange.

As you have read, Department of Highways' engineers continue to insist that the ramps of the interchange can be made safe in winter only by installing heating coils to control icing conditions. We have not yet secured the agreement of the Federal Highway Administration to sharing the cost. It is too much for Kentucky to absorb, but a federal decision may prevent the heating coils, if they refuse to fund the $1.5 million in cost required for installation.

There is also work to be done on Interstate 275 in northern Kentucky. It is needed to keep this bypass route moving ahead. Specifically, we plan to take bids on the superstructure of the Licking River bridge and a grade-and-drain project, 1.7 miles from U.S. 25 to Horse Branch.

The Department of Highways is readying these projects, on I-64 and I-275, to be put into a letting as soon as possible. And we are counting on a substantial Appalachian program this year, perhaps as much as $75 million. This program was not affected by lack of highway legislation in 1972. Construction projects will be undertaken on sections of KY 61 and KY 80, both west of U.S. 27, and on U.S. 23 and U.S. 119 in eastern Kentucky.

I am sure you would like to have some idea what our total construction program may amount to in 1973. To give you a number requires that we make certain assumptions about federal aid: We must assume that Congress passes and the President signs a highway bill with reasonable promptness. We must assume that Kentucky receives about the same amount for obligation next fiscal year that we were told we could expect for the current fiscal year. This means we would count on $58 million this year, and the same amount next. We are also assuming all this money would be released for obligation in 1973. On this basis, and not including routine surfacing and resurfacing projects, we can look forward to lettings of $175 to $200 million. A nice neighborhood! And it's a neighborhood I expect the highway program will be living in for the next few years.

The interstate program is now on its last lap. Nationally, 80 percent of its total mileage is open to traffic. In Kentucky we have 585 miles in service. Of the remainder, all but fifty-eight miles are already under construction. Considering the cost of highway-debt retirement, which reaches $72 million next fiscal year, it is most unlikely that we will be able to take on additional indebtedness for other construction.

What does all this mean to the highway industry? Let me give you a few facts, as I see them, and a few impressions. Instead of volume, I believe highway contractors are going to have to concentrate on quality. This may very well result in more costly construction, but I believe the climate of the times requires it. We—and I am speaking of both my side of the table, the administrators of highway programs, and yours, the highway builders—are going to face more intense and more critical public scrutiny than we have ever had in the past.

The time was, not too long ago, when any highway project was such welcome news that few citizens, if any, could be found to protest against it. Nowadays, urban projects—and more and more of our work is urban—are more apt to meet with resistance than applause. Why? Because the benefits of these projects are conferred primarily on those who do not live in the affected area, and the benefits may be several years ahead. On the other hand, the inconvenience and damage is immediate and local, keenly felt by those citizens in an area where highway construction is going on. These are the people we must persuade to support highway projects.

The professional staff of the Department of Highways tells Charlie Pryor and me that they expect our employers, the public, are going to demand more attention in the following situations: The flow of traffic through construction sites must be improved, both for safety's sake and efficiency. Environmental nuisances must be controlled. Finally, everyone involved—administrators, engineers, and contractors—must work to reduce the unreasonably long time required to bring a new road into being. It is difficult to find acceptable explanations for the six-to-eight-year period before a new highway is born.

I know no better way to resist the critics than with quality performance. The best public relations in the long run is the best service.

When the people of Kentucky and the nation are convinced that their highway program is meeting their needs intelligently and effectively, we will no longer need fear for our programs. We can go ahead, planning and building the roads Kentucky wants, needs, and deserves.

It certainly doesn't hurt to let our congressional delegation know what we think those wants and needs are. Just before Christmas, Senator Huddleston and six congressmen met at the mansion to discuss the highway program. I can tell you they were delighted to have our advice—the first time it had been presented so effectively, they said—and assured us of their collective support for a federal highway program that will face up to Kentucky's transportation problems. I only wish we had a President who was truly interested in recognizing our needs.

I have tried to keep these remarks brief—for a very good reason. I'll see you at the pool!

---

1. Charles Pryor, commissioner of highways, for more information see speech from March 24, 1973, in the Reorganization section, p. 125.

2. John Anthony Volpe (1908–   ), ambassador; president, John A. Volpe Construction Company (1933–1960), chairman of the board (1960–1969); Governor of Massachusetts (1961–1963, 1965–1969); United States secretary of transportation (1969–1973); ambassador to Italy (1973–1977). Who's Who in America, 1974–1975 (Chicago, 1975), 2:3173.

CYNTHIANA ACCESS ROUTE
Cynthiana / April 9, 1973

THIS may seem to most of you like a hastily called meeting, but let me assure you that since the first of March I've been trying to visit you on my own initiative to discuss some of your interests.[1] Several months ago, a number of you who are present now visited me in Frankfort to discuss a subject that has long concerned this community —an improved route to Interstate 75. Even before that session, John Swinford and Wilson Palmer[2] had spent a considerable amount of time in the Capitol with the same project in mind.

I'm probably more familiar with Cynthiana and Harrison County than you think. Tommy Preston,[3] who's still homesick, keeps me up to date, and both Wilson and John are frequent visitors on matters pertaining to your community. I'm also aware of your frustrations. For fifteen years at least, an access route to I-75 has been on your minds. Three Governors who preceded me promised relief, yet when I was a candidate for Governor nothing had happened, and you had pretty much resigned yourselves that nothing would happen, no matter what was said in the future. I honestly believe you would have preferred during that period one of the Governors coming here to level with you, to say although he promised help, he simply couldn't do it because of other priorities. At least you would have had an answer.

The improvement of U.S. 62 between Cynthiana and Georgetown has been pretty tough to wrestle. There are many high-priority road projects throughout Kentucky. There are limited funds, and this is even more so today because of two factors. First, Congress failed to pass a highway bill last session. This has denied us part of a construction season and inflation means delayed construction will eventually take more money than anticipated. The other reason is that Kentucky's highway-bonded indebtedness has soared. When I assumed office as Governor, the state was already obligated to make increased payments throughout my term. As an example, during the 1970–1971 fiscal year, the figure amounted to $35 million. For 1971–1972 it went to $44 million; then to $60 million for 1972–1973 fiscal year; and in the 1973–1974 fiscal year it will go over $72 million. These were prior obligations which I must satisfy.

There is a lot of self-reliance in this community. I say this as the highest compliment I can pay you as individuals. The dividends from your self-reliance are quite visible, especially since the very late fifties and very early sixties. In my opinion, such an attitude will continue, and I want to assist. I want to be a part because this community has been good to me. You furnished me with a floor leader in the House who fought hard for many programs which I personally felt would be in the best interest of all Kentucky. You furnished me with a state senator, who very quietly on many occasions successfully carried the ball for us at the other end of the hall. What this points out is whenever people with the same concerns work together, progress is made.

Let's continue working together. In this regard I am announcing today that my administration is going to take the first steps toward what you have been promised, and disappointed in, for the past fifteen years. We will begin immediately the first stage of rebuilding U.S. 62, starting at this end. I want to be very candid and tell you that if U.S. 62 ever is improved, it must be done in stages, as I indicated to your delegation last year in Frankfort. Now what have we already done and what will we do right now? We have already completed preliminary engineering on a portion of the route between U.S. 27 and the Russell Cave Pike. We will carry out engineering from the Russell Cave Pike toward Georgetown to determine future staging plans. I have allocated additional funds for the widening and resurfacing of the first four miles as stage one. That construction project begins at once.

After such a long wait, and probably loss of hope, you're going to see definite progress. This isn't another pledge. This is one man keeping his word to you, because the papers are already signed and sufficient funds have been set aside for phase one.

I have over two and a half years remaining and as far as Wendell Ford is concerned, we're going to maintain this attitude of working together in your best interest during the next thirty-two months. I hope today is an indication of that.

---

1. Press conference.
2. John Swinford (1932–   ), Democrat from Cynthiana; Kentucky House of Representatives (1962–1975), majority floor leader (1972–1974). *Kentucky General Assembly 1974* (Frankfort, n.d.), p. 27. Wilson Palmer (1917–   ), Democrat from Cynthiana; insurance and real estate broker, farmer; Kentucky Senate (1962–1970, 1972–1974). *Kentucky General Assembly 1972* (Frankfort, n.d.), p. 9.
3. Tommy Preston, for more information see speech from June 25, 1973, in the Tourism section, p. 474.

REMOVAL OF TOLLS FROM
TWO INTERCHANGES
Louisville / May 25, 1973

WHEN I campaigned for Governor, certain commitments were made. They were made with two thoughts in mind: first, with the personal thought that each commitment was necessary for the progress of Kentucky and second, with the personal determination that my word would be my bond.

Upon assuming office, the direction of a new administration became clear to those who would participate in the activities of state government. As a first priority, I wanted to begin keeping my commitments, rather than waiting until later in my term. After twelve months, approximately 85 percent of the commitments had been attended to, and today I am here for the expressed purpose of continuing this effort.

One of the promises made during my campaign, and made in this county, related to the removal of the tolls from the ramps of the Outer Loop and Fern Valley interchanges of the Kentucky Turnpike. In all candor, few believed this would be accomplished, and even fewer believed it could be accomplished this early. It is therefore my pleasure to announce that before noon (unless the press keeps me here for questions) those tolls will be lifted, because I'm going from here to take that first sign down myself. Not only does this ease a monetary burden to the commuters, it relieves traffic congestion that has probably been in the craw of most at one time or the other during rush hours.

Let's go further. There are other significant announcements which hopefully will be received with the same enthusiasm we have in making them. I have instructed Highway Commissioner Jim Gray[1] to assign the highest priority to construction of the section of the Jefferson Freeway extending through and from the interchange on the Kentucky Turnpike to and through the interchange at Preston Street, KY 61. The estimated cost of this project is $16 million. This project is already under design and progress has been made toward preparing plans. Commissioner Gray has assured me that the date of the public hearing will be moved up to November of this year and that the Bureau of Highways will start the right-of-way process in 1974.

For another project, we have authorized and provided funding for construction of the Outer Loop Interchange and 2.9 miles of the Outer Loop from the Turnpike to Old Shepherdsville Road. The interchange and road construction will add up to $10 million. In addition, we are going to reconstruct Old Shepherdsville Road from the Outer Loop to West Beuchel, a project covering 3.7 miles and costing approximately $5 million. You are probably aware that the section of the Old Shepherdsville Road immediately adjoining Appliance Park is already under design. What has now been authorized, and funded, will eliminate hopscotching on this road through reconstruction all the way.

Any of you keeping notes will see that these programs add up to $31 million. These are estimates, but from my experience with cost estimates, I feel safe in saying they will be no less than $31 million. Every one of these roads will have a minimum of four lanes with a median. Every mile will be constructed to modern standards. Periodically, I speak of the need to work together. In Louisville and Jefferson County, as well as throughout Kentucky, we have experienced a refreshing approach to solving the problems of people through cooperation. The construction announcements I am now making are a direct result of such cooperation. Your state administration is pleased to acknowledge the high degree of cooperation, input, and financial assistance provided by Jefferson County. Judge Hollenbach[2] has committed county government to a share of $7.5 million of the $31 million in projects I have outlined. He and Scott Gregory[3] have worked hard on the arrangements we can announce today. I am truly sorry that Judge Hollenbach cannot be with us, just as I regret the absence of Jim Gray. Jim's father died late yesterday afternoon, and Judge Hollenbach is out of town due to the illness of his father.

The problems of Kentucky's major metropolitan area can best be dealt with when all levels of government—and often the very important private sector—are working together for solutions. We find this in Judge Hollenbach, Mayor Burke,[4] and the leadership of the business community. As you have read and heard, we have reorganized transportation activities in state government as a major phase in the total reorganization. Transportation Secretary Elijah Hogge[5] has been given a massive responsibility, because his boundaries are extensive. But he and his staff join me as individuals who want your community, and the many others throughout our great state, to be much better than they were previously. Today is another illustration that we mean what we say, because action is backing up words. If there are questions from the press, we will try to answer them. Afterwards, I invite all of you to go with me to the Fern Valley Interchange ramp where we will officially free the tolls and start dismantling procedures.

---

1. Jim Gray, for more information see speech from March 24, 1973, in the Reorganization section, p. 125.

2. Louis J. "Todd" Hollenbach, Jefferson County judge, for more information see speech from November 27, 1973, in the Health and Welfare section, pp. 205–6.

3. Scott S. Gregory (1932–   ), Louisville; former director, Jefferson County Works Department; former Jefferson County engineer; executive assistant to Jefferson County Judge Hollenbach. Telephone interview with Gregory's office, August 3, 1976.

4. Frank Welsh Burke, former mayor of Louisville, for more information see speech from November 27, 1973, in the Health and Welfare section, p. 206.

5. Elijah Hogge, for more information see speech from March 24, 1973, in the Reorganization section, p. 125.

DEDICATION OF HOPKINSVILLE
BYPASS
Hopkinsville / June 29, 1973

BEING in Hopkinsville today to participate in the dedication of this newly completed bypass gives me a great deal of satisfaction. I realize how much this three-mile stretch of highway can contribute to Hopkinsville's future development by relieving downtown traffic congestion. It will help bring new life to your city by allowing it to "breathe" and grow in a more orderly fashion.

At first, much of the highway traffic was routed down the main streets of Kentucky towns. Streets became clogged with tourists, many of them trying to get house trailers through narrow downtown streets. Local customers couldn't even get to the stores, and tourists avoided these towns as much as possible. It was about this time that the word "bypass" suddenly became a good word. Townspeople discovered that too much traffic was as bad as not enough. Many of them sent delegations to Frankfort to request a bypass that would relieve the downtown congestion. Now that many Kentucky towns have bypasses, the residents have discovered that the improved flow of traffic is bringing more business to town than ever before.

Hopkinsville is ideally situated to benefit from an efficient, well-designed highway system. It is on the axis of major north-south and east-west routes. It is near one of the nation's largest inland water resorts. It is near one of the largest military bases in the United States.[1] It is the county seat of Christian County, one of the Commonwealth's most fertile counties. Your city has almost unlimited growth possibilities.

I have the pleasure of announcing to you another highway improvement that will tie Hopkinsville into the interstate system. On July 19 the contract will be let for the 9.5-mile resurfacing of U.S. 41A from the southern city limits of Hopkinsville to just this side of Fort Campbell. The estimated cost of this project, more than $400,000, tells you

that major improvements are scheduled for the Fort Campbell Highway, and I am pleased to bring this news. This road has always been
important to Hopkinsville, and with the completion of I-24, its importance will increase. Cutting the ribbon for the first quadrant of
your city's bypass will open the way to bigger and better things for
Hopkinsville. It is a privilege to be here today in the dedication of a
vital link in the chain of orderly social and economic progress for this
fine city. I join in your vision of a much better tomorrow and have every
reason to believe that if we maintain a certain philosophy, there will
indeed be a much better tomorrow. This philosophy is, "coming together is a beginning, keeping together is progress, and working
together is success." I believe today is a perfect indication of this
philosophy in action.

---

1. Governor Ford is referring to the Kentucky Lake–Lake Barkley resort
area and to nearby Fort Campbell.

RIBBON-CUTTING CEREMONIES
FOR I-64
Frankfort and Lexington / August 30, 1973

I'VE always been told the longer you wait for something, the more you
appreciate it.[1] That certainly is the case today for all of us who have
waited for this much-needed section of Interstate 64 to be completed.
Though this stretch of road only covers 17.3 miles, a seemingly small
distance, it is so very important to all of Kentucky. Just what will this
road mean to Frankfort and Franklin County? It will offer a safe and
direct route to Lexington. It will connect with Interstate 75 near Lexington, serving routes both to the north and south. It will provide a
bypass for much of the daily commuter traffic, which has been forced
to use either U.S. 60 or 421 in the past and thus alleviate some of our
city's traffic congestion and safety hazards which traffic volume has
created.

But this stretch is much more than a Frankfort-to-Lexington road.
It is one of the final links in Interstate 64, which stretches across Kentucky from the West Virginia line in Boyd County to the Indiana border

in Jefferson County. Communities and industries across the state, from Louisville to Ashland, will be served by this link. Goods transported by trucks will arrive faster. Tourists traveling by car will arrive safer.

Only two more sections of I-64 remain to be finished. One is a nine-mile stretch in Carter County, which should be completed later this year. The other is the massive Ninth Street interchange in Louisville, now under construction and due to be ready in 1975. All of Kentucky will be brought closer by this road. We've waited three years for it to be opened. Now I am ready to put this new road to work. And as we do, let us dedicate it to the service and safety of the people of Kentucky and the nation.

There is no doubt that the unretouched beauty of the Bluegrass which this new highway reveals will certainly make a lasting impression on all who travel it.[2] We are pleased that this road captures so much of central Kentucky's natural beauty. But we are even prouder of something else—the fact that this stretch of Interstate 64 should be one of the safest roadways in the state. Many communities in central Kentucky will share the benefits of this new road, which directly serves four counties. I know the people of Lexington and Versailles are especially glad to see this stretch opened.

In recent months, we have been made increasingly aware of the hazards that exist on U.S. 60 between Lexington and Versailles. Suburban development and increased usage, by both large trucks and passenger cars, have resulted in tremendous congestion on the old road, creating serious traffic hazards, matters we have been working on with dispatch to correct. Even though U.S. 60 will always be a major artery, much of the traffic that has been forced to use U.S. 60 will now be attracted to I-64, which can better handle such volume. And a substantial part of the diverted traffic will undoubtedly be heavy equipment, such as big trucks. This new section of I-64 will not solve all of U.S. 60's problems, but it is bound to help.

With the opening of this road, Kentucky's highways will have an even finer reputation than they now enjoy among out-of-state guests, many of whom take the time to write back and tell us they were impressed. Communities, industries, visitors will all share the benefits this highway has to offer. Most importantly though, this section of I-64 will offer safe and efficient passage to the people of Kentucky and the nation.

---

1. This portion of the address was given by Governor Ford at the Frankfort ceremonies.

2. This portion of the address was given by Governor Ford at the Lexington ceremonies.

LEXINGTON CHAMBER OF COMMERCE LUNCHEON
Lexington / August 30, 1973

As many of you know, last week I took my office to the State Fair in Louisville to find out what people expect from state government. Before that, we were in northern Kentucky for the same purpose. The response was overwhelming. Hundreds of people visited the office each day. And if there was one thing I learned from the experience, it is that Kentuckians are concerned about their roads. They realize that an efficient and well-developed transportation network is essential for community growth. They are exactly right. You've heard the slogan, "Highways help people." Highways do help people—they are important economic factors to our state.

We have already had two ceremonies to open this new section of Interstate 64, one many have anxiously awaited. As I said earlier, this new road is one of the final links in I-64 that stretches from Louisville past Ashland. Communities across the state, especially Lexington and central Kentucky, will be served by this safe and efficient highway. You only have to look across the Commonwealth to see the remarkable growth that has taken place in community after community where interstate highways and parkways were placed in service.

Lexington, since finding itself at the crossroads of Interstates 64 and 75 as well as the Blue Grass and Mountain parkways, has seen its growth accelerate in a fashion no one would have dreamed possible two decades ago. It seems all roads lead to Lexington, and nearby communities—Versailles, Richmond, Winchester, Georgetown, Frankfort, to name only a few—have shared in Lexington's growth and prosperity.

Central Kentucky will feel the benefits of the new link of interstate we opened today. Recreational opportunities, such as the new State Horse Park, will be more readily available than ever before for the people of this area and the many out-of-state tourists who visit Kentucky each year. We have various resources in this section of the state, and we want to share this wealth with others. Educational, cultural, recreational, and other resources abound here.

I want to point out that our interstate system, and all of our highways, are carefully planned to protect the land through which they traverse. At the same time, they are designed to provide the best service possible where that service is needed.

With the opening of this new highway, we now have 606 miles of interstate highways. Only 132 miles remain to be completed. And we're pushing on with this program. You may recall that when federal highway funds were impounded, when there was no highway bill, I committed $37 million, 100 percent state money, to keep our interstate system on schedule. It was a calculated risk that worked. Kentucky is becoming a crossroads state. We are a bridge between the industrial Midwest and the markets of the South and East. The Commonwealth is in the center of a twenty-eight-state distribution area which reaches the northern manufacturing belt, the eastern seaboard, and the southern gulf ports. This area contains 73 percent of the nation's population, 73 percent of its personal income, and 81 percent of its manufacturing employment. These figures are important, because they can have a real impact on our business future.

Our interstate and parkway systems enable Kentuckians to utilize these resources to the fullest, opening the doors of Kentucky to surrounding states. But a state's transportation system needs much more than just superhighways. Just as important are the secondary routes I call "get-to-it" roads. These are the roads that must be safe and decent for the buses that carry our schoolchildren. These are the roads that must be free of hazards for the farmer when he takes his tobacco to market. These are the roads that must not be cause for worry when a man leaves for work. These are the roads that must be properly maintained and renovated in order to meet the highest safety standards.

Transportation is an all-inclusive program today, which is a major reason we believe reorganization of the Transportation Department will be of such immense benefit to Kentucky. For the first time, a fully coordinated approach to the entire transportation picture is possible. This means less delay and a better job in the future. In transportation it is essential that we prepare for tomorrow's demands today. It is a big order. But we—your state government and Department of Transportation—are committed to filling it.

You are concerned about what is being done. Here is some information that will be of interest to you. During fiscal year 1972–1973, $6,282,685 was spent by the Kentucky Bureau of Highways in Lexington-Fayette County. Four major traffic-operational programs for improving capacity and safety are under way in Lexington at a cost of more than $919,000. Projects such as this are designed to improve the "get-to-it" roads by widening lanes and installing new traffic signals. The major project presently in progress in Lexington involves construction of a new parking lot and providing access to the new Commonwealth Stadium on Cooper Drive. This project will be completed by September 15, the day Kentucky opens its football season.

Two landscaping projects, one on New Circle Road and the other on Tates Creek Road, also are nearing completion. Other projects include the right-of-way phase which has been started for work on the Lexington-Paris road; an extension of Newtown Pike from West Main to Euclid Avenue and South Limestone Street under design; a nearly completed design for a new bridge to be constructed on the Leestown Pike near the cemetery; a nearly completed design for a bridge on High Street, U.S. 60; and a design under way for new State Horse Park interchange on Interstate 75 at the Ironworks Pike.

I-64 DEDICATION LUNCHEON
Grayson / November 21, 1973

NEXT week, this administration will mark the end of its first two years in office. The past twenty-four months have reaffirmed my contention that Kentuckians are interested in roads. They are concerned because they realize that an efficient, well-developed transportation network is essential for community and statewide growth. And they are exactly right. You've heard the slogan, "Highways help people." Highways do help people; they are important economic stimulators to our state.

Anyone looking across the Commonwealth can see the remarkable growth that has taken place in community after community where interstate highways, parkways, and other good roads were placed in service. But today that growth is threatened. And it's a very real and present threat that is not disguised. It is the energy crisis. As you know, right now my staff and I are involved in preparation of the budget for the next biennium. We must address ourselves to two funds—the general fund and the road fund. We are faced with the very real possibility of an acute decrease in road-fund revenue, which is produced by highway tolls, the sale of gasoline and new cars, truck and auto licenses, and driving certificates and permits.

Quite frankly, we cannot now predict with desired accuracy how much revenue the state will be able to derive from these sources during the next two years because of the current fuel shortage. The energy crisis has served notice that we must be very cautious in any plans we make. At the same time, we must try to anticipate what the effect will be. It is obvious we cannot count on any immediate direction from Washington. The President's advisers are poles apart about which course to follow. His energy adviser and the Secretary of the Interior are calling for gas rationing. In the opposite corner the Economic Council chairman, Treasury Secretary, and Commerce Secretary all regard rationing as an administrative nightmare which should be resisted.[1] They believe a rise in fuel prices and a steep surtax would discourage unnecessary consumption. By the time this group ever gets around to reaching agreement, it may be too late, unless the man at the top sets firm directions.

The energy crisis could also have a drastic impact on our state's economy in other areas. Our tourism industry, a $634 million business last year, will suffer. Large-scale unemployment could result if stores and factories are forced to shut down. All of this lends credit to the fact that we have been able to live within our budget the past two years, that we even showed a surplus, and that we didn't rush out and spend our federal revenue-sharing funds. But this also tells us that we will have to be even more conservative in our planning and spending in the coming years.

We have already survived some very trying circumstances in road building during the last twenty-four months. You may recall that when federal highway funds were impounded, when there was no highway bill, I committed $37 million, 100 percent state money, to keep our interstate system on schedule. It was a calculated risk that worked. In addition, with rising inflation, we have had to live with accelerated construction costs.

Now, more than ever before, with a new crisis at hand, we must continue to take a careful approach to the future, if we are to be able to keep our commitment to wise and resourceful government. This is essential if we are to continue to keep Kentucky's roads properly maintained and renovated in order to meet the highest safety standards.

This highway (I-64) underscores the importance of good roads. Not only does it draw people in many communities closer together and serve as an economic stimulus to the entire state, it also will relieve much congestion and provide increased safety for the road it will complement, U.S. 60, and your other "get-to-it" roads. These are the roads that must be safe and decent for the buses that carry our school-children. These are the roads that must be free of hazards for the farmer when he takes his crops to market. These are the roads that must not be cause for worry when a man leaves for work.

Transportation is an all-inclusive program today, which is a major reason we believe our reorganization and development of the transportation department will be of such immense benefit to Kentucky. For the first time, a full-coordinated approach to the entire state transportation picture is possible. This means less delay and a better performance in the future. This means your state will be as prepared as humanly possible to meet the demands of the energy crisis, as well as other unexpected events dictated by the federal government.

In transportation, it is essential that we plan for tomorrow's demands today—a big order. But we, your state government, and Department of Transportation, are committed to filling it. I know today has been in your minds for a long time, because opening this link means so much to your community. Progress moves at various speeds, but when the destination is reached, we can see progress, just as we do this hour.

---

1. President Nixon's energy adviser was William E. Simon; his secretary of the interior was Rogers Morton. The chairman of the Economic Council was Herbert Stein; the treasury secretary was George P. Schultz, and the commerce secretary was Frederick B. Dent.

SPECIAL REPORT ON COAL ROADS
Frankfort / August 23, 1974

KENTUCKY's contribution to the national energy problem and its impact on transportation systems will be the subject of a special report to the federal Bureau of Highways.[1] The plan was initiated Thursday during a meeting in Washington between Governor Wendell Ford and Norbert Tiemann,[2] administrator of the federal Bureau of Highways. Ford told Tiemann that a "unique situation" had developed because of increased national demands for Kentucky coal. "We're having to cope with massive reconstruction and repair of many roads and highways now becoming lengthy routes for truck transportation of coal," Ford said. "Kentucky is being called upon to supply fossil fuel, which places unprecedented maintenance requirements beyond the state's capabilities," the Governor added.

Tiemann said he, as a former Governor, could fully appreciate the state's position and would work with Ford toward a solution. During their conference Ford and Tiemann agreed that the Kentucky Department of Transportation would provide total truck counts and weights on coal truck routes; establish dollar needs for reconstruction of damaged routes; furnish short-term and long-term figures of funds necessary to maintain roads used in industrial haul, giving estimates of state contributions and anticipated needs for federal dollars; and detail truck routes to be used in movement of energy supplies.

Tiemann told Ford he was interested in Kentucky's plans on industrial routes, based on 1974 legislation, and suggested this information be included in the report to identify additional state efforts toward solving the problem. The Bureau of Highways administrator also noted that Kentucky had the nation's first energy-research-and-development program under way and asked Ford for a complete analysis of Kentucky's initiative in this area of meeting a national demand. "I again found former Governor Tiemann keenly aware of state problems, and left the meeting convinced that if there is any way possible to secure federal assistance we will be given top priority," Ford said. The Governor said he believed there are other possible related programs for future implementation, including a federal public-works plan for energy-producing areas where road building would become a primary undertaking. Ford said he had notified the Kentucky Department of Transportation to begin its report at once.

----

1. Press release.

2. Norbert Tiemann (1924–), Lincoln, Nebraska; Governor of Nebraska (1967–1970); federal highway administrator (1973–1977). *Who's Who in American Politics, 1975–1976,* 5th ed. (New York, 1975), p. 930.

DEMOCRATIC PARTY
LEADERSHIP

KENTUCKY PRESS ASSOCIATION
Frankfort / January 22, 1972

YOUR role as professional journalists prompts a close association with government at all levels, including the evaluation of leadership. You express this through editorials, by-lined columns, and news articles appropriately designated as commentary. This is your right, this is your duty. It is also your duty and responsibility to evaluate and offer opinion based on a gathering of every relevant piece of material available which pertains to your subject of interest. Every politician, every person in government who faces the public spotlight, "thinks press." This is a fact of life. This is a very natural reaction.

As Governor of the Commonwealth of Kentucky, I am also the leader of my political party. Such a position comes in addition to the constitutional requirement, and privilege, that I serve as the chief executive of all who are residents of our great state. My first and foremost concern is working for the betterment of our state and all its people. This will be my concern for the entire four years I am in office as Governor.

In harmony with this concern is a much broader implication. State government progresses, or regresses, by virtue of action, or lack of action, from the federal government. The need for a close kinship between Washington and Frankfort is by no means marginal in today's complex society—a society where so many lives are directly affected by decisions made locally, but predicated on decisions handed down from the national level. The need for a close kinship is critical. Many of the programs to be advanced by my administration will be directly affected by the man who sits in the chair of the President of the United States.

Each time there is a presidential campaign and election, our political history grows more complicated. As our state and nation mature, as population increases, and as economics become more and more a household anxiety, the tie between federal, state, and local government tightens. As our most perplexing difficulties continue in Southeast Asia and elsewhere, as mankind draws on the products of God and nature, and as science and technology determine our everyday activities, we find evidence of rapid growth in this massive involvement with government at the highest peak.

As Governor, I am duty-bound in effecting the best possible degree of coordination between my office and the federal government. I would be remiss by having any other intention. As Governor, just as you in the journalistic field, I must analyze the potential leadership of our nation. I do so without emotion, but with a careful, self-controlled approach to the implications of my action.

In 1972 the American people will determine who is to be President. They will determine whether or not Mr. Nixon is to be replaced. I believe, as conscientiously and firmly as humanly possible, that he must be, if our potential, our hopes, and our ambitions are to bear fruit. But this personal feeling is insufficient. There must be an alternative, a candidate worthy of the awesome responsibilities and power of the presidency. Simply endorsing an individual because he appears as the one who can win is not enough. Waiting to endorse a sure nominee is irresponsible if one's motives are directed to the best interests of his state, as mine are. Refusing to take a stand is a mark of unworthiness for your Governor. And yes, it would be easy to follow the results of the first seven tests—New Hampshire, Florida, Illinois, Wisconsin, Rhode Island, Massachusetts, and Pennsylvania. It would be easy to wait, to feel the atmosphere of public opinion based on these early primaries. I am not seeking the easy road.

The Democratic party's list of presidential contenders dictates a most judicious examination. I have, for quite some time, studied the capabilities, qualifications, and qualities of those who are now announced candidates or may ultimately find themselves in the competitive arena. I am today endorsing Senator Edmund Muskie of Maine.[1] I will labor without hesitation or reservation for his nomination and election, but more importantly, for the causes he will advance in behalf of every Kentuckian.

Next Wednesday morning, in Frankfort, Senator Muskie and I will conduct a joint press conference just before he leaves to begin building his organization in Florida. At that conference I plan to give elaboration to my endorsement. So, bringing this closer to the journalist's terminology, you might consider the endorsement today my scoop. Wednesday, I shall submit a first editorial.[2]

---

1. Edmund Sixtus Muskie (1914–   ), Waterville, Maine; attorney; Maine House of Representatives (1948–1951), floor leader (1949–1951); Governor of Maine (1955–1959); United States Senator (1959–   ), assistant majority whip (1966–   ); Democratic vice presidential nominee (1968). *Who's Who in American Politics, 1975–1976* (New York, 1975), p. 675.

2. Governor Ford welcomed Senator Muskie to Frankfort on January 26, 1972, with an address not included in this volume.

JEFFERSON-JACKSON DAY DINNER,
GEORGIA DEMOCRATIC PARTY
Atlanta, Georgia / February 14, 1972

By inviting me to address this gathering of Georgia Democrats, you have offered a tribute which I deeply appreciate. I am sure our companionship can grow into a long and mutually rewarding association. From the people of Kentucky, I bring greetings. Come to the Bluegrass state anytime where you will find warm enthusiasm for your visit, where you will always be welcome, no matter the length of your stay. What is said here tonight, along with the degree of your response, can be the continuation of a movement we started in Kentucky early last year—a movement to dump Richard Nixon!

The dump-Nixon idea was a major theme in my campaign for Governor. We offered a strong case against the present Republican administration as well as the Republican forces firmly entrenched in our own statehouse. We launched our dump-Nixon campaign with full knowledge that he had carried Kentucky by 65,000 votes in 1968, with sober understanding that Kentucky had elected both of its United States Senators from the GOP ranks, and with no underestimation of the power which would be exerted by the Governor through his close alliance with President Nixon. But we chose our course because it was the right course. Kentuckians responded! Next November Americans will respond accordingly. And I expect the great state of Georgia to be in the thick of that fight.

With the Republicans asking us to keep them in power after the mess they have made of things, it's a little like the boy who murdered his mama and daddy. He threw himself on the court's mercy on the grounds that he was an orphan. By the way, you've heard about the new drink? A GOP Cocktail? It's called Savings on the Rocks. The Nixon economic game plan seems to be a system of checks and balances—unemployment checks and declining balances! Lincoln once said you can't fool all the people all the time. Of course, honest Abe lived a long time before Nixon was born. Someone asked me what I thought about the company President Nixon keeps. I said I didn't think much of it. He can't decide which Chinese restaurant to patronize— Formosa or Mainland; he has turned his press problems over to Spiro Agnew; Bebe Rebozo is in charge of fun and games; and Martha Mitchell does all the talking![1] Someone came up with a great way to improve Martha's image. First you make a tape. Then you put it over her mouth. Seriously, Martha comes out with some refreshing statements. She's one part of the Nixon administration no one has been able to put a "Top Secret" stamp on.

The President has a new plan for eliminating the opposition. He's going to put Spiro in every golf and tennis tournament sponsored by the Democrats! Actually, the Republican party doesn't have a firm plan. It's more like an X-rated movie—you don't know what's coming off next! In all fairness though, the Republicans are trying. Yesterday a plane flew over Washington and dropped five million leaflets. The handbills said, "Richard Nixon is against pollution."

Well, it's fun to take pokes at your opposition. And I'm here tonight hopefully to fire you up. Knowing the enthusiasm of Georgia Democrats, this isn't going to be a very tough job at all. The dump-Nixon movement is important for numerous reasons. Despite a few laudable initiatives on the international front, even somewhat on the domestic front, the cold, hard facts remain. President Nixon has not delivered his campaign and inaugural pledges—to win peace, straighten out the economy, or bring us together again. Excessive military spending and our commitment to the arms race leave no doubt that without a change in philosophy, there is little hope for serious attention to our long-neglected social needs. While an $82 billion military budget gives attention to support-of-war industry jobs, this is certainly not the answer to our long-range economic difficulties. We have an administration giving only lip service to the problems of equity among men, poverty, urban decay, rural exodus, consumerism, the protection of our environment, and the plight of the independent farmer.

As citizens, just as we are Democrats, we must be concerned about the frightening trend toward centralization of power in the executive branch, executive influence over the judicial branch, governmental manipulation of the communications media, and suppression of individual liberties. While a candidate four years ago, Mr. Nixon drew from a passage by Thomas Jefferson, who wisely said that the concentration of power within federal government is, in the end, the great enemy of liberty. Unfortunately, Mr. Nixon spoke through insincerity.

Stewart Alsop, in a recent article very fair to the President, nevertheless asked: "He didn't bring us together. Why does 1972 look like his year?"[2] I want to amplify this and then briefly discuss the answer to Mr. Alsop's burning question. When Mr. Nixon was running, he did indeed promise to bring us together. His pledge was one of enormous dimension, yet it was a firm commitment. Regrettably, he has not fulfilled his commitment. I don't believe, nor do I think you believe, Richard Nixon is the person who can truly bring us together. He has failed to instill confidence both in government and in those who lead government. This absence of confidence erodes the very foundations of our governmental system, the greatest system known to man. Within the Democratic party there are leadership capabilities to restore confidence. For this reason, among many others, we must put a Democrat in the White House this year!

There are other broken promises to give cause for alarm. Over two major television networks in September of 1968, Mr. Nixon the candidate said: "I plan a streamlined federal system with a return to the states, cities, and communities of decision-making powers rightfully theirs." My friends, it isn't happening. The paper thicket within federal government grows more intense. As the needs of states, cities, and communities for a return of both federal support and decision-making processes expand, in reality we find the opposite. The distance between Washington and where you live has increased.

Two months before his statement on communities, Mr. Nixon the candidate uttered another expression designed to instill support. Now we recognize the hollow echoes of his words. He talked about the economy, our most painful dilemma at this time, and obviously the subject he is totally ill equipped to handle. Mr. Nixon noted that the national debt was expanding, in his words, "still spreading distortions throughout the economy." Looking at that situation now, we didn't know how fortunate we were in '68.

What of today? The Nixon budget carried with it a $40 billion deficit, the greatest in history. His promise to allow the dollar to recover much of its strength was futile. The dollar in your pocket right now will buy twenty-one cents less in groceries than when Mr. Nixon assumed office. No wonder you had to pay so much for this dinner tonight!

On the farm front, the President has perhaps stumbled more frequently than in any other endeavor. I recall his campaign literature which said he wanted to appoint a Secretary of Agriculture who will explain the farmer's problems to the President. What happened? The President wound up appointing a geologist from New York City as his first Secretary of Agriculture. That man didn't pan out, so we now have a theorist.[3] No wonder the farmer is discouraged. No wonder the farmers of America are going to rise up in unparalleled solidarity to elect a Democrat President next November!

In his nomination acceptance speech, Mr. Nixon offered the American people this gem: "We've had enough of big promises and little action." That one statement will haunt the President from now until Election Day, for instead of its being his criticism, it has become his creed. Government by political expediency is distasteful. The Republicans in Kentucky tried this approach during the last four years, and our citizens reacted in indignation. We found it easy to enlist our people in the dump-Nixon movement, for they were tired of big promises and little action. They were tired of an administration that treaded water for three years, then attempted a marathon swim the final twelve months, the period of our political campaign. Aren't you tired of Richard Nixon treading water on every major issue until a political year?

Nineteen seventy-two will be the year of the GOP propagandist. You may as well prepare for the heaviest concentration of political maneuvering this nation has ever experienced. Frankly, I am appalled that our President would establish timetables on Vietnam, the economy, taxes, health and welfare, and other measures in order to gain his best image just before the voters go to the polls. This is exactly what is happening. If a new dance emerges in '72, it will have to be called the Dick Nixon Shuffle. I am reminded of another Nixonism. He said he did not believe the American people should be forced to choose between unemployment and un-American controls. Apparently he hasn't reviewed his campaign rhetoric, since we have both unemployment and controls.

Finally, the Nixon of today says it is un-American to criticize his peace efforts, contending that our criticism only lessens the chances of peace in Southeast Asia. This attitude proves how conveniently forgetful the President is. For in discussions of the conduct of the war, as a candidate, Mr. Nixon found nothing wrong with vocal disagreement. He admitted to being "the most consistent critic of our policy in Vietnam." What a difference a change in status makes.

Our task is monumental. The Democrats must go one-on-one against the most powerful political machine ever assembled in America. Our course is pitted with obstacles. The Republican administration will exercise every muscle at its disposal to convince you when necessary that red is purple, that cold is heat, and that night is day. This will be the propaganda effort, and unless we in the Democratic party ensure an informed citizenry and encourage others to be aware of what really is going on, then we can expect four more years of the Nixon policy—foreign and domestic. It's up to you. The challenge is yours, beginning right now.

Flying into Atlanta earlier this evening, I thought of your eighth wonder of the world, Stone Mountain, and how it can symbolize the Democratic party. With 16 billion cubic feet of exposed granite, Stone Mountain is nature's way of reminding us of the powerful force beyond our control or influence. America's voters are an equally powerful force. No control or influence can make the electorate act against its will if you and I clearly illustrate the issue at hand. Last fall Kentucky's gubernatorial campaign was the only one in this country where Democratic and Republican philosophies were in contest. The Democrats won. The same can happen nationally next November!

---

1. Spiro Theodore Agnew (1918–   ), attorney; governor of Maryland (1967–1969); vice president of the United States (1969–1973). *The New Columbia Encyclopedia* (New York, 1975), p. 34. Charles Gregory "Bebe" Rebozo (1912–   ), Key Biscayne, Florida; banker, chairman of the board of the Key Biscayne Bank (1964–   ); president of Monroe Land Title Co., Washwell Inc., Fisher Island, Inc. Rebozo is a close friend of Richard Nixon. *Who's Who in America, 1974–1975* (Chicago, 1975), 2: 2540. Martha Elizabeth Beall Jennings Mitchell (1918–1976), wife of former Attorney General John Mitchell. Ibid., p. 2174.

2. Stewart Johonnot Alsop (1914–1975), Washington, D.C.; magazine columnist; *New York Herald Tribune* (1945–1958); national affairs contributing editor, *Saturday Evening Post* (1958–1962), Washington editor (1962–1968); columnist for *Newsweek* (1968–1975). *Who's Who in America, 1974–1975* (Chicago, 1975), 1:52.

3. Nixon appointed Dr. Clifford M. Hardin as his first secretary of agriculture in 1969. Earl Lauer Butz succeeded him in 1971. Clifford Morris Hardin (1915–   ), chancellor, University of Nebraska, (1945–1969); secretary of the United States Department of Agriculture (1969–1971); vice chairman of the board, Ralston Purina Corporation (1971–   ). *Who's Who in America, 1976–1977* (Chicago, 1976), p. 1327.

MUSKIE UNION LEADERSHIP DINNER
Rock Hill, South Carolina / March 24, 1972

HAD you visited Kentucky during the last two months while our General Assembly was in session, you would have noticed a state administration attitude very favorable to labor. I am proud of this. I am pleased with our record in behalf of the workingman. The 1972 session of our Legislature distinguished itself in your brotherhood's cause. We removed completely the oppressive 5 percent sales tax on groceries.

We passed a strong minimum wage bill, made great strides in workmen's compensation, and deleted the waiting requirement for unemployment compensation. We brought a generic drug law to Kentucky, one of the very first of its kind in this nation. Collective bargaining received a solid boost.

These enactments are mentioned as a preface to your request for a political address. And I might add that as Lieutenant Governor four years ago, I led the fight against a Republican administration to abolish the sales tax on prescription medicine. There is no personal reason or desire to offer these facts as a vehicle for self-applause. This limited background is presented to illustrate how labor and public officials can work together in the best interest of people. My decisions, as they pertain to any national election, would therefore give full consideration to labor. The record is clear.

It is an honor to represent Edmund Muskie this evening. I endorsed the Senator several weeks ago and am actively working for his nomination. You are weighing all sides in what is a most critical election year. I have done the same. I did so first in consideration of my state, and next in consideration of all other citizens throughout America. We have in the Senator from Maine a man who has demonstrated exceptional leadership in areas of mutual concern. His credentials are impressive on the subject of jobs. He coauthored the payroll-tax reform bill, which would reduce federal taxes paid by 63 million low- and middle-income Americans for Social Security and increase benefits for present and future Social Security beneficiaries.

He has brought unparalleled leadership into the environmental arena, just as he has brought leadership into the hard questions of our cities. We find a distinguished record in the health fields, in equal opportunity, and in the war on crime and drugs. He was the original sponsor of the Emergency Employment Act of 1971, a battle he won over a 1970 Richard Nixon veto. He has sponsored legislation to help create new jobs and train people to fill them.

Last May Senator Muskie said in Detroit: "It is time to abolish the concept of unemployment in America. Unemployment occurs when there are more people to work than things to do. But there are plenty of tasks in our society for every pair of willing hands in our economy." This has been a prevailing attitude throughout his public-service career. He was a job man as Governor. He is a job man as Senator. He will be a job man as President.

Every barometer points to the economy as a prime determining factor in the voting results of this country next fall. Only yesterday the federal government offered us more bad news from the consumer price index. Grocery prices soared 1.9 percent for the greatest single-month increase since March of 1958. It is disturbing to note—and I say to you, let others know—that so far in the four months of phase two, living costs have risen at an annual rate of 4.9 percent, greater than the 4.1 percent rate in the six months before the August freeze.

You don't want any more of the Republican mess and neither do I! We were promised price stability and prosperity. We have been given 6 percent inflation, 6 percent unemployment, the first trade deficit since 1893, an astronomical balance-of-payments deficit, a world monetary crisis, and forced devaluation of the dollar.

Who then can best lead us from misguided Republican domination? In my opinion, that person is Edmund Muskie. Through twenty-five years of public service, he has emerged as the one man with the weight and experience to be President. He is the logical candidate in what will become a tedious task in divesting a strongly entrenched GOP political machine from its death grip on America.

He is neither packaged nor programmed. He has characteristics we all possess, and if at times they have created widespread public attention, they have also shown us a human being who has human emotions, who is willing to admit his mistakes, and who isn't afraid to fight back when the odds are against him.

A few months ago the Eugene, Oregon, *Register-Guard* said it about as well as anyone when that paper commented: "Muskie seems as authentic as the stereotyped politician seems phony." So I say to you, look hard at Muskie. He brings the best of two requirements—a candidate ready for the office of President and a candidate who can win that office. You stand for political awareness. Unlike so many who are deceived by propaganda or who simply do not rely on factual information, you make it a point to be fully informed. This is one reason why America needs labor's influence—to tell it as it is! We must strengthen our determination to know what is really going on in government if we are to react as intelligent citizens.

During my campaign for Governor of Kentucky, I often referred to a growing absence of confidence in government and in those who lead government. Another theme of my campaign was the dump-Nixon movement. Such a thrust was made with full knowledge of Mr. Nixon's 65,000 victory margin in our state in 1968. This was with full knowledge that he had two Republican United States Senators and a Republican Governor very close to President Nixon. But the conditions clearly pointed to Republican mismanagement, just as they do today on a national level. Our economic headaches had become worse; our farm community had been ignored; our citizens were growing sick and tired of words rather than deeds, just as we are today when examining the national picture.

We had experienced one of the highest unemployment rates in years when the decade of the sixties began. Unemployment was near 12 percent of our work force. Then we elected a Democratic President, and in a year the unemployment rate dropped by one-fourth. Under Democratic Governors and Presidents conditions improved. Unfortunately, the Republicans showed up again. Our unemployment rate had gone to a low of 4.2 percent, but it didn't take long for the Republicans to ruin that figure.

So, with the tremendous help given by many, including labor, I plunged into the political ring to return Kentucky's statehouse to the people. We didn't mince words. We offered a program, we shot straight, and we put the blame where it should have been put—right in the laps of the Republicans—and the people responded.

In this presidential year, you can render an invaluable service by driving ahead in the dump-Nixon movement. You can help put the skids under an administration that for three years has failed to follow the creed that government exists to serve people. You can expose the GOP con game as one filled with rhetoric.

You can expect the most comprehensive effort imaginable from the GOP in its pursuit of favorable headlines. Every statistic benefiting the present administration will be hurled at us. This election year will bring us the most dramatic sidestepping of the facts we have ever seen. No doubt we can expect improvement, temporary improvement. Mr. Nixon will use every device at his disposal to have improvement when election day draws near. He must do this to survive. The Nixon camp will pull every trick out of its well-stuffed bag to create an improved atmosphere.

They say, if you hear the same old tune over and over again, you will begin singing it yourself. Well, we've heard the tune, but I don't believe it's sinking in. No group can do more than you. You have the advantage of close communication within your fraternity. You know the economic picture. You are in constant touch with your membership. And when a man's paycheck buys less, no amount of promising from any administration eases that man's burden. Without your participation and the determined involvement of others, a look into the future might go like this, as reported by a newscaster three years from now:

President Richard Nixon today announced phase eight of his economic program to get this country moving. Predicting a better year than last,

Mr. Nixon called for patience on the part of the people. Elsewhere, the Stock Market ended its lengthy and steady decline after banks said they wouldn't raise interest rates beyond 9 percent. Analysts saw the halt in steady declines as a seasonal adjustment, since it has been almost a full season since there was any good news from Wall Street. In a special message to Congress this afternoon, the Vice President, speaking for Mr. Nixon who is vacationing at his Montana White House after spending last weekend at his New Mexico White House, said: "It's time to stop harping and give thanks that we are only asking approval to increase the current fiscal-year deficit by $60 billion." The Vice President said this was considerably less than expected. There is a bright spot on the horizon though. Home building is on the upswing. The President has announced plans to construct Nevada, South Carolina, and New York White Houses.

And finally in the headlines, continued investigations into the ITT case have produced another memo from Dita Beard.[1] President Nixon said he thinks the one found sticking out of his middle desk drawer is the authentic one. Mr. Nixon says he is sure this will clear up any misunderstanding that has existed for three years!

I touch on a most serious matter, using a light approach. I do so to illustrate the seriousness. I do so in no disrespect to the Office of the President, rather only to say in conclusion that there are many things you can do in the months ahead to prevent this type of newscast in 1975. We cannot afford four more years of Richard Nixon. The people of my state served him first notice only last November. The people of this nation will serve final notice through the polls next November. And our strongest ammunition is Ed Muskie![2]

---

1. Dita Davis Beard (1918–   ), lobbyist for International Telephone and Telegraph; former employee of the National Association of Broadcasters. Beard is the alleged author of a memorandum which tied ITT's contributions to the 1972 Republican Convention with the settlement of three antitrust suits against the company. *New York Times*, March 6, 1972.

2. Governor Ford delivered a similar address to the International Union of Electricians, Radio, and Machine Workers District Conference on May 12, 1972, which is not included in this volume.

KENTUCKY DEMOCRATIC CONVENTION
Frankfort / June 3, 1972

FOUR years ago, the Kentucky Democratic party was recoiling from defeat. The luster of a once-vibrant organization had dimmed. Our financial status was critical. All but a determined few lacked optimism. Even more distressing to Democrats, and shortly thereafter to Republicans, was the realization that human needs would fall prey to inept and callous leadership from a Governor who played his tune only to the special interests.

Our party, which had served mankind so well for twenty years, was at a crossroad—unsure, unstable, and unaccustomed to its new and unpleasant role. Yet during the early days of disarray, there were those who rallied to a cause for survival. They plunged into a fight for rejuvenation with more grit, more sweat, and more self-sacrifice than the Kentucky Democratic party had seen since its birth. The odds were enormous. Voices of gloom cried out to the winds, while searching for someone to lead them back into a political environment where victory was not just a daydream.

Adding to our burdens were the known riches which poured into the Republican coffers from strong-arm tactics deplored by a responsible electorate. The great majority of Kentuckians were treated as sixth-class citizens by a Governor whose forked tongue uttered mumbo-jumbo except at tax-collection time. Then his words came out loud and clear. "Give! Give!" shouted Louie Nunn. And he took, without mercy, from those least able to pay.

Today, as I keynote this convention, the terrible drama of the past four years has passed. It has passed because of those who refused to accept the consequences of defeat because more and more willing hands joined to pick up the pieces. Many of you must feel a sense of pride in your personal contributions of time, energy, and money which have restored our party to prominence. This is what the Kentucky Democratic party is all about—vitality through personal commitment. No political organization can survive with a johnny-come-lately form of leadership at any level. The heritage, growth, and stability of our reconstituted party is a direct result of those who were willing to begin in a laboring role and earn their way through the ranks with one thought in mind, that is, building a dynamic organization truly serving the needs of all the people. Without the strong fibers of aggressive party faithfuls, this convention would be clouded with the frets and misfortunes of 1968.

It is time, my fellow Democrats, to forge ahead even more. There is no place in Kentucky for the Louie Nunns, the Dita Beards,[1] and the Richard Nixons! There is no place for political domination as experienced the last four years where needed state projects were delayed until a political year to be used for political gain! There is no place for gross mismanagement which resulted in our necessary seizure and rehabilitation of insurance companies to protect stockholders and policyholders. There is no place for anyone who would turn his head from the obvious by disregarding the security of those making investments in building and loan companies, having good faith that their state government would guarantee protection, and waking up to find that such was not the case.

These are Louie Nunn messes this administration must clean up! There is no place for executive dictatorship, for those elected officials who would permit special favor to private interests through the use of state equipment and monies as we have found at Gobbler's Knob on Kentucky Lake.[2] There is no place for an attitude directly in opposition to the merit-system law, where mass firings without proper cause have cost you nearly a million dollars. I know Wendell Ford has been criticized for moving too slowly in patronage. I want Democrats who are qualified, and who will work, to have jobs in this administration, and they will! But I am not going to cost the taxpayers of this state what Louie Nunn did by violating the merit-system law.

There is no place for high-elected officials who cater to a patronage-riddled probation and parole system which undermines the very security of our families and properties. There is no place for the ridiculous antics of those who would go so far as to buy nearly eleven-hundred-dollars worth of parts for horse-drawn mowing equipment! That's right! While Louie was flying around in his expensive jet that could land only at a handful of Kentucky airports, his Highway Department was buying pieces for horse-drawn mowing equipment. In contrast, during the very few months of this administration, through proper management, by eliminating waste, our Highway Department has been able to contract for an additional $4 million of resurfacing of roads which otherwise couldn't have been repaired if the practices of yesterday were continued. The appalling record of the previous administration is surfacing every day—unpaid bills, broken promises, special favors, and an attitude that perpetuates unsound government policy!

Louie didn't just run roughshod. He embarrassed Kentucky. Our largest annual event, the Kentucky Derby—and what was the story all over the world? Dita Beard! Rumors of political deals and a black eye to every Kentuckian who has any sense of pride in his state.

Only a united Democratic party can prevent a repeat of what happened during the reign of Louie Nunn. And only a united Democratic party in Kentucky and throughout this nation can prevent a continuation of the domestic failures of Richard Nixon. The same man who put this state in reverse wants to be a U.S. Senator. The Nixons and the Beards want him in Washington, and I do too! But not in any capacity as a public official! I want Dee Huddleston[3] to be the next U.S. Senator!

Nor does someone who served Governor Nunn so faithfully, until he saw the real Louie Nunn [Bob Gable[4]], want him to be Senator, and his public testimony gives you reasons why. It's simple why Richard Nixon wants Louie in Washington. Anyone who can fool the public like Louie did is needed in the Nixon administration, because that's what you and I have been getting from Trickie Dick these last four years. He has misled us on the economy, and you housewives feel it as much as anyone. He has misled us on Vietnam so many times we don't know which way he will turn next. Nixon indicted himself; any man who couldn't stop the war in four years should not be President.

Because we are the party of the people, we are the party of progress. Where is the Republican progress in our welfare mess? Where is Republican progress in our tax loophole mess? Where is Republican progress in urban problems? And above all, where is Republican progress in the plight of our farmers? It isn't there; it hasn't been since Nixon took office; and it won't emerge if he wins again.

We must protect the threats to employment. We must erase the fears of pollution, we must restore the confidence of the troubled, the disillusioned, and the fearful. There is no other course than unity. The Democratic party has found unity in sincere debate just as it has found unity in common cause. Let us therefore set ourselves to this task. Let us give the power back to the people from Maine to California. Let us be Democrats with a very large "D," and let us go to Miami as a force that must be considered on all counts, in order that in the final analysis, America becomes a place of honor in the hearts of every man, woman, and child living here or abroad.

---

1. Dita Beard, ITT lobbyist, for more information see speech from March 24, 1972, in this section, p. 581.

2. For more information on the Gobbler's Knob controversy, see speech from May 19, 1972, in the Tourism section, pp. 460–61.

3. Walter "Dee" Huddleston, United States Senator, for more information see speech from September 28, 1972, in the Reorganization section, p. 98.

4. Robert E. Gable (1934–), Stearns; corporation executive; commissioner, Department of Parks (1967–1970); director, Kentucky Travel Coun-

cil (1969–1970); unsuccessful Republican candidate for Governor (1975). *The Public Papers of Governor Louie B. Nunn, 1967–1971*, ed. Robert F. Sexton (Lexington, 1975), p. 102.

STATE DEMOCRATIC
WOMEN'S CLUBS LUNCHEON
Lexington / October 7, 1972

I want to talk about decency in politics and government. This is the end to which you, as a political organization, must always work. This is the end to which we, as public officials, must always aspire. There is no decency, I said no decency, in politics or government when the evils of deceit, misrepresentation, shady deals, hidden incomes, or distortions of the truth are allowed to prevail.

Yet, the only way this can be stopped is through an aroused public, an enraged public, a public that says to those who participate in or condone such activities, "This will not continue." Decency is lost when we, as citizens, shut our eyes to international wheat sales at large profits to selected friends of a national administration. Decency is lost when a legitimate investigation into the bugging and surveillance of a party headquarters is brushed aside by those who ask for our trust. Decency is lost when a candidate for office will distort his opponent's legitimate positions on issues of importance. Decency is lost when a person's hard-earned savings aren't protected, when land is destroyed, when people can't believe because of broken promises.

I think you understand the point here. This election campaign offers example after example of what I am talking about. But only on November 7 will we know whether or not the message is clear enough. Here is where your role is so vital to the safeguards of decency. It all boils down to communications. You have the strongest arguments imaginable in behalf of Kentucky and its people. But you can't help Dee Huddleston, or Carl Perkins, or John Breckinridge, or Bill Natcher, or Ron Mazzoli, or Frank Stubblefield unless you communicate with others.[1] Their records, their achievements, and their sense of responsibility are all earmarked by decency, and I am proud to be associated politically with such outstanding Kentuckians.

Your organization, by being well informed on the candidates and issues, can reach thousands upon thousands of voters because you are in the precincts on a day-by-day basis. Communicate! Let the truth be known. For ten months now I've been trying to clean up the mess Louie Nunn left in Frankfort. And you know, a lot of eyes are being opened because we're doing things differently, and it's working. We're returning a sense of decency and respect to state employment. The people of Kentucky will be better served by those who have jobs in state government because what we're doing is placing a value on performance, rather than on their financial standing with the Democratic party.

There have been a number of breaks with the past, and there will be more. One which in my opinion is as significant as any is the prohibition of assessments. It isn't being permitted. Good politics is good government, and good government is good politics. We're communicating directly to state employees throughout Kentucky in a series of meetings being conducted by individuals representing me. We're telling them: your job-standing is not based on donations to the party or to any campaign. It's based on the quality of work you do for Kentucky. We're telling them, in no uncertain terms, that they will not be coerced into making a contribution, and if they are, it won't be by any representative of the Ford administration or the Democratic party, and if they are, I want to know about it.

The day of employee shakedowns is over! We're telling employees that the money they have been forced to give in the past would be better spent on clothing for their children or food for their tables. This is Wendell Ford's directive and I know J. R. Miller agrees with me 100 percent.[2] During the previous administration, big brother shadowed over state employees with piercing eyes and keen ears directly from the Governor's Office. Political professionals loaded the payrolls of state government under Louie Nunn, and the taxpayers shelled out for his corps of cronies whose only duty was a game of politics.

You won't find these people in my office. You won't find every department having their own political contact men as was the case with my predecessor. Some politicians may think we're, well, crazy! I disagree. I don't think the public appreciates the attitude as expressed by one Republican political appointee who left shortly after I took office when he said, "I didn't work under the Republicans, I don't intend to do so under the Democrats." I hope, and I believe very sincerely, that this new atmosphere in bringing dignity to employees of state government will inspire them to support this philosophy. If so, they will support what we stand for, what men such as Dee Huddleston and the other candidates I mentioned stand for. They will have more reason to endorse enthusiastically our candidates at the polls.

Unlike the hundreds of thousands of taxpayer dollars spent by the Nunn administration to play politics, we're saying this is the party's responsibility. The party is picking up the bill. Obviously this puts an added burden on our state party. But we're willing to accept that burden rather than impose it on the taxpayers of Kentucky. I like the game of politics as well as anyone. I want to restore honor to politics, to prove to the public that they can indeed have confidence in their public officials.

Upon assuming office, I listed the commitments made by me during the campaign for Governor. These commitments are being kept—the removal of the sales tax on grocery store food; the reorganization of state government; the construction of badly needed roads; legislation passed to protect consumers. These and many other examples of Wendell Ford's keeping his word are also examples of Dee Huddleston's keeping his word. His leadership and integrity are without question. I've worked with both candidates for the U.S. Senate. I know that Dee will make an outstanding Senator. Honestly! I know that Dee wants to ensure that same degree of decency and credibility in government. I also know that when the public fully examines the record of Dee and the record of his opponent, the choice will be easy. Kentuckians want a man opposed to a national sales tax. That's Dee Huddleston. Kentuckians want a man who isn't ashamed of his campaign contributors. That's Dee Huddleston. Kentuckians want a man who is independent, not a rubber stamp for anybody else except the people. That's Dee Huddleston. Kentuckians want a man who tells the truth. That's Dee Huddleston. Kentuckians want a man who respects the farmer, the laborer, the ideas of the young, and the wishes of the elderly. That's Dee Huddleston. These are the qualities found in Breckinridge, Perkins, Stubblefield, Mazzoli, and Natcher. How badly do you want these Kentucky qualities to continue? How badly do you want the Kentucky Democratic party to grow in strength, in stature, in respect? I'm laying it on the line right now. I challenge you to do more than you have ever done in your life for those who will carry our state's needs to Washington.

You do this, and the most surprised individuals in Kentucky on November 7 will be the Republicans, who have already started celebrating their victory. And the most surprised person of all will be Louie Nunn, who is trying to ride all the way to Washington on the coattails of another. I don't blame him though; with a record like Louie's he has to hitchhike. Louie Nunn is the greatest enemy to the truth. Louie is using the same tactics he used in his race for Governor in 1967—radio ads with religious overtones, pitting race against race, sections of the state against sections. Tactics such as this are opposed by such prominent Republicans as John Sherman Cooper and Tim Lee Carter.[3]

---

1. Walter "Dee" Huddleston, for more information see speech from September 28, 1972, in the Reorganization section, p. 98. Carl D. Perkins (1912–   ), Knott County; attorney (1941–1948); counsel, State Department of Highways (1948); United States House of Representatives (1949–   ), chairman, House Education and Labor Committee. *Who's Who in American Politics, 1975–1976*, 5th ed. (New York, 1975), p. 729. John Bayne Breckinridge (1929–   ), Lexington; attorney; Kentucky House of Representatives (1956–1959); Kentucky attorney general (1960–1964, 1968–1972); United States House of Representatives (1973–   ); member of numerous Kentucky agencies. Ibid., p. 101. William H. Natcher (1909–   ), Bowling Green; attorney; federal conciliation commissioner, Western Kentucky District (1936–1937); Warren County attorney (1937–1949); United States House of Representatives (1953–   ); former president, Young Democrat Clubs of Kentucky. Ibid., p. 679. Romano Mazzoli, for more information see speech from January 14, 1972, in the Reorganization section, pp. 94–95. Frank A. Stubblefield (1907–   ), Murray; United States House of Representatives (1959–1974). *Who's Who in American Politics, 1975–1976*, 5th ed. (New York, 1975), p. 903.

2. James R. Miller, state Democratic party chairman, for more information see speech from August 16, 1973, in this section, pp. 595–97.

3. John Sherman Cooper (1901–   ), Somerset; attorney; Kentucky House of Representatives (1928–1930); Pulaski County judge (1930–1938); circuit judge (1945–1946); United States Senator (1947–1949, 1953–1955, 1957–1973); United States ambassador to East Germany (1974–1976). *Who's Who in American Politics, 1975–1976*, 5th ed. (New York, 1975), p. 192. Tim Lee Carter (1910–   ), Tompkinsville; physician; United States House of Representatives (1965–   ). Ibid., p. 151.

FRANKLIN COUNTY
YOUNG DEMOCRATS FISH FRY
Frankfort / May 24, 1973

LAST night in Washington, Senate Majority Leader Mike Mansfield told party supporters that he was never more proud to be a Democrat than at that moment.[1] I feel the same way. But like other members of my party, I recognize how much more important it is today than ever before to purify, renew, and strengthen the political processes of this nation. Here is where the Democratic party has a major advantage. We are the party of inclusion, not exclusion. We have a heritage of responsiveness to the masses, rather than being traditionally for only a selected few. We don't disregard human needs, violate the checks and balances as provided through the executive, legislative, and judicial system, or try to establish a monarchy whereby the grass roots is never heard or even considered.

In Kentucky, the Democratic party has witnessed a response from the people, and that response has made us stronger than ever before. Our people-to-people fund-raising must be considered a monumental success. The election of Dee Huddleston was a public mandate in view of an overwhelming presidential advantage. The signs in future races have never been more favorable.

Yet we can bask in glory, sit back with a relaxed air of success, and roll in the warm tides of victory, and suddenly find ourselves vulnerable. We can believe that Watergate gives us the key to unrestricted gains in the next few years, and while our opponents are most hurt by this sad and messy chapter in history, the spin-offs do affect everyone in politics and government. At such times all politics, all government, becomes suspect.[2] We must show America that there are far more decent politicians than crooks; that there are far more officeholders with the right intentions than the wrong intentions.

Mistakes are made. There are errors in judgment. It happens in industry as well as politics, business as well as government, in professions as well as trades. But the immortal Dante tells us that divine justice weighs the sins of the cold-blooded and the sins of the warm-hearted on different scales. This is what everyone must recognize. There is a difference, a vast difference, in the spirit of error.

Politics becomes better for our communities, state, and nation whenever more people are involved. I have often asked, "If those who are good and decent, honest and forthright, refuse to participate, then whose fault is it when government and our political system fail?" It's the holier-than-thous who sit on the sidelines and criticize. It's the uninformed who have fiction rather than fact, rumor rather than substance, and a sense of irresponsibility rather than realization of what really is at stake. It's the person who isn't willing to fight the wars in the precinct trenches first and to take a leadership role second. It's the person who puts self-glory above his party, above the people who are to be represented, and above the land that has given him so much.

Your presence here tonight is another indication that Kentucky Democrats are on the right road, will stay on that road with a level head, and want to restore the people's faith, not only in politics and government but in themselves. This is not a time for Democrats to lean on Watergate. This is more of a time for Democrats to continue building for the future, to maintain the confidence and credibility in our philosophy and in ourselves, and to reaffirm to all others that what we do is born of sincerity, concern, honor, and trust.

---

1. Michael J. Mansfield (1916–   ), Missoula, Montana; miner, mining engineer, history professor; United States House of Representatives (1943–1953); United States Senator (1953–1977), Senate Democratic whip (1957–1961), majority leader (1961–1977); member, Democratic Executive Committee. *Who's Who in American Politics, 1975–1976*, 5th ed. (New York, 1975), p. 583.

2. Governor Ford discussed the Watergate theme in greater detail in an earlier address to the Paducah Democratic Rally on April 23, 1973. In this speech, not found in this volume, the Governor said: "It would be easy for a Democrat to jump on the Watergate scandal for no other reason than headline hunting. This, in my opinion, is wrong. What we have learned thus far goes much deeper into the very structure of our political and governmental way of life. We are on the brink of collapse in public confidence, and as a result, the entire political structure is affected."

DEMOCRATIC REGISTRATION DRIVE
Frankfort / July 7, 1973

ON numerous occasions I have been proud to be one of you, a Kentucky Democrat. But today is a special day for me. I have the great honor of being your Governor on the day when we, as a party, keep another public commitment—a commitment to start the construction of a permanent State Democratic Headquarters Building, that is paid for and belongs to the people's party, the Democratic party.

At no other time in modern American history would such a ceremony be more meaningful in Kentucky or anywhere else in our great country as now. For in no other time in American history has there been such a crying need for politicians, public officeholders, and political parties to perform on their promises. For confidence in our political system is on the brink of destruction. For confidence in our very system of government is in serious jeopardy. The people of Kentucky— the people of America—desperately need to be able to believe.

Many of you here tonight, and other Democrats from all across our state, some four years ago this month decided the answer to sound government and honest politics was based on the one premise that government and party policy had to be returned to the people. We put together a party legislative platform, and we promised we would keep our word. And amid the clamor of the doubting Thomases, the cynics, and the self-appointed authorities, we kept our word as a party.

One year later we promised the people of Kentucky tax reform, reorganization of state government, and a long list of programs for the people of Kentucky. And amid the clamor from the same cynics, the same doubting Thomases and self-appointed authorities, we kept our word to the people of Kentucky. During this same period, we as a party promised to rebuild our party—to take the party back to the grass roots, to the people. We organized a full-time staff. We had workshops in Frankfort and all across the state. We said to every Democrat in this state—this is your party, you must participate, you must guide it, you must finance it, you must make its policy, for if you don't, it will not be the instrument of the people as it was organized and conceived to be. Well, the same cynics, doubting Thomases, and self-appointed judges started their same clamor. But we are succeeding, we are keeping our word. The eyes of the nation are on you, you Kentucky Democrats, because we have, together, gone back to our individual members to organize, to elect a U.S. Senator, and to elect additional congressmen in the face of the most awesome and corrupt political machine ever assembled in our nation's capital.

We have organized in every county and community in our state to finance our party at the grass roots where it belongs, to reverse the modern trend of financing political parties that has culminated in the mess in Washington. We are organizing, as proved by our reregistration[1] meetings today, to build the broadest possible base for our party. All these accomplishments—this new direction—has taken and will continue to take hard work. And I want today, publicly, to let the cynics, the doubting Thomases, and self-appointed judges know that they may continue their clamor if they wish, but we are going to stay on our course. For, in my judgment, the very future of our political system and our form of government depends on grass-roots support and on the kind of hard work you have been willing to give so unselfishly.

During my term as Lieutenant Governor and now as your Governor, I have tried with every ounce of my ability and energy to do those things that my party mandated. And let me say, no public official has ever had greater support from the rank-and-file members of his party. Don't worry about the cynics. You are on the right track, and we are proving it each day.

Today we proved it again by breaking ground for a monument to the thousands of Kentucky Democrats who believe in, and have proven, that our political system can still work, who have proven that a party can be organized, financed, and operated in a broad-based democratic manner.[2] I cannot express to you how proud I am to be one of you— a Democrat—a Kentucky Democrat.

---

1. Reregistration was necessitated by a change in the Kentucky laws (Senate Bill 162, "An Act Relating to Elections and Registration") of the prior year which had required each voter to register again after the registration rolls were wiped clean. The new law required this reregistration to take place before the 1973 elections.

2. On July 14 the Governor said, "I guess we learned one thing for sure, and that is, not to be more open than the law requires. For as you know, we only had to report $200,000 out of the over $800,000 raised. The truth of the matter is we had nothing to hide. We were so proud of the thousands of Democrats who worked so hard to return the financing of our party to where it belongs, with the rank-and-file individual members, that we simply reported every dime we received. I personally am extremely pleased by the results of our party's fund-raising effort. If you compare our efforts and openness to the Republican party of Kentucky, I believe every Kentuckian

should be pleased. We have started in a new direction, and I hope our controversy with the clerk of the Senate has not damaged our chances to continue in the future. I personally would like to see our fund-raising efforts compared in detail to the Republican party fund-raising in Kentucky, so that the people of Kentucky can be the judge." The "controversy" referred to by Governor Ford resulted from a full report submitted to the Clerk of the Senate on the monies collected by the Democratic party of Kentucky. Only a portion of the funds collected was used for Senator Huddleston's campaign, and technically only that portion would have had to be reported to the Clerk of the United States Senate.

DIVISION II CIRCUIT JUDGESHIP
Frankfort / July 23, 1973

It is my firm belief that the people of Owensboro and Daviess County are entitled to the facts regarding the Division II Circuit Judgeship.[1] This matter pertains to a vacancy created by the death of the Honorable Dan M. Griffith and the subsequent process of a replacement for his position.[2]

After assuming office, I developed a procedure to be followed in cases where it was necessary for the Governor to appoint a Circuit Judge. I used this procedure for the Division II Circuit Judgeship just as I had in other districts. I received the names of two attorneys who were interested in serving. There were no other applications or names submitted to me. Those names were then forwarded to the Kentucky Bar Association for screening and review. The Kentucky Bar Association later gave me its report, stating that both individuals were qualified, competent men of integrity who would make fine judges.

Immediately thereafter, I received a letter from one of the applicants, asking that his name be withdrawn. The name was withdrawn. I then conferred with Daviess County Democratic chairman, William M. Kuegel,[3] informing him of the procedure. He fully understood the orderly steps which had thus far been taken and concurred in my selection of Calvin Ray Robinson who had been recommended both locally and by the State Bar as extremely well qualified.[4] Mr. Kuegel personally assured me that he agreed with the procedure and went further to assure me that the Democratic Committee would nominate unanimously Mr. Robinson for the November election.

The county chairman then called upon Mr. Robinson and assured him that he would support his nomination and that the committee would, in fact, nominate him. Following this assurance, on July 6, I announced that effective July 23, I would appoint Mr. Robinson as Circuit Judge.

Last week, through news reports, I learned that the county committee nominated someone other than Mr. Robinson as the Democratic candidate for the November election. This was absolutely in contradiction to what the county chairman had personally assured both Mr. Robinson and myself.

On Thursday, July 19, Mr. Kuegel told me that he had met with certain members of the committee prior to Wednesday, July 18, the date of the Executive Committee meeting, and knew full well what would take place at the meeting. If Mr. Kuegel had advised me of the desire of the committee, I could have asked them to postpone the meeting thirty days, which would have given me the opportunity to submit the name the committee desired to the State Bar Association for their evaluation. For I have no reason to dictate to any local committee, let alone my home county. My only interest is to see that the people have the best we can offer in our judicial system and those who determine the direction for improvement in law and order.

Under the circumstances, Mr. Robinson has asked that I not appoint him to fill the existing vacancy. Unfortunately, the incident will be extremely costly to Mr. Robinson, since he understood the local support was there and had made plans to assume the Judgeship and close his law practice.

In view of the situation, and Mr. Robinson's request, I do not plan to appoint a successor. Certainly, I would not place either the local Bar or Kentucky Bar Association in the embarrassing position of judging a person who had already been nominated by the local party committee. Instead, I will ask the Court to assign judges whenever necessary during the brief period until the citizens by vote in November make their wishes known. The people are perfectly capable of rendering a proper decision, and whomever the candidates might be in that election, I know the right choice will be made through the voting process.

---

1. Press release.

2. Dan M. Griffith (1906–1973), Owensboro; attorney; commonwealth attorney (1946–1962); circuit judge, division II. *Kentucky State Bar Association Portraits and Biographical Sketches of the Members* (Louisville, 1967), p. 48.

3. William Martin Kuegel (1924–), Owensboro; farmer; chairman, Daviess County Democratic party (1959–). *Who's Who in American Politics, 1975–1976*, 5th ed. (New York, 1975), p. 522.

4. Calvin Ray Robinson (1927–), Owensboro; attorney; master commissioner, Daviess County Circuit Court; past president, Daviess County Bar Association. *Kentucky State Bar Association Portraits and Biographical Sketches of the Members*, p. 54.

J. R. MILLER RETIREMENT
Frankfort / August 16, 1973

J. R. MILLER has been a loyal supporter and strong advocate of Democratic party philosophy throughout his lifetime.[1] An outspoken, hardworking, and unselfish leader in my political career, he possesses a tremendous capacity for organization. His energies are seemingly without limit, and the motivating force behind J. R. Miller has been a series of goals which have benefited both our party and the citizens of this state.

For some time I knew of J.R.'s desire to step down from the chairmanship of the Kentucky Democratic party. His tenure has been lengthy, considering the magnitude of work involved. He has been concerned with party matters when he would rather be with his family, when he would rather be involved in business, and when he would rather be enjoying some of the comforts of life where pressures and demands are replaced by relaxation and recreation.

The contributions J. R. Miller has made to the success and growth of the Kentucky Democratic party are registered in those goals which have been attained.

You have just heard of his wish, as well as his decision to place that wish aside at this particular time. I respect both, though neither am I at all surprised that he would want to stand up and be counted in the matter of an allegation against one of his employees and the party to which he has dedicated so much of his time and resources. Allegations are a dime a dozen, and it is irresponsible to even remotely associate guilt unless facts bear out the charge. Allegations without foundation bring harm to innocent people, and this is wrong.

When certain charges were made by William Grissom,[2] I obtained the record of events from the Bureau of Highways and have continued to examine every possible aspect of this case as it might relate to an agency of state government. At the same time, Chairman Miller conducted his own investigation since the Democratic party was named by Mr. Grissom. First, it should be known that there has been no communication between Democratic Headquarters and the Bureau of Highways in appraisal matters.

Next, it comes as no surprise that agencies of the federal government have reared their heads. I have talked with Governor after Governor and found federal agencies busy investigating Democratic administrations throughout the country. Certain federal officials don't hesitate to leak their activities in order to gain a political headline. I will say in defense of the FBI that it had no idea someone else would make a public issue out of their activities before they could ascertain the facts requested of them. But just look how this one allegation has mushroomed within the corridors of the present national administration— from the federal Bureau of Highways to the Justice Department to the U.S. Attorney to the FBI. If this is real justice in action, where individuals or a political party would be tried strictly on innuendo, then I suggest no person is safe from unreasonable public attack and unwarranted abuse, especially when the political end might justify the means.

I welcome any responsible investigation. But I hope the proof of innocence will be as visible to the public as is the implication of wrongdoing, whenever any allegation is made and then disseminated by the media. I suggest that what will be found is this: a man, who during the last administration, received over $108,000 in twenty-seven months for state appraisal business wanted more. His price was too high, and he was rejected. If Mr. Grissom had gotten his price, there would have been no complaint. Some have tried to make it appear that he had a job taken away with our award going to a friend. The significant point is that we saved nearly $4,000 by not giving Mr. Grissom the job. In trying to do what is right, this administration is turned upon, with H. K. Taylor being made the scapegoat.

If this is the burden one must accept for trying to operate state government on a sound basis, then I welcome the abuse, because I believe the public can see through the smokescreen which has been made thicker by a national administration that desperately wants to overshadow the Watergate headlines with articles about Democrats, no matter the credibility.

It is also interesting that Mr. Grissom has contracts with several federal agencies, including the Justice Department. Even beyond that, our investigation has questioned procedures conducted by some career employees over a period of twenty years that have always been sanctioned by the federal Bureau of Highways. I wonder if federal agencies aren't really investigating their own procedures, trying to find a state administration on which to lay the blame.

---

1. James R. Miller (1916–   ), Owensboro; public utility executive; past member, State Board of Agriculture and State Board of Economic Development; past president, Owensboro-Daviess County Chamber of Commerce and Owensboro Jaycees; former chairman, state Democratic party (1968–1973); member, Democratic Executive Committee. *Kentucky Lives*, ed. Hambleton Tapp (Hopkinsville, 1966), p. 361.

2. William H. Grissom (1920–   ), Glasgow; real estate broker, appraiser, and developer; mayor of Glasgow (1957–1961); president of Glasgow Chamber of Commerce (1961). Telephone interview with Grissom.

SENATE RACE ANNOUNCEMENT
Frankfort / March 22, 1974

SOMEONE, a newsman if I recall correctly, commented that Wendell Ford has, for many years, followed a set pattern of taking matters as they come, placing each in order, and not letting one interfere with another. I suppose this is a pretty accurate analysis, because I have always tried to approach decisions in a systematic way. Despite repeated speculation, daily questions, and the obvious amount of conversation about the United States Senate race in 1974, I did not allow that topic to "buck the line," so to speak, against priorities of state government.[1] My option was to continue the business at hand—budget preparation, the energy crisis, key bills such as reorganization and energy research and development, and the many other daily activities which have been important to Kentucky during the past few months.

In the last few days, I have assessed the Senate race. I have discussed it with my family, with as many individuals as possible who could reflect grass-roots sentiment. I have talked with my staff and cabinet. Certainly, I have been aware of the encouragement and urging of individuals from throughout Kentucky. There has been strong insistence from many friends elsewhere. In addition, I have evaluated the twenty-seven months thus far in office as Governor, and have projected our establishment of new programs, as well as the continuation of existing programs. Then I took a careful look at the problems facing both Kentucky and this nation, trying to evaluate those sources where specific problems began, or were compounded, as well as those sources where they can be solved.

At the state level, I honestly believe we have provided unprecedented services to the citizens since December 1971. Perhaps more significant is the fact that we have structured numerous programs for the long-range future of Kentucky. This consideration was made in behalf of children, of those who would have something special to look forward to—a state where economic strength makes their life better; a state where the quality of life in all its phases exceeds that of others.

But there is one factor which gives Governors and local officials the most trouble. Again and again an undisputed fact keeps returning. It's called "isolation." There is an isolated federal bureaucracy where certain elected and appointed officials are totally out of touch with the mainstream of America. States can go just so far in helping the citizens. I have always maintained that government at any level exists to serve people. When this doesn't happen, there must be change. As a state senator, Lieutenant Governor, and Governor, I believe the major advantage I have had in government responsibility has been retaining a closeness with the general public. You have heard me say before that the nation's Governors are the best conduit from the grass roots to Capitol Hill. This is why I have encouraged stronger participation by Governors in national affairs, both governmental and political. The attitude we have as Governors must prevail elsewhere, if Kentucky and this country are to fully gain from our democratic system. I can cite you example after example of nonresponsiveness at the federal level. But much more important is doing something positive about it.

I want to try! My decision, therefore, is to run for the United States Senate. In my opinion, and in the opinion of those who have urged my candidacy, the Senate is now the best place where I can work for Kentucky and, in fact, carry forward and further the progress we have under way in this great state.

It's time we represent the people of our state as U.S. Senators, rather than having someone who represents a national administration and who is out of touch with the needs of the housewife, the laborer, the elderly, the young, the businessman, the disadvantaged, and the neglected. Governors' problems today are increased by a paralyzed federal government. These problems are far different now than they were six years ago, and they will be different in the future. But the crux of the matter is responding to the people; people for whom I have served in three capacities. If they believe I can do more as United States Senator, I am willing.

I am proud of my administration, of the credibility which has been established by doing those things which I said, as a candidate for Governor, I would do. Should the voters select me next November, Lieutenant Governor Carroll[2] will continue the progress, the programs, and the direction state government has achieved. He has assured me of this.

So the challenge is mine, by asking the voters of Kentucky to put me to work as their United States Senator, just as they put me to work as a state senator, Lieutenant Governor, and Governor. And I will make my first campaign commitment right now. If it is humanly possible to work any harder than I have in these capacities, I will do so, because my only desire is the best interest of all Kentucky.[3]

---

1. In a statement issued on January 17, 1973, not included in this volume, Ford refused to clarify his position on the 1974 Senate race. He claimed the gubernatorial responsibilities were of top priority. The Governor, however, did add: "You know, nothing changes faster than Kentucky weather and Kentucky politics. This is early 1973, not a time when responsible people dwell first on elections and second on the people's business. I have always felt that good politics is good government. If you concentrate on good government, the politics will take care of itself."

2. Julian M. Carroll (1931–   ), Frankfort; attorney; member of Kentucky House of Representatives (1962–1972); lieutenant governor of Kentucky (1971–1974); governor of Kentucky (1974–   ).

3. Early in the campaign, Ford's opponent, incumbent Senator Marlow Cook, became involved in a legal dispute concerning a technical error in filing for candidacy. On several occasions in April 1974, Ford repeated his desire to face Cook in the fall election. He stated on April 29: "The people of Kentucky deserve no less than a vigorous campaign where political philosophy and performance offer a clear choice in candidates. I do not want to be a U.S. Senator by default—the voice of the people is much more important." This speech is not included in this volume.

DOWNTOWN LIONS CLUB LUNCHEON
Louisville / October 15, 1974

THREE weeks from today Kentuckians will speak with more force than any impact my opponent and I have collectively made in campaign addresses! This is how it should be. The last word is yours, not ours. For me, this has been a restricted campaign—one necessarily so, due to the fact I have felt it proper to be Governor first, a candidate second. But when opportunities such as this have been available, I have tried to address myself to issues relating to existing conditions within our society, plus others which can profoundly influence the future of our children and our children's children. Only through a positive approach, through evaluation of the records, and through the expression of one's philosophy can a candidate, in my opinion, fully communicate with the public.

You may recall that as a candidate for Governor, I met with citizens throughout Kentucky to establish priorities for our state. Louisville and Jefferson County are a good example. The people here were instrumental in developing a program for this area. That program has been given full-scale attention. These ideas or priorities do not belong only to Wendell Ford. They belong to you, because you were willing to participate, you understood local needs, and you expressed your desires for the future.

Quickly, let's review what has happened and is happening in this area. The new teaching hospital, renovation of the fairgrounds and Freedom Hall, home rule, a new civic center and exhibition hall downtown, the Vocational-Technical Institute, full recognition of U of L into the state system, and a major vocational training center associated with Jefferson Community College.

There are also the removal of tolls from the Kentucky Turnpike here, state-local revenue-sharing, expansion at Southwest Jefferson Community College, and $31 million in road projects for southern and southwestern Jefferson County alone. Work is progressing on the Jefferson Freeway—a massive, slow, and expensive necessity, but it is progressing. I can add the removal of the sales tax on food, the Kentucky Low Income Housing Authority, additional circuit judges, and expansion at Tom Sawyer Park.

These and many other items are commitments which were made. But more importantly, they represent commitments kept. I offer these points for one reason. Without citizen cooperation and without citizen support which gave me a chance to carry out these programs, I could not cite them. So the credit goes to you and people like you, and this is what government ought to understand, that elected officials are in office to serve in a partnership with the people. This same attitude can prevail in Washington. It's the same attitude I want to carry a step further in helping restore confidence in our federal government.

Let me reflect on some of the priorities I think the next Congress should consider: First is prompt enactment of a comprehensive tax-reform package to remove the current inequities in our tax system. The working men and women who are bearing the brunt of inflation do not need an additional 5 percent surtax. They need tax relief, not more taxes. Loopholes, which permit privileged few, the huge oil companies, and the multinational corporations, to escape paying their share of the tax burden, must be plugged. Congress must take a hard line on federal expenditures and cut nonessential programs. We can tighten the belt on federal spending and at the same time provide funds to those productive segments of the economy hardest hit by inflation. Up to now, this hasn't occurred.

Steps must be taken to cope with the shortages of materials in our country. This is not a demand inflation. This is a cost-push inflation, caused by shortages, by the lack of demand in places where there should be demand, and by overdemand where it needs to be decreased. Another urgent need is for the development of a comprehensive national energy policy. The President's proposal did not offer much long-term direction in this area, except repeating a call for Americans to drive less and appointing our sixth energy czar. There is no doubt that this country must accelerate the domestic production of oil and speed up the development of new energy sources. Kentucky stands ready to make a significant contribution toward the goal of energy self-sufficiency through coal—through coal liquefaction and gasification, or turning coal into oil and pipeline gas. We now have the first-of-its-kind energy research and development program in the nation. If Kentucky can do it, so can America.

The next Congress also needs to speed up action on a program of national health insurance. Such a program must provide relief for those who incur lengthy, catastrophic illnesses. We must take a hard look at the various proposals now before Congress, especially as to cost and benefits provided. In developing a national health-insurance program, we should consider what is the best coverage for the people, then determine how it should be funded, to what extent, and from what source of revenue. Our Social Security system cannot bear the entire burden. But the guarantee of a free choice of doctors and preserving the doctor-patient relationship are paramount, just as is the guarantee that any system will not be controlled by a federal bureaucracy.

The farm economy determines our national economy. Production incentives, new markets, accelerated research in techniques and products, a more equitable credit system, and input by the farmers themselves are all necessary to stimulate this vital portion of our society. A recent mistake was that the farmer was not invited to the President's economic summit for his input. The new Congress also needs to consider reform of our welfare system. When you read of someone earning $13,000 a year and still receiving welfare, you know something is out of balance. Reform of the welfare system has been discussed for years, but we have seen little action. Inequities have mounted, the bureaucracy has grown, and costs have increased. Reform in this area should be approached on the basis of what is best for the people who need help. We've done something about it in Kentucky. We're taking 400 persons off welfare rolls each month because they have been able to find a job and earn their own way with respect. These are just a few of the priorities to which the next Congress must direct its attention. They are not Wendell Ford's priorities, but the priorities of the people of Kentucky and America.

The other day someone asked why Governors should serve in the House or Senate. One good reason, in my opinion, is that we're with people from all walks of life every morning, noon, and night, seven days a week, twelve months each year. We hear their voices, we see their plight, we relate to their needs. We haven't been isolated from the grass roots. We've stayed out in the grass roots! And I believe any Governor will tell you that after having to operate a state through the trying times of recent years, we're ready to carry your message to Washington. The priorities I have mentioned—your priorities—have come through loud and clear these past thirty-three months! Time, unfortunately, limits discussion of priorities and program items. If any of you desire, I am willing to entertain your questions, but let me emphasize a point that many politicians seemingly want to keep from the public.

I don't have all the answers! But I'm willing to work, to listen, to encourage your input, and represent Kentucky in Washington. I have no desire to go up there, slam my door, swell up with Potomac Fever, and forget those who sent me and for what purpose. Harry Truman once warned of this, and I believe his admonition is well advised.[1]

---

1. In a post-primary statement issued on May 28, 1974, Governor Ford outlined his campaign strategy. He said: "I pledge tonight to every Ken-

tuckian—Democrat, Republican, and Independent—that I will work as hard as humanly possible to be the best Governor possible between now and January. My campaign for the United States Senate will have to come second to that of my responsibilities as Governor. Yet whenever possible, I intend to wage a hard, straightforward, and aggressive campaign, based on the issues most important to the people of Kentucky." The speech is not included in this volume.

KENTUCKY AND THE NATION

JAYCEES EXECUTIVES CLUB
Washington, D.C. / April 29, 1972

It would be inappropriate for me to stand here, as part of you and as the chief executive of my state, if I failed to dwell on the theme of our meeting. So if you will permit some personal references and reflections, I would like to respond, to respond with pride, appreciation, and reverence, to the question: "What is right about America?"

When a boy from Yellow Creek with only a high school education can experience the countless blessings, as I have, such a theme is easily magnified into other relevant questions: "What is good about America?" "How fortunate are we to be Americans?" or "Why not show your pride in America?" America puts few silver spoons in the mouths of babes but extends unlimited golden opportunities for those who are willing to accept her bountiful offerings. Like a thoughtful parent, this country gives unparalleled love to its children, whether they be short or tall, ugly or handsome, rich or poor. Like a responsible parent, this country asks for self-sacrifice, personal initiative, a willingness to work, and an understanding of others. Like a rewarding parent, America will recognize any sincere ambition, any determination to improve one's self, or any effort that is made in behalf of others. And as a strict parent, America does not condone the dissipation of one's potential, the absence of one's integrity, or the laziness of one's activities.

My good fortune as a farm boy was to have an environment whereby these expectations were made very clear by my family, because they understood and taught me what America offered and expected. This then has been the springboard for Wendell Ford, whose good fortune has been found in opportunity, rather than in handout. There must be a whole lot right about America when that opportunity lets someone travel the road from Yellow Creek to this spot today. I find the fact especially true because there were no family riches, in the sense of material grants, yet there were doors which could be opened if I would be willing to open them. Jaycees also showed me many things that were right about America.

There is much right about America when political chance comes to someone who really hopes for a role in public service, as only government can provide. In no other place can you do more for people. In politics just as in Jaycees, the odds were heavy, and there was always the underdog role. During these early remarks, I asked your permission for personal references. This was done only for self-expression in behalf of the American opportunity. There are many stories such as mine which are far more impressive. America has been good to us, and this is what's right about our country—her goodness, her generosity, her challenges to anyone with a determined spirit, and her constant, gentle shoves stimulating the great majority of her children to that determined spirit.

You know, it isn't unusual for a Baptist to give testimony! It does the soul good. I am appreciative of your invitation to give testimony for a land that said to a rural youth from western Kentucky, "There's the road, start walking, and if you get over the bumps and obstacles, your trip will be filled with rewards." I pray that I never forget the many rewards. I pray that I always remember my debt to America, a continued personal investment which just might extend this country's benevolence to others.

NATIONAL ASSOCIATION
OF INSURANCE COMMISSIONERS
Lexington / May 8, 1972

It is always a pleasure as Governor of the Commonwealth of Kentucky to welcome visitors to our state. But on this occasion, there are two reasons why I am especially happy to extend a hand of hospitality. First, we are entering a new tourist era, kicked off by the Kentucky Derby, and one which will bring millions of people from all over the world to this state. Our guests are important to Kentucky. You are important to Kentucky, and I want you to feel at home during your stay here. The second reason for me to express pleasure about today is the realization that I am among members of my own business fraternity. As a former (and future!) insurance agent, I am well aware of the impact insurance, with all of its ramifications, has upon the individual citizens of this state and every state in the union.

Your profession is one of service to people, and this is really what government is all about, serving people rather than forcing people to serve government.

The office I hold must direct itself to the problems confronting all

Kentuckians, rather than any particular group. It is gratifying to know there are people in this room resolved to study and provide solutions affecting some of the most vital interests of Kentuckians. The economic impact insurance has upon the life of each citizen is, in many instances, awesome. This fact must be weighed in your every deliberation. The Kentucky Legislature, which meets biennially, convenes less than a month after the Kentucky Governor takes office. The time within which any Kentucky Governor has to prepare and present to that Legislature his program for the first biennium is too brief a period of time. So it was at the beginning of 1972. However, I can announce that this administration adopted and had enacted at the 1972 session of the General Assembly the National Association of Insurance Commissioners' Model Act relating to insurance holding company systems, the National Association of Insurance Commissioners' Model Act relating to the guarantee fund for property and casualty insurers, and the reenactment of the "Kentucky Fair Plan," which without legislative action, would have expired in Kentucky at the end of 1972.[1]

As Lieutenant Governor of Kentucky, I was president of the Legislative Research Commission when that group undertook the study of Kentucky insurance laws, and drafted and presented to the 1970 Legislature the new Kentucky Revised Insurance Code.[2] This code, good as it is, is not perfect and there are some changes which should be made. To this end, we will appreciate your suggestions and advice during the remainder of the year. In looking at the program you have scheduled for this annual meeting, it is interesting to see the areas you are bringing under study.

Certainly it should be the goal of every regulator to acquire for the consuming public adequate protection with the least interference of freedom of enterprise. Achieving this delicate balance is the true measure of the effectiveness of your regulations. Also relating to this, it is my understanding that statutory accounting by life insurance companies has been proven to be dependable, because it is based on the premise of showing the degree of solvency of a life insurance company. However, I understand it has been less than a perfect tool for reflecting useful insurance company earnings as a going concern for the purpose of considerations for investments.

It is my firm conviction that the insurance industry can best be regulated by the various states. The federal government, perhaps in recognition of this concept, allowed the states to implement the Phase II guidelines, as they applied to the rate regulations of the insurance industry. Such action was proper. Therefore, it is also proper that you have devoted a portion of your program to this subject. I challenge you to administer this program in such a way that continuing state regulation of the insurance industry will be justified.

In campaigning throughout Kentucky, a candidate who truly listens learns the problems of the people of this state. Having recently successfully concluded a campaign which took me to all parts of Kentucky, I am aware of a general dissatisfaction with the present automobile reparation system. It is an appropriate subject at this time for discussion. We have a special problem relative to this matter since our Constitution states, "The General Assembly shall have no power to limit the amount to be recovered for injuries resulting in death or for injury to person or property."[3] The Kentucky General Assembly has ordered an in-depth study of no-fault insurance during 1972–1973. I have directed individuals on my staff to keep abreast of all developments in the area of automobile reparation and to keep me continually informed. This can mean a legislative program in 1974 which will provide Kentuckians the best possible solution to the dilemma of no-fault.

It is my hope that in the future you will have occasion to look to the ever-increasing problems that are developing in workmen's compensation, and particularly in the field of occupational diseases. In Kentucky, as is true in all coal-producing states, black lung presents an ever-increasing problem. We must minimize the possibility of contracting this disease. We must ensure that the miner who does contract it is adequately compensated for his loss of ability to earn a living. We must achieve a fair distribution of the cost of such insurance, and yet we must make certain that the coal-producing industry, which now includes many operators who are at best marginal in their endeavor, is not so overburdened with this expense that they are driven out of production. I challenge you in the insurance industry to provide us with answers for this dire crisis that is developing.

---

1. See an act "relating to Insurance Holding Company System," which was approved March 13, 1972. *Acts of the General Assembly of the Commonwealth of Kentucky, 1972,* Chapter 52 (S.B. 93), pp. 165–74. See also an act "relating to insurance," which was approved March 25, 1972. Ibid., Chapter 137 (S.B. 91), pp. 591–603. Also of interest is an act "relating to the establishment of Fair Plan to make essential Property Insurance available to all qualified applicants," which was approved March 15, 1972. Ibid., Chapter 65 (S.B. 92), pp. 257–62.

2. See an act "providing the Kentucky Insurance Code," which was approved March 30, 1970. *Acts of the General Assembly of the Commonwealth of Kentucky, 1970,* Chapter 301 (S.B. 253), pp. 1004–445.

3. This is a direct quote from Section 54 of the Kentucky Constitution.

INDUSTRY LUNCHEON
New York / May 9, 1972

IN some respects you might equate my appearance today as one of a man with a split personality! For if this were the Christmas season, your description of my attitude could properly be that of Ebenezer Scrooge and Santa Claus! After my first 150 days as the chief executive of the Commonwealth of Kentucky, I feel it is incumbent upon me to address you in a complex philosophical vein. As Scrooge, there are self-admitted motivating factors of opportunism for my state. I want more from you and from people like you, because we won't be satisfied unless our business lot is vastly improved. This is a Kentucky necessity. As Santa, I intend to see that the Governor's Office is more accessible, more responsive, and more enlightened to your economic posture than any of our fifty states. I'll take a chance on an advertising pun and say, "Try us, you'll like us!" Without our becoming better acquainted, both interests would suffer. This is why I have brought key members of a new administration to New York. They have the same goals for Kentucky as do I. Each will play a specific role in achieving new dimensions for the Bluegrass state.

Some of you have been involved with similar luncheons, in which other Kentucky Governors participated. Therefore, the challenge to me is one of proving sincerity. If nothing else is accomplished right now, other than being candid and illustrating the true reason we are associated with state government, this will indeed be a successful venture. Let me express appreciation for this occasion to talk about Kentucky, about our economic status, our resources for profitable production, about the direction of government already, and about my views of government in the years ahead.

Kentucky's economic position and structure underwent a substantial transformation during the decade of the sixties. As a member of the Governor's staff early in that decade, later as a state senator and then as Lieutenant Governor, I was directly involved in the foundation process for which the thrust of this administration is committed. Personal income of Kentuckians increased by $5.1 billion during that period. Per-capita income went up by $1,500. This sharp improvement in the economic position of Kentuckians enabled them to live better, work better, and consume more of the nation's abundance. It also made possible marked improvements in the quality and quantity of human resources essential in a modern society. Kentucky has moved strongly toward the mainstream of the nation's financial and social structure. More opportunities for work with better pay was the primary reason for our rapidly improved position. Two hundred and sixty thousand non-agricultural jobs were added in Kentucky between 1960 and 1970; 80,000 of these were in manufacturing. This 46 percent gain in manu-facturing jobs was more than triple the country's industrial growth rate.

Firms represented here today have contributed immeasurably to our industrial and economic growth because you selected Kentucky. On the other hand, Kentucky's resources have added to the black ink side of your profit and loss statement.

Why should you choose to produce in Kentucky? Here are but a few reasons. Kentucky occupies an excellent geographical location at the center of a twenty-eight state distribution area with more than 70 per-cent of the nation's population, jobs, and income. We have a magnifi-cent system of highways blending interests with parkways into an integrated net, which puts Kentucky in close interstate transit time with major production, consumption, and distribution centers. My admin-istration will now concentrate on what I have termed "get-to-it roads." You have asked for such a priority. Rail trunklines generally run paral-lel to the interstates. Our rivers offer heavy barging as a part of the overall transportation system. Our multimillion-dollar efforts to con-struct port and riverfront facilities are already under way.

Kentucky's labor supply is plentiful and extremely productive. There is no substitute for a rural background in creating the under-standing of an honest day's work. Already one of the finest vocational-technical educational systems in America, Kentucky's is destined to improve even more for two reasons—first, impact of my budget, and second, because our people seek vocational training.

Electrical power is readily available in large quantities at competitive prices. Water, both surface and underground, is abundantly available. Our livability, recreation, natural scenery, and opportunity for relax-ation in today's hectic times are unsurpassed.

The Kentucky business climate encourages profitable operations. Regulations on business and industry are realistic. The tax system is balanced, fairly and professionally administered in a fair and efficient manner.

I cannot overemphasize this undisputed fact: There is an adminis-tration receptive to your needs. There are communities in every section of the state whose welcome mat is not a facade, but rather a blend of readiness and anxiousness to please. These resources, keystones to growth, are available. On March 17 the Kentucky General Assembly adjourned. Passed was an executive budget reflective of an optimistic administration. Our legislative programs contain measures of national significance. Specifically, I want to touch on a few actions which are concurrent with the basics of industry and business.

Educational improvement is a major element in my legislative package. Elementary and secondary education received the greatest attention. This ranged from the provisions for 2,600 new classroom units to dramatic steps in special education; from a statewide kindergarten program to what will become a $35 million-plus technical institute with emphasis on the medical occupations. One hundred and ninety-five new vocational units were authorized and funded for the biennium; teachers were provided long overdue benefits; and a comprehensive educational program to have far-reaching influence on our statewide system has been given the highest priority in the Department of Education. In higher education, two new four-year institutions were added to the system. We are restructuring our higher education coordinating agency in order to bring improved planning, management control, and budgetary matters into a new focus as dictated by tomorrow. This has great implications for more effective use of our higher education dollars, a subject with which I am sure you are familiar.

In the field of criminal justice, we have started with the policeman on the beat and moved through every phase relating to crime and the courts to such an extent that other states have already asked for our blueprints. A 300 percent increase in state dollars, from 2.1 million to 6.7 million, brings to bear an additional 19 million federal dollars on the critical problem of law and order. We have instituted a state revenue-sharing plan to upgrade police officers. In many respects, we don't have the problems experienced elsewhere. We're taking steps now to ensure they never occur.

In the field of supporting economic growth we have provided additional loan funds for the development of industrial sites and building construction, increased funding for local airport development, passed legislation expediting construction of sewerage disposal systems throughout the state, and have taken steps to provide more effective assistance to local governments. I have already mentioned our riverport and highway-impact plans. We have also started state-local revenue-sharing for urban street construction and maintenance.

Environmental pollution control is a major issue facing all of us. The emotional overtones make solutions even more complex, as you know. We are facing up to our responsibilities, not through emotion but in the most businesslike and environmentally conscious way humanly possible. New legislation consolidating all environmental-control functions will be a remedy to a thus-far inadequate system, and the responsibility is placed squarely on the shoulders of the Governor. This, in my judgment, is where it belongs. Now people can get answers without being pitched from pillar to post. And we will have undelayed data from experts representing the technical disciplines.

We will be strict, yet reasonable. We fully intend to protect adequately the health and welfare of our citizens and, as well, our natural resources. Our attitude will parallel that of any responsible industry. This means basing decisions on reason, whereby rational men can arrive at conclusions which are fair to all considerations. This means scrutinizing both the environmental impact and the economic impact, to carefully weigh benefits and costs.

As for the cost of doing business in Kentucky, we remain in an enviable position, yet we altered our tax structure. A University of Kentucky study is under way to provide full facts comparing the soundness of Kentucky's competitive position. We expect the results early this summer. Several serious studies of revenue and finance demonstrated conclusively that within the past few years Kentucky's tax system had weighed heavily on the individual. Correction of this inequity was important. Maintaining our coveted competitive position received particular emphasis. We removed the 5 percent sales tax from food, placed a severance tax on coal amounting to 4 percent or 30 cents per ton, and changed the corporate income tax by removing the deductibility of the federal corporate income tax and reducing the tax rate to 4 percent of the first $25,000 taxable income and to 5.8 percent of income in excess of $25,000. Previously the rates had been 5 and 7 percent.

The Kentucky general fund will receive approximately $16 million more in corporate income taxes in fiscal 1973, but the net increase to corporations will be about $8.3 million due to the deductibility clause under the federal tax. This adjustment actually equals only 0.25 percent of wages paid by manufacturing firms alone. Corporate income taxes in Ohio, South Carolina, Tennessee, Virginia, West Virginia, Georgia, North Carolina, Michigan, and New York, to name a few states, exceed that of Kentucky's. We increased our gasoline tax from seven to nine cents per gallon—an absolutely necessary step to continue a system of highways vitally important to business and industry. This is a national pattern since all states are facing similar headaches with their road building and repair expenses.

The conduct of state government, as I view it, is much like the conduct of your business. This is exactly the basis on which we are operating. My first budget shows a decline in the percentage costs of state government. We are now beginning a massive reorganization of state government to accomplish three goals: the halt of a rapidly spiraling personnel growth in government; the bringing of government closer to the people in order to provide better and faster service; and the abolition of bureaucratic strongholds contributing to an outlandish waste of taxpayers' money.

Yes, a lot has happened in just 150 days. We want you to be a part of what will happen the next forty-three months. We want to listen, and we will listen to you, for the cornerstone placed by a new administration is worthless unless there is ultimately full and proper community growth. We can't have that without new businesses and industries. In conclusion, let me add this thought. While we are striving to acquire manufacturing additions, we are also placing a high priority on regional offices. Modern communication and transportation, the executive's demand for tranquil living, and the strategic location of Kentucky make our state ideal for regional bases. You have been patient and generous by allowing a somewhat lengthy report. This is our knock on your door. Now, let's sit down and start some serious talking—anytime, anyplace, on any subject of interest to you![1]

---

1. In an address to the Kentucky Society the same day in New York, Governor Ford again praised the Commonwealth—stressing its history, its famous sons and daughters, and its favorable location.

COUNCIL OF STATE GOVERNMENTS
Atlanta, Georgia / May 11, 1972

FROM the tobacco wars of the early 1900s to the famous feuds between mountain families, the antics of boatmen on the Ohio, and the assassination of Governor Goebel, crime in Kentucky has been the subject of writers and historians. They have even romanticized crime. We still occasionally find criminal acts romanticized, as in the case of the man known as "D. B. Cooper" who some months ago parachuted out of a Boeing-727 with $200,000 in ransom. But the very fact that crime and violence in America grew by 180 percent in the decade of the sixties while our population increased only by 13 percent made it an everyday unromantic fact of life for most Americans.

For the first time in polling history, the Gallup Poll announced in early 1968 that crime and lawlessness topped the list of domestic concerns in the minds of Americans. That finding was confirmed less than a month ago—except that the number of Americans who are now afraid to go out on the streets at night has grown from 31 percent to 45 percent.

The actual amount of crime we experience and our fear of it serve to diminish the quality of American life today. For that reason, we must take hold of our future by finding effective ways to deal with criminal behavior while maintaining the liberties upon which this country is founded. I would like to see the decade of the seventies, in contrast to the sixties, remembered for its intelligent response to the problems of crime and justice in society.

We have taken some first steps in Kentucky. But before I describe them, let me call your attention to the responsibility of state government—both the legislative and executive branches—in this field. Shortly after the first Gallup Poll (but not, of course, because of it) the Congress of the United States passed the Omnibus Crime Control and Safe Streets Act. In it, states were encouraged to create planning agencies for criminal justice, and federal funds were available in "bloc grants" for implementation of the resulting state plans. Primary responsibility for reducing crime and improving justice was therefore turned over to the states and such regional or local planning councils as established. Then, in 1971, the Safe Streets Act was amended not only to encourage, but to require, further state participation.

The states were organized to provide a "cash" match to qualify for those federal funds allocated to state agencies. And the states were further required to assist localities by raising 25 percent of the local matching share. In a way Congress said that if we, the states, are going to exercise an unprecedented authority over federal funds, we are going to have to devote some of our own resources to the goals and tasks for which the federal monies are earmarked. Accordingly, state legislatures are now on the spot for more than ideas.

As some of you may know, the Kentucky General Assembly meets for sixty days every two years. The recently concluded sixty-day session did more in the area of criminal justice than any previous Legislature in the history of our Commonwealth. We responded to the 1971 congressional amendments to the Safe Streets Act by initiating a state-to-local revenue-sharing program for law-enforcement and criminal-justice agencies. Over the next biennium $6.7 million was allocated to our Crime Commission for the purpose of matching an estimated $19 million in federal funds. This means we will provide the full matching share for both state and local law-enforcement agencies that qualify for funds under the bloc-grant program. With departmental increases recommended in my budget and accepted by our Legislature, we actually increased the percentage of our state budget going to law and justice from 4.4 percent in 1972 to 5.5 percent in 1973.

It was my judgment that if we were to begin seriously to move from rhetoric to effective action in the war on crime, we had to look at the entire system of criminal justice and beyond. What this means is facility construction. My budget has provided for a 150-bed forensic psychiatric hospital to serve mentally disturbed inmates now in our prisons. This project alone will cost $4.9 million the first two years. This also means early action in the awarding of grants to communities of all sizes to make sweeping changes in the war against crime. During the first 150 days of office, we have provided money totaling about $3 million for regional crime council staffs, evidence collection units, educational programs for judges, area training facilities, information networks, and delinquency programs, to name but a few priorities. When assuming office as Governor, I inherited two hellholes—Eddyville and LaGrange. These prisons turn an amateurish young first offender into a professional. They are overcrowded, understaffed, and not conducive to rehabilitation. I employed a young Corrections Commissioner,[1] highly qualified, willing to be innovative, and who has proven elsewhere his capability to make Kentucky's Corrections System a national model. It's his department with no political pressure. But it has the full support of the Governor.

In the police field, we initiated a salary-incentive law which will offer local police a 15 percent salary increase when new training, education, and operational standards are met. Basic-recruit training, one week of annual in-service training, and a high-school degree may now be expected of police in Kentucky. Moreover, the state will offer a 50-50 match, up to $500, for localities paying salary increases for college and graduate-school credits.

The standards will be real. Operational standards, including participation in the uniform crime-reporting system, will be set by our Crime Commission according to the size and location of each department. Training will be geared to the level and experience of the enrolled officers, and as a result, we expect uniform, fair enforcement of our criminal laws. As a matter of fact, it seems to me that state government, state Legislatures specifically, have for too long passed state criminal laws without a proper interest in the uniformity and fairness of their application.

In the area of courts, our 1972 Assembly passed a new penal code and the first public defender law in Kentucky.[2] The penal code was three-and-one-half years in the making. It was the first comprehensive revision ever of our massive criminal law. Three hundred and six provisions are continued in the code, and no two men are going to agree on anything that massive. What we did find agreement about, however, was our objective—to plug loopholes, to grade offenses according to severity, to drop obsolete statutes, and to define each offense rather than rely upon common law. You might be interested to know that the state planning agency—we call it our Crime Commission—actually set up and completed the drafting job itself. The total cost was under $50,000, but the benefit to Kentuckians is invaluable.

In the future, we will attempt to prevent the unexamined growth of our criminal law by creating a criminal law revision committee that will study and fit all new crimes and penalties into the code. If nothing else, the code and this committee represent our admission that the law must grow and develop not only as technology changes and new offenses are defined but also as public attitudes and social standards change.

You will see from the chart before you that six major laws were enacted that should change the course of corrections and offender rehabilitation in the years to come. Lower-court judges in Kentucky have been faced with the choice of either suspending sentence or imprisoning convicted misdemeanants. Now they will have some intelligent options: 1) They may choose to place a minor offender on probationary supervision through the state Department of Corrections; 2) They may decide to hold the man in jail at night or on weekends, while permitting him to work at other times; or 3) They may choose to parole a misdemeanant after he has served a portion of his sentence. We found the lack of alternatives a serious deterrent to effective judicial handling of men who were too often on their way to major crime. We found it desirable also to offer work release to felons and to require supervision of all felons leaving our prison system. In the past year, Kentucky's parole board released only 60 percent of all those leaving our prison system. The other 40 percent, presumably unqualified for parole, were permitted to walk out of Eddyville's door with twenty dollars, a suit, and a bus ticket and no professional supervision.

None of this would have made much actual difference, however, if we hadn't provided the matching appropriations to implement the laws and if we had not declared that patronage would no longer play a role in the selection and retention of parole board members, as well as probation and parole officers. Where will we go in the future? Certainly we want to evaluate further our judicial structure, the effectiveness of part-time prosecutors, and the advisability of speeding justice by requiring trial within thirty or sixty days of arrest.

If I have been remiss today, it may be that I have not given adequate credit where it is due. An independent and professional staff of a state planning agency can be invaluable. The involvement of members of the Legislature on the agency's supervisory board will ease the way toward legislative action. Judiciary and appropriations committee members are usually the most concerned, of course.

I want to conclude with several observations about the Legislature and its critical position on the ladder of success we will try to climb in the seventies toward the reduction of crime in America. First, significant reform may be deferred or defeated by legal impediments. No money, for example, would have authorized work release in Kentucky. Second, the very nature of the legislative process subjects the tunnel vision of idealistic reformers to the hard light of public discussion and debate: a liberalized abortion provision in the penal code did not stand up under scrutiny. And, third, our Legislatures are vital because they can sustain ideas and reforms after the zeal of the reformer has waned. In other words, the Legislature can institutionalize ideas and operations which might not otherwise outlive the original practitioner.

---

1. Corrections commissioner, Charles J. Holmes, for more information see speech from September 7, 1972, in the Public Safety section, p. 270.

2. See an act "relating to the Kentucky Penal Code, to be known as the Kenton-Moloney Code of Criminal Justice," which was approved on March 27, 1972. *Acts of the General Assembly of the Commonwealth of Kentucky, 1972*, Chapter 385 (H.B. 197), pp. 1653–783.

JOINT CONFERENCE WITH GOVERNOR MATTHEW WELSH
Louisville / October 31, 1972

NUMEROUS problems facing our states today are not within the confines of a geographic boundary.[1] Environmental pollution, drug traffic, other crimes and detriments to society don't stop at a state line or a river's edge. On a positive note, our ability to improve conditions for our own citizens is often enhanced through partnership arrangements with other states.

Historical economic development along the Ohio River has given rise to many communities on both shores. With the growing flexibility in transportation, these communities have become less separated and more involved in their relationship with across-the-river sister-cities. Kentucky and Indiana illustrate this type of growth in two common SMSA (standard metropolitan statistical areas) categories. The Louisville SMSA and the Evansville SMSA show a combined population of over one million persons. It is only logical that governing bodies, responsible for their respective peoples, work together in a common cause benefiting all, no matter which side of the river they live on.

I have slightly over three years remaining in my term as Governor of the Commonwealth. I am genuinely concerned about interstate cooperation in dealing with problems which know no state lines. Yet I also know that Kentucky won't be able to do much on its own unless there is a similar philosophy in the Indiana statehouse. Matt Welsh has this same philosophy.[2] His term as Governor has been acknowledged as one of the best in Indiana's history. The endorsements for Matt Welsh's campaign have come from many people, and today I want to add my endorsement to his bid for the governorship of Indiana.

If Kentucky and Indiana are going to come together for the purpose of solving our shared problems, we are going to need the proven leadership of Governor Welsh. With his experience and commitment, I am confident that our states will be able to make great inroads toward better interstate cooperation. There are several technical means by which states can reach cooperative agreements: joint conferences and associations, bistate and multistate agreements and understandings, reciprocal statutes and uniform state laws for more formal cooperation, and the most formal arrangement: interstate compact.

Any or all of these general means for interstate cooperation rest on one crucial element—conviction of intent. If two states merely go through the motions of interstate cooperation, the ultimate result will be failure. In endorsing my friend today, I want to reemphasize the conviction of my administration in this common need. We will always work closely with Indianapolis in achieving the kind of cooperation that will result in a better quality of life for the people on both sides of the river, and in this regard we look forward to a progressive association with Governor Welsh.[3]

---

1. Press conference.
2. Matthew Epson Welsh (1912–   ), Democrat from Indianapolis; attor-

ney; member of Indiana House of Representatives (1941–1944); member of Indiana Senate (1955–1960); Governor of Indiana (1961–1965); Democratic nominee for Governor of Indiana (1972). *Who's Who in American Politics, 1975–1976,* 5th ed. (New York, 1975), p. 984.

3. On March 7, 1972, Governor Ford was named to the five-member Campaign Committee of Democratic Governors. He endorsed Welsh as a friend and as a Democratic campaigner.

PROPOSED REPORT BY
NATIONAL WATER COMMISSION
Washington, D.C. / January 10, 1973

THE real significance of this report cannot be determined by piecemeal analysis of the more than 300 recommendations. Some of these recommendations we do not oppose. They deal with topics which have been recognized generally as being problems with apparent solutions. The conclusions and recommendations for other, more controversial subjects are frequently hedged by a qualifier such as "except where there is unusual social need." Also, many of the recommendations are predicated on assumed adoption of others which precludes specific selection and rejection.

In order to get a clear understanding of the significance of the report findings, it is necessary to relate them to past federal activities in the field of water-resources development. It then becomes evident that adoption of the proposals generally would be a reversal of long-standing national water policies. Specifically, the requirement that all costs be borne by direct recipients of benefits is a throwback. This reversal would be the withdrawal of federal responsibility for water-resource development. Such responsibility would be shifted to states and regional organizations for planning and funding.

In seeking to understand why the recommended policies in the report are in such conflict with past and current policies, it appears one explanation may be the origin of the data on which the report is based. The background studies for the report are published in sixty-two volumes, each devoted to a specific topic, the great majority of which were prepared by specialized academically associated authors. One can conclude that such an academic analysis could be blind to the value of water-resource developments resulting from federal policies which have prevailed during the past five decades. Few would deny that our national interest has been well served by these projects.

One test of the wisdom of the recommended policies is to visualize the results had they prevailed since the 1920s. Many attempts prior to that decade by states and local organizations to provide for navigation, flood control, and drainage had been failures. Most such projects, limited in scope by the capabilities of the developers, were underdesigned and ineffective. Most were abandoned, and some of the attempts at flood protection had resulted in failure and catastrophe. Had this continued, where would this country be today?

The effect of federal-government interest is demonstrated by the development of the greatest inland waterway system in the world along the Ohio and Mississippi rivers and their tributaries. This system serves all elements of our society. It includes the area in the central United States recognized to have the greatest potential for industrial development in the country. This area, from Pennsylvania to Missouri, from the Great Lakes to the Gulf, could be the Ruhr Valley of America. One cannot see the wisdom in limiting the growth of this industrial expansion so beneficial to all by adoption of these recommendations.

Acts of Congress during the 1920 and 1930 decades recognized the need for the responsibility of the federal government to participate actively in navigation and flood-damage prevention projects. Subsequent Acts of Congress expanded the federal effort to include provisions for water supply, water quality, recreation, fish and wildlife, and other water-development needs.

This congressional acceptance of federal responsibility came by way of the democratic process of responding to the expressed wishes of the electorate. The nature and extent of appropriate federal assistance was carefully evaluated by the Congress. The Hoover Commission, Kerr Committee, and others explored this matter thoroughly and furnished policy guidance for congressional actions which followed. In light of these events, it appears unduly presumptive for the National Water Commission to summarily reject policies so carefully derived in the wisdom of Congress as representative of the people's wishes.

The older Kentuckian, by assuming that most of the water developments he has seen would not have occurred under the presently recommended policies, can test their wisdom by reflecting on conditions as he knew them in the 1920s and 1930s. He could remember the steamboats stranded on the sandbars in the Ohio River during July and August. He would know that neither the massive tows now plying the river nor the huge industries they serve would exist had the federal government not provided the navigation facilities. He could remember the devastation of the 1937 flood at Louisville and other cities along the river. He would know that without federal assistance for reservoirs to reduce flood flows and build local floodwalls at the communities, development would have been limited drastically and the citizenry would still live in constant dread of the inevitable flood.

The Kentuckian, young or old, who visits the beautiful state parks at the federally developed lakes and enjoys the boating and fishing there, can well realize that neither would have been available had federal assistance not been rendered for their implementation. In this respect it is proper to know that federal assistance for water-related recreation is supported in the report. Of course the costs of this water use, taken alone, can readily be retrieved through user fees. However, very few of these projects could have been justified without including other uses such as flood control, power, or navigation.

It would appear reasonable to assume that adoption of a federal policy to disengage from water-resource developments would presage similar policy with regard to land preservation and reclamation. The report refers to "excess productive capacity of agriculture" in support of its recommendation to discontinue federal support of water projects for agricultural purposes. In this context, the reflective Kentuckian might well remember the eroded hillsides in the 1930s which have since been replaced by productive pastureland by federal assistance through U.S. Department of Agriculture programs. This is mentioned only in general support of the need for continued recognition that both land and water are national resources, of national interest and concern, and beyond the limited capabilities of state and local governments.

Kentucky is a water-rich state and is, of course, opposed to any policy that would limit the development of its potential in water resources. Kentucky has more than 1,400 miles of streams improved for navigation, including more than two-thirds of the Ohio River. The Mississippi forms its western boundary. Six tributary streams in Kentucky feed water traffic into the Ohio. Average annual rainfall of forty-six inches provides for continued utilization and development of the streams to the economic and social betterment of the citizenry. We note that all but one of the commissioners are from the semiarid west and we must feel that the deemphasis of water developments in their recommendations may not reflect the true value to the nation of continued development of the vast water resources of the central states.

Implementation of the general policy reflected in the commission's recommendations also would shift the principal responsibility for water-resource developments from Congress to the executive branch.

It appears advisable that Congress retain its present prerogatives in both authorization and funding of water projects. Otherwise, the voice of the people cannot be properly expressed. Adoption of the changed policy would further strengthen the executive branch's practice of withholding appropriated funds for budgetary purposes and circumventing the people's desires as expressed through their duly elected representatives.

Other federal programs involve expenditures of vast amounts of money for the social and economic betterment of the nation. Housing programs, urban renewal, disaster relief measures, highways, Amtrak, urban mass transit, etc., are not predicated on the premise that the identifiable beneficiaries bear the total costs. Blanket adoption of the policies proposed by the commission would be contrary to the generally accepted practice of federal responsibility for development of the nation's economy and wipe away the potential for further progress in making the beneficial use of our water resources.

One further point serves to underscore what I can only assume to be a lack of serious thought in advancing such a philosophy regarding our water resources. If such a policy could ever be justified, certainly it could not be now. We have seen what a difference federal and congressional leadership has meant in development of our water resources. But our problems may be even more severe at this time than ever in our history.

Not only is water itself necessary to human life and provides a source of food, it provides this nation with outstanding and low-cost transportation facilities, recreation facilities, low-cost power generation, waste disposal, and various other assets. At a time when an increasing population is demanding clean water in adequate supplies, along with more of all the other "products" of water, how can this commission propose to remove the federal government, especially Congress, from its role of leadership in developing and managing this vital resource?

The report is voluminous, and time has not permitted an in-depth study. However, it is my feeling that it is unclear on several points and this could even be a dangerous document if accepted unquestioningly by those in a position to decide its fate. A recommendation is made that those receiving benefits from water resource development projects should pay for the construction and maintenance of such facilities. Obviously, that means some form of user fees for tugboats and towing companies. Does it also mean that pleasure boats must pay? I assume it does. Does this report recommend that a city drawing its water supply from a reservoir must pay for the cost of building and maintaining the reservoir? Does it mean that a city must also pay for a navigational dam on our rivers, if the dam provides a better pool and flow to handle treated waste pumped into the river? Apparently it does.

One final, vital question is how much authority and control over water resources would go to states or regional compacts along with responsibilities for collecting user fees and financing? I do not think any state likes to assume financial and management responsibility while leaving control in the hands of the federal government. On the other hand, it could be chaos if individual states had the ability to control water resources within their boundaries. For example, I have pointed out that two-thirds of the mighty Ohio River lies within the official boundaries of the Commonwealth of Kentucky. I raise these questions because they must be answered. If they have been answered in the report, they must also be answered more clearly in open and public hearings.

In summary, we believe that the policies contained in the report's recommendations are regressive and contrary to the best interests of Kentucky, the midwestern states, and the nation as a whole. The only reason for the existence of a federal government is to provide the ability for a nation of people to do collectively what they cannot do individually or to assume responsibility for development of resources whose direct and indirect benefits are not exclusive to one state. If water resources are not of enough benefit to merit continued congressional and federal attention, then I know of no other reason that is important enough to merit this attention. We may as well disband the federal government and exist as fifty separate and independent states, able to negotiate our own treaties or compacts. I wonder what Thomas Jefferson or Abraham Lincoln would think of that.

YALE POLITICAL UNION
New Haven, Connecticut / February 22, 1973

LET us look at those governing versus the governed. I say "versus" because there is an increasing awareness of a competitive attitude between those who govern and those being governed.

Historians and students of government and politics have long argued whether or not our present system will survive the rigors of ever-changing social, economic, and political pressures. Like many who are involved in the operation of our governmental structure, I believe there are mechanical changes requiring attention which would make it more responsive. But beyond mechanical alterations, there is a greater threat to the effective functioning of this system. It is the public concept of elected officials. By examining one's performance in office, which departs from that same individual's campaign positions, we can make some valid predictions. Certainly, technical and theoretical mechanics are important, but there is another factor which will have a lasting impact.

Survival of the political and governmental design, as we now know it, is more influenced by citizen confidence and trust in elected officials. And I refer to elected officials at all levels! Disappearing confidence and trust pose a very real danger of our entering into an era whereby external and internal stresses threaten the collapse of the system we now have. The key question is, "When does this manifest itself to the breaking point?"

In our country, one result of a disgruntled public attitude has been thus far periodic replacement of individuals or of one political party's control by another. What happens though, when a majority of our citizens lose confidence in both major political parties? Forming another political organization to reflect collective views has been advanced previously. I doubt its effectiveness, especially if the reason for the absence of trust is not party philosophy or issues, but wholesale loss of confidence in elected officials period!

In times of economic and social stability, the prospects are lessened. It becomes a different matter, however, when there is a combination of serious economic and social stresses and loss of overall confidence in public officials as a group. Never underestimate the necessity for citizen respect. In essence, the system is dependent directly on a trust relationship—that there should be no difference between the governing and the governed. After all, who must properly influence those who are governing?

If my premise is correct, the survival and strengthening of our political system can only be attained by officials who live up to their own public positions advanced as candidates and implemented through subsequent public action. A more intelligent America, a more conscious America, one where there is constant media focus on public figures, means we will have a more alert citizenry. Going further, it means there is a tendency for the citizenry to react much more in the future than it has in the past.

Permit one example of this problem. Admittedly, it may be too early for complete judgment, but here is an illustration with the highest public visibility in our country. In his second Inaugural Address, President Nixon said: "We have the chance today to do more than ever before in our history to make life better in America—to ensure better education, better health, better housing, better transportation, a cleaner environment—to restore respect for law, to make our communities more livable—and to ensure the God-given right of every American to full and equal opportunity." I like this commitment. Yet in just one month after he uttered those words, executive action is caving in the roof on items he mentioned.

In tonight's debate on the Tenth Amendment, you might incorporate the wisdom of Chief Justice Taney, author of the "dual federalism" doctrine.[1] Said Taney, "The object and end of all government is to promote the happiness and prosperity of the community by which it is established, and it can never be assumed that the government intended to diminish its power of accomplishing the end for which it was created." I might also remind you that Justice Taney did not always adhere to his own philosophy in decision pronouncements.

Throughout my years in the political arena, I have espoused a creed that says in fewer words what Taney intended: "The only reason for the existence of government, at any level, is to serve people." Mr. Nixon indicated this posture in his Inaugural Address. Yet people programs, education, the environment, health, housing, transportation, law and order—all face a reduction of federal attention as evidenced by the executive budget and Nixon priority scale.[2] The burden is being placed on states and local communities without corresponding resources to enhance the social conditions of our people. This tactic has today drawn the battle lines between Congress and the President. Never before has Congress faced a stronger challenge to maintain the status and integrity of its own institution.

Clearly, the assumption by Mr. Nixon of increased executive powers dictates serious debate. Impoundment of funds, usurping the wishes of Congress, redirection of priorities, and the issuance of guidelines and regulations contrary to congressional intent make one wonder how Mr. Nixon interprets the duties of his office—especially that which says, "He shall from time to time give to the Congress Information of the State of the Union and recommend to their Consideration such Measures as he shall judge necessary and expedient."[3]

This tactic will also draw battle lines with the Governors. If you look at history, you will find that years ago the Governors lost not only public confidence but federal confidence. This brought about the transfer of policy and money decisions to the federal level. Hence, the governorship as an institution has gone through a period of no public confidence. It has taken a half-century to regain what was lost. Many of the transfers became successful because they involved an institutional adjustment over a long period of time. Now Mr. Nixon indicates he wants a reversal of policy. Yet Mr. Nixon's failing is in his methods— the overnight redirection of vitally important programs that cannot be sustained by the states.

The President may think he has the right answer in health programs, but in my state, I am faced with the removal of financing for physician training for Appalachia and for minority groups where there is a severe shortage of doctors. The Nixon budget dictates this. The President may think he has the right direction for housing development, but in Kentucky, we are stunned by the elimination of federal support for home-owner assistance on new low-income subsidized-housing programs. The President calls in his Inaugural message for more self-reliance, then eliminates all federal support for public, school, and university library programs—one of the very foundations of self-reliance. In one breath, Mr. Nixon praised the present system. In the next he said we must shift from the old policies. How can there be public confidence in such rhetoric? Hence, the role of Governors broadens. Faced with the necessity to influence Congress in trying to regain in our states' losses of resources, we must also consider the time element.

It has taken forty years for the federal government to develop social-service capabilities that Mr. Nixon is now asking the states to take over in four months. Obviously, there is no way to adjust. I would be the first to agree that many of our programs have been mired in lengthy delay and excessive funding. But you do not merely abandon those programs serving people because there are imperfections. And if you do relegate them to a different governmental structure, you have the responsibility of assisting that structure. Are the Nixon proposals states' rights in reverse? Perhaps not, but the new burdens imposed on states by the executive budget and the Nixon philosophy give a clear mandate to all Governors that their presence in Washington affairs could be the final hope of preventing what I believe will soon become a rapid decline in public confidence and trust in elected officials.

What I fear most is the inability of states to adapt so rapidly and, therefore, the harm that will come to so many innocent people. This lessens trust, even when the fault is elsewhere. Our last election provided both institutional and personal mandates from the people. Mr. Nixon's was personal. However, a different mandate arose in behalf of Congress and the Governors, and while we must consider how many Americans failed to vote in 1972, we cannot ignore the insistence given by those who did cast ballots. In my opinion, Mr. Nixon is using his personal mandate to make institutional decisions, and this is wrong. Certainly, we all want reduced spending, elimination of waste, and a stronger delivery of services from government to the people. A proper redirecting of government nevertheless is best accomplished when we follow the federal system, because through the federal system we can absorb institutional change.

I am concerned that the President is not operating as if this is a federal system. He is talking about institutional changes, but his actions aren't in terms of institutional decisions, rather they are personal decisions. In cold hard facts, he isn't recommending, he is implementing!

The Governors, I sincerely feel, are not going to shy away from their added burdens and responsibilities. Neither are they going to sit back and allow public confidence to erode because of actions by the presidency. The governorship once experienced such an erosion of trust and to a great extent has finally overcome it. I suggest the Nixon attitude might lead the office of the presidency in the same direction unless both the Congress and the Governors stand firm.

We can stand firm—to better accomplish what the American people want and deserve and prevent the wrecking of a political and governmental system through public disappointment.

---

1. Roger Brooke Taney (1777–1864), Maryland; jurist, statesman; attorney general of the United States (1831–1833); United States secretary of the treasury (1833–1834); chief justice of the Supreme Court (1836–1864). Among the most important decisions of the Taney Court were *Dred Scott* v. *Sanford, Charles River Bridge* v. *Warren Bridge, Ableman* v. *Booth,* and *Ex parte Merryman. Concise Dictionary of American Biography* (New York, 1964), pp. 1042–43.

2. Governor Ford again noted the discrepancy between Nixon's words and deeds in a speech on February 27, 1973, before the Senate Subcommittee on Intergovernmental Relations, not included in this volume.

3. This is a quote from Article II, section three, of the United States Constitution.

KENTUCKY READY-MIXED CONCRETE ASSOCIATION
Louisville / March 9, 1973

I ADDRESS you today as responsible members of the business community who are interested in your governments, whether they be local, state, or federal. Whatever the behavior of elected officials might be—and I use the term "behavior" as it applies to the conduct of office—such deeds, in some manner, touch your lives, either directly or indirectly.

Probably never before in the history of these United States has there been greater public attention focused on the Republican administration of President Nixon and the Democratic majorities in Congress. We find such expressions as "drawn battle lines," "a showdown," "test of strength," and numerous others used in describing the predictions of governmental observers. Countless words have already been uttered and written concerning the differences in philosophy, the differences in priorities, now being expressed by both sides.

Governors are involved, hopefully not speaking as partisans—though I will admit the elements of political rhetoric have already been recorded—but rather as conduits whereby the voices of their constituents might be heard. As Governor of Kentucky, I have expressed my opinions, based I trust and pray, on the wishes of the vast majority of Kentuckians. In this day, this era, this particular time, Governors cannot fulfill their executive roles from a cocoon in the state capitol. Federal domination of state and local programs impels Governors to exercise their leadership in Washington, armed with the facts as they relate to their respective states. But beyond that, Governors must reflect the thinking, the wishes, and the needs of grass-roots America. The time has come for Governors to take the voice of grass-roots communication to Washington. The time has come to make this voice heard at congressional hearings so that federal policy becomes people's policy. The time has come to make the voice of the people heard in the formation of multistate compacts and agreements. We must break down the barriers of communication between the governed and the governing, and this is becoming a major responsibility of state executive offices throughout the country.

Impoundment has become almost a household word. Certainly it is a word generating considerable attention among public officials, attention sparked by fear at times, by misunderstanding at times, and by serious interest at all times. Thomas Jefferson was the first President to impound funds—$50,000 in 1803, which Congress had provided for gunboats on the Mississippi. Since that date, other Presidents have impounded monies, allocated by congressional authority. Under President Nixon, at least $12 billion appropriated by Congress was impounded during his first term.

Yet while both Democratic and Republican chief executives have utilized what they consider, and I question, their privilege of impounding funds, there is a clear difference in what Mr. Nixon has done and threatens to do, and in what others have decreed in the past. The record of impoundments since Thomas Jefferson shows presidential action pertaining to defense or war spendings. In contrast, Mr. Nixon has used the ax of impoundments on people-programs, while increasing his defense budget, while increasing his commitments to aid foreign countries, and while confusing the American public with carefully worded scripts which, without a doubt, do not reflect the true impact of his budget.

Let there be absolutely no misunderstanding—I fully support holding the line on federal spending. Yet I do not approve of a hardware-oriented budget which sacrifices education, health, housing, and the millions of Americans who are unable to care for themselves. I fully support reducing the federal deficit; yet I do not consider it fiscally responsible to transfer the deficit to the states and local communities. The budget does exactly that.

I fully support the practice of states' assuming many programs now controlled by the federal government and am ready to begin whatever task is required to effect this change. Yet there is absolutely no logic in ignoring an orderly process and the provisions for financial support. In effect, the President is saying, "You take on the programs, but we will rake in the taxes." And I fully endorse attempts to eliminate waste which can be found in many programs. This is one reason why I do want the states to take on a greater role in program administration, since we can accomplish the job at less cost to the taxpayer than can Washington.

The original intent of revenue-sharing, along with an orderly transfer of responsibilities, would provide this without bringing on chaos. But now even the original intent of revenue-sharing has been changed by the White House. It is a confusing issue, but the truth must be understood by our citizens. You don't have to take Wendell Ford's word for it. Study the budget yourself, analyze the consequences, and read the impartial studies which are now available.

What we are really talking about is reflected in the argument of impoundments. The U.S. Constitution outlines certain presidential duties by saying: "He shall from time to time give to the Congress Information of the State of the Union, and recommend to their Consideration such Measures as he shall judge necessary."[1] Note the word recommend. What other role does a President have under the Constitution in the appropriations process beyond his power of veto and the responsibility of recommending? In the context of impoundments, I seriously doubt if he is privileged to usurp the intent of Congress. Granted, in our complex society, presidential alternatives have increased over the years. But this specific matter goes to the heart of constitutional intent, where certain rights are carefully guarded by the legislative and judicial branches. The simple fact is that funds authorized and appropriated by Congress are being isolated from the people for whom they are intended, though not by presidential veto. The power of the purse is one of the most basic powers of the legislative branch. Therefore, neither reason nor precedent supports impounding of funds, if we are to have checks and balances in our system of government.

Impoundments have touched Kentucky—in our highway program, in our ability to clean up our streams as required by the federal government, and in our ability to plan where budgeting dictates the course of action.

So what is the answer? A first attempt to conclude this debate will come in Congress, though I predict the ultimate decision will be vested within the courts. One fact is without challenge. We must settle this argument quickly. Because government has grown too complicated and complex already, as evidenced by so much confusion, the man on the street experiences continuous difficulty in trying to understand intelligently what is going on.

---

1. This is a quote from Article II, section three, of the United States Constitution.

PRESS BREAKFAST STATEMENT
Washington, D.C. / September 20, 1973

BEFORE any questions, allow me an observation that is heard frequently, a charge that isn't intended as political and a suggestion that has been seldom, if ever, publicly advanced. There are various issues facing America which must be approached in a nonpolitical vein. Although I am a Democratic Governor from Kentucky and serve as chairman of the National Democratic Governors' Caucus,[1] my message today is intended to cross party boundaries, because the economy touches every citizen in this nation—our economic plight! Housewives pinch pennies because of it, farmers are confused over it, businessmen find themselves appalled with it, and those on fixed incomes are paralyzed from it. Our economic status is more dangerous than Watergate and certainly is not even remotely the result of Watergate, despite some political trivia from the White House. It threatens us both abroad and domestically.

Economic woes have been the hallmark of the Nixon presidency, and for some unknown reason orderly steps to ease the burden have been bypassed for knee-jerk reactions. The result? Scatter shots at a multitude of targets with a record number of misses. Thus, the economic mess is compounded, and waning confidence in White House leadership has become more evident in all sectors of our society.

The latest issue of *U.S. News and World Report* hints at the real problem by saying: "Never before has peacetime inflation been attacked with such a combination of weapons." Obviously, the wrong weapons have been pulled from Mr. Nixon's arsenal. The absence of logic is prevailing, and more so, the absence of any coordinated economic program places states in the unenviable position of having to cope with an illness where there can be only partial medication—the states' own resources.

Kentucky is a good example. Less than two years ago we faced the challenge of unemployment, low per-capita income, terrific competition for new business, and of trying to overcome the frustration of an agricultural industry, abandoned by the previous administration— Republican I might add. Upon assuming office, I instituted a tax reform, including the removal of a 5 percent sales tax on food. Little did we realize then the added positive impact that one would have in less than twenty-four months! My opponents called me irresponsible, said our reforms and projected biennial surplus of three-plus million dollars wouldn't hold, and contended we could not fund an aggressive two-year program in the manner I chose to pursue.

In the first eighteen months, we tripled the national rate of unemployment decline, doubled the national rate of increase in nonagricultural jobs, initiated a comprehensive agricultural plan which is already paying dividends, and in the first quarter of this year led forty-seven other states in increased per-capita income. Not since before World War II, and in many instances never, has this happened in Kentucky. As for a surplus, we'll have at least $140 million—$54 from growth, plus $86 in revenue-sharing that we are drawing interest on until our Legislature meets. The $54 million is directly tied to our state's economic gains, plus over a $12 million saving in state government operating expenses—money budgeted in 1972 but unneeded because of prudent management.

A healthy economy nationally would have propelled us even further. Inflation, a dollar worth twenty cents less than when Mr. Nixon took office, sharply increased gold prices, a confusing stock market, fantastic interest rates, and all the other economic mutations we are experiencing point to the heart of Mr. Nixon's problem. He has refused, since taking office, to establish firm, domestic economic priorities. This he must do before any significant change for the better is experienced.

Let me ask a question. Why, if you put 100 economists in a room to discuss this subject, do you get 100 different answers? Because the President has yet to identify domestic economic priorities, they have no official direction! In almost five years we have not benefited from this desperately needed leadership. There is no doubt in my mind that we have the talent, the resources, the technical acumen, and the common sense to solve any problem. But we are at a critical point in history by virtue of the President's abdicating his responsibility by not setting national domestic priorities in a clear-cut manner in order that a proper assault against economic misfortune might be initiated. The economy simply cannot be managed without priorities that serve the interests of all the people. With priorities fully defined, there would be less disagreement among economists, and we could get on with the business of easing the concerns you and I hear each day.

So along with the criticism, I offer a strong plea to the President. Only he and his closest advisers can establish domestic priorities, because only they have the total information needed to map out a progressive course for this nation.

I fully realize there are no simple solutions, and politicians or public officials who always have the ready answer only contribute to the temperature and humidity of Washington. But I do offer a course of action as a beginning, along with the understanding that alterations of our balance of trade overseas must increase, and we must stop trying to solve problems at the expense of the middle- and low-income families and those on fixed incomes. Tied to these must be tax reform to get us out of our classical overinvestment boom. Our national wealth has no direction, and the President can remedy this.

---

1. Governor Ford was picked unanimously by a thirty-one state membership as the chairman of the Democratic Governors' Caucus on June 4, 1973. Ten days later Governor Ford's office announced that the Governor had also been selected by Robert Strauss, National Democratic party chairman, to serve on a sixteen-member Advisory Planning Committee for the 1974 midterm conference.

REPORT AT SOUTHERN
GOVERNORS' CONFERENCE
Point Clear, Alabama / September 24, 1973

ONE of the major topical concerns expressed last December for attention by the Committee on Law Enforcement, Justice, and Public Safety was the forthcoming congressional action on the future of the Safe Streets Act and criminal justice monies available to the states through the Law Enforcement Assistance Administration.[1]

Several of us here today testified or had testimony presented before congressional committees, considering this legislation. Our testimony in support of this legislation reflected some fairly uniform positions on funding and program principles which we believed to be critical in turning the corner on crime in our respective states. For example, 1972 saw a national reduction of approximately 3 percent in the rate of crime. In Kentucky alone, crime was reduced by 8 percent. This was the first reduction in our crime rate since World War II, and there was an actual decrease of 5,000 serious crimes.

Our testimony supported the bloc-grant concept and systemwide planning at the state level. The bloc-grant concept embodied in the Safe Streets Act was not merely a forerunner of revenue-sharing. It was also a gradual and orderly means of returning federal tax dollars to the states. Systemwide planning at the state level has proven to be a vital element in the coordination of decision-making, resource allocation, and response to common problems. The problems of the criminal justice system are interdependent because crime is a complex matter. It can only be solved by an integrated strengthening of the entire criminal justice system, from the policeman on the beat through the courts, corrections, probation, and parole.

Stewardship and program discretion by the states were challenged this year with proposed amendments to the legislation which would have required a certain percentage of the money allocated to a state to be spent in a specified program area. Many of us again responded by working through our state's congressional delegations to see that these amendments were deleted. We were successfully persistent in this effort because of our belief in accountability at the state level.

One of the most important ingredients in any criminal justice program is credibility. If the people don't believe that the system is capable of protecting their well-being, property, and rights, they are going to shrug it off and go their own way. We all know the unhappy consequences of the law's failure to meet the just expectations of those governed by it; law loses its stabilizing influence. At best the results are alienation and lack of trust in the legal system. At worst, there is violence and unrest.

Crime commissions, criminal justice planning agencies, and law-enforcement commissions in our respective states have been putting the money where crime must be fought. A review of fiscal years 1969 through 1972 indicates that state planning agencies have allocated almost 65 percent of all local funds to high crime areas. State planning agencies have dealt realistically with standards for criminal justice. Southern states have developed standards which are resulting in better trained, equipped, and educated policemen who are now more able to effectively deal with crime on the streets. These standards are also enhancing the proper police image.

In Kentucky, one of the most innovative programs to come out of the 1972 General Assembly was a 15 percent salary-educational incentive supplement going to over 2,600 local policemen. Only after a ten-month ordeal with the Federal Pay Board and Cost of Living Council did Kentucky finally have an opportunity to implement this program. Ours was not a mere request for increased salaries. It was a unique state response to the problem of crime and justice and represented for Kentucky a significant milestone in achieving statewide minimum educational standards for police.

Other topics which have been raised for consideration by the Committee on Law Enforcement, Justice, and Public Safety have led the committee to propose a seminar or spotlight conference for this fall. The committee has tentatively selected November 16 and 17 for such a conference. The members of this committee believe, geographically, it would be better to hold this seminar in Atlanta. The proposed agenda includes topics of importance to the respective states of the Southern Governors' Conference. They range from new federal resources for state and local law-enforcement to problems in state administration of the Safe Streets Act, to organized crime in the states, to the reorganization of state government in meeting the crime problem, to an insight into the true causes of crime.

Our committee urges each member state to take advantage of what promises to be an extremely comprehensive spotlight conference. The new LEAA administrator has agreed to be present along with some of the most outstanding experts in the criminal justice field.

---

1. "The Law Enforcement Assistance Administration (LEAA) was established June 19, 1968, by the Omnibus Crime Control and Safe Streets Act of 1968 (84 Stat. 197, as amended by 84 Stat. 1880; 42 U.S.C. 3701) as amended by the Crime Control Act of 1973 (87 Stat. 197). LEAA is under the general authority of the Attorney General."

"The purpose of LEAA is to assist State and local governments to reduce crime." "The block-grant concept embodied in the legislation implies that more authority and power should be shifted to State and local levels of government in order to decentralize operations of the Federal Government." *United States Government Manual 1975/1976*, revised May 1, 1975 (Washington, D.C., 1975), pp. 321–23.

FEDERAL TAX REDUCTION
Frankfort / April 22, 1974

GOVERNOR Wendell H. Ford today urged the nation's Democratic Governors to endorse his resolution calling for a federal tax reduction to help those in low, middle, or fixed income brackets.[1] Ford spoke in behalf of a program to grant tax relief for those he termed "most adversely affected by a continuing and surging inflation."

He said the present Republican national administration's domestic policies have led "to the highest inflation rate since the early 1950s while economic growth in America has fallen by the largest rate in sixteen years." "These are facts," Ford stressed, "backed up by alarming economic reports, but more importantly felt by the millions of Americans who are in the crunch of inflation." He said the country was in a "borderline recession" with prospects almost nil for improvement under the national administration's domestic economic policies.

Last March in Washington, Ford quizzed President Nixon's top economic adviser, Herbert Stein, chairman of the President's economic council.[2] When Ford advocated tax reduction, Stein said he considered it a low priority of the Nixon administration. "This is the basic difference between Democratic and Republican economic philosophies," Ford said. "Those least able to carry the nation's tax burden are in the low, middle, or fixed income brackets, yet the Republican economic plan hits this group the hardest. We must have an alternative to prevent any continuation of the present course."

Ford called on his colleagues to publicly support tax relief now. He said he favored the concept advocated by Senators Walter Mondale, Ted Kennedy, and Hubert Humphrey.[3] "In fact, I am in favor of going further," Ford added. He said a $5.9 billion tax reduction would help those earning up to $15,000 a year. Eighty-two percent of those assisted in the total package fall in the $15,000 or less income brackets. Ford explained there would be an option of a $190 tax credit for taxpayers and each dependent, or a raise in the personal exemption rate of from $750 to $825, whichever is most beneficial in individual cases.

"I strongly urge the Senate of the United States to move at once on this plan and believe the Governors must put their unqualified support behind it. Otherwise, the economic stagnation we have experienced and are finding more unbearable each month will create even more domestic chaos," Ford emphasized.

He said the program would provide three positive results without delay: 1) Stimulation of a sluggish economy by generating more dollars in the economic mainstream; 2) granting tax relief to those most in need; 3) enhancing new jobs thereby stemming the rise in unemployment.

---

1. Statement prepared for Governor Ford and read and/or delivered to the press by a staff member.
2. Herbert Stein (1916–   ), Silver Springs, Maryland; economist, author; economist and research director for the Council on Economic Development

(1945–1967); member of President's Council of Economic Advisers (1969–1974). *Who's Who in Government 1972–1973* (Chicago, 1972), p. 486.

3. Walter Frederick Mondale (1928–   ), Minnesota; attorney; attorney general of Minnesota (1960–1964); United States Senator (1965–1976), chairman of various Senate subcommittees; vice president of the United States (1977–   ). *Who's Who in Government, 1972–1973* (Chicago, 1972), p. 353. Edward Moore Kennedy (1932–   ), Hyannisport, Massachusetts; attorney, author; United States Senator (1963–   ), former assistant majority leader; president of Joseph P. Kennedy, Jr. Foundation (1961–   ). *Who's Who in America, 1974–1975* (Chicago, 1975), 1:1677. Hubert Horatio Humphrey, Jr. (1911–1978), Minneapolis, Minnesota; pharmacist, professor, administrator; mayor of Minneapolis (1945–1948); United States Senator (1949–1965, 1971–1978), majority whip (1961–1965); vice president of the United States (1965–1969); member of numerous councils and committees. Ibid., 1:1523.

NATIONAL ASSOCIATION
OF COUNTIES CONVENTION
Miami, Florida / July 16, 1974

LET me start out in a cynical way—Listen to the theme of your conference: "Counties and states in partnership for the people." Now that's pretty high-sounding for a group of politicians and public officials. It's like window dressing, as though you hired a public relations expert to paint a do-gooder picture. Yes, sir! Your theme has a real American ring to it. You know all the old expressions about apple pie, motherhood, and the flag.

So how many citizens around this country really are convinced that you care about a partnership for the people? I believe the number is growing. I believe there is indeed more caring than ever before, and no one in this room has to apologize for wanting a county-state partnership which will help people. The reason I began in a cynical manner was to make a point. For too long, a *de facto* separation of government at all levels, spurred on by a huge, impersonal federal bureaucracy, isolated one government from another. In turn, people were often left out in the cold, with the governed feeling the pains of great distance from those who were governing.

People had a right to become hardened, cynical, and doubtful. Themes fell, and rightfully so, on deaf ears. But times are changing because states and local governments have redirected their courses in a partnership. While the climate needs much more warmth, the chill factor is being removed. States and local governments have had to initiate cooperative ventures in view of federal abandonment of programs, of curtailments and impoundments. A more interested general public seeks closer relationships. And in my opinion, officials in state capitols, courthouses, municipal buildings, and county seats are finding this discovery better for all concerned—a better way to make things work.

The positive response to this conference indicates why I am optimistic. Yours is the very group of individuals which must meet in a common cause of improving government responsiveness to the citizens. Thus the theme we hear does have merit, based on activity. I am optimistic because of what is happening in Kentucky, as well as the philosophy put to work by Governors in other states who want a closer association with local governments. I suggest we all have an obligation to bring this same attitude to our highest plateau of government in Washington. How well we perform can have a positive effect. The degree of proof we submit through action rather than words can cause Washington to reevaluate its own posture of isolation. There is no question that the closer government and people become, the better served citizens will be. After all, the only reason for the existence of government, at any level, is to serve people. The future of our political and governmental systems depends on a total adaptation of this attitude. Those governed expect no less; those who govern responsibly want no less.

How then can states and counties strengthen a partnership? First, leadership is derived from both entities. Obviously, due to circumstances, states must initiate most of the action. However, counties must be willing and ready to respond. Perhaps what we have accomplished in Kentucky, far from perfect or far from being complete, will illustrate how local and state units can work together. Over the years I detected a frustration in local officials' attempts to deal effectively with state government, a frustration affecting people who rely on services in their home areas, as well as from the state. This is why reorganization of state government became a priority issue when I became Governor. We consolidated over sixty departments and agencies, plus more than 240 boards and commissions into eight program cabinets. We moved to program budgeting where accountability is meaningful to the General Assembly and public. There still are kinks, some rough spots, but you should know that Kentucky state government hadn't been reorganized in thirty-six years. We placed an emphasis on the future. If we must administer new federal programs, we won't have to create new divisions. Of particular interest to your domains though may be the concentration given to local government.

Attached directly to the executive department is an Office for Local Government, created to give your counterparts a direct line of communication to the state. It is local government's support group, on call at anytime to assist in a great variety of programs and problems. Whether it be bookkeeping, grant application assistance, engineering help, or practically any other technical and administrative advice, the Office for Local Government is mobilized to respond. A multiple revenue-sharing system has been developed. Part of our gasoline tax is sent back for street and road improvements, where local officials make the decisions. A police educational/salary incentive plan, where the state supplements local police officers' salaries if they attain specific educational standards, is now provided. This gives better-trained, better-educated, and better-qualified security. Coal-producing counties receive a portion of state fees to be used any way local officials see fit. They also receive a portion of the coal severance-tax surplus, again to be used for various development projects, determined locally. This year, $5.5 million in surplus goes to the counties. The state will pick up the cost for the operation of circuit courts, thus freeing additional funds at local levels. And we increased jurors' pay $7.50 per day.

We have a new procedure whereby 100 percent of Kentucky's share of BOR grants will be directed straight into local communities.[1] Normally only 40 percent of these funds would be designated. Home-rule legislation, providing local governments with increased powers and responsibilities, means added responsiveness to those directly affected. Home rule and local option mean the input has more credibility, because you know your own situation much better than does your state government, just as state government understands its needs and problems much better than Washington.

We also gave county officials permanent cost-of-living increases, showing our confidence in the caliber of the men and women who are taking on greater responsibilities. Three other firsts deserve mention. Our new Pollution Abatement Authority has enabled local communities to obtain to date an additional $20 million for water and sewer projects. The state now provides funds for training and equipping volunteer fire departments and also pays workmen's compensation for these volunteers. And the state has provided training and equipment for community volunteer rescue squads. These are but a few of the new programs in partnership with local units. Others include, for instance, making up losses in federal funds which would have seriously crippled county operations. We have fifteen Area Development Districts in Kentucky, operated primarily by interested citizens and officials. This year we made up the 38.6 percent reduction at the federal level of funds, so the work of such districts would not be hampered. We did this for local libraries, for schools, and in other service delivery systems.

In every instance, our attempt has been to create an orderly, properly timed transition of authority and programs to the counties. States can be of help rather than hindrance, and the dollars go further when there are fewer middlemen. Hopefully, we are on the right track. There is excellent leadership in our counties with good representation here this morning. For that leadership to be fully utilized, the resources of state government have to be ready and willing to provide the incentive, the administrative link between federal and local governments, and the funding. Responses by counties give us confidence, perhaps because we have confidence in those who administer closest to the people.

---

1. "The Bureau of Outdoor Recreation was created April 2, 1962. Under the act of May 28, 1963 (16 U.S.C. 4601), the Bureau is responsible for promoting coordination and development of effective programs relating to outdoor recreation." *United States Government Manual 1973/74* (Washington, D.C., 1974), p. 275.

LEXINGTON KIWANIS CLUB
Lexington / September 17, 1974

SEVEN weeks from today, the voters of Kentucky will select their United States Senator for the next six years. I recognize that you are involved, and vitally concerned, with the future well-being of your community, state, and country. You deserve a candid and frank discussion of the issues in this race. Throughout the course of this campaign, I have tried to address these issues in a positive, forthright manner.

No matter how you look at it, one issue stands out above the rest—the economy. This is uppermost in the minds of Kentuckians, certainly with the retired and those on low and middle incomes. It reaches out into business, agriculture, professions, industry, and, without any question, right into your own homes. This is an issue which concerns the role of credit, the rate of federal spending, commodity shortages, soaring costs, and an increasing threat of real and severe unemployment. This is an issue which isn't going away overnight.

We are not on the verge of a recession, we are in a recession. The economic policies of the national administration have brought our economy to its most serious plateau since the Great Depression. Consumer prices are up 11 percent in the last year. The real level of spendable earnings is down 5.5 percent. National unemployment is at 5.6 percent and threatening to go higher. Real industrial production is down. Interest rates are the highest since the Civil War. The number of people below the poverty line has increased by 300,000. Farmers are paying more for what they use and are getting less of the agricultural dollar. Our international balance of payments is running at a deficit and threatens to get out of hand completely. Commodities and minerals are in severely short supply. The latest wholesale price index shows that prices jumped 3.9 percent last month. Items that cost $100 wholesale in 1967 now cost $167.40. I don't even have to talk about the stock market.

For six years we have heard talk from Washington about the economy. But we have seen very little sound, positive action or consistent policy. Fiscal and monetary policies were designed to have the economy booming at 1972 election time, setting the stage for the price explosion beginning in the winter of 1972. The federal budget was in a $14.3 billion deficit in fiscal 1973, when it should have been in balance. Price-wage policies lurched from extreme to extreme. The guideposts were scrapped at the beginning of 1969, to be followed by two-and-a-half years of a do-nothing policy, followed by the imposition of full wage and price controls, followed by a dismantling in phases one to five. These unpredictable swings in policy created instability in business and consumer expectations, distortions and shortages.

In all honesty, the entire blame cannot be placed on a lack of federal policy. The worldwide crop failure of 1972–1973, the Arab oil embargo and high pricing of oil, the inadequate expansion of industrial capacity in some of our basic industries, and the strength of the worldwide business cycle upswing of the last two years, all contributed to the development of the price explosion and other economic ills. But we have seen here in Kentucky that positive action and sound policy is a vital element. We—and I'm talking about you and me working together—must be doing something right, because Kentucky's economic trends have remained strong. Kentucky's growth rate in total non-agricultural employment and in the manufacturing sector has been well above the national average. Per-capita income increases have been above the national average. Unemployment has been below the national average. Appropriations in the operation of state government were conserved, thereby enabling us to have a surplus. We have achieved additional surpluses, paving the way for vitally needed programs in a variety of areas. In comparing Kentucky's economy with the nation, we must note our tax base. We made several changes to create a more equitable structure, and the facts show this has strengthened our state's economy.

The nation needs stronger economic policies to cope with our current difficulties. We must act vigorously, and act soon, to promote employment, to lift the poor toward an acceptable standard of living, to improve the structure of the economic system, to reform the federal tax system, and to keep interest rates at tolerable levels. This is not a "demand" inflation. This is a "cost push" inflation caused by shortages, by the lack of demand in places where there should be demand, and by overdemand in places where it needs to be decreased. There are no quick solutions to the present inflation. We must have a steady improvement in the inflation rate without plunging the economy into a deeper recession. Wages and profits are out of balance after the drop in real earnings and the surge of profits, so a catch-up period of unit-labor costs is in sight. Finished-goods prices do not yet fully reflect the surge of raw material costs. The shortages of capacity in some of our basic industries cannot be relieved quickly. Stabilizing food stocks are gone, and this summer's drought has hurt the food-price outlook. Foreign resource supplies are insecure.

Under these conditions, the attempt to produce a quick end to inflation through high interest rates and slashed budgets alone is likely to push unemployment beyond 7 percent, to cut the incomes of all groups, and to set loose the downward spiral of recession. The central tasks of policy are to restrain demand carefully without overkill, to take numerous other steps to reduce the near-term inflation outlook, and to improve the permanent structure of the economy.

We need to recast our policy, to get away from treating all problems by applying rigid formulas to every situation alike. In this context, I would like to discuss a few ideas of my own. Federal expenditures must be kept under control and managed with a better sense of priorities. The Congress now has the machinery to share in a bipartisan program to control the budget growth. Wasteful expenditures in all areas must stop. We should try to balance the federal budget for 1976. Only if recession slashes federal tax collections could a substantial deficit be justified.

However, there are extreme limitations in using the budget alone to combat inflation. Inflation would be cut only by an estimated one-tenth of 1 percent if federal spending were reduced by $5 billion. If we are going to have a tight fiscal policy, the Federal Reserve System is going to have to take a good hard look at monetary policy. Serious consideration should be given to the imposition of direct credit restraint for specified business borrowing and specified consumer-installment loans. Some segments of our economy have been experiencing an "overinvestment boom." This has driven interest rates up and absolutely denied credit to others. A further cause for concern in this regard is the highly extended condition of the money-center and many large regional banks, which means a lack of ready money.

The Federal Reserve cannot shirk its responsibility to assure reasonable credit to all sectors of the economy. The strong borrowers, the largest corporations, are able to meet their credit needs, while housing, small business, and municipalities are cut back. The Federal Reserve should directly limit the expansion of bank loans if their growth is excessive. It should assure a fair allocation of bank credit by imposing bank requirements that vary according to the distribution of a bank's loans, mortgages, and other assets. Federal tax policy in recent years has shifted the burden from the wealthy and large corporations to those on low and middle income and to the small businessman. To cite a few figures since 1968: While after-tax disposable personal income has risen 63 percent, after-tax corporate earnings have risen 80 percent, the maximum federal income tax rate has fallen from 70 percent to 50 percent on earned income. But the personal taxes (federal income and Social Security) for the average family have risen. A family with $13,000 in taxable income has had its tax rate raised from 27 percent to 32 percent.

The loss of real income by a wage earner is an especially serious aspect of the current economic situation. Tax relief for the retired, those on low and middle incomes, the farmer and small businessman must be a first priority. This is based on equity and also to reduce pressures for severe upward adjustments in wage rates that would add to inflation. Tax relief should not result in reduced revenue collections, but should be replaced by increasing taxes from other sources, including excess corporate profit taxes, closing loopholes on high-income groups and overseas operations.

Tougher treatment of foreign oil production to stop subsidizing foreign oil producers and to make domestic exploration and production more attractive is necessary. Domestic international sales corporations which encourage the export of scarce commodities and jobs, and which cost the taxpayers hundreds of millions of dollars, should be abolished.

If unemployment continues to rise, I'd like to see a public service employment program put into action. This program, designed for community betterment, should be administered at the state and local levels, matching personnel and program needs. It should be triggered to expand, contract, and terminate with specific levels of unemployment. The unemployment we now have in our economy is not chiefly a reflection of recession or a deficiency in aggregate economic demand, but a reflection of the national administration's neglect of a very important social need—the need of our young people and minorities for training in job skills and for assistance in obtaining a job.

Wendell Ford doesn't have all the answers. Neither Wendell Ford nor any other individual is going to solve every problem alone. But Wendell Ford believes that our objectives—yours and mine—are the same: a better community, a better state, a better country, and a better life for our children and our children's children. We are going to differ on various issues, yet we all agree that a complete presentation of facts is necessary in order to reach a decision.

ROTARY CLUB LUNCHEON
Louisville / October 24, 1974

ONE subject I would like to discuss this afternoon parallels your fourth avenue of service, as enumerated in the object of Rotary. You, of course, are familiar with "the advancement of international understanding, good will, and peace through a world fellowship of business and professional men united in the ideal of service."[1]

Rotary is not a political organization, nor does it exert pressure upon governments. There is no party line to bind individual judgments of members. These and other facts are spelled out quite clearly in the story of Rotary. However, there is collective as well as individual power in Rotary. A similar theory can be applied to government's role in advancing international understanding. I would like to see our nation aggressively enter into shared programs with other countries on matters such as medical research, pollution abatement, conservation, and other scientific achievements which pertain to humanitarian ventures.

A logical question you might ask is: "Aren't we already doing this?" The answer is yes, but unfortunately in a fragmented, limited, and less-than-desirable manner. Within our own federal structure, we find hit-and-miss propositions between the U.S. and foreign nations in the area of shared humanitarian programs. I would not criticize the intent. I do seriously question whether or not the procedure is orderly, sufficient, and able to achieve maximum results.

We lack coordination—not only internal but external coordination. A moment ago I mentioned collective as well as individual power. Let's apply this idea to shared humanitarian programs. Collective power would be the total input by various countries in solving a technical problem. Individual power would come from the private sectors working in conjunction with government. My theory calls for greater attention and assistance from the federal government, without greater domination. Hence, advancing international understanding, goodwill, and peace rests with a spirit of harmony and unselfishness where governments and the grass roots merge into a common cause. The key is what mechanism is adopted. Right now there seems to be an absence of push—for want of a better word—where lip service and organizational charts overshadow results.

Look at the United Nations, one possibility for expanded leadership and positive action if the United States will give that push and other member countries will join in. The U.N. has a social, humanitarian, and cultural committee. There is an Economic and Social Council. Under specialized agencies, we have the World Health Organization, the U.N. Educational, Scientific, and Cultural Organization, and the United Nations International Children's Emergency Fund. Where is the coordination? Where is there program justification in view of the time, money, and purpose of such groups? America can offer a new direction, utilizing and therefore strengthening the U.N. purpose.

Around the world there are untapped resources of talent, technology, and training, where peoples of all countries can benefit. Bringing this huge reservoir of knowledge together, allowing the gears to fully mesh, and providing the tools for beneficial results is a target for closer aim. This, in my opinion, does not call for another federal bureaucracy. It does call for a central clearinghouse to ensure those conditions for a cooperative venture among different governments and different technical societies. We can exercise the leadership to guarantee this central clearinghouse. We can inspire other countries to join us. We can generate responsiveness from the private sectors if they are assured that there will be sufficient funding for the duration of their particular research; there will be charters between or among countries interested in the same goals and willing to participate to reach these goals; there will not be governmental interference once a project is adopted, approved, and under way; and that the results will be shared for the well-being of citizens in all lands as the central theme. If, for instance, the United States and five other countries apply their resources to the elimination of a certain disease, we take these steps: America seeks those who privately specialize in that disease and offers a coordinated research system with the five other countries. Cost-sharing formulas are adopted, both from governments and from foundations.

The clearinghouse, which is primarily a citizens' technical commission to establish priorities, initiates the program in cooperation with governments, and monitors the research. Perhaps this clearinghouse would be in the United Nations. If so, liaison could be established with a congressional committee devoted to international humanitarian ventures. Participating countries would have similar patterns to follow. And we get on with the business of helping people.

This is not the polished formula. But I feel it does offer food for thought and can be refined into a working system of international cooperation. America cannot continue to buy friendship through pocketbook diplomacy, but America can certainly take the lead in a process involving widespread activity which says to the world, "Let's join in making the quality of life much better for all."

Right now there is something missing in our numerous research and development activities, both here and abroad. Somehow we must have the mechanism to constantly provide collective findings in those arenas of mutual interest. Today it's piecemeal at best. But I believe we can take this idea, expand and refine it, then move in a direction whereby eventually, it will pass the test of humanitarian service, where there is no duplication of time, effort, and money among nations.

---

1. This is a quote from the Rotary Club's Constitution.

RESIGNATION

RESIGNATION STATEMENT
Frankfort / December 27, 1974

EARLIER today Senator Marlow Cook[1] resigned from the United States Senate, thus creating an interim vacancy. Although scheduled Senate sessions have been concluded in the ninety-third Congress, it is proper and in the appropriate course of guaranteeing full representation for Kentucky that this vacancy be filled immediately. As you know, several members of the Senate have either resigned or announced their intentions to do so before January 3.

I am, therefore, resigning as Governor of the Commonwealth of Kentucky effective tomorrow. Lieutenant Governor Carroll[2] will assume the duties and responsibilities of Governor. He will appoint me to fill the unexpired Senate term, a position I accept until January 3 when I become a United States Senator by virtue of the November 5 election.

I appreciate Senator Cook's consideration as all Kentuckians should, because he contributes to the seniority standing of a new Senator from Kentucky which is in the best interest of the Commonwealth of Kentucky.

All of our plans, those of my office and those of Lieutenant Governor Carroll's office, have been directed toward an orderly transition. We are in good shape for this change, although our time table does move forward somewhat. We do have to clear our respective offices, and this will require staff work next week. In order to answer some anticipated questions let me make the following remarks:

Mr. Cook's resignation becomes effective at midnight. My appointment would follow my resignation and the Lieutenant Governor's assumption of his new office, and it will carry tomorrow's date. Although the ninety-fourth Congress begins work on January 3, members will not be sworn in until January 14, retroactive to the actual day they took office, whether it be January 3 or in my case December 28. We have temporary office space in the Dirksen Senate Office Building on the fourth floor and will move into those facilities immediately after January 3. Appointments other than what have been announced, plans for regional offices in Kentucky, and committee assignments will be the subject of later announcements as details are completed.

My office staff here will remain to conclude the mechanics of moving. Mrs. Ford and I will remain in the Mansion until sometime next week—arrangements which have been made between Governor Carroll and myself. Senator Cook's staff will remain in the present status through January 2. Senator Cook and I have talked once since the election. We had a very cordial conversation by telephone and discussed a number of matters, both of a personal and a professional nature.

As I conclude three years as Governor, there are many thoughts. Three years ago Kentucky was without many services and programs vitally needed by the people of all regions. I believe dramatic progress has been made, especially at a time in our nation's history where the economic and domestic barriers have never been more restrictive. There is temptation for instant analysis of my administration. I seriously doubt if anyone can offer a thorough, factual, and balanced analysis without ample time to see so many of our programs develop. For it is a matter of fact that much of the direction has been in assuring long-range advantages to our people while providing immediate improvements. We have accomplished a number of firsts—firsts not only for Kentucky but the nation, and these especially will have their impact in years to come. I hope and expect they will prove of immense benefit.

---

1. Marlow Cook, for more information see speech from September 6, 1974, in the Legislative Messages and Statements section, p. 88.

2. Julian Carroll, for more information see speech from March 22, 1974, in the Democratic Party Leadership section, p. 599.

APPENDIX 1
The Ford Administration

Following the pattern of the first volume in this series the editor requested Thomas L. Preston to prepare the following analysis of the Ford administration from a participant's perspective. Preston was concurrently Special Assistant to the Governor for Information and Communication and Commissioner of Public Information for twenty-two months and in the former position for the remainder of the Governor's term.

Any analysis of the Ford administration should include far more than statistics, chronological events, and commentary on state program management. However, space dictates brevity in this compendium, a restrictive factor in view of the Governor's significant tenure before his election to the United States Senate.

Wendell Ford was an imaginative architect and builder of both immediate and long-range resources for the Commonwealth; several were unprecedented not only in Kentucky but also in the nation.

Anyone can gain access to old files or clippings such as *Louisville Courier-Journal* editorials about the Ford budget ("A Document with a Heart," and "imaginative in response to human needs . . . fiscally sound"), but what about the work, concern, patience, frustration, and rationale surrounding those budgets? Historically, administrations are judged, to a great degree, on legislative programs forged through the budget process.

To examine Governor Ford the man, to equate attitude with action, or to correlate his philosophy of government to services performed will reveal a political leader who kept his word. He recorded every pledge made while running for office. Those notes were given top priority while he shaped both biennial budgets; more than 85 percent of his campaign promises were satisfied in the first budget, the remainder in the second.

He said he would remove the sales tax from food and did. He said the cumbersome and rapidly expanding state government would be reorganized. It was. He wanted to link more closely government and people. A series of executive decisions accomplished this—revenue-sharing for counties, establishment of the Office for Local Government in the executive branch, spearheading legislation permitting home rule, taking state government directly to the citizenry.

His reorganization of state government was extensive—the first since 1936. It required over two years, was resisted initially by certain entrenched bureaucrats and a few pressure groups, but in the final analysis the success was apparent even to prior doubting Thomases. Certainly, every item in the reorganization plan was not perfect. There were rough edges, in the Human Resources Cabinet for instance—an unwieldy operation—but the Associated Press acknowledged a halt to the spiraling growth of state employment after reorganization. Consistently, each budget for the administration of state government required a lower percentage. Equally important, the management of state government required less money than appropriated.

Kentuckians were to pay less taxes and receive more benefits from state services because of tax reform, economic stimulations, and reorganization. For instance, the severance tax imposed on coal was directed primarily to non-Kentuckians, since more than 85 percent of our coal is purchased by out-of-state entities. Yet, the removal of the sales tax on food helped all Kentuckians.

A fourteen-hour day for the Governor was routine, sixteen hours frequent, and an eighteen-hour work schedule not uncommon during his three-plus years in office. He held a deep conviction that the privilege of administering demanded a personal commitment to give far more time, energy, and attention to duty than normally expected in other endeavors. Vacations almost were nonexistent—even mini-breaks from the arduous tasks were rare—much to the chagrin of his immediate staff! That group was small in numbers, sometimes too limited in size for the ever-increasing demands of citizens. Governor Ford considered the pomp and circumstances of office, which provide seemingly unlimited fringe benefits, incompatible with his view of the role a public official should embrace.

A typical day would find him arising before 6 A.M., checking overnight reports, getting the news, and preparing to leave the Mansion before 7:30. He often was first in the office which meant he frequently made the coffee always available for visitors and staff. With early telephone calls out of the way, the Governor normally devoted the 8–10 A.M. period to dictation, review of mail, and quick conferences with assistants. Citizens and government officials then had appointments with the Governor until noon, or whenever completed. A quick lunch (sandwich and coffee) at his desk was commonplace. If in Frankfort the entire day he would work until 7 or 7:30 P.M., then stroll alone, carrying one or two crammed briefcases, back to the Mansion for a quiet dinner with Mrs. Ford. Television, reading, and relaxed conversation usually followed, but it was rare indeed if another private study session didn't occur around 10 o'clock, lasting until after midnight.

Travel altered the daily routine. Overwhelmed by invitations for personal appearances and meetings, he judiciously guarded his time in order to accommodate as many as humanly possible. If he had to travel out of state on business, or appear somewhere in Kentucky at night, he would remain in the Capitol as late as possible. Still, the work ethic prevailed; he would use travel—by auto or plane—as an uninterrupted period for reviewing reports, writing memos, reading mail, dictating messages, and making last-minute notes on speeches.

Overnight excursions were highlighted by a cheeseburger and french fries in a small hotel room; up before sunrise; completion of scheduled business by early afternoon if possible; and back in the Capitol for several more hours before returning to the Mansion. It wasn't a schedule many would enjoy. Wendell Ford did.

An oft-repeated expression, "The only reason for the existence of government at any level is to serve people," was more than a political or administrative theme.

One needs only a casual perusal. Perhaps no measure of the man was more impressive than his influence on the state's economy. Not since the beginning of World War II, and in many cases not ever, had the Commonwealth's economic growth of 1972–1973 been matched. This occurred despite the energy crisis, soaring national inflation, including recessionary aftershocks.

For the first time in history a true billion-dollar farm economy was recorded. It quickly soared to a billion and a quarter. Per-capita income for Kentuckians increased faster than the national average. At one period Kentucky fared better than forty-seven other states. There was a 4.2 percent unemployment when the national average was over 8 percent.

These results were not just happenstance. A carefully designed blueprint to achieve economic stimulation merged internal and external forces to enhance industrial expansion, energy supplies, spendable income, reverse investment, and public confidence.

There were numerous firsts during the Ford administration, but the most noteworthy was his leadership toward the first energy research and development program for any state in the country. This $50 million venture was directed primarily to expansion of coal by-products which would generate clean synthetic fuels through gasification and liquefaction. After becoming United States Senator, he saw the results with the construction of a liquefaction plant near Ashland and with the accelerated efforts toward high BTU gasification facilities in western Kentucky plus several low BTU plants in other regions of the state.

Governor Ford's successful plan to upgrade the status of local police officers was another first for the nation. Stressing continuing education and making available state funds for salary incentives if certain educational standards were met, he fought the federal government and won when his program seemed doomed to the arbitrary restrictions of wage controls.

In consumer protection, he was publicly credited for advocating and passing the "most progressive and strongest consumer protection legislative package in America," applauded by business and consumers alike, a rare achievement.

Medical and health care, for some inexplicable reason, is probably one of the most underpublicized aspects of the Ford administration. He successfully obtained a state/private facility for research into aging where related applications are expected to enhance the productivity of older citizens. He funded the $33 million Louisville Teaching Hospital, funded the University of Kentucky Medical School's Division of Family Practice—a long overdue need—and secured hard-to-get federal dollars for the Norton's Infirmary to provide additional medical care for children. He established new programs to equalize further the available medical manpower to all regions of Kentucky. Retarded children were a special emphasis. He funded the yet-to-be constructed multiple-handicapped facility. Governor Ford developed the first plans to support volunteer rescue squads throughout Kentucky; he worked out an emergency delivery system in the Louisville area, tying in with Fort Knox to furnish medical evacuation service by helicopter for accident and other victims. He found the monies for all of these and many other new services while still leaving a surplus of more than $147 million when he became Senator.

The Governor's emphasis on conservation and the environment was strong. Only a few examples illustrate the magnitude of this issue: saving Six Mile Island near Louisville, the first Wild Rivers Act, the nation's first Orphan Land Reclamation Program, massive increases in funding for more strip-mine inspectors and in equipment for that division, creation of the Department for Natural Resources and Environmental Protection, stronger surface-mining laws, and fair but firm enforcement of those laws.

He recognized the importance of agriculture by keeping another promise—reviving the Governor's Council on Agriculture and establishing the Kentucky Farmers' Advocate who received executive support directly from the Governor's Office. His interest, perhaps stemming from his own farm background, influenced growth in farm exports, livestock exhibitions, new marketing procedures, and exchanges of production information to keep farmers posted on new trends.

Education was another area for both innovation and increased support. Normally a topic of widespread publicity, education received a degree of attention from the Governor that resulted in a little-known fact, but one of significance: During the Ford administration, state government funding to elementary and secondary education was the ninth best in America.

This did not include the millions provided in the Ford budget to correct an old deficiency—the teachers' retirement system, long abandoned and debt ridden. Governor Ford not only ensured Kentucky's share, he also put into motion a program that would place the system back into the solvency column.

Other areas of education which felt the Ford boost were the beginning of a statewide kindergarten system, the more than doubling of special education classroom units, provision of funds to construct new vocational schools in various sections of the state, and the restructuring of the Council on Public Higher Education.

The University of Louisville was brought fully into the state system of higher education while the University of Kentucky received necessary support to maintain its status as the state's major university. Kentucky State College gained university recognition while all regional universities were able to meet essential responsibilities through both Ford budgets.

Finally, the human side of the administration was one where dollars, bricks, and other physical or fiscal considerations were secondary. At no time was this more evident than in April 1973, when a series of tornadoes killed and injured hundreds of Kentuckians, leaving destruction in the hundreds of millions of dollars.

In less than a dozen hours after the first tornado hit, Governor Ford had mobilized more than 5,000 state employees who traveled wherever necessary to assist victims of the state's worst natural tragedy. The Governor established a command post in his office to direct personally rescue and disaster-relief operations involving both state and federal agencies. Except for on-site inspections he worked from his office almost on a constant basis for nearly ten days until matters became more settled. To those unfamiliar with the man, his performance was beyond expectations. To those around the Governor, it was typical of his regard for a responsibility, a Commonwealth, and, most importantly, a people.

APPENDIX 2

Organization Chart of Kentucky State Government at the End of the Ford Administration

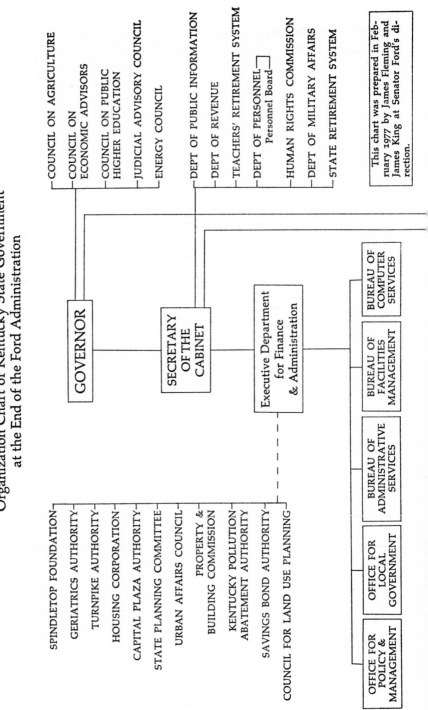

- COUNCIL ON AGRICULTURE
- COUNCIL ON ECONOMIC ADVISORS
- COUNCIL ON PUBLIC HIGHER EDUCATION
- JUDICIAL ADVISORY COUNCIL
- ENERGY COUNCIL
- DEPT OF PUBLIC INFORMATION
- DEPT OF REVENUE
- TEACHERS' RETIREMENT SYSTEM
- DEPT OF PERSONNEL — Personnel Board
- HUMAN RIGHTS COMMISSION
- DEPT OF MILITARY AFFAIRS
- STATE RETIREMENT SYSTEM

GOVERNOR

SECRETARY OF THE CABINET

Executive Department for Finance & Administration

- SPINDLETOP FOUNDATION
- GERIATRICS AUTHORITY
- TURNPIKE AUTHORITY
- HOUSING CORPORATION
- CAPITAL PLAZA AUTHORITY
- STATE PLANNING COMMITTEE
- URBAN AFFAIRS COUNCIL
- PROPERTY & BUILDING COMMISSION
- KENTUCKY POLLUTION ABATEMENT AUTHORITY
- SAVINGS BOND AUTHORITY
- COUNCIL FOR LAND USE PLANNING

OFFICE FOR POLICY & MANAGEMENT

OFFICE FOR LOCAL GOVERNMENT

BUREAU OF ADMINISTRATIVE SERVICES

BUREAU OF FACILITIES MANAGEMENT

BUREAU OF COMPUTER SERVICES

This chart was prepared in February 1977 by James Fleming and James King at Senator Ford's direction.

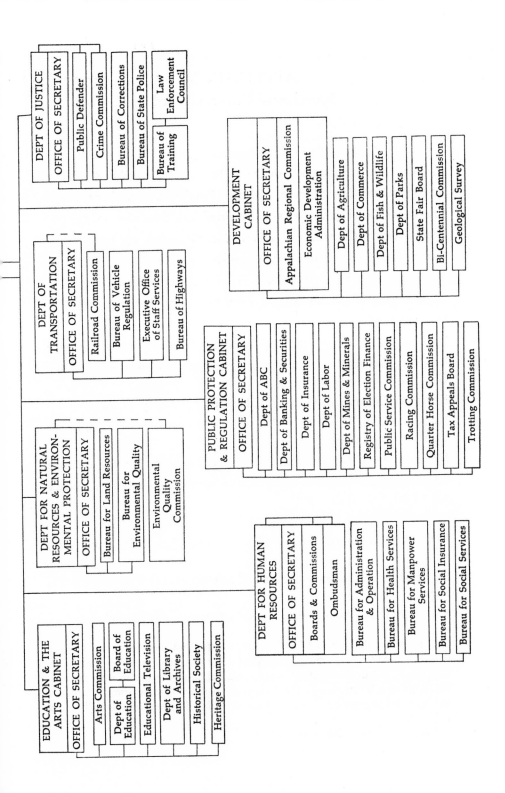

EDUCATION & THE ARTS CABINET
OFFICE OF SECRETARY
- Arts Commission
- Dept of Education / Board of Education
- Educational Television
- Dept of Library and Archives
- Historical Society
- Heritage Commission

DEPT FOR NATURAL RESOURCES & ENVIRONMENTAL PROTECTION
OFFICE OF SECRETARY
- Bureau for Land Resources
- Bureau for Environmental Quality
- Environmental Quality Commission

DEPT OF TRANSPORTATION
OFFICE OF SECRETARY
- Railroad Commission
- Bureau of Vehicle Regulation
- Executive Office of Staff Services
- Bureau of Highways

DEPT OF JUSTICE
OFFICE OF SECRETARY
- Public Defender
- Crime Commission
- Bureau of Corrections
- Bureau of State Police
- Bureau of Training
- Law Enforcement Council

DEVELOPMENT CABINET
OFFICE OF SECRETARY
- Appalachian Regional Commission
- Economic Development Administration
- Dept of Agriculture
- Dept of Commerce
- Dept of Fish & Wildlife
- Dept of Parks
- State Fair Board
- Bi-Centennial Commission
- Geological Survey

PUBLIC PROTECTION & REGULATION CABINET
OFFICE OF SECRETARY
- Dept of ABC
- Dept of Banking & Securities
- Dept of Insurance
- Dept of Labor
- Dept of Mines & Minerals
- Registry of Election Finance
- Public Service Commission
- Racing Commission
- Quarter Horse Commission
- Tax Appeals Board
- Trotting Commission

DEPT FOR HUMAN RESOURCES
OFFICE OF SECRETARY
- Boards & Commissions
- Ombudsman
- Bureau for Administration & Operation
- Bureau for Health Services
- Bureau for Manpower Services
- Bureau for Social Insurance
- Bureau for Social Services

APPENDIX 3
Speeches of Governor Ford

INAUGURAL ADDRESS, Frankfort, December 7, 1971*

1972 OPENING OF THE MARCH OF DIMES, Frankfort, December 8, 1971

GOVERNOR BERT COMBS PICTURE HANGING, Frankfort, December 10, 1971

CHRISTMAS TREE LIGHTING CEREMONY, Frankfort, December 11, 1971

PRELEGISLATIVE CONFERENCE, Gilbertsville, December 13, 1971*

OWENSBORO APPRECIATION DAY, Owensboro, December 15, 1971

REMOVAL OF POLITICAL PATRONAGE, Frankfort, December 18, 1971*

COAL SEVERANCE TAX DISPOSITION, Frankfort, December 31, 1971*

STATE OF THE COMMONWEALTH ADDRESS, Frankfort, January 4, 1972*

STRIP MINERS' VISIT TO TALK OVER PROBLEMS, Frankfort, January 4, 1972

BOWLING GREEN-WARREN COUNTY CHAMBER OF COMMERCE, Bowling Green, January 7, 1972*

KENTUCKY CHAMBER OF COMMERCE, Lexington, January 12, 1972*

LOUISVILLE AREA CHAMBER OF COMMERCE CONGRESSIONAL FORUM, Louisville, January 14, 1972*

MADISONVILLE CHAMBER OF COMMERCE, Madisonville, January 15, 1972

LOUISVILLE AREA CHAMBER OF COMMERCE LUNCHEON, Louisville, January 17, 1972*

JOBS FOR VETERANS PROGRAM, Louisville, January 18, 1972*

KENTUCKY COUNCIL OF COOPERATIVES LUNCHEON, Louisville, January 20, 1972*

SENATOR JOHN SHERMAN COOPER RETIREMENT, Frankfort, January 21, 1972

KENTUCKY PRESS ASSOCIATION, Frankfort, January 22, 1972*

This listing of Governor Ford's speeches does not include, as the volume does not, the speeches which he made as overt campaign speeches during his race for a seat in the United States Senate against the incumbent, Senator Marlow Cook. Even though the campaign speeches contain some references to his record as governor, they were not considered as part of Wendell Ford's public papers as governor.

* Address is included in this volume.

JEFFERSON COUNTY CRIMINAL JUSTICE GRANT, Frankfort, January 25, 1972*

EXPO '72 (YOUTH FOR CHRIST), Frankfort, January 26, 1972

SENATOR EDMUND MUSKIE WELCOME, Frankfort, January 26, 1972

BUDGET MESSAGE, Frankfort, February 3, 1972*

UNITED AUTO WORKERS COUNCIL, Indianapolis, Ind., February 6, 1972

FLORIDA TILE COMPANY EXPANSION DEDICATION, Lawrenceburg, February 7, 1972

BOY SCOUTS OF AMERICA ANNUAL REPORT, Frankfort, February 9, 1972

JEFFERSON-JACKSON DAY DINNER, GEORGIA DEMOCRATIC PARTY, Atlanta, Georgia, February 14, 1972*

COMMENT ON INSURANCE COMPANY SEIZURE, Frankfort, February 16, 1972*

CONSUMER PROTECTION BILL SIGNING, Frankfort, February 17, 1972

BUDGET—SEVERANCE TAX, Frankfort, February 21, 1972

SEVERANCE TAX STATEMENT, Frankfort, February 21, 1972*

KENTUCKY STATE POLICE CADETS CLASS NUMBER 44, Frankfort, February 25, 1972

HOUSE BILL 236: RESPONSE TO WHAS COMMENT, Frankfort, March 9, 1972

STATEMENT RE: BUDGET PASSAGE, Frankfort, March 15, 1972*

DRUGS AT EDDYVILLE PENITENTIARY, Paducah, March 17, 1972

OFFICE OF MINORITY BUSINESS ENTERPRISES, Frankfort, March 17, 1972*

HOUSE BILL 294: CLERICAL ERROR IN COMPLETION OF THIS BILL, Frankfort, March 20, 1972

INTERSTATE STREAMS, Frankfort, March 20, 1972

KENTUCKY HIGHWAY CONFERENCE, Lexington, March 20, 1972*

FRANKFORT-FRANKLIN COUNTY CHAMBER OF COMMERCE, Frankfort, March 23, 1972

WILD RIVERS BILL, Frankfort, March 23, 1972

MUSKIE UNION LEADERSHIP DINNER, Rock Hill, South Carolina, March 24, 1972*

KENTUCKY STATE POLICE CADETS CLASS NUMBER 46, Frankfort, March 27, 1972

SUPERVISORY PERSONNEL OF STATE POLICE, Frankfort, March 27, 1972*

STATE PAYMENT OF UTILITY RELOCATION, Frankfort, March 27, 1972*

JOHN Y. BROWN, Frankfort, March 30, 1972

STATEMENT RE: SPECIAL SESSION, Frankfort, March 30, 1972*

VOTING LAW REVISION, Frankfort, March 30, 1972

CRIME COMMISSION GRANTS, Frankfort, April 12, 1972*

EMPLOYMENT OF TOM EWELL, Frankfort, April 12, 1972

MARKLAND DAM HIGHWAY BRIDGE, Warsaw, April 12, 1972*

KENTUCKY EDUCATION ASSOCIATION, Louisville, April 14, 1972*

TRAVEL CONFERENCE, Louisville, April 14, 1972*

CIVITAN CLUB, Northern Kentucky, April 15, 1972

KENTUCKY FEDERATION OF WOMEN'S CLUBS, Lexington, April 18, 1972*

TREMCO MANUFACTURING COMPANY GROUND BREAKING, Barbourville, April 18, 1972

THOROUGHBRED CLUB OF AMERICA, Lexington, April 19, 1972*

FEDERAL REGULATION OF THE OHIO, Frankfort, April 24, 1972*

LEXINGTON KIWANIS CLUB, Lexington, April 25, 1972*

JAYCEES EXECUTIVES CLUB, Washington, D.C., April 29, 1972*

NATIONAL ASSOCIATION OF INSURANCE COMMISSIONERS, Lexington, May 8, 1972*

INDUSTRY LUNCHEON, New York, New York, May 9, 1972*

THE KENTUCKY SOCIETY, New York, New York, May 9, 1972

COUNCIL OF STATE GOVERNMENTS, Atlanta, Georgia, May 11, 1972*

KENTUCKY BROADCASTERS ASSOCIATION, Louisville, May 12, 1972*

INTERNATIONAL UNION OF ELECTRICIANS, RADIO, AND MACHINE WORKERS DISTRICT CONFERENCE, Clarksville, Indiana, May 12, 1972

KENTUCKY WESLEYAN COLLEGE, Owensboro, May 13, 1972*

TRIBUTE TO J. A. GOLDFARB, Frankfort, May 15, 1972

INDUSTRY APPRECIATION LUNCHEON, Louisville, May 18, 1972*

KENTUCKY JUNIOR ACHIEVEMENT BANQUET, Louisville, May 18, 1972

GOBBLER'S KNOB, Gilbertsville, May 19, 1972*

TRAFFIC SAFETY PRESS CONFERENCES, Seven Different Locations, May 22, 1972

COOPERATIVE OFFICE PRACTICE PROGRAM LUNCHEON, Frankfort, May 25, 1972*

LIVERMORE HIGH SCHOOL ALUMNI ASSOCIATION, Livermore, May 27, 1972

POST WHITE HOUSE CONFERENCE ON AGING, Louisville, May 30, 1972*

INTERLAKE INCORPORATED, Newport, May 31, 1972*

FRANKFORT HIGH SCHOOL COMMENCEMENT, Frankfort, June 1, 1972

KENTUCKY DEMOCRATIC CONVENTION, Frankfort, June 3, 1972*

SPECIAL SESSION, Frankfort, June 8, 1972*

NATIONAL GOVERNORS' CONFERENCE REPORT TO PRESS ON HOUSTON CONFERENCE, Frankfort, June 9, 1972

GIRLS' STATE (not delivered in person), Frankfort, June 16, 1972

GREATER CINCINNATI AIRPORT DEDICATION, Covington, June 16, 1972

THE STATES' ROLE IN THE ENERGY CRISIS VERSUS ENVIRONMENTAL QUALITY, Bismarck, North Dakota, June 26, 1972*

STRIP MINING RECLAMATION NATURAL RESOURCES, Frankfort, August 1, 1972

KENTUCKY TURNPIKE ANNOUNCEMENT, Louisville, August 9, 1972*

KENTUCKY STATE FAIR, Louisville, August 17, 1972*

BANANA FESTIVAL LUNCHEON, Fulton, August 18, 1972

LINCOLN FOUNDATION, INC., Frankfort, August 28, 1972*

INTERIM REPORT ON STRIP MINING, Frankfort, August 30, 1972*

LOUISVILLE CENTRAL AREA, Louisville, August 31, 1972*

STRIP MINING LAWS PRESS CONFERENCE, Frankfort, September 1, 1972

TRAFFIC SAFETY PRESS CONFERENCE, n/a, September 1, 1972

SOUTHERN GOVERNORS' CONFERENCE, Hilton Head, South Carolina, September 5, 1972*

KENTUCKY COUNCIL ON CRIME AND DELINQUENCY, Louisville, September 7, 1972*

CERTIFICATE OF NEED BOARD, Frankfort, September 8, 1972

CONSUMER ADVISORY COUNCIL APPOINTMENT, Frankfort, September 8, 1972

KENTUCKY BANKERS ASSOCIATION, French Lick, Indiana, September 12, 1972

KING'S DAUGHTERS HOSPITAL GROUND BREAKING, Frankfort, September 13, 1972

BOY SCOUT ROUND-UP, Lexington, September 14, 1972

INTRODUCTION OF ROGERS MORTON AT THE KENTUCKY HISTORICAL SOCIETY LUNCHEON, Pleasant Hill, September 15, 1972

SALES TAX REMOVAL, Frankfort, September 21, 1972

HORSE PARK PRESS CONFERENCE, Lexington, September 26, 1972

ISRAEL'S TWENTY-FIFTH ANNIVERSARY CELEBRATION, Louisville, September 26, 1972

INDUSTRIAL RESOURCES REVIEW, Prestonsburg, September 27, 1972*

KENTUCKY MUNICIPAL LEAGUE, Cadiz, September 28, 1972*

COOPERATIVE MONTH KICKOFF BREAKFAST, Frankfort, October 2, 1972

CHAMBER OF COMMERCE GOVERNOR'S TOUR, Louisville, October 3, 1972

CHAMBER OF COMMERCE GOVERNOR'S TOUR, Shively, October 3, 1972*

CHAMBER OF COMMERCE GOVERNOR'S TOUR, Covington, October 4, 1972*

CHAMBER OF COMMERCE GOVERNOR'S TOUR, Lexington, October 5, 1972*

WILLARD WADE DAY, Park Hills, October 5, 1972

BOOTS RANDOLPH GOLF COURSE DEDICATION, Cadiz, October 7, 1972

STATE DEMOCRATIC WOMEN'S CLUBS LUNCHEON, Lexington, October 7, 1972*

CRIME COMMISSION LUNCHEON, Louisville, October 13, 1972

KENTUCKY WELFARE ASSOCIATION, Louisville, October 13, 1972*

STUDENT PROGRAM ON KENTUCKY (SPOKE), Lexington, October 14, 1972

RIVERVIEW-HOBSON HOUSE ASSOCIATION DEDICATION, Bowling Green, October 16, 1972

MASONIC GRAND LODGE OF KENTUCKY ANNUAL COMMUNICATION, Louisville, October 17, 1972

OFFICE OF PUBLIC DEFENDER, Louisville, October 17, 1972*

LAW ENFORCEMENT CENTER GROUND BREAKING, Richmond, October 18, 1972

KENTUCKY OCCUPATIONAL HEALTH AND SAFETY, Louisville, October 18, 1972*

PRESENTATION OF LIBRARY CHECK, Frankfort, October 19, 1972

New Plant of Nicolet Paper Company, Nicholasville, October 19, 1972

Introduction of Senator Thomas F. Eagleton, Morehead, October 20, 1972

Annual Session of Eastern Star Grand Chapter, Louisville, October 23, 1972

Sheehan Bridge and Paducah Firemen Training Announcement, Paducah, October 23, 1972

Governor's Presidential Conference on Exporting and Export Financing, Louisville, October 26, 1972*

Revolving Fund to Reclaim Orphan Strip Mine Banks, Morganfield, October 26, 1972*

Housing Corporation, Louisville, October 31, 1972*

Joint Conference with Governor Matthew Welsh, Louisville, October 31, 1972*

Charleston Bottoms Power Generating Station Ground Breaking, Maysville, November 1, 1972*

General Contractors' Association Luncheon, Lexington, November 3, 1972

Public Assistance Adjustments, Frankfort, November 3, 1972*

Farm-City Week Kickoff Luncheon, Frankfort, November 8, 1972

Natural Bridge State Park Association, Slade, November 10, 1972*

Governor's Annual Conservation Achievement Award Dinner, Louisville, November 11, 1972*

Opening of the Patton Museum, Fort Knox, November 11, 1972*

Introduction of Adolph Rupp, Louisville, November 20, 1972*

Reorganization (1), Frankfort, November 28, 1972*

National Jaycee Seminar, Washington, D.C., November 30, 1972

Scott County Courthouse Rededication, Georgetown, December 2, 1972

Capital Chapter of National Secretaries Association, Frankfort, December 5, 1972*

Smithsonian Institution 1973 Showcase, Announcement of American Folklife Festival, Frankfort, December 7, 1972

Christmas Tree Lighting Ceremony, Frankfort, December 11, 1972

KENTUCKY ASSOCIATION OF SCHOOL ADMINISTRATORS, Louisville, December 11, 1972*

PRESENTATION BEFORE THE PAY BOARD, Washington, D.C., December 14, 1972*

GREEN RIVER PARKWAY DEDICATION, Bowling Green, December 15, 1972*

GREEN RIVER PARKWAY DEDICATION, Hartford and Beaver Dam Interchange, December 15, 1972*

GREEN RIVER PARKWAY DEDICATION, Morgantown Interchange, December 15, 1972*

GREEN RIVER PARKWAY DEDICATION, Owensboro, December 15, 1972*

POLICE INCREASES IN SALARY—PAY BOARD, Frankfort, December 21, 1972

OWENSBORO HOMEBUILDERS ASSOCIATION, Owensboro, December 22, 1972

REORGANIZATION: DEPARTMENT FOR NATURAL RESOURCES AND ENVIRONMENTAL PROTECTION, Frankfort, January 3, 1973*

MARSHALL COUNTY CHAMBER OF COMMERCE ANNUAL MEMBERSHIP DINNER, Gilbertsville, January 8, 1973

HUNTER FOUNDATION GRADUATION CEREMONIES FOR TRAINEES, Lexington, January 9, 1973

LEXINGTON LIONS CLUB, Lexington, January 10, 1973

PROPOSED REPORT BY NATIONAL WATER COMMISSION, Washington, D.C., January 10, 1973*

KENTUCKY PRESS ASSOCIATION, Louisville, January 12, 1973

KENTUCKY OCCUPATIONAL PROGRAM KICKOFF, Frankfort, January 16, 1973*

STATEMENT ON THE DEATH OF PRESIDENT LYNDON B. JOHNSON, Frankfort, January 22, 1973

KENTUCKY HIGHWAY CONTRACTORS ASSOCIATION, Acapulco, Mexico, January 22, 1973*

VIETNAM CEASE-FIRE, Frankfort, January 25, 1973

MOVE TO LEXINGTON OF ISLAND CREEK COAL COMPANY, Lexington, January 29, 1973

ANNUAL CHAMBER OF COMMERCE BANQUET, Lebanon, January 29, 1973*

STATEMENT TO U.S. SENATE COMMITTEE ON INTERIOR AND INSULAR AFFAIRS, Washington, D.C., February 6, 1973*

COUNCIL ON AGRICULTURE, Frankfort, February 7, 1973*

INTERNAL REVENUE SERVICE RULING ON PRUDENTIAL BUILDING AND LOAN ASSOCIATION, Frankfort, February 7, 1973

ANNUAL GOVERNOR'S CONFERENCE ON TOURISM, Lexington, February 7, 1973*

PAY BOARD RULING, Frankfort, February 8, 1973

LIONS CLUB DISTRICT CONVENTION, Frankfort, February 11, 1973

NATIONAL FARM MACHINERY SHOW: OPENING OF STATE FAIR, Louisville, February 14, 1973

LOUISVILLE JAYCEES, Louisville, February 15, 1973

AUDUBON COUNCIL OF BOY SCOUTS OF AMERICA DINNER, Hopkinsville, February 16, 1973

WINCHESTER-CLARK COUNTY CHAMBER OF COMMERCE, Winchester, February 19, 1973*

COMMENTS TO KENTUCKY CONGRESSIONAL DELEGATION, Washington, D.C., February 21, 1973*

YALE POLITICAL UNION, New Haven, Connecticut, February 22, 1973*

NATIONAL ASSOCIATION OF REGIONAL COUNCILS, Minneapolis, Minnesota, February 25, 1973*

STATEMENT TO U.S. SENATE SUBCOMMITTEE ON INTERGOVERNMENTAL RELATIONS, Washington, D.C., February 27, 1973

DEDICATION OF AGRICULTURE SCIENCE BUILDING SOUTH, Lexington, March 2, 1973

REORGANIZATION: HUMAN RESOURCES, Frankfort, March 2, 1973*

KENTUCKY MOTHERS ASSOCIATION, Louisville, March 3, 1973

DEMOCRATIC GOVERNORS' DAY ANNUAL DINNER, Greenville, South Carolina, March 5, 1973

KENTUCKY READY-MIXED CONCRETE ASSOCIATION, Louisville, March 9, 1973*

ENVIRONMENTAL QUALITY COMMISSION, Frankfort, March 12, 1973*

OWENSBORO COUNCIL FOR RETARDED CHILDREN, Owensboro, March 12, 1973*

ANNUAL CONVENTION OF THE KENTUCKY SCHOOL BOARDS ASSOCIATION, Louisville, March 13, 1973*

BROWN CHALLENGE GIFT, Frankfort, March 15, 1973*

REORGANIZATION: TRANSPORTATION, Frankfort, March 16, 1973*

ANNUAL MEETING OF KENTUCKY ASSOCIATION OF HIGHWAY ENGINEERS, Lexington, March 24, 1973*

AMBULANCE REGULATIONS, Frankfort, March 26, 1973*

TESTIMONIAL DINNER FOR ALEX WILLIAMS, Lexington, March 28, 1973

NATIONAL ELEMENTARY SCHOOL GUIDANCE CONFERENCE, Louisville, March 29, 1973*

MEETING OF STATE MANPOWER COUNCIL, Frankfort, March 30, 1973*

YOUNG AND ADULT FARMER RECOGNITION, Hopkinsville, March 30, 1973

GIRL SCOUT FRIENDSHIP DAY, Frankfort, March 31, 1973

KENTUCKY DENTAL ASSOCIATION ANNUAL MEETING, Louisville, April 2, 1973

ASARCO INDUSTRY SITE, Frankfort, April 3, 1973

ENVIRONMENTAL AWARENESS STATEWIDE SEMINAR, Frankfort, April 3, 1973

OWENSBORO-DAVIESS COUNTY INDUSTRIAL FOUNDATION LUNCHEON, Owensboro, April 4, 1973*

PINKERTON TOBACCO PLANT SITE RIBBON-CUTTING, Owensboro, April 4, 1973

RIVER REGION MENTAL HEALTH-MENTAL RETARDATION BOARD, Louisville, April 4, 1973*

HAZARD-PERRY COUNTY CHAMBER OF COMMERCE, Hazard, April 6, 1973

INDUSTRY APPRECIATION WEEK ANNUAL LUNCHEON, Louisville, April 6, 1973*

SENATORS' RURAL DEVELOPMENT CONFERENCE, Lexington, April 6, 1973

BROOKSVILLE LIONS CLUB ANNUAL BASKETBALL BANQUET, Brooksville, April 9, 1973

CYNTHIANA ACCESS ROUTE, Cynthiana, April 9, 1973*

KENTUCKY SCHOOL FOR THE DEAF, 150TH ANNIVERSARY AND DEDICATION CEREMONY, Danville, April 10, 1973

LUNCHEON HONORING RETURN OF PRISONERS OF WAR, Louisville, April 10, 1973

KENTUCKY JAYCEES AWARDS LUNCHEON, Frankfort, April 11, 1973

YOUTH WEEK CEREMONIES AND SIGNING OF PROCLAMATION, Frankfort, April 11, 1973

KENTUCKY STATE FAIR BOARD AND LOUISVILLE CHAMBER OF COMMERCE, Louisville, April 12, 1973

MAYSVILLE CHAMBER OF COMMERCE, Maysville, April 12, 1973

COMMISSION ON ALCOHOL AND DRUG PROBLEMS, Frankfort, April 13, 1973*

INTERNATIONAL UNION OF ELECTRICIANS, RADIO, AND MACHINE WORKERS DISTRICT CONFERENCE, Clarksville, Indiana, April 14, 1973

KENTUCKY PLUMBING INDUSTRY WEEK KICKOFF DINNER DANCE, Frankfort, April 14, 1973

JASPER CORPORATION NEW PLANT SITE, Fordsville, April 16, 1973

PRESIDENT'S LUNCHEON OF THE KENTUCKY HOSPITAL ASSOCIATION, Louisville, April 17, 1973*

THOROUGHBRED CLUB OF AMERICA, Lexington, April 18, 1973

GREEN RIVER AREA DEVELOPMENT DISTRICT, Owensboro, April 25, 1973*

REORGANIZATION: COMPUTER OPERATIONS, Frankfort, April 25, 1973*

INTERNAL REORGANIZATION OF DEPARTMENT FOR FINANCE AND ADMINIS-TRATION, Frankfort, April 26, 1973*

PRESS CONFERENCE WITH ROBERT STRAUSS, Frankfort, April 27, 1973

KENTUCKY THOROUGHBRED BREEDERS ASSOCIATION, Louisville, May 3, 1973*

MURRAY STATE UNIVERSITY COMMENCEMENT, Murray, May 4, 1973*

COMMISSION ON WOMEN, Frankfort, May 8, 1973*

APPRECIATION LUNCHEON FOR BEN FLORA, RETIRING SCHOOL SUPERINTEN-DENT, Bellevue, May 8, 1973

ENVIRONMENTAL PROTECTION AGENCY MEETING, Washington, D.C., May 9, 1973*

HOUSING AND URBAN DEVELOPMENT MEETING, Washington, D.C., May 9, 1973

AMERICAN PUBLIC HEALTH ASSOCIATION SOUTHERN BRANCH AND KENTUCKY PUBLIC HEALTH ASSOCIATION, Louisville, May 11, 1973*

GOVERNOR'S DAY IN ASHLAND, Ashland, May 11, 1973*

PUBLIC DEFENDERS SEMINAR LUNCHEON, Lexington, May 11, 1973*

WESTERN KENTUCKY UNIVERSITY COMMENCEMENT, Bowling Green, May 12, 1973

EASTERN KENTUCKY UNIVERSITY COMMENCEMENT, Richmond, May 13, 1973

BLACK LUNG BENEFITS, Frankfort, May 21, 1973*

KENTUCKY DAY, WEEK OF THE EAGLES, Fort Campbell, May 21, 1973

KENTUCKY'S WESTERN WATERWAYS ANNUAL MEETING, Cadiz, May 21, 1973*

OWENSBORO ROTARY CLUB, Owensboro, May 23, 1973*

FRANKLIN COUNTY YOUNG DEMOCRATS FISH FRY, Frankfort, May 24, 1973*

SOMERSET HIGH SCHOOL COMMENCEMENT, Somerset, May 25, 1973

REMOVAL OF TOLLS FROM TWO INTERCHANGES, Louisville, May 25, 1973*

JUNE DAIRY MONTH KICKOFF LUNCHEON, Lexington, June 1, 1973*

POLICE PAY INCENTIVE SUPPLEMENTARY PAY—PRESS CONFERENCE, Frankfort, June 11, 1973

POLICE TRAINING AND EDUCATIONAL INCENTIVE PROGRAM, Frankfort, June 11, 1973

REMARKS TO KENTUCKY STATE POLICE (video tape), Frankfort, June 13, 1973*

CLARK EQUIPMENT COMPANY PLANT GROUND BREAKING, Georgetown, June 20, 1973

CONFERENCE ON LOCAL GOVERNMENT PROBLEMS, Louisville, June 21, 1973*

NORTH AMERICAN LIVESTOCK SHOW AND EXPOSITION, Louisville, June 21, 1973*

KENTUCKY GAS ASSOCIATION, Lexington, June 22, 1973*

FESTIVAL OF AMERICAN FOLKLIFE, Frankfort, June 25, 1973*

KENTUCKY PEACE OFFICERS ASSOCIATION CONVENTION, Owensboro, June 27, 1973*

POKE SALLET FESTIVAL, Harlan, June 27, 1973

COMMONWEALTH CLEANUP KICKOFF, Winchester, June 28, 1973

FORT BOONESBOROUGH RECONSTRUCTION GROUND BREAKING, Richmond, June 28, 1973

DEDICATION OF HOPKINSVILLE BYPASS, Hopkinsville, June 29, 1973*

HOPKINSVILLE CIVIC LUNCHEON, Hopkinsville, June 29, 1973

KENTUCKY STATE POLICE TWENTY-FIFTH ANNIVERSARY BANQUET, Frankfort, June 29, 1973

TWENTY-FIFTH ANNIVERSARY OF THE KENTUCKY DEPARTMENT OF COMMERCE, Frankfort, July 2, 1973*

AMERICAN LEGION OF KENTUCKY ANNUAL STATE CONVENTION, Covington, July 7, 1973

DEMOCRATIC REGISTRATION DRIVE, Frankfort, July 7, 1973*

BOY SCOUT FUND-RAISING VARMINT DINNER, Henderson, July 13, 1973

DIVISION II CIRCUIT JUDGESHIP, Frankfort, July 23, 1973*

GOVERNOR'S COUNCIL ON AGRICULTURE COMMITTEES, Frankfort, July 24, 1973*

KICKOFF PREVIEW FOR THE KENTUCKY '74 CELEBRATION, Frankfort, July 26, 1973*

KENTUCKY MAGISTRATES AND COMMISSIONERS ANNUAL CONVENTION, Owensboro, July 27, 1973

RESIGNATION OF CHARLES OWEN FROM CRIME COMMISSION, Frankfort, July 31, 1973

CAMPBELL COUNTY SENIOR CITIZENS ANNUAL PICNIC, Melbourne, August 1, 1973*

ECONOMIC FACTORS AND BUDGET SURPLUS, Frankfort, August 3, 1973*

TWENTY-FIFTH ANNUAL SUMMER SCHOOL OF UNITED AUTO WORKERS, REGION 3, Bloomington, Indiana, August 5, 1973

CENTRAL CITY CENTENNIAL, Central City, August 6, 1973

ANNOUNCEMENT OF NEW FIRESTONE PLANT, Henderson, August 6, 1973

MERIT SYSTEM EXPANSION, Frankfort, August 6, 1973*

KENTUCKY ASSOCIATION OF CHIEFS OF POLICE FIRST ANNUAL CONFERENCE, Lexington, August 9, 1973*

KENTUCKY STATE FAIR, Louisville, August 10, 1973

NORTHERN KENTUCKY STATE GOVERNMENT DAYS, Covington, August 15, 1973

J. R. MILLER RETIREMENT, Frankfort, August 16, 1973*

BANANA FESTIVAL LUNCHEON, Fulton, August 17, 1973

KENTUCKY CHAMBER OF COMMERCE STATE FAIR LUNCHEON, Louisville, August 21, 1973*

KENTUCKY FARM BUREAU DAY, Louisville, August 22, 1973

PROGRAM BUDGET PILOT EFFORT, Frankfort, August 27, 1973*

BUDGET SEMINAR, Frankfort, August 29, 1973*

HUMAN RESOURCES CABINET ANNOUNCEMENT, Frankfort, August 29, 1973*

RIBBON-CUTTING CEREMONIES FOR I-64, Frankfort and Lexington, August 30, 1973*

LEXINGTON CHAMBER OF COMMERCE LUNCHEON, Lexington, August 30, 1973*

REAPPORTIONMENT STATEMENT, Frankfort, August 30, 1973

STATEMENT ON ROCK FESTIVAL, Frankfort, August 30, 1973

STATEMENT ON THE SIGNING OF THE UNITED MINE WORKERS AND EASTOVER MINING COMPANY CONTRACT, Frankfort, August 30, 1973

ACREAGE FEES FOR STRIP MINING AND DISASTER CHECKS, Frankfort, September 10, 1973*

BOY SCOUT FUND-RAISING BARBECUE, Lexington, September 11, 1973

REORGANIZATION: DEPARTMENT OF JUSTICE, Frankfort, September 11, 1973*

KENTUCKY COUNCIL ON CRIME AND DELINQUENCY CONFERENCE, Louisville, September 12, 1973*

REORGANIZATION: CABINET FOR DEVELOPMENT AND CABINET FOR EDUCATION AND THE ARTS, Frankfort, September 13, 1973*

KENTUCKY FAIR AND EXPOSITION CENTER, Louisville, September 17, 1973

PRESS BREAKFAST STATEMENT, Washington, D.C., September 20, 1973*

KENTUCKY MUNICIPAL LEAGUE BANQUET, Louisville, September 21, 1973*

STULL'S SEED FIELD DAY LUNCH, Sebree, September 21, 1973*

REPORT AT SOUTHERN GOVERNORS' CONFERENCE, Point Clear, Alabama, September 24, 1973*

KENTUCKY NATIONAL GUARD DINING-IN, Louisville, September 29, 1973

COOPERATIVE MONTH KICKOFF BREAKFAST, Frankfort, October 1, 1973

OUTWOOD STATE HOSPITAL, Frankfort, October 1, 1973

SAINT MATTHEWS BUSINESS ASSOCIATION ANNUAL DINNER MEETING, Louisville, October 1, 1973

CHAMBER OF COMMERCE GOVERNOR'S TOUR, Richmond, October 2, 1973*

CHAMBER OF COMMERCE GOVERNOR'S TOUR, Pineville, October 2, 1973*

EPISCOPAL CHURCH CONVENTION, Louisville, October 3, 1973

CHAMBER OF COMMERCE GOVERNOR'S TOUR, Breaks, Virginia, October 3, 1973*

CHAMBER OF COMMERCE GOVERNOR'S TOUR, Paintsville, October 4, 1973*

INSTALLATION OF DR. JAMES G. MILLER, Louisville, October 5, 1973*

STATEMENT ON THE AGNEW RESIGNATION, Frankfort, October 10, 1973

INTRODUCTION OF SLIDE PRESENTATION FOR INDUSTRIAL TOUR, Frankfort, September 12, 1973

SUPPORT OF HENRY HOWELL OF VIRGINIA (tape), Frankfort, October 12, 1973

KENTUCKY COAL ASSOCIATION ANNUAL MEETING, Lexington, October 12, 1973*

BURLEY AND DARK LEAF TOBACCO EXPORT ASSOCIATION CONVENTION LUNCHEON, Louisville, October 15, 1973*

REORGANIZATION: DEPARTMENT OF PUBLIC INFORMATION, Frankfort, October 15, 1973*

PRAYER BREAKFAST WELCOME, Frankfort, October 16, 1973

INTRODUCTION OF SENATOR HAROLD HUGHES AT PRAYER BREAKFAST, Frankfort, October 16, 1973

DAVIESS COUNTY STATE VOCATIONAL-TECHNICAL SCHOOL DEDICATION, Owensboro, October 18, 1973*

FARM TOUR DINNER, Owensboro, October 18, 1973*

MADISONVILLE COMMUNITY COLLEGE DEDICATION, Madisonville, October 18, 1973*

KENTUCKY BROADCASTERS ASSOCIATION, Frankfort, October 19, 1973

EARLE CLEMENTS DAY, Morganfield, October 20, 1973

L & N ANNOUNCEMENT, Frankfort, October 23, 1973

TAX CUT (tape), Frankfort, October 31, 1973

LOUISVILLE AREA CHAMBER OF COMMERCE CONGRESSIONAL FORUM, Louisville, November 9, 1973

ANNOUNCEMENT OF LEXINGTON CIVIC CENTER, Lexington, November 10, 1973*

GOVERNOR'S ANNUAL CONSERVATION ACHIEVEMENT AWARD DINNER, Louisville, November 10, 1973

CRIME COMMISSION GRANTS, Frankfort, November 12, 1973

INSTALLATION OF DR. DENO CURRIS, Murray, November 12, 1973*

APPROPRIATION AND REVENUE BUDGET SEMINAR, Louisville, November 13, 1973*

YMCA ANNUAL DINNER, Frankfort, November 13, 1973

COUNTY JUDGES ASSOCIATION ANNUAL MEETING, Louisville, November 15, 1973

CRIMINAL JUSTICE SEMINAR, Atlanta, Georgia, November 16, 1973*

RESPONSE TO TEACHER-PROMOTED LETTERS FROM STUDENTS, Frankfort, November 20, 1973

I-64 DEDICATION LUNCHEON, Grayson, November 21, 1973*

SOUTHERN POLICE INSTITUTE, Louisville, November 21, 1973

LOUISVILLE CHAMBER OF COMMERCE, Louisville, November 27, 1973*

MARCH OF DIMES CONFERENCE, Louisville, November 30, 1973

PRELEGISLATIVE CONFERENCE, Gilbertsville, December 3, 1973*

KENTUCKY FARM BUREAU, Louisville, December 4, 1973*

FARM PRESS AND RADIO BANQUET, Frankfort, December 6, 1973

UNITED AUTO WORKERS LEGISLATIVE CONFERENCE, Frankfort, December 7, 1973

CHRISTMAS TREE LIGHTING CEREMONY, Frankfort, December 9, 1973

ENERGY RESEARCH AND DEVELOPMENT, Frankfort, December 14, 1973

DEDICATION CEREMONY OF HENRY CLAY LAW OFFICE RESTORATION, Lexington, December 15, 1973

STATEMENT OF CHAIRMAN OF DEMOCRATIC NATIONAL GOVERNORS' CAUCUS, Frankfort, December 20, 1973

KENTUCKY STATE POLICE CADETS CLASS No. 48, Frankfort, December 21, 1973

STATEMENT RE: CONSUMER PROTECTION AND REGULATION CABINET, Frankfort, January 2, 1974*

TIME REALIGNMENT REQUEST APPROVAL, Frankfort, January 4, 1974

STATE OF THE COMMONWEALTH ADDRESS, Frankfort, January 8, 1974*

1974 GENERAL ASSEMBLY BICENTENNIAL SALUTE, Frankfort, January 9, 1974*

BICENTENNIAL CELEBRATION '74 (mailed statement to *Jefferson Reporter*), January 16, 1974

ENERGY MESSAGE, Frankfort, January 16, 1974*

KENTUCKY HEART FUND KICKOFF LUNCHEON, Frankfort, January 21, 1974

BUDGET ADDRESS, Frankfort, January 22, 1974*

TROOPER OF THE YEAR ANNUAL RECOGNITION PROGRAM, Louisville, January 23, 1974

KENTUCKY CHAMBER OF COMMERCE LEGISLATIVE CONFERENCE, Louisville, January 24, 1974

MAYOR DAVID A. PARISH (radio spot), Madisonville, January 26, 1974

KENTUCKY JAYCEE LEGISLATIVE CONFERENCE LUNCHEON, Frankfort, January 29, 1974

EAGLE SCOUT RECOGNITION AND AWARDS CEREMONY, Frankfort, February 3, 1974

POLLUTION ABATEMENT AUTHORITY CHECK PRESENTATION, Frankfort, February 4, 1974

TRUCKERS' STRIKE STATEMENT, Frankfort, February 4, 1974*

TRUCKING SITUATION: CALL-OUT OF NATIONAL GUARD, Frankfort, February 5, 1974*

SPEED LIMIT, HOUSE BILL 184 SIGNING, Frankfort, February 6, 1974

LOUISVILLE PUBLIC SCHOOLS ASSEMBLY INAUGURAL, Louisville, February 9, 1974*

COUNCIL ON AGRICULTURE SYMPOSIUM, Louisville, February 13, 1974*

HAZARD HEART FUND TELETHON (tape), Frankfort, February 13, 1974

NATIONAL FARM MACHINERY SHOW, Louisville, February 13, 1974

CLAY WADE BAILEY STATEMENT, Frankfort, February 19, 1974

STATE OFFICE BUILDING DEDICATION, Owensboro, February 19, 1974*

LAMBDA CHI ALPHA FRATERNITY FOUNDERS' DAY, Lexington, March 2, 1974

ENERGY CONSERVATION ACTION PLAN, Frankfort, March 4, 1974*

KENTUCKY'S RESPONSE TO THE ENERGY SHORTAGE (mailed to the National Governors' Conference), March 7 and 8, 1974

SIGMA ALPHA EPSILON FOUNDERS' DAY DINNER, Lexington, March 8, 1974

STATEMENT RE: SENATE BILL 45, Frankfort, March 14, 1974*

BICENTENNIAL COMMISSION LUNCHEON, Frankfort, March 15, 1974

ENERGY BILL SIGNING—HOUSE BILL 251, Frankfort, March 15, 1974

SENATE RACE ANNOUNCEMENT, Frankfort, March 22, 1974*

WINCHESTER-BOONESBOROUGH ROAD KY 627 GROUND BREAKING, Winchester, March 25, 1974

WINCHESTER GROUND BREAKING CEREMONY LUNCHEON, Winchester, March 25, 1974

LEXINGTON JAYCEES AND CHAMBER OF COMMERCE JOINT MEETING, Lexington, March 26, 1974

JESSAMINE COUNTY SENIOR CITIZENS PROGRAM (radio spot), Nicholasville, March 27, 1974

MARTIN LUTHER KING, JR., DAY—HOUSE BILL 78 SIGNING, Frankfort, April 1, 1974

OPEN MEETINGS—HOUSE BILL 100 SIGNING, Frankfort, April 1, 1974

LOUISVILLE VOCATIONAL-TECHNICAL INSTITUTE GROUND BREAKING, Louisville, April 3, 1974*

APRIL TORNADO RELIEF, Frankfort, April 5, 1974*

SOUTH-CENTRAL KENTUCKY RADIO CRUSADE FOR TORNADO VICTIMS, Frankfort, April 11, 1974

DEDICATION OF FOSTER HALL HOME AND SCHOOL, Owensboro, April 20 1974

FEDERAL TAX REDUCTION, Frankfort, April 22, 1974*

TENNESSEE-TOMBIGBEE WATERWAY PROJECT, Frankfort, April 22, 1974

BARREN RIVER AREA DEVELOPMENT DISTRICT, Lucas, April 23, 1974*

KENTUCKY ENERGY CONSERVATION CONFERENCE, Louisville, April 24, 1974*

KENTUCKY JAYCEES AWARDS LUNCHEON, Frankfort, April 24, 1974

RED RIVER PROJECT, Frankfort, April 24, 1974*

INDUSTRIAL COAL CONFERENCE, Lexington, April 25, 1974*

NATIONAL TURF WRITERS ANNUAL BANQUET, Louisville, May 1, 1974

U. S. GRANT BRIDGE AND RIBBON-CUTTING CEREMONY, Portsmouth, Ohio, May 1, 1974

RAGÚ FOODS, INC., NEW PLANT SITE, Frankfort, May 2, 1974

THOROUGHBRED BREEDERS OF KENTUCKY ANNUAL AWARDS LUNCHEON, Louisville, May 2, 1974

KENTUCKY FEDERATION OF WOMEN'S CLUBS, Louisville, May 7, 1974

INDUSTRY APPRECIATION ANNUAL LUNCHEON, Louisville, May 8, 1974*

HANCOCK COUNTY CHAMBER OF COMMERCE ANNUAL DINNER MEETING, Hancock County, May 9, 1974

FAMILY PRACTICE/STUDENT HEALTH SERVICE BUILDING DEDICATION, Lexington, May 11, 1974

NORTON CHILDREN'S HOSPITAL DEDICATION, Louisville, May 11, 1974

BRESCIA COLLEGE COMMENCEMENT, Owensboro, May 12, 1974*

GOAL FOR COAL CONFERENCE, Russellville, May 14, 1974

KENTUCKY WEEKLY NEWSPAPER ASSOCIATION, Lexington, May 17, 1974

FIRESTONE RUBBER COMPANY NATIONAL BOARD OF DIRECTORS MEETING, Bowling Green, May 21, 1974

FRANKFORT BICENTENNIAL EXPO '74 KICKOFF, Frankfort, May 24, 1974

HORSE PARK PRESS CONFERENCE, Lexington, May 24, 1974

INTRODUCTION OF SENATOR WILLIAM PROXMIRE AT KENTUCKY BAR ASSOCIATION BANQUET, Louisville, May 24, 1974

CUMBERLAND FALLS CHAIRLIFT, Frankfort, May 28, 1974*

OWENSBORO HIGH SCHOOL COMMENCEMENT, Owensboro, June 6, 1974

REVENUE AND APPROPRIATIONS REPORT, Frankfort, June 6, 1974*

CHANGE IN TRANSPORTATION SECRETARY, Frankfort, June 6, 1974

KENTUCKY NATIONAL GUARD RETREAT, Fort Knox, June 7, 1974

SHIVELY INTERCHANGE OPENING, Shively, June 7, 1974

ALL AMERICAN MOVERS INVESTIGATION, Frankfort, June 12, 1974

KIWANIS CLUB, Ashland, June 12, 1974*

BICENTENNIAL RUN FOR GLORY, Frankfort, June 13, 1974

LOCAL GOVERNMENT ISSUES ANNUAL CONFERENCE, Louisville, June 13, 1974

KENTUCKY GIRLS STATE, Frankfort, June 14, 1974

MIDDLESBORO STATE GOVERNMENT DAY, Middlesboro, June 17, 1974

SOMERSET STATE GOVERNMENT DAY, Somerset, June 18, 1974

LEXINGTON CIVIC CENTER GROUND BREAKING, Lexington, June 21, 1974

OUTWOOD REPLACEMENT, Frankfort, June 21, 1974*

VETERANS OF FOREIGN WARS AND LADIES AUXILIARY JOINT SESSION, Louisville, June 21, 1974

MANCHESTER CENTER GRANT, Manchester, July 3, 1974

DEDICATION OF KING'S DAUGHTERS MEMORIAL HOSPITAL, Frankfort, July 7, 1974

COAL UTILIZATION CONFERENCE, COUNCIL OF STATE GOVERNMENTS, Louisville, July 10, 1974

FRANKFORT CIVIC CLUBS JOINT MEETING, Frankfort, July 10, 1974*

COLUMBUS-BELMONT STATE PARK BICENTENNIAL BARBECUE, Columbus, July 11, 1974

HICKMAN COUNTY COURTHOUSE HISTORICAL MARKER DEDICATION, Clinton, July 11, 1974

HICKMAN COUNTY LIBRARY GROUND BREAKING, Clinton, July 11, 1974

ANNOUNCEMENT OF COAL GASIFICATION PLANT, Frankfort, July 13, 1974*

NATIONAL ASSOCIATION OF COUNTIES CONVENTION, Miami, Florida, July 16, 1974*

KENTUCKY AGRICULTURAL EXPORT CONFERENCE LUNCHEON, Louisville, July 17, 1974*

STATEMENT ON THE DEATH OF REPRESENTATIVE JAY LOUDEN, Frankfort, July 17, 1974

NATIONAL CONFERENCE OF APPELLATE COURT CLERKS ANNUAL BANQUET, Louisville, July 18, 1974

HOPKINSVILLE STATE GOVERNMENT DAY LUNCHEON, Hopkinsville, July 19, 1974

PRESENTATION OF CHECK TO AREA DEVELOPMENT DISTRICT, Frankfort, July 22, 1974

STATEMENT ON MINE PICKETING, Frankfort, July 22, 1974*

MADISONVILLE STATE GOVERNMENT DAY, Madisonville, July 30, 1974*

SECOND AREA MEETING OF THE KENTUCKY ASSOCIATION OF CONSERVATION DISTRICTS, Henderson, July 31, 1974*

MOREHEAD STATE UNIVERSITY SUMMER COMMENCEMENT, Morehead, August 1, 1974*

SEVERANCE TAX CONFERENCE, Frankfort, August 1, 1974*

BICENTENNIAL FLAG DAY CEREMONY, Frankfort, August 5, 1974

KENTUCKY ASSOCIATION OF SCHOOL ADMINISTRATORS, Louisville, August 5, 1974

CAMPBELL COUNTY SENIOR CITIZENS ANNUAL PICNIC, Melbourne, August 7, 1974

STATEMENT ON THE DEATH OF REPRESENTATIVE BROOKS HINKLE, Frankfort, August 8, 1974

BOWLING GREEN KIWANIS CLUB, Bowling Green, August 8, 1974*

STATEMENT ON THE RESIGNATION OF PRESIDENT RICHARD NIXON, Lexington, August 8, 1974

JEFFERSON COMMUNITY COLLEGE LEARNING RESOURCES CENTER GROUND BREAKING, Louisville, August 13, 1974

KENTUCKY FIREMEN'S ASSOCIATION, Shively, August 13, 1974*

BOOKMOBILE CELEBRATION, Louisville, August 15, 1974

KENTUCKY STATE FAIR, Louisville, August 15, 1974

LAMBDA CHI ALPHA FRATERNITY NATIONAL CONVENTION, Knoxville, Tennessee, August 15, 1974

BANANA FESTIVAL LUNCHEON, Fulton, August 16, 1974

SAVAGE DAYS, Providence, August 17, 1974

HART COUNTY JUDGE PRESENTATION—CLEANUP PROGRAM, Munfordville, August 19, 1974

STATE GOVERNMENT DAY, Munfordville, August 19, 1974*

STATEMENT ON THE VICE PRESIDENTIAL NOMINATION OF NELSON ROCKEFELLER, Frankfort, August 20, 1974

OWEN HAMMONS TESTIMONIAL DINNER, Louisville, August 22, 1974

STATEMENT ON THE DANIEL BOONE TREATMENT CENTER, Frankfort, August 23, 1974*

SPECIAL REPORT ON COAL ROADS, Frankfort, August 23, 1974*

LIVESTOCK EXPOSITION CENTER GROUND BREAKING, Murray, August 26, 1974

HICKMAN NATIONAL GUARD ARMORY GROUND BREAKING, Hickman, August 27, 1974

KNOWLTON BROTHERS PLANT DEDICATION, Madisonville, August 28, 1974

ACREAGE FEES FOR STRIP MINING, Frankfort, August 29, 1974

STATEMENT ON THE RED RIVER GORGE DAM (UPI), Frankfort, August 30, 1974

CASEY COUNTY AIRPORT DEDICATION, Liberty, August 30, 1974

FORT BOONESBOROUGH STATE PARK DEDICATION, Boonesboro, August 30, 1974*

MORGAN COUNTY SCHOOL DEDICATION, West Liberty, August 31, 1974*

ANDERSON COUNTY LIBRARY DEDICATION, Lawrenceburg, September 4, 1974

ASHLAND OIL EXPANSION, Frankfort, September 4, 1974*

SIX MILE ISLAND PURCHASE, Louisville, September 6, 1974

STATEMENT RE: EXCESS FUNDS, Frankfort, September 6, 1974*

OPENING OF SEVENTH ANNUAL GAS LIGHT FESTIVAL, Jeffersontown, September 7, 1974

HENDERSON AREA MENTAL HEALTH CENTER DEDICATION, Henderson, September 8, 1974

STATEMENT ON PRESIDENT FORD'S PARDON OF PRESIDENT NIXON, Frankfort, September 8, 1974

ALL-KENTUCKY PRODUCTS BREAKFAST, Louisville, September 13, 1974*

FLAVO-RICH MILK PLANT GROUND BREAKING, I-75 and Daniel Boone Parkway, September 17, 1974

LEXINGTON KIWANIS CLUB, Lexington, September 17, 1974*

FISHER-PRICE TOY COMPANY DEDICATION, Murray, September 19, 1974

LOGAN COUNTY COURTHOUSE DEDICATION, Russellville, September 21, 1974

STATEMENT ABOUT SENATOR EDWARD KENNEDY, Frankfort, September 23, 1974

UNITED AUTOMOBILE WORKERS RETIREES PICNIC, Louisville, September 23, 1974*

CHAMBER OF COMMERCE GOVERNOR'S TOUR, Bowling Green, September 25, 1974

CHAMBER OF COMMERCE GOVERNOR'S TOUR, Somerset, September 25, 1974

LEXINGTON CHAMBER OF COMMERCE CONGRESSIONAL FORUM, Lexington, September 25, 1974

DEDICATION OF NEW WELCOME CENTER, I-65 at Kentucky-Tennessee Line, September 26, 1974*

ASHLAND STATE POLICE POST DEDICATION, Ashland, September 27, 1974

SOUTHWEST JEFFERSON COUNTY HOSPITAL GROUND BREAKING, Louisville, September 28, 1974

EASTERN KENTUCKY UNIVERSITY NEW HEALTH SERVICES GROUND BREAKING LUNCHEON, Richmond, September 30, 1974

COOPERATIVE MONTH KICKOFF BREAKFAST, Frankfort, October 1, 1974

INTRODUCTION OF HAROLD K. JOHNSON AT PRAYER BREAKFAST, Frankfort, October 2, 1974

BROWNING MANUFACTURING PLANT GROUND BREAKING, Morehead Industrial Foundation, Morehead, October 3, 1974

KENTUCKY ASSOCIATION OF CONSERVATION DISTRICTS ANNUAL CONVENTION, Louisville, October 3, 1974

KENTUCKY NATIONAL GUARD DINING-IN, Louisville, October 5, 1974*

SOUTHERN REGIONAL EDUCATION BOARD, Lexington, October 8, 1974*

MASONIC GRAND LODGE OF KENTUCKY ANNUAL COMMUNICATION, Louisville, October 15, 1974

DOWNTOWN LIONS CLUB LUNCHEON, Louisville, October 15, 1974*

BOONE ARMORY DEDICATION, Frankfort, October 17, 1974

CARTER COUNTY (tape), Frankfort, October 17, 1974

EASTERN STAR GRAND CHAPTER ANNUAL SESSION, Louisville, October 21, 1974

INDUSTRIAL LUNCHEON, Owensboro, October 22, 1974

OPPORTUNITY CENTER WORKSHOP EXPANSION GROUND BREAKING, Owensboro, October 22, 1974

MARSHALL COUNTY SENIOR CITIZENS FACILITY GROUND BREAKING, Benton, October 23, 1974

ROTARY CLUB LUNCHEON, Louisville, October 24, 1974*

"SOUND OFF" COLUMN (*Louisville Times*), Frankfort, October 24, 1974

BRESCIA COLLEGE HEARING DEFECT CENTER GROUND BREAKING, Owensboro, November 21, 1974

LOUISVILLE DOWNTOWN NEW CONVENTION CENTER GROUND BREAKING, Louisville, November 21, 1974

BAPTIST HOSPITALS IN KENTUCKY FIFTIETH ANNIVERSARY CELEBRATION, Louisville, November 24, 1974

STATEMENT ON LEAA GRANTS, Frankfort, December 2, 1974*

CHRISTMAS TREE LIGHTING CEREMONY, Frankfort, December 8, 1974

IDA LEE WILLIS GARDEN DEDICATION, Frankfort, December 15, 1974

RESIGNATION STATEMENT, Frankfort, December 27, 1974*

INDEX